Critical Studies
in Organization
and Bureaucracy

Critical Studies in Organization and Bureaucracy

Edited by Frank Fischer — pol. science
and Carmen Sirianni — sociologist

Temple University Press
PHILADELPHIA

Temple University Press, Philadelphia 19122
© 1984 by Temple University. All rights reserved
Published 1984
Printed in the United States of America

Library of Congress Cataloging in Publication Data
Main entry under title:

Critical studies in organization and bureaucracy.

   Includes bibliographical references.
   1. Bureaucracy—Addresses, essays, lectures.
2. Organization—Addresses, essays, lectures.
I. Fischer, Frank, 1942–   . II. Sirianni, Carmen.
HD38.4.C74   1984   302.3′5   83–24305
ISBN 0–87722–344–0 (pbk.)
ISBN 0-87722-343-2

Contents

About the Editors / ix
Preface / xi

**Organization Theory and Bureaucracy:
A Critical Introduction,** Frank Fischer and Carmen Sirianni / 3

PART I. Classical Problems: Critical and Mainstream Perspectives / 21

1. **Bureaucracy,** Max Weber / 24
2. **The Spirit of Bureaucracy** and **Beyond Bureaucracy: The Paris Commune,** Karl Marx / 40
3. **Oligarchy,** Robert Michels / 48
4. **Trade Unions, Factory Councils, and Workers' Control of Production,** Antonio Gramsci / 64
5. **Scientific Management,** Frederick W. Taylor / 68
6. **The Real Meaning of Taylorism,** Harry Braverman / 79
7. **Human Relations and the Informal Organization,** Fritz J. Roethlisberger and William J. Dickson / 86
8. **Three Patterns of Bureaucracy,** Alvin W. Gouldner / 96

PART II. Forms of Control and the Division of Labor / 107

9. **Forms of Control in the Labor Process: An Historical Analysis,** Richard C. Edwards / 109
10. **Machine Technology and Workplace Control: The U.S. Post Office,** Peter Rachleff / 143

11. The Taylorization of Police Work, Sid Harring / 157
12. Ideology and Organization Theory, Frank Fischer / 172
13. Technocratic Administration and Educational Control,
    Beverly H. Burris and Wolf V. Heydebrand / 191

PART III. Structures and Practices / 211

14. The Rationing of Services in Street-Level Bureaucracies,
    Michael Lipsky / 213
15. Organizing Consent on the Shop Floor:
    The Game of Making Out, Michael Burawoy / 231
16. Women and Power in Organizations,
    Rosabeth Moss Kanter / 241
17. Female Tokenism in the Volunteer Army,
    Michael L. Rustad / 269
18. Normal Accident at Three Mile Island,
    Charles Perrow / 287

PART IV. System and Conflict / 307

19. The Political Economy of American Bureaucracy,
    Susan S. Fainstein and Norman I. Fainstein / 309
20. The Department of Defense and
    the Military-Industrial Establishment:
    The Politics of the Iron Triangle, Gordon Adams / 320
21. Class and Politics in the Organization
    of Public Administration:
    The U.S. Department of Labor, Nancy DiTomaso / 335
22. Bureaucracy and the Regulation of Health
    and Safety at Work: A Comparison of
    the U.S. and Sweden, Steven Kelman / 356

PART V. Organizational Alternatives and Social Change / 375

23. **Worker Ownership, Participation, and Control: Toward a Theoretical Model,** *William Foote Whyte and Joseph R. Blasi* / 377
24. **Collective Organization and the National State: The Kibbutz Model,** *Paula Rayman* / 406
25. **Work Reform and Quality Circles in Japanese Industry,** *Robert Cole* / 421
26. **Barriers to Organizational Democracy in Public Administration,** *Michael P. Smith* / 453
27. **Feminism and the Forms of Freedom,** *Jane Mansbridge* / 472
28. **Participation, Opportunity, and Equality: Toward a Pluralist Organizational Model,** *Carmen Sirianni* / 482

About the Editors

Frank Fischer teaches in the department of political science and the graduate program in public administration at Rutgers University in Newark, New Jersey. His teaching and research span a range of interests, from the theory and methodology of public policy and organizational analysis to political economy, public employment policies, and the politics of urban service bureaucracies. The author of *Politics, Values, and Public Policy: The Problem of Methodology*, he is completing a sequel entitled *Beyond Technocracy: Essays on Knowledge, Power, and Bureaucracy*. In addition, he has served as a policy analyst and consultant on organizational issues for several government agencies and a major research foundation. Before joining the Rutgers faculty, he taught at an alternative college of the State University of New York and at New York University, where he received his doctoral degree.

Carmen Sirianni teaches graduate and undergraduate courses in the sociology of organizations and work at Northeastern University in Boston. He is the author of *Workers Control and Socialist Democracy: The Soviet Experience*, and co-editor (with James E. Cronin) of *Work, Community, and Power: The Experience of Labor*. He has written articles on the comparative dynamics of democratization of the state and economy, and is currently working on a book entitled *Equality and Democracy in the Division of Labor: Theoretical Reconstructions*. Before joining the Northeastern faculty, he taught at Brandeis University and the State University of New York at Binghamton, where he received his doctoral degree.

Preface

Over the past decade, it has become increasingly evident that the study of organizations is confronting a theoretical crisis. For one thing, the sophisticated empirical methodologies of organization theory have failed to explain many of the most important problems in the organizational world. For another, the dominant models of organization have been heavily criticized for their rationalistic, conservative bias. Organization theory, in the view of many, has often unreflectively served to support the bureaucratic status quo, particularly the dominant hierarchial patterns of managerial power.

In the academic world, the signs of this crisis are now widely discussed. The theoretical literature of sociology and political science, as well as the practical journals of business and public administration, is filled with essays on organizational failures. More recently, the popular press has also begun to chronicle the problems of organization and bureaucracy. In the face of growing concern about declining productivity, inferior quality, and conflict-ridden employee relations, the failures of organizational management are now frequently front page news. Even more telling, the topic of management has climbed to the top of the best-seller book list.

In recognition of this organizational malaise, our book is designed to contribute to the search for more adequate organizational approaches. It is founded upon our conviction that good theory must be grounded in practical empirical realities. We have thus shunned the heavy theoretical orientation that characterizes much of the literature in the field and have turned instead to specific organizational issues in empirical settings. In our view, theoretical renewal can be achieved only by developing insights gleaned from the generally neglected facts of organizational life. To facilitate this process, we have presented a series of relevant critical studies that explore these issues. In particular, they focus on the role of power, social control, political economy, women in organizations, alienation and technology, cooperative work arrangements, and organizational democracy. These topics are examined in a broad range of organizational contexts: from the industrial workplace and the corporate boardroom to the Department of Labor and the nuclear power plant, from the university and the social services agency to the post office and the Department of Defense, from the kibbutz and the consciousness-raising group to quality control circles and worker-owned factories.

The selection of essays for an anthology is always fraught with troublesome choices. In the essays that follow, we have sought to avoid ideological distinctions that separate the range of viewpoints expressed. Instead, our guiding principle has been to select studies that enhance the reader's ability to think critically about the issues and problems confronting organizational participants. To this end, the book begins with a section on classical theory, which presents some of the great debates that continue to inform organizational analysis, and follows in subsequent sections with readable cases of specific organizations (primarily in American society) drawn from a critical perspective.

While we have focused on cases and problems at the expense of theory construction, it is important to stress our debt to the critical tradition in the social sciences. Though no more unified or comprehensive than its mainstream competitors, the critical tradition has existed in the social sciences from the beginning. Over the past decade or two, this tradition has undergone a dramatic renewal in the field of organization theory. Not only has it generally revived interest in the study of organizations in the social sciences, but it has also refocused attention on such problems as organizational power, bureaucratic control, class conflict, alienation, gender, and political economy. We have borrowed heavily from this emerging perspective, presenting a selection of some of its recent contributions.

We have tried throughout to keep a wide range of students in mind. As a result, the book can be used by students of organization and bureaucracy in sociology and political science, as well as those in administratively oriented professional programs that require study of organizational behavior. As either primary text or supplemental reading, it speaks to the issues raised in professionally oriented public administration programs, labor and management studies, and human and social services.

Finally, editing a book of this kind necessarily involves assistance and advice from many friends and colleagues. While it is impossible to mention all who have been involved, we would like to single out a number of people for special thanks. Two in particular were most important: Jane Barrett and Andrea Walsh both steadily supplied editorial insight, as well as constant encouragement and support. To them, we wish to acknowledge our deeply felt personal gratitude.

Also, we want to thank Jennifer French, Lew Friedland, Alan Mandell, Paula Rayman, Wolf Heydebrand, Nancy DiTomaso, John Forester, Joel Rogers, Michael Smith, and Gordon Adams. Each offered useful comments at various stages along the way.

F.F.
C.S.
Thanksgiving Day 1983

**Critical Studies
in Organization
and Bureaucracy**

Organization Theory and Bureaucracy: A Critical Introduction

Frank Fischer and Carmen Sirianni

The concept of bureaucratic organization, which condenses a development of almost two centuries of social and political analysis, was a focus of interest for many of the classical theorists, including Max Weber, Karl Marx, John Stuart Mill, Gaetano Mosca, and Robert Michels. By the mid-twentieth century, it had become one of the most important concepts of modern social and political life. In the 1930s, writers began to speak of the "managerial revolution" and the coming "bureaucratization of the world." Today, terms such as the "bureaucratic phenomenon" or "organizational America" are commonplace in social science literature.[1]

Organizational America is something of a paradox. On the one hand, the efficiencies of large-scale organizations have made possible the unprecedented material growth of the twentieth century; on the other hand, the scope of their power and influence has come to threaten our basic social and political values, particularly individual freedom. While George Orwell's classic on "big brother" appears premature in 1984, no one can deny the disturbing growth of centralized bureaucratic control that pervades more and more areas of modern life. In the face of giant corporations and big government, with access to technological surveillance and centralized data banks, Bertram Gross has characterized these modern trends as "friendly fascism."[2] At times, the term has a ring of credence.

For modern capitalist systems the problem poses itself as a unique ideological embarrassment. As the progeny of Adam Smith's eighteenth-century philosophy of the free market, as well as the nineteenth-century belief in "rugged individualism," the rise of large-scale bureaucratic capitalism is a perverse anomaly. "Organization man" has replaced the free-market entrepreneur, but we are still guided by various conceptions of market capitalism. Even though most people have come to accept large-scale organization as a "necessary evil," they accept it only because of the material abundance with which it is associated. More difficult to justify or rationalize are the interrelated social and political realities of this phenomenon. The internal work environments of these bureaucracies produce dull and alienating social relations; centralized government and the corporate system pose political dangers for our traditional concepts of democracy. In the face of these fundamental tensions, theorists such as Juergen Habermas have spoken of a potential "crisis of legitimacy."[3]

Socialist systems have fared no better. Large-scale organization and its techniques of planning have permitted socialist regimes to rapidly industrialize underdeveloped regions of the world, often bringing impressive material achievements. However, much that passes as modern socialism has, at the same time, produced an authoritarian form of bureaucratic collectivism generally unknown to liberal capitalist systems. Given the fact that liberation from the capitalist state has long been the rallying call of socialism, this harsh reality is a fundamental embarrassment. For one thing, there is no shortage of literature on the tyrannies of social and political life under a bureaucratic police state and its "new class."[4] For another, the economic irrationalities of centralized directive planning have become increasingly clear not only to democratic and socialist oppositions, but also to many within the economic, administrative, and political apparatuses as well.[5]

In view of the dimensions of the problem, it is surprising to see how little agreement exists about the conceptual foundations of organization theory. For example, one writer has found more than ten different competing definitional criteria for the term bureaucracy.[6] Given the level of conceptual confusion, another has gone so far as to suggest that the term be banished from social science literature.[7] In view of the omnipresence of the bureaucratic revolution in twentieth century life, this is indeed an intellectually troublesome state of affairs. One might say that the conventional literature of organization theory is characterized by something of a paradox: As the importance of bureaucratic organization has grown in modern society, our ability to conceptualize and explain this phenomenon has continued to decline.

Recognition of the problem has begun to grow over the past ten or fifteen years. Many scholars in the field have begun to express an uneasiness about the theoretical and epistemological status of organizational analysis. Ironically, as the methodologies of organizational analysis have become more sophisticated, they have been less successful in solving the practical problems confronting organizational participants.

Perrow, for example, argues that over the past seventy years it is fair to say that our theories have been explaining realities that don't exist.[8] In his view, the sophisticated empirical methodologies of organizational sociology explain only a small percentage of the variance found in the organizational world. Similarly, in political science it is common to speak of an "intellectual crisis" in the theory of public administration.[9] More recently, this concern has spread beyond sociologists and political scientists to include administrative theorists. For instance, pointing to a "crisis in organizational science," Susman and Evered capture the dilemma in these words:

> Many of the findings in our scholarly management journals are only remotely related to the real world of practicing managers and to the actual issues with which members of organizations are concerned, especially when the research has been carried out by the most rigorous methods of the prevailing conception of science.[10]

While no adequate theory has yet to emerge to explain the failures of organization theory, a new breed of theorists has begun to revitalize the conceptual machinery of the field. Engaged in what can broadly be construed as the search for a "critical" perspective, the competing concepts and methodologies of these writers often differ as much as they converge. In general, however, they tend to merge around two major themes. All share a common disdain for the traditionally dominant organizational paradigm stressing "rational efficiency" and its variants. All urge that primary emphasis be placed on the problems of power, politics, and control.

It is difficult to list all of the criticisms that have been leveled at the rational paradigm. Aiken and Zey-Ferrell, for example, have enumerated as many as twelve different dimensions that have come under attack, while others such as Goldman have organized the criticisms around a few central themes.[11] Common to all of the approaches is a concern over the conservative/elitist bias of organizational theory, a general absence of social class analysis, a failure to connect the organization to the political economy of the larger social and historical context, a general neglect of political and bureaucratic power, and the ideological uses of scientific organizational analysis.

The rational paradigm of organization theory in its classic form views the organization as an instrument of efficiency. An organization is viewed as a rationally designed means for the explicit realization of given goals. As a central theoretical concept, bureaucratic structure is understood to be a means for improving efficiency. Alvin Gouldner, in one of the seminal critiques of the rational model, put the issue this way:

> The rational model assumes that decisions are made on the basis of a rational survey of the situation, utilizing certified knowledge with a deliberate orientation to an expressly codified legal apparatus. The focus is, therefore, on the legally prescribed structure—i.e., the formally "blue-printed" patterns—since these are more largely subject to deliberate inspection and rational manipulation.[12]

Traditionally, this rational model has been characterized as a "mechanistic" perspective. As Gouldner further explains, "it views the organization as a structure of manipulable parts, each of which is separately modifiable with a view to enhancing the efficiency as a whole." Thus, modifications of the organization can be introduced through rational planning based on scientific managerial analysis. Applying the "natural laws" of organizational science, the proper scientific design of elite administrative planners will produce a cooperative harmony of organizational interests.

The origins of the rational model are not difficult to locate. In this country, the pioneering research that initiated the discipline was closely intertwined with the rise of corporate capitalism and its bureaucratic mode of organization. Men such as Frederick W. Taylor, Elton Mayo, and Chester Barnard were all dedicated students of business efficiency with close ties to the industrial community.

Taylor's work on "scientific management" is often posited as the formal beginning of the rational model.[13] Generally identified with "time and motion" studies and the "organization chart," Taylor's efforts were aimed to achieve greater efficiency through physical analysis of work in production-oriented organizations. For Taylor, the key to greater efficiency is to be found in the division of labor and the formal rules or principles that govern it. The task of scientific management is to uncover the single most efficient method of organizing and, through a proper division of labor, bring the employees in line with it. Emphasizing a clear-cut division of labor, scientific management has stressed the study of functional specialization, unity of command, centralized decision making, top-down authority, and a narrow span of control.

In addition to Taylor, the study of the formal (rational) aspects of organization has also been greatly influenced by the theory of bureaucracy put forward by the German sociologist Max Weber.[14] Generally considered to be the father of modern organizational sociology, Weber was not concerned with a theory of organizational management per se, though his emphasis clearly resembles the tenets of scientific management. In this respect, seven basic similarities are apparent between Weber's theory of bureaucracy and Taylor's concepts of hierarchy and specialization. For Weber, bureaucratic organization is defined by (1) a division of labor with clearly defined authority relationships and responsibilities, (2) offices organized into a hierarchy or chain of command, (3) managerial offices selected from technical qualifications determined by education and examination, (4) rules and regulations governing the conduct of work, (5) impersonality between management and employees, (6) career-oriented officials receiving fixed salaries, and (7) in the case of government administrators, administrative appointments rather than the election of department heads.

This convergence of the hierarchical models of bureaucratic administration of Taylor and Weber and the work that has evolved in this tradition has often been referred to as the "machine model" of organization. Its fundamental assumptions have been succinctly captured in these words:

> The individual had to adjust to the organization; the design of the physical structure—the anatomy of the organization—came first and, indeed, was the principal consideration. This was the "organization" and efficiency depended upon the proper initial arrangements and later readjustments of the "parts," that is, the organizational subdivisions.[15]

While Weber, unlike Taylor, was a scholar rather than a consultant to industry, his theory also has had a major influence on the search for a rational basis for large-scale organization. Where Taylor focused on the physical dimensions of production, Weber emphasized the problem of authority. For Weber, authority is the cornerstone of any organization. It directs the organization toward its goal: It imposes order on chaos.

Of primary concern to Weber was the replacement of dominant "old-world" forms of organizational authority based on tradition and charismatic leadership with a "rational-legal" type of authority, which would facilitate the emergence of modern capitalism in Germany.[16] Authority founded upon tradition was inefficient for free-market competition because leadership was based on continuity rather than competence; charismatic leadership was inefficient because of its reliance on emotion and mystique instead of fixed rules and routines. In contrast, the "legal-rational" type of authority is linked to clearly defined, procedurally-determined rules and regulations; they are designed to coordinate the relationships among the various administrative units and to direct them collectively toward the efficient accomplishment of organizational goals. Obedience and compliance of subordinates is connected to legal-like rules rather than particular persons. Subordinates obey commands from their superiors, but superiors also comply with regulations. Authority, thus, is anchored to the rules governing the rational pursuit of goals. And this, it is important to recognize, links with scientific management, where the task is to uncover the rules governing the rational pursuit of goals.

For Weber, the bureaucracy fitting the rational-legal model represented the purest form of administration. This ideal model succeeded in becoming a basic analytical or conceptual foundation of modern organization theory. As one writer put it, "combination or alloys would appear in practice but Weber wanted to characterize an ideal type for the purposes of theoretical analysis."[17]

Mainstream writers have found many flaws with the rationalistic model and, over the past few decades, have spawned numerous schools as a response to its failures. The first and most famous of these efforts was the human relations movement advanced by Elton Mayo,[18] Fritz Roethlisberger, and William Dickson (see Part I, Chapter 7). Although Mayo and his followers accepted the basic model of scientific management, the human relations school of organization theory was largely a response to the limitations imposed by Taylor's overly mechanistic physical orientation to work. Generally presented as an effort to bring the more complex social and psychological variables into play, their main contributions were the introduction of behavioral science techniques and the conceptualization of the informal social group, as contrasted with Taylor's formal model. While human relations psychology is still credited with important conceptual advances, as a general approach it fell into disrepute. For many of its critics, it devolved in practice into a narrowly oriented manipulative technique employed by personnel managers (Part II, Chapter 12).

Following human relations theory, there has been a substantial flow of research designed to demonstrate the dysfunctions and inefficiencies of the narrow emphasis of both scientific management and human relations theory. Among the early classics in this effort were Merton's work on the relation of organization to personality, Blau's study of the informal rules of a government agency, Selznick's classic analysis of leadership in the Tennessee Valley Authority (TVA), and Gouldner's study of labor-management relations in a gypsum factory (Part I, Chapter 8).[19]

Since the rapid growth of organizational science after World War II, most organization theorists have had less of a pro-business bias than their predecessors in scientific management or human relations research. In the language of social science, most of this work is viewed as an attempt to find a more suitable conceptualization for linking social and technical variables, often dubbed the "socio-technical system." Following the empirical canons of "social science," researchers seek to maintain a "value-free" intellectual orientation. From this perspective, they purport only to seek the universal scientific postulates that explain how organizations actually work. Any bias that exists in the work of these theorists tends to be found in the assumptions that inform their methodologies (Part II, Chapter 12).

During this period, a number of theoretical approaches have emerged. Among the most important have been those of structural and institutional sociologists (Etzioni and Selznick), organizational humanists in psychology (Argyris and McGregor), and decision theorists in political science (March and Simon).[20] To date, however, a synthesis capable of combining the full range of social and technical variables for which theorists must account has yet to emerge.

With the unfolding complexity of organization theory, the discipline has increasingly taken on an interdisciplinary perspective, combining the efforts of sociologists, psychologists, political scientists, and administrative theorists. To accommodate this burgeoning expansion, in the 1970s many turned to systems theory and its step-cousin, contingency theory. This move represented a search for a wider framework to encompass the multiplicity of social and technical variables that require incorporation in a more comprehensive model of organizational explanation. In this respect, it has often merged with the dominant Parsonian model of structural-functional explanation, with its emphasis on the relation of subdivisions of an organization to its system as a whole.[21]

Beyond the emphasis on incorporating the social and technical dimensions of organization into a complex model, "open" systems theory has drawn attention to the role of the organization's external environment. Much theory in recent years has tried to explain internal organizational change as a response or adjustment to environmental changes. The product of these efforts has been the development of "contingency theory," designed to show how different types of environments—open and closed, turbulent or placid—require different types of internal managerial structures. Therefore, some organizational environments dictate the introduction of hierarchical structures (of, say, scientific management), while others might require participatory models (of, say, human relations theory or organizational humanism). For many in the mainstream, the contingency approach represents a major advance in the attempt to bridge the gap between theory and practice through a situational logic.

In spite of the voluminous literature on the dysfunctions and inefficiencies of the rational model, as well as the attempts to supply a theoretical alternative, mainstream theory is still fundamentally linked to the assumptions of the rational model. The operating assumption underlying mainstream theory is that modern organizations can be *reasonably* rational, if not ideally rational in the scientific sense of the term. Classical rationality, with its criteria of economy, efficiency, stability, and prediction, predominates. In this regard, the work of the human relations psychologists and decision theorists, the systems and contingency approaches, and so forth, can all properly be described by Perrow as "Neo-Weberian" models."[22] Even though each is critical of the Weberian model, none can be said to jettison its basic contours. They have, in short, only sought to offset its simplicities. In all these theories, implicitly or explicitly, the function of the manager and the social scientist is to replace "irrationality" with formally rational actions. Moreover, underneath this assumption is the belief that better managers and better social scientists will keep less irrationality from creeping in. Over the past twenty-five years, however, the efforts of managers and social scientists have not been major success stories.

Today, in fact, the failures of management theory are often the subject of much public discussion. For example, concern about the country's falling rate of productivity has drawn much attention in the press to the provocative thesis of Harvard Business School professors Robert Hayes and William Abernathy.[23] Rather than blaming our economic problems on the standard scapegoats, unionization and worker apathy, they attribute them to bad management practices. For them, our difficulties are rooted in management's failure to set the conditions conducive to innovation and productivity. Moreover, such arguments have drawn attention to the successes of the worker-oriented managerial styles of Japanese companies, our leading industrial competitors. Especially important is Japan's use of "quality control circles" (Part V, Chapter 25).

Economists Samuel Bowles, David Gordon, and Thomas Weisskopf point to the same problem but offer a much more scathing indictment.[24] Rather than blaming the decline of the United States economy on bad management practices per se, they attribute the situation to corporate management's political motives. According to them, faced with a breakdown in the postwar system, management has sacrificed efficiency and innovation in a struggle to maintain tight control over its power. The result of techniques such as excessive supervision, underemployment, anti-unionism, induced recessions, and corporate flight has been increasing inefficiencies, falling productivity, and corporate waste. For these economists, the solution lies in a radical turn to industrial democracy and worker self-management.

What, then, does a critical perspective offer as an alternative? The place to begin is with the problem itself.

For the critical theorist, mainstream writers have confused the rational model of efficient administrative behavior with organizational rationality itself. Essentially, the problem stems from the conventional theorists' unwillingness to look beyond the managerial point of view. The result has been an organization theory dominated by the issues of technical and administrative efficiency. Research questions, as Albrow illustrates, are now posed largely from the vantage point of the administrators—the most powerful members of the bureaucracy.[25]

There are a number of factors that have contributed to this bias, but surely one of the most significant has been management's ability to make substantial financial contributions to organizational research. Since workers never have the kinds of financial resources available to management, management has had a very large voice in shaping the direction of organizational studies. Along with the general political and cultural biases that favor management under capitalism, the effects of this influence on research has cultivated an assumption that managers are the only ones that *really* count. Consequently, researchers have primarily obtained their data and orientation to organizational problems from the administrative frame of reference. Thus, the managerial perspective has largely become *the* definition of the organization; rational organization is misconstrued as administrative efficiency.

Nowhere are the limits of this one-dimensional conception of rationality more evident than in the study of labor problems. Failing to see more than one logic of rationality in the workplace,[26] mainstream theory frequently confuses management's interests and motives with those of the full range of organizational participants. The classic illustration of this problem is the managerial interpretation of unionization. Instead of identifying the rationality of unionization as the product of legitimate needs and interests, work behavior that fails to conform to management's conception of rationality is commonly interpreted as dysfunctional or deviant.

From this vantage point, the search for a critical theory of organizations can be understood as an attempt to offset this narrow efficiency-oriented conception of organizational rationality. Much of the critical perspective can be interpreted as a search for a broader conception of rationality. Organizations, in this regard, must be defined as something more than instruments for getting the work done (i.e., as means for the production and delivery of goods and services, material and immaterial). Antecedent to the problem of efficient work, organizations must be conceptualized as tools for the pursuit of personal, group, or class interests. The task of a critical organizational perspective is to theoretically situate work structures within a larger framework of sociopolitical interests. In this regard, Collins's distinction between political and productive labor provides a useful analytical construct.

Collins argues that organizational work, for analytical purposes, must be divided into two types of labor: political and productive.[27] Productive labor refers to those activities, routines, and rules that pertain to the implementation of the organization's everyday work decisions. As the most concrete, technically oriented dimension of the organization, the productive work system can be empirically described in significant detail through various measurement techniques of the social sciences. These techniques can be used to analyze task content, to examine formal and informal procedures, to compare educational and salary scales, to document recruitment patterns, to count supervisory personnel, to measure the efficiency of inputs and outputs, and so forth. Most mainstream organizational research has focused on the analysis of these production-oriented dimensions of work organization and bureaucracy.

Political labor, on the other hand, is the primary emphasis of critical organizational theorists. Without obscuring the problem of efficiency, the task here is to cast the productive system within the organization's governing framework of power and interests. The principal commodities of political labor—power and interests—are embodied in the organization's administrative or managerial system. Directed by a dominant coalition or managerial elite, the administrative structure is an internal political hierarchy. In contrast to the actual conduct of productive work, the function of the administrative system is to set the conditions under which production is appropriated, controlled, and distributed—in political terms, to determine what is produced and who gets it. Thus, from top to bottom the division of political labor spans the system to shape and control production according to a specific configuration of economic and social interests. The upper executive stratum deals with the broad issues of institutional policy (production goals, systemic coordination, wage scales, etc.). Middle managers and shop-floor supervisors are more directly involved in the control of productive labor; as members of a centralized political team, they translate top-level policy priorities into objective workplace practices. Their methods range from simple coercion to the sophisticated techniques of scientific management and human relations psychology—job design, task evaluation, personnel review.

Because both forms of labor—political and productive—are generally performed at the same time, they are often difficult to distinguish. For example, the executive of a municipal hospital who intervenes in a dispute about the location of the hospital's new treatment center for drug addiction is delivering the service while settling a clash between political and organizational interests. But the executive is usually thought of as engaging in a single act: "running the program."

The critical organization theorist attempts to sort out this reality by looking for the fundamental tensions between political and productive labor. Given the political control of administration over labor in a class society, bureaucratic structure is built on an enduring conflict between the two organizational dynamics. One of the most classic statements of this tension is Michels' "Iron Law of Oligarchy."[28] From his study of political party organizations, Michels argued that there is an inevitable and unrestrained tendency toward conflict between efficiency (productive labor) and the organizational interests (political labor) of the managerial elite. While the elite will continue to act in the name of organizational efficiency, the outcome of the conflict will always further its own interests. Writing more recently in the Marxist tradition, Braverman has similarly argued that production in capitalist organizations is never simply organized to conform to the logic of efficiency and technology: Organization follows whatever path best allows management to prevent workers from controlling their own work, as well as the distribution of production (Part I, Chapter 6).

One of the most useful perspectives for analyzing the conflict between political and productive labor is that of political economy. While there is no well-defined approach to the political economy of organizations, there is a disparate but growing collection of theorists that have begun to move the critical perspective in this direction. Central to this research is an emphasis on examining internal organizational conflicts (work stoppages, distribution of incentives and rewards, design of work control, collective bargaining, and ideological differences) within the larger context of political-economic conflicts in the society (class struggle, unemployment, racism, inequality, labor politics).[29] By directing attention to external social and political forces, political economy is theoretically well-equipped to address the larger societal implications of bureaucratic power.

Bureaucracy has emerged from its internal role in the productive system as a central institutional mechanism of the larger political economy. For Weber as well as Marx, bureaucracy fundamentally evolves in a class society as an instrument for social and political domination. Politically, its role is to organize and conduct economic and social affairs in a manner that perpetuates the existing power configuration of social class relations. Bureaucracy, in this regard, serves as a political buffer between the ruling elites and the working class population. Control of bureaucracy thus emerges as a major issue for class politics (Part IV, Chapters 19 and 21).

However, like class conflict in general, struggle over bureaucratic control is fraught with political contradictions. Besides the internal conflicts over control of the labor process, bureaucracy has also engendered long-standing issues pertaining to its external political control. In this respect, two interrelated problems, often referred to as the "bureaucracy problem" and the rise of the "new class," are particularly significant.

For as long as the activities of large-scale organizations have been chronicled, observers have recorded the manifestations of the "bureaucracy problem": the ubiquitous tendency of the executive stratum or power elite of the organization to disengage itself from the interests that initially mandated it (i.e., the policy initiatives of the ruling regime or the profitability of a capitalist's investment).[30] The bureaucracy problem thus refers to the tendency of the executive stratum to displace the organization's original mandated goals in the course of its own struggle for power and control. In short, the personal goals of the executive stratum slowly displace those mandated by external political elites. As a result, external bureaucratic politics initiate a subtle but critical tension between the ruling class and their middle-class "functionaries," the professional-managerial "classes." Positioned between the interests of capital and labor, the professional-managerial stratum is located in a strategic political position. The leverage it derives from this middle echelon provides a potential for emerging as a "new class" in the larger struggle for political control of society.[31]

In general, the critical perspective differs sharply from mainstream approaches on major theoretical assumptions. Five themes commonly distinguish critical from mainstream theories: emphasis on the elitist character of modern organizations, attention to the issues of social class conflict, focus on power as the primary currency of organizational dynamics, stress on the social and historical context of action, and use of nonpositivistic methodologies.

An elitist theory of administrative control underlies the mainstream emphasis on the rational model of organizational analysis. To be sure, there is nothing new about the elitist character of organizations, past or present. In fact, in his classic formulation of the "Iron Law of Oligarchy," Michels argued that there is no escape from elitism as organizations grow large. As he put it, "He who says organization says oligarchy."[32] (Part I, Chapter 3.)

Today the oligarchic structure of bureaucratic organization is commonly accepted—and even legitimated—by most conventional analysts. Ignoring the classic struggles between labor and management that gave shape to modern bureaucratic structures (Part II, Chapter 9), mainstream writers emphasize the technical imperatives of industrialization in their explanation of bureaucratic centralization. In view of their elaborate technical and administrative training, managers emerge from such an analysis as the most valuable members of the organizational system. Only managers, not workers, can plan and oversee the technical complexity of modern organizational processes.

Throughout the history of bureaucratic studies, the elitist perspective has always had its critics. For example, in response to the inevitability of oligarchy, others have argued that elitist theories overlook the political and economic presuppositions of organizational leadership in the past. Critics ranging from John Stuart Mill to Karl Marx (Part I, Chapter 2) have argued that an active worker's role is not only possible but is a requirement of the good society. Where Mill maintained that worker participation is an essential ingredient for the development of democratic values,[33] Marx asserted that industrial democracy would evolve under socialism. For Marx, oligarchy would end when the "state apparatus" was abolished. Under communism, the "administration of people" would be replaced by the "administration of things." In the good society, life would be organized around the cooperative decentralized structure of the commune. From these perspectives, the professional and technocratic justifications of managerial power are primarily ideological rationalizations designed to advance and protect the interests of the administrative stratum (Part II, Chapters 12 and 13). In the final section of the book (Part V), attention is devoted to the development of nonelitist, worker-managed organizations. These range from a discussion of an American plywood firm and an Israeli kibbutz to the analysis of feminist collectives.

The challenge to the elitist theory of organization from the critical perspective is motivated by an underlying analysis of social class relations. Conventional organization theorists, of course, recognize the presence of social class differences: Workers and managers receive unequal pay for different tasks and responsibilities; family class background plays an important part in the determination of adult work roles; hierarchial conflict between administrators and workers is a fundamental aspect of organizational processes. But seldom does conventional analysis confront these issues on their own terms. As Goldman states, "Underneath this recognition of organizational conflicts, most theorists assume that the fundamental interests of workers and managers are neither contradictory nor antagonistic."[34] If we assume, as rational model theorists do, that the interests of corporations (or government bureaucracies) and the men and women who work for them are commonly shared, we can never get to the bottom of the class character of bureaucratic organization. Without a critical class analysis, conflicts between owners/managers and workers/unions are generally misinterpreted as dysfunctional "bureaucratic" conflicts. In this light, it is difficult to see that the resolution of many of these class conflicts may lie in the transformation of the social relations of work rather than simply bureaucratic modifications.

Explanations resting on elitism and class analysis must be driven by the concepts of power and control. Seldom are these concepts anything more than implicit in the rational model of organization. If power and control are analyzed at all, it is generally in terms of "influence and authority," the organizationally based power of management or organizational elites. As Aiken and Zey-Ferrell state, "Almost never are domination, subjugation, coercion, manipulation, or the extortion of one group or class of organizational members by a more powerful group or class analyzed."[35] This type of analysis, which is not within the institutionally based definition of authority, is therefore not considered especially relevant to bureaucracies. But these are very real aspects of power. Domination is one of the primary functions of institutionally based systems of authority, such as a hierarchy of offices and positions, control by rules and regulations, or monopoly of knowledge by "experts." Weber himself clearly recognized this.

Placing power and control at the center of organizational studies has pervasive consequences for analysis. These concepts became overriding issues in organizational analysis, rather than just two more concepts among many (the division of labor, functionalization, expertise, communication, and so forth). From the point of view of power and control, we address the central political-economic questions of organizational analysis throughout the book: How does the dominant coalition develop and maintain its control (Part II)? What are the dysfunctions and inefficiencies of the dominant modes of bureaucratic power, particularly as they affect different groups or classes (Part III)? How does the internal distribution of power interact with the dominant modes of authority in the society as a whole (Part IV)? What are the prospects for an alternative distribution of organizational power (Part V)?

To confront power, conflict, and control on their own terms, it is essential to examine them in their specific social, political, and historical contexts (Part II, Chapters 9, 12, and 13). In most mainstream studies, organizations appear to evolve by a continual and gradual process of technological and administrative "rationalization." Management's responsibility in this process is primarily to monitor and facilitate the sociotechnical adjustments dictated by technological change. Thus, as Goldman states, "There is little cause to explain how and why a firm or an industry's historically critical decisions were made by capitalists or managers and the reciprocal relationship between these decisions and the problems of the larger economy or workers' activities." Likewise, "The historic roots of government agencies and the conditions that led to their beginnings are only infrequently seen as important or as influencing current practices."[36] (Part IV, Chapter 21). Instead, organizational problems are conceptualized as atemporal and unchanging technical-administrative issues. The lack of historical perspective freezes analysis into the present and reifies the goals of the status quo. In this regard, organizational goals often appear to emerge from the organizations themselves rather than from the critical decisions of the dominant coalitions or managements that structured the organization.

Clegg maintains that organizations must be analyzed as complex "structures-in-motion" that are "historically constituted entities" designed for control of the labor process. Organizational structure must be understood as a complex set of social relations that are historical products of both class conflict and the changing patterns of capitalism. Clegg states:

> Major changes in the organization of the labor process thus take on a historically rational evolution. They emerge as responses by dominant economic agents (i.e., dominant coalitions) within organizations to changed conditions of accumulation. In order to try to construct more profitable conditions, economic agents effect reorganization. New underlying principles of organization are tried, widely adopted, and accepted as the rules for particular aspects of the labor process. The genesis and adoption of these rules are not random, but are historically conditioned by fundamental movements.[37]

The need for attention to social, political, and historical contexts raises the issue of methodology. Emphasis on context requires that we reject the traditional mainstream emphasis on value-neutral, universal laws of organizational structure and functioning that apply in every context to all organizations—business firms, hospitals, public agencies, and so forth. Without context, theory ideologically glosses over, disguises, or buttresses the organizational inequalities and hierarchical power that critical analysts seek to explain.

The idea of universal explanations (or generalizations), borrowed from an outdated conception of the natural sciences, is behind the modern theorist's search for a general theory of organizations, particularly those of the systems theorist. As Aiken and Zey-Ferrell argue, "This assumption is easily integrated into the systems perspective in an attempt to develop a general theory of organizations. . . . At the base of these sets of principles or causal relationships is the assumption that there is one best way for the structure and functioning of all organizations."[38] Thus, like its earliest ancestors, the updated rational model of the systems perspective also explains changes or conflicts in the organization in terms of a lack of integration or fit between organizational parts. Not only is such a "mechanistic" perspective normatively problematic, its statistical correlations tell us almost nothing about why organizational phenomena occur, under what circumstances, or through which types of mediating processes.

Once we recognize the importance of context, the need to focus major attention on case studies becomes apparent. Central to a critical methodology is the necessity to move back and forth between theoretical explanation and practical case studies. Generally this involves supplementing empirical research with interpretive methodologies such as historical and contextual analysis, phenomenological "action" research, and participant observation. Such methodologies frequently pose sophisticated epistemological issues that clash with the canons of mainstream research. While the tasks of methodological innovation are beyond the scope and purpose of this book, we have sought to facilitate the critical project by emphasizing specific contextual issues of organizational life. Moreover, to offset the fact that most books on the subject—both mainstream and critical—are dominated by abstract theoretical discussions, we have sought to shift the emphasis toward the concrete.

Theory, however, is by no means absent from this book. While we have assumed no specific theoretical orientation within the critical perspective, the essays in the book have been loosely selected to convey the crucial issues of power, class conflict, and political economy. In our view, adoption of a specific perspective at this point in the evolution of a critical theory of organizations would prematurely cut off the need for further theoretical discussion. It is our belief that critical thinkers, both classical and contemporary, have yet to fully and adequately respond to the challenges raised by traditional or mainstream theory, particularly those by Weber and Michels.

Part I, "Classical Problems: Critical and Mainstream Perspectives," is the principal theoretical section of the book. To give the reader an appreciation of the tensions that underlie the need for a critical perspective, we have contrasted critical and mainstream orientations. In this regard, the rationalistic or mainstream perspectives of Weber, Michels, Taylor, Roethlisberger, and Dickson are contrasted with such critical challengers as Marx, Gramsci, Gouldner, and Braverman. No attempt, of course, has been made here to present a comprehensive picture of the classical problems. Given the limitations of space, we chose to underscore as sharply as possible the issues that separate these two perspectives. The purpose is to set the stage for the discussion that follows.

Primary emphasis in the subsequent sections is designed to provide both the student and the analyst with a set of social and political insights into the conflict-prone character of organizational processes. Toward this end, we have attempted to amass a wide range of specific topics, including management strategies, union conflicts, government regulation, women's power and representation, the uses of social science techniques, the management of nuclear technology, educational administration, social services delivery, work in the military, and occupational health and safety on the job. These topics are discussed in cases that are drawn from both the private and public sectors. The significance of each essay is briefly described in the introductions that precede the sections in which they appear.

Notes

1. James Burnham, *The Managerial Revolution* (New York: Day, 1941); Bruno Rizzi, *La Bureaucratisation du Monde* (Paris: Hachette, 1939).
2. Bertram Gross, *Friendly Fascism* (New York: Evans, 1980).
3. Juergen Habermas, *Legitimation Crisis* (Boston: Beacon Press, 1973).
4. Milovan Djilas, *The New Class* (New York: Praeger, 1957); George Konrad and Ivan Szelenyi, *Intellectuals on the Road to Class Power*, Andrew Arato and Richard Allen, trans. (New York: Harcourt Brace Jovanovich, 1979).
5. Alec Nove, *Political Economy and Soviet Socialism* (London: Allen & Unwin, 1979); John Burns, "Soviet Study Urges Relaxing Controls to Revive Economy," *New York Times*, 8 Aug. 1983, sec. A, pp. 1 and 4.
6. Richard H. Hall, "The Concept of Bureaucracy: An Empirical Assessment," *American Journal of Sociology* 69 (July 1963): 32–40.
7. Martin Albrow, *Bureaucracy* (New York: Praeger, 1970).
8. Charles Perrow, "Organizational Theory in a Society of Organizations" (Paper presented at the Annual Meeting of the American Sociological Association, Boston, Sept. 1979).
9. Vincent Ostrom, *The Intellectual Crisis in American Public Administration* (University, Ala.: University of Alabama Press, 1974).
10. Gerald I. Susman and Roger D. Evered, "An Assessment of the Scientific Merits of Action Research," *Administrative Science Quarterly* 23 (Dec. 1978): 582–603.
11. Mary Zey-Ferrell and Michael Aiken, eds., *Complex Organizations: Critical Perspectives* (Glenview, Ill.: Scott, Foresman & Co., 1981), 1–21; Paul Goldman, "Sociologists and the Study of Bureaucracy: A Critique of Ideology and Practice," *The Insurgent Sociologist* 3, no. 1 (Winter 1978): 21–30.
12. Alvin Gouldner, "Organizational Analysis," in R. K. Merton, L. Broom, and L. S. Cottrel, Jr., eds., *Sociology Today* (New York: Basic Books, 1959), 404–405.
13. Frederick Winslow Taylor, *Scientific Management* (New York: Harper and Row, 1911).
14. Max Weber, *The Theory of Economic and Social Organization* (New York: Oxford University Press, 1947).
15. Felix and Lloyd Nigro, *Modern Public Administration* (New York: Harper and Row, 1973), 94.
16. S. M. Miller, ed., *Max Weber* (New York: Thomas Y. Crowell Co., 1963).
17. Daniel Wren, *The Evolution of Management Thought* (New York: Ronald Press, 1972), 230.

18. Elton Mayo, *The Human Problems of an Industrial Civilization* (New York: Macmillan, 1933).

19. Robert K. Merton, "Bureaucratic Structure and Personality," *Social Forces* 18 (May 1940): 560–568; Peter M. Blau, *The Dynamics of Bureaucracy* (Chicago: The University of Chicago Press, 1955); Philip Selznick, *TVA and the Grass Roots* (Berkeley: University of California Press, 1949); and Alvin W. Gouldner, *Patterns of Industrial Bureaucracy* (New York: Free Press, 1954).

20. Amitai Etzioni, *Modern Organizations* (Englewood Cliffs, N.J.: Prentice-Hall, 1964); Philip Selznick, *Leadership in Administration* (New York: Harper and Row, 1957); Chris Argyris, *Integrating the Individual and the Organization* (New York: John Wiley, 1964); Douglas McGregor, *The Human Side of Enterprise* (Cambridge: MIT Press, 1960); and James G. March and Herbert A. Simon, *Organizations* (New York: Wiley, 1958).

21. On systems theory and the contingency approach, see Fred Luthans, *Organizational Behavior* (New York: McGraw-Hill, 1981) and Talcott Parsons, "A Sociological Approach to the Theory of Organizations," *Structure and Process in Modern Societies* (Glencoe, Ill.: Free Press, 1964), 16–58.

22. Charles Perrow, *Complex Organizations* (Glenview, Ill.: Scott, Foresman and Co., 1972), 145–176.

23. Robert H. Hayes and William J. Abernathy, "Managing Our Way to Economic Decline," *Harvard Business Review* (July–Aug., 1980): 67–77; Leslie Wayne, "Management Gospel Gone Wrong," *New York Times*, 30 May 1982, sec. 3, p. 1.

24. Samuel Bowles, David M. Gordon, and Thomas E. Weisskopf, *Beyond the Wasteland: A Democratic Alternative to Economic Decline* (New York: Doubleday, 1983).

25. Martin Albrow, "The Study of Organizations—Objectivity or Bias," *People and Organizations*, Graeme Salaman and Kenneth Thompson, eds. (London: Longman, 1973), 396–413.

26. On the logics of organizational action, see Lucien Karpik, ed., *Organization and Environment* (Beverly Hills, Ca.: Sage, 1978).

27. Randall Collins, *The Credential Society* (New York: Academic Press, 1979).

28. Robert Michels, *Political Parties* (Chicago: Free Press, 1949).

29. For general discussions of the political economy approach, see Richard Colignon and David Cray, "New Organizational Perspectives: Critiques and Critical Organizations, in Zey-Ferrell and Aiken, *Complex Organizations*, 100–116; Gibson Burrell and Gareth Morgan, *Sociological Paradigms and Organizational Analysis* (London: Heinemann, 1979), 365–392; and Stuart Clegg and David Dunkerley, *Organization, Class and Control* (London: Routledge and Kegan Paul 1980). In addition to selections that follow in this book, also see Alain Touraine, *The Post-Industrial Society* (New York: Random House, 1971); Paul Goldman and Donald R. Van Houten, "Bureaucracy and Domination: Managerial Strategy in Turn-of-the-Century American Industry," in Zey-Ferrell and Aiken, *Complex Organizations*, 189–216; Frances Fox Piven and Richard Cloward, *Poor People's Movements* (New York: Pantheon, 1977); Philip Green, "Prolegomena to a Democratic Theory of the Division of Labor," *The Philosophical Forum* 14, nos. 3–4 (Spring–Summer 1983): 263–295; and Edward S. Greenberg, "Industrial Self-Management and Political Attitudes," *American Political Science Review* 75 (March 1981): 29–42.

30. Bengt Abrahamsson, *Bureaucracy or Participation: The Logic of Organization* (Beverly Hills, Ca.: Sage Publications, 1977), 15–82.

31. Alvin W. Gouldner, *The Future of the Intellectuals and the Rise of the New Class* (New York: Oxford University Press, 1979) and Pat Walker, ed., *Between Labor and Capital* (Boston: South End Press, 1979).

32. Michels, *Political Parties*.

33. John Stuart Mill, *Collected Works*, J. M. Robson, ed. (Toronto: University of Toronto Press, 1965).

34. Goldman, "Sociologists and the Study of Bureaucracy," 26.

35. Zey-Ferrell and Aiken, *Complex Organizations*, 16.

36. Goldman, "Sociologists and the Study of Bureaucracy," 22.

37. Stuart Clegg, "Organization and Control," *Administrative Science Quarterly* 26 (Dec. 1981): 551.
38. Zey-Ferrell and Aiken, *Complex Organizations*, 16.

PART I

Classical Problems: Critical and Mainstream Perspectives

This section presents a selection of classic discussions of bureaucracy and organization. Because many of the issues they raise have been discussed in the general introduction, only a few words of clarification are necessary.

Max Weber's essay is probably the most well-known classic of all, and it set the stage for most subsequent thinking. It is no accident that such a major contribution on bureaucracy came out of Germany; the Prussian bureaucracy was renowned the world over and had provided the context for Hegel and Marx's analyses in the nineteenth century. In this selection, Weber discusses the general features of the bureaucratic type, some of the reasons for its development, its advantages over previous types of organization, and why, once established, it is extremely difficult to destroy. While Weber himself favored legislative controls over bureaucracies, he was quite pessimistic about the long-term prospects for reigning in bureaucratic power.

Karl Marx, though usually not considered a theorist of organization per se, had a number of acute insights into bureaucracy, and his general analysis on social development provided a point of reference for many of the debates that were to follow. In his discussion of the "spirit of bureaucracy" from 1843, Marx develops a stinging critique of the Prussian bureaucracy. Though written in the dense philosophical style of his youth, Marx's basic points are clear enough. Bureaucracy, obsessed with its power and its formalism, views the world as an object to be administered and extends its tentacles as far as it is able to reach. Marx notes bureaucracy's formal characteristics: hierarchy and secrecy. He explains how the levels of the bureaucracy mutually deceive each other; how bureaucrats, concerned above all with their own careers, mask their own interests as general interests of state; and how the bureaucratic meaning of things is often quite different from the real meaning. Marx's own hopes for the complete elimination of bureaucracy are more fully revealed in his discussion of the radically democratic organizational features that he perceived in the Paris Commune, the municipal system that was developed by the mass of Parisian citizens in rebellion against their own centralized and insensitive state in 1871. The Paris Commune subsequently became the symbol of an alternative form of participatory government for many radicals throughout the world.

Robert Michels directly addressed himself to Marx and attempted to show that real democracy in organizations is impossible, although many social struggles would continue to dress themselves in its mantle. Based on his analysis of the Social Democratic party and the trade unions under the kaiser, Michels argues that oligarchy, or rule by a clique of leaders who do all they can to protect their own position in the organization, is inevitable. For profound organizational and pyschological reasons, oligarchy asserts itself as an "iron" sociological law.

Antonio Gramsci, a young Marxist later recognized as one of Italy's true intellectual giants of the twentieth century, wrote around the same time as Max Weber, Robert Michels, and Frederick Taylor. Also concerned with the bureaucratization of the trade unions, Gramsci developed an analysis of new forms of factory organization that had appeared in Italy and elsewhere, the factory councils. Gramsci saw these organizations as truly innovative forms of democracy and workers' power, and argued that a truly democratic transformation of society implied workers directly participating in and controlling the production process itself. Written in the heat of a major confrontation between labor and capital in post–World War I Italy, Gramsci's analysis has become the focal point for many subsequent debates on workers' participation and economic democracy.

Much of the labor turmoil in the early decades of this century, in both Europe and the United States, was a motivating concern behind the next essay. Frederick Taylor, known as the father of scientific management, developed a set of principles for what he considered the best and most efficient way to organize production. While few adopted Taylor's views totally, they did have a profound impact on organization thinking and on the reality of work organization in the lives of many people. Taylor argued not only that management should have complete authority over the organization of work, but also that tasks should be simplified and fragmented as much as possible and that the brain work should be concentrated in the hands of management.

In the 1970s, after it became clear that Taylorist principles, far from dead, had even spread to various forms of white collar work, Harry Braverman undertook a reevaluation of the significance of Taylorism. His study was particularly timely, in light of the rising degree of dissatisfaction among both blue- and white-collar workers not only in the United States, but in many other major industrial countries. Since its publication in 1974, Braverman's analysis has become a classic, and perhaps the most cited piece, in the study of the modern workplace. Braverman attempts to show that the real meaning of Taylorism lies not in some neutral organizational precepts about efficiency, but in the struggle by management to secure control over the workplace and to lower the cost of labor. The fragmentation of work and the separation of conception and execution are not inevitable features of the modern workplace and advanced technology, but reflect management's interest in profit and control.

In a classic essay of the human relations school, Roethlisberger and Dickson develop an analysis of the organization as having both a human and a technical side, an informal as well as a formal one. On the basis of their famous studies at the Hawthorne Plant of Western Electric, the authors argue that the network of personal relations and the "nonrational" sentiments are crucial for understanding what makes an organization function—and what makes workers often resist the demands of management. Although the value of human relations theory has been much debated (Part II, Chapter 12), there can be little doubt that Roethlisberger and Dickson alerted organization theory to the necessity for studying the informal human side of organizations as well as the formal and technical features.

In the final selection, Alvin Gouldner, a major figure in the revival of critical thinking in American sociology, addresses himself to the various types of bureaucracy in industrial settings. The three types (mock, representative, and punishment-centered) reflect different degrees of agreement or conflict between workers and management. The values legitimating them are different, and the consequences of violating them also vary. Gouldner's analysis attempts to expand Weber's theory by uncovering those aspects of bureaucracy that concern human relations, consent, and democratic process in addition to authority, efficiency, and expertise.

1
Bureaucracy

Max Weber

Characteristics of Bureaucracy

Modern officialdom functions in the following specific manner:

I. *There is the principle of fixed and official jurisdictional areas, which are generally ordered by rules, that is, by laws or administrative regulations.*

1. The regular activities required for the purposes of the bureaucratically governed structure are distributed in a fixed way as official duties.
2. The authority to give the commands required for the discharge of these duties is distributed in a stable way and is strictly delimited by rules concerning the coercive means, physical, sacerdotal, or otherwise, which may be placed at the disposal of officials.
3. Methodical provision is made for the regular and continuous fulfillment of these duties and for the execution of the corresponding rights; only persons who have the generally regulated qualifications to serve are employed.

In public and lawful government these three elements constitute "bureaucratic authority." In private economic domination, they constitute bureaucratic "management." Bureaucracy, thus understood, is fully developed in political and ecclesiastical communities only in the modern state, and, in the private economy, only in the most advanced institutions of capitalism. Permanent and public office authority, with fixed jurisdiction, is not the historical rule but rather the exception. This is so even in large political structures such as those of the ancient Orient, the Germanic and Mongolian empires of conquest, or of many feudal structures of state. In all these cases, the ruler executes the most important measures through personal trustees, table-companions, or court-servants. Their commissions and authority are not precisely delimited and are temporarily called into being for each case.

Reprinted from *From Max Weber: Essays in Sociology*, edited and translated by H. H. Gerth and C. Wright Mills. Copyright 1946 by Oxford University Press, Inc.; renewed 1973 by Hans H. Gerth. Reprinted by permission of the publisher.

II. *The principles of office hierarchy and of levels of graded authority mean a firmly ordered system of super- and subordination in which there is a supervision of the lower offices by the higher ones.* Such a system offers the governed the possibility of appealing the decision of a lower office to its higher authority, in a definitely regulated manner. With the full development of the bureaucratic type, the office hierarchy is monocratically organized. The principle of hierachical office authority is found in all bureaucratic structures: in state and ecclesiastical structures as well as in large party organizations and private enterprises. It does not matter for the character of bureaucracy whether its authority is called "private" or "public."

When the principle of jurisdictional "competency" is fully carried through, hierarchical subordination—at least in public office—does not mean that the "higher" authority is simply authorized to take over the business of "lower." Indeed, the opposite is the rule. Once established and having fulfilled its task, an office tends to continue in existence and be held by another incumbent.

III. *The management of the modern office is based on written documents ("the files"), which are preserved in their original or draught form.* There is, therefore, a staff of subaltern officials and scribes of all sorts. The body of officials actively engaged in a "public" office, along with the respective apparatus of material implements and the files, make up a "bureau." In private enterprise, "the bureau" is often called "the office."

In principle, the modern organization of the civil service separates the bureau from the private domicile of the official, and, in general, bureaucracy segregates official activity as something distinct from the sphere of private life. Public monies and equipment are divorced from the private property of the official. This condition is everywhere the product of a long development. Nowadays, it is found in public as well as in private enterprises; in the latter, the principle extends even to the leading entrepreur. In principle, the executive office is separated from the household, business from private correspondence, and business assets from private fortunes. The more consistently the modern type of business management has been carried through the more are these separations the case. The beginnings of this process are to be found as early as the Middle Ages.

It is the peculiarity of the modern entrepreneur that he conducts himself as the "first official" of his enterprise, in the very same way in which the ruler of a specifically modern bureaucratic state spoke of himself as "the first servant" of the state.[1] The idea that the bureau activities of the state are intrinsically different in character from the management of private economic offices is a continental European notion and, by way of contrast, is totally foreign to the American way.

IV. *Office management, at least all specialized office management— and such management is distinctly modern—usually presupposes thorough and expert training.* This increasingly holds for the modern executive and employee of private enterprises, in the same manner as it holds for the state official.

V. *When the office is fully developed, official activity demands the full working capacity of the official, irrespective of the fact that his obligatory time in the bureau may be firmly delimited.* In the normal case, this is only the product of a long development, in the public as well as in the private office. Formerly, in all cases, the normal state of affairs was reversed: Official business was discharged as a secondary activity.

VI. *The management of the office follows general rules, which are more or less stable, more or less exhaustive, and which can be learned.* Knowledge of these rules represents a special technical learning which the officials possess. It involves jurisprudence, or administrative or business management.

The reduction of modern office management to rules is deeply embedded in its very nature. *The theory of modern public administration, for instance, assumes that the authority to order certain matters by decree—which has been legally granted to public authorities—does not entitle the bureau to regulate* the matter by commands given for each case, but only to regulate the matter abstractly. This stands in extreme contrast to the regulation of all relationships through individual privileges and bestowals of favor, which is absolutely dominant in patrimonialism, at least in so far as such relationships are not fixed by sacred tradition.

The Position of the Official

All this results in the following for the internal and external position of the official:

I. *Office holding is a "vocation."* This is shown, first, in the requirement of a firmly prescribed course of training, which demands the entire capacity for work for a long period of time, and in the generally prescribed and special examinations which are prerequisites of employment. Furthermore, the position of the official is in the nature of a duty. This determines the internal structure of his relations in the following manner: Legally and actually, office holding is not considered a source to be exploited for rents or emoluments, as was normally the case during the Middle Ages and frequently up to the threshold of recent times. Nor is office holding considered a usual exchange of services for equivalents, as is the case with free labor contracts. Entrance into an office, including one in the private economy, is considered an acceptance of a specific obligation of faithful management in return for a secure existence. It is decisive for the specific nature of modern loyalty to an office that, in the pure type, it does not establish a relationship to a *person*, like the vassal's or disciple's faith in feudal or in patrimonial relations of authority. Modern loyalty is devoted to impersonal and functional purposes. Behind the functional purposes, of course, "ideas of culture-values" usually stand. These are *ersatz* for the earthly or supra-mundane personal master: ideas such as "state," "church," "community," "party," or "enterprise" are thought of as being realized in a community; they provide an ideological halo for the master.

The political official—at least in the fully developed modern state—is not considered the personal servant of a ruler. Today, the bishop, the priest, and the preacher are in fact no longer, as in early Christian times, holders of purely personal charisma. The supra-mundane and sacred values which they offer are given to everybody who seems to be worthy of them and who asks for them. In former times, such leaders acted upon the personal command of their master; in principle, they were responsible only to him. Nowadays, in spite of the partial survival of the old theory, such religious leaders are officials in the service of a functional purpose, which in the present-day "church" has become routinized and, in turn, ideologically hallowed.

II. *The personal position of the official is patterned in the following way:*

1. Whether he is in a private office or a public bureau, the modern official always strives and usually enjoys a distinct *social esteem* as compared with the governed. His social position is guaranteed by the prescriptive rules of rank order and, for the political official, by special definitions of the criminal code against "insults of officials" and "contempt" of state and church authorities.

The actual social position of the official is normally highest where, as in old civilized countries, the following conditions prevail: a strong demand for administration by trained experts; a strong and stable social differentiation, where the official predominantly derives from socially and economically privileged strata because of the social distribution of power; or where the costliness of the required training and status conventions are binding upon him. The possession of educational certificates—to be discussed elsewhere[2]—are usually linked with qualification for office. Naturally, such certificates or patents enhance the "status element" in the social position of the official. For the rest this status factor in individual cases is explicitly and impassively acknowledged; for example, in the prescription that the acceptance or rejection of an aspirant to an official career depends upon the consent ("election") of the members of the official body. This is the case in the German army with the officer corps. Similar phenomena, which promote this guild-like closure of officialdom, are typically found in patrimonial and, particularly, in prebendal officialdoms of the past. The desire to resurrect such phenomena in changed forms is by no means infrequent among modern bureaucrats. For instance, they have played a role among the demands of the quite proletarian and expert officials (the *tretyj* element) during the Russian revolution.

Usually the social esteem of the officials as such is especially low where the demand for expert administration and the dominance of status conventions are weak. This is especially the case in the United States; it is often the case in new settlements by virtue of their wide fields for profit-making and the great instability of their social stratification.

2. The pure type of bureaucratic official is *appointed* by a superior authority. An official elected by the governed is not a purely bureaucratic figure. Of course, the formal existence of an election does not by itself mean that no appointment hides behind the election—in the state, especially, appointment by party chiefs. Whether or not this is the case does not depend upon legal statutes but upon the way in which the party mechanism functions. Once firmly organized, the parties can turn a formally free election into the mere acclamation of a candidate designated by the party chief. As a rule, however, a formally free election is turned into a fight, conducted according to definite rules, for votes in favor of one of two designated candidates.

In all circumstances, the designation of officials by means of an election among the governed modifies the strictness of hierarchical subordination. In principle, an official who is so elected has an autonomous position opposite the superordinate official. The elected official does not derive his position "from above" but "from below," or at least not from a superior authority of the official hierarchy but from powerful party men ("bosses"), who also determine his further career. The career of the elected official is not, or at least not primarily, dependent upon his chief in the administration. The official who is not elected but appointed by a chief normally functions more exactly, from a technical point of view, because, all other circumstances being equal, it is more likely that purely functional points of consideration and qualities will determine his selection and career. As laymen, the governed can become acquainted with the extent to which a candidate is expertly qualified for office only in terms of experience, and hence only after his service. Moreover, in every sort of selection of officials by election, parties quite naturally give decisive weight not to expert considerations but to the services a follower renders to the party boss. This holds for all kinds of procurement of officials by elections, for the designation of formally free, elected officials by party bosses when they determine the slate of candidates, or the free appointment by a chief who has himself been elected. The contrast, however, is relative: Substantially similar conditions hold where legitimate monarchs and their subordinates appoint officials, except that the influence of the followings are then less controllable.

Where the demand for administration by trained experts is considerable, and the party followings have to recognize an intellectually developed, educated, and freely moving "public opinion," the use of unqualified officials falls back upon the party in power at the next election. Naturally, this is more likely to happen when the officials are appointed by the chief. The demand for a trained administration now exists in the United States, but in the large cities, where immigrant votes are "corralled," there is, of course, no educated public opinion. Therefore, popular elections of the administrative chief and also of his subordinate officials usually endanger the expert qualification of the official as well as the precise functioning of the bureaucratic mechanism. It also weakens the dependence of the officials upon the hierarchy. This holds at least for the large administrative bodies that are difficult to supervise. The superior qualification and integrity of federal judges, appointed by the president, as over against elected judges in the United States is well known, although both types of officials have been selected primarily in terms of party considerations. The great changes in American metropolitan administrations demanded by reformers have proceeded essentially from elected mayors working with an apparatus of officials who were appointed by them. These reforms have thus come about in a "Caesarist" fashion. Viewed technically, as an organized form of authority, the efficiency of "Caesarism," which often grows out of democracy, rests in general upon the position of the "Caesar" as a free trustee of the masses (of the army or of the citizenry), who is unfettered by tradition. The "Caesar" is thus the unrestrained master of a body of highly qualified military officers and officials whom he selects freely and personally without regard to tradition or to any other considerations. This "rule of the personal genius," however, stands in contradiction to the formally "democratic" principle of a universally elected officialdom.

3. Normally, the position of the official is held for life, at least in public bureaucracies; and this is increasingly the case for all similar structures. As a factual rule, *tenure for life* is presupposed, even where the giving of notice or periodic reappointment occurs. In contrast to the worker in a private enterprise, the official normally holds tenure. Legal or actual life-tenure, however, is not recognized as the official's right to the possession of office, as was the case with many structures of authority in the past. Where legal guarantees against arbitrary dismissal or transfer are developed, they merely serve to guarantee a strictly objective discharge of specific office duties free from all personal considerations. In Germany, this is the case for all juridical and, increasingly, for all administrative officials.

Within the bureaucracy, therefore, the measure of "independence," legally guaranteed by tenure, is not always a source of increased status for the official whose position is thus secured. Indeed, often the reverse holds, especially in old cultures and communities that are highly differentiated. In such communities, the stricter the subordination under the arbitrary rule of the master, the more it guarantees the maintenance of the conventional seigneurial style of living for the official. Because of the very absence of these legal guarantees of tenure, the conventional esteem for the official may rise in the same way as, during the Middle Ages, the esteem of the nobility of office[3] rose at the expense of esteem for the freemen, and as the king's judge surpassed that of the people's judge. In Germany, the military officer or the administrative official can be removed from office at any time, or at least far more readily than the "independent judge," who never pays with loss of his office for even the grossest offense against the "code of honor" or against social conventions of the salon. For this very reason, if other things are equal, in the eyes of the master stratum the judge is considered less qualified for social intercourse than are officers and administrative officials, whose greater dependence on the master is a greater guarantee of their conformity with status conventions. Of course, the average official strives for a civil-service law, which would materially secure his old age and provide increased guarantees against his arbitrary removal from office. This striving, however, has its limits. A very strong development of the "right to the office" naturally makes it more difficult to staff them with regard to technical efficiency, for such a development decreases the career-opportunities of ambitious candidates for office. This makes for the fact that officials, on the whole, do not feel their dependency upon those at the top. This lack of a feeling of dependency, however, rests primarily upon the inclination to depend upon one's equals rather than upon the socially inferior and governed strata. The present conservative movement among the Badenia clergy, occasioned by the anxiety of a presumably threatening separation of church and state, has been expressly determined by the desire not to be turned "from a master into a servant of the parish."[4]

4. The official receives the regular *pecuniary* compensation of a normally fixed *salary* and the old age security provided by a pension. The salary is not measured like a wage in terms of work done, but according to "status," that is, according to the kind of function (the "rank") and, in addition, possibly, according to the length of service. The relatively great security of the official's income, as well as the rewards of social esteem, make the office a sought-after position, especially in countries which no longer provide opportunities for colonial profits. In such countries, this situation permits relatively low salaries for officials.

5. The official is set for a "*career*" within the hierarchical order of the public service. He moves from the lower, less important, and lower paid to the higher positions. The average official naturally desires a mechanical fixing of the conditions of promotion: if not of the offices, at least of the salary levels. He wants these conditions fixed in terms of "seniority," or possibly according to grades achieved in a developed system of expert examinations. Here and there, such examinations actually form a character *indelebilis* of the official and have lifelong effects on his career. To this

is joined the desire to qualify the right to office and the increasing tendency toward status group closure and economic security. All of this makes for a tendency to consider the offices as "prebends" of those who are qualified by educational certificates. The necessity of taking general personal and intellectual qualifications into consideration, irrespective of the often subaltern character of the educational certificate, has led to a condition in which the highest political offices, especially the positions of "ministers," are principally filled without reference to such certificates. . . .

Technical Advantages of Bureaucratic Organization

The decisive reason for the advance of bureaucratic organization has always been its purely technical superiority over any other form of organization. The fully developed bureaucratic mechanism compares with other organizations exactly as does the machine with the non-mechanical modes of production.

Precision, speed, unambiguity, knowledge of the files, continuity, discretion, unity, strict subordination, reduction of friction and of material and personal costs—these are raised to the optimum point in the strictly bureaucratic administration, and especially in its monocratic form. As compared with all collegiate, honorific, and avocational forms of administration, trained bureaucracy is superior on all these points. And as far as complicated tasks are concerned, paid bureaucratic work is not only more precise but, in the last analysis, it is often cheaper than even formally unremunerated honorific service.

Honorific arrangements make administrative work an avocation and, for this reason alone, honorific service normally functions more slowly; being less bound to schemata and being more formless. Hence it is less precise and less unified than bureaucratic work because it is less dependent upon superiors and because the establishment and exploitation of the apparatus of subordinate officials and filing services are almost unavoidably less economical. Honorific service is less continuous than bureaucratic and frequently quite expensive. This is especially the case if one thinks not only of the money costs to the public treasury—costs which bureaucratic administration, in comparison with administration by notables, usually substantially increases—but also of the frequent economic losses of the governed caused by delays and lack of precision. The possibility of administration by notables normally and permanently exists only where official management can be satisfactorily discharged as an avocation. With the qualitative increase of tasks the administration has to face, administration by notables reaches its limits—today, even in England. Work organized by collegiate bodies causes friction and delay and requires compromises between colliding interests and views. The administration, therefore, runs less precisely and is more independent of superiors; hence, it is less unified and slower. All advances of the Prussian administrative organization have been and will in the future be advances of the bureaucratic, and especially of the monocratic, principle.

Today, it is primarily the capitalist market economy which demands that the official business of the administration be discharged precisely, unambiguously, continuously, and with as much speed as possible. Normally, the very large, modern capitalist enterprises are themselves unequalled models of strict bureaucratic organization. Business management throughout rests on increasing precision, steadiness, and, above all, the speed of operations. This, in turn, is determined by the peculiar nature of the modern means of communication, including, among other things, the news service of the press. The extraordinary increase in the speed by which public announcements, as well as economic and political facts, are transmitted exerts a steady and sharp pressure in the direction of speeding up the tempo of adminstrative reaction towards various situations. The optimum of such reaction time is normally attained only by a strictly bureaucratic organization.[5]

Bureaucratization offers above all the optimum possibility for carrying through the principle of specializing administrative functions according to purely objective considerations. Individual performances are allocated to functionaries who have specialized training and who by constant practice learn more and more. The "objective" discharge of business primarily means a discharge of business according to *calculable rules* and "without regard for persons."

"Without regard for persons" is also the watchword of the "market" and, in general, of all pursuits of naked economic interests. A consistent execution of bureaucratic domination means the leveling of status "honor." Hence, if the principle of the free-market is not at the same time restricted, it means the universal domination of the "class situation." That this consequence of bureaucratic domination has not set in everywhere, parallel to the extent of bureaucratization, is due to the differences among possible principles by which polities may meet their demands.

The second element mentioned, "calculable rules," also is of paramount importance for modern bureaucracy. The peculiarity of modern culture, and specifically of its technical and economic basis, demands this very "calculability" of results. When fully developed, bureaucracy also stands, in a specific sense, under the principle of *sine ira ac studio*. Its specific nature, which is welcomed by capitalism, develops the more perfectly the more the bureaucracy is "dehumanized," the more completely it succeeds in eliminating from official business love, hatred, and all purely personal, irrational, and emotional elements which escape calculation. This is the specific nature of bureaucracy and it is appraised as its special virtue.

The more complicated and specialized modern culture becomes, the more its external supporting apparatus demands the personally detached and strictly "objective" *expert*, in lieu of the master of older social structures, who was moved by personal sympathy and favor, by grace and gratitude. Bureaucracy offers the attitudes demanded by the external apparatus of modern culture in the most favorable combination. As a rule, only bureaucracy has established the foundation for the administration of a rational law conceptually systematized on the basis of such enactments as the latter Roman imperial period first created with a high degree of technical perfection. During the Middle Ages, this law was received along with the bureaucratization of legal administration, that is to say, with the displacement of the old trial procedure which was bound to tradition or to irrational presuppositions, by the rationally trained and specialized expert. . . .

The Concentration of the Means of Administration

The bureaucratic structure goes hand in hand with the concentration of the material means of management in the hands of the master. This concentration occurs, for instance, in a well-known and typical fashion, in the development of big capitalist enterprises, which find their essential characteristics in this process. A corresponding process occurs in public organizations.

The bureaucratically led army of the Pharaohs, the army during the later period of the Roman republic and the principate, and, above all, the army of the modern military state are characterized by the fact that their equipment and provisions are supplied from the magazines of the war lord. This is in contrast to the folk armies of agricultural tribes, the armed citizenry of ancient cities, the militias of early medieval cities, and all feudal armies; for these, the self-equipment and the self-provisioning of those obliged to fight was normal.

War in our time is a war of machines. And this makes magazines technically necessary, just as the dominance of the machine in industry promotes the concentration of the means of production and management. In the main, however, the bureaucratic armies of the past, equipped and provisioned by the lord, have risen when social and economic development has absolutely or relatively diminished the stratum of citizens who were economically able to equip themselves, so that their number was no longer sufficient for putting the required armies in the field. They were reduced at least relatively, that is, in relation to the range of power claimed for the polity. Only the bureaucratic army structure allowed for the development of the professional standing armies which are necessary for the constant pacification of large states of the plains, as well as for warfare against far-distant enemies, especially enemies overseas. Specifically, military discipline and technical training can be normally and fully developed, at least to its modern high level, only in the bureaucratic army.

Historically, the bureaucratization of the army has everywhere been realized along with the transfer of army service from the propertied to the propertyless. Until this transfer occurs, military service is an honorific privilege of propertied men. Such a transfer was made to the native-born unpropertied, for instance, in the armies of the generals of the late Roman republic and the empire, as well as in modern armies up to the nineteenth century. The burden of service has also been transferred to strangers, as in the mercenary armies of all ages. This process typically goes hand in hand with the general increase in material and intellectual culture. The following reason has also played its part everywhere: The increasing density of population, and therewith the intensity and strain of economic work, makes for an increasing "indispensability" of the acquisitive strata[6] for purposes of war. Leaving aside periods of strong ideological fervor, the propertied strata of sophisticated and especially of urban culture as a rule are little fitted and also little inclined to do the coarse war work of the common soldier. Other circumstances being equal, the propertied strata of the open country are at least usually better qualified and more strongly inclined to become professional officers. This difference between the urban and the rural propertied is balanced only where the increasing possibility of mechanized warfare requires the leaders to qualify as "technicians."

The bureaucratization of organized warfare may be carried through in the form of private capitalist enterprise, just like any other business. Indeed, the procurement of armies and their administration by private capitalists has been the rule in mercenary armies, especially those of the Occident up to the turn of the eighteenth century. During the Thirty Years' War, in Brandenburg the soldier was still the predominant owner of the material implements of his business. He owned his weapons, horses, and dress, although the state, in the role, as it were, of the merchant of the "putting-out system," did supply him to some extent. Later on, in the standing army of Prussia, the chief of the company owned the material means of warfare, and only since the peace of Tilsit has the concentration of the means of warfare in the hands of the state definitely come about. Only with this concentration was the introduction of uniforms generally carried through. Before then, the introduction of uniforms had been left to a great extent to the arbitrary discretion of the regimental officer, with the exception of individual categories of troops to whom the king had "bestowed" certain uniforms, first, in 1620, to the royal bodyguard, then, under Frederick II, repeatedly.

Such terms as "regiment" and "battalion" usually had quite different meanings in the eighteenth century from the meanings they have today. Only the battalion was a tactical unit (today both are); the "regiment" was then a managerial unit of an economic organization established by the colonel's position as an "entrepreneur." "Official" maritime ventures (like the Genoese *maonae*) and army procurement belong to private capitalism's first giant enterprises of far-going bureaucratic character. In this respect, the "nationalization" of these enterprises by the state has its modern parallel in the nationalization of the railroads, which have been controlled by the state from their beginnings.

In the same way as with army organizations, the bureaucratization of administration goes hand in hand with the concentration of the means of organization in other spheres. The old administration by satraps and regents, as well as administration by farmers of office, purchasers of office, and, most of all, administration by feudal vassals, decentralize the material means of administration. The local demand of the province and the cost of the army and of subaltern officials are regularly paid for in advance from local income, and only the surplus reaches the central treasure. The enfeoffed official administers entirely by payment out of his own pocket. The bureaucratic state, however, puts its whole administrative expense on the budget and equips the lower authorities with the current means of expenditure, the use of which the state regulates and controls. This has the same meaning for the "economics" of the administration as for the large centralized capitalist enterprise.

In the field of scientific research and instruction, the bureaucratization of the always existing research institutes of the universities is a function of the increasing demand for material means of management. Liebig's laboratory at Giessen University was the first example of big enterprise in this field. Through the concentration of such means in the hands of the privileged head of the institute, the mass of researchers and docents are separated from their "means of production," in the same way as capitalist enterprise has separated the workers from theirs.

In spite of its indubitable technical superiority, bureaucracy has everywhere been a relatively late development. A number of obstacles have contributed to this, and only under certain social and political conditions have they definitely receded into the background. . . .

The Permanent Character of the Bureaucratic Machine

Once it is fully established, bureaucracy is among those social structures which are the hardest to destroy. Bureaucracy is the means of carrying "community action" over into rationally ordered "societal action." Therefore, as an instrument for "societalizing" relations of power, bureaucracy has been and is a power instrument of the first order—for the one who controls the bureaucratic apparatus.

Under otherwise equal conditions, a "societal action," which is methodically ordered and led, is superior to every resistance of "mass" or even of "communal action." And where the bureaucratization of administration has been completely carried through, a form of power relation is established that is practically unshatterable.

The individual bureaucrat cannot squirm out of the apparatus in which he is harnessed. In contrast to the honorific or avocational "notable," the professional bureaucrat is chained to his activity by his entire material and ideal existence. In the great majority of cases, he is only a single cog in a ever-moving mechanism which prescribes to him an essentially fixed route of march. The official is entrusted with specialized tasks and normally the mechanism cannot be put into motion or arrested by him, but only from the very top. The individual bureaucrat is thus forged to the community of all the functionaries who are integrated into the mechanism. They have a common interest in seeing that the mechanism continues its functions and that the societally exercised authority carries on.

The ruled, for their part, cannot dispense with or replace the bureaucratic apparatus of authority once it exists. For this bureaucracy rests upon expert training, a functional specialization of work, and an attitude set for habitual and virtuoso-like mastery of single yet methodically integrated functions. If the official stops working, or if his work is forcefully interrupted, chaos results, and it is difficult to improvise replacements from among the governed who are fit to master such chaos. This holds for public administration as well as for private economic management. More and more the material fate of the masses depends upon the steady and correct functioning of the increasingly bureaucratic organizations of private capitalism. The idea of eliminating these organizations becomes more and more utopian.

The discipline of officialdom refers to the attitude-set of the official for precise obedience within his *habitual* activity, in public as well as in private organizations. This discipline increasingly becomes the basis of all order, however great the practical importance of administration on the basis of the filed documents may be. The naive idea of Bakuninism of destroying the basis of "acquired rights" and "domination" by destroying public documents overlooks the settled orientation of *man* for keeping to the habitual rules and regulations that continue to exist independently of the documents. Every reorganization of beaten or dissolved troops, as well as the restoration of administrative orders destroyed by revolt, panic, or other catastrophes, is realized by appealing to the trained orientation of obedient compliance to such orders. Such compliance has been conditioned into the officials, on the one hand, and, on the other hand, into the governed. If such an appeal is successful it brings, as it were, the disturbed mechanism into gear again.

The objective indispensability of the once-existing apparatus, with its peculiar, "impersonal" character, means that the mechanism—in contrast to feudal orders based upon personal piety—is easily made to work for anybody who knows how to gain control over it. A rationally ordered system of officials continues to function smoothly after the enemy has occupied the area; he merely needs to change the top officials. This body of officials continues to operate because it is to the vital interest of everyone concerned, including above all the enemy.

During the course of his long years in power, Bismarck brought his ministerial colleagues into unconditional bureaucratic dependence by eliminating all independent statesmen. Upon his retirement, he saw to his surprise that they continued to manage their offices unconcerned and undismayed, as if he had not been the master mind and creator of these creatures, but rather as if some single figure had been exchanged for some other figure in the bureaucratic machine. With all the changes of masters in France since the time of the First Empire, the power machine has remained essentially the same. Such a machine makes "revolution," in the sense of the forceful creation of entirely new formations of authority, technically more and more impossible, especially when the apparatus controls the modern means of communication (telegraph, et cetera) and also by virtue of its internal rationalized structure. In classic fashion, France has demonstrated how this process has substituted *coups d'état* for "revolutions": all successful transformations in France have amounted to *coups d'état*. . . .

The Power Position of Bureaucracy

Everywhere the modern state is undergoing bureaucratization. But whether the *power* of bureaucracy within the polity is universally increasing must here remain an open question.

The fact that bureaucratic organization is technically the most highly developed means of power in the hands of the man who controls it does not determine the weight that bureaucracy as such is capable of having in a particular social structure. The ever-increasing "indispensability" of the officialdom, swollen to millions, is no more decisive for this question than is the view of some representatives of the proletarian movement that the economic indispensability of the proletarians is decisive for the measure of their social and political power position. If "indispensability" were decisive, then where slave labor prevailed and where freemen usually abhor work as a dishonor, the "indispensable" slaves ought to have held the positions of power, for they were at least as indispensable as officials and proletarians are today. Whether the power of bureaucracy as such increases cannot be decided *a priori* from such reasons. The drawing in of economic interest groups or other non-official experts, or the drawing in of nonexpert lay representatives, the establishment of local, inter-local, or central parliamentary or other representative bodies, or of occupational associations—these *seem* to run directly against the bureaucratic tendency. How far this appearance is the truth must be discussed in another chapter rather than in this purely formal and typological discussion. In general, only the following can be said here:

Under normal conditions, the power position of a fully developed bureaucracy is always overtowering. The "political master" finds himself in the position of the "dilettante" who stands opposite the "expert," facing the trained official who stands within the management of administration. This holds whether the "master" whom the bureaucracy serves is a "people," equipped with the weapons of "legislative initiative," the "referendum," and the right to remove officials, or a parliament, elected on a more aristocratic or more "democratic" basis and equipped with the right to vote a lack of confidence, or with the actual authority to vote it. It holds whether the master is an aristocratic, collegiate body, legally or actually based on self-recruitment, or whether he is a popularly elected president, a hereditary and "absolute" or a "constitutional" monarch.

Every bureaucracy seeks to increase the superiority of the professionally informed by keeping their knowledge and intentions secret. Bureaucratic administration always tends to be an administration of "secret sessions": In so far as it can, it hides its knowledge and action from criticism. Prussian church authorities now threaten to use disciplinary measures against pastors who make reprimands or other admonitory measures in any way accessible to third parties. They do this because the pastor, in making such criticism available, is "guilty" of facilitating a possible criticism of the church authorities. The treasury officials of the Persian shah have made a secret doctrine of their budgetary art and even use secret script. The official statistics of Prussia, in general, make public only what cannot do any harm to the intentions of the power-wielding bureaucracy. The tendency toward secrecy in certain administrative fields follows their material nature: Everywhere that the power interests of the domination structure toward *the outside* are at stake, whether it is an economic competitor of a private enterprise, or a foreign, potentially hostile polity, we find secrecy. If it is to be successful, the management of diplomacy can only be publicly controlled to a very limited extent. The military administration must insist on the concealment of its most important measures; with the increasing significance of purely technical aspects, this is all the more the case. Political parties do not proceed differently, in spite of all the ostensible publicity of Catholic congresses and party conventions. With the increasing bureaucratization of party organizations, this secrecy will prevail even more. Commercial policy, in Germany for instance, brings about a concealment of production statistics. Every fighting posture of a social structure toward the outside tends to buttress the position of the group in power.

The pure interest of the bureaucracy in power, however, is efficacious far beyond those areas where purely functional interests make for secrecy. The concept of the "official secret" is the specific invention of bureaucracy, and nothing is so fanatically defended by the bureaucracy as this attitude, which cannot be substantially justified beyond these specifically qualified areas. In facing a parliament, the bureaucracy, out of a sure power instinct, fights every attempt of the parliament to gain knowledge by means of its own experts or from interest groups. The so-called right of parliamentary investigation is one of the means by which parliament seeks such knowledge. Bureaucracy naturally welcomes a poorly informed and hence a powerless parliament—at least in so far as ignorance somehow agrees with the bureaucracy's interests. . . .

Notes

1. Frederick II of Prussia.
2. Cf. *Wirtschaft und Gesellschaft* (Tübingen, 1922), pp. 73 ff. and part II [German editor's note].
3. *Ministerialen*.
4. Written before 1914 [German editor's note].
5. Here we cannot discuss in detail how the bureaucratic apparatus may, and actually does, produce definite obstacles to the discharge of business in a manner suitable for the single case.
6. *Erwerbende Schichten*.

2
The Spirit of Bureaucracy *and* Beyond Bureaucracy: The Paris Commune
Karl Marx

The Spirit of Bureaucracy

The "state formalism" of bureaucracy is the "state as formalism," and Hegel has described it as such formalism. Since this "state formalism" constitutes itself as an actual power and becomes its own *material* content, it is obvious that "bureaucracy" is a web of *practical* illusions or the "illusion of the state." The spirit of bureaucracy is thoroughly Jesuitical and theological. The bureaucrats are the state's Jesuits and theologians. Bureaucracy is the priest's republic.

Since bureaucracy is the "state as formalism" in its *essence*, it is also the state as formalism in its *purpose*. For bureaucracy the actual purpose of the state therefore appears as a purpose *against* the state. The spirit of bureaucracy is the "formal state spirit." Bureaucracy makes the "formal state spirit" or the *actual* spiritlessness the categorical imperative. Bureaucracy considers itself the ultimate finite purpose of the state. Since bureaucracy converts its "formal" purposes into its contents, it everywhere comes in conflict with "real" purposes. It is, therefore, compelled to pass off what is formal for the content and the content for what is formal. The purposes of the state are changed into purposes of bureaus and vice versa. Bureaucracy is a circle no one can leave. Its hierarchy is a *hierarchy of information*. The top entrusts the lower circles with an insight into details, while the lower circles entrust the top with an insight into what is universal, and thus they mutually deceive each other.

Bureaucracy is the imaginary state beside the real state, the spiritualism of the state. Hence everything has a double meaning, a real and a bureaucratic meaning, just as knowledge and also the will are something double, real, and bureaucratic. What is real is dealt with in its

---

"The Spirit of Bureaucracy" is reprinted from *Writings of the Young Marx on Philosophy and Society*, edited by Loyd Easton and Kurt Guddat (Garden City: Doubleday, 1967), 185–187, with permission from the editors.

"Beyond Bureaucracy: The Paris Commune" is reprinted from *Writings on the Paris Commune*, by Karl Marx and Friedrich Engels, edited by Hal Draper (New York: Monthly Review Press, 1971), 69–78, by permission of the publisher.

bureaucratic nature, in its otherworldly spiritual essence. Bureaucracy possesses the state's essence, the spiritual essence of society, as its *private property*. The universal spirit of bureaucracy is the *secret*, the mystery sustained within bureaucracy itself by hierarchy and maintained on the outside as a closed corporation. The open spirit and sentiment of patriotism, hence, appear to bureaucracy as a *betrayal* of this mystery. So *authority* is the principle of its knowledge, and the deification of authority is its *sentiment*. But within bureaucracy *spiritualism* becomes a *crass materialism*, the materialism of passive obedience, of faith in authority, of the *mechanism* of fixedly formal activity, fixed principles, views, and traditions. For the individual bureaucrat the state's purpose becomes his private purpose of *hunting for higher positions* and *making a career* for himself. In one respect he views actual life as something *material*, for *the spirit of this life has its separate existence* in bureaucracy. Bureaucracy, therefore, must aim to make life as material as possible. In another respect, life insofar as it becomes the object of bureaucratic treatment is material for him, for his spirit is not his own, his purpose lies outside, his particular existence is the existence of the bureau. The state then only exists in various fixed bureau-spirits whose connection is subordination and passive obedience. *Actual* knowledge seems lacking in content, just as actual life seems dead, since this imaginary knowledge and this imaginary life pass for real. So the bureaucrat must treat the actual state Jesuitically, no matter whether this Jesuitism is conscious or unconscious. It is necessary, though, that the Jesuitism, aware of its antithetical position, then achieves self-consciousness and becomes intentional.

While the bureaucracy is in one sense this crass materialism, its crass spiritualism is shown in its trying *to do everything*, that is, in its making *will* the causa prima, because it is merely *active* particular existence, derives its content externally, and thus can demonstrate its existence only through forming and limiting this content. For the bureaucrat the world is a mere object of his concern. . . .

Beyond Bureaucracy: The Paris Commune

On the dawn of the 18th of March, Paris arose to the thunderburst of "Vive la Commune!" What is the Commune, that sphinx so tantalising to the bourgeois mind?

> "The proletarians of Paris," said the Central Committee in its manifesto of the 18th March, "amidst the failures and treasons of the ruling classes, have understood that the hour has struck for them to save the situation by taking into their own hands the direction of public affairs. . . . They have understood that it is their imperious duty and their absolute right to render themselves masters of their own destinies, by seizing upon the governmental power."

But the working class cannot simply lay hold of the ready-made State machinery, and wield it for its own purposes.

The centralised State power, with its ubiquitous organs of standing army, police, bureaucracy, clergy, and judicature—organs wrought after the plan of a systematic and hierarchical division of labour—originates from the days of absolute monarchy, serving nascent middle-class society as a mighty weapon in its struggles against feudalism. Still, its development remained clogged by all manner of mediaeval rubbish, seignorial rights, local privileges, municipal and guild monopolies and provincial constitutions. The gigantic broom of the French Revolution of the eighteenth century swept away all these relics of bygone times, thus clearing simultaneously the social soil of its last hindrances to the superstructure of the modern State edifice raised under the First empire, itself the offspring of the coalition wars of old semi-feudal Europe against modern France. During the subsequent *régimes* the Government, placed under parliamentary control—that is, under the direct control of the propertied classes—became not only a hotbed of huge national debts and crushing taxes; with its irresistible allurements of place, pelf, and patronage, it became not only the bone of contention between the rival factions and adventurers of the ruling classes; but its political character changed simultaneously with the economic changes of society. At the same pace at which the progress of modern industry developed, widened, intensified the class antagonism between capital and labour, the State power assumed more and more the character of the national power of capital over labour, of a public force organised for social enslavement, of an engine of class despotism. After every revolution marking a progressive phase in the class struggle, the purely repressive character of the State power stands out in bolder and bolder relief. The Revolution of 1830, resulting in the transfer of Government from the landlords to the capitalists, transferred it from the more remote to the more direct antagonists of the working men. The bourgeois Republicans, who, in the name of the Revolution of February, took the State power, used it for the June massacres, in order to convince the working class that "social" republic meant the Republic ensuring their social subjection, and in order to convince the royalist bulk of the bourgeois and landlord class that they might safely leave the cares and emoluments of Government to the bourgeois "Republicans." However, after their one heroic exploit of June, the bourgeois Republicans had, from the front, to fall back to the rear of the "Party of Order"—a combination formed by all the rival fractions and factions of the appropriating class in their now openly declared antagonism to the producing classes. The proper form of their joint-stock Government was the *Parliamentary Republic*, with Louis Bonaparte for its President. Theirs was a *régime* of avowed class terrorism and deliberate insult toward the "vile multitude." If the Parliamentary Republic, as M. Thiers said, "divided them (the different fractions of the ruling class) least," it opened an abyss between that class and the whole body of society outside their spare ranks. The restraints by which their own divisions had under former *régimes* still checked the State power, were removed by their union; and in view of the threatening upheaval of the proletariat, they now used that State power mercilessly and ostentatiously as the national war-engine of capital against labour. In their uninterrupted crusade against the producing masses they were, however, bound not only to invest the executive with continually increased powers of repression, but at the same time to divest their own parliamentary stronghold—the National Assembly—one by one, of all its own means of defence against the Executive. The Executive, in the person of Louis Bonaparte, turned them out. The natural offspring of the "Party-of-Order" Republic was the Second Empire.

The empire, with the *coup d'état* for its certificate of birth, universal suffrage for its sanction, and the sword for its sceptre, professed to rest upon the peasantry, the large mass of producers not directly involved in the struggle of capital and labour. It professed to save the working class by breaking down Parliamentarism, and, with it, the undisguised subserviency of Government to the propertied classes. It professed to save the propertied classes by upholding their economic supremacy over the working class; and, finally, it professed to unite all classes by reviving for all the chimera of national glory. In reality, it was the only form of government possible at a time when the bourgeoisie had already lost, and the working class had not yet acquired, the faculty of ruling the nation. It was acclaimed throughout the world as the saviour of society. Under its sway, bourgeois society, freed from political cares, attained a development unexpected even by itself. Its industry and commerce expanded to colossal dimensions; financial swindling celebrated cosmopolitan orgies; the misery of the masses was set off by a shameless display of gorgeous, meretricious and debased luxury. The State power, apparently soaring high above society, was at the same time itself the greatest scandal of that society and the very hotbed of all its corruptions. Its own rottenness, and the rottenness of the society it had saved, were laid bare by the bayonet of Prussia, herself eagerly bent upon transferring the supreme seat of that *régime* from Paris to Berlin. Imperialism, is, at the same time, the most prostitute and the ultimate form of the State power which nascent middle-class society had commenced to elaborate as a means of its own emancipation from feudalism, and which full-grown bourgeois society had finally transformed into a means for the enslavement of labour by capital.

The direct antithesis to the empire was the Commune. The cry of "social republic," with which the Revolution of February was ushered in by the Paris proletariat, did but express a vague aspiration after a Republic that was not only to supersede the monarchical form of class-rule, but class-rule itself. The Commune was the positive form of that Republic.

Paris, the central seat of the old governmental power, and, at the same time, the social stronghold of the French working class, had risen in arms against the attempt of Thiers and the Rurals to restore and perpetuate that old governmental power bequeathed to them by the empire. Paris could resist only because, in consequence of the siege, it had got rid of the army, and replaced it by a National Guard, the bulk of which consisted of working men. This fact was now to be transformed into an institution. The first decree of the Commune, therefore, was the suppression of the standing army, and the substitution for it of the armed people.

The Commune was formed of the municipal councillors, chosen by universal suffrage in the various wards of the town, responsible and revocable at short terms. The majority of its members were naturally working men, or acknowledged representatives of the working class. The Commune was to be a working, not a parliamentary, body, executive and legislative at the same time. Instead of continuing to be the agent of the Central Government, the police was at once stripped of its political attributes, and turned into the responsible and at all times revocable agent of the Commune. So were the officials of all other branches of the Administration. From the members of the Commune downwards, the public service had to be done at *workmen's wages*. The vested interests and the representation allowances of the high dignitaries of State disappeared along with the high dignitaries themselves. Public functions ceased to be the private property of the tools of the Central Government. Not only municipal administration, but the whole initiative hitherto exercised by the State was laid into the hands of the Commune.

Having once got rid of the standing army and the police, the physical force elements of the old Government, the Commune was anxious to break the spiritual force of repression, the "parson-power," by the disestablishment and disendowment of all churches as proprietary bodies. The priests were sent back to the recesses of private life, there to feed upon the alms of the faithful in imitation of their predecessors, the Apostles. The whole of the educational institutions were opened to the people gratuitously, and at the same time cleared of all interference of Church and State. Thus, not only was education made accessible to all, but science itself freed from the fetters which class prejudice and governmental force had imposed upon it.

The judicial functionaries were to be divested of that sham independence which had but served to mask their abject subserviency to all succeeding governments to which, in turn, they had taken, and broken, the oaths of allegiance. Like the rest of public servants, magistrates and judges were to be elective, responsible, and revocable.

The Paris Commune was, of course, to serve as a model to all the great industrial centres of France. The communal *régime* once established in Paris and the secondary centres, the old centralised Government would in the provinces, too, have to give way to the self-government of the producers. In a rough sketch of national organisation which the Commune had no time to develop, it states clearly that the Commune was to be the political form of even the smallest country hamlet, and that in the rural districts the standing army was to be replaced by a national militia, with an extremely short term of service. The rural communes of every district were to administer their common affairs by an assembly of delegates in the central town, and these district assemblies were again to send deputies to the National Delegation in Paris, each delegate to be at any time revocable and bound by the *mandat impératif* (formal instructions) of his constituents. The few but important functions which still would remain for a central government were not to be suppressed, as has been intentionally mis-stated, but were to be discharged by Communal, and therefore strictly responsible agents. The unity of the nation was not be broken, but, on the contrary, to be organised by the Communal Constitution and to become a reality by the destruction of the State power which claimed to be the embodiment of that unity independent of, and superior to, the nation itself, from which it was but a parasitic excrescence. While the merely repressive organs of the old governmental power were to be amputated, its legitimate functions were to be wrested from an authority usurping pre-eminence over society itself, and restored to the responsible agents of society. Instead of deciding once in three or six years which member of the ruling class was to misrepresent the people in Parliament, universal suffrage was to serve the people, constituted in Communes, as individual suffrage serves every other employer in the search for the workmen and managers in his business. And it is well known that companies, like individuals, in matters of real business generally know how to put the right man in the right place, and, if they for once make a mistake, to redress it promptly. On the other hand, nothing could be more foreign to the spirit of the Commune than to supersede universal suffrage by hierarchic investiture.

It is generally the fate of completely new historical creations to be mistaken for the counterpart of older and even defunct forms of social life, to which they may bear a certain likeness. Thus, this new Commune, which breaks the modern State power, has been mistaken for a reproduction of the mediaeval Communes, which first preceded, and afterwards became the substratum of, that very State power. The Communal Constitution has been mistaken for an attempt to break up into a federation of small States, as dreamt of by Montesquieu and the Girondins, that unity of great nations which, if originally brought about by political force, has now become a powerful coefficient of social production. The antagonism of the Commune against the State power has been mistaken for an exaggerated form of the ancient struggle against over-centralisation. Peculiar historical circumstances may have prevented the classical development, as in France, of the bourgeois form of government, and may have allowed, as in England, to complete the great central State organs by corrupt vestries, jobbing councillors, and ferocious poor-law guardians in the towns, and virtually hereditary magistrates in the counties. The Communal Constitution would have restored to the social body all the forces hitherto absorbed by the State parasite feeding upon, and clogging the free movement of, society. By this one act it would have initiated the regeneration of France. The provincial French middle class saw in the Commune an attempt to restore the sway their order had held over the country under Louis Philippe, and which, under Louis Napoleon, was supplanted by the pretended rule of the country over the towns. In reality, the Communal Constitution brought the rural producers under the intellectual lead of the central towns of their districts, and these secured to them, in the working men, the natural trustees of their interests. The very existence of the Commune involved, as a matter of course, local municipal liberty, but no longer as a check upon the, now superseded, State power. It could only enter into the head of a Bismarck, who, when not engaged on his intrigues of blood and iron, always likes to resume his old trade, so befitting his mental calibre, of contributor to *Kladderadatsch* (the Berlin *Punch*), it could only enter into such a head, to ascribe to the Paris Commune aspirations after that caricature of the old French municipal organisation of 1791, the Prussian municipal constitution which degrades the town governments to mere secondary wheels in the police-machinery of the Prussian State. The Commune made that catchword of bourgeois revolutions, cheap government, a reality, by destroying the two greatest sources of expenditure—the standing army and State functionarism. Its very existence presupposed the non-existence of monarchy, which, in Europe at least, is the normal incumbrance and indispensable cloak of class-rule. It supplied the Republic with the basis of really democratic institutions. But neither cheap Government nor the "true Republic" was its ultimate aim; they were its mere concomitants.

The multiplicity of interpretations to which the Commune has been subjected, and the multiplicity of interests which construed it in their favour, show that it was a thoroughly expansive political form, while all previous forms of government had been emphatically repressive. Its true secret was this. It was essentially a working-class government, the produce of the struggle of the producing against the appropriating class, the political form at last discovered under which to work out the economic emancipation of labour. . . .

Except on the last condition, the Communal Constitution would have been an impossibility and a delusion. The political rule of the producer cannot coexist with the perpetuation of his social slavery. The Commune was therefore to serve as a lever for uprooting the economical foundations upon which rests the existence of classes, and therefore of class-rule. With labour emancipated, every man becomes a working man, and productive labour ceases to be a class attribute.

It is a strange fact. In spite of all the tall talk and all the immense literature, for the last sixty years, about emancipation of Labour, no sooner do the working men anywhere take the subject into their own hands with a will, than uprises at once all the apologetic phraseology of the mouthpieces of present society with its two poles of Capital and Wages Slavery (the landlord now is but the sleeping partner of the capitalist), as if capitalist society was still in its purest state of virgin innocence, with its antagonisms still undeveloped, with its delusions still unexploded, with its prostitute realities not yet laid bare. The Commune, they exclaim, intends to abolish property, the basis of all civilisation! Yes, gentlemen, the Commune intended to abolish that class-property which makes the labour of the many the wealth of the few. It aimed at the expropriation of the expropriators. It wanted to make individual property a truth by transforming the means of production, land and capital, now chiefly the means of enslaving and exploiting labour, into mere instruments of free and associated labour.—But this is Communism, "impossible" Communism! Why, those members of the ruling classes who are intelligent enough to perceive the impossibility of continuing the present system—and they are many—have become the obtrusive and full-mouthed apostles of co-operative production. If co-operative production is not to remain a sham and a snare; if it is to supersede the Capitalist system; if united co-operative societies are to regulate national production upon a common plan, thus taking it under their own control, and putting an end to the constant anarchy and periodical convulsions which are the fatality of Capitalist production—what else, gentlemen, would it be but Communism, "possible" Communism?

The working class did not expect miracles from the Commune. They have no ready-made utopias to introduce *par décret du peuple*. They know that in order to work out their own emancipation, and along with it that higher form to which present society is irresistibly tending by its own economical agencies, they will have to pass through long struggles, through a series of historic processes, transforming circumstances and men. They have no ideals to realise, but to set free the elements of the new society with which old collapsing bourgeois society itself is pregnant. In the full consciousness of their historic mission, and with the heroic resolve to act up to it, the working class can afford to smile at the coarse invective of the gentlemen's gentlemen with the pen and inkhorn, and at the didactic patronage of well-wishing bourgeois-doctrinaires, pouring forth their ignorant platitudes and sectarian crotchets in the oracular tone of scientific infallibility.

When the Paris Commune took the management of the revolution in its own hands; when plain working men for the first time dared to infringe upon the Governmental privilege of their "natural superiors," and, under circumstances of unexampled difficulty, performed their work modestly, conscientiously, and efficiently—performed it at salaries the highest of which barely amounted to one-fifth of what, according to high scientific authority, is the minimum required for a secretary to a certain metropolitan school board—the old world writhed in convulsions of rage at the sight of the Red Flag, the symbol of the Republic of Labour, floating over the Hôtel de Ville.

3
Oligarchy

Robert Michels

Democracy is inconceivable without organization. A few words will suffice to demonstrate this proposition.

A class which unfurls in the face of society the banner of certain definite claims, and which aspires to the realization of a complex of ideal aims deriving from the economic functions which that class fulfills, needs an organization. Be the claims economic or be they political, organization appears the only means for the creation of a collective will. Organization, based as it is upon the principle of least effort, that is to say, upon the greatest possible economy of energy, is the weapon of the weak in their struggle with the strong.

The chances of success in any struggle will depend upon the degree to which this struggle is carried out upon a basis of solidarity between individuals whose interests are identical. In objecting, therefore, to the theories of the individualist anarchists that nothing could please the employers better than the dispersion and disaggregation of the forces of the workers, the socialists, the most fanatical of all the partisans of the idea of organization, enunciate an argument which harmonizes well with the results of scientific study of the nature of parties.

We live in a time in which the idea of cooperation has become so firmly established that even millionaires perceive the necessity of common action. It is easy to understand, then, that organization has become a vital principle of the working class, for in default of it their success is *a priori*

Reprinted from *Political Parties*, by Robert Michels (New York: Free Press, 1964), 61–62, 65–73, 167–168, 170–173, 187, 354, 364–371, by permission of Macmillan Publishing Co. Copyright 1962 by The Crowell-Collier Publishing Co.

impossible. The refusal of the worker to participate in the collective life of his class cannot fail to entail disastrous consequences. In respect of culture and of economic, physical, and physiological conditions, the proletarian is the weakest element of our society. In fact, the isolated member of the working classes is defenseless in the hands of those who are economically stronger. It is only by combination to form a structural aggregate that the proletarians can acquire the faculty of political resistance and attain to a social dignity. The importance and the influence of the working class are directly proportional to its numerical strength. But for the representation of that numerical strength organization and coordination are indispensable. The principle of organization is an absolutely essential condition for the political struggle of the masses.

Yet this politically necessary principle of organization, while it overcomes that disorganization of forces which would be favorable to the adversary, brings other dangers in its train. We escape Scylla only to dash ourselves on Charybdis. Organization is, in fact, the source from which the conservative currents flow over the plain of democracy, occasioning their disastrous floods and rendering the plain unrecognizable. . . .

It is obvious that such a gigantic number of persons belonging to a unitary organization cannot do any practical work upon a system of direct discussion. The regular holding of deliberative assemblies of a thousand members encounters the gravest difficulties in respect of room and distance; while from the topographical point of view such an assembly would become altogether impossible if the members numbered ten thousand. Even if we imagined the means of communication to become much better than those which now exist, how would it be possible to assemble such a multitude in a given place, at a stated time, and with the frequency demanded by the exigencies of party life? In addition must be considered the physiological impossibility even for the most powerful orator of making himself heard by a crowd of ten thousand persons.[1] There are, however, other reasons of a technical and administrative character which render impossible the direct self-government of large groups. If Peter wrongs Paul, it is out of the question that all the other citizens should hasten to the spot to undertake a personal examination of the matter in dispute, and to take the part of Paul against Peter.[2] By parity of reasoning, in the modern democratic party, it is impossible for the collectivity to undertake the direct settlement of all the controversies that may arise.

Hence the need for delegation, for the system in which delegates represent the mass and carry out its will. Even in groups sincerely animated with the democratic spirit, current business, the preparation and the carrying out of the most important actions, is necessarily left in the hands of individuals. It is well known that the impossibility for the people to exercise a legislative power directly in popular assemblies led the democratic idealists of Spain to demand, as the least of evils, a system of popular representation and a parliamentary state.[3]

Originally the chief is merely the servant of the mass. The organization is based upon the absolute equality of all its members. Equality is here understood in its most general sense, as an equality of like men. In many countries, as in idealist Italy (and in certain regions in Germany where the socialist movement is still in its infancy), this equality is manifested, among other ways, by the mutual use of the familiar "thou," which is employed by the most poorly paid wage-laborer in addressing the most distinguished intellectual. This generic conception of equality is, however, gradually replaced by the idea of equality among comrades belonging to the same organization, all of whose members enjoy the same rights. The democratic principle aims at guaranteeing to all an equal influence and an equal participation in the regulation of the common interests. All are electors, and all are eligible for office. The fundamental postulate of the *Déclaration des Droits de l'Homme* finds here its theoretical application. All the offices are filled by election. The officials, executive organs of the general will, play a merely subordinate part, are always dependent upon the collectivity, and can be deprived of their office at any moment. The mass of the party is omnipotent.

At the outset, the attempt is made to depart as little as possible from pure democracy by subordinating the delegates altogether to the will of the mass, by tieing them hand and foot. In the early days of the movement of the Italian agricultural workers, the chief of the league required a majority of four-fifths of the votes to secure election. When disputes arose with the employers about wages, the representatives of the organization, before undertaking any negotiations, had to be furnished with a written authority, authorized by the signature of every member of the corporation. All the accounts of the body were open to the examination of the members, at any time. There were two reasons for this. First of all, the desire was to avoid the spread of mistrust through the mass, "this poison which gradually destroys even the strongest organism." In the second place, this usage allowed each one of the members to learn bookkeeping, and to acquire such a general knowledge of the working of the corporation as to enable him at any time to take over its leadership.[4] It is obvious that democracy in this sense is applicable only on a very small scale. In the infancy of the English labor movement, in many of the trade unions, the delegates were either appointed in rotation from among all the members, or were chosen by lot.[5] Gradually, however, the delegates' duties became more complicated; some individual ability becomes essential, a certain oratorical gift, and a considerable amount of objective knowledge. It thus becomes impossible to trust to blind chance, to the fortune of alphabetic succession, or to the order of priority, in the choice of a delegation whose members must possess certain peculiar personal aptitudes if they are to discharge their mission to the general advantage.

Such were the methods which prevailed in the early days of the labor movement to enable the masses to participate in party and trade-union administration. Today they are falling into disuse, and in the development of the modern political aggregate there is a tendency to shorten and stereotype the process which transforms the led into a leader—a process which has hitherto developed by the natural course of events. Here and there voices make themselves heard demanding a sort of official consecration for the leaders, insisting that it is necessary to constitute a class of professional politicians, of approved and registered experts in political life. Ferdinand Tönnies advocates that the party should institute regular examinations for the nomination of socialist parliamentary candidates, and for the appointment of party secretaries.[6] Heinrich Herkner goes even farther. He contends that the great trade unions cannot long maintain their existence if they persist in entrusting the management of their affairs to persons drawn from the rank and file, who have risen to command stage by stage solely in consequence of practical aptitudes acquired in the service of the organization. He refers, in this connection, to the unions that are controlled by the employers, whose officials are for the most part university men. He foresees that in the near future all the labor organizations will be forced to abandon proletarian exclusiveness, and in the choice of their officials to give the preference to persons of an education that is superior alike in economic, legal, technical, and commercial respects.[7]

Even today, the candidates for the secretaryship of a trade union are subject to examination as to their knowledge of legal matters and their capacity as letter-writers. The socialist organizations engaged in political action also directly undertake the training of their own officials. Everywhere there are coming into existence "nurseries" for the rapid supply of officials possessing a certain amount of "scientific culture."

. . . It is undeniable that all these educational institutions for the officials of the party and of the labor organizations tend, above all, towards the artificial creation of an *élite* of the working class, of a caste of cadets composed of persons who aspire to the command of the proletarian rank and file. Without wishing it, there is thus effected a continuous enlargement of the gulf which divides the leaders from the masses.

The technical specialization that inevitably results from all extensive organization renders necessary what is called expert leadership. Consequently the power of determination comes to be considered one of the specific attributes of leadership, and is gradually withdrawn from the masses to be concentrated in the hands of the leaders alone. Thus the leaders, who were at first no more than the executive organs of the collective will, soon emancipate themselves from the mass and become independent of its control.

Organization implies the tendency to oligarchy. In every organization, whether it be a political party, a professional union, or any other association of the kind, the aristocratic tendency manifests itself very clearly. The mechanism of the organization, while conferring a solidity of structure, induces serious changes in the organized mass, completely inverting the respective position of the leaders and the led. As a result of organization, every party or professional union becomes divided into a minority of directors and a majority of directed.

It has been remarked that in the lower stages of civilization tyranny is dominant. Democracy cannot come into existence until there is attained a subsequent and more highly developed stage of social life. Freedoms and privileges, and among these latter the privilege of taking part in the direction of public affairs, are at first restricted to the few. Recent times have been characterized by the gradual extension of these privileges to a widening circle. This is what we know as the era of democracy. But if we pass from the sphere of the state to the sphere of party, we may observe that as democracy continues to develop, a backwash sets in. With the advance of organization, democracy tends to decline. Democratic evolution has a parabolic course. At the present time, at any rate as far as party life is concerned, democracy is in the descending phase. It may be enunciated as a general rule that the increase in the power of the leaders is directly proportional with the extension of the organization. In the various parties and labor organizations of different countries the influence of the leaders is mainly determined (apart from racial and individual grounds) by the varying development of organization. Where organization is stronger, we find that there is a lesser degree of applied democracy.

Every solidly constructed organization, whether it be a democratic state, a political party, or a league of proletarians for the resistance of economic oppression, presents a soil eminently favorable for the differentiation of organs and of functions. The more extended and the more ramified the official apparatus of the organization, the greater the number of its members, the fuller its treasury, and the more widely circulated its press, the less efficient becomes the direct control exercised by the rank and file, and the more is this control replaced by the increasing power of committees. Into all parties there insinuates itself that indirect electoral system which in public life the democratic parties fight against with all possible vigor. Yet in party life the influence of this system must be more disastrous than in the far more extensive life of the state. Even in the party congresses, which represent the party-life seven times sifted, we find that it becomes more and more general to refer all important questions to committees which debate *in camera*.

As organization develops, not only do the tasks of the administration become more difficult and more complicated, but, further, its duties become enlarged and specialized to such a degree that it is no longer possible to take them all in at a single glance. In a rapidly progressive movement, it is not only the growth in the number of duties, but also the higher quality of these, which imposes a more extensive differentiation of function. Nominally, and according to the letter of the rules, all the acts of the leaders are subject to the ever vigilant criticism of the rank and file.

In theory the leader is merely an employee bound by the instruction he receives. He has to carry out the orders of the mass, of which he is no more than the executive organ. But in actual fact, as the organization increases in size, this control becomes purely fictitious. The members have to give up the idea of themselves conducting or even supervising the whole administration, and are compelled to hand these tasks over to trustworthy persons specially nominated for the purpose, to salaried officials. The rank and file must content themselves with summary reports, and with the appointment of occasional special committees of inquiry. Yet this does not derive from any special change in the rules of the organization. It is by very necessity that a simple employee gradually becomes a "leader," acquiring a freedom of action which he ought not to possess. The chief then becomes accustomed to dispatch important business on his own responsibility, and to decide various questions relating to the life of the party without any attempt to consult the rank and file. It is obvious that democratic control thus undergoes a progressive diminution, and is ultimately reduced to an infinitesimal minimum. In all the socialist parties there is a continual increase in the number of functions withdrawn from the electoral assemblies and transferred to the executive committees. In this way there is constructed a powerful and complicated edifice. The principle of division of labor coming more and more into operation, executive authority undergoes division and subdivision. There is thus constituted a rigorously defined and hierarchical bureaucracy. In the catechism of party duties, the strict observance of hierarchical rules becomes the first article. The hierarchy comes into existence as the outcome of technical conditions, and its constitution is an essential postulate of the regular functioning of the party machine.

It is indisputable that the oligarchical and bureaucratic tendency of party organization is a matter of technical and practical necessity. It is the inevitable product of the very principle of organization. Not even the most radical wing of the various socialist parties raises any objection to this retrogressive evolution, the contention being that democracy is only a form of organization and that where it ceases to be possible to harmonize democracy with organization, it is better to abandon the former than the latter. Organization, since it is the only means of attaining the ends of socialism, is considered to comprise within itself the revolutionary content of the party, and this essential content must never be sacrificed for the sake of form.

In all times, in all phases of development, in all branches of human activity, there have been leaders. It is true that certain socialists, above all the orthodox Marxists of Germany, seek to convince us that socialism knows nothing of "leaders," that the party has "employees" merely, being a democratic party, and the existence of leaders being incompatible with democracy. But a false assertion such as this cannot override a sociological law. Its only result is, in fact, to strengthen the rule of the leaders, for it serves to conceal from the mass a danger which really threatens democracy.

For technical and administrative reasons, no less than for tactical reasons, a strong organization needs an equally strong leadership. As long as an organization is loosely constructed and vague in its outlines, no professional leadership can arise. The anarchists, who have a horror of all fixed organization, have no regular leaders. In the early days of German socialism, the *Vertrauensmann* (homme de confiance) continued to exercise his ordinary occupation. If he received any pay for his work for the party, the remuneration was on an extremely modest scale, and was no more than a temporary grant. His function could never be regarded by him as a regular source of income. The employee of the organization was still a simple workmate, sharing the mode of life and the social condition of his fellows. Today he has been replaced for the most part by the professional politician, *Berzirksleiter* (U.S. ward-boss), etc. The more solid the structure of an organization becomes in the course of the evolution of the modern political party, the more marked becomes the tendency to replace the emergency leader by the professional leader. Every party organization which has attained a considerable degree of complication demands that there should be a certain number of persons who devote all their activities to the work of the party. The mass provides these by delegations, and the delegates, regularly appointed, become permanent representatives of the mass for the direction of its affairs.

For democracy, however, the first appearance of professional leadership marks the beginning of the end, and this, above all, on account of the logical impossibility of the "representative" system, whether in parliamentary life or in party delegation. . . .

Those who defend the arbitrary acts committed by the democracy, point out that the masses have at their disposal means whereby they can react against the violation of their rights. These means consist in the right of controlling and dismissing their leaders. Unquestionably this defense possesses a certain theoretical value, and the authoritarian inclinations of the leaders are in some degree attenuated by these possibilities. In states with a democratic tendency and under a parliamentary regime, to obtain the fall of a detested minister it suffices, in theory, that the people should be weary of him. In the same way, once more in theory, the ill-humor and the opposition of a socialist group or of an election committee is enough to effect the recall of a deputy's mandate, and in the same way the hostility of the majority at the annual congress of trade unions should be enough to secure the dismissal of a secretary. In practice, however, the exercise of this theoretical right is interfered with by the working of the whole series of conservative tendencies to which allusion has previously been made, so that the supremacy of the autonomous and sovereign masses is rendered purely illusory. The dread by which Nietzsche was at one time so greatly disturbed, that every individual might become a functionary of the mass, must be completely dissipated in face of the truth that while all have the right to become functionaries, few only possess the possibility.

With the institution of leadership there simultaneously begins, owing to the long tenure of office, the transformation of the leaders into a closed caste.

Unless, as in France, extreme individualism and fanatical political dogmatism stand in the way, the old leaders present themselves to the masses as a compact phalanx—at any rate whenever the masses are so much aroused as to endanger the position of the leaders.

The election of the delegates to congresses, etc., is sometimes regulated by the leaders by means of special agreements, whereby the masses are in fact excluded from all decisive influence in the management of their affairs. These agreements often assume the aspect of a mutual insurance contract. In the German Socialist Party, a few years ago, there came into existence in not a few localities a regular system in accordance with which the leaders nominated one another in rotation as delegates to the various party congresses. In the meetings at which the delegates were appointed, one of the big guns would always propose to the comrades the choice as delegates of the leader whose "turn" it was. The comrades rarely revolt against such artifices, and often fail even to perceive them. Thus competition among the leaders is prevented, in this domain at least; and at the same time there is rendered impossible anything more than passive participation of the rank and file in the higher functions of the life of the party which they alone sustain with their subscriptions.[8] Notwithstanding the violence of the internecine struggles which divide the leaders, in all the democracies they manifest vis-á-vis the masses a vigorous solidarity. "They perceive quickly enough the necessity for agreeing among themselves so that the party cannot escape them by becoming divided."[9] This is true above all of the German social democracy, in which, in consequence of the exceptional solidity of structure which it possesses as compared with all the other socialist parties of the world, conservative tendencies have attained an extreme development.

When there is a struggle between the leaders and the masses, the former are always victorious if only they remain united. At least it rarely happens that the masses succeed in disembarrassing themselves of one of their leaders. . . .

There is no indication whatever that the power possessed by the oligarchy in party life is likely to be overthrown within an appreciable time. The independence of the leaders increases concurrently with their indispensability. Nay more, the influence which they exercise and the financial security of their position become more and more fascinating to the masses, stimulating the ambition of all the more talented elements to enter the privileged bureaucracy of the labor movement. Thus the rank and file becomes continually more impotent to provide new and intelligent forces capable of leading the opposition which may be latent among the masses.[10] Even today the masses rarely move except at the command of their leaders. When the rank and file does take action in conflict with the wishes of the chiefs, this is almost always the outcome of a misunderstanding. The miners' strike in the Ruhr basin in 1905 broke out against the desire of the trade-union leaders, and was generally regarded as a spontaneous explosion of the popular will. But it was subsequently proved beyond dispute that for many months the leaders had been stimulating the rank and file, mobilizing them against the coal barons with repeated threats of a strike, so that the mass of the workers, when they entered on the struggle, could not possibly fail to believe that they did so with the full approval of their chiefs.

It cannot be denied that the masses revolt from time to time, but their revolts are always suppressed. It is only when the dominant classes, struck by sudden blindness, pursue a policy which strains social relationships to the breaking-point, that the party masses appear actively on the stage of history and overthrow the power of the oligarchies. Every autonomous movement of the masses signifies a profound discordance with the will of the leaders. Apart from such transient interruptions, the natural and normal development of the organization will impress upon the most revolutionary of parties an indelible stamp of conservatism.

The thesis of the unlimited power of the leaders in democratic parties, requires, however, a certain limitation. Theoretically the leader is bound by the will of the mass, which has only to give a sign and the leader is forced to withdraw. He can be discharged and replaced at any moment. But in practice, as we have learned, for various reasons the leaders enjoy a high degree of independence. It is none the less true that if the Democratic Party cannot dispense with autocratic leaders, it is at least able to change these. Consequently the most dangerous defect in a leader is that he should possess too blind a confidence in the masses. The aristocratic leader is more secure than the democratic against surprises at the hands of the rank and file. It is an essential characteristic of democracy that every private carries a marshal's baton in his knapsack. It is true that the mass is always incapable of governing; but it is no less true that each individual in the mass, in so far as he possesses, for good or for ill, the qualities which are requisite to enable him to rise above the crowd, can attain to the grade of leader and become a ruler. Now this ascent of new leaders always involves the danger, for those who are already in possession of power, that they will be forced to surrender their places to the newcomers. The old leader must therefore keep himself in permanent touch with the opinions and feelings of the masses to which he owes his position. Formally, at least, he must act in unison with the crowd, must admit himself to be the instrument of the crowd, must be guided, in appearance at least, by its goodwill and pleasure. Thus it often seems as if the mass really controlled the leaders. But whenever the power of the leaders is seriously threatened, it is in most cases because a new leader or a new group of leaders is on the point of becoming dominant, and is inculcating views opposed to those of the old rulers of the party. It then seems as if the old leaders, unless they are willing to yield to the opinion of the rank and file and to withdraw, must consent to share their power with the new arrivals. If, however, we look more closely into the matter, it is not difficult to see that their submission is in most cases no more than an act of foresight intended to obviate the influence of their younger rivals. The submission of the old leaders is ostensibly an act of homage to the crowd, but in intention it is a means of prophylaxis against the peril by which they are threatened—the formation of a new élite. . . .

As soon as the new leaders have attained their ends, as soon as they have succeeded (in the name of the injured rights of the anonymous masses) in overthrowing the odious tyranny of their predecessors and to attaining to power in their turn, we see them undergo a transformation which renders them in every respect similar to the dethroned tyrants. Such metamorphoses as these are plainly recorded throughout history. In the life of monarchical states, an opposition which is headed by hereditary princes is rarely dangerous to the crown as an institution. In like manner, the opposition of the aspirants to leadership in a political party, directed against the persons or against the system of the old leaders, is seldom dangerous. The revolutionaries of today become the reactionaries of tomorrow. . . .

The principle that one dominant class inevitably succeeds to another, and the law deduced from the principle that oligarchy is, as it were, a preordained form of the common life of great social aggregates, far from conflicting with or replacing the materialist conception of history, completes that conception and reinforces it. There is no essential contradiction between the doctrine that history is the record of a continued series of class struggles and the doctrine that class struggles invariably culminate in the creation of new oligarchies which undergo fusion with the old. The existence of a political class does not conflict with the essential content of Marxism, considered not as an economic dogma but as a philosophy of history; for in each particular instance the dominance of a political class arises as the resultant of the relationships between the different social forces competing for supremacy, these forces being of course considered dynamically and not quantitatively.

Leadership is a necessary phenomenon in every form of social life. Consequently it is not the task of science to inquire whether this phenomenon is good or evil, or predominantly one or the other. But there is great scientific value in the demonstration that every system of leadership is incompatible with the most essential postulates of democracy. We are now aware that the law of the historic necessity of oligarchy is primarily based upon a series of facts of experience. Like all other scientific laws, sociological laws are derived from empirical observation. In order, however, to deprive our axiom of its purely descriptive character, and to confer upon it that status of analytical explanation which can alone transform a formula into a law, it does not suffice to contemplate from a unitary outlook those phenomena which may be empirically established; we must also study the determining causes of these phenomena. Such has been our task.

Now, if we leave out of consideration the tendency of the leaders to organize themselves and to consolidate their interests, and if we leave also out of consideration the gratitude of the led towards the leaders, and the general immobility and passivity of the masses, we are led to conclude that the principal cause of oligarchy in the democratic parties is to be found in the technical indispensability of leadership.

The process which has begun in consequence of the differentiation of functions in the party is completed by a complex of qualities which the leaders acquire through their detachment from the mass. At the outset, leaders arise *spontaneously*; their functions are *accessory* and *gratuitous*. Soon, however, they become *professional* leaders, and in this second stage of development they are *stable* and *irremovable*.

If follows that the explanation of the oligarchical phenomenon which thus results is partly *psychological*; oligarchy derives, that is to say, from the psychical transformations which the leading personalities in the parties undergo in the course of their lives. But also, and still more, oligarchy depends upon what we may term the *psychology of organization itself*, that is to say, upon the tactical and technical necessities which result from the consolidation of every disciplined political aggregate. Reduced to its most concise expression, the fundamental sociological law of the political parties (the term "political" being here used in its most comprehensive significance) may be formulated in the following term: "It is organization which gives birth to the dominion of the elected over the electors, of the mandataries over the mandators, of the delegates over the delegators. Who says organization, says oligarchy."

Every party organization represents an oligarchical power grounded upon a democratic basis. We find everywhere electors and elected. Also we find everywhere that the power of the elected leaders over the electing masses is almost unlimited. The oligarchical structure of the building suffocates the basic democratic principle. That which *is* oppresses *that which ought to be*. For the masses, this essential difference between the reality and the ideal remains a mystery. Socialists often cherish a sincere belief that a new *élite* of politicians will keep faith better than did the old. The notion of the representation of popular interests, a notion to which the great majority of democrats, and especially the working-class masses of the German-speaking lands, cleave with so much tenacity and confidence, is an illusion engendered by a false illumination, is an effect of mirage. In one of the most delightful pages of his analysis of modern Don Quixotism, Alphonse Daudet shows us how the "brav' commandant" Bravida, who has never quitted Tarascon, gradually comes to persuade himself, influenced by the burning southern sun, that he has been to Shanghai and has had all kinds of heroic adventures.[11] Similarly the modern proletariat, enduringly influenced by glib-tongued persons intellectually superior to the mass, ends by believing that by flocking to the poll and entrusting its social and economic cause to a delegate, its direct participation in power will be assured.

The formation of oligarchies within the various forms of democracy is the outcome of organic necessity, and consequently affects every organization, be it socialist or even anarchist. Haller long ago noted that in every form of social life relationships of dominion and of dependence are created by Nature herself.[12] The supremacy of the leaders in the democratic and revolutionary parties has to be taken into account in every historic situation present and to come, even though only a few and exceptional minds will be fully conscious of its existence. The mass will never rule except *in abstracto*. Consequently the question we have to discuss is not whether ideal democracy is realizable, but rather to what point and in what degree democracy is desirable, possible, and realizable at a given moment. In the problem as thus stated we recognize the fundamental problem of politics as a science. Whoever fails to perceive this must, as Sombart says, either be so blind and fanatical as not to see that the democratic current daily makes undeniable advance, or else must be so inexperienced and devoid of critical faculty as to be unable to understand that all order and all civilization must exhibit aristocratic features.[13] The great error of socialists, an error committed in consequence of their lack of adequate psychological knowledge, is to be found in their combination of pessimism regarding the present, with rosy optimism and immeasurable confidence regarding the future. A realistic view of the mental condition of the masses shows beyond question that even if we admit the possibility of moral improvement in mankind, the human materials with whose use politicians and philosophers cannot dispense in their plans of social reconstruction are not of a character to justify excessive optimism. Within the limits of time from which human provision is possible, optimism will remain the exclusive privilege of utopian thinkers.

The socialist parties, like the trade unions, are living forms of social life. As such they react with the utmost energy against any attempt to analyze their structure or their nature, as if it were a method of vivisection. When science attains to results which conflict with their apriorist ideology, they revolt with all their power. Yet their defense is extremely feeble. Those among the representatives of such organizations whose scientific earnestness and personal good faith make it impossible for them to deny outright the existence of oligarchical tendencies in every form of democracy, endeavor to explain these tendencies as the outcome of a kind of atavism in the mentality of the masses, characteristic of the youth of the movement. The masses, they assure us, are still infected by the oligarchic virus simply because they have been oppressed during long centuries of slavery, and have never yet enjoyed an autonomous existence. The socialist regime, however, will soon restore them to health, and will furnish them with all the capacity necessary for self-government. Nothing could be more antiscientific than the supposition that as soon as socialists have gained possession of government power it will suffice for the masses to exercise a little control over their leaders to secure that the interests of these leaders shall coincide perfectly with the interests of the led. This idea may be compared with the view of Jules Guesde, no less antiscientific than anti-Marxist (though Guesde proclaims himself a Marxist), that whereas Christianity has made God into a man, socialism will make man into a god.[14]

The objective immaturity of the mass is not a mere transitory phenomenon which will disappear with the progress of democratization *au lendemain du socialisme*. On the contrary, it derives from the very nature of the mass as mass, for this, even when organized, suffers from an incurable incompetence for the solution of the diverse problems which present themselves for solution—because the mass *per se* is amorphous, and therefore needs division of labor, specialization, and guidance. "The human species wants to be governed; it will be. I am ashamed of my kind," wrote Proudhon from his prison in 1850.[15] Man as individual is by nature predestined to be guided, and to be guided all the more in proportion as the functions of life undergo division and subdivision. To an enormously greater degree is guidance necessary for the social group.

From this chain of reasoning and from these scientific convictions it would be erroneous to conclude that we should renounce all endeavors to ascertain the limits which may be imposed upon the powers exercised over the individual by oligarchies (state, dominant class, party, etc.). It would be an error to abandon the desperate enterprise of endeavoring to discover a social order which will render possible the complete realization of the idea of popular sovereignty. In the present work, as the writer said at the outset, it has not been his aim to indicate new paths. But it seemed necessary to lay considerable stress upon the pessimist aspect of democracy which is forced on us by historical study. We had to inquire whether, and within what limits, democracy must remain purely ideal, possessing no other value than that of a moral criterion which renders it possible to appreciate the varying degrees of that oligarchy which is immanent in every social regime. In other words, we have had to inquire if, and in what degree, democracy is an ideal which we can never hope to realize in practice. A further aim of this work was the demolition of some of the facile and superficial democratic illusions which trouble science and lead the masses astray. Finally, the author desired to throw light upon certain sociological tendencies which oppose the reign of democracy, and to a still greater extent oppose the reign of socialism.

The writer does not wish to deny that every revolutionary working-class movement, and every movement sincerely inspired by the democratic spirit, may have a certain value as contributing to the enfeeblement of oligarchic tendencies. The peasant in the fable, when on his death-bed, tells his sons that a treasure is buried in the field. After the old man's death the sons dig everywhere in order to discover the treasure. They do not find it. But their indefatigable labor improves the soil and secures for them a comparative well-being. The treasure in the fable may well symbolize democracy. Democracy is a treasure which no one will ever discover by deliberate search. But in continuing our search, in laboring indefatigably to discover the undiscoverable, we shall perform a work which will have fertile results in the democratic sense. We have seen, indeed, that within the bosom of the democratic working-class party are born the very tendencies to counteract which that party came into existence. Thanks to the diversity and to the unequal worth of the elements of the party, these tendencies often give rise to manifestations which border on tyranny. We have seen that the replacement of the traditional legitimism of the powers-that-be by the brutal plebiscitary rule of Bonapartist parvenus does not furnish these tendencies with any moral or aesthetic superiority. Historical evolution mocks all the prophylactic measures that have been adopted for the prevention of oligarchy. If laws are passed to control the dominion of the leaders, it is the laws which gradually weaken, and not the leaders. Sometimes, however, the democratic principle carries with it, if not a cure, at least a palliative, for the disease of oligarchy. When Victor Considérant formulated his "democratico-pacificist" socialism, he declared that socialism signified, not the rule of society by the lower classes of the population, but the government and organization of society in the interest of all, through the intermediation of a group of citizens; and he added that the numerical importance of this group must increase *pari passu* with social development.[16] This last observation draws attention to a point of capital importance. It is, in fact, a general characteristic of democracy, and hence also of the labor movement, to stimulate and to strengthen in the individual the intellectual aptitudes of criticism and control. We have seen how the progressive bureaucratization of the democratic organism tends to neutralize the beneficial effects of such criticism and such control. None the less it is true that the labor movement, in virtue of the theoretical postulates it proclaims, is apt to bring into existence (in opposition to the will of the leaders) a certain number of free spirits who, moved by principle, by instinct, or by both, desire to revise the base upon which authority is established. Urged on by conviction or by temperament, they are never weary of asking an eternal "Why?" about every human institution. Now this predisposition towards free inquiry, in which we cannot fail to recognize one of the most precious factors of civilization, will gradually increase in proportion as the economic status of the masses undergoes improvement and becomes more stable, and in proportion as they are admitted more effectively to the advantages of civilization. A wider education involves an increasing capacity for exercising control. Can we not observe every day that among the well-to-do the authority of the leaders over the led, extensive though it be, is never so unrestricted as in the case of the leaders of the poor? Taken in the mass, the poor are powerless and disarmed vis-à-vis their leaders. Their intellectual and cultural inferiority makes it impossible for them to see whither the leader is going, or to estimate in advance the significance of his actions. It is, consequently, the great task of social education to raise the intellectual level of the masses, so that they may be enabled, within the limits of what is possible, to counteract the oligarchical tendencies of the working-class movement.

In view of the perennial incompetence of the masses, we have to recognize the existence of two regulative principles: 1. The *ideological* tendency of democracy towards criticism and control; 2. The *effective* counter-tendency of democracy towards the creation of parties ever more complex and ever more differentiated—parties, that is to say, which are increasingly based upon the competence of the few.

To the idealist, the analysis of the forms of contemporary democracy cannot fail to be a source of bitter deceptions and profound discouragement. Those alone, perhaps, are in a position to pass a fair judgment upon democracy who, without lapsing into dilettantist sentimentalism, recognize that all scientific and human ideals have relative values. If we wish to estimate the value of democracy, we must do so in comparison with its converse, pure aristocracy. The defects inherent in democracy are obvious. It is none the less true that as a form of social life we must choose democracy as the least of evils. The ideal government would doubtless be that of an aristocracy of persons at once morally good and technically efficient. But where shall we discover such an aristocracy? We may find it sometimes, though very rarely, as the outcome of deliberate selection; but we shall never find it where the hereditary principle remains in operation. Thus monarchy in its pristine purity must be considered as imperfection incarnate, as the most incurable of ills; from the moral point of view it is inferior even to the most revolting of demagogic dictatorships, for the corrupt organism of the latter at least contains a healthy principle upon whose working we may continue to base hopes of social resanation. It may be said, therefore, that the more humanity comes to recognize the advantages which democracy, however imperfect, presents over aristocracy, even at its best, the less likely is it that a recognition of the defects of democracy will provoke a return to aristocracy. Apart from certain formal differences and from the qualities which can be acquired only by good education and inheritance (qualities in which aristocracy will always have the advantage over democracy—qualities which democracy either neglects altogether, or, attempting to imitate them, falsifies them to the point of caricature), the defects of democracy will be found to inhere in its inability to get rid of its aristocratic scoriæ. On the other hand, nothing but a serene and frank examination of the oligarchical dangers of democracy will enable us to minimize these dangers, even though they can never be entirely avoided.

The democratic currents of history resemble successive waves. They break ever on the same shoal. They are ever renewed. This enduring spectacle is simultaneously encouraging and depressing. When democracies have gained a certain stage of development, they undergo a gradual transformation, adopting the aristocratic spirit, and in many cases also the aristocratic forms, against which at the outset they struggled so fiercely. Now new accusers arise to denounce the traitors; after an era of glorious combats and of inglorious power, they end by fusing with the old dominant class; whereupon once more they are in their turn attacked by fresh opponents who appeal to the name of democracy. It is probable that this cruel game will continue without end.

Notes

1. Roscher, p. 351.
2. Louis Blanc, "L'état dans une démocratie," *Questions d'aujourd'hui et de demain* (Paris: Dentu, 1880), vol. iii, p. 144.
3. Cf. the letter of Antonio Quiroga to King Ferdinand VII, dated January 7, 1820 (Don Juan van Halen, *Mémoires*, Renouard, Paris, 1827, Part II, p. 382).
4. Egidio Bernaroli, *Manuale per la constituzione e il funzionamento delle leghe dei contadini*, Libreria Soc. Ital., Rome, 1902, pp. 20, 26, 27, 52.
5. Sidney and Beatrice Webb, *Industrial Democracy* (German edition), Stuttgart, 1898, vol. i, p. 6.
6. Ferdinand Tönnies, *Politik und Moral*, Neaer Frankfort Verlag, Frankfort, 1901, p. 46.
7. Heinrich Herkner, *Der Arbeiterfrage*, Guttentag, Berlin, 1908, 5th ed., pp. 116, 117.
8. Similar phenomena have been observed in party life in America (Ostrogorsky, *La Démocratie*, vol. 2, p. 196).
9. Trans. from Antoine Elisée Cherbuliez, *Théorie des Garantis constitutionelles* (Paris: Ab. Cherbuliez, 1838), vol. 2, p. 253.
10. Thus Pareto writes: "If B [the new élite] took the place of A [the old élite] by slow infiltration, and if the social circulation is not interrupted, C [the masses] are deprived of the leaders who could incite them to revolt." (Trans. from Vilfredo Pareto, *Les Systèmes socialistes*, Giard and Brière, Paris, 1892, vol. i, p. 35).
11. Alphonse Daudet, *Tartarin de Tarascon*, Marpon et Flammarion, Paris, 1887, p. 40.
12. Ludwig von Haller, *Restauration der Staatswissenschaften*, Winterthur, 1816, vol. i, pp. 304 et seq.

13. Werner Sombart, *Dennoch!* (Jena: Fischer, 1900), p. 90. Cf. also F. S. Merlino, *Pro e contro il Socialismo*, pp. 262 et seq.
14. Jules Guesde, *La Problème et la Solution*, Libr. du Parti Socialiste, Paris, p. 17.
15. Charles Gide et Charles Rist, *Histoire des Doctrines économiques depuis les Physiocrates jusqu'à nos jours*, Larose et Tenin, Paris, 1909, p. 709.
16. Victor Considérant, *Principes du Socialisme. Manifeste de la Démocratie au xix Siècle*, Librairie Phalanstérienne, Paris, 1847, p. 53.

4

Trade Unions, Factory Councils, and Workers' Control of Production

Antonio Gramsci

The trade union is not a predetermined phenomenon. It *becomes* a determinate institution, i.e. it takes on a definite historical form to the extent that the strength and will of the workers who are its members impress a policy and propose an aim that define it.

Objectively, the trade union is the form which labour as a commodity is bound to assume in a capitalist system, when it organizes itself in order to control the market. This form consists in an office staffed by functionaries, organizational technicians (when they can be called technicians), specialists (when they can be called specialists) in the art of concentrating and guiding the workers' forces in such a way as to establish a favourable balance between the working class and the power of capital.

The development of trade-union organization is characterized by two facts: 1. the union embraces an ever increasing number of workers; 2. the union concentrates and generalizes its scope until the movement's power and discipline is focused in a central office. This office becomes divorced from the masses it has regimented, and removes itself from the eddies and currents of fickle whims and foolish ambitions that are to be expected in the excitable broad masses. The union thus acquires the ability to negotiate agreements and take on responsibilities. In this way it obliges the employer to acknowledge a certain legality in his dealings with the workers, a legality that is conditional on his faith in the union's *solvency*

Reprinted from *Selections from Political Writings, 1910–1920*, by Antonio Gramsci (London: Lawrence and Wishart, 1977), 265–268, by permission of the publisher.

and its capacity to secure respect for contracted obligations from the working masses.

The emergence of an industrial legality is a great victory for the working class, but it is not the ultimate and definite victory. Industrial legality has improved the working class's standard of living but it is no more than a compromise—a compromise which had to be made and must be supported until the balance of forces favours the working class. If the trade-union officials regard industrial legality as a necessary, but not a permanently necessary compromise; if they deploy all the means at the union's disposal to improve the balance of forces in favor of the working class; and if they carry out all the spiritual and material preparatory work that will be needed if the working class is to launch at any particular moment a victorious offensive against capital and subject it to its law—then the trade union is a tool of revolution, and union discipline, even when used to make the workers respect industrial legality, is revolutionary discipline.

The relations which should prevail between the trade unions and Factory Councils need to be judged in the light of the following question: what is the nature and value of industrial legality?

The Council is the negation of industrial legality: it strives at all times to destroy it, to lead the working class to the conquest of industrial power and make it the source of industrial power.[1] The union represents legality, and must aim to make its members respect that legality. The trade union is answerable to the industrialists, but only in so far as it is answerable to its own members: it guarantees to the worker and his family a continuous supply of work and wages, i.e. food and a roof over their heads. By virtue of its revolutionary spontaneity, the Factory Council tends to spark off the class war at any moment; while the trade union, by virtue of its bureaucratic form, tends to prevent class war from ever breaking out. The relations between the two institutions should be such that a capricious impulse on the part of the Councils could not result in a set-back or defeat for the working class; in other words, the Council should accept and assimilate the discipline of the union. They should also be such that the revolutionary character of the Council exercises an influence over the trade union, and functions as a reagent dissolving the union's bureaucracy and bureaucratism.

The Council strives at all times to break with industrial legality. The Council consists of the exploited and tyrannized masses who are obliged to perform servile labour: as such, it strives to universalize every rebellion and give a resolutive scope and value to each of its acts of power. The union, as an organization that is jointly responsible for legality, strives to universalize and perpetuate this legality. The relations between union and Council should create the conditions in which the break with legality, the working-class offensive, occurs at the most opportune moment for the working class, when it possesses that minimum of preparation that is deemed indispensable to a lasting victory.

The relations between unions and Councils cannot be stabilized by any other device than the following: the majority of a substantial number of the electors to the Council should be organized in unions. Any attempt to link the two institutions in a relation of hierarchical dependence can only lead to the destruction of both.

If the conception that sees the Councils merely as an instrument in the trade-union struggle takes material form in a bureaucratic discipline and a hierarchical structure in which the union has direct control over the Council, then the Council is sterilized as a force for revolutionary expansion—as a form of the actual development of the proletarian revolution, tending spontaneously to create new modes of production and labour, new modes of discipline and, in the end, a communist society. Since the rise of the Council is a function of the position that the working class has achieved in the sphere of production, and a historical necessity for the working class, any attempt to subordinate it hierarchically to the union would sooner or later result in a clash between the two institutions. The Council's strength consists in the fact that it is in close contact—indeed identified—with the consciousness of the working masses, who are seeking their autonomous emancipation and wish to put on record their freedom of initiative in the creation of history. The masses as a whole participate in the activity of the Council, and gain a measure of self-respect in the process. Only a very restricted number of members participate in the activity of the trade union; its real strength lies in this fact, but this fact is also a weakness that cannot be put to the test without running very grave risks.

If, moreover, the unions were to lean directly on the Councils, not to dominate them, but to become their higher form, then they would reflect the Council's own tendency to break at all times with industrial legality and unleash the final phase of the class war. The union would lose its capacity to negotiate agreements, and would lose its role as an agent to regulate and discipline the impulsive forces of the working class.

If its members establish a revolutionary discipline in the union, a discipline which the masses see as being necessary for the triumph of the workers' revolution and not as slavery to capital, this discipline will undoubtedly be accepted and made its own by the Council. It will become a natural aspect of the Council's activity. If the union headquarters becomes a center for revolutionary preparation, and appears as such to the masses by virtue of the campaigns it succeeds in launching, the men who compose it and the propaganda it issues, then its centralized and absolutist character will be seen by the masses as a major revolutionary strength, as one more (and a very important) condition for the success of the struggle to which they are committed all the way.

In Italian conditions, the trade-union official sees industrial legality as a permanent state of affairs. Too often he defends it from the same perspective as the proprietor. He sees only chaos and willfulness in everything that happens amongst the working masses. He does not universalize the worker's act of rebellion against capitalist discipline as rebellion; he perceives only the physical act, which might in itself be trivial. Thus the story of the "porter's raincoat" has been as widely disseminated and has been interpreted by stupid journalists in the same way as the myth of the "socialization of women in Russia." In these conditions, the trade-unon discipline can be nothing other than a service rendered to capital; in these conditions any attempt to subordinate the Councils to the trade unions can only be judged as reactionary.

The communists would like the revolutionary act to be, as far as possible, a conscious and responsible act. Hence they would like to see the choice of the moment in which to launch the working-class offensive (to the extent that such a moment can be chosen) resting in the hands of the most conscious and responsible section of the working class—the section organized in the Socialist Party and playing the most active part in the life of the organization. For this reason, the communists could not possibly want the union to lose any of its disciplinary energy and systematic centralization.

By forming themselves into permanently organized groups within the trade unions and factories, the communists need to import into these bodies the ideas, theses and tactics of the IIIrd International; they need to exert an influence over union discipline and determine its aims; they need to influence the decisions of the Factory Councils, and transform the rebellious impulses sparked off by the conditions that capitalism has created for the working class into a revolutionary consciousness and creativity. Since they bear the heaviest historical responsibility, the communists in the Party have the greatest interest in evoking, through their ceaseless activity, relations of interpenetration and natural interdependence between the various working-class institutions. It is these relations that leaven discipline and organization with a revolutionary spirit.

Note

1. In Gramsci's scheme, the factory Council was the organization that represented all workers regardless of trade or level of skill. It strove at the factory level to achieve democratic control of everyday work tasks and eventually of all production, and not merely higher wages and shorter hours (the trade union orientation). Its aim was to release the creative initiative of all workers, and to prepare them technically and culturally to eventually run the larger society in a democratic, egalitarian manner.

5
Scientific Management
Frederick W. Taylor

The writer has found that there are three questions uppermost in the minds of men when they become interested in scientific management.

First. Wherein do the principles of scientific management differ essentially from those of ordinary management?

Second. Why are better results attained under scientific management than under the other types?

Third. Is not the most important problem that of getting the right man at the head of the company? And if you have the right man cannot the choice of the type of management be safely left to him?

One of the principal objects of the following pages will be to give a satisfactory answer to these questions. . . .

Before starting to illustrate the principles of scientific management, or "task management" as it is briefly called, it seems desirable to outline what the writer believes will be recognized as the best type of management which is in common use. This is done so that the great difference between the best of the ordinary management and scientific management may be fully appreciated.

In an industrial establishment which employs say from 500 to 1000 workmen, there will be found in many cases at least twenty to thirty different trades. The workmen in each of these trades have had their knowledge handed down to them by word of mouth, through the many years in which their trade has been developed from the primitive condition, in which our far-distant ancestors each one practised the rudiments of many different trades, to the present state of great and growing subdivision of labor, in which each man specializes upon some comparative small class of work.

The ingenuity of each generation has developed quicker and better methods for doing every element of the work in every trade. Thus the methods which are now in use may in a broad sense be said to be an

---

Reprinted from "The Principles of Scientific Management," in *Scientific Management*, by Frederick Winslow Taylor, (New York: Harper & Row, 1939), 30–48, 57–60, by permission of the publisher. Copyright 1911 by Frederick W. Taylor; renewed in 1939 by Louise M. S. Taylor.

evolution representing the survival of the fittest and best of the ideas which have been developed since the starting of each trade. However, while this is true in a broad sense, only those who are intimately acquainted with each of these trades are fully aware of the fact that in hardly any element of any trade is there uniformity in the methods which are used. Instead of having only one way which is generally accepted as a standard, there are in daily use, say, fifty or a hundred different ways of doing each element of the work. And a little thought will make it clear that this must inevitably be the case, since our methods have been handed down from man to man by word of mouth, or have, in most cases, been almost unconsciously learned through personal observation. Practically in no instances have they been codified or systematically analyzed or described. The ingenuity and experience of each generation—of each decade, even, have without doubt handed over better methods to the next. This mass of rule-of-thumb or traditional knowledge may be said to be the principal asset or possession of every tradesman. Now, in the best of the ordinary types of management, the managers recognize frankly the fact that the 500 or 1000 workmen, included in the twenty to thirty trades, who are under them, possess this mass of traditional knowledge, a large part of which is not in the possession of the management. The management, of course, includes foremen and superintendents, who themselves have been in most cases first-class workers at their trades. And yet these foremen and superintendents know, better than anyone else, that their own knowledge and personal skill falls far short of the combined knowledge and dexterity of all the workmen under them. The most experienced managers therefore frankly place before their workmen the problem of doing the work in the best and most economical way. They recognize the task before them as that of inducing each workman to use his best endeavors, his hardest work, all his traditional knowledge, his skill, his ingenuity, and his goodwill—in a word, his "initiative," so as to yield the largest possible return to his employer. The problem before the management, then, may be briefly said to be that of obtaining the best *initiative* of every workman. And the writer uses the word "initiative" in its broadest sense, to cover all of the good qualities sought for from the men.

On the other hand, no intelligent manager would hope to obtain in any full measure the initiative of his workmen unless he felt that he was giving them something more than they usually receive from their employers. Only those among the readers of this paper who have been managers or who have worked themselves at a trade realize how far the average workman falls short of giving his employer his full initiative. It is well within the mark to state that in nineteen out of twenty industrial establishments the workmen believe it to be directly against their interests to give their employers their best initiative, and that instead of working hard to do the largest possible amount of work and the best quality of work for their employers, they deliberately work as slowly as they dare while they at the same time try to make those over them believe that they are working fast.[1]

The writer repeats, therefore, that in order to have any hope of obtaining the initiative of his workmen the manager must give some *special incentive* to his men beyond that which is given to the average of the trade. This incentive can be given in several different ways, as, for example, the hope of rapid promotion or advancement; higher wages, either in the form of generous piecework prices or of a premium or bonus of some kind for good and rapid work; shorter hours of labor; better surroundings and working conditions than are ordinarily given, etc., and, above all, this special incentive should be accompanied by the personal consideration for, and friendly contact with, his workmen which comes only from a genuine and kindly interest in the welfare of those under him. It is only by giving a special inducement or "incentive" of this kind that the employer can hope even approximately to get the "initiative" of his workmen. Under the ordinary type of management the necessity for offering the workman a special inducement has come to be so generally recognized that a large proportion of those most interested in the subject look upon the adoption of some one of the modern schemes for paying men (such as piece work, the premium plan, or the bonus plan, for instance) as practically the whole system of management. Under scientific management, however, the particular pay system which is adopted is merely one of the subordinate elements.

Broadly speaking, then, the best type of management in ordinary use may be defined as management in which the workmen give their best *initiative* and in return receive some *special incentive* from their employers. This type of management will be referred to as the management of "*initiative and incentive*" in contradistinction to scientific management, or task management, with which it is to be compared.

The writer hopes that the management of "initiative and incentive" will be recognized as representing the best type in ordinary use, and in fact he believes that it will be hard to persuade the average manager that anything better exists in the whole field than this type. The task which the writer has before him, then, is the difficult one of trying to prove in a thoroughly convincing way that there is another type of management which is not only better but overwhelmingly better than the management of "initiative and incentive."

The universal prejudice in favor of the management of "initiative and incentive" is so strong that no mere theoretical advantages which can be pointed out will be likely to convince the average manager that any other system is better. It will be upon a series of practical illustrations of the actual working of the two systems that the writer will depend in his efforts to prove that scientific management is so greatly superior to other types. Certain elementary principles, a certain philosophy, will however be recognized as the essence of that which is being illustrated in all of the practical examples which will be given. And the broad principles in which the scientific system differs from the ordinary or "rule-of-thumb" system are so simple in their nature that it seems desirable to describe them before starting with the illustrations.

Under the old type of management success depends almost entirely upon getting the "initiative" of the workmen, and it is indeed a rare case in which this initiative is really attained. Under scientific management the "initiative" or the workmen (that is, their hard work, their good-will, and their ingenuity) is obtained with absolute uniformity and to a greater extent than is possible under the old system; and in addition to this improvement on the part of the men, the managers assume new burdens, new duties, and responsibilities never dreamed of in the past. The managers assume, for instance, the burden of gathering together all of the traditional knowledge which in the past has been possessed by the workmen and then of classifying, tabulating, and reducing this knowledge to rules, laws, and formulæ which are immensely helpful to the workmen in doing their daily work. In addition to developing a *science* in this way, the management take on three other types of duties which involve new and heavy burdens for themselves.

>These new duties are grouped under four heads:
>*First.* They develop a science for each element of a man's work, which replaces the old rule-of-thumb method.
>*Second.* They scientifically select and then train, teach, and develop the workman, whereas in the past he chose his own work and trained himself as best he could.
>*Third.* They heartily cooperate with the men so as to insure all of the work being done in accordance with the principles of the science which has been developed.
>*Fourth.* There is an almost equal division of the work and the responsibility between the management and the workmen. The management take over all work for which they are better fitted than the workmen, while in the past almost all of the work and the greater part of the responsibility were thrown upon the men.

It is this combination of the initiative of the workmen, coupled with the new types of work done by the management, that makes scientific management so much more efficient than the old plan.

Three of these elements exist in many cases, under the management of "initiative and incentive," in a small and rudimentary way, but they are, under this management, of minor importance, whereas under scientific management they form the very essence of the whole system.

The fourth of these elements, "an almost equal division of the responsibility between the management and the workmen," requires further explanation. The philosophy of the management of "initiative and incentive" makes it necessary for each workman to bear almost the entire responsibility for the general plan as well as for each detail of his work, and in many cases for his implements as well. In addition to this he must do all of the actual physical labor. The development of a science, on the other hand, involves the establishment of many rules, laws, and formulæ which replace the judgment of the individual workmen and which can be effectively used only after having been systematically recorded, indexed, etc. The practical use of scientific data also calls for a room in which to keep the books, records,[2] etc., and a desk for the planner to work at. Thus all of the planning which under the old system was done by the workman, as a result of his personal experience, must of necessity under the new system be done by the management in accordance with the laws of the science; because even if the workman was well suited to the development and use of scientific data, it would be physically impossible for him to work at his machine and at a desk at the same time. It is also clear that in most cases one type of man is needed to plan ahead and an entirely different type to execute the work.

The man in the planning room, whose specialty under scientific management is planning ahead, invariably finds that the work can be done better and more economically by a subdivision of the labor; each act of each mechanic, for example, should be preceded by various preparatory acts done by other men. And all of this involves, as we have said, "an almost equal division of the responsibility and the work between the management and the workman."

To summarize: Under the management of "initiative and incentive" practically the whole problem is "up to the workman," while under scientific management fully one-half of the problem is "up to the management."

Perhaps the most prominent single element in modern scientific management is the task idea. The work of every workman is fully planned out by the management at least one day in advance, and each man receives in most cases complete written instructions, describing in detail the task which he is to accomplish, as well as the means to be used in doing the work. And the work planned in advance in this way constitutes a task which is to be solved, as explained above, not by the workman alone, but in almost all cases by the joint effort of the workman and the management. This task specifies not only what is to be done but how it is to be done and the exact time allowed for doing it. And whenever the workman succeeds in doing his task right, and within the time limit specified, he receives an addition of from 30 per cent to 100 percent to his ordinary wages. These tasks are carefully planned, so that both good and careful work are called for in their performance, but it should be distinctly understood that in no case is the workman called upon to work at a pace which would be injurious to his health. The task is always so regulated that the man who is well suited to his job will thrive while working at this rate during a long term of years and grow happier and more prosperous, instead of being overworked. Scientific management consists very largely in preparing for and carrying out these tasks.

The writer is fully aware that to perhaps most of the readers of this paper the four elements which differentiate the new management from the old will at first appear to be merely high-sounding phrases; and he would again repeat that he has no idea of convincing the reader of their value merely through announcing their existence. His hope of carrying conviction rests upon demonstrating the tremendous force and effect of these four elements through a series of practical illustrations. It will be shown, first, that they can be applied absolutely to all classes of work, from the most elementary to the most intricate; and second, that when they are applied, the results must of necessity be overwhelmingly greater than those which it is possible to attain under the management of initiative and incentive.

The first illustration is that of handling pig iron, and this work is chosen because it is typical of perhaps the crudest and most elementary form of labor which is performed by man. This work is done by men with no other implements than their hands. The pig-iron handler stoops down, picks up a pig weighing about 92 pounds, walks for a few feet or yards and then drops it onto the ground or upon a pile. This work is so crude and elementary in its nature that the writer firmly believes that it would be possible to train an intelligent gorilla so as to become a more efficient pig-iron handler than any man can be. Yet it will be shown that the science of handling pig iron is so great and amounts to so much that it is impossible for the man who is best suited to this type of work to understand the principles of this science, or even to work in accordance with these principles without the aid of a man better educated than he is. And the further illustrations to be given will make it clear that in almost all of the mechanic arts, the science which underlies each workman's act is so great and amounts to so much that the workman who is best suited actually to do the work is incapable (either through lack of education or through insufficient mental capacity) of understanding this science. This is announced as a general principle the truth of which will become apparent as one illustration after another is given. After showing these four elements in the handling of pig iron, several illustrations will be given of their application to different kinds of work in the field of the mechanic arts, at intervals in a rising scale, beginning with the simplest and ending with the more intricate forms of labor.

One of the first pieces of work undertaken by us, when the writer started to introduce scientific management into the Bethlehem Steel Company, was to handle pig iron on task work. The opening of the Spanish War found some 80,000 tons of pig iron placed in small piles in an open field adjoining the works. Prices for pig iron had been so low that it could not be sold at a profit, and it therefore had been stored. With the opening of the Spanish War the price of pig iron rose, and this large accumulation of iron was sold. This gave us a good opportunity to show the workmen, as well as the owners and managers of the works, on a fairly large scale the advantages of task work over the old-fashioned day work and piece work, in doing a very elementary class of work.

The Bethlehem Steel Company had five blast furnaces, the product of which had been handled by a pig-iron gang for many years. This gang, at this time, consisted of about seventy-five men. They were good, average pig-iron handlers, were under an excellent foreman who himself had been a pig-iron handler, and the work was done, on the whole, about as fast and as cheaply as it was anywhere else at the time.

A railroad switch was run out into the field, right along the edge of the piles of pig iron. An inclined plank was placed against the side of a car, and each man picked up from his pile a pig of iron weighing about 92 pounds, walked up the inclined plank and dropped it on the end of the car.

We found that this gang were loading on the average about 12½ long tons per man per day. We were surprised to find, after studying the matter, that a first-class pig-iron handler ought to handle between 47 and 48 long tons per day, instead of 12½ tons. This task seemed to us so very large that we were obliged to go over our work several times before we were absolutely sure that we were right. Once we were sure, however, that 47 tons was a proper day's work for a first-class pig-iron handler, the task which faced us as managers under the modern scientific plan was clearly before us. It was our duty to see that the 80,000 tons of pig iron was loaded onto the cars at the rate of 47 tons per man per day, in place of 12½ tons, at which rate the work was then being done. And it was further our duty to see that this work was done without bringing on a strike among the men, without any quarrel with the men, and to see that the men were happier and better contented when loading at the new rate of 47 tons than they were when loading at the old rate of 12½ tons.

Our first step was the scientific selection of the workman. In dealing with workmen under this type of management, it is an inflexible rule to talk to and deal with only one man at a time, since each workman has his own special abilities and limitations, and since we are not dealing with men in masses, but are trying to develop each individual man to his highest state of efficiency and prosperity. Our first step was to find the proper workman to begin with. We therefore carefully watched and studied these seventy-five men for three or four days, at the end of which time we had picked out four men who appeared to be physically able to handle pig iron at the rate of 47 tons per day. A careful study was then made of each of these men. We looked up their history as far back as practicable and thorough inquiries were made as to the character, habits, and the ambition of each of them. Finally we selected one from among the four as the most likely man to start with. He was a little Pennsylvania Dutchman who had been observed to trot back home for a mile or so after his work in the evening about as fresh as he was when he came trotting down to work in the morning. We found that upon wages of $1.15 a day he had succeeded in buying a small plot of ground, and that he was engaged in putting up the walls of a little house for himself in the morning before starting to work and at night after leaving. He also had the reputation of being exceedingly "close," that is, of placing a very high value on a dollar. As one man whom we talked to about him said, "A penny looks about the size of a cart-wheel to him." This man we will call Schmidt.

The task before us, then, narrowed itself down to getting Schmidt to handle 47 tons of pig iron per day and making him glad to do it. This was done as follows. Schmidt was called out from among the gang of pig-iron handlers and talked to somewhat in this way:

"Schmidt, are you a high-priced man?"

"Vell, I don't know vat you mean."

"Oh yes, you do. What I want to know is whether you are a high-priced man or not."

"Vell, I don't know vat you mean."

"Oh, come now, you answer my questions. What I want to find out is whether you are a high-priced man or one of these cheap fellows here. What I want to find out is whether you want to earn $1.85 a day or whether you are satisfied with $1.15, just the same as all those cheap fellows are getting."

"Did I vant $1.85 a day? Vas dot a high-priced man? Vell, yes, I was a high-priced man."

"Oh, you're aggravating me. Of course you want $1.85 a day—everyone wants it! You know perfectly well that that has very little to do with your being a high-priced man. For goodness' sake answer my questions, and don't waste any more of my time. Now come over here. You see that pile of pig iron?"

"Yes."

"You see that car?"

"Yes."

"Well, if you are a high-priced man, you will load the pig iron on that car tomorrow for $1.85. Now do wake up and answer my question. Tell me whether you are a high-priced man or not."

"Vell—did I got $1.85 for loading dot pig iron on dot car tomorrow?"

"Yes, of course you do, and you get $1.85 for loading a pile like that every day right through the year. That is what a high-priced man does, and you know it just as well as I do."

"Vell, dot's all right. I could load dot pig iron on the car tomorrow for $1.85, and I get it every day, don't I?"

"Certainly you do—certainly you do."

"Vell, den, I was a high-priced man."

"Now, hold on, hold on. You know just as well as I do that a high-priced man has to do exactly as he's told from morning till night. You have seen this man here before, haven't you?"

"No, I never saw him."

"Well, if you are a high-priced man, you will do exactly as this man tells you tomorrow, from morning till night. When he tells you to pick up a pig and walk, you pick it up and you walk, and when he tells you to sit down and rest, you sit down. You do that right straight through the day. And what's more, no back talk. Now a high-priced man does just what he's told to do, and no back talk. Do you understand that? When this man tells you to walk, you walk; when he tells you to sit down, you sit down, and you don't talk back at him. Now you come on to work here tomorrow morning and I'll know before night whether you are really a high-priced man or not."

This seems to be rather rough talk. And indeed it would be if applied to an educated mechanic, or even an intelligent laborer. With a man of the mentally sluggish type of Schmidt it is appropriate and not unkind, since it is effective in fixing his attention on the high wages which he wants and away from what, if it were called to his attention, he probably would consider impossibly hard work.

What would Schmidt's answer be if he were talked to in a manner which is usual under the management of "initiative and incentive"? say, as follows:

"Now, Schmidt, you are a first-class pig-iron handler and know your business well. You have been handling at the rate of 12½ tons per day. I have given considerable study to handling pig iron, and feel sure that you could do a much larger day's work than you have been doing. Now don't you think that if you really tried you could handle 47 tons of pig iron per day, instead of 12½ tons?"

What do you think Schmidt's answer would be to this?

Schmidt started to work, and all day long, and at regular intervals, was told by the man who stood over him with a watch, "Now pick up a pig and walk. Now sit down and rest. Now walk—now rest," etc. He worked when he was told to work, and rested when he was told to rest, and at half-past five in the afternoon had his 47½ tons loaded on the car. And he practically never failed to work at this pace and do the task that was set him during the three years that the writer was at Bethlehem. And throughout this time he averaged a little more than $1.85 per day, whereas before he had never received over $1.15 per day, which was the ruling rate of wages at the time in Bethlehem. That is, he received 60 per cent higher wages than were paid to other men who were not working on task work. One man after another was picked out and trained to handle pig iron at the rate of 47½ tons per day until all of the pig iron was handled at this rate, and the men were receiving 60 percent more wages than other workmen around them.

The writer has given above a brief description of three of the four elements which constitute the essence of scientific management: first, the careful selection of the workman, and, second and third, the method of first inducing and then training and helping the workman to work according to the scientific method. Nothing has as yet been said about the science of handling pig iron. The writer trusts, however, that before leaving this illustration the reader will be thoroughly convinced that there is a science of handling pig iron, and further that this science amounts to so much that the man who is suited to handle pig iron cannot possibly understand it, nor even work in accordance with the laws of this science, without the help of those who are over him.

The law is confined to that class of work in which the limit of a man's capacity is reached because he is tired out. It is the law of heavy laboring, corresponding to the work of the cart horse, rather than that of the trotter. Practically all such work consists of a heavy pull or a push on the man's arms, that is, the man's strength is exerted by either lifting or pushing something which he grasps in his hands. And the law is that for each given pull or push on the man's arms it is possible for the workman to be under load for only a definite percentage of the day. For example, when pig iron is being handled (each pig weighing 92 pounds), a first-class workman can only be under load 43 percent of the day. He must be entirely free from load during 57 percent of the day. And as the load becomes lighter, the percentage of the day under which the man can remain under load increases. So that, if the workman is handling a half pig weighing 46 pounds, he can then be under load 58 per cent of the day, and only has to rest during 42 per cent. As the weight grows lighter the man can remain under load during a larger and larger percentage of the day, until finally a load is reached which he can carry in his hands all day long without being tired out. When that point has been arrived at this law ceases to be useful as a guide to a laborer's endurance, and some other law must be found which indicates the man's capacity for work.

When a laborer is carrying a piece of pig iron weighing 92 pounds in his hands, it tires him about as much to stand still under the load as it does to walk with it, since his arm muscles are under the same severe tension whether he is moving or not. A man, however, who stands still under a load is exerting no horse-power whatever, and this accounts for the fact that no constant relation could be traced in various kinds of heavy laboring work between the foot-pounds of energy exerted and the tiring effect of the work on the man. It will also be clear that in all work of this kind it is necessary for the arms of the workman to be completely free from load (that is, for the workman to rest) at frequent intervals. Throughout the time that the man is under a heavy load the tissues of his arm muscles are in process of degeneration, and frequent periods of rest are required in order that the blood may have a chance to restore these tissues to their normal condition.

To return now to our pig-iron handlers at the Bethlehem Steel Company. If Schmidt had been allowed to attack the pile of 47 tons of pig iron without the guidance or direction of a man who understood the art, or science, of handling pig iron, in his desire to earn his high wages he would probably have tired himself out by eleven or twelve o'clock in the day. He would have kept so steadily at work that his muscles would not have had the proper periods of rest absolutely needed for recuperation, and he would have been completely exhausted early in the day. By having a man, however, who understood this law, stand over him and direct his work, day after day, until he acquired the habit of resting at proper intervals, he was able to work at an even gait all day long without unduly tiring himself.

Now one of the very first requirements for a man who is fit to handle pig iron as a regular occupation is that he shall be so stupid and so phlegmatic that he more nearly resembles in his mental make-up the ox than any other type. The man who is mentally alert and intelligent is for this very reason entirely unsuited to what would, for him, be the grinding monotony of work of this character. Therefore the workman who is best suited to handling pig iron is unable to understand the real science of doing this class of work. He is so stupid that the word "percentage" has no meaning to him, and he must consequently be trained by a man more intelligent than himself into the habit of working in accordance with the laws of this science before he can be successful.

The writer trusts that it is now clear that even in the case of the most elementary form of labor that is known, there is a science, and that when the man best suited to this class of work has been carefully selected, when the science of doing the work has been developed, and when the carefully selected man has been trained to work in accordance with this science, the results obtained must of necessity be overwhelmingly greater than those which are possible under the plan of "initiative and incentive."

Notes

1. The writer has tried to make the reason for this unfortunate state of things clear in a paper entitled "Shop Management," read before the American Society of Mechanical Engineers.

2. For example, the records containing the data used under scientific management in an ordinary machine shop fill thousands of pages.

6
The Real Meaning of Taylorism

Harry Braverman

First Principle

"The managers assume . . . the burden of gathering together all of the traditional knowledge which in the past has been possessed by the workmen and then of classifying, tabulating, and reducing this knowledge to rules, laws, and formulae. . . ."[1] We have seen the illustrations of this in the cases of the lathe machinist and the pig-iron handler. The great disparity between these activities, and the different orders of knowledge that may be collected about them, illustrate that for Taylor—as for managers today—no task is either so simple or so complex that it may not be studied with the object of collecting in the hands of management at least as much information as is known by the worker who performs it regularly, and very likely more. This brings to an end the situation in which "Employers derive their knowledge of how much of a given class of work can be done in a day from either their own experience, which has frequently grown hazy with age, from casual and unsystematic observation of their men, or at best from records which are kept, showing the quickest time in which each job has been done."[2] It enables management to discover and enforce those speedier methods and shortcuts which workers themselves, in the practice of their trades or tasks, learn or improvise, and use at their own discretion only. Such an experimental approach also brings into being new methods such as can be devised only through the means of systematic study.

This first principle we may call the *dissociation of the labor process from the skills of the workers*. The labor process is to be rendered independent of craft, tradition, and the workers' knowledge. Henceforth it is to depend not at all upon the abilities of workers, but entirely upon the practices of management.

Reprinted from *Labor and Monopoly Capital*, by Harry Braverman (New York: Monthly Review Books, 1974), 112–121, by permission of the publisher.

Second Principle

"All possible brain work should be removed from the shop and centered in the planning or laying-out department. . . ."[3] Since this is the key to scientific management, as Taylor well understood, he was especially emphatic on this point and it is important to examine the principle thoroughly.

In the human, as we have seen, the essential feature that makes for a labor capacity superior to that of the animal is the combination of execution with a conception of the thing to be done. But as human labor becomes a social rather than an individual phenomenon, it is possible—unlike in the instance of animals where the motive force, instinct, is inseparable from action—to divorce conception from execution. This dehumanization of the labor process, in which workers are reduced almost to the level of labor in its animal form, while purposeless and unthinkable in the case of the self-organized and self-motivated social labor of a community of producers, becomes crucial for the management of purchased labor. For if the workers' execution is guided by their own conception, it is not possible, as we have seen, to enforce upon them either the methodological efficiency or the working pace desired by capital. The capitalist therefore learns from the start to take advantage of this aspect of human labor power, and to break the unity of the labor process.

This should be called the principle of the *separation of conception from execution*, rather than by its more common name of the separation of mental and manual labor (even though it is similar to the latter, and in practice often identical). This is because mental labor, labor done primarily in the brain, is also subjected to the same principle of separation of conception from execution; mental labor is first separated from manual labor and, as we shall see, is then itself subdivided rigorously according to the same rule.

The first implication of this principle is that Taylor's "science of work" is never to be developed by the worker, always by management. This notion, apparently so "natural" and undebatable today, was in fact vigorously discussed in Taylor's day, a fact which shows how far we have traveled along the road of transforming all ideas about the labor process in less than a century, and how completely Taylor's hotly contested assumptions have entered into the conventional outlook within a short space of time. Taylor confronted this question—why must work be studied by the management and not by the worker himself; why not *scientific workmanship* rather than *scientific management?*—repeatedly, and employed all his ingenuity in devising answers to it, though not always with his customary frankness. In *The Principles of Scientific Management*, he pointed out that the "older system" of management makes it necessary for each workman to bear almost the entire responsibility for the general plan as well as for each detail of his work, and in many cases for his implements as well. In addition to this he must do all of the actual physical labor. The development of a science, on the other hand, involves the establishment of many rules, laws, and formulae which replace the judgment of the individual workman and which can be effectively used only after having been systematically recorded, indexed, etc. The practical use of scientific data also calls for a room in which to keep the books, records, etc., and a desk for the planner to work at. Thus all of the planning which under the old system was done by the workman, as a result of his personal experience, must of necessity under the new system be done by the management in accordance with the laws of the science; because even if the workman was well suited to the development and use of scientific data, it would be physically impossible for him to work at his machine and at a desk at the same time. It is also clear that in most cases one type of man is needed to plan ahead and an entirely different type to execute the work.[4]

The objections having to do with physical arrangements in the workplace are clearly of little importance, and represent the deliberate exaggeration of obstacles which, while they may exist as inconveniences, are hardly insuperable. To refer to the "different type" of worker needed for each job is worse than disingenuous, since these "different types" hardly existed until the division of labor created them. As Taylor well understood, the possession of craft knowledge made the worker the best starting point for the development of the science of work; systematization often means, at least at the outset, the gathering of knowledge which *workers already possess*. But Taylor, secure in his obsession with the immense reasonableness of his proposed arrangement, did not stop at this point. In his testimony before the Special Committee of the House of Representatives, pressed and on the defensive, he brought forth still other arguments:

> I want to make it clear, Mr. Chairman, that work of this kind undertaken by the management leads to the development of a science, while it is next to impossible for the workman to develop a science. There are many workmen who are intellectually just as capable of developing a science, who have plenty of brains, and are just as capable of developing a science as those on the managing side. But the science of doing work of any kind cannot be developed by the workman. Why? Because he has neither the time nor the money to do it. The development of the science of doing any kind of work always required the work of two men, one man who actually does the work which is to be studied and another man who observes closely the first man while he works and studies the time problems and the motion problems connected with this work. No workman has either the time or the money to burn in making experiments of this sort. If he is working for himself no one will pay him while he studies the motions of some one else. The management must and ought to pay for all such work. So that for the workman, the development of a science becomes impossible, not because the workman is

not intellectually capable of developing it, but he has neither the time nor the money to do it and he realizes that this is a question for the management to handle.[5]

Taylor here argues that the systematic study of work and the fruits of this study belong to management for the very same reason that machines, factory buildings, etc., belong to them; that is, because it costs labor time to conduct such a study, and only the possessors of capital can afford labor time. The possessors of labor time cannot themselves afford to do anything with it but sell it for their means of subsistence. It is true that this is the rule in capitalist relations of production, and Taylor's use of the argument in this case shows with great clarity where the sway of capital leads: Not only is capital the property of the capitalist, but *labor itself has become part of capital.* Not only do the workers lose control over their instruments of production, but they must now lose control over their own labor and the manner of its performance. This control now falls to those who can "afford" to study it in order to know it better than the workers themselves know their own life activity.

But Taylor has not yet completed his argument: "Furthermore," he told the Committee, "if any workman were to find a new and quicker way of doing work, or if he were to develop a new method, you can see at once it becomes to his interest to keep that development to himself, not to teach the other workmen the quicker method. It is to his interest to do what workmen have done in all times, to keep their trade secrets for themselves and their friends. That is the old idea of trade secrets. The workman kept his knowledge to himself instead of developing a science and teaching it to others and making it public property."[6] Behind this hearkening back to old ideas of "guild secrets" is Taylor's persistent and fundamental notion that the improvement of work methods by workers brings few benefits to management. Elsewhere in his testimony, in discussing the work of his associate, Frank Gilbreth, who spent many years studying bricklaying methods, he candidly admits that not only *could* the "science of bricklaying" be developed by workers, but that it undoubtedly *had been:* "Now, I have not the slightest doubt that during the last 4,000 years all the methods that Mr. Gilbreth developed have many, many times suggested themselves to the minds of bricklayers." But because knowledge possessed by workers is not useful to capital, Taylor begins his list of the desiderata of scientific management: "First. The development—by the management, not the workmen—of the science of bricklaying."[7] Workers, he explains, are not going to put into execution any system or any method which harms them and their workmates: "Would they be likely," he says, referring to the pig-iron job, "to get rid of seven men out of eight from their own gang and retain only the eighth man? No!"[8]

Finally, Taylor understood the Babbage principle better than anyone of his time, and it was always uppermost in his calculations. The purpose of work study was never, in his mind, to enhance the ability of the worker, to concentrate in the worker a greater share of scientific knowledge, to ensure that as technique rose, the worker would rise with it. Rather, the purpose was to cheapen the worker by decreasing his training and enlarging his output. In his early book, *Shop Management*, he said frankly that the "full possibilities" of his system "will not have been realized until almost all of the machines in the shop are run by men who are of smaller calibre and attainments, and who are therefore cheaper than those required under the old system."[9]

Therefore, both in order to ensure management control and to cheapen the worker, conception and execution must be rendered separate spheres of work, and for this purpose the study of work processes must be reserved to management and kept from the workers, to whom its results are communicated only in the form of simplified job tasks governed by simplified instructions which it is thenceforth their duty to follow unthinkingly and without comprehension of the underlying technical reasoning or data.

Third Principle

The essential idea of "the ordinary types of management," Taylor said, "is that each workman has become more skilled in his own trade than it is possible for any one in the management to be, and that, therefore, the details of how the work shall best be done must be left to him." But, by contrast: "Perhaps the most prominent single element in modern scientific management is the task idea. The work of every workman is fully planned out by the management at least one day in advance, and each man receives in most cases complete written instructions, describing in detail the task which he is to accomplish, as well as the means to be used in doing the work.... This task specifies not only what is to be done, but how it is to be done and the exact time allowed for doing it.... Scientific management consists very largely in preparing for and carrying out these tasks."[10]

In this principle it is not the written instruction card that is important.* Taylor had no need for such a card with Schmidt, nor did he use one in

---

*This despite the fact that for a time written instruction cards were a fetish among managers. The vogue for such cards passed as work tasks became so simplified and repetitious as to render the cards in most cases unnecessary. But the concept behind them remains: it is the concept of the direct action of management to determine the process, with the worker functioning as the mediating and closely governed instrument. This is the significance of Lillian Gilbreth's definition of the instruction card as "a self-producer of a predetermined product."[11] The worker as producer is ignored; management becomes the producer, and its plans and instructions bring the product into existence. This same instruction care inspired in Alfred Marshall, however, the curious opinion that from it,

many other instances. Rather, the essential element is the systematic pre-planning and pre-calculation of all elements of the labor process, which now no longer exists as a process in the imagination of the worker but only as a process in the imagination of a special management staff. Thus, if the first principle is the gathering and development of knowledge of labor processes, and the second is the concentration of this knowledge as the exclusive province of management—together with its essential converse, the absence of such knowledge among the workers—then the third is the *use of this monopoly over knowledge to control each step of the labor process and its mode of execution*.

As capitalist industrial, office, and market practices developed in accordance with this principle, it eventually became part of accepted routine and custom, all the more so as the increasingly scientific character of most processes, which grew in complexity while the worker was not allowed to partake of this growth, made it ever more difficult for the workers to understand the processes in which they functioned. But in the beginning, as Taylor well understood, an abrupt psychological wrench was required.* We have seen in the simple Schmidt case the means employed, both in the selection of a single worker as a starting point and in the way in which he was reoriented to the new conditions of work. In the more complex conditions of the machine shop, Taylor gave this part of the responsibility to the foremen. It is essential, he said of the gang bosses, to "nerve and brace them up to the point of insisting that the workmen shall carry out the orders exactly as specified on the instruction cards. This is a difficult task at first, as the workmen have been accustomed for years to do the details of the work to suit themselves, and many of them are intimate friends of the bosses and believe they know quite as much about their business as the latter."[13]

Modern management came into being on the basis of these principles. It arose as theoretical construct and as systematic practice, moreover, in the

---

workers could learn how production is carried on: such a card, "whenever it comes into the hands of a thoughtful man, may suggest to him something of the purposes and methods of those who have constructed it."[12] The worker, in Marshall's notion, having given up technical knowledge of the craft, is now to pick up the far more complex technical knowledge of modern industry from his task card, as a paleontologist reconstructs the entire animal from a fragment of a bone!

*One must not suppose from this that such a psychological shift in relations between worker and manager is entirely a thing of the past. On the contrary, it is constantly being recapitulated in the evolution of new occupations as they are brought into being by the development of industry and trade, and are then routinized and subjugated to management control. As this tendency has attacked office, technical, and "educated" occupations, sociologists have spoken of it as "bureaucratization," an evasive and unfortunate use of Weberian terminology, a terminology which often reflects its users' view that this form of govenment over work is endemic to "large-scale" or "complex" enterprises, whereas it is better understood as the specific product of the capitalist organization of work, and reflects not primarily scale but social antagonisms.

very period during which the transformation of labor from processes based on skill to processes based upon science was attaining its most rapid tempo. Its role was to render conscious and systematic, the formerly unconscious tendency of capitalist production. It was to ensure that as craft declined, the worker would sink to the level of general and undifferentiated labor power, adaptable to a large range of simple tasks, while as science grew, it would be concentrated in the hands of management.

Notes

1. Frederick Taylor, *The Principles of Scientific Management* (New York: 1967), 36.
2. Ibid., 22.
3. Frederick Taylor, "Shop Management," *Scientific Management* (New York and London: 1947), 98–99.
4. Taylor, *Principles of Scientific Management*, 37–38.
5. "Taylor's Testimony before the Special House Committee," Taylor, *Scientific Management*, 235–236.
6. Taylor, Ibid.
7. Taylor, Ibid., 75, 77.
8. Taylor, *Principles of Scientific Management*, 62.
9. Taylor, "Shop Management," *Scientific Management*, 105.
10. Taylor, *Principles of Scientific Management*, 39, 63.
11. Lillian Gilbreth, "The Psychology of Management (1914)," *The Writings of the Gilbreths*, William R. Spriegel and Clark E. Myers, eds. (Homewood, Ill.: 1953), 404.
12. Alfred Marshall, *Industry and Trade* (London: 1919, 1932), 391–393.
13. Taylor, "Shop Management," *Scientific Management*, 108.

7
Human Relations and the Informal Organization
Fritz J. Roethlisberger and William J. Dickson

The Two Major Functions of an Industrial Organization

An industrial organization may be regarded as performing two major functions, that of producing a product and that of creating and distributing satisfactions among the individual members of the organization. The first function is ordinarily called economic. From this standpoint the functioning of the concern is assessed in such terms as cost, profit, and technical efficiency. The second function, while it is readily understood, is not ordinarily designated by any generally accepted word. It is variously described as maintaining employee relations, employee good will, cooperation, etc. From this standpoint the functioning of the concern is frequently assessed in such terms as labor turnover, tenure of employment, sickness and accident rate, wages, employee attitudes, etc. The industrial concern is continually confronted, therefore, with two sets of major problems: (1) problems of external balance, and (2) problems of internal equilibrium. The problems of external balance are generally assumed to be economic; that is, problems of competition, adjusting the organization to meet changing price levels, etc. The problems of internal equilibrium are chiefly concerned with the maintenance of a kind of social organization in which individuals and groups through working together can satisfy their own desires.

Ordinarily an industrial concern is thought of primarily in terms of its success in meeting problems of external balance, or if the problems of internal equilibrium are explicitly recognized they are frequently assumed to be separate from and unrelated to the economic purpose of the enterprise. Producing an article at a profit and maintaining good employee relations are frequently regarded as antithetical propositions. The results of the studies which have been reported indicated, however, that these two sets of problems are interrelated and interdependent. The

---

Reprinted from *Management and the Worker*, by Fritz J. Roethlisberger and William J. Dickson (Cambridge: Harvard University Press, 1939), 552–562, by permission of the publisher.

kind of social organization which obtains within a concern is intimately related to the effectiveness of the total organization. Likewise, the success with which the concern maintains external balance is directly related to its internal organization.

A great deal of attention has been given to the economic function of industrial organization. Scientific controls have been introduced to further the economic purposes of the concern and of the individuals within it. Much of this advance has gone on in the name of efficiency or rationalization. Nothing comparable to this advance has gone on in the development of skills and techniques for securing cooperation, that is, for getting individuals and groups of individuals working together effectively and with satisfaction to themselves. The slight advances which have been made in this area have been overshadowed by the new and powerful technological developments of modern industry.

The Technical Organization of the Plant

In looking at an industrial organization as a social system it will first be necessary to examine the physical environment, for this is an inseparable part of any organization. The physical environment includes not only climate and weather, but also that part of the environment which is owned and used by the organization itself, namely, the physical plant, tools, machines, raw products, and so on. This latter part of the factory's physical environment is ordered and organized in a certain specified way to accomplish the task of technical production. For our purposes, therefore, it will be convenient to distinguish from the human organization this aspect of the physical environment of an industrial plant and to label it the "technical organization of the plant." This term will refer only to the logical and technical organization of material, tools, machines, and finished product, including all those physical items related to the task of technical production.

The two aspects into which an industrial plant can be roughly divided—the technical organization and the human organization—are interrelated and interdependent. The human organization is constantly molding and recreating the technical organization either to achieve more effectively the common economic purpose or to secure more satisfaction for its members. Likewise, changes in the technical organization require an adaptation on the part of the human organization.

The Human Organization of the Plant

In the human organization we find a number of individuals working together toward a common end: the collective purpose of the total organization. Each of these individuals, however, is bringing to the work situation a different background of personal and social experiences. No two individuals are making exactly the same demands of their job. The demands a particular employee makes depend not only upon his physical needs but upon his social needs as well. These social needs and the sentiments associated with them vary with his early personal history and social conditioning as well as with the needs and sentiments of people closely associated with him both inside and outside of work.

The Individual

It may be well to look more closely at the sentiments the individual is bringing to his work situation. Starting with a certain native organic endowment the child is precipitated into group life by the act of birth. The group into which the child is born is not the group in general. The child is born into a specific family. Moreover, this specific family is not a family in isolation. It is related in certain ways to other families in the community. It has a certain cultural background—a way of life, codes and routines of behavior, associated with certain beliefs and expectations. In the beginning the child brings only his organic needs to this social milieu into which he is born. Very rapidly he begins to accumulate experience. This process of accumulating experience is the process of assigning meanings to the socio-reality about him; it is the process of becoming socialized. Much of the early learning period is devoted to preparing the child to become capable of social life in its particular group. In preparing the child for social participation the immediate family group plays an important role. By the particular type of family into which the child is born he is "conditioned" to certain routines of behavior and ways of living. The early meanings he assigns to his experience are largely in terms of these codes of behavior and associated beliefs. As the child grows up and participates in groups other than the immediate family his leanings lose, although never quite entirely, their specific family form. This process of social interaction and social conditioning is never-ending and continues from birth to death. The adult's evaluation of his surroundings is determined in a good part by the system of human interrelations in which he has participated.

The Social Organization of the Plant

However, the human organization of an industrial plant is more than a plurality of individuals, each motivated by sentiments arising from his own personal and private history and background. It is also a social organization, for the members of an industrial plant—executives, technical specialists, supervisors, factory workers, and office workers—are interacting daily with one another and from their associations certain patterns of relations are formed among them. These patterns of relations, together with the objects which symbolize them, constitute the social organization of the industrial enterprise. Most of the individuals who live among these patterns come to accept them as obvious and necessary truths and to react as they dictate. Both the kind of behavior that is expected of a person and the kind of behavior he can expect from others are prescribed by these patterns.

If one looks at a factory situation, for example, one finds individuals and groups of individuals who are associated at work acting in certain accepted and prescribed ways toward one another. There is no complete homogeneity of behavior between individuals or between one group of individuals and another, but rather there are differences of behavior expressing differences in social relationship. Some relationships fall into routine patterns, such as the relationship between superior and subordinate or between office worker and shop worker. Individuals conscious of their membership in certain groups are reacting in certain accepted ways to other individuals representing other groups. Behavior varies according to the stereotyped conceptions of relationship. The worker, for example, behaves toward his foreman in one way, toward his first-line supervisor in another way, and toward his fellow worker in still another. People holding the rank of inspector expect a certain kind of behavior from the operators—the operators from the inspectors. Now these relationships, as is well known from everyday experiences, are finely shaded and sometimes become complicated. When a person is in the presence of his supervisor alone he usually acts differently from the way he acts when his supervisor's supervisor is also present. Likewise, his supervisor acts toward him alone quite differently from the way he behaves when his own supervisor is also there. The subtle nuances of relationship are so much a part of everyday life that they are commonplace. They are taken for granted. The vast amount of social conditioning that has taken place by means of which a person maneuvers himself gracefully through the intricacies of these finely shaded social distinctions is seldom explicitly realized. Attention is paid only when a new social situation arises where the past social training of the person prevents him from making the necessary delicate interpretations of a given social signal and hence brings forth the "socially wrong" response.

In the factory, as in any social milieu, a process of social evaluation is constantly at work. From this process distinctions of "good" and "bad," "inferior" and "superior," arise. This process of evaluation is carried on with simple and ready generalizations by means of which values become attached to individuals and to groups performing certain tasks and operations. It assigns to a group of individuals performing such and such a task a particular rank in the established prestige scale. Each work group becomes a carrier of social values. In industry with its extreme diversity of occupations there are a number of such groupings. Any noticeable similarity or difference, not only in occupation but also in age, sex, and nationality, can serve as a basis of social classification, as, for example, "married women," the "old-timer," the "white-collared" or clerical worker, the "foreign element." Each of these groups, too, has its own value system.

All the patterns of interaction that arise between individuals or between different groups can be graded according to the degree of intimacy involved in the relationship. Grades of intimacy or understanding can be arranged on a scale and expressed in terms of "social distance." Social distance measures differences of sentiment and interest which separate individuals or groups from one another. Between the president of a company and the elevator operator there is considerable social distance, more for example than between the foreman and the benchworker. Social distance is to social organization what physical distance is to physical space. However, physical and social distance do not necessarily coincide. Two people may be physically near but socially distant.

Just as each employee has a particular physical location, so he has a particular social place in the total social organization. But this place is not so rigidly fixed as in a caste system. In any factory there is considerable mobility or movement. Movement can occur in two ways: the individual may pass from one occupation to another occupation higher up in the prestige scale; or the prestige scale itself may change.

It is obvious that these scales of value are never completely accepted by all the groups in the social environment. The shop worker does not quite see why the office worker, for example, should have shorter hours of work than he has. Or the newcomer, whose efficiency on a particular job is about the same, but whose hourly rate is less than that of some old-timer, wonders why service should count so much. The management group, in turn, from the security of its social elevation, does not often understand what "all the fuss is about."

As was indicated by many of the studies, any person who has achieved a certain rank in the prestige scale regards anything real or imaginary which tends to alter his status adversely as something unfair or unjust. It is apparent that any move on the part of the management may alter the existing social equilibrium to which the employee has grown accustomed and by means of which his status is defined. Immediately this disruption will be expressed in sentiments of resistance of the real or imagined alterations in the social equilibrium.

From this point of view it can be seen how every item and event in the industrial environment becomes an object of a system of sentiments. According to this way of looking at things, material goods, physical events, wages, hours of work, etc., cannot be treated as things in themselves. Instead they have to be interpreted as carriers of social value. The meanings which any person in an industrial organization assigns to the events and objects in his environment are often determined by the social situation in which the events and objects occur. The significance to an employee of a double-pedestal desk, of a particular kind of pencil, or of a handset telephone is determined by the social setting in which these objects appear. If people with double-pedestal desks supervise people with single-pedestal desks, then double-pedestal desks become symbols of status or prestige in the organization. As patterns of behavior become crystallized, every object in the environment tends to take on a particular social significance. It becomes easy to tell a person's social place in the organization by the objects which he wears and carries and which surround him. In these terms it can be seen how the introduction of a technical change may also involve for an individual or a group of individuals the loss of certain prestige symbols and, as a result, have a demoralizing effect.

From this point of view the behavior of no one person in an industrial organization, from the very top to the very bottom, can be regarded as motivated by strictly economic or logical considerations. Routine patterns of interaction involve strong sentiments. Each group in the organization manifests its own powerful sentiments. It is likely that sometimes the behavior of many staff specialists which goes under the name of "efficiency" is as much a manifestation of a very strong sentiment—the sentiment or desire to originate new combinations—as it is of anything strictly logical.

This point of view is far from the one which is frequently expressed, namely, that man is essentially an economic being carrying around with him a few noneconomic appendages. Rather, the point of view which has been expressed here is that noneconomic motives, interests, and processes, as well as economic, are fundamental in behavior in business, from the board of directors to the very last man in the organization. Man is not merely—in fact is very seldom—motivated by factors pertaining strictly to facts or logic. Sentiments are not merely things which man carries around with him as appendages. He cannot cast them off like a suit of clothes. He carries them with him wherever he goes. In business or elsewhere, he can hardly behave without expressing them. Moreover, sentiments do not exist in a social vacuum. They are the product of social behavior, of social interaction, of the fact that man lives his life as a member of different groups. Not only does man bring sentiments to the business situation because of his past experiences and conditioning outside of business, but also as a member of a specific local business organization with a particular social place in it he has certain sentiments expressing his particular relations to it.

According to this point of view, every social act in adulthood is an integrated response to both inner and outer stimuli. To each new concrete situation the adult brings his past "social conditioning." To the extent that this past social conditioning has prepared him to assimilate the new experience in the culturally accepted manner, he is said to be "adjusted." To the extent that his private or personal view of the situation is at variance with the cultural situation, the person is called "maladjusted."

The Formal Organization of the Plant

The social organization of the industrial plant is in part formally organized. It is composed of a number of strata or levels which differentiate the benchworker from the skilled mechanic, the group chief from the department chief, and so on. These levels are well defined and all the formal orders, instructions, and compensations are addressed to them. All such factors taken together make up the formal organization of the plant. It includes the systems, policies, rules, and regulations of the plant which express what the relations of one person to another are supposed to be in order to achieve effectively the task of technical production. It prescribes the relations that are supposed to obtain within the human organization and between the human organization and the technical organization. In short, the patterns of human interrelation as defined by the systems, rules, policies, and regulations of the company, constitute the formal organization.

The formal organization of an industrial plant has two purposes: it addresses itself to the economic purposes of the total enterprise; it concerns itself also with the securing of cooperative effort. The formal organization includes all the explicitly stated systems of control introduced by the company in order to achieve the economic purposes of the total enterprise and the effective contribution of the members of the organization to those economic ends.

The Informal Organization of the Plant

All the experimental studies pointed to the fact that there is something more to the social organization than what has been formally recognized. Many of the actually existing patterns of human interaction have no representation in the formal organization at all, and others are inadequately represented by the formal organization. This fact is frequently forgotten when talking or thinking about industrial situations in general. Too often it is assumed that the organization of a company corresponds to a blueprint plan or organization chart. Actually, it never does. In the formal organization of most companies little explicit recognition is given to many social distinctions residing in the social organization. The blueprint plans of a company show the functional relations between working units, but they do not express the distinctions of social distance, movement, or equilibrium previously described. The hierarchy of prestige values which tends to make the work of men more important than the work of women, the work of clerks more important than the work at the bench, has little representation in the formal organization; nor does a blueprint plan ordinarily show the primary groups, that is, those groups enjoying daily face-to-face relations. Logical lines of horizontal and vertical co-ordination of functions replace the actually existing patterns of interaction between people in different social places. The formal organization cannot take account of the sentiments and values residing in the social organization by means of which individuals or groups of individuals are informally differentiated, ordered, and integrated. Individuals in their associations with one another in a factory build up personal relationships. They form into informal groups, in terms of which each person achieves a certain position or status. The nature of these informal groups is very important, as has been shown in the Relay Assembly Test Room and in the Bank Wiring Observation Room.

It is well to recognize that informal organizations are not "bad," as they are sometimes assumed to be. Informal social organization exists in every plant, and can be said to be a necessary prerequisite for effective collaboration. Much collaboration exists at an informal level, and it sometimes facilitates the functioning of the formal organization. On the other hand, sometimes the informal organization develops in opposition to the formal organization. The important consideration is, therefore, the relation that exists between formal and informal organizations.

To illustrate, let us consider the Relay Assembly Test Room and the Bank Wiring Observation Room. These two studies offered an interesting contrast between two informal working groups; one situation could be characterized in almost completely opposite terms from the other. In the Relay Assembly Test Room, on the one hand, the five operators changed continuously in their rate of output up and down over the duration of the test, and yet in a curious fashion their variations in output were insensitive to many significant changes introduced during the experiment. On the other hand, in the Bank Wiring Observation Room output was being held relatively constant and there existed a hypersensitivity to change on the part of the worker—in fact, what could almost be described as an organized opposition to it.

It is interesting to note that management could draw from these studies two opposite conclusions. From the Relay Assembly Test Room experiment they could argue that the company can do almost anything it wants in the nature of technical changes without any perceptible effect on the output of the workers. From the Bank Wiring Observation Room they could argue equally convincingly that the company can introduce hardly any changes without meeting a pronounced opposition to them from the workers. To make this dilemma even more striking, it is only necessary to recall that the sensitivity to change in the one case occurred in the room where no experimental changes had been introduced whereas the insensitivity to change in the other case occurred in the room where the operators had been submitted to considerable experimentation. To settle this question by saying that in one case the situation was typical and in the other case atypical of ordinary shop conditions would be to beg the question, for the essential difference between the two situations would again be missed. It would ignore the social setting in which the changes occurred and the meaning which the workers themselves assigned to the changes.

Although in both cases there were certain informal arrangements not identical with the formal setup, the informal organization in one room was quite different from that in the other room, especially in its relation to the formal organization. In the case of the Relay Assembly Test Room there was a group, or informal organization, which could be characterized as a network of personal relations which had been developed in and through a particular way of working together; it was an organization which not only satisfied the wishes of its members but also worked in harmony with the aims of management. In the case of the Bank Wiring Observation Room there was an informal organization which could be characterized better as a set of practices and beliefs which its members had in common—practices and beliefs which at many points worked against the economic purposes of the company. In one case the relation between the formal and informal organization was one of compatibility; in the other case it was one of opposition. Or to put it another way, collaboration in the Relay Assembly Test Room was at a much higher level than in the Bank Wiring Observation Room.

The difference between these two groups can be understood only by comparing the functions which their informal organizations performed for their members. The chief function of the informal group in the Bank Wiring Observation Room was to resist changes in their established routines of work or personal interrelations. This resistance to change, however, was not the chief function of the informal group in the Relay Assembly Test Room. It is true that at first the introduction of the planned changes in the test room, whether or not these changes were logically in the direction of improvement, was met with apprehension and feelings of uneasiness on the part of the operators. The girls in the beginning were never quite sure that they might not be victims of the changes.

In setting up the Relay Assembly Test Room with the object of studying the factors determining the efficiency of the worker, many of the methods and rules by means of which management tends to promote and maintain efficiency—the "bogey," not talking too much at work, etc.—were, in effect, abrogated. With the removal of this source of constraint and in a setting of heightened social significance (because many of the changes had differentiated the test room girls from the regular department and as a result had elevated the social status within the plant of each of the five girls) a new type of spontaneous social organization developed. Social conditions had been established which allowed the operators to develop their own values and objectives. The experimental conditions allowed the operators to develop openly social codes at work and these codes, unhampered by interference, gave a sustained meaning to their work. It was as if the experimenters had acted as a buffer for the operators and held their work situation steady while they developed a new type of social organization. With this change in the type of social organization there also developed a new attitude toward changes in their working environment. Toward many changes which constitute an unspecified threat in the regular work situation the operators become immune. What the Relay Assembly Test Room experiment showed was that when innovations are introduced carefully and with regard to the actual sentiments of the workers, the workers are likely to develop a spontaneous type of informal organization which will not only express more adequately their own values and significances but also is more likely to be in harmony with the aims of management.

Although all the studies of informal organization at the Hawthorne Plant were made at the employee level, it would be incorrect to assume that this phenomenon occurs only at that level. Informal organization appears at all levels, from the very bottom to the very top of the organization.[1] Informal organization at the executive level, just as at the work level, may either facilitate or impede purposive cooperation and communication. In either case, at all levels of the organization informal organizations exist as a necessary condition for collaboration. Without them formal organization could not survive for long. Formal and informal organizations are interdependent aspects of social interaction.

Note

1. C. I. Barnard, *The Functions of the Executive* (Cambridge: Harvard University Press, 1938), 223–24.

8
Three Patterns of Bureaucracy
Alvin W. Gouldner

1. Mock Bureaucracy: The "No-Smoking" Rule

Analysis of the plant rules can begin by turning to the "no-smoking" regulations. As comments of people in the plant emphasized, one of the most distinctive things about this rule was that it was a "dead letter." Except under unusual circumstances, it was ignored by most personnel.

Thus, while offering a cigarette to a worker, one of the interviewers asked:

> What about the "No-Smoking" signs? They seem to be all over the place, yet everyone seems to smoke.

> (Laughing) Yes, these are *not really Company rules*. The fire insurance writers put them in. The office seems to think that *smoking doesn't hurt anything*, so they don't bother us about it. That is, of course, until the fire inspector (from the insurance company) comes around. Then as soon as he gets into the front office, they call down here and *the word is spread round for no smoking*.

The workers particularly seemed to enjoy the warning sent by the front office, for they invariably repeated this part of the story. For example, another worker remarked:

> We can smoke as much as we want. When the fire inspector comes around, *everybody is warned earlier*. . . . The Company doesn't mind.

Since under ordinary circumstances no one attempted to enforce this rule, it entailed little or no tension between workers and management. On the contrary, the situation was one which strengthened solidarity between the two groups. Their joint violation of the no-smoking rule, and their cooperative effort to outwit the "outsider," the insurance company, allied them as fellow "conspirators."

It seems evident from the above quotations that *one* of the things leading to rejection of the no-smoking rule, by workers and management

---

Reprinted from *Patterns of Industrial Bureaucracy*, by Alvin W. Gouldner (Glencoe, Ill.: Free Press, 1954), pp. 182–87, 187–89, 207, 212–14, 216–17, by permission of Macmillan Publishing Co. Copyright 1954 by The Free Press; renewed 1982 by Alvin Gouldner.

alike, was that this regulation was initiated by an *outside* group. The workers usually distinguished between rules voluntarily initiated by the Company or plant management and those which, for one or another reason, management was compelled to endorse. Nonetheless, there were certain rules with which workers complied, even though local management was not viewed as responsible for their introduction.

One of these regulations governed the mining of gypsum ore. It specified that different "checks" (which were little numbered placards) had to be placed on each load of gypsum that was sent up from the mine. As a miner explained:

> You get a 'Number 1' check for General Gypsum and a 'Number 5' for royalty. They (the Company) have to pay ten cents a ton to everyone whose land they use. You can see *they're not doing this 'cause they want to; it's got to be done this way.*

Though [it presented] something of a nuisance, miners were ready to conform to this rule, and did so, despite the fact that it sprang from "outside" pressure. They conformed because the system enabled them to "check up" on their tonnage output and, since their earnings were geared to this, on their income.

Enforcement of the no-smoking rule would, of course, subject workers to an annoyance which, for some of them, was more than trifling. To demand that a man give up smoking would be much like asking him to stop chewing his fingernails. As a surface painter said:

> You can't stop a man from smoking. He has to. *It keeps him from getting nervous.* You just can't stop a man from smoking if he wants to.

Had conformance to this rule been demanded, a powerful and clear-cut legitimation would have been needed. As the above painter added:

> Safety is another story. The men won't resist that. *It's for their own good. They don't want accidents, if they can help it.* It's not like smoking.

Similarly, the labor relations director at the main office remarked:

> In plants where there is a *real danger of fire*, the men can be gotten to give up smoking.

In this plant, though, since there was little flammable material around, workers could see "no good reason" why they should stop smoking. In other words, workers do not believe that management has the right to institute *any* kind of a rule, *merely because they have the legal authority to do so*. A rule must also be legitimate in terms of the group's *values*, and will be more readily accepted if it is seen as furthering their own ends. Workers rejected the no-smoking rule, in part, because it could not be justified by rational considerations; it did not effectively attain something *they* valued and wanted.

This, however, was only a part of the picture. What would have happened, or what did people in the situation believe would happen, if the no-smoking rule would be enforced? Enforcement of the rule was generally expected to *sharpen* status distinctions within the plant. This was suggested, for example, by the comments of a foreman, who was explaining why the no-smoking rule was ignored:

> You see, they got a permit to smoke in the office. *The men feel if they can smoke up there, they can smoke down here* (in the factory).

In brief, enforcement of the no-smoking rule would heighten the visibility of existent status differences, allowing to one group obvious privileges denied to another. This relates to the "screening function" of the rules, and their role in blurring unacceptable status distinctions. Apparently, where enforcement of rules *unveils* status distinctions, as in this case, rather than masking them, the rule is neglected.

There is a difference between this situation and the "check" system in the mine. When miners conformed to the check regulation, their status was not impaired. Quite the contrary; for an important attribute of their status, namely their income, was made all the more secure by conforming to the checking rules. Conformance to the no-smoking regulations, however, would threaten, not fortify, the status of most production workers and even their supervisors.

Only on one occasion did management seek compliance with the no-smoking rule. This occurred when the insurance inspector made his tour through the plant. The worker who violated the rule *at this time* was bombarded with sharp criticism by his peers. As one board worker complained:

> There are a few guys who didn't even stop smoking when the inspector comes around. They are troublemakers, and *we let them know where they get off*.

During these routine inspections, as in the routine conduct of the "checking" system in the mine, workers viewed management's enforcement of the rule as compelled; that is, "they're not doing this 'cause they want to." The inspection was *not* seen as an occasion joyfully seized upon by management to increase its control over the workers. On the other hand, workers who "*violated*" the no-smoking rule under ordinary conditions were not viewed by supervisors as "troublemakers" giving vent to their hostilities. Instead, workers who smoked were viewed as being in the grip of an uncontrollable "human" need, for smoking was presumably required to quell their "nervousness."

Briefly, then, the no-smoking rule is a pattern possessing the following fairly obvious characteristics:

1. Usually, the rule was neither enforced by plant management nor obeyed by workers.

2. As a rule, it engendered little tension and conflict between the two groups and in fact seemed to enhance their solidarity.
3. Both the customary violation of the rule, as well as the occasional enforcement of it, were buttressed by the informal sentiments and behavior of the participants.

As point "two" above suggests, this pattern was partly anchored in the "leeway function" of the rules. That is, informally friendly and cooperative attitudes toward management were evoked insofar as management *withheld* enforcement of the rules. While the above discussion has already suggested some clues as to *how* this pattern was brought about, it will be helpful to wait and consider other rules before a summary analysis, which sifts out the underlying variables, is attempted.

This pattern has been called "mock bureaucracy," for many of the bureaucratic cues were present—rules, posters calling for their enforcement, and inspections—but in the ordinary day-to-day conduct of work, this bureaucratic paraphernalia was ignored and inoperative. In terms of the plant's recognized work divisions or departments, it is evident that the mine, rather than the surface factories, more closely approximated mock bureacracy. Finally, it may be noted that "mock bureaucracy" was the organizational counterpart of the "indulgency pattern." The indulgency pattern refers to the criteria in terms of which the plant was judged by workers as "lenient" or "good." Together, these criteria comprised an implicit description of mock bureaucracy. To put it the other way around, mock bureaucracy refers to the kind of social relations that emerge if the norms of the indulgency pattern are administratively implemented.

2. Representative Bureaucracy: The Safety Rules

The safety operations comprised a sphere which was more bureaucratically organized than any other in the plant. This was not, of course, the only respect in which safety regulations differed from other rules; nevertheless, it is a key factor that deserves consideration.

As a preliminary indication of the high degree of bureaucracy in this sphere, attention may be given first to the sheer quantity of rules included under the heading of safety. These were more numerous and complex than rules governing any other distinctive activity. There were, for example, sizeable lists of safety regulations which applied to the plant as a whole, while there were others which applied only to specific divisions of the factory. Thus, in the mine, there were specific rules concerning the use and handling of dynamite caps. In the mill, there were rules specifying the manner in which the large dehydrating vats were to be cleaned out. Still other rules, indicating proper procedure to be followed if a tool fell into the mixture, applied only to the board building.

Not only was the system of safety rules complex, but considerable stress was placed upon conformity to them. Unlike the no-smoking rules, the safety regulations were not a "dead letter." Specific agencies existed which strove energetically to bring about their observance. These agencies placed continual pressure upon both workers and management, and sought to orient the two groups to the safety rules during their daily activities. For example, the Company's main office officially defined accident and safety work as one of the regular responsibilities of foreman and supervisors. As the Company's safety manual asserted:

> The foreman must accept the responsibility for the accidents that occur in his department . . . (and) he should be provided with the *knowledge* (sic) he needs to carry it out. (Our emphasis—A. W. G.)

A complex system of "paper work" and "reports," so symptomatic of developed bureaucracy, was centered on the safety program. Thus, in the event that a compensable accident occurred, foremen were directed to prepare a complete report. The safety manual specified the detailed information which this report had to contain: (1) the specific unsafe condition involved in the accident; (2) the specific unsafe working practice committed by the injured worker or some other employee; (3) what the foreman had done, or recommended should be done, to prevent a similar accident.

In addition to these reports, records were also kept of *all* first aid cases. Both accident reports and first aid records were given regular and careful review by a "safety engineer" who worked out of the Company's main office.

Another instrument designed for generating conformance to the safety program was the closely planned and regularly conducted "safety meeting." Usually, this was presided over by the "safety and personnel manager" employed by the local plant. Such meetings were supposed to limit themselves to a thorough examination of the accidents which had occurred, the analysis of the outstanding accident-producing practices and conditions in the plant, and the suggestion of ways and means of correcting them. Actually, as will be noted later, the meetings sometimes discussed other subjects having little connection with safety work.

A final indication of the extent to which safety work was bureaucratized is that it was organized by, and was the responsibility of, a specific, continually existent office, 'the safety and personnel manager" in the plant. On the basis of his *superior and specialized knowledge*, he was expected to detect unsafe acts or conditions in the plant, and to call them to the attention of the appropriate foreman.

No other ongoing program in the plant was as highly bureaucratized. The "no-absenteeism" rule, for example, was not backed up with anything like the careful system of statistics and reports which were prepared for accidents. In fact, there were no absenteeism statistics kept in the plant. No other program in the plant had the galaxy of rules, special meetings, posters, inspections, or special supervisors in the main office and local plant. Indeed, until Peele's arrival, the only thing that the men in the plant thought of as "rules" were the safety regulations. As one foreman said: "It is the one thing they really work on."

3. Punishment-Centered Bureaucracy:
The No-Absenteeism Rule

"Punishment-centered bureaucracy" is distinguished from "mock" and "representative" bureaucracy in that responses to deviations take the form of *punishments*. This particular type is composed of two subpatterns, depending on *who* exercises the punishment and who receives it. In one case, management utilizes punishments, directing them against workers. In the other case, workers subject management to punishments when the latter deviates. The first case can be called the "disciplinary" pattern. The second subtype can be termed the "grievance" pattern, for the union-grievance machinery is one of the most commonly used instruments by means of which workers inflict punishments on management.

[We focus here on the "disciplinary" pattern, the best example of which was the "no-absenteeism" rule, whose violations were specifically punished.]

Management on all levels of authority was hostile to absenteeism. While workers had varying feelings about the no-absenteeism rule, few of them welcomed it. Since we are not paid for time off, some workers asked rhetorically, why should management complain? As was already emphasized, absenteeism was traditionally valued by the miners, and they solidly closed their ranks to squash a challenge to this ancient prerogative. Many values important to workers were satisfied by absenteeism: for example, they could spend more time with their families, repair their homes, do spring plowing, hunt and fish, visit around, get drunk, or just rest. It was also a personalized and individual way of giving vent to dissatisfactions that arose in the course of working. At any rate, absenteeism was one way workers realized values that at any given moment might be more important to *them* than management's need for regular, predictable production.

The social status of worker and management alike was involved in the tug-of-war centering around the no-absenteeism rule. The foreman who was short-handed, due to absenteeism or any other reason, faced the danger of being unable to fill his production quota. No one in the plant was exempt from meeting this obligation, for "production comes first." Supervisors enforced the no-absenteeism rule, partly, therefore, because it enabled them to satisfy their chief status-obligation, keeping production going.

The no-absenteeism regulation also meant that the worker had to *account* for what he did *outside* of the plant. Under this rule the worker had, in effect, to receive his supervisor's permission to go to a wedding, attend a funeral, or stay home with a sick relative, whom he must now prove was really sick. The no-absenteeism rule challenged the workers' control over a wide range of out-of-plant behavior, bringing it within the purview of the foreman. As such, the rule was experienced as an extension of managerial power into an illegitimate area.

When the worker returned from an absence, the supervisor had to decide whether the worker's behavior was punishable. He was not formally interested in the causes of absenteeism, as he was of accidents, with the object of removing them. The investigation of an absence simply determined whether or not a worker would be punished.

The supervisor operated on the assumption that some absences were not "excusable." He believed that they evidenced the worker's "irresponsibility," marking him as a person who knowingly and deliberately evaded his obligations. The supervisor did not assume, as he did with respect to safety violations, that the absent worker was unwittingly careless, or ignorant of the requirements. As one foreman said emphatically:

> They know God-damned well they're not supposed to be out without a good excuse. What can we do with them but get tough?

Workers responded in much the same way when they felt that the requirements of the "bidding system" had been evaded by supervisors. Since the bidding rules had been incorporated into the contract and since, time and again, the union committee had called these provisions to management's attention, their neglect tended to be viewed as malicious and deliberate. As one mill worker said in such a situation, *"They're just asking for trouble."* Like management, workers responded by getting "tough." The rules, therefore, served to legitimate the punishment of those deemed to be *willfully* deviant and deliberately aggressive.

In fine, then, the punishment-centered bureaucratic pattern was characterized by the following features:

1. The rules about which the pattern was organized were *enforced*, but primarily by *one group*, either workers or management, rather than by both.
2. Adjustment to the rules was not attained by ignoring them, nor by "educating" the deviant or involving him in the rule's administration, but by *punishing* him.
3. The pattern was associated with considerable conflict and tension.

It may now be clear that this pattern was given its name because it is organized around the punishment-legitimating functions of bureaucratic rules, and is intimately associated with "close supervision."

Summary of Factors Associated with the Three Patterns of Bureaucracy

Mock	Representative	Punishment-Centered
	1. Who Usually Initiates the Rules?	
The rule or rules are imposed on the group by some "outside" agency. *Neither* workers nor management, neither superiors nor subordinates, identify themselves with or participate in the establishment of the rules or view them as their own. e. g.—The "no-smoking" rule was initiated by the insurance company.	*Both* groups initiate the rules and view them as their own. e. g.—Pressure was exerted by union *and* management to initiate and develop the safety program. Workers and supervisors could make modifications of the program at periodic meetings.	The rule arises in response to the pressure of *either* workers or management, but is *not jointly* initiated by them. The group which does not initiate the rule views it as imposed upon it by the other. e. g.—Through their union the workers initiated the bidding system. Supervisors viewed it as something to which the Company was forced to adhere.
	2. Whose Values Legitimate the Rules?	
Neither superiors nor subordinates can, ordinarily, legitimate the rule in terms of their own values.	Usually, *both* workers and management can legitimate the rules in terms of their own key values. e. g.—Management legitimated the safety program by tying it to *production*. Workers legitimized it via their values on personal and bodily welfare, maintenance of income, and cleanliness.	*Either* superiors or subordinates alone consider the rule legitimate; the other may concede on grounds of expediency, but does not define the rule as legitimate. e. g.—Workers considered the bidding system "fair," since they viewed it as minimizing personal favoritism in the distribution of jobs. Supervisors conformed to it largely because they feared the consequences of deviation.

Summary of Factors Associated with the Three Patterns of Bureaucracy—*Continued*

Mock	Representative	Punishment-Centered

3. Whose Values Are Violated by Enforcement of the Rules?

Enforcement of the rule violates the values of *both groups*.

   e. g.—If the no-smoking rule were put into effect, it would violate the value on "personal equality" held by workers and supervisors, since office workers would still be privileged to smoke.

Under most conditions, enforcement of the rules entails violations of *neither* group's values.

   e. g.—It is only under comparatively *exceptional* circumstances that enforcement of the safety rules interfered with a value held by management, say, a value on production.

Enforcement of the rules violates the values of only one group, *either* superiors or subordinates.

   e. g.—The bidding rules threatened management's value on the use of skill and ability as criteria for occupational recruitment.

4. What Are the Standard Explanations of Deviations from the Rules?

The deviant pattern is viewed as an expression of "uncontrollable" needs or of human nature."

   e. g.—People were held to smoke because of "nervousness."

Deviance is attributed to ignorance or well-intentioned *carelessness*—i. e., it is an unanticipated byproduct of behavior oriented to some other end, and thus an "accident." This we call a "utilitarian" conception of deviance.

   e. g.—Violation of the safety rule might be seen as motivated by concern for production, rather than by a deliberate intention to have accidents. If, for example, a worker got a hernia, this might be attributed to his ignorance of proper lifting technique.

In the main, deviance is attributed to *deliberate* intent. Deviance is thought to be the deviant's *end*. This we call a "voluntaristic" conception of deviance.

   e. g.—When a worker was absent without an excuse, this was *not* viewed as an expression of an uncontrollable impulse, or as an unanticipated consequence of other interests. It was believed to be *willful*.

5. What Effects Do the Rules Have upon the Status of the Participants?

Ordinarily, deviation from the rule is status-enhancing for workers and management *both*. Conformance to the rule would be status-impairing for both.

e. g.—Violation of the no-smoking rule tended to minimize the visibility of status differentials, by preventing the emergence of a privileged stratum of smokers.

Usually, deviation from the rules impairs the status of superiors *and* subordinates, while conformance ordinarily permits both a measure of status improvement.

e. g.—The safety program increased the prestige of workers' jobs by improving the cleanliness of the plant (the "good housekeeping" component), as well as enabling workers to initiate action for their superiors through the safety meetings. It facilitated management's ability to realize its production obligations, and provided it with legitimations for extended control over the worker.

Conformance to or deviation from the rules leads to status gains *either* for workers or supervisors, but not for both, and to status losses for the other.

e. g.—Workers' conformance to the bidding system allowed them to escape from tense relations with certain supervisors, or to secure jobs and promotions without dependence upon supervisory favors. It deprived supers of the customary prerogative of recommending workers for promotion or for hiring.

6. Summary of Defining Characteristics or Symptoms

(a) Rules are neither enforced by management nor obeyed by workers.
(b) Usually entails little conflict between the two groups.
(c) Joint violation and evasion of rules is buttressed by the informal sentiments of the participants.

(a) Rules are both enforced by management and obeyed by workers.
(b) Generates a few tensions, but little overt conflict.
(c) Joint support for rules buttressed by informal sentiments, mutual participation, initiation, and education of workers and management.

(a) Rules enforced by either workers or management, and evaded by the other.
(b) Entails relatively great tension and conflict.
(c) Enforced by punishment and supported by the informal sentiments of *either* worker or management.

PART II

Forms of Control and the Division of Labor

The essays in this section are concerned with managerial strategies designed to control the labor process. From Taylorism and the human relations school to modern technocratic approaches, they show that organization theory has suffered from a conservative managerial bias. Much of organization theory (presented as "neutral" principles for structuring of a "natural" harmony of interests between labor and management) has in fact supported—both wittingly and unwittingly—management's struggle to dominate working-class interests on the shop floor, especially to lower the costs of labor. For these writers, the division of labor, conceptualized as a separation and fragmentation of the planning and execution of work processes, is as much a tool of social control as a technique for efficiency. In mainstream theory, organizational efficiency is typically portrayed as the product of an innate logic of workplace technologies; from the critical perspective, it is seen to follow the path that best maintains the dominant managerial patterns of hierarchical control.

In the first essay, Richard Edwards analyzes the labor process as the site of the historic confrontation between capital and labor. Responding to theoretical issues raised by Braverman's theory of workforce degradation, Edwards seeks to preserve and reformulate the role of class conflict in the analysis of labor processes. As a political economist, he offers a political interpretation of the control systems introduced to govern the immediate processes of industrial production. In a historical context, he focuses primarily on the evolution of technical and bureaucratic control mechanisms as managerial responses to the continuing struggle over control of the division of labor. The result is a dialectical conception of workplace conflict. The unfolding logic of capitalism creates new circumstances for both management and labor which become the source of new possibilities and constraints in the continuing organizational struggle.

Edwards' piece is followed by two essays that document the processes of technical and bureaucratic control, one in the United States Postal

Service and the other in modern city police departments. While not written with Edwards' specific concept of technical control in mind, Peter Rachleff's essay portrays the attempt of postal management, with the introduction of new technology to sort mail, to undercut the successes of postal workers' unions in the early 1970s. Offering a unique glimpse of workplace struggles in the public sector, the essay examines congressional and managerial responses to the postal workers' nationwide strike during the Nixon administration. Illustrating how machine technologies helped postal administrators disrupt informal workplace groups, increase control through large-scale reorganization, as well as undermine postal unions, Rachleff stresses both the economic dysfunctions and human alienation resulting from wholesale automation. Throughout the discussion, worker opposition to mechanization and reorganization are contrasted with the objectives of postal service officials.

Sid Harring's contribution documents the value of Braverman's analysis of scientific management in major urban police departments. Harring asserts that the move toward centralized bureaucratic planning of the individual officer's work has significantly strengthened the control of police professionalization. "Deprofessionalization" is examined in terms of the restructuring of the patrol function, the use of civilians, the introduction of automation, the training of police managers, and the use of incentives or performance pay to undercut police unionization. The unique role of the police function in the social class structure is emphasized.

Frank Fischer's essay portrays the managerial bias that has shaped the development of social science's contribution to organizational analysis, both its theory and methodology. Focusing on the contribution of organizational psychology and the human relations school in the development of modern organization theory, he demonstrates the ideological support that theory has provided for management throughout its history of struggle with labor over industrial workplace control. Fischer concludes by pointing to the contemporary uses of psychological techniques to combat unionization in both private and public sector organizations.

Finally, Beverly Burris and Wolf Heydebrand argue that the structure of control in higher education has evolved historically through theocratic, professional, and bureaucratic forms and is now evolving toward a technocratic mode of administrative control. Presented as an emergent historical and structural synthesis of professional and bureaucratic forms of control, technocratic administration is rooted in the methodologies of managerial and social science "expertise." Burris and Heydebrand associate it with greater emphasis on systematic long-range planning through quantification of inputs and outputs, the introduction of computerized decision-making systems, and the growing "deprofessionalization" of teaching. The essay concludes with the discussion of the technocratic implications of the 1980 Supreme Court ruling against the faculty union of Yeshiva University.

9
Forms of Control in the Labor Process: An Historical Analysis
Richard C. Edwards

For the last several years, discussions of the labor process have tended to take as their starting point Harry Braverman's *Labor and Monopoly Capital*. Most writers have accepted Braverman's thesis of the degradation of work; a few have criticized it. Yet despite the book's brilliant insights, the weaknesses in its analysis are becoming increasingly visible. Most important are the following:

1. The book fails to take account of labor responses to the new forms of "degraded" work that employers have developed. In Braverman's story, new, fragmented, de-skilled methods of work are developed and implemented by capitalists, with drastic effects on workers but with little apparent resistance. No impact results from what resistance does occur. Unions play no role, and there is no class struggle.
2. The book accepts or seems to accept writings on management theory as evidence for actual developments on the shop or office floor. The most important example is Braverman's reading of Frederick Taylor's writings as though they described real processes rather than simply Taylor's thinking and theories. The book has therefore taken what are clearly ideological sources of information and treated them as though the processes they describe were real.
3. The book's basic premise of "de-skilling" remains problematical. It seems clear that de-skilling has occurred in the traditional craft trades, including the machinists' tradition out of which Braverman himself came. It also seems correct to emphasize the tendency for capitalists to replace high-skill (or more precisely, high-wage) labor with low-skill (low-wage) labor whenever possible. Nonetheless, the development of both the forces and relations of production continually throw up new products, new technologies, and a demand for re-skilled, especially educated labor as well as de-skilled

---

Originally appeared as "The Social Relations of Production at the Point of Production." Reprinted from *Work and Labor*, a special issue of *The Insurgent Sociologist* 8, nos. 2–3 (Fall 1978): 109–125, by permission of the publisher.

labor. Thus accumulation must be seen as simultaneously de-skilling and re-skilling the labor force. Rather than the simple, one-way process that Braverman describes, we must recognize this more complicated, two-way movement.

Admitting this point immediately changes our analysis of the trends in the composition of the American working class. The historical tendency can no longer be the simple one of the creation of an ever-increasing mass of unskilled or low-skilled workers. Rather, craft work declines, educated labor emerges, and the overall impact on the working class—whether it is becoming more homogeneous or more differentiated—is at least ambiguous.

4. The book fails to be clear as to whether modern techniques of production (carrying with them their inherent de-skilling, degradation of work, etc.) are inevitable consequences of technical economies of scale. The most consistent reading of the book, I would argue, would necessarily interpret the new methods of production as more efficient. In part, of course, the new methods simply permit (in Braverman's theory) the use of low-skill workers, but this begs the central question of whether such techniques do not also result in higher productivity. If this reading is accurate, then the demise of craft and other production in which workers have a knowledge of the entire production process is sad but "progressive." Capitalism is only the messenger, the vehicle for these necessary advances in society's productive capacity. Yet this reading seems quite at odds with the vitriol that Braverman displays when he records management's quest for control, and his suggestion, in several places, that degradation results from the specifically capitalist organization of production.

5. The book fails to make any distinctions between monopoly capital and non-monopoly capital. Indeed, the "monopoly capital" of the title turns out to be monopoly capital*ism*, i.e., capitalism in the present period. Yet how the book's analysis relates to monopoly capitalism rather than simply to capitalism remains entirely unclear. There is no evidence or reasoning introduced to suggest that monopoly capital in particular impinges upon the labor process in any way different from contemporary non-monopoly capital—or, for that matter, different from an earlier competitive capital. Of course the more recent managers are more sophisticated than (e.g.) their 19th-century counterparts, but the transition to monopoly capitalism does not seem to have altered the *logic* of the labor process.

6. While the book appears to provide an historical argument, starting with the development of management ideas in the 19th century and

pursuing their realization in the present, in fact there exists no real historical content to the analysis. For example, between Taylorism and the present came, among other historical processes, the organization of workers in the mass production industries into industrial unions. This historic achievement, the goal of the labor and left-wing movements for the preceding several decades, does not in any way impinge on Braverman's "historical" argument.

These six omissions (and others) are serious flaws indeed in any analysis of the labor process. Just as Paul Baran and Paul Sweezy in *Monopoly Capital* excise the sphere of production from their analysis of modern capitalism, so it seems Harry Braverman has left class conflict out of his analysis of the labor process. The relations of production simply unfold as ever more systematic (and horrifying) applications of the Babbage principle. This rather mechanical logic is all the more surprising since it was Braverman himself who insisted that Marx's distinction between labor and labor power (between work done and the capacity to do work) was the essential starting point for any analysis of the labor process. But surely the relevance of this distinction is precisely the workers' ability—individually, in small groups, and collectively—to resist and in consequence to re-shape employers' schemes to transform labor power into labor. Workers do not have unlimited power, but then neither do capitalists, and Braverman's story needs to be amended to take account of the real constraints on capitalists.

In this paper I cannot deal with all these issues, but I will try to suggest an alternative formulation of the dynamics of the labor process which begins to get at some of the problems in Braverman's analysis.[1] The central departure from Braverman's analysis can be quite simply stated. Whereas Braverman concerned himself primarily with the *technical* aspects of the development of the labor process—"technical" in the sense of workers' relations to the physical process of production—my analysis will focus on the developing *social* relations of production at the point of production. This analysis, rather than contradicting Braverman's work, instead incorporates and builds upon it. The 20th century has witnessed the emergence of two divergent tendencies: (1) the development of production technology has tended to abolish old craft skills and obliterated distinctions among work tasks, . . . thereby also reducing skills distinctions among workers; but (2) the development of the social relations of the workplace has tended to create new divisions (and institutionalize pre-existing ones) based on the social organization of the workplace. As a result, the working class has become both more homogeneous as a mass of machine operatives and re-divided by the social organization of production. What Braverman leaves out is the capitalist firm as a social system, one embodying technical and social relations of production. This is what must be studied if we are to understand the dynamics of the labor process and the formation of the modern American working class. The rest of this paper is devoted to providing a sketchy and schematic framework for such an investigation.

1. The Labor Process

Capitalists are in business to make profits, and to do that they organize society's production. They begin by converting their funds for investment (money capital) into the raw materials, labor, machinery, etc., needed for production; they organize the labor process itself, whereby the constituents of production are transformed into useful products or services; and then, by selling the products of labor, they re-convert their property back to money form. If the money capital obtained at the end of this cycle exceeds that invested initially, the capitalists have earned a profit.

Each step in this sequence is fraught with uncertainties, and none more so than production itself. In organizing the labor process, employers seek to carry out two very different tasks. The first is what might be termed the coordination of social production. Any production process that involves many persons must be consciously directed so that each person's labor meshes with or contributes to the labor of the other producers. Such coordination is required in all societies.

The second task derives more particularly from the class nature of the capitalist labor process. Employers not only coordinate, they must also compel. They must compel because, while workers produce the firm's output, it is capitalists who own or appropriate the output. Capitalists must therefore convince workers, through means subtle or brutal, to produce goods that they (the capitalists) will profit from. That is, capitalists must seek to convert the labor power they have purchased in the marketplace into useful labor under conditions in which the possessor of the labor power has little to gain from providing useful labor. Indeed, competition among capitalists makes such compulsion not merely a matter of individual choice or greed but rather an economic necessity. Capitalists are forced to extract as much useful labor from their workers as possible; those employers who fail to do so or do it badly will usually be driven out of business.

What employers strive to achieve is minimum *per unit* costs of production. After all, it is the total unit cost that is deducted from the selling price to yield the "residual," the capitalist's profit. Profit maximizing, particularly if it is intensified and enforced by market competition, thus sets in motion a continuing search for new methods of production, new sources of labor, new ways of organizing the labor process that will reduce unit costs. In this search, the capitalist has few biases: whatever reduces unit costs and increases profits is seized upon.

It must be noted, however, that de-skilling and the increasing use of low-skill, low-wage labor is only *one* avenue for reducing unit costs. Consider in particular that portion of total unit costs that derives from the labor input, i.e., the unit labor cost. This portion of the firm's costs clearly depends upon two quantities: the price (wage) or labor power, and the productivity of labor power. Minimizing one of these elements (e.g., the wage) does not minimize their ratio. Specifically, it may pay the firm to pay a wage higher than the least possible wage if the result is a more than proportionate increase in productivity. Of course, if wages can be reduced with effect on, or with an increase in, productivity, then cutting wages will be profit-maximizing; but if lower wages bring forth lower productivity, then the profit-maximizing strategy depends on the magnitudes involved.

This distinction between minimizing wages and minimizing per unit labor costs is not simply a point in theory; as should become clear below, the history of the labor process in the 20th century cannot be understood without it. This distinction assumes such importance because labor, unlike all the other ingredients of production, does not come available to capitalists as a purchasable commodity. Labor power can be bought, but between the purchase of labor power and the real appropriation of useful labor comes a wedge; the will, motivation, and consciousness of the worker drastically affect the work force's productivity. Hence the employer's second task in organizing production: the extraction of labor from labor power.

This second task must be understood as one which applies primarily to the firm's workforce at large, or at least to substantial portions of it. For any individual or any small group of workers, wider market mechanisms come into play. Any worker who produces significantly less than the "norm," or indeed who produces less than the most eager substitute among the unemployed, will simply be replaced; here, the market and the "reserve army" enforce production levels. But as I argue below, the use of the reserve-army sanction as a "first-resort" mechanism for extracting labor has produced resistance to the limitations on capitalists as well as obedience from workers. In all cases the employer's prerogative to hire and fire remains the ultimate sanction, but, especially among big employers, different methods serve to organize work on a day-to-day basis.

In some cases, the second task may be trivial. It is trivial, for example, if employers can directly contract for labor rather than labor power. If it is possible to specify in advance all of the duties to be performed, then the employer can simply purchase the product or service of labor. Likewise, employers may pay only for work actually done if each worker's output is independent; here, piece-rate pay may compel adequate production. Other workplace schemes may be directed towards the same end.

In general, however, capitalists have found it neither practical nor profitable to rely on such devices. Only rarely can every worker's duties be exhaustively specified when the worker is hired. Piece-rate pay has limited application and frequently engenders conflict over the rates themselves. In both cases, evaluation of whether the contracted work was properly done raises further problems. Moreover, such workers are likely to be using company-provided tools or machinery, so even if a "slow" worker receives a low wage, the capitalist cannot be indifferent to the under-utilization of the capital. Other schemes (profit sharing, distributing company stock to workers, more elaborate incentive schemes) also fail. Most importantly, all these devices founder because their targets, the workers, retain their ability to resist. Typically, then, the second task—extracting work from employees who have no direct stake in profits—remains to be carried out in the workplace itself.

The social division into workers and capitalists thereby lays the foundation for continuing conflict in the labor process, as employers attempt to extract the maximum effort from workers [who] necessarily resist their bosses' impositions. Conflict ensues over how work shall be organized, what work pace shall be established, what conditions producers must labor under, what "rights" workers shall enjoy, how the various employees of the enterprise shall relate to each other. The workplace becomes a perpetual battleground.

The struggle in the workplace has a closely-intertwined parallel in the bargaining that goes on in the marketplace. Here conflict concerns wages, as labor and capital contend over the reward for the laborer's time. Sometimes this bargaining occurs collectively (e.g., between unions and industry representatives); at other times it takes an individual form (between job applicant and employer). At times wage bargaining creates a crisis; at other times it assumes an entirely pacific form. But here too the clash of interests persists.

Thus, in the old slogan, "a fair day's work for a fair day's pay," both elements become matters of conflict. "A fair day's work" is as much an issue for bargaining, resistance, and struggle as is the "fair day's pay." The old Wobbly demand said it more cogently if less completely: "Good Pay or Bum Work!"

The "war" on the shop and office floor may take many forms. At times it is open warfare, mutually joined; more commonly, it is a cold war, or some variant of guerrilla operations and peaceful co-existence. Frequently it is not consciously recognized as battle at all. The combatants sometimes perceive the clash in class terms, but more often they view it within an individual or small-group framework. But whether acute or dormant, the conflict remains.

Conflict in the labor process occurs under definite historical circumstances—or, what is the same, within a specific economic and social context. Most importantly, production is part of the larger process of capital accumulation, i.e., the cycle of investment of prior profits, organization of production, sale of produced commodities, realization of profits (or loss), and reinvestment of profits. This process constitutes the fundamental dynamic of a capitalist economy. But capital accumulation, while it remains the basic theme, gets played out with substantial variations. A whole set of factors—the degree of competition among capitalists, the size of corporations, the extent of trade union organization, the level of class consciousness among workers, the impact of governmental policies, the speed of technological change, and so on—influence the nature and shape and pace of accumulation. Taken together, these various forces provide both possibilities and constraints for what can occur within the workplace. What was possible or successful in one era may be impossible or disastrous in another. Conflict at work, then, must be understood as a product both of the strategies or wills of the combatants and of definite conditions not wholly within the grasp of either workers or capitalists. As Marx put it, "People make their own history, but they do not make it just as they please; they do not make it under circumstances chosen by themselves, but under circumstances directly found, given, and transmitted from the past."[2]

Conflict occurs within definite limits imposed by a social and historical context, yet this context rarely yields a precise determination of work organization. After technological constraints, the discipline of the market, and other forces have been taken into account, there remains a certain indeterminacy to the labor process. This "space" for the working out of workplace conflict is particularly evident within the large corporation, where "external" constraints have been reduced to a minimum. Here especially, the essential question remains: how shall work be organized?

Outside the firm, relations between capitalists and workers take the form of demanders and suppliers of the commodity "labor power;" that is, the "equality" of market relations prevails. Inside the firm, relations between capitalists and workers take the form of boss and bossed; that is, a *system of control* prevails. Any system of control must embody three elements: (1) the direction of work tasks, (2) the evaluation of the work done, and (3) the rewarding and disciplining of workers.

I distinguish below between three historically important and essentially quite different ways of organizing these three elements. The first is what I term "simple control": capitalists exercise power openly, arbitrarily, and personally (or through hired bosses who act in much the same way). Simple control formed the organizational basis of 19th century firms and continues today in the small enterprises of the more competitive industries. The second is "technical control": the control mechanism is embedded in the physical technology of the firm, designed into the very machines and other physical apparatus of the workplace. The third is "bureaucratic control": control becomes embedded in the social organization of the enterprise, in the contrived social relations of production at the point of production. These last two systems of control constitute "structural" forms of control, in the sense that the exercise of power becomes institutionalized in the very structure of the firm and is thus made impersonal. Structural control, as explained below, provides the rationale for the organization of workplace[s] in big corporations today.

This typology of control embodies both the pattern of historical evolution and the array of contemporary methods for organizing work. On the one hand, each form of control corresponds to a definite stage in the development of the "representative" or most important firms, and so the systems of control correspond to or characterize stages of capitalism. On the other hand, capitalist production has developed unevenly, with some sectors pushing far in advance of other sectors, and so each type of control exists alongside the others in the economy today.

Since the transformation of the workplace in the 20th century is largely a story of the organization of work in large corporations in the advanced countries, I restrict the discussion below to that topic. Workers in small firms, as well as most large corporations' employees in Third World countries, continue to face older, more direct, less institutionalized forms of control.

The labor process becomes an arena of class conflict. Faced with chronic resistance to their efforts to compel production, employers over the years have attempted to resolve the matter by reorganizing, indeed revolutionizing, the labor process itself. Their goal remains profits; their strategies aim at establishing structures of control at work. That is, capitalists have attempted to organize production in such a way as to minimize workers' opportunities for resistance and even to alter workers' perceptions of the desirability of opposition. Work has been organized, then, to contain conflict. In this endeavor employers have sometimes been successful.

2. Towards New Systems of Control

The conditions of work in capitalist enterprises have changed as capitalism itself has changed. In both cases, evolution has not overturned the fundamental relations that exist between capitalist and worker. But just as capitalism has proceeded from a competitive to a monopoly phase, so also have the organization of workers in production and the circumstances of their employment passed from one developmental stage to another. And it is important to note that the latter process has occurred largely as a result of the class nature of capitalist production, rather than as the result of anything "inevitable" or "natural" in either technology or the operation of large organizations.

During the 19th century much production was still carried on by skilled craftsmen, who established their own working conditions, protected the quality of their products, and limited access to their industry through craft rules, customs, apprenticeships, and the like. They were subject to market forces, of course, yet within the unit of production they themselves or their craft traditions served to organize the labor process. But as a population dependent on wages emerged, capitalists could increasingly out-compete petty producers by taking control of the labor process directly. Production itself, as well as the sale of commodities, became organized by capitalists.

Most 19th-century businesses were small and subject to relatively tight discipline from competition in their product markets. The typical firm had few resources and little energy to invest in creating more sophisticated management structures. A single entrepreneur, usually flanked by a small coterie of foremen and managers, ruled the firm. They exercised power personally, intervening often in the labor process to exhort workers, bully and threaten them, reward good performance, hire and fire on the spot, favor loyal workers, and generally act as despots, benevolent or otherwise. They had a direct stake in promoting production, and they combined both incentives and sanctions in an idiosyncratic and unsystematic mix. There was little structure to how power was exercised, and workers tended to be treated arbitrarily. Since workforces were small and the boss was both close and powerful, workers had little chance collectively to oppose his rule. Generally, workers could do little more than attempt to protect dying craft traditions or engage in informal efforts to restrict output.

In terms of the three elements of a control system listed above, analysis shows that each element tended to reveal simply another feature of the personal relation between capitalist (or other bosses) and workers. In specifying what tasks were to be done, the boss directly delineated the jobs and assigned workers to them. Where production involved unstandardized or batch-type processes, this direction typically involved continuous supervision, as in gang-labor. Where production was routinized, personal direction still involved assignment and reassignment of workers to different work stations. Evaluations also occurred continuously and could scarcely be distinguished from direction; certainly few separate evaluation procedures existed. Rewarding and disciplining tended to be somewhat more structured (firms often established wages schedules, for example), yet even here the arbitrary and unconstrained power of the capitalist to punish workers meant that workers were constantly subject to personal rule. Control was, in effect, a system of direct and immediate tyranny, from which little relief was possible. Indeed, those outside the factory gates—the reserve army—stood as ready replacements for any workers who rebelled against such tyrannical power.

This system of *simple control* survives today in the small-business sector of the American economy. It has necessarily been amended by the passage of time and by borrowings of management practices from the more advanced corporate sector, but it retains its essential principles and mode of operation. We readily see it in the mom-and-pop grocery store, but it is also apparent in small manufacturing concerns. For example, a small guitar factory in Kansas employs some 50–60 workers, all of whom know the owner well. Indeed, the owner acts as "head workman" in some cases, occasionally building the specialized one-of-a-kind guitars ordered by show-business celebrities. The workers build the more standardized instruments, each doing a small operation on the 10 or so guitars produced every day. In directing their labor, in evaluating their performance, in rewarding and disciplining them, the owner (and the few other bosses present) rely on the personal relations of the factory to control work. The impact of simple control can also be seen in a Boston-area electronics plant, a plant employing some 500 workers. As described by Ann Bookman, the owner and the top-level foreman rule the roost in direct personal ways, exhorting or threatening workers to produce more, watching closely how hard workers work, assigning workers to easy or tough work stations depending on the foreman's fancy, and handing out or withholding pay raises, permission to take time off, overtime, etc., as rewards and disciplines.[3] Once again, personal despotism rules the workplace.

The system of simple control is not the principal organizing device in today's corporate sector. Toward the end of the 19th century, tendencies toward concentration of capital undermined the practice; some firms grew too large for effective simple control. As firms began to employ thousands of workers, the distance between capitalists and workers expanded and the intervening space was filled by growing numbers of foremen, general foremen, supervisors, superintendents, and other petty managers. The unplanned, willy-nilly expansion of intermediate bosses produced an exaggerated harshness on the shop floor—what one observer has aptly termed "the foreman's empire."[4] Here, foreman and hired bosses ruled nearly without restraint, assuming most of the powers formerly exercised by the entrepreneur. They hired and fired, assigned work, set pay rates, disciplined recalcitrants, and drove the work pace. They acted as petty tyrants, dispensing and withholding the various sanctions at their command.

But whereas immediate tyranny had been more or less successful when conducted by entrepreneurs (or foremen close to them), the system did not work well when staffed by hired bosses. The new bosses were caught in the middle of intensifying workplace conflict. On one side, foremen came into conflict with the employers. The new bosses exercised many of the workplace powers of entrepreneurs, but they nonetheless remained hired hands, not capitalists. The interests of capitalists and petty bosses diverged, and foremen began to use their power for their own ends. Owners experienced increasing difficulty in controlling production through these unreliable intermediaries. Sometimes termed "organizational uncoupling," substitution of the foreman's interests for those of the capitalist understandably destroyed the foreman's allegiance to the system.

On the other side, and undoubtedly more serious, the foremen also came into increasingly serious conflict with the workers. Intensified competition—"cutthroat" competition, as it was known—among manufacturers led them to press ever harder in their efforts to extract greater production from their workers. But the firm's workforce had grown much bigger, and with expansion and speed-up came increased consciousness. Then, too, the entrepreneur had profited directly from increased productivity, and a small capitalist's success often derived as much from eliciting cooperation and loyalty from his employees as from exercising the whip. But for foremen, no comparable incentive existed, and the historical evidence demonstrates that simple control via hired bosses produced brutal, severe punishment, abusive supervision, and few positive compensations. The industrial regime had become harsher, and the mix of incentives and sanctions had swung to nearly total reliance on the negative.

These developments inside the firm both reflected and interacted with a broader reorganization occurring throughout the American economy: the transition from the small-business, competitive capitalism of the 19th century to the corporate monopoly capitalism of the 20th. The driving force of capital accumulation pushed successful firms first to merge and then to attempt to make their new positions profitable. This tendency toward centralization increasingly produced a dichotomy in the economy's industrial structure. Big firms with great market power dominated most major industries, while small firms with little market power survived in their interstices and along their periphery. The dual economy was born.

The transition also unleashed powerful oppositional forces. The maturing labor movement and an emergent Socialist Party organized the first serious challenge to capitalist rule. From the Homestead and Pullman strikes at the beginning of the period to the great 1919–1920 steel strike that closed it, workers fought with their bosses over control of the actual process of production. Intensifying conflict in society at large and the specific contradictions of hierarchical control in the workplace combined to produce an acute "crisis of control" on the shop floor.

The large corporations fashioned the most far-reaching response to this crisis. During the conflict, big employers joined small ones in supporting direct repression of their adversaries. But the large corporations also began to move in systematic ways to reorganize work. They confronted the most serious problems of control, but they also commanded the greatest resources with which to attack the problems. Their size and substantial market power released them from the tight grip of short-run market discipline and made possible for the first time planning in the service of long-term profits. Their initial steps—welfare capitalism, scientific management, company unions, industrial psychology, etc. constituted experiments, trials with serious errors inherent in them, but useful learning experiences nonetheless. In retrospect, these efforts appear as beginnings in the corporations' larger project of establishing more secure control over the labor process.

The new methods of organization that big employers developed were more formalized, more consciously contrived, more structured; they were, in fact, *structural* forms of control. Two possibilities existed: the more formal, consciously contrived controls could be embedded either in (1) the physical structure (technology) of the labor process, or in (2) its social structure. In time, employers used both. They found the advantages of structural control (whether in its technical or social variant) to be two-fold. On the one hand, it made the control system less visible to workers, more hidden and institutional; control became a product not of capitalist employment relations, but rather of "technology" or the scale of "modern industry." On the other hand, structural control provided a means for controlling the "intermediate layers," those extended lines of supervision and power.

Technical control tended to emerge out of the employer's attempts to control conflict in the "bluecollar" or production operations of the firm, whereas bureaucratic control grew out of similar conflicts in the burgeoning "white-collar" or administrative functions. Yet, as I argue below, no such simple identification is possible today. The incompleteness of technical control and the increasingly factory character of administrative work has largely obliterated such distinctions.

3. Technical Control

How something is produced is in large part dictated, of course, by the nature of the product and by the known and available technologies for producing it. Thus lumbering tends to be dispersed in the forests while auto assembly is concentrated indoors, building jet-liners tends to involve a stationary work-object while radio-assembly uses a moving line. In this sense, considerations of the physical efficiency of a technique—for example, the number of times steel has to be reheated as it is processed—distinguish superior from inferior methods. Yet these types of technical considerations by themselves are insufficient for determining what technologies will actually be used.

It is well known that most industries face a variety of possible techniques, and that the relative costs or required inputs will influence which technology is chosen. For example, steel-making can be performed in huge automated factories with much machinery and little labor, as can be seen now in the advanced countries where labor is expensive; or it can be produced in primitive hearths, with greater labor inputs and less machinery, as, for example, in some underdeveloped countries today or in the advanced countries 75 years ago, where machinery is or was expensive. Thus, *within* the known and available technologies, considerable choice is possible.

What is less well known is that there is an important social element in the development and choice of technique as well[, j]ust as it is true that firms confront a range of techniques which tend to provide greater or lesser possibilities for control over their workforces. That is, capitalists may prefer one technique over another because it gives them a strengthened hand in transforming labor power into useful labor. The preferred technique need not be more efficient, but it must be more *profitable*. What is profitable depends on the extent to which purchased commodities (including labor power) result in salable output. Consider, for example, two production techniques, A and B. Technique A is highly efficient, permitting three workers to produce 10 units per day, but it also gives workers substantial power to set their own pace. Technique B is less efficient, permitting three workers to produce at most 8 units per day, but the technology establishes this pace as an invariant daily rate. The two techniques are identical with respect to the per unit use of other inputs. If we take as the "labor input" the labor actually done, the first technique is more efficient. However, if technique A's workers use their control over the labor process to limit how much useful labor they tender in each working day, they do not affect the efficiency of the technique but they do affect the level at which it can be run. For example, they may actually produce only 7 units a day. Technique A remains the more efficient one, but technique B becomes more profitable, since for the same *purchased* inputs, the capitalist winds up with more output in technique B.

Thus, while it remains true that capitalists undoubtedly seek those technologies which are most profitable, we now must admit that there are several considerations which enter into the calculations of profitability. One is physical efficiency, the ratio of the physical output to the material inputs; another is the cost of the various inputs and the value of outputs; yet a third is the extent to which any technology provides managers leverage in transforming labor power into labor done. The way in which the third consideration—control—came to be considered is revealing of the whole process which has revolutionized work in the capitalist era.

Technical control involves designing machinery and planning the flow of work to minimize the labor/labor-power problem. This process occurs simultaneously with the attempt to maximize the purely physically based possibilities for achieving efficiencies. Thus a social dimension—the inherent class nature of capitalist production—is added to the evolution of technology.

Technical control is "structural" in the sense that it is embedded in the technological structure or organization of production. Technical control can be distinguished from simple mechanization, which merely increases the productivity of labor without altering the elements of control. Thus, for example, use of an electric rather than manual typewriter increases the speed with which a secretary works, but it does not alter how the secretary is directed to the new task, how his or her work is evaluated, or what the rewards or disciplining will be. Mechanization often brings with it technical control, as the worker loses control of the pace or sequence of tasks, but this consequence must nearly always be understood to be the result of the *particular* (capitalist) design of the technology and not as an inherent characteristic of machinery *in general*.

Technical control may also be distinguished from simple machine pacing, although the latter may be considered simply as technical control applied to the individual worker. Machine pacing occurs whenever a worker must respond to, rather than set, the pace at which the machinery is being operated. Building a production pace into machinery has long been a tactic used by employers to try to gain control of the labor process. Yet so long as the machinery affects just one worker or one work team, the conflict over pace and rhythm continues to revolve around and focus on these workers and their boss. For example, such machinery typically can in fact be operated at various speeds, and in this sense it requires bonus schemes, piece-rates, incentive pay, etc., to set the pace. Even where machinery has only one speed, boss and workers can nonetheless agree to turn it off for rest periods, if the machinery in question utilizes only workers in this workplace. The social organization surrounding such machine pacing continues to be that of simple control.

Technical control only emerges when the entire production process of the plant, or large segments of the plant, are based on a technology which paces and directs the labor process. In this case, the pacing and direction of work transcend the particular workplace and are thus beyond the power of even the immediate boss; control here is truly "structural."

Toward the end of the 19th century, the crisis created by the contradiction of simple control set off a search for more powerful and sophisticated mechanisms. This experimentation, often identified with "scientific management" or "Taylorism," both went far beyond the theories and stopped far short of the often silly applications put forward by Frederick Taylor and his followers. In essence, although the scientific management movement self-consciously adopted the rhetoric of mechanical engineering, the actual contribution of Taylor and his followers to the design of machinery was quite small. Yet in the plants and offices of the large corporations, the notion of technical control was by no means ignored. The advantages of continuous flow production beckoned.

While all the corporations at the turn of the century groped toward new structures to control their workers, each firm and each industry faced somewhat different circumstances. In some, the product—whether blast furnace heat, a harvester, or a railroad sleeping car—seemingly involved single-unit or small-batch production; here employers saw little chance to exploit technical possibilities for control, although they did engage in a titanic struggle to break the power of the skilled crafts workers. In these industries simple control was solidified, and the corporations turned to the bribes of bonus schemes, incentive pay, and welfare capitalism to create a more sophisticated control structure. But in other industries, notably meat-packing, electrical products, and autos, the flow of production was more direct. There technology was first recognized as a basis for wider, *structural* control.

Textile manufacturers in the 19th century had developed the basis for technical structuring of the first of the three elements of any control system, the technical direction of the work tasks. The other elements of the control system were less well worked out. In these mills, workers found themselves yoked to machinery which determined their work pace. There was little room for resistance in the workplace, and, lacking a strong union, the workers accepted the work or left.

Meat-packing was another early industry to adopt continuous-flow production—this time as a disassembly line. When Swift, Armour, and other Chicago packers began using refrigeration to revolutionize slaughtering and meat-packing, the old shop-based, small-batch techniques of the abattoir gave way to continuous flow. Investigating the packing houses for a British medical journal, one observer put it as follows:

> Outside the big factory buildings there are long, inclined, boarded passages up which the animals are driven. Thus the pigs are brought up to the height of the second floor. As they enter the main building each pig is caught by one of the hind legs. With rope and loop-knot and hook it is slung up, the head downwards and the neck exposed, at a convenient height for the slaughterer to strike. With great rapidity the suspended pigs are pushed on to a sort of passage about four feet broad where their throats are slashed open as they pass along. . . . Within less than a minute the dying pig reaches a long tank full of scalding water and in this the palpitating body is thrown. . . . Standing in the damp and steam, men armed with long prongs push the swine along. By the time when the hogs have floated down to the other end of the boiling-water tank they are sufficiently scalded for the bristles to be easily extracted. They are now put on a moveable counter or platform and as the hogs pass along other workers scrape the bristles off their backs. . . . At a subsequent stage the body is opened and the intestines are removed.[5]

From the perspective of control, the benefits of such production were immediate and obvious. By establishing the pace at which hogs were driven up the passages and onto the slaughter platform, managers could set the pace of work for the entire workforce. There were, of course, limits, both physical and worker-imposed ones, but each supervisor no longer has primary responsibility for directing the workers. Instead, the line now determined the pace, and the foreman had merely to get workers to follow that pace. Our observer makes this point quite explicit:

> When [the animal is] strung up, the machinery carries [it] forward and men have to run after it to cut its throat, while others follow with great pails to catch the blood; and all this without interrupting the dying animal's journey to . . . the next process of manufacture. . . . On they go from stage to stage of manufacture and the men have to keep pace with them.[6]

Thus by 1905 the essentials of continuous flow production, including the possibilities for controlling workers, were established in meat-packing.

With each worker fixed to a physical location in the production process, contact between and among workers nearly ceased. Whereas before workers had made the workday pass more quickly by talking, reading to each other, etc., now each worker simply tended his or her machine. Of particular interest to their employers was the fact that workers had little opportunity to discuss common grievances, compare foremen, exchange views on pay rates or job conditions, etc. Thus, despite their physical proximity, workers had little chance to communicate.

But if continuous flow production appeared first in textiles, meat-packing, lamp-production, and elsewhere, it was the Ford assembly line which brought the technical direction of work to its fullest potential. The automobile industry had its origin in the bicycle plants, where each team (a skilled mechanic and his helpers) performed all the operations necessary to assemble bicycles from separate parts. Carried over into auto plants, this organization slowly gave way as the assembly process began to be broken into parts; each team now added only a limited range of parts to the product, which was then passed on to another team. But it was not until the Highland Park plant opened in 1913 that the endless conveyor finally abolished the craft pretensions of the Ford workers.

The Ford line resolved technologically the essential first task of any control system: it provided unambiguous direction as to what operation each worker was to perform next, and it established the pace at which the worker was forced to work. Henry Ford himself emphasized this aspect of the line by stating as one of his three principles of "progressive manufacture": "The delivery of work instead of leaving it to the workmen's initiative to find it."[7]

Ford might well have added that the line's "delivery of work" also relieved his foremen of having to push work onto the workers, as was the case in simple control. H. L. Arnold studied the plant in great detail in

1914, and his report provides an excellent source for understanding how the new methods worked out in practice. Ford introduced the first chain-driven "endless conveyor" to assemble magnetos, and Arnold (and co-author L. F. Faurote) wrote, "The chair drive [i.e., continuous assembly] proved to be a very great improvement, hurrying the slower men, holding the fast men back from pushing work on to those in advance, and acting as an all-around adjustor and equalizer."[8]

The Ford line created a "technological necessity" in the sequence of tasks which were to be performed. Despite the fact that many assembly sequences were physically possible, no choice attached to the order in which workers did their jobs: the chassis or magneto or engine under construction came past a worker's station, lacking the part inventoried at that station; it would soon move on to other stations where it would gain every other part. The obvious necessity of adding the part in question at this station was thus established. Arnold and Faurote expressed this point as follows:

> Minute division of operations is effective in labor-cost reducing in two ways: first, by making the workmen extremely skillful, so that he does his part with no needless motions, and secondly, by training him to perform his unvaried operation with the least possible expenditure of will-power, and hence with the least brain fatigue.[9]

Thus the line hemmed in the worker, establishing a situation in which only one task sequence was possible.

Similarly, the line established a "technological presumption" in favor of the line's work pace. Struggle between workers and bosses over the transformation of labor power into labor done was no longer a simple and direct *personal* confrontation; now the conflict was mediated by the production technology itself. Workers had to oppose the pace of the line, not the (direct) tyranny of their bosses. The line thus established a technically-based and technologically-repressive mechanism to be used to keep workers at their tasks.

The substitution of technical for human direction and pacing of work simultaneously revolutionized the relation between foreman and workers. Arnold and Faurote explained that

> [The Highland Park plant] has applied team work [i.e., division of labor] to the fullest extent, and by this feature in conjunction with the arrangement of successive operations in the closest proximity, so as to minimize transportation and to *maximize the pressure of flow of work, it succeeds in maintaining speed without obtrusive foremanship*.[10]

The line eliminated "obtrusive foremanship," that is, close supervision in which the foreman simultaneously directed production, inspected and approved work, and disciplined workers. In its place, the line created a situation in which the foreman was relieved of responsibility for the first element of the control system. This change marked an important first step away from the simple control model which granted the foreman all the prerequisites of an "entrepreneur" within his own shop. Instead, the line brought with it the first appearance of structural control.

The importance of this change is indicated by the small number of "straw-bosses" and foremen needed to supervise the Ford workplace. In 1914 about 15,000 workers were employed at all the Ford plants. Leaving aside the top management, this large force was overseen by just 255 men ranking higher than "workman," including: 11 department foremen, 62 job foremen, 84 assistant foremen, and 98 sub-foremen (straw-bosses). Thus there was one foreman (all ranks) for each 58 workers, an impossible ratio except in a situation in which the foremen no longer directed the sequence of pacing of work.[11]

The foreman in technical control is thus transformed into an *enforcer* of the requirements and dictates of the technical structure. On the assembly line he or she monitors workers to keep them at their tasks—the foreman no longer is busy initiating tasks. The foreman penalizes exceptions to the normal flow of work, rather than personally directing that flow. Moreover, this enforcement is seen as being required by the larger structure. Exceptional circumstances aside, the foreman cannot personally be held responsible for the oppressiveness of the production process. If the legitimacy of the line is accepted, then the necessity for the foreman's job follows. The actual power to control work is thus vested in the line itself rather than in the person of the foreman, and the power relations are made more invisible. Instead of control appearing to flow from boss to workers, control emerges from the much more impersonal "technology."

Technical control has since come to be based upon a much more sophisticated technology, of course, than that which was available when the Ford line was introduced. The most dramatic changes in technology have occurred as a result of the invention of new devices to control or "program" machinery, including the increasingly pervasive linking of mini- or micro-computers to machines. Yet rather than producing qualitative differences, this new technology is best understood as simply expanding the potential contained in the concept of technical control.

But technical control by itself was not a sufficient advance over simple control to resolve the crisis of control within the firm, and it is not difficult to see why. Technical control provided the possibility of embedding in the technical structure the first element of all control systems (progressively directing the worker to further tasks), but it did little to change the second and third elements (evaluating work performance and enforcing compliance). In early forms of technical control, for example, supervisors had the power to discharge workmen immediately and at will. The second and third elements of control changed little.

Thus technical control by itself was not destined to be the ultimate wrinkle in corporate control. For one thing, it still left open the issue of how to motivate workers. If anything, the Ford plants represented a step *backwards* on this score, since the massive layoffs needed to "discipline" those workers who failed to produce according to the line's speed provoked increasingly intense hostility and resistance. The carrot was largely absent, the stick ever-present. The chief weapon, often even a first-resort disciplining device, was the "reserve army of the unemployed." Less drastic penalties (docking pay, suspension, etc.) also existed, but their usefulness varied directly with the potency of the supervisor's major sanction, dismissal. The only real motivator in this system was the worker's fear of being sacked.

But if dismissal was to be feared, either as a threat or as a fact, it was necessary that there be many substitute workers able and available to fill the jobs. The lack of plausible replacements was precisely what had given the old skilled workers their power, and had led, by way of reaction, to their demise. Similarly, in times of tight labor markets (such as during war), workers were relatively confident both that replacements could not easily be found and that, if fired, workers could find other jobs.

Thus, in technical control no less than in simple control, employers had a powerful incentive to make their workers as interchangeable and substitutable as possible. The continuing mechanization eroded the need for skills anyway, making the workforce more uniformly composed of unskilled and semi-skilled machine operatives. But the strictly *control* aspects of work reorganization contributed a further impetus to the homogenizing process.

The tendency to create a common (and degraded) status for all workers was evident in the labor policies of the early Ford plants. The famous Five Dollar Day which Ford announced in 1914 seemed to be a real advance, since $5 was substantially above other wages being paid to factory labor. Yet the higher wage was not essential for filling the company's vacancies; although it did create an enormous labor surplus. The day after the announcement there were 10,000 people outside the gates clamoring for jobs; for months afterward, as Francesca Maltese reports, the job-seekers "continued to clog the entrances to Ford's employment offices."[12] The lesson was not lost on the people employed inside the gates: the Company would have no trouble finding replacements for recalcitrant workers.

Similarly, other Ford labor policies attempted to generate a "ready reserve" of surplus labor. Thus it is no coincidence that the first large-scale entry of blacks into northern industrial employment was in the Ford plants. By 1926 Ford employed 10,000 black workers, over 90 percent of Detroit's black industrial labor force. The Company cast its net even further, drawing into potential employment the physically handicapped (generously labelled "substandard men"), young boys, and others. It was energetic in establishing a recruiting bureau to attract workers from other cities. Thus technical control both continued the need for surplus labor as a ready disciplinarian, and strengthened its derivative, the increasing substitutability and homogenizing of the labor force.

The attempt to generate highly visible pools of surplus labor was a response to the crisis of control on the shop floor, and it affected primarily the blue-collar workers. But technical control's influence extended also to the lower-level clerical staff, and here technical control introduced a new stimulus towards homogenization.

The corporation in part addressed the problem of controlling the white-collar staff by reorganizing their work along the lines of technical control. The routinization of clerical work has been extensively investigated elsewhere, and it need not be repeated here.[13] The essential point is that many clerical workers—those performing key-punching, typing of forms, and other standardized operations—were transformed into operatives of simple machines. Given the nearly universal nature of high school education by 1930, they could easily be replaced, and they became subject to the discipline of the reserve army. They had been reduced to the level of homogeneous labor.

But even as the new system solved some of the corporation's labor problems, it created other and more serious ones. Technical control yoked the entire firm's labor force (or each of the major segments thereof) to a common pace and pattern of work set by the productive technology. In so doing, technical control resolved for the individual workplace and the individual foreman the problem of translating labor power into labor. But it did so at the cost of raising this conflict to the plant-wide level. Thus the basic conflict was *displaced*, not eliminated.

At first this displacement was not realized. Throughout the 1910's and even more so during the relatively conflict-free 1920's, technical control appeared to have decisively turned the power balance in favor of the capitalists. Individual sabotage, disputes between workers and their foremen, and grumbling over wages continued, of course, but these could be managed and the power of technology drove the work pace.

The flaw in this naïveté was exposed dramatically and at heavy costs to the capitalists. Irving Bernstein describes what happened in the auto plants.

> On December 28 [1936] a sudden sit-down over piece-rate reductions in one department in Cleveland swept through the plant and 7000 people stopped work; Chevrolet body production came to a complete halt. On December 30 the workers in Flint sat down in the huge Fisher One and the smaller Fisher Two plants. Combined with the stoppage in Cleveland, this forced the closing of Chevrolet and Buick assembly operations in Flint. On December 31 the UAW sat down at Guide Lamp in Anderson, Indiana. . . . By the end of the first week of the new year, the great General Motors automotive system had been brought to its knees.[14]

The cost of lifting the shop-floor conflict out of the individual workplace and raising it to the plant-wide level was not apparent. Technical control linked together the plant's workforce, and when the line stopped, every worker necessarily joined the strike. Moreover, in a large, integrated manufacturing operation, such as auto production, a relatively small group of disciplined unionists could cripple an entire system by shutting down a part of the line.

Technical control thus took relatively homogeneous labor—unskilled and low-skilled workers—and technologically linked them together in production. This combination proved to be exceptionally favorable for building unions. The Flint strike was not the first sit-down, nor were such strikes confined to plants with moving lines. But the sit-downs were most effective in the mass-production industries of autos, electrical products, rubber, and textiles. More broadly, "quickie" sit-downs (strikes of a few minutes or an hour or two), sabotage, wildcats, and other labor actions were much more effective in plants organized according to technical control.

The CIO success of the 1930's clearly resulted in part from wider factors not considered here: the depression, the increasing concentration of industry, the conscious activity of militant union organizers. Yet the rise of industrial unionism was also significantly a response to technical control, and it marked the beginning of an effective limitation on that system.

These limits were nowhere more clearly revealed than at GM's Lordstown (Ohio) Vega plant several decades later.[15] GM had come to Lordstown with the intention of achieving a dramatic speedup in output. Its strategy was two-pronged. First, GM re-designed the plant and machinery to accommodate production at roughly 100 cars per hour (one every 36 seconds); this rate represented a 40 percent increase over the one-a-minute average that prevailed in most of its plants. Second, the company recruited a new labor force, one without long traditions of struggle to restrict industrial output. The plan didn't work.

The 1972 revolt at Lordstown gained much publicity and even notoriety, and justifiably so, but mostly the event attracted attention for the wrong reasons. On one side, Lordstown was declared atypical (and hence not really worrisome) because of the youthfulness of the workers (average age 24), because of the plant's counter-culture ambience, and because of the workforce's lack of industrial experience and discipline. On the other side, Lordstown was heralded as the new wave of working-class revolt for precisely the same reasons. Yet what really should have been noted was that Lordstown may have represented technical control's final gasp as an ascendant control system. The most advanced industrial engineering went into the design of the plant, but only resistance and the breakdown of control came out. Undoubtedly youth, counter-culture, and lack of industrial conditioning contributed to GM's problems, but it is precisely for such populations that technical control is designed.

Machine-pacing and de-skilling through use of "smart" machines continue, and it is even expanding in the lower-level clerical occupations. Moreover, in the "new" areas of investment—the U.S. South and the Third World, for example—technical control remains a first principle for factory organization. Equally, in the economy's small-firm periphery such organization remains important. But technical control can never again by *itself* constitute an adequate control system for the core firm's main industrial labor force.

Indeed, in its principal areas of application, technical control has evolved into a more mixed system, with unions playing a decisive (even if limited) role. The second and third elements of control become *jointly* administered by management and unions (with unions as junior partners). Evaluation and reward/discipline become matters for mutual determination in accordance with collectively bargained rules, procedures, and protections. Arbitrary dismissal and other punishments are limited by arbitration and grievance machinery; job "rights" become contractual obligations rather than "privileges" dispensed by bosses; wages and benefits are established within an overall contract structure. Technical control thus becomes supplemented, in the unionized sector of industry, by the elaborate administrative mechanisms achieved by unions to protect workers from the ravages of the earlier, more pure system of technical control.

The resistance engendered by technical control set off a new search for methods of controlling the workplace. In firms like IBM, Polaroid, Xerox, Gillette, and others, management devised a different system of structural control, this time based on the social or organizational structure of the firm. The result is what is here termed *bureaucratic control*.

4. Bureaucratic Control

The defining feature of bureaucratic control is the institutionalization of hierarchical power. "Rule of law"—the firm's law—replaces "rule by supervisor command" in the direction of work tasks, in the principles for evaluation of those tasks, and in the exercise of the firm's power to enforce compliance. Work activities become defined and directed by a set of work criteria: the rules, procedures, and expectations governing particular jobs. Thus for the individual worker, his or her job tends to be defined more by formalized job descriptions or "work criteria" attached to the job (or, more precisely, by the interpretation given to those criteria by his or her supervisor and higher levels of supervision) than by specific orders, directions, and whims of the supervisor. Moreover, it is against those criteria that the worker's performance is measured. Finally, company rules and procedures carefully spell out the penalties for poor performance and, more importantly, the rewards for adequate performance.

The criteria contain both written and unwritten requirements, and the essential characteristic is just that the worker is able to ascertain them and that they are highly stable. The firm no longer alters the worker's tasks and responsibilities by having the supervisor tell the worker to do something different; rather, it "creates a new job" or "redefines the job." From these criteria derive the "customary law" notions of "equity" or "just cause" in firing, promotion, and job assignment.

Top-echelon management retain their control over the enterprise through their ability to determine the rules, set the criteria, establish the structure, and enforce compliance. For the latter concern (enforcing compliance), bureaucratic organization again marked a departure from simple control. In simple control, power is vested in individuals and exercised arbitrarily according to their discretion, but with bureaucratic control power becomes institutionalized by vesting it in official positions or roles and permitting its exercise only according to prescribed rules, procedures, and expectations. Rules governing the exercise of power become elements of the work criteria defining supervisor's jobs. Superiors as well as subordinates become accountable to top-down control; the system thus broadens its reach to the "intervening layers" of petty officials.

Work activities can never be completely specified by job criteria in advance, and "rule of law" can never completely replace "rule of command" in an hierarchical enterprise. Some situations or problems always arise which need to be handled in an *ad hoc*, particularistic way, and so supervisors can never be content merely to evaluate and never to instigate. The shift to bureaucratic control must therefore be seen as a shift toward relatively greater dependence on institutionalized power, and bureaucratic control comes to exist alongside and be reinforced by elements of simple control. Bureaucratic control becomes, then, the predominant system of control, giving shape and logic to the firm's organization, although not completely eliminating elements of simple control.

The imposition of bureaucratic control in the monopoly firm had four specific consequences for the social relations of the firm.

1. The power relations of hierarchical authority were made invisible, submerged and embedded in the structure and organization of the firm, rather than visible and openly manifest in personal, arbitrary power.
2. Bureaucratic control, because of its emphasis on formal structure and status distinctions, made it possible to differentiate jobs more finely. Organizational as well as technical (i.e., production) aspects of jobs defined their status. Each job appeared more unique and

individualized by its particular position in the finely graded hierarchical order, by the job criteria which specified work activities, and by its distinct status, power, responsibilities, and so on. Elements of the social organization of the firm which differentiated between jobs were emphasized, while those which created commonality diminished.

These two changes tended to erode the bases for common worker opposition. Increasingly the individual worker came to face an impersonal and massive organization more or less alone. In general, the work environment became less conducive to unions and strike or other opposition activities. In those bureaucratized industries where unions remained (or were subsequently organized), more and more the unions accepted the organization of work and directed their energies toward non-control issues (wages, fringe benefits, and procedures for promotion, hiring, and firing). Even where unions turned their attention to the work activities themselves, their efforts were mainly defensive, directed toward making the job criteria more explicit and openly articulated; while this tended to undermine the authority of arbitrary foremen, it strengthened the legitimacy of the overall structure. As the common bases of work experience declined, so did the possibility for united worker action concerning control over work.

3. The role of the supervisor was transformed from that of active instigator, director, and overseer of work activities to that of monitor and evaluator of the worker's performance. The superior now judged the subordinate's work according to the work criteria. Moreover, the supervisor's own work—his or her use of sanctions, for example—became subject to much greater evaluation and control from above.
4. Bureaucratic control has made possible, and indeed fostered, career ladders and institutional rewards for tenure and seniority within the firm—that is, what labor market economists have called "internal labor markets." These mechanisms by which job vacancies are filled—for example, job bidding systems, regularized promotion procedures requiring periodic supervisors' evaluations, customs restricting job access to apprentices or assistants, and "management development" programs—all tend to tie the worker to continued employment in the firm. Good jobs up the job ladder become available only for workers who stay with the firm. In all these ways, the firm structures relations so that identification with the company pays off, while resistance is penalized.

This new system of control appears in modified or partial form in many corporations, but it is seen most clearly in the "modern management" firms that have consciously planned it. Polaroid is a good illustration.[16]

Each job within the Polaroid plants has been analyzed and summarized in an "approved description" (or, in the case of salaried employees, an "exempt compensation survey"). Such descriptions, in addition to stating pay, location, and entry-requirement characteristics for each job, set forth in considerable detail the tasks which the worker must perform. That is, the company writes down in these descriptions the rules, procedures, and expectations that I have referred to more broadly as "work criteria."

One such description is that for the job of a machine operator who assembles SX-70 film. All the regular duties of such operatives are set forth in considerable detail, including the operation of the "automatic assembly machine," responsibility for "clearing jams" and making adjustments, monitoring the machine's output, maintaining the machine, etc. In addition, precise direction is given for responsibilities in the event of the crew chief's absence (the operative is responsible). Finally, even the "irregular" duties are spelled out: training new operators, conducting special tests for management to improve productivity or quality, and so on.

It might be thought that the company would find it profitable to make such a careful listing of duties and responsibilities only for management or skilled positions. But the job description indicates that "SX-70 Film Assembly Operator" is rated only at the level of PCV-13; from the company's wage schedule one can see that roughly half of the hourly workers—not to mention the salaried employees—have higher-level jobs.

The content of each job, what the worker is supposed to do while at work, is thus formalized and made explicit and routine in these "approved descriptions." In contrast to simple control, where bosses assign work tasks by command, or to technical control, where sequencing is engineered into the machinery, bureaucratic control at Polaroid directs production through work criteria. In large part these are *written* rules and directives. They may also include unwritten procedures that the company inculcates during training programs. But what is central is that whatever their form, they emanate from the contrived formal organizational structure of the firm.

Of course bureaucratic control never fully replaces direct and personal command, and Polaroid's compensation manual is careful to point out that any approved description "does not attempt to define all elements of a position. It defines Main Function, Regular Duties, and Irregular Duties." Implicitly, Irregular Duties or even the occasional Exceptional Circumstances may require efforts outside the job description, and as we shall see, the evaluation procedure permits plenty of scope for supervisors to reinforce cooperation in such matters.

Yet the fact that bureaucratic specification of tasks is less than complete should not obscure the tremendous importance of what it does do.

The fine division and stratification of Polaroid's workers, in combination with the carefully articulated job descriptions (work criteria), establish each job as a distinct slot with clearly defined tasks and responsibilities. A presumption of work and its specific content—that is, a presumption of what constitutes a "fair day's work"—has been established.

Directing the worker is only the first control-system element. At Polaroid, great attention is given to the second element as well. Polaroid appraises every worker's performance on a regular schedule. Undoubtedly supervisors on the job consistently monitor, assess, and reprimand or praise workers as production occurs. Yet more formally, at least once per year, supervisors must evaluate each worker's performance.

Polaroid's bureaucratic control immediately provides the structure for evaluation. Workers are evaluated on the tasks and duties laid out in the job description. Although (e.g.) the significance of any particular task or the severity of the assessment undoubtedly varies with the supervisor, the job description provides a limited, explicit, and set basis for rating each worker's performance.

The criteria, and what the worker is supposed to do on the job, are known by both worker and boss; so also is the evaluation. Evaluation is an open process, with the final supervisor's rating available for the worker's inspection.

Formalizing and making explicit the basis for evaluation also in turn permit Polaroid's first-line and intermediate supervisors to be evaluated themselves. Their appraisals of subordinates can be subjected to higher-up scrutiny.

For example, a "production manager" at Polaroid normally supervises 10 to 25 production workers. In addition to directing and monitoring production, he or she must "interpret and administer personnel policies. Select, train, and evaluate individual and team performance. Initiate actions on merit increases, promotions, transfers, disciplinary measures." Yet in all these activities the production manager reports to a "general supervisor—production" whose job it is to "select and train first-line supervisors. Evaluate performance of supervisors and determine actions on salary and promotion. Review and approve supervisor determinations on merit increases, promotions, disciplinary measures." Hence the first-line supervisor's room for maneuver is restricted by the imposition of inspection by higher command.

The content as well as the form of Polaroid's evaluation provides insight into its control system. Each worker is rated in each of four equally important categories on a seven-point scale, with the seven levels defined as performances appropriate to the seven pay steps built into each job classification. Of the four categories, only the fourth ("skill and job knowledge") deals with whether the employee is capable of doing the assigned job. One category treats the quantity of work done. The remaining two categories—"quality" (meaning the worker's dependability and thoroughness) and "work habits and personal characteristics"—are concerned with work behavior rather than actual production achieved. These categories rate the degree to which the employee is responding appropriately to the work criteria and to the bureaucratic organization of the workplace.

A separate category in the evaluation checks up on "attendance and punctuality." Here mere judgments are not enough, and the form demands more precise information: a space is left for percentages and frequencies. Once again Polaroid is not measuring output but instead compliance with rules.

The formal system of evaluation does not perfectly mirror the actual system, of course, and personality clashes, favoritism, and personal jealousies often occur. Yet formalizing evaluation—making it periodic and written, basing it on established criteria, opening it to the employee's inspection, subjecting it to higher scrutiny—tends to limit and constrain the arbitrariness of the system.

Within the bureaucratic control system, as in any control system, it is insufficient simply to set out the tasks and later check to see whether they have been done; capitalists require rewards and sanctions to elicit or compel behavior in accord with their needs. Polaroid's policies demonstrate the considerable advance in sophistication and subtlety which bureaucratic control allows over prior systems.

The company's power to hire and fire underlies its ability to get purchased labor power transformed into labor done. This power comes into play in a couple of ways. Insubordination and other explicit "violations of company rules and of accepted codes of proper behavior" (to use the company's language) can trigger immediate dismissal. Dismissal also threatens workers who get bad evaluations. The company states that the evaluations are designed to weed out "mediocrity," and, of course, "mediocre" job performance is determined by how faithfully the worker fulfills the work criteria. In addition to periodic reviews—new employees after three months, older workers at least once a year—both old and new workers are on almost continuous probation. So the penalty for failing to comply with stated performance standards is readily evident.

Yet even though bureaucratic control at Polaroid continues the historic capitalist right to deprive workers of their livelihood, this power has been re-shaped by the bureaucratic form. Exceptional violations aside, workers can be dismissed only if, after receipt of written warnings specifying the improper behavior, they continue to "misbehave." Moreover, higher supervisory approval is required and any grievance can be appealed. Thus even the process of dismissal has become subjected to the rule of (company) law.

If bureaucratic control has re-shaped the power to fire (and other negative sanctions), it has brought even greater change by introducing elaborate positive rewards to elicit cooperation from the workers. At

Polaroid, the structure of rewards begins with the seven possible pay steps within each job. Each of these steps represents a five-percent increment over the previous pay. After having been hired into a particular job, the worker is expected in a period of months to pass through the first two ("learning") steps. What is actually to be learned is not so much job skills as "work habits, attendance, attitude, and other personal characteristics" which Polaroid sees as necessary for dependable performance. Moreover, the learning may occur more on the side of the company (learning whether the new worker has acquired the proper work habits through prior schooling or jobs) than on the part of the employee.

As he or she demonstrates "mastery" of the "normal work routine," the worker moves up into the middle three ("experienced") pay steps. At these levels, work "quality can be relied on," the worker is "reliable," and "good attendance [has been] established;" or more simply, "personal characteristics are appropriate to the job." Progress is by no means automatic, but the worker who tries reasonably hard, who makes little trouble, and is an "average performer" moves, in time, through these steps.

Finally, there remain the final two ("exceptional") pay steps for workers who set "examples . . . to others in methods and use of time" and who suggest ways of "improving job methods" and "increasing effectiveness of the group." These workers need to show "cooperation, enthusiasm, [and exceptional] attitude." Supervisors are reminded that there must be "special justification for 'outstanding' ratings such as these."

The pay steps within each job classification thus establish a clear reward (up to 30 percent higher pay) for workers who obey the rules, follow the work criteria, cooperate, and in general do their jobs without creating difficulty. Yet the pay scales within job classifications are merely a prelude to rewards available to those who move up the corporate hierarchy—that is, who transfer to new job categories.

"It is [Polaroid's] general policy to fill job openings by promotion from within the Company. . . ." The mechanism for filling jobs is a posting system. The company lists each job, along with skill requirements and other job characteristics, on bulletin boards. Employees wishing to move to the new job can "bid" for the job, setting in motion a process of application, interview, and selection. Unlike many union plants, Polaroid's selection is not based solely on seniority, although "seniority should always be considered." Instead, jobs are filled by "the persons considered to be among the most qualified;" qualifications include, among other things, work habits and attendance.

Thus, through the posting system, Polaroid's 15 hourly and 10 salaried grades of jobs come to represent a second scale of rewards for the enterprising employee. Although no employee can realistically expect to start at the bottom and rise to the top—such stories better support myth than represent reality—the salary differential nonetheless suggests the range of rewards available to the employee who accepts the system: the top pay, at $160,644 annually (in 1975), is over 28 times the lowest pay of $5678 per year. More to the point, the top hourly pay ($9.26) more than triples the bottom ($3.01), and the pay of the 30-35 percent of the firm's workforce which is salaried rises from the top hourly pay.

Yet even the within-job and between-job differentials do not complete the positive incentives which Polaroid dangles before its workers. Every employee who stays at the job for five years earns an additional five-percent bonus. Seniority is also a factor in being able to obtain job transfers and promotions. Finally, the company's lay-off policy is based on an elaborate "bumping" system in which seniority is the key criterion. For example, during the 1975 recession nearly 1600 employees were laid off; employees in departments where there was no work bumped less senior workers in other departments or even in other plants.

Polaroid's structure thus provides tremendous rewards—higher pay, more rights, greater job security—to workers who accept the system and seek, by individual effort, to improve their lot within it. Moreover, the considerable rewards to workers who stay long periods at Polaroid insure that this identification will be a long-term affair. Organizing efforts to build a union at Polaroid have failed due in large measure to this structure.

To be understood fully, Polaroid's organization of its workers must be seen as a system—a structure in which power is institutionalized and the various elements of control fit together. Most importantly, it is the sytem which directs work, monitors performance, and rewards cooperation or punishes recalcitrance. Insofar as it works, people only carry out roles that the system assigns them, with circumscribed responsibilities and "proper" modes of behavior. By contrivance, Polaroid's exercise of power has been embedded in the firm's social relations.

One of the clearest manifestations of the systematic character of control is the elimination of arbitrary and capricious rule by bosses. Most importantly, supervisors' treatment of their underlings, including their evaluation of workers' performance, is subjected to scrutiny and is regulated by higher-ups. That treatment is also constrained from below, as workers have rights: they can file a grievance when they feel the rules are not being followed, they can inspect their supervisors' evaluations of them, they can demand explanations when they have been passed over for a job they bid on. Except for the highest echelons (where people can change the system itself), superiors as well as subordinates are enmeshed in the system.

A second feature of Polaroid's system is worth emphasizing. As its major way of motivating workers, the company has explicitly moved away from reliance on negative sanctions, on penalizing failure, and moved toward positive incentives, toward rewarding cooperation. All elements of control—not only rewards but the very structure of jobs and the process of evaluation as well—have been bent to make these incentives efficacious. This feature is especially striking relative to prior systems of control. Of course for troublemakers or chronic slackers the sack is still always available; but the attractions of the sophisticated range of promotions, step pay raises, seniority bonuses, and other positive rewards work for most employees.

The positive incentives, the relief from capricious supervision, the right to appeal grievances and bid for jobs, the additional job security from seniority—all these make the day-by-day worklife of Polaroid's workers more pleasant. They function as an elaborate system of bribes, and like all successful bribes, they are attractive. But they are also corrupting. They push workers to pursue their self-interests in a narrow way as individuals, and they stifle the impulse to struggle collectively for those same self-interests.

All this elaboration of job titles and rules and procedures and rights and responsibilities is, of course, neither accidental nor benevolent on Polaroid's part. It is simply a better way to do business. As workers are isolated from each other and as the system is made distinct from bosses who supervise it, the basic capitalist-worker relation tends to shrink from sight. The capitalist's power has been effectively embedded in the firm's organization.

For a time, bureaucratic control appeared to have resolved the problem of control—it was the first system without contradictions. Indeed, at present the corporations that have carried it furthest have been quite successful in forestalling unionism and in containing worker resistance. Yet this success is deceptive. While the opposition to bureaucratic control remains more a potential than a pressing reality, it is growing and already we can begin to see the main lines of attack. This opposition appears as the demand for workplace democracy.[17]

Workers' response to bureaucratic control, in the U.S. at least, has resulted primarily in individual and small-group discontent rather than collective action. This individualistic opposition emerges in part from the failure of the labor movement to challenge new forms of control. In the absence of a well-articulated critique, the systemic roots of experiences producing individual resentment remain obscure. The lack of a collective response can also be partially traced, however, to the inherent properties of bureaucratic control; its stratification and re-division of workers makes collective action more difficult. Workers' failure to respond collectively is, then, a measure of bureaucratic control's success in dividing workers. Together with the lack of a self-conscious movement challenging it, bureaucratic control has resulted in individual, not collective, opposition.

Thus bureaucratic control has created among American workers vast discontent, dissatisfaction, resentment, frustration, and boredom with their work. We do not need to recount here the many studies measuring alienation: the famous HEW-commissioned report, *Work in America*, among other summaries, has already done that. It argued, for example, that the best index of job satisfaction or dissatisfaction is a worker's response to the question: "What type of work would you try to get into if you could start all over again?" A majority of both white-collar workers and blue-collar workers—and an increasing proportion of them over time—indicated that they would choose some different type of work. This overall result is consistent with a very large literature on the topic.[18] Rising dissatisfaction and alienation among workers, made exigent by their greater job security and expectation of continuing employment with one enterprise, directly create problems for employers (most prominently, reduced productivity).

Individual or small-group opposition cannot by itself, however, seriously challenge employer control. Such opposition has existed throughout the history of capitalism without posing a real problem. Only the *collective* power of workers can effectively threaten the organized power of capitalists. Moreover, productivity loss by itself is not so serious either, since capitalists depend on average, not peak, productivity. What makes the rising individual frustration with capitalist control a source of potentially revolutionary change is the fact that an *alternative, higher-productivity* method of organizing work beckons. That truth emerges from the many experiments with worker self-management. An astonishingly high proportion of such experiments result in (a) relaxing of management's prerogative to make the rules, and (b) higher productivity.[19] The former is the peril that capitalists face in introducing workers' management; the latter is the lure, and it has proved to be a powerful attraction.

Capitalists themselves are led, even forced, to introduce the very schemes that threaten their grip. They have been the most important force behind actual experiments in workplaces. They have sponsored innumerable efforts in job enrichment, job enlargement, Scanlon Plans, worker self-management, worker-employer co-management, etc. Thus the logic of accumulation increasingly drives capitalists to try to unlock the potential productivity which lies inside economically secure producers who both identify with their enterprise and govern their work activities themselves. They try to obtain this higher output "on the cheap," by granting limited amounts of each of the needed components: some security within the overall capitalist context of insecurity, partial identification with work within the relations of private ownership, and limited self-government within authoritarian enterprise.

The trouble is that a little is never enough. Just as some job security leads to demands for guaranteed lifetime wages, so some control over workplace decisions raises the demand for industrial democracy. Thomas Fitzgerald, Director of Employee Research and Training at GM's Chevrolet Division and a former GM first-line supervisor, stated this point directly; Fitzgerald explained to the readers of the *Harvard Business Review* that, once workers begin participating,

> the subjects of participation . . . are not necessarily restricted to those few matters that management considers to be of direct, personal interest to employees. . . . [A plan cannot] be maintained for long without (a) being recognized by employees as manipulative or (b) leading to expectations for wider and more significant involvement—"Why do they only ask us about plans for painting the office and not about replacing this old equipment and rearranging the layout?" Once competence is shown (or believed to have been shown) in say, rearranging the work area, and after participation has become a conscious, officially sponsored activity, *participators may very well want to go to topics of job assignment, the allocation of rewards, or even the selection of leadership. In other words, management's present monopoly [of control] can in itself easily become a source of contention.*[20]

That this concern is no idle threat is evident from an incident in the 1960's at Polaroid. The company set up a special worker-participation project involving some 120 film-pack machine operators. The production requirements did not seem especially promising for the experiment; making the new film packs called for high-quality operation of complex machinery in the face of a pressing deadline. Workers on the project spent one hour each day in special training, two hours doing coordinating work, and five hours operating the machinery. According to Polaroid's "organization development" consultant, the film was brought into production on time, and "most people think we would never have gotten it out otherwise." Nonetheless, the experiment was liquidated, not for efficiency reasons but rather because democracy got out of hand. Ray Ferris, the company's training director, explained: "[The experiment] was *too* successful. What were we going to do with the supervisors—the managers? We didn't need them anymore. Management decided it just didn't want operators that qualified."[21]

5. The Present Situation

The social relations of the workplace can only be understood as a product of an on-going dialectic. The unfolding logic of the accumulation process creates new circumstances for both capitalists and workers, circumstances embodying both new constraints and new possibilities. On the one hand, capitalists are pushed by competition to seek new ways to reduce unit labor costs at the same time that the concentration of capital gives them new resources with which to conduct this search. On the other hand, workers are subject to new forms of control while they continually press for their needs based on what they experience, what they perceive, what they think possible. Together, capitalists and workers clash in the sphere of production over the general issue of the transformation of labor power into labor. More concretely, capitalists and workers struggle over the pace of work, workplace "rights," issues of safety, relief from the immediacy of the reserve army sanction, and myriad other specific aspects of capitalist production.

This history of accumulation and class conflict provides and "transmits from the past" definite circumstances which impinge upon the present. Contemporary labor processes are subject to three quite distinct sets of the social relations of production at the point of production: simple control, technical control, and bureaucratic control. Each system contains within it important variations on the general theme of the exploitation of wage-labor.

The existence of distinct systems of control in the labor process has far-reaching implications for the formation of the modern American working class. For one thing, the nature of workers' resistance to workplace tyranny differs markedly depending upon the organization of the workplace. In simple control, workers tend to struggle against the effects of boss's personal despotism. In technical control with joint management/union administration, workers resist the technically-imposed production pace as well as struggle for expansion and enforcement of the collectively-bargained "rights." In bureaucratic control, workers are beginning to press for the introduction of workplace democracy. Thus, in these workplace-specific struggles, the needs and demands of workers turn out to be quite different because the manner of the workers' exploitation also differs.

The effects of these divisions in the labor process extend far beyond the workplace. They provide an immediate basis for the oft-noted segmentation of labor markets and the more widely observed division (or "fractionalizing") of the American working class. They even, I argue elsewhere, impart a new (i.e., post-1945) dynamic to American politics.[22]

This, then, is the element of the labor-process dialectic that Braverman misses. Technical aspects of production—de-skilling, degradation of work, creation of a mass of machine-operatives, etc.—can only be understood within this simultaneous development of the social relations of production. For, fundamentally, capitalism is not driven by technology but rather by the imperatives of appropriating surplus labor.

Notes

1. See my *Contested Terrain: The Transformation of the Workplace In the 20th Century* (New York: Basic Books, 1979) for a more extended treatment.
2. Karl Marx, *The Eighteenth Brumaire of Louis Bonaparte*, in Robert C. Tucker, ed., *The Marx-Engels Reader* (New York: Norton, 1972), 457.

3. Ann Bookman, *The Process of Political Socialization Among Women and Immigrant Workers* (unpublished Ph.D. thesis, Harvard University, 1977).
4. Daniel Nelson, *Managers and Workers* (Madison, Wisc.: University of Wisconsin Press, 1975), Ch. III.
5. *The Lancet*, no. 4246 (January 14, 1905), 120.
6. *Ibid.*, 122.
7. Henry Ford, "Progressive Manufacture," *Encyclopedia Britannica* (Cambridge: Cambridge University Press, 1927).
8. H. L. Arnold and L. F. Faurote, *Ford Methods and the Ford Shops* (New York: The Engineering Magazine Co., 1915).
9. *Ibid.*, 245.
10. *Ibid.*, 6, 8 (emphasis added).
11. *Ibid.*, 2, 46.
12. Francesca Maltese, "Notes Towards a Study of the Automobile Industry," in R. Edwards, M. Reich, and D. Gordon, eds., *Labor Market Segmentation* (Lexington, Mass.: D. C. Heath, 1975).
13. See Harry Braverman, *Labor and Monopoly Capital* (New York: Monthly Review Press, 1974).
14. Irving Bernstein, *Turbulent Years: A History of the American Worker, 1933-1941* (Boston: Houghton Mifflin, 1970), 524-525.
15. Stanley Aronowitz, *False Promises* (New York: McGraw-Hill, 1972), Ch. 1.
16. All quotations, data, etc., concerning Polaroid are taken from internal documents that the company made available to me.
17. I consider here only the workplace-oriented opposition. In *Contested Terrain* I consider the broader and potentially more revolutionary opposition, rooted in bureaucratic control, that appears in the political sphere.
18. See, for example, Special Task Force to the Secretary of Health, Education, and Welfare, *Work in America* (Washington, D.C.: U.S. Government Printing Office, 1972), and Harold Sheppard and Neal Herrick, *Where Have All the Robots Gone?* (New York: Free Press, 1972).
19. See David Jenkins, *Job Power* (New York: Doubleday, 1973), and Juan Espinosa and Andrew Zimbalist, *Economic Democracy* (New York: Academic Press, 1978).
20. Thomas Fitzgerald, "Why Motivation Theory Doesn't Work," *Harvard Business Review*, July-August 1971, 42 (emphasis added).
21. In Jenkins, op. cit., 313-315.
22. See my *Contested Terrain*.

10
Machine Technology and Workplace Control: The U.S. Post Office
Peter Rachleff

The availability, development, and introduction of new technologies has long provided management with a powerful weapon in its quest to control workplaces. The implementation of various machine technologies has helped management disrupt workers' informal workplace organization, reorganize production, routinize work, increase the office's control over the shop, and undermine trade unionism. In the past decade, labor and social historians, radical economists, and sociologists have helped shed light on this process. Among the more important studies have been those of Harry Braverman,[1] Dan Clawson,[2] Andrew Zimbalist,[3] Joan Greenbaum,[4] David Montgomery,[5] Richard Edwards,[6] Stephen Marglin,[7] Bryan Palmer,[8] and Jeremy Brecher.[9]

Most of these studies are grounded in research in the private sector—the steel industry, the auto industry, data processing, machine shops, the manufacture of electrical products, longshoring, and others. An examination of the United States Postal Service since its reorganization in the early 1970s demonstrates that similar forces have been at work in the public sector as well. Postal management turned to wholesale reorganization in the face of growing demands and militancy on the part of postal workers in the late 1960s and early 1970s. The replacement of human labor by machines and the regimentation of remaining labor processes through machines became the order of the day. Postal facilities were relocated from urban centers to concrete parking lots in suburbia. Management designed and introduced new technologies that disrupted work groups and social networks of support within postal facilities, reorganized production, and centralized management's control. The quality of work and of the nation's mail service plummeted; however, the introduction of these new technologies served management by significantly shifting the

---

This is a revision of an article that first appeared in *Radical America* 16, nos. 1–2 (Jan.–April 1982): 79–90, and is reprinted by permission of the editors.

balance of power in its direction. This is the story that emerges from transcripts of congressional oversight hearings (held annually to review the United States Postal Service's budget) and from interviews with management officials, research and development staffers, union officials, and rank-and-file postal workers from all over the country.

For nearly two hundred years, the United States Post Office had functioned as a federal agency and as such had been largely immune from the pressures for higher profits and capital accumulation facing business enterprises. The delivery of the nation's mail relied almost exclusively on manual labor, with management in the hands of political appointees. Congress determined policies governing the Post Office Department, established appropriations for running it, and evaluated its performance. In July 1971, with the passage of the Postal Service Reorganization Act, all of this changed. Once seemingly immune to goals of business and distant from the havoc created by new technology, in the decade of the 1970s the postal service now moved into the economic mainstream.

As the volume of all mail more than doubled between 1940 and 1970, and first-class mail tripled in volume, the postal service compensated by adding to its workforce, becoming the second largest employer in the entire country. Postal facilities became increasingly crowded with both mail and workers, and the quality both of service and of working conditions went steadily downhill. In 1969 a postal-union official told a House of Representatives committee:

> The average mail handler working in one of these poorly lit, dirty, cluttered, depressing and inefficient operations, usually bears the brunt of the Post Office's backwardness. He finds himself lugging around an 85- to 100-pound sack that could be transported far more efficiently and easily by machines operated by mail handlers. Many of our major post offices are so inadequate for today's needs that mail handlers and other postal employees are literally falling all over one another trying to get their job done.

In 1970, this deterioration of the postal service came to a head for both management and workers. Drawing strength and confidence from the movement of public-employee unionism in the 1960s, rank-and-file postal workers, from mail handlers to letter carriers, defied their national union leaders and launched a nationwide wildcat strike. For one week, the nation's mail was disrupted as postal workers held firm and, in some cities, threatened to expand their strike to other dissatisfied public employees. Administrators, meanwhile, had become convinced—some before, some during the strike—that full-scale "reorganization," wedded to massive capital improvements, mechanization, and "modernization," was the solution to their problems.

Postal workers were united in their quest for significant wage increases. At the time, their average annual income fell well below the Department of Labor's minimum standards for a family of four. There were even stories of full-time workers receiving public assistance. Postal workers had no intention of going back to work, whatever their union leaders told them, until they got their due. It did not take long for management to make conciliatory noises, as even Wall Street tottered on the brink of shutdown. President Nixon told the public that postal workers had been underpaid for the past twenty-three years. Within the halls of Congress, rumors of substantial wage increases were leaked out. Even then, even after all this talk, it took the deployment of 25,000 federal troops into the New York City postal facilities—the very center of the strike—to finally push postal workers back to the job.

Postal management, for its part, was thinking beyond the immediate termination of the strike to full-scale reorganization. An elaborate plan took shape, whose implementation would change the postal service from top to bottom. Part of this plan was, first, the convincing of union officials that their members' demands for decent wages and working conditions could only be met through reorganization and mechanization, and then, secondly, to use the union leaders to convince their members of the same. Over the 1970s, the first would prove easier to accomplish than the second.

In 1971, a new semi-independent United States Postal Service was born, with a new "nonpolitical" management structure and new corporate goals. The new USPS was given "broad borrowing authority," the right to float bonds to finance capital improvements. "Efficiency," cost-cutting, attrition, mechanization, productivity, and "self-sufficiency" became the watchwords of the new management. Here, then, was the ultimate answer to the threat which had been posed in the 1970 national wildcat.

One of the first steps taken by USPS was to seek binding collective bargaining agreements with a limited number of nationwide trade unions, along industrial rather than craft lines. With rapid job transformation and work reorganization in the offing, postal management knew that an industrial-union structure would prove more amenable to the job loss and transfers that would result. The agreements also specifically denied postal workers the right to strike. A highly formalized grievance procedure with arbitration as the final step was negotiated for solving questions that arose under the contracts. Each agreement contained a "management rights" clause patterned after those in private industry. It read, in part:

> The Employer shall have the exclusive right, subject to the provisions of this Agreement and consistent with applicable laws and regulations:
> A. To direct employees of the Employer in the performance of official duties;
> B. To hire, promote, transfer, assign, and retain employees in positions within the Postal Service and to suspend, demote, discharge, or take other disciplinary actions against such employees;
> C. To maintain the efficiency of the operations entrusted to it;

D. To determine the methods, means, and personnel by which such operations are to be conducted.

In short, the USPS was given a free hand to "reorganize" postal work as it saw fit.

Mechanization was seen as the way to reduce the total labor costs of the USPS, which management feared would outstrip its ability to pay—especially in light of the wage concessions that had been necessary to end the 1970 wildcat. Many hoped that mechanization would eventually bring immunity to the disruption of strikes. Frederick R. Kappel, then chair of the USPS Board of Governors, was asked by a congressional committee in early 1973:

> Q: What would we do if we had an occurrence of the strike of a couple of years ago? Do we have any machinery now that would work any better than we had before?

Mr. Kappel responded:

> A: No, we do not. I do not know what you could do about it. I think we have some mechanization, but it only feeds into a place where there isn't any, and I think we are still in a very serious condition should a strike occur.

Zip codes, originally intended primarily for use by large-volume mailers, were now promoted for adoption by all users of the postal service. Postal management also began a long—and ongoing—campaign for relative uniformity in envelope and postcard dimensions. The focus of management's attention rested on dreams of a mechanized post office. Peter Dorsey, then the regional postmaster for New York and later the USPS's primary strategist in its mechanization campaign, told a congressional committee in 1973: "I suppose the ideal thing would be to have a long conglomeration of equipment hooked up sequentially where you could dump raw mail in one end and have it come out sorted to the carrier at the other end."

The early 1970s saw the piecemeal introduction of such notions, with chaotic and catastrophic results. New machines were installed in antiquated and overcrowded postal facilities in major cities. Moe Biller, then president of the New York Metro local postal workers union, told a congressional committee in 1973:

> The mechanization program, which runs into billions, will yet prove the biggest bust of all. You can't quarrel with the idea of mechanization in 1973, just as we're all for motherhood and against sin. Let's look at the New York experience in this regard. The introduction of letter-sorting machines into the general post office, a building built in 1910. That is a crying shame. The noise is unbearable. The machines are not cleaned enough; frequently there are paper lice. . . . The workers on these machines have mostly nightwork and most of them work weekends even though, initially, management advertised these jobs as mostly weekends off. Management's comment? The people must be where the mail is.

At the same time, during the early seventies, the new postal management also adopted the strategy of reducing total labor costs through attrition, actively encouraging early retirement and even imposing a hiring freeze in 1972. They sought quick results, and they got them: 55,000 postal employees opted for early retirement. In New York for example, total postal personnel fell by 13 percent between 1970 and 1973. Needless to say, such across-the-board reductions failed to mesh with the mechanization program and created even more chaos in the postal service. Letter carriers certainly didn't have their loads lightened. With their ranks reduced, they found their routes lengthened, their traditional work patterns disrupted by such directives as crossing lawns rather than walking on sidewalks, and their actual work observed by timekeepers and monitored by devices in their vehicles. Local union officials across the country reported an increase in heart attacks among letter carriers. Inside postal facilities, the reduced work forces were called upon to put in long overtime hours, actually increasing labor costs of many facilities. New York regional postmaster Peter Dorsey admitted to Congress in 1973: "We may have gone too far, we were hell bent on saving money as opposed to service." James H. Rademacher, then president of the National Association of Letter Carriers, summed it all up in his testimony before the same committee: "We can state without fear of contradiction by the general public that the level of mail service is at the worst stage in history and the quality of the nation's mail service is the poorest it has ever been." Indeed, no one contradicted him.

By 1973, the business-oriented management of the new USPS had introduced new machines in existing postal facilities with high mail volumes and had reduced their total workforce through an attrition campaign. All observers, inside and outside the postal service, were agreed: the immediate results had been disastrous. The USPS was no closer to "self-sufficiency" than it had been in 1970 at its establishment. The quality of mail service had become a national scandal. And working conditions inside postal facilities had deteriorated even further. Despite the no-strike clause in the contract, management feared another major disruption of the nation's mails upon the contract's expiration in 1973. Apparently, the business-oriented management's new strategies had backfired all around.

In this context, postal management moved to drastically reorganize the postal system, seeking to *create* large accumulations of mail in specific locations. A single, centralized facility would process all the originating mail for a given geographical region. And the entire range of new mail-handling and processing machines would be installed in these new buildings, constructed according to new, "modular" specifications. Similar plans were laid for the construction of twenty-one new bulk-mail facilities, which would transform the handling of parcels and other non-first-class items. Peter Dorsey, now promoted to senior assistant postmaster general for operations despite his problem in New York, reported in 1974:

> Inside a Bulk Mail Center or Auxiliary Service Facility we will replace today's manual single sorting operations with high-speed machine processing designed to maintain a continuous flow of mail through the facility. Our aim is to reverse the present 80 percent manual, 20 percent mechanical ratio in processing bulk mail. . . .
>
> Put very simply, the basic idea behind the national Bulk Mail Service is to centralize mail processing so that it is more efficient to utilize mechanization.

Thus relocation and mechanization became inseparable strategies as postal management moved to put the service on a more businesslike basis. Without relocation to concentrate the mails, mechanization would not be profitable—and without mechanization, relocation would make no sense at all.

Having reorganized the workplace and the whole mail-handling system, management established standards for the output expected from each type of job within the post office. It also prescribed the most "efficient" methods for performing individual tasks. Now it resorts to discipline or discharge for those who fail to meet the standards or refuse to follow established methods.

In the short span of one decade the U.S. Post Office Department, a federal agency which provided an essential service, was reorganized, and in the process of that reorganization it acquired new goals.

The Postal Service Moves to the Suburbs

It was part of postal management's overall strategy to locate many of the new facilities for accumulating mail outside of central cities. Publicly, postal officials offered a range of weak excuses for this major decision. Traffic was too congested in central cities, they argued, and it would slow the transportation of mail to and from the new facilities. But it turned out that many of the new locations were on major commuter arteries, and no less prone to traffic tie-up than urban streets. Land was too expensive in the cities, they also argued. But then they went out and paid exorbitant sums for suburban acreage. Of course, under the new United States Postal Service structure, they did not really have to convince anyone of the justice of their argument. What was behind their strategic relocation of major postal facilities?

The center of the 1970 wildcat had been in the major postal facilities in large cities. In Detroit, Pittsburgh, Philadelphia, and New York, some 50 to 75 percent of the workers—and strikers—had been black. Moving to the suburbs was designed to alter the composition of the workforces at the major postal facilities. Forest Park, Illinois, for example, was selected as the site for a new facility to replace the major Chicago center. In the old post office, a majority of the employees were black. In Forest Park, a lengthy commute from South Chicago, there were no black families—not one. It was unlikely that many black postal workers would make the transfer. Similar concerns were voiced in city after city.

The suburban location of the new facilities would alter the composition of the workforce in other ways as well. Many workers would choose not to transfer, either seeking jobs elsewhere in the postal system or retiring altogether. Administrators would thus have considerable latitude in hiring new workers or reassigning veteran workers, and, with their strengthened hand, could shape the workforce more in accordance with their own preference and needs. An added weapon, of course, was that workers transferring in had to be able to master the operation of new machinery. The location of new facilities at some distance from the currently operating centers therefore gave management a tremendous opportunity to reorganize the workforces inside the centers of the postal system.

But the implications of this relocation extended even further, for it simultaneously undermined two major sources of postal workers' strength. With the reorganization of work and the workforce which accompanied relocation, informal work groups which had developed over many years were suddenly torn apart. Men and women who had come to trust and understand each other would never work together again. Moving to a new facility was an individual decision, and many chose not to go. Even accepting reassignment offered little promise of keeping work groups together, for the new machines in the new facilities demanded a reorganization of the work itself. Management in the new, mechanized facilities could thus operate, at least initially, with little concern for the workplace powers developed by experienced work groups.

The impact of relocation was even more wide-ranging. Traditionally, the bars, taverns, and restaurants surrounding a large workplace have served as centers of socializing and discussion by the workers employed there. These establishments, and the neighborhood within which they are located, have been a critical element to whatever strengths their patrons and residents exercised at work. The old, central-city postal facilities were situated within such a framework, one which helped consolidate and extend the postal workers' immediate work-group relationships. But the new facilities were constructed "in the middle of nowhere," surrounded by miles of concrete in every direction.

The new postal facilities were not located in the heart of any neighborhoods, surrounded by various social institutions. Nor have such institutions developed. Most postal workers live too far away from the new facilities to be willing to add to their time away from home by hanging around after work. The prospect of an hour's drive in heavy traffic is enough to sour any man or woman on relaxed socializing.

One postal worker gave the following account of a postal relocation in Pennsylvania:

> The GMF is on the outskirts of town. While the facility is only 2.5 miles from the old building, the setting is totally different. The old building is three blocks from the center of Lancaster. A convenience store and sandwich shops are literally across the street or around the corner. Banks and stores in the downtown area can be walked to during lunch break or after work. Numerous bars and taverns are within walking distance.
>
> In contrast, the GMF is surrounded by acres of grass and farmland. There is no store or sandwich shop within walking distance. Employees are thus subtly encouraged to stay in the building. Except for the administrative offices, there are no windows in the building. The building consists of a one story, 156,000 square foot concrete slab. The warehouse atmosphere is cold and sterile.

Postal management officials have designed these bleak facilities in such a way as to maximize their control over workers. The results are strikingly similar to a prison yard. (Postal workers noted that even the newly remodeled facilities in central cities look very much like fortresses and prisons.)

On the basis of efficiency and financial return on the dollars invested, however, the relocation strategy did not make a particularly good showing. The bulk mail centers soon became the subject of much public criticism. In February 1979 the nationally syndicated columnist Jack Anderson sent one of his staff into a bulk mail center as a postal employee and then published the following impressions, under the headline "BULK MAIL CENTER: AUTOMATED NIGHTMARE."

> The bulk mail center is a machine-powered world modeled after Charlie Chaplin's movie, "Modern Times." Automated carts filled with mail run along trolley tracks, heedless of parcels that fall off and people who get in the way. Overhead trays carry mail through the building, tipping their contents into chutes on command from the control room.
>
> Operators in the control room can tell how the mail is moving by watching the flow on video screens. Unfortunately the screens don't show the plight of a worker frantically trying to load a truck as fast as the conveyor belt spews the mail out. It also doesn't show the assemblyline workers who can't keep pace with the relentless machines and can't shut off or slow down the conveyor belt. The parcels often spill off the belt onto the floor, where they may remain for days.
>
> Employees at the Washington center have their own wry slogan: "You mail 'em, we maul 'em." It's not the humans who are doing the mauling, though; it's the machines. Like the sack shake-out rig that empties parcels—including those marked "Fragile—Glass"—from mail sacks and lets them fall four feet onto a belt.

Packages that get jammed in the automatic conveyors are ripped apart. Attempts are made to patch them up, but the many Humpty Dumpty irreparables end up in a parcel graveyard—a room designated "loose in the mail" and off-limits to all but a few employees. Our reporter got inside for a look around, and found thousands of items from books to homemade Christmas presents. There were so many books that they had been arranged by topic on metal shelves. . . .

The billion-dollar bulk mail system was supposed to save the Postal Service $300 million a year. Recent estimates have now reduced the potential savings to $40 million—a return of 4 percent on the money invested.

Nor is there any evidence that the bulk mail system saves time. A package en route from El Paso to Midland, Tex., for example, is sent 1,483 miles out of the way to be processed by a bulk mail center.

When Machines Replace People

Traditionally, mail had been sorted manually by experienced clerks, working in "teams" around a shared table. Each person had to memorize complex sorting "schemes," and all were able to gain virtually 100-percent accuracy. A great deal of pride and experience went into learning "schemes," and tight-knit informal work groups developed within the post office. All this was wiped out by the introduction of letter-sorting machines (LSMs).

Now clerks sit before keyboards and screens. Letters—already faced, cancelled, and placed in position—appear on the screen at the rate of one per second. Reading the zip code, the clerk then types the appropriate code on the keyboard. Each clerk sits, fixated before the automatically placed screen, in a separate cubbyhole. Communication with workmates is virtually impossible. The LSMs are very noisy—so noisy that many operators contend they exceed OSHA noise levels. At any rate, the level of noise presents a major obstacle to normal conversation. But that doesn't concern postal management, since normal conversation among LSM operators is prohibited in most facilities.

The new LSMs rely on electronic memory banks, which allow operators to sort mail into an immediate 277 separations, far superior to the 77 which had been standard under the manual-sort system. The new machines reduce the number of sorts necessary overall, and, intermeshed with the accumulation of mail volumes in a limited number of locations, their use made possible a significant reduction in the sorting workforce employed in mail processing. The LSM alone, according to postal management, was at least 57 percent more productive than the manual sorting system.

Nowhere in management's productivity claims did it count the human toll. LSM operators have complained of hearing loss, eyesight impairment, and various stress-related disorders. Some even developed serious personal problems as a result of the job.

> I hated the job and everything about it so much, that I took it out (unwittingly) on those around me. When I finally bid off that dehumanizing LSM, my wife told me how completely different I was and how thankful she was I had gotten off—and then she told me she didn't know how much more she could have taken had I stayed on the machine: only then did I learn how close I had come to ruining my marriage.

The letter-sorting machine was not introduced alone. Rather it was interfaced with a host of other innovations, which brought mail processing close to a continuous flow operation. Mechanical cullers, face-cancellers, and edgers fed mail into the LSMs. Operators processed letters at the rate of one every second, and trays were automatically swept, the letters bagged for transportation to their post office of destination. The labor needed for first-class mail handling dropped sharply.

Postal management was—and still is—very interested in yet another innovation which could be interfaced with the LSM, further boosting productivity and displacing labor. This technological wonder—the optical character reader, or OCR—has long held a particular fascination for postal management. The San Francisco sectional center manager pulled no punches when he told a congressional committee in 1973: "The only piece of machinery that we have no problem with is the OCR. But as long as you put a human being at one of those LSMs, we do have a problem because it is getting this human being adjusted to the machinery."

While there are technical problems to be overcome before the OCR can be introduced on a system-wide basis, when it does come the OCR will eliminate the LSM operator's job.

This, then, is the modern facility where most first-class mail is processed. Clearly, it has cost postal workers a great deal. Interestingly, it has not seemed to solve the USPS's problems. More mail than ever is sent through private carriers. Overnight delivery remains a pipe dream for most first-class mail. Postal rates have continued to climb, while the goal of "self-sufficiency" remains as elusive as ever. Missent mail floats throughout the system. But there is no denying that this reorganization has strengthened postal management's hand vis-a-vis its employees. In this sense, and in no other, the reorganization of first-class mail processing can be termed a "success."

The second main area of postal reorganization and mechanization has been bulk mail. Changes in this area have proven even more disastrous for postal workers.

In the early 1970s, the new management of the USPS earmarked more than $1 billion for the construction of a complete, integrated, mechanized bulk mail system. Twenty-one BMCs and eleven Auxiliary Service Facilities were to be constructed by the mid-1970s. Here, as with the relocation of major postal facilities, management's public justification was questionable. The stated goal was to win back the parcel-post business which had been lost to UPS and other private carriers. However, a study commissioned by the Postal Service itself in 1973 had concluded that, even if it worked perfectly, the new bulk-mail system, with its complicated rerouting of packages over thousands of miles between facilities, would never be competitive with UPS within a 600-mile range of delivery—precisely the area in which UPS has captured the largest share of USPS business. Even before the new bulk-mail system became operational, then, it was clear to postal management that it could not magically recapture the lost business.

But this did not deter postal management. The new system—with its centralized control, relocation of centers to suburban areas, recomposition of the workforce, and reorganization of work—remained attractive to them. Despite a series of construction delays and equipment failure, the new system was put into operation in the later 1970s. George R. Cavell, the first program director of the Bulk Mail Processing Department, explained to Congress what was supposed to happen in each facility:

> The equipment in question consists of high-speed sorting machines into which parcels are introduced from a series of automatic induction units. When the machinery is running, unsorted parcels are brought on conveyors to employees who, by operating simple keyboards, feed the zip code of each package into a computer. Once a package has been through this key code operation, it is automatically transferred to one of a number of shallow trays mounted on chair-driven carriages. These trays move by at a rate of 160 per minute, and, following an oval path, carry the packages past a series of slides each of which leads to a different collection point. The computer "remembers" which individual collection point each package is destined for, and as the tray comes up to the particular slide into which its package should be deposited, the computer activates a tripping device that tilts the tray and lets the parcels slide out.

It sounds pretty smooth. But in 1976, Representative Charles Wilson opened his subcommittee's hearings on the Bulk Mail System by calling it, "a dream gone sour, or, more appropriately, a management blunder of the first magnitude, which will cost the American public millions of dollars."

Witnesses told Wilson's subcommittee of packages caught between conveyor rollers, parcels being run over by containers, small parcels being damaged in induction unit slides by heavier parcels, and packages being smashed upon dropping from sack shake-out machines. William Anderson, deputy director of the General Government Division of the GAO, which had just released its study of the bulk mail system, testified: "We believe much of the damage is caused by the equipment in the centers. Unlike the other problems the Postal Service may have, the personnel have very little to do with this one. It's just a case of the machinery."

Missent and misdirected parcels remained a much larger percentage of total volume than was expected as well. Instead of the targeted maximum of 5 percent, for example, the Washington, D.C., regional facility was rarely below 10 percent in 1975 and 1976, and occasionally above 20 percent.

The BMC's were also quite unsafe. Accident rates were high from the day the centers opened, and they have remained high to the present day. In 1978, for example, USPS figures ranged between twelve and fourteen injuries per million work hours, triple the nationwide average. The brand new buildings with brand new machinery were proving as unsafe as the old, antiquated facilities which were being closed. GAO investigator William Anderson testified in 1976:

> The walkways are really tough to stick to and then these towveyors are moving downward. There are a lot of instances, and I know we had to dodge them all over the place walking through the plant here. The work floor is just so crowded, and these things are coming sporadically and if you don't keep your—if you're not intent all the time on trying to spot a coming towveyor, I can understand how people can be getting hurt.

It is unfortunate indeed that frequently the public placed the responsibility for postal services inefficiencies on the postal employees rather than on poor management and ineffective machinery. Employees who have traditionally prided themselves on both speed and accuracy in handling the nation's mails have thereby been hit hard from both sides. The new technology has eliminated jobs and degraded those that remain. And when the new technology fails, the workers get blamed.

Summoning up the USPS's success in making the mails more efficient, one union leader made the following critique in 1976:

> What has $3 billion in plant and mechanization accomplished? The Bulk Mail System cost $1 billion and high speed letter sorting machines, and other mechanization cost nearly $2 billion. Let's look at the Postal Service when it was labor intensive. During that time, missent, misdirected and damaged mail amounted historically to about ½ of 1 percent of the volume during the decade preceding the Postal Reorganization Act of 1970. Today the Bulk Mail System damage rate is 1 percent and the missent is approximately 5 percent. This error rate is machine error, not human error. In the letter sorting machine operation the error rate (machine) is 4 percent.

Who now thinks of "self-sufficiency" as a feasible goal for the USPS? Postal rates increase, subsidies increase, and postal service remains a public laughing stock. It is now important to ask ourselves why these have been the results of the new strategies of postal management.

One is tempted to answer the question glibly by dismissing the USPS's condition as merely another typical example of government bureaucracy in action. To be sure, instances of mismanagement, ignorance, stupidity, and perfidy can be cited ad infinitum. But, was there not a method to this madness? Are there not some long-run advantages to management which will outweigh the costs and confusion which we have noted? It seems so.

The one critical, shared feature of the measures taken by the new business-oriented management was that they all attacked postal workers' sources of power. Not only was the workforce reduced and the postal unions tightly restricted, but the attack also targeted the informal work groups, the neighborhoods around the postal facilities, and the once-crucial importance of the workers' skill and knowledge to the daily operations of the postal service. Work was simplified, mechanized, routinized, and subjected to the automatic pace of machines and the centralized control of management. Parking lots look like prison yards, surrounded by high gates. Management's concern with gaining control dictated the strategies which have resulted in the continuing deterioration of the quality of postal service, but these same strategies now place management in the driver's seat for determining, without challenge or interruption, the future of the postal service.

Use of machine technology has put postal management in the driver's seat for the moment; however, it also has generated new levels of opposition and awareness among postal workers and their unions. At the national level, officials of the American Postal Workers Union (APWU) and the National Association of Letter Carriers (NALC) have begun discussing a merger of their organizations. Local union officials from both organizations have launched a variety of collaborative ventures, from classes on "labor and technology" for shop stewards to public demonstrations. Rank-and-file groups have published local level shop newspapers and have laid the foundation for national networks. Some have promoted the dissemination of information and critical analyses on management strategies, from machine technologies to quality circles and participation schemes. And some of these rank-and-file groups have affiliated themselves with similar groups from other industries, within both the public and private sectors. These concerns have given birth to new visions of the role of machine technologies in the organization of work, the purpose of this industry, and the nature of its management. An editorial in a rank-and-file paper from Maryland, for instance, concluded:

> We would run the PO democratically. The first step would be the elimination of all craft distinctions, and the equalization of salaries for all postal workers. All supervisory and managerial positions would be filled by democratic vote, all would be subject to recall, and would receive salaries no higher than the rest of the workers. . . . All rules and regulations concerning work, salary, etc. would be decided democratically. . . . The postal service would remain as the property of the people of the US, run and operated by the workers as a non-profit service to the public.[10]

Notes

1. Harry Braverman, *Labor and Monopoly Capital: The Degradation of Work in the Twentieth Century* (New York: Monthly Review Press, 1974).
2. Dan Clawson, *Bureaucracy and the Labor Process: The Transformation of U.S. Industry, 1860–1920* (New York: Monthly Review Press, 1980).
3. Andrew Zimbalist, *Case Studies on the Labor Process* (New York: Monthly Review Press, 1979).
4. Joan Greenbaum, *In the Name of Efficiency: Management Theory and Shopfloor Practice in Data-Processing Work* (Philadelphia: Temple University Press, 1979).
5. David Montgomery, *Workers Control in America* (Cambridge: Cambridge University Press, 1979).
6. Richard Edwards, *Contested Terrain: The Transformation of the Workplace in the Twentieth Century* (New York: Basic Books, 1979).
7. Stephen A. Marglin, "What Do Bosses Do?" *Review of Radical Political Economics* 6, no. 2 (Summer 1974): 33–60.
8. Bryan Palmer, "Class, Conception and Conflict: The Thrust for Efficiency, Managerial Views of Labor, and the Working Class Rebellion, 1903–1922," *Review of Radical Political Economics* 7, no. 2 (Summer 1975): 31–49.
9. Jeremy Brecher, "Uncovering the Hidden History of the American Workplace," *Review of Radical Political Economics* 10, no. 4 (Winter 1978): 1–23.
10. Editorial by Dan Betman, *Union Dispatch*, Prince Georges, Md., local of APWU. The editorial continued in these words: "[Our] proposal is really very simple. Get rid of the current make-up of the Postal Service, the PMG, the Board of Governors, the whole mess. In its place, turn over the operation and running of the Postal Service to the only people who know how to run it correctly—the people who do the work day in and day out. This could be done by working through the Union structure. Let the Congress stake us to just three years Postal Subsidy to cover the period of reorganization, and we would be breaking even at the end of those 3 years.

"The problem with the PO isn't the hopeless situation of trying to provide a cheap, efficient service to the people and it is not with the workers themselves. The real problem is with top management who sit down in L'Enfant Plaza in air conditioned and carpeted offices and play around with computers, adding machines, pushing a lot of paper and juggling a lot of figures. The problem is that they don't know the first thing of what it is like on the workroom floor, of what it is like actually trying to move the mail. The average worker on the floor knows more about his/her job than any so-called "expert" and there is nothing that cannot be learned by the workers about the rest of the operations. . . .

"The problem with the PO is not the workers. The problem is the system under which the PO is run. Even the politicians who are hell-bent upon destroying the Postal Service say this. Their solution is give it away to business and the public and workers be damned. We see the same problem but offer a different solution, one that can provide a cheap, reliable service to the public and safeguard our welfare, our safety and our livelihood. So, Mr. PMG, give away the postal service, not to those who only want to use it for their own profit, but to those who are the only ones capable enough and caring enough to do the job."

11
The Taylorization of Police Work

Sid Harring

The focus of most sociological work on police institutions, from radical as well as liberal sociologists, is on the police work product: arrests, racism, crime control methods, police killings, methods of providing services, and so on. This emphasis on what the police do is the central focus of most major works. For example, Egon Bittner (1980) argues that the social service (or "Florence Nightingale") function of the police is in sharp contradiction with the crime control ("Willie Sutton") function. Jerry Skolnick (1966) focuses instead on a contradiction between legality and the necessity to control crime, often by illegal methods.

Harry Braverman's seminal work, *Labor and Monopoly Capital* (1974), entirely ignored in sociology of police circles, makes it clear that it is important to study the nature of the organization of police work as well: what the police are, as well as what the police do. Police work is, after all, a complex work role as much as it is anything else. We can expect, accordingly, that contradictions in the organization of police work will have important influences on the outcomes of police work, ultimately affecting crime control, levels of violence (both legitimate and illegitimate), and the police institution's public service function.

Radical sociologists, while concerned with the police institution in general, as well as with the sociology of work in general, have not bridged these two areas to look in depth at the sociology of police work. Robert

---

Reprinted from "Taylorization of Police Work: Prospects for the 1980s," *The Insurgent Sociologist* 10, no. 4—11, no. 1 (Summer–Fall 1981): 25–32, by permission of the publisher.

A note on method: I want to credit my students with informing me of the process of Taylorization in the New York City Police Department. I then proceeded backwards, from student information and my own reading of Braverman to the literature on police productivity. To make this material useful to others, I have documented most of the changes referred to, mostly with references to the Law Enforcement Assistance Administration (LEAA) or other police literature, but a few pieces of information were provided by students and were not corroborated in the literature. Rather than cite students' names or termpapers, I have simply included these facts without citations. I believe all this information to be accurate. While much of this paper describes the New York City situation, the main tendency described is a national one.

Reiner's *The Blue-Coated Worker* (1978), a detailed and important study of the British police officer and his work, is the one exception to this. This work, however, is not properly a model for American research because, appearing only slightly after Braverman's work, it was not informed by the power of that analysis, nor, of course, by the dozens of works that have followed in Braverman's path. This is not a criticism of Reiner, and American sociologists of the police would do well to consult his later work, as well as *The Blue-Coated Worker*.

This analysis will be primarily descriptive. It is intended to document what Braverman called the "Taylorization" of police work and what Marx called the "degradation" of human work under monopoly capitalism. This is done here for an explicit purpose: to demonstrate that much of the "police problem" that conservatives, liberals, and radicals are perhaps partially agreed upon has to do not with the work product of the police—their crime control, public order, and social service functions—but with the transformation of police work since the late 1960s.

To show how this applies to a single issue, take the idea of "professionalizing the police." The idea has been around since the 1880s but was popularized under that term in the 1920s. In the late 1960s, it was backed by over one million man-years of college credits financed by the Law Enforcement Assistance Administration (LEAA). It now is universally regarded to be in deep trouble (Bernstein, 1977; Jacobs, 1978). *Law Enforcement News, Police Chief*, and similar journals continue to use the rhetoric of "professionalization"; but the scholarly journal *Police Science and Administration* seldom lets an issue go by without an article on the problem of "professionalism" and its failure really to take hold in police institutions.

This should not puzzle anyone who has read *Labor and Monopoly Capital*. The drive toward "professionalization" moved forward for political reasons having to do with legitimation; the fiscal crisis fostered a tendency toward Taylorization in all areas of public service employment. While the police institution historically has lagged behind other public institutions in this respect, this move to take control of the individual officer's work product from above has strengthened police administrators and greatly undermined the ideal of "professionalization" which carries with it, by definition, greater control over one's work product—in sharp contradiction to the steadily reduced control that individual officers have on a day to day basis. Taylorization, the process of breaking down police work into a number of simpler elements under the control of police administrators, is the opposite of professionalization. Police officers, unlike teachers, social workers, and more established professional occupations, were not first professionalized and then Taylorized; they experienced both at the same time, with strongly negative organizational consequences.[1]

I. The Taylorization of Police Work

Any police administrator will proclaim that it is impossible to Taylorize police work and will deny vigorously that this ever occurs. This denial, however, is contradicted by the literature on police Taylorization, backed by a number of experimental programs in reorganizing police work, often financed by the Police Foundation or by LEAA. The major work in this field is by Joan Wolfle and John Heaphy, *Readings on Productivity in Policing* (1975), published by the Police Foundation. LEAA offers three detailed guides to this literature, complete with abstracts of each published work to make the reading of productivity literature more efficient: *Police Productivity* (1978), *Police Management* (1978), and *Police Manpower Management* (1980). The major productivity proposals, discussed below, are often resisted by the police rank-and-file, except in cities with weak traditions of rank-and-file organizations (especially in the South and West).

The LEAA's interest clearly establishes that Taylorization is not just a regional phenomenon, somehow associated with the fiscal crises of Eastern cities. While many of the specific attempts at Taylorization clearly involve those cities, the "Reaganomics" of reduced public expenditure at all levels without sacrifice in areas such as national defense and criminal justice carries within it the kind of logic that supports such efforts. Experiments at police Taylorization have in fact, occurred nationwide, a fact easily determined by study of the above bibliographies. Equally obvious, it is not LEAA interest alone that makes police Taylorization an important issue, for the LEAA is often out of touch with local police matters. Rather, current nationwide policy focuses on improved management and fiscal restraint in public services, policies that facilitate Taylorization at the local level.

1.A. Restructuring the Patrol Function

Our image of police work clearly places the patrol function at the center of the work role with good reason: 60 percent, 70 percent, or even 80 percent of patrolmen spend their work time riding around in patrol cars (or walking), looking for "suspicious" behavior, checking "suspicious" places, and generally "keeping their eye" on things. Not surprisingly, then, the patrol function is the key to police productivity studies. The first, the *Kansas City Preventive Patrol Experiment* (1974), centered on an empirical examination of the effectiveness of police patrols. The results of this study are well-known. They seem to indicate, though by no means conclusively, that the patrol function has no direct effect on crime rates. Similar studies, in rapid-fire succession, showed that one-man cars were as effective as two-man cars and no more dangerous, that "response time" was not an important factor in clearing crimes, and that "team policing" was more effective than traditional beat-patrol methods (Gay and Schack, 1977; Kelling, 1978). These studies all coincided with the fiscal crisis and provided a rationale, often denied, for reducing patrols by reducing the size of the police force.

Police unions have insisted, then and now, that a vigorous patrol function is at the core of good police work and have resisted all such cuts. This position is not difficult to understand. First, the result of this productivity measure was not to improve the working conditions of the rank-and-file but to make them worse. Layoffs occurred in several cities and were threatened in others. Police hours were already worse than those in almost any other occupation, with the possible exception of transportation. Shift structures became more complex, to cover for reduced manpower, and more disruptive of personal lives. Second, and perhaps more important, patrolmen like the work of patrolling. It allows a high degree of initiative and autonomy; and partners remain together for years in an intimate work situation (which, by the way, fully explains their resistance to one-man patrol cars).

Here it may be useful to include a historical note on police patrolling as the core of police work. There is no inherent link between policing and the practice of patrolling. Rather, the patrol-based police force is the second distinct form of policing to emerge in America; it is linked to particular policing problems that may well be obsolete in the future. The first American form of policing was the "watch-force," a small corps of "watchmen" assigned to protect specifically designated pieces or agglomerations of property. This form was dominant until it evolved into the patrol function between the 1840s and the 1870s in most Eastern and Midwestern cities. The patrol function shifted from a passive "watching" of property to an aggressive "patrolling" of people. This arose as the problem of socialization of urban workers extended beyond the factory to all parts of the city. The police became a key institution in the reproduction of the labor process, maintaining some form of labor discipline all over the city.[2]

This function held strong until after World War II, when a complex range of other social institutions finally were able to integrate American workers into the generally accepted patterns of labor discipline more effectively than the police. (This does not imply, of course, that the class struggle was obviated—only that the form of class struggle changed.) Police patrol since the 1950s has been "soft" and quite possibly largely wasteful and inefficient because it is no longer needed for its original purpose.[3]

The exception to this trend has been the policing of Black and Hispanic communities and perhaps a few isolated sections of downtown districts where vice is concentrated (like New York City's 42nd Street). But even here the function changed. The police role was no longer the reproduction of the working class by temporarily disciplining a reluctant group of workers. It became the safekeeping of a permanent population of surplus workers: technically "surplus" or the "industrial reserve," in Marxist terms, but an army that no policymakers ever expect to use. Criminologists identified with the "new utilitarian" school provide the social rationale that these people cannot be changed, just dominated. Obviously, aggressive police patrolling methods can be one way of doing this; but they are not necessarily even the most efficient. These neighborhoods do not need to be patrolled, only occupied. Other neighborhoods only need to be "protected."

This "protection" function lends itself well to another form of policing: reactive policing, which is much cheaper than patrolling. In this form, the patrolman becomes an "appendage" of a communication system, summoned by a citizen phone call via a radio dispatcher's message. The public, in effect, does its own watching. The "correct" number of officers is sent, in the "correct" priority. This still leaves the officer room for "professional" judgment in how to handle the case when he arrives, but this is a far cry from his former ability to "run" his own patrol operation in his own sector.

1.B. Civilianization

If fewer patrolmen are needed for the patrol function, it might be expected that this would lead to improved professional advancement, as patrol officers are transferred to other types of police work. The irony is that the opposite is true: the range of other types of work open to individual officers is dropping, as jobs formerly held by police officers are civilianized.

Formerly, ten or so years in a patrol car could easily lead to an inside job, even if it did not lead to promotion. At an increasing rate, virtually every city in America is replacing patrolmen with civilians in these inside jobs—clerical workers, telephone operators, specialists (photographers, fingerprint technicians, evidence specialists, computer technicians)—for one clear reason: lower cost. High police salaries and twenty-year pension plans, combined with unlimited sick days and strong unions, make police labor very expensive. New York City estimates that civilians cost from one-third to one-half the cost of a police officer, even for tasks of equal skill.

As a result, answering emergency phone calls, once a good job for older officers who didn't want patrol work, has become a bad job for young, mostly Black or Hispanic men and women. New York City's police department faces a serious problem with low morale and a high turnover rate among its emergency operators. This is reflected in emergency service, as a new group must be trained continuously, remaking old errors that experienced officers would be less likely to make.[4]

Again, ironically, it is not only the less skilled clerical jobs that are being civilianized and removed from the career alternatives of a police officer. As police departments have become more administratively complex, highly skilled professional jobs have opened up. These, too, go to civilians because, while LEAA paid for a great amount of college education, it paid primarily for education in "criminal justice" rather than for highly technical skills such as computer science, business administration, psychology, or the physical sciences.

Civilianization also fundamentally alters the class base of a police department's workforce. Now Blacks, Hispanics, and women, long barred from careers on police forces, often work beside officers who are male, white, and paid two or three times their salary. These workers are not organized into the patrolmen's unions, and it is not far-fetched to predict that some day a strike of civilian workers will shut down a major police department, as well as win wage concessions approaching the salaries of uniformed officers. Departments once perhaps 10 percent civilian now are approaching 25 percent civilian. The New York police department has a goal of converting 500 jobs (about 4 percent of the force) from patrolmen to civilians each year (*Chief*, Feb. 6, 1981:3). What happens to the 500 officers each year? Some retire; others are kicked out of inside jobs and back into patrol cars often after years at desk jobs.[5]

Perhaps more threatening to the patrolman's work is the civilianization of the patrol function itself. As that function is defined as less important, it can be delegated to less-trained workers. San Francisco already has put CETA workers on buses as "monitors"—trained by the police department over the objections of the police patrolmen's union. New York has 6,800 auxiliaries, who are trained by the police department and wear uniforms, but carry clubs instead of guns. These volunteers patrol streets and parks and summon the police if they see the need (*New York Times*, Dec. 28, 1980:36). Citizen groups like New York's Guardian Angels perform a similar function. The Transit Patrolmen's Union is opposed to the Guardian Angels, and there has been tension and conflict between the two groups. Similarly, the PBA opposes the use of auxiliaries. The reason is obvious: the example that civilians can handle the patrol job itself undermines the professional image that the police institution fosters.

Perhaps the greatest tendency toward civilianization is in the second largest police function after general patrol: traffic work, normally occupying between 10 percent and 20 percent of an urban police department's patrolmen. The meter maids of the 1950s and 1960s have given way to civilian traffic officers, with thick ticket books but no guns. In Manhattan, traffic officers, in distinctive brown uniforms, are much more visible than regular patrolmen, directing traffic, towing cars away, and writing tickets. These officers are much more likely to be young, Black, Hispanic, or female than regular patrolmen, and, like clerical workers in police jobs, earn about one-third to one-half of a police officer's pay, including all fringe benefits.

In Marxist terms, what has been described is known as "increasing the division of labor." The general and interesting work of a police officer increasingly is being broken down into single function tasks, with specialists hired in specific task lines. While an officer might previously have done 911 emergency telephone work, traffic work, desk work, and night patrol over a few years of a 20-year career, now all those tasks except night patrol increasingly are outside of the police role. This not only sets up isolated and alienating low pay "careers" for civilians; it has the same effect on the police officer. He is left simply a "patrolman." But even his patrol work has been modified; the level of autonomy is reduced as the independent patrol is succeeded by a "response" type of patrol, not entirely unlike the work of the fire department. Instead of going from fire to fire, the patrolman will go from felony crime to felony crime: highly dangerous work, much more tightly controlled by a dispatcher and senior officer than patrol work currently is.

1.C. Automation

It might surprise many people to learn that the police officer's job is vulnerable to automation. The propaganda behind the professional model, coupled with television, conveys a person-oriented view of policing such that it could not possibly be automated. But as Braverman notes, the whole history of capitalist organization of work has been aimed at tying human workers more and more closely to machines that greatly increase the workers' productivity and, at the same time, virtually control their work (Marx's "appendage of the machine" argument).

Police officers' work is especially vulnerable for two reasons.

First, much of the work has to do with information-gathering, surveillance, and communications functions that are prone to automation.

Second, the police institution has lagged far behind other public agencies, not to mention private industry, in using modern, primarily computer-based equipment and techniques. For example, police equipment for keeping records of arrests is notoriously unreliable, while the airlines' equipment for keeping records of plane reservations is efficient and accurate. The police have "gotten by" by belatedly adopting antiquated equipment, and even then not learning how to use it properly. This "backwater" quality of police adopting new technology reflects the inadequate management abilities of managers come up through the ranks with little formal training, coupled with intensely conservative organizational management practices and a fiscal crisis that has made great new capital expenditures impossible. New York's 911 system uses antiquated surplus airline phone-answering and reservation equipment, cheap but not the best for the task.

The possibilities for fully electronic applications in police work are endless. Television cameras, monitored at a central location, can patrol lonely streets and subway stations. One officer or civilian can monitor hundreds of locations and electronically dispatch officers where needed. In Philadelphia, this approach already serves to reduce the kinds of subway crime for which New York is famous (*New York Times*, Jan. 1981). Similarly, police officers with full access to computer information banks can recall immense amounts of information to help them with investigations or with field interrogations of "suspicious" persons.

Furthermore, computers can organize police work itself. The most advanced of these programs, currently being introduced by the police administration in Los Angeles, is the Electronic Command and Control System (ECCS). Financed by a special $20 million bond issue approved by the voters (after an earlier request was rejected and the amount pared down), the system will effectively tie patrol cars into a computerized response system. A central computer, located in a bomb-proof command center six stories under the civic center, can match citizen calls for assistance with available cars, ordering the most readily available car to respond. The computer can also keep track of each patrol car, noting its assignment and the time such an assignment takes. The patrol cars are fitted with computer terminals which have typewriter-like keyboards, similar to those used by airline reservation desks. These allow improved communication between headquarters and the officers on the beat because they bypass the police radio, a slow and cumbersome device that greatly restricts the amount of information that can be transmitted in a short period of time. A continuous exchange of information can flow between patrol cars and the computer, providing the officer on the beat with much more information about stolen car reports and the like, but also providing headquarters with much more information about and control over the officers on the beat. Eliminated because of its cost was a computerized mapping system that would have monitored the location of each car on a grid. Although the computer technically is capable of ordering police patrols to respond to situations as they develop, the dispatch system is termed "computer assisted" because a dispatcher studies the computer and actually gives the order, avoiding rank-and-file resistance to being "ordered around" by a computer.[6]

This system is currently full of bugs. For example, the police shift structure is so complex that the computer has difficulty keeping track of the men on duty; and civilian computer programmers have little knowledge of police operations, as attempts to train patrolmen for this were abandoned in Kansas City and not attempted in Los Angeles.

There is no question, however, that computerization is applicable to many stages of police work. There also is no question that this computerization leads to increased management control over the police labor process.

This goes to the heart of police work: crime solving. A recent study suggests that it is not the professional skills of patrolmen and detectives or even the "street smart" savvy that they acquire which solves crimes. Rather, it is effective information-collection and analysis, which is amenable to computerization. This emphasis shifts police crime control measures away from professionalism and creativity and relocates them downtown in computerized record-keeping operations. Police management controls this data and determines how it is "worked" for felony convictions (Greenwood, 1976).

This threatens the detective role, the ultimate crime-solving police role. Obviously, it does not eliminate the detective as we know him. Rather, it removes much of his control over his work. This process, by the way, began five to ten years ago. Formerly, New York detectives worked in fixed geographic areas and took on all kinds of cases. Detectives now work in highly specialized areas organized by type of crime; thus, a detective may work for many years on a succession of truck hijackings. He may be more efficient this way, but the work is much less interesting than it was when a wide variety of criminal problems came along.

1.D. Management of Police Organization

One of the factors holding back the rate of Taylorization of police work has doubtless been the police managers' resistance to change. The quality of management in police organizations is probably worse than in any other public sector area. We must be careful not to explain this with the anti-working class argument that this inefficiency arises because the police institution produces its own management; so does General Motors. Rather, police managers are poorly trained, learning "on the job" skills rather than modern methods of public administration. This policy functioned, in the past, to reduce class conflict within the police institution. Captains and lieutenants could pass themselves off as "one of the boys" who knew first-hand the patrolmen's problems. This idea of "one class—all blue" neatly tied in with the "professional" model of policing. But it is an idea that is not really consistent with the current need for productivity in police work. There are indications that lines are being drawn between management and the rank-and-file in police departments.

Part of the reason for this turns on the adoption of unpopular work measures described above. Part also stems from a change in traditional upward mobility patterns in police departments. Since the late 1960s, mobility in police departments has been highly problematic for a number of reasons. The fiscal crisis, on one level, simply reduced the number of promotions that a city could afford. In New York, there simply are no more detectives' slots, and there haven't been for years. But new methods also changed the nature of police management. Formerly, large numbers of first level supervisors were necessary: "roundsmen" in the late 19th century, "sergeants" later, now often "lieutenants." Officers on the beat now can be supervised partially by modern communication methods. In addition, the rules for promotions have changed. Exams that used to require little more than memorizing regulations now include essay questions about the causes and prevention of delinquency. Promotions are much more difficult to predict. Similarly, affirmative action regulations have delayed or limited promotions of many white officers, by far the largest number of patrolmen.

There has never been much mobility within police departments. Even under the best conditions, probably nine out of ten patrolmen retired at their entry rank. But this symbolized an important notion of professionalism and equality, and the institution is not the same without it. Blocked mobility opportunities sharpen differences between management and the rank-and-file, exactly at the point of most intense movement toward Taylorization. This makes productivity language more palatable to administrators who might not have been receptive several years ago. Police management does not originate productivity schemes; these are foisted on the institution from outside. In New York, these policies originate with the banks, which require reduced city expenditure. The spending cuts are allocated among all city agencies, raising productivity standards among all city workers.

1.E. Wages and Hours

Wages are chiefly relevant for radicals in that they are one measure of the capitalists' exploitation of workers' labor. Public employees usually do not produce products with value; hence the value of their work cannot be measured this way. Police officers are well-paid in comparison to other government employees of similar education and experience. Organizational solidarity and strong unions with a tradition of militancy keep wages high. In July, 1980, when New York's city government employee unions settled for an 8 percent raise, the police union refused a united front strategy and instead insisted on bargaining separately, with a strike threat to establish clearly that they were entitled to more pay. They finally settled for a symbolic 8½ percent, preserving their point. This was justified primarily on the basis of the danger of police work. Formerly, great opportunities for overtime kept real wages even higher. This is now greatly reduced in New York, but unlimited sick leave still permits higher wages: the same pay for less work.

Work hours have been a greater point of contention with management. The hours of peak demand for police services do not correspond readily to any shift system. Traditionally, the day shift (8 a.m. to 4 p.m.) has very few officers assigned to it, usually older men with seniority. The 4 p.m. to midnight shift and the midnight to 8 a.m. shift involve virtually all of the patrol force. Crime patterns are not so regular, peaking between 7 p.m. and 2 a.m., and then only on certain days, especially weekends. Officers are best not used on set shifts but relocated at the convenience of management. Various plans have called for fourth shifts: 6 p.m. to 2 a.m., overlapping two other shifts, or even fifth shift combinations. These may be convenient for management, but they play havoc with the personal lives of police officers. Work hours may vary from day to day, with numerous court appearances breaking up much of the "free" time. Police unions have opposed many attempts to change work hours, seeing these measures as disguised devices to increase productivity without increasing pay. For the police, hours of work are a form of productivity increase since, by definition, the work turns on public visibility on the streets.

Not to be overlooked, though not tested on a widespread basis, are experiments to tie police pay to performance in Flint, Michigan, and Orange County, California. Quantitative measures of improved efficiency were tied to pay bonuses, trying to get more policing per officer from an eight hour shift. Such measures are reminiscent of the old "police service for fee" system in the days of the night watch. The kinds of manipulation possible under such a system, by both the rank-and-file and management, are limitless. This is pure Frederick Winslow Taylor, with his Schmidt, the German pig iron hauler who, for a few cents more a day, could do many times the work of the other men (Greiner, 1974; Braverman, 1974:102–106).

In summarizing this material on the Taylorization of police work, it is important to underscore the idea that these are tendencies currently being promoted in major U.S. cities. Often, in individual cities, these methods are primitive and underutilized because of rank-and-file resistance, backward administrators, or a combination of both. Cities facing sharp fiscal problems have had more incentive to move faster, which is why New York's Mayor Koch is taking a strong stand on improving the productivity of all city workers, including the police (*Chief*, Feb. 6, 1981:1, 3). But it is an important tendency with roots in the rebellions of the late 1960s and President Johnson's task force report on the police (President's Commission, 1967). It is critically important for all sociologists of the police to understand this tendency, as it surely will be accelerated at a rapid pace in the 1980s.

II. Implications of the Taylorization of Police Work

Radicals do not study Taylorization because it is intrinsically of interest, but rather because the organization of work is a critical force in mobilizing working class people to political action. It is the capitalists' control over the labor process that shapes the working class consciousness and gives it form; and in turn, it is that control that makes a capitalist a capitalist. Mere legal ownership of the means of production is worthless without control of the work process and the labor force, or without the ability to appropriate the product of the work as well as organize it.

Theoretically, the case of public workers is different because they do not produce goods or services that are sold by capitalists. Rather they deal in "public services," often popular services with a great deal of public contact. As Taylorization moves rapidly to public service areas, it is useful to recall that the great attraction of public service work has been that public employers, while they often paid less, offered better working conditions precisely because they were not capitalists. The work pace was more human, the intrinsic rewards of "public service" higher. As cities become more indebted to bankers demanding private management techniques in return for continued debt-servicing, city workers become directly organized by capitalists who seek to provide public service with the same forms of organization of work with which they run banks or factories. City workers generally resist this process.

The police present a special problem because of their function as social control within the established order. Thus far, we have focused on the police work organization as if it were the same as any other form of work organization. It is not, as anyone knows who watched New York PBA President Vincent Caruso on television, urging PBA members to shoot first and aim to kill, after New York's eighth police officer in one year was killed. This kind of action is unparalleled in any other kind of union; it is a far cry from resisting productivity speedups.

This "hired gun" model has led some to argue that the patrolman is not a worker at all but a member of the petty bourgeoisie because of high salaries and ideology, paid a "premium" extracted from the working class and claiming "professional" status (Greer, 1978).

This analysis is in error. Most of its assumptions are fallacious: salaries are comparable to those of the unionized, skilled working class; political ideology often is that of workers with parallel salaries and skill; and the claim to "professionalization" simply is not real: it is a legitimation device.

The key to resolving the contradiction between the class basis of policing and the class of police officers is that these workers sell their work product to another class, which uses it to its own ends. Obviously, this leads to many contradictions, but these are handled through such legitimating devices as "the rule of law," the "public service" ("velvet glove" or "Florence Nightingale") functions of the police, public images of dangerous criminals, and badges and uniforms.

One of the major reasons for studying Taylorization of the police institution is to undermine the notion that the police somehow are immune from the dehumanizing experiences of other workers. In turn, Taylorization carries within itself divisive seeds which undermine police solidarity, dividing the rank-and-file from police administrators and civilian workers from both the rank-and-file and the administrators. These make the police institution less effective and may in fact force city managers to move faster with Taylorization to cover the gap. This in turn may well drive the police rank-and-file closer to other city workers and the working class generally.

No one would deny that New York faces a serious "police crisis," in large part due to Taylorization of police work. Changes in police work, shifts, and promotion structures in recent years have seriously undermined any notion among the rank-and-file of being "professionals." Virtually all of the police officers attending John Jay College, a bastion of the ideal of police "professionalism," are officers with 10 to 15 years of service, who are getting degrees in order to get off the police force as 15 or 20 year retirement time approaches. They explicitly are *not* getting their degrees to further "professional" ideals or advance their careers.

Ten or more years ago, the situation was the opposite. The major source of police alienation in New York is the structure of police work. Changes since the 1960s have made it less interesting; and opportunities for advancement are seen as minimal because of promotion freezes and affirmative action. Some of the complaints of police in the 1960s, "lack of public support" for example, either are entirely missing (obviously, much of the public supports the police all it can in most situations), or are greatly diminished. Police alienation, formerly rooted in relations with the public, increasingly is generated by the organization of work in the police institution itself, although a poor public image still is a problem. It takes more than badges and neat blue uniforms to create an "esprit de corps.". . .

It is precisely here that this analysis of the Taylorization of police work should provide us with some clues to understanding what is happening and increasingly will be happening with the police in the 1980s. The "crime problem," fueled by all the vicious "law and order" rhetoric of the late 1960s and early 1970s, has gotten much worse, paralleling rapid economic downturns. This spread in criminal behavior, along with high energy costs, unemployment, and wage cuts through inflation, now emerges simply as another "inevitable" consequence of monopoly capitalism, generally accepted without all the "law and order" rhetoric. It is, however, still available as an organizing tool for future use.

The police institution faces the impossible task of reducing the crime rate, or at least of providing some measure of personal and public safety, at a time when this is impossible. This inevitably means that the police institution will face great popular pressure for order, alongside pressure for social stability in a declining economic situation. This increased effort will come at a time when the institution will face high levels of internal alienation, unheard of during the middle-to-late 1960s when we saw a great deal of police solidarity. . . .

The creation of a significant class division, along with already significant racial division, within police departments could greatly accelerate this. The patrolmen, while well-organized into unions and sensing increasing class differences between themselves and police administrators, historically have been conservative, although Taylorization has produced more militancy around traditional workers' issues. The growing numbers of civilians in police work lack this conservative tradition and come from more union-minded segments of the population, especially Blacks, women and young people. As yet, there is no significant labor militancy among this group, but they are likely to organize.

... For criminologists and for sociologists of the law and the police institution, these contradictions will help to explain much of the current crisis in policing, the sharp decline in the trend towards "professionalism" (though this may be accompanied by an increase in the *rhetoric* of "professionalism"). They also will help to illustrate some of the tendencies to which we should be alert in our future research.

Notes

1. The best historical treatment of problems of police administration can be found in President's Commission, *Task Force Report* (1967: ch. 3).
2. On the evolution of patrol practices, see Harring (forthcoming).
3. I want to make clear here that this characterization of contemporary police patrol practicies as "soft" is my own. It refers not to police violence or lack thereof but to the use of the police patrols affirmatively to shape urban behavior. This notion was central to the original policy decisions to shift from a "watch-type" force to a patrol-type force. It seems to me now that the patrol form has been continued with much less emphasis on the idea that police patrol can control and discipline urban life. Rather, it is a crime watch, often leading to eight full hours of patrol, by two officers, with no significant citizen contact or only a few service calls.
4. Three of my students have worked as interns at 911, New York's emergency police number. All information on 911 is from their reports and from conversations with them.
5. It is important to note here that these 500 jobs per year are being civilianized, not eliminated. Hence, this is not a function of cutbacks or layoffs.
6. In May, 1977, Gerda Ray and I spent one week in Los Angeles working in the police library on the fifth floor of Parker Center, LAPD headquarters. Gerda was especially interested in ECCS, and this interest was rewarded with a tour of the emergency command center. This information was collected during several informal interviews there.

It is important to note that this system is unique in American law enforcement. Given the obvious applicability of computerization to police work, the failure of other cities to follow this model is significant. The reasons for this failure are numerous, but two stand out: high start-up costs in a time of budget cuts, and rank-and-file resistance.

References

Bernstein, Susie (1977). *The Iron Fist and the Velvet Glove*, Second ed. Oakland: Center for Research on Criminal Justice.
Bittner, Egon (1980). *The Functions of the Police in Modern Society*, Second ed. Cambridge: Oelgeschlager, Gunn & Hain.
Braverman, Harry (1974). *Labor and Monopoly Capital*. New York: Monthly Review Press.

The Chief, The Civil Employee's Weekly. New York.
Gay, W. C. & Schack, S. (1977). *Improving Patrol Productivity*, Vol 1: *Routine Patrol.* Washington, D.C.: Law Enforcement Assistance Administration.
Greenwood, Peter W. (1976). *The Criminal Investigation Process.* Santa Monica: Rand Corporation.
Greer, Edward (1978). *Big Steel.* New York: Monthly Review Press.
Greiner, J.M. (1974). *Tying City Pay to Performance.* Washington: Labor-Management Relations Service.
Harring, Sid (forthcoming). *Policing a Class Society.*
Jacobs, James (1978). "At LEEP's End," *Journal of Police Science and Administration.*
Johnson, Bruce (1976). "Taking Care of Labor," *Theory and Society.*
Kelling, George (1978). "Police Field Services and Crime: The Presumed Effects of a Capacity," *Journal of Police Science and Administration.*
———(1974). *The Kansas City Preventive Patrol Experiment.* Washington, D.C.: The Police Foundation.
Law Enforcement Assistance Administration (1980). *Police Manpower Management: A Selected Bibliography.* Washington, D.C.
———(1978). *Police Management: A Selected Bibliography.* Washington, D.C.
———(1978). *Police Productivity: A Selected Bibliography.* Washington, D.C.
Kansas City Police Department (1978). *Response Time Analysis—Executive Summary.* Kansas City.
New York Times
President's Commission on Law Enforcement and Administration of Justice (1967). *Task Force Report: The Police.* Washington, D.C.: U.S. Government Printing Office.
Reiner, Robert (1980). "Fuzzy Thoughts: The Police and Law and Order Politics," *Sociological Review* 28, 2 (May): 377–413.
———(1978). "The Police in the Class Structure," *British Journal of Law and Society* 5 (Winter): 166–84.
———(1978). *The Blue Coated Worker: A Sociological Study of Police Unionism.* Cambridge: Cambridge University Press.
Skolnick, Jerome (1966). *Justice Without Trial.* New York: John Wiley.
Spring 911. New York Patrolmen's Benevolent Association Newspaper.
Wolfle, Joan and Heaphy, John (1975). *Readings on Productivity in Policing.* Washington, D.C.: The Police Foundation.

12
Ideology and Organization Theory

Frank Fischer

During the past two decades an increasing number of writers have turned their attention to the ideological role of the social sciences.[1] In general, this work has evolved from an epistemological critique of the social sciences dominant methodology, empiricism. Such critiques range from an assault on the traditional "value-neutral" conception of an empirical science, which rules out social and political evaluation, to an attempt to locate an interest in sociotechnical control within social science methodology itself.[2] Various writers have ascribed ideological consequences to such a methodology ranging from a bias toward social stability and the status quo to political domination and repression.

One of the areas of social science that has come under relatively sharp criticism is the field of organizational theory. The purpose of this discussion is to illustrate the ideological character of one major component of organization theory, organizational psychology and the human relations school.

Ideology and Authority

To put the issue bluntly, organizational psychology emerged to facilitate the bureaucratic processes of twentieth century corporate capitalism. As unabashed students of industrial efficiency and stable work relations, its first theorists laid the groundwork for a discipline designed to supplement and support the bureaucratic mode of authority and control. Since then the study of organizational behavior has never swung far from the narrowly defined objectives of corporate organization. Always closely affiliated with a school of business or an institute of labor relations, the discipline has emerged as one of the most well-financed but carefully insulated areas of social research.

The outcome, as Paul Goldman explains, is an organization theory that has "by its assumptions and procedures systematically narrowed its field of inquiry and, consequently, presented an incomplete and distorted picture of organizational reality."[3] Similarly, Alasdair MacIntyre maintains that the methodology of organization theory itself has become the ideology of bureaucratic authority. In his words, organizational science represents little more than an "ideological expression of that same organizational life which the theorists are attempting to describe."[4] For both Goldman and MacIntyre, the result of this narrowed field of interest is an elite-oriented, ahistorical theory that is insulated from the critical concepts of social and political theory, particularly the concepts of power, authority, and class.

By distorting the picture of workplace realities, organization theory has taken on the standard functions of an ideology, in both the descriptive and pejorative meanings of the term. As a workplace ideology, organization theory has conventionally represented a managerial "world view." In this sense, it has programmatically embodied the interests, values, and objectives of the professional-managerial classes.

For example, Daniel Bell defines ideology in programmatic terms as "a way of translating ideas into action" and explains a "*total* ideology" as "an all inclusive system of comprehensive reality," which includes "a set of beliefs, infused with passion, that seeks to transform the way of life."[5] A total ideology, as such, is a program or plan of action based on an explicitly systematic model or theory of how society works, which is held with more confidence (passion) than the evidence for the theory or model warrants.

It is when we raise this issue of warrantability that an ideology loses its descriptive or nonjudgmental function and takes on a pejorative connotation. In the pejorative sense, the term is used when agents in the society are deluded about themselves, their position in society, or their interests. Juergen Habermas, for instance, speaks of an ideology as a "world picture" that stabilizes or legitimizes authority and domination.[6] It is by virtue of the fact that it supports or justifies reprehensible social institutions, unjust social practices, relations of repressive authority, exploitation or domination that a form of consciousness is an ideology.

Ideologies in organizations, in this regard, must be understood as efforts to justify the struggle for power and authority. Generated by conditions of conflict and contradiction, Reinhard Bendix has defined the function of organizational ideologies as "attempts by leaders of enterprises to justify the privilege of voluntary action and association for themselves, while imposing upon all subordinates the duty of obedience and of service to the best of their ability."[7]

The objective here is to offer an interpretive sketch of the ideological functions of organizational psychology and the human relations movement. Bringing the perspective of the political and social theorist to bear on an "applied" social science, the purpose is to show how the human relations movement, cloaked in the garb of scientific warrantability, has served to ideologically translate images of repressive authority into a widely accepted form of workplace consciousness.

Authority in Organization Theory

For Max Weber, the founder of modern organizational sociology, the problems of power and authority lay at the very heart of bureaucratic organization. Weber's principal objective was essentially to both describe and legitimate the replacement of "old world" forms of state authority based on traditional and charismatic leadership with a "rational-legalistic" mode of authority that facilitated industrial development.[8]

Based on emotion and mystique, rather than calculation and orderly change, the traditional and charismatic forms of monarchial and clerical authority thwarted the development of profit maximizing in the wider society. In place of these earlier forms, Weber sought to both describe and promote an alternative mode of authority based on fixed rules and routines, which he called "legal-rational" authority. As the foundation of managerial power in both state and industrial organizations, rational authority is linked to clearly defined, procedurally determined rules and regulations for coordinating relationships among administrative units.

For analytical purposes, Weber posited an ideal model of bureaucracy as the quintessential form of legal-rationalistic authority. This legal-rationalistic model represented the purest form of administrative control. As an analytical construct, it emerged as the basic conceptual foundation of organizational analysis. Contemporary theory, however, has underplayed Weber's emphasis on authority as a form of *power*, stressing instead the *efficient* aspects of legal rationalistic authority. In a turn from Weber's social and political perspective on bureaucracy, the modern literature has adopted a narrower orientation: Bureaucratic administration is represented more as a model of technical efficiency than as a form of power and domination.

At this point, Weber's conception of bureaucracy as a model of efficiency converges with the emerging "value-neutral" science of management, designed to uncover the efficient rules governing the rational pursuit of goals. In the process, Weber's modern-day followers have underplayed his original concept of authority. Shunning his broad political perspective on entrepreneurial legitimation, they have restricted the concept of authority to an emphasis on its functional contribution to efficient organization practices, such as the uses of hierarchy, technical competence, and leadership.

Organizational Authority and Class Conflict

Bendix is one of the few theorists in the mainstream literature who has maintained Weber's early emphasis on power and authority. Based on a comparative examination of managements' justifications for workplace authority in major industrial countries, Bendix defines the function of a management ideology this way:

> [S]uch ideologies interpret the facts of authority and obedience so as to neutralize or eliminate the conflict between the few and the many in the interest of a more effective exercise of authority. To do this, the exercise of authority is either denied altogether on the ground that the few merely order what the many want; or it is justified with the assertion that the few have qualities of excellence which enable them to realize the interest of the many.[9]

In the United States, the problem of legitimating management assumed special import. Managers in the United States faced a particular dilemma or contradiction. On the one hand, democratic ideologies stress liberty and equality for all. On the other, large masses of workers had to submit to the arbitrary authority of the enterprise's managers, backed up by local and national police forces and legal power, for ten to twelve hours a day, six days a week. Moreover, in face of this fact, the workers' right to form unions of their own was severely limited or simply prohibited.

The problem, as Bendix put it, was this: How could a managerial elite legitimate its own privileges while imposing a harsh subservience upon its subordinates? The solution was sought at the level of symbols. Designed as "weapon(s) . . . in the struggle for industrialization," managerial ideologies emerged to confer advantage upon the privileged capitalist class.

Prior to industrialization, managers took little interest in the attitudes of their workers. Only when workers became antagonistic did early industrialists intervene in the work process. And then, to stem the tide of rebellion, they principally relied upon the prerogatives of ownership, backed by the physical force of the state. After the turn of the century, however, there was a dramatic turn to the promulgation of managerial ideologies to foster the compliance of labor. In this phase of the struggle, as DiTomaso points out, the loyalty of the worker, or at least the pretension of loyalty, becomes as important as doing a good job.[10] Rather than only specifying rules and regulations to govern various work situations, managerial ideologies function to promote an atmosphere or attitude of loyalty. As Bendix explains, they are aimed at the "spirit" rather than the letter of the rules.

The purpose of the remaining discussion is to illustrate the role of one managerial ideology—human relations theory—in class conflict at the level of the workplace.

Scientific Authority and Class Conflict

In the textbook conception of the human relations movement, its task has been to compensate for the empirical deficiencies of scientific management through the introduction of behavioral science methods and techniques.[11] Accepting the basic postulates of classical organization theory, the neoclassical human relations school sought to empirically build the *human* element into Frederick Taylor's "machine model" of management. In this regard, human relations psychologists attempted to scientifically modify Taylorism by introducing the role of individual behavior and the concept of the "informal group."

In addition to the general introduction of behavioral science methodology, the lasting theoretical contribution of neoclassical human relations theory clearly has been its conceptualization of informal group processes. In contrast to the focus upon formal hierarchial structures within scientific management, neoclassical theory emphasized informal work groups, defined as the natural social groups that emerge in the workplace. Unaccounted for by the formal "table of organization," such groupings appear, according to human relations theory, as a response to the worker's social need to associate with others. Generating an internal culture of norms for group conduct, the informal group can serve as an agency for worker identification, socialization, and control.

From the viewpoint of management, the informal group operates as a system of status and communication capable of thwarting managerial policy and control. In this respect, human relations theorists have often sought ways to coordinate the activities of the formal and informal organizations. William Scott puts it this way:

> Management should recognize that the informal organization exists, nothing can destroy it, and so the executive might just as well work with it. Working with the informal organization involves not threatening its existence unnecessarily, listening to opinions expressed for the group by the leaders, allowing group participation in decision-making situations, and controlling the grapevine by prompt release of accurate information.[12]

What none of this says is that in practice human relations psychology actually took hold as a response to the earlier successes of labor unions by the 1920s. Mainstream theorists are correct to see human relations as a response to the limitations of scientific management, but not for the reasons of science alone. Rather than a theoretical problem in experimental design, we must first look at human relations in the context of scientific management's experience with worker unrest.

By 1915, there was growing opposition to Taylorism and scientific management. One result was a major strike against scientific management practices at the government's Watertown Arsenal. The strike prompted extensive congressional hearings that elevated Taylorism to the level of national concern.

At the root of the problem was the issue of workplace control. As Harry Braverman and Dan Clawson have illustrated, to properly understand scientific management, it is essential to penetrate its scientific rhetoric and to recognize it as a response to labor's authority over actual work processes.[13] Above all else, scientific management emerged as a managerial strategy to gain greater control of the workplace during the labor struggles that accompanied rapid industrialization, especially from 1880 to 1920.

Fundamentally, Taylor recognized that capitalists could never win the struggle with labor under the divided authority that characterized nineteenth century workplace organization. As long as capitalists continued to take for granted that the workers' craft organizations would retain control of the details of the labor process, they were forced to depend on the voluntary cooperation and active initiatives of these workers. Taylor recognized that capitalists had to conceive and implement an alternative organization of production. That clearly became the task of scientific management. The functions of the scientific management expert were twofold. First, they were to enter the workplace to learn (through time and motion studies) what the *workers* already knew: how to plan and direct the details of the work process. Second, through managerial planning and analysis, Taylorites were to employ this newly gained knowledge to "efficiently" redesign the production process under *management* control.

Although Taylorism in the standard textbook is presented only as a stage in the scientific evolution of organization theory, its *real* contribution was less the development of scientific techniques for measuring work processes than the construction of a new mode of organizational control. In fact, according to Clawson, Taylor never conducted anything that approximated a scientific experiment. Thus, while Taylorism was able to show productivity increases, there is little basis for telling whether such increases resulted from *improved* work procedures or were merely obtained by speeding up the existing practices.

Scientific management's primary contribution to the work process was thus to wrest authority from the craft organizations of the nineteenth century and to place it in the hands of a newly emerging profession of management. As a set of *practical* procedures for the shop floor, however, it was less than a success. Labor found fault with it for political reasons, while management troubled over its technical failures. From management's point of view, Taylorites had properly identified the issue of workplace authority, but as Richard Edwards put it, they "had not found quite the right mechanism."[14] The human relations movement can be understood as the culmination of a series of interrelated attempts to find the "right mechanism." Early interest in human relations by industrialists can, in fact, be interpreted as a response to the upsurge of organized labor, significantly facilitated by hostilities toward Taylorism itself.

Hugo Munsterberg's industrial psychology was the earliest forerunner of the human relations movement. As father of the newly emerging discipline, Munsterberg couched his 1913 book, *Psychology and Industrial Efficiency*, in language borrowed from Taylor's *Principles of Scientific Management*. Writing at the height of national interest in scientific management, Munsterberg's purpose was to elevate the study of human behavior to the same level of concern. The central focus of his book was to develop psychological techniques to identify the "best possible man" for the job.[15] Despite major opposition by many industrialists to psychological techniques, others began to recognize the need for the development of a "scientific personnel management" as a logical extension to Taylorism.

With the increasing pace of labor instability in the second decade of the century, particularly reflected in the problems of work stoppages, absenteeism, and turnover, this concern was expressed in the emergence of specialists to aid line managers in the selection and testing of workers, as well as to perform other functions such as the administration of wages. The development of such specialists was one of the first steps in the widespread growth of the personnel department as a primary organizational function. Munsterberg's industrial psychology set the agenda, touching off study in vocational counseling and placement testing in both business and public administration.

Industrial psychology and the "personnel movement" received big pushes during both World War I and its aftermath. Facilitated by discussion between Munsterberg and government officials—including President Wilson, as well as the secretaries of both Commerce and Labor—psychological techniques were widely put to use during the government's war efforts. Not only were soldiers tested and selected by psychological techniques, such methods were also extended to job analysis and problems of morale. After the war, facing the enormous task of making a transition to a peacetime economy, military and government psychologists were turned loose to work on the problems of industrial personnel. Psychological consulting firms developed into a thriving business.

During the same period, another approach gave credibility to the importance of the human dimension of organization, or what came to be known as the "labor problem." Dubbed "welfare capitalism," it involved bribing workers with selected nonjob benefits to undercut the militance created by the oppressive, alienating conditions of factory work, especially those associated with the newly emerging system of assembly line production.[16]

Henry Ford, the founder of "welfare capitalism," startled the industrial world in 1914 with the announcement of a bold and unprecedented program.[17] To both win the loyalty of his workers and spur productivity, Ford agreed to more than double hourly production wages. Ford's "welfare" scheme was, however, largely designed to undercut a growing labor crisis wrought by assembly-line techniques, which were introduced to the industrial world by Ford himself. While the assembly line dramatically increased the rate of production, it had the simultaneous effect of increasing the ranks of the unions, particularly the ranks of the militant Industrial Workers of the World (IWW) at the Ford plant.

Ford's pay increase solved his basic labor problem. Because the new wage scale was so much higher than prevailing wages, it enlarged the pool of labor from which the company could choose. Moreover, because workers were now anxious to hang on to their jobs, it was easier for the plant to increase the pace of production. But this was only the beginning. To further insure labor tranquility, Ford required participating workers to submit to the ministrations of his "Sociological Department." Basically, this meant that workers agreed to permit one or more of the department's one hundred investigators—or "advisors"—to inspect their homes for cleanliness, to monitor their drinking habits, to investigate their sex lives, and generally to insure that their leisure time was used "properly."

Heralded as a success by the business community, Ford's experiment proved a point. If management would devote time, effort, and a little money to the consideration of the human element of business, production and profits would rise. It was at least equivalent to the introduction of better machinery.

The lesson was not wasted on the larger community. Organizations of prominent industrialists (such as the National Civic Federation) incorporated "welfare capitalism" into their strategies for "harmonizing" the interests of labor and capital. Designed to combat a combination of tight labor markets and socialist union militance (both of which threatened military production in the coming World War), the capitalist welfare program "represented a sophisticated, well-financed, and widely implemented plan for controlling labor."[18] It continued well into the mid-1920s.

Closely related to the idea of welfare capitalism was the concept of the "company union." The chief stimuli for company unions were the labor settlements negotiated during the war. While army psychologists were busy developing techniques for selection and control, the government mandated companies to introduce "work councils" or "plans of representation" in the hope of stemming the dramatic rise of labor militance threatening to cripple military production. After the United States entered the war, President Wilson established the War Labor Board and a new labor policy mandating worker council participation in labor-management arbitration. In exchange for peace, specifically a moratorium on strikes, labor was guaranteed the right to organize and bargain collectively through the representation plan.[19]

However, the policy had a loophole. Because the law was vague on the type of labor organization permitted by the War Labor Board, big companies turned eagerly to a new experiment, the "company union." To meet the War Labor Board's requirement for a "work council" or "plan of representation," many large corporations quickly set up their own company-controlled unions before real unions could be established.

The idea of a company union was simple: Establish a formal grievance procedure within the context of rigorously defined limits. Given a channel for expression of legitimate grievances, "loyal" workers would not be driven to join a labor union. As such, these channels represented a substantial roadblock to independent unions, as well as extensive possibilities for company propaganda. The administration of the company plan became an important function for the newly emerging personnel departments.

During the war, the government's War Industry Board set up special procedures to facilitate and promote the training of "employment managers," often essential for the administration of the company union. In all plants manufacturing munitions, war supplies, and ships, the government mandated the existence of a personnel department. Although "labor administration" had begun to slowly emerge before the war, the managerial requirements generated by the war were the primary catalyst behind the full-scale appearance of personnel departments. Their functions included recruiting, testing, selection, training, discipline, grievance procedures, research, company unions, and welfare provisions. One writer estimates that over two hundred departments were added during this period.[20]

Although the company council and the personnel department were too transparent to stifle the intense workplace conflicts of the depression era, they were highly effective in delaying unionism during the postwar decade. Furthermore, they offered valuable lessons that advanced the human relations movement, the most important of which was the legacy of the grievance procedure. Corporate capitalists came to realize that formal grievance appeals procedures were actually quite useful. Rather than a threat to management prerogatives, they could be used to protect management's authority. Not only did they permit the company to redress individual grievances at little cost, such procedures also focused attention on individual cases rather than on company policy itself. Often this prevented grievances from festering into union militance.

From these activities—psychological testing, personnel administration, welfare capitalism, and company unions—emerged a growing recognition of the value of the human element, particularly in regard to the use of grievance procedures and the supervision of workers' needs. Yet these practical techniques were not provided with theoretical underpinnings until the final development that cinched the success of the human relations movement: the Hawthorne experiments and the writings of Elton Mayo.

The Hawthorne studies, usually posited as the starting point for the human relations tradition in conventional theory, were initiated and publicly financed by the congressionally chartered National Research Council of the National Academy of Sciences.[21] At the outset, the project began as an experiment in scientific management at the Western Electric Company near Chicago, a plant well known for its opposition to organized labor. The purpose of the Hawthorne experiments was to determine the effects of lighting on work performance.

To summarize a lengthy and complex set of investigations, the light experiments were conducted on two groups of women. One group was placed in a test room where the intensity of illumination was varied, and the other group worked in a control room with a supposedly constant environment. The investigation was to determine the specific conditions governing work efficiency.

The results were baffling to the researchers: Productivity increased in both rooms. The predicted correlations between lighting and output in the test room were thus undermined. In fact, to the astonishment of the investigators, the production of the women in the test room continually increased whether the lighting level was raised, was retained at the original level, or even was reduced so low that the workers could barely see. Obviously, some variables in the research were not being held constant under experimental controls. Something besides the level of illumination was causing the change in productivity.

That something turned out to be the "human" variable. After additional experiments, Elton Mayo theorized that the variations were a function of the changing "mental attitude" of the group. The subjects in the test room of the experiment, as it turned out, had formed an "informal" social group that enjoyed the attention of the supervisors and developed a sense of participation in the project. Believing that they had been specially chosen to participate in an important experiment, the women in the test group informally banded together to provide the researchers with their best performance, even in the face of worsening physical conditions.

From all the theories about the Hawthorne studies, the most important finding for management has been recognition of the *supervisory* climate. Mayo hypothesized that the experimenters, having taken an interest in the workers, had assumed the role of de facto supervisors. This led to a second series of studies designed to examine the effects of supervision. Largely under the direction of a Harvard research team headed by Fritz Roethlisberger and William Dickson, these experiments initiated an "interviewing program" to further explore the connection between morale and supervision.

With the aim to improve supervisory techniques, the researchers sought to reeducate shop floor supervisors by teaching them to play the role accidently assumed by the experimenters in the original light studies. During this second phase, counselors were appointed to the various departments under investigation. No educational or professional experience was required, though the company gave them in-plant training. The principal requirement for counselors was that they be well liked by the people in the department. The counselor's function was to deal with the worker's *attitudes* toward their problems, but not the problems themselves. As Loren Baritz explained, "Regardless of all the technical gobbledygook that has been written about the function of the counselor, it all simmers down to a plain injunction that he was to listen to any problem of any employee, good worker or not; that he was not to give advice or argue; and that he should make no promises about remedial action."[22]

In short, the counselor, who was not to be guided by a problem or efficiency-oriented approach, was just to listen to the employee. According to a Western Electric publication, the counselor "was to watch constantly for signs of unrest and to try to assuage the tension of the worker by discussion before the unrest became active." Counselors were to try to dilute or redirect dissatisfaction by helping the employees to think along "constructive lines." Through this process of adjusting people to situations, rather than situations to people, management hoped that absenteeism, low production, high turnover, grievances, and militant unionism could be reduced, if not avoided.

In addition, the company hoped to achieve a secondary benefit from the counseling program. One of the major themes throughout its interest in the role of counseling, as Baritz stated, "was that a well-trained counselor would be a likely candidate for promotion to a supervisory position, and it was thus hoped that counseling would . . . provide a recruitment pool for managerial positions."[23] In short, the counseling program could serve as a managerial screening device.

The Hawthorne studies probably remain the most widely analyzed and discussed experiments in the history of the social sciences. Many have criticized the findings for methodological errors; writers such as Alex Carey have argued that no valid generalizations emerge from the experiments, while others such as Paul Blumberg maintain that the Harvard researchers failed to see the real implications of their experiments.[24] As Donald Wren points out, however, most of the complaints have generally missed the over-arching implications of the study: Regardless of their validity, the experiments opened up "new vistas" for supervision. Management could train supervisors to establish a harmonious work climate, free of idiosyncratic, personal authority.[25] This link between supervision, morale, and productivity became the foundation of academic human relations theory.

For Mayo, the Hawthorne studies offered nothing less than a foundation for a new *political* vision of industrial civilization. Basic to his philosophy was the view that twentieth century industrial institutions were organized for conflict rather than cooperation. Class politics under capitalism, as he saw it, was nothing more than a "confused struggle of pressure groups [and] power blocs." In his own conception of the ideal community, small cooperative social groupings would replace the lost need for community.

Mayo maintained that the cooperation of individuals and groups is the supreme principle of the ideal community. Cooperation, he wrote, is a "balanced relation between various parts of the organization, so that the avowed purpose for which the whole exists [defined as the 'common interest'] may be conveniently and continuously fulfilled." Where there are different group interests, even certain inevitable conflicts, their elimination is merely a matter of "intelligent organization that takes careful account of all the group interests involved."[26]

Much of Mayo's political and social theorizing was based on a "psychopathological" analysis of industrial life. Essentially, he argued that workers tend to be motivated by emotions and generalized feelings, while management acts on the basis of logic and rationality. Unable to find satisfactory outlets for the expression of personal dissatisfactions in their work lives, workers became preoccupied with latent "pessimistic reveries," which are manifestly expressed as an apprehension of authority, restriction of output, and a variety of other forms of behavior that reduce morale and output. According to Mayo, industrial society, as presently organized, leads to the social maladjustment of workers and eventually to obsessively irrational behavior, including the formation of adversarial unions.

For Mayo, social class conflict is thus a "deviation" from the normal state of human actions and attitudes. For instance, he argued that "Marx detested 'the bourgeoisie' on grounds that will someday probably be shown to have been personal." Similarly, he described labor leaders as psychological deviates: "These men had no friends. . . . They had no capacity for conversation. . . . They regarded the world as a hostile place. . . . In every instance the personal history was one of social privation—a childhood devoid of normal and happy association in work and play with other children."[27]

Class conflict was therefore little more than a primitive expression of human imperfections. In Mayo's ideal community, there would be no need for political confrontations between labor and capital: "Where cooperation is maintained between the individual and his group, the group and the union, the union and management, the personal sense of security and absence of discontent in the individual run high."[28]

The remedy for class conflict is the proper application of psychological techniques. The objective is to eliminate class tensions through the development of "social skills" education. With the proper introduction of human relations–oriented supervisors and psychological counselors, workers' desires for recognition, security, and the expression of grievances would be adequately fulfilled, obviating the need for union representation altogether.

For Mayo, as well as later Mayoists, the obligation for cooperation always remains in the hands of the management.[29] As the embodiment of logic and rationality, management always knows best. Its interests are thus presented as synonymous with the interests of the organization and society as a whole. For this reason, according to Baritz, Mayo only bothered to discuss the role of unions twice in all his writings.

Given the implications of his theory, Mayo was eager to justify human relations research to corporate management. From his academic post at the Harvard Graduate School of Business, he sought to convince top management that he knew their problems, understood their needs, and sympathized with their goals. Human relations techniques were presented as a means for discovering the true causes of management's problems, which could be revealed by nondirective psychological skills training. As Baritz stated, "Management was encouraged and instructed to enter not only the intellectual, social, and financial lives of the workers, but through counseling, to expose their most personal thoughts and aspirations."[30] In short, management's problems were caused more by management's failure to convert the worker to its point of view than by labor's failure to understand the principles of cooperation.

Given the managerial bias of his theory, it didn't take long for Mayo to find staunch supporters. By the 1940s, his work was widely viewed as the theoretical successor to scientific management. In industry generally, as Peter Drucker and others have pointed out, the human relations philosophy was widely adopted as the creed of the modern personnel department.[31] By the 1950s, groups such as the American Management Association asserted that human relations skills and supervisory training were the most important ingredients of good workplace management. Moreover, a quick look at the curriculum of any contemporary management program, not to mention industrial psychology departments, will attest to the enduring value of the conviction.

As the theoretical capstone of the human relations movement, Mayo's work succinctly expressed the culmination of a thirty-year search for the "right mechanism," from the rise of industrial psychology and personnel administration to the development of company unions and welfare capitalism. From the foregoing discussion, it is clear that Mayo's contribution was much more than an empirical step in the evolution of modern organization theory. Regardless of the experimental orientation of the

Hawthorne studies, Mayo's most profound contribution was to lift the findings to the level of a managerial *ideology*.

Not only does human relations philosophy offer a justification for the dominance of management over labor, it also provides psychological techniques for blurring the realities of workplace control. As a managerial world view it posits the logical, "rational" authority of management over the "irrational," psychologically immature behavior of workers and their unions. Management is the agent of cooperation, while unions are the embodiment of social and political conflict.

In programmatic terms, human relations ideology masks a strategy to stabilize or legitimate managerial authority and domination. Through the manipulation of the organization's psychological climate, the purpose is to promote an atmosphere or attitude of loyalty to management. Although never stated formally, the specific objective is to blur the worker's consciousness of the general issues of power, authority, and class; particular unjust practices; and repression.[32] Depicting the union as an external interloper between the worker and management, workers are socialized to accept a paternalistic conception of "management-knows-best." In psychological terms, management portrays the all-knowing, benevolent father who offers guidance and protection to his children, the workers.

Finally, human relations theory, like ideologies in general, came to be accepted with more confidence than the evidence would warrant. This is attested to by the number of studies that have shown the Hawthorne experiments to be either unscientific or inconclusive at best. As Carey put it after his detailed study of the purported evidence, one wonders "how it is possible for studies so nearly devoid of scientific merit, and conclusions so little supported by the evidence, to gain so influential and respected a place within the scientific disciplines and to hold this place so long?"[33]

The answer is found in the theory's ideological appeal, especially to those who have generally funded organizational research. No one has more succinctly expressed this appeal than Michael Rose. Describing Mayoism as the "twentieth century's most seductive managerial ideology," Rose has captured its appeal in these words: "What, after all, could be more appealing than to be told that one's subordinates are nonlogical; that their uncooperativeness is a frustrated urge to collaborate; that their demands for cash mark a need for your approval; and that you have a historic destiny as a broker of social harmony?"[34]

In 1949, the United Auto Workers' (UAW) monthly education magazine expressed the union's hostility to human relations: "The Prophet is Elton Mayo, a Harvard University professor who has been prying into the psychiatric bowels of factory workers since around about 1925 and who is the Old Man of the movement." Further satirizing management's devotion to Mayoism, they continued:

The Bible is the book, the Human Problems of an Industrial Civilization. The Holy Place is the Hawthorne Plant of the Western Electric Company (the wholly owned subsidiary of one of the nation's largest monopolies, the AT and T). At Hawthorne, Ma Bell, when she wasn't organizing company unions, allowed Professor Mayo to carry on experiments with a group of women workers for nine years.[35]

Criticizing Mayo's assertion that the women produced more because of the expressed interest the supervisors and psychologists took in their personal problems, they sarcastically concluded that his finding "is the greatest discovery since J. P. Morgan learned that you can increase profits by organizing a monopoly, suppressing competition, raising prices and reducing production." While the union's view offers little to refine our understanding of the human relations approach, it does help to convey the labor-management tensions that it was designed to address.

Beyond the UAW, however, the human relations school was greeted by labor with relative silence. Given the fact that human relations techniques were motivated by a desire to undercut the growth of unionism, it is surprising that they never elicited the full outcry that was accorded to Taylorism. In part, this was probably because psychological techniques are more subtle than the industrial engineer's stopwatch. The human relations approach, therefore, appears as a less explicit threat and in many quarters may have passed over the heads of union leaders. Another reason may be the fact that by the 1940s the leaders of organized labor had substantially moved toward a more conciliatory relationship with management. Unions, as a result of Gomper's legacy, concentrated on wage gains and left workplace authority to management.

By 1960, human relations theory was on the wane. As modern organization theory began to shift its emphasis to top-level managerial concerns such as strategic planning and systems analysis, the human relations tradition was seemingly relegated to a story in the history of organization theory. To the degree that its contribution lived on, it was subsumed under specialized areas of industrial and personnel psychology.

During the 1970s, however, when recessionary conditions began to put new pressures on corporate profit margins, management urgently unleashed the most explicit offensive against trade unions since the 1930s. In the process, the traditional concerns of human relations practitioners began again to surface on the managerial agenda. This time the issues were pressed by a new breed of organizational experts. These new consultants, specializing in an updated application of human relations techniques, have assisted management in a sophisticated form of employee manipulation and union-busting to tighten administrative control. Combining the techniques of behavioral psychology and industrial relations, these "human relations consultants" now constitute a small industry. It is estimated by labor sources that they are presently assisting management to oppose about two-thirds of all union organizing drives, including efforts in both the private and public sectors.[36]

As in the Mayoist tradition, their approach is grounded in a basic ideological opposition to the labor movement. Emphasizing a new vision of "humanistic" workplace relations, introduced by an "enlightened" and "benevolent" management, conflict between workers and management is to be eliminated by good communications and improved supervision. Through a variety of techniques designed to socialize and "indoctrinate" workers to management's point of view, particularly during union-organizing drives, these specialists (like their predecessors) often establish the informal group as the central focus of their assault.

According to these consultants, up to ninety percent of all organizing drives are initiated by informal employee groups rather than by union organizers. Recognizing that unionization is the product of troubles that first find expression in the organization's informal groups, such modern-day consultants are quick to advise management on the merits of an internal grievance process to undercut such channels of communication. As with the earlier human relations movement, the purpose is to isolate and stifle dissatisfaction before it festers to the widespread dissent that fosters unionization.

Contrary to the history of the earlier period, however, unions are more cognizant of the impact of these procedures. In recent years, union charges that such consultants are abusing the nation's labor laws prompted the House Education and Labor Committee's subcommittee on labor-management relations to conduct hearings in 1979 that linked such consultants to unfair labor practices and union busting.[37]

Concluding Perspectives

Max Horkheimer wrote that "the surface appearance or even the thesis of a doctrine rarely offers a clue to the role it plays in society."[38] The developments presented here clearly show that organization theory can be offered as evidence to substantiate his premise. In sharp contrast to an objective science of organizational behavior, what emerges from the history of organizational psychology is a picture of ideological corruption. Both wittingly and unwittingly, organizational psychology has evolved into a tool of manipulation and control in the ongoing struggle for command of the workplace.

The example of human relations theory thus demonstrates the need for a *political* theory of organizational science. While the articulation of such a theory is beyond the scope of the present essay, from the foregoing analysis it is nonetheless possible to specify a number of factors that must be included in such a theory. Consider, for example, the relationship between organizational expertise and class politics.

An adequate theory of the role of organizational expertise must begin with the premise that knowledge has become a critical resource in the politics of class struggle, both inside and outside the workplace. In an age of bureaucratic organizations, characterized by hierarchy and functional compartmentalization, the very premises that determine political consciousness and class conflict are significantly shaped by the control of knowledge and information. Therefore, political scientists and sociologists must examine organizational psychology not only for its contribution to work processes, but also for its critical force in shaping the political attitudes and actions of the working classes.

Second, in the elaboration of such a theory, one must recognize the complexity of the role of organizational expertise in the larger class struggle between capital and labor.[39] Men like Mayo were more than "tools" of capitalist power. While human relations psychology, like scientific management, has helped to mitigate the capitalists' conflicts with labor, it must be perceived as the commodity of a *new* class vying for position in the evolving world of bureaucratic capitalism.

Here we can benefit from Stark's analysis of scientific management.[40] Like scientific management, human relations theory must be understood as an emergent ideology of organizational psychologists bent upon earning a niche for themselves in the structures of modern industrial society. Positioned between capital and labor, they have sought the basis for a new professional recognition and autonomy by mediating class conflict. In this regard, Baritz, too, has shown that industrial and human relations psychologists required little prodding by the leaders of industry and government. Like the industrial engineers before them, they sought to legitimate themselves as members of a new professional-managerial strata. The justification for the role was to be provided by the experimental knowledge of human relations research developed by the industrial and organizational psychology community. Appeals to the "objective" laws of human behavior provided the basic ideological underpinnings for the psychologist's autonomy; psychological measurement offered the necessary data for display of their expertise; and the newly developed departments of personnel administration established an organizational base of operations.

Finally, a few comments should be made about the role of government. From the foregoing discussion, it is clear that the federal government has consistently sponsored the development of managerially biased organizational techniques. Thus, the focus of labor relations policy should be extended beyond its primary emphasis on collective bargaining to include government's role in shaping specific workplace practices. Like the scientific management approach introduced at the government's Watertown Arsenal, the major strides in the development of industrial psychology, personnel management, and company unions were facilitated by the government's war efforts and later through public financing, as exemplified by the Hawthorne studies. Today, the research offices of the federal government, particularly those of the army and navy, remain among the most significant financial contributors to organizational research.

Consideration of these various elements leads to the following conclusion: If organization theory is to contribute to the construction of a socially just society, it must more directly confront the political motivations that shape its uses. In the realm of practice, social scientists must begin with the understanding that theory does not directly dictate practice. Unable to control the implications of their own work, they must recognize that even the most humanistic techniques can be employed to further unjust ends. Only with such caveats clearly in mind can organizational theorists realistically hope to address the need for legitimate practical reforms.

Notes

1. See, for example, Robin Blackburn, ed., *Ideology in Social Science* (London: Fontana, 1972).
2. On the critique of "value-neutrality," see Frank Fischer, *Politics, Values, and Public Policy: The Problem of Methodology* (Boulder, Co.: Westview Press, 1980). For an attempt to locate an interest in sociotechnical control in social science methodology, see Herbert Marcuse, *One-Dimensional Man* (Boston: Beacon Press, 1964).
3. Paul Goldman, "Sociologists and the Study of Bureaucracy: A Critique of Ideology and Practice," *The Insurgent Sociologist* 3 (Winter 1978): 21.
4. Alasdair MacIntyre, "Social Science Methodology as the Ideology of Bureaucratic Authority," *Through the Looking-Glass*, ed. by Maria J. Falco (Washington: University Press of America, 1979), 42.
5. Daniel Bell, "The End of Ideology in the West," *The End of Ideology Debate*, ed. by Chaim I. Waxman (New York: Funk and Wagnalls, 1968), 88, 96.
6. Juergen Habermas, *Toward a Rational Society* (Boston: Beacon Press, 1970).
7. Reinhard Bendix, *Work and Authority in Industry* (New York: John Wiley, 1956), xxiii; Michael E. Urban, "Bureaucracy, Contradiction, and Ideology in Two Societies," *Administration and Society* 10, no. 1 (May 1978): 49–85.
8. Max Weber, *The Theory of Economic and Social Organization* (New York: Oxford University Press, 1947).
9. Bendix, *Work and Authority in Industry*, 13.
10. Nancy DiTomaso, "The Organization of Authority in the Capitalist State," *Journal of Political and Military Sociology* 6 (Fall 1978): 189–204.
11. William G. Scott, "Organization Theory: An Overview and Appraisal," *Organizations*, ed. by Joseph A. Litterer (New York: John Wiley, 1969), 15–28.
12. Ibid, 20.
13. Harry Braverman, *Labor and Monopoly Capital* (New York: Monthly Review Press, 1974); Dan Clawson, *Bureaucracy and the Labor Process* (New York: Monthly Review Press, 1980), 47.
14. Richard Edwards, *Contested Terrain* (New York: Basic Books, 1979), 104.
15. Donald A. Wren, *The Evolution of Management Thought* (New York: Ronald Press, 1972), 195–208.

16. Stuart Brandeis, *American Welfare Capitalism, 1880-1940* (Chicago: University of Chicago Press, 1976).
17. Loren Baritz, *The Servants of Power: A History of the Use of Social Science in American Industry* (Middletown, Conn.: Wesleyan University Press, 1960), 32-35; Braverman, *Labor and Monopoly Capital*, 149.
18. Edwards, *Contested Terrain*, 95.
19. Ibid., 105-10.
20. Henry Eilburt, "The Development of Personnel Management in the United States," *Business History Review* 33 (Autumn 1959): 345-64.
21. Baritz, *Servants of Power*, 76-116; Wren, *Evolution of Management Thought*, 275-299.
22. Baritz, *Servants of Power*, 105.
23. Ibid.
24. Alex Carey, "The Hawthorne Studies: A Radical Criticism," *American Sociological Review* 32 (June 1974): 403-16; Paul Blumberg, *Industrial Democracy* (New York: Schocken Books, 1976), 14-46; A. J. M. Sykes, "Economic Interest and the Hawthorne Researchers," *Human Relations* 18 (August 1965): 253-63.
25. Wren, *Evolution of Management Thought*, Chap. 13 and 14.
26. Elton Mayo, *The Social Problems of an Industrial Civilization* (London: Routledge, 1949), 128; Mayo, *The Political Problems of Industrial Civilization* (Cambridge: Harvard University Printing Office, 1947).
27. Mayo, *The Social Problems of an Industrial Civilization*, 24; Baritz, *Servants of Power*.
28. Mayo, *The Social Problems of an Industrial Civilization*, 111.
29. For a good illustration of the anti-trade union interpretation of the Hawthorne findings, see T. North Whitehead, *Leadership in a Free Society* (Cambridge: Harvard University Press, 1936), 155.
30. Baritz, *Servants of Power*, 115.
31. Peter Drucker, *The Practice of Management* (New York: Harper and Row, 1954), 273-88.
32. For a discussion of how the vocabulary of human relations experts blurs the facts of organizational power, see C. Wright Mills, "The Contributions of Sociology to Studies of Industrial Relations," *Proceedings of the First Annual Meeting of Industrial Relations Association* (1948), 212-13.
33. Carey, "Hawthorne Studies," 403.
34. Michael Rose, *Industrial Behaviour: Theoretical Development Since Taylor* (London: Allen Lane, 1975), 124.
35. Baritz, *Servants of Power*, 114-15.
36. See, for example, Steve Lagerfeld, "The Pop Psychologist as Union Buster," *American Federationist* (November 1981): 6-12; Damon Stetson, "New Kind of Law Firm Keeping Labor at Bay," *New York Times*, 25 October 1981, 53.
37. Committee on Education and Labor, House of Representatives Oversight Hearings before the Subcommittee on Labor-Management Relations, *Pressures in Today's Workplace*, 96th Congress, 1st session (Washington, D.C.: GPO, 1979), 4 volumes.
38. Max Horkheimer, *The Eclipse of Reason* (New York: Oxford University Press, 1947), 85.
39. For an illustration of a Marxist attempt to explain organizational psychology in terms of the larger class struggle between capital and labor, see Walter R. Nord, "The Failure of Current Applied Behavioral Science—A Marxian Perspective," *The Journal of Applied Behavioral Science* 10, no. 4 (October, November, December 1974): 557-78.
40. David Stark, "Class Struggle and the Transformation of the Labor Process: A Relational Approach," *Theory and Society* 9 (January 1980): 102.

13
Technocratic Administration and Educational Control

Beverly H. Burris and Wolf V. Heydebrand

The technocratic administration of higher education was formally inaugurated when the U.S. Supreme Court, in a 5 to 4 decision on February 20, 1980, held that the full-time faculty members of Yeshiva University were managerial employees in addition to being professional employees of the university. The decision bars university professors and their faculty unions from engaging in collective bargaining with private institutions of higher education.

Furthermore, this decision implies that the traditional line of demarcation between professional and administrative work is no longer valid or, at least, that it has become seriously blurred. This integration of professional and managerial functions under one unified organizational system, whose imperatives and problems are to a large extent granted priority over those of specialized departments, schools, groups, or individual interests within it, is integrally related to the extensive application of system-wide criteria of work performance: efficiency, productivity, and cost-effectiveness. This ascent of educational systems-management is based on scientific-technical knowledge and appropriate technology and relies heavily on instrumental rationality, forecasting, and long-term planning in order to achieve its goal of efficient and nonconflictual systems engineering. This is the form of institutional control that we term "technocratic administration."

Educational control structures serve to facilitate the control and administration of three distinct but interrelated levels of organization: individual institutions of education, the overall educational system, and the relationship between educational institutions and other social institutions, particularly the occupational sector. Technocratic administration emerged after certain earlier control structures were superseded; theocratic boards of trustees, professional status groups, and bureaucracy have all been influential in determining the structure of institutions

---

Reprinted from J. Wilson (Ed.), *New Directions for Higher Education: Management Science Applications to Academic Administration*, no. 35 (San Francisco: Jossey-Bass, September 1981), by permission of the publisher.

of higher education. An analysis of this historical process is therefore crucial to an understanding of both technocracy and contemporary institutions of higher education. Our historical review will culminate in a more detailed analysis of the Yeshiva case. Finally, we will discuss the implications of our analysis for the concept of technocracy, for theories of organizational control, and for the contemporary situation of higher education.

1636–1850: Theocracy and Early Capitalism

Education was a priority of the early American settlers. Harvard College was established in 1636 in the midst of the founding of the new society. However, the fear of academic freedom was strong, and the early colleges and schools were clearly dominated by the ruling theocracy. This subordination of educational purpose to religion and law was evident in the wording of the Massachusetts Act of 1642, which gave legal sanction to education while carefully circumscribing its function: "Children must learn to read and understand the principles of religion and the capital laws of the country" (Rippa, 1967, p. 45). Basic literacy was to be achieved through the "dame schools," which used scriptural tests, religious primers, and stringent discipline to achieve this purpose. The early colleges and Latin schools, however, were for the purpose of advanced theological instruction for the ministerial elite. Material production was home-based, and necessary skills (including early professional skills, such as medicine) were taught either within the family or by a vestigial apprenticeship system (Cremin, 1970; Bailyn, 1960; Bowles and Gintis, 1976). The salient social hierarchy was a theocratic one, and the bifurcation of the educational system into primary schools and elite colleges corresponded to the social division between the ministers and the members of the congregation. In this period, an early division of labor into mental and manual labor was combined with the power of religion to create a clearly defined social hierarchy.

The administrative control structure of the early colleges was a board of trustees drawn from the ministerial elite of whichever religious denomination had founded the college. These trustees then hired a president and a small faculty, to whom they delegated authority but supervised closely. The early American colleges were thus structured like chartered corporations, in direct contrast to the traditional European model of intellectual craft guilds, in which "faculty (and sometimes students) banded together in guilds, attempted to govern themselves through collegial principles, and maneuvered as best they could against the somewhat removed officials of state and church" (Clark, 1978, p. 104).

If the administrative control structure of the individual American college was unusually strong, the coordination and control of the overall system was unusually weak. In the late eighteenth and nineteenth centuries, as the theocracy eroded, the rise of entrepreneurial capitalism was complemented by entrepreneurial expansion of the educational system. The Enlightenment, the fight for political independence, and the growth of trade and mercantilism shaped societal priorities away from religious absorption and towards secularization and utilitarianism. Different types of colleges proliferated in a rather haphazard manner, with the organizational death rate as high as the birth rate: "In the Darwinian struggle, the form was gradually strengthened and . . . the control mechanism of a private board was perfected" (Clark, 1978, p.105). Businessmen also began to replace ministers on many boards of trustees.

As theocracy gave way to the Enlightenment and early capitalism, the internal administrative structure of the colleges became modified. Educational priorities shifted from conserving knowledge to expanding it, and the power of the faculty compared to the board correspondingly increased. Disputes between the faculty and the board over governance issues had occurred periodically throughout the colonial period, with the faculty failing to achieve appreciable autonomy (Brubacher and Rudy, 1958, p. 29). However, in 1825–26, the Harvard faculty mounted a drive to gain seats on the governing board, which, although failing in its immediate objective, did result in a restructuring of Harvard's governance model. The compromise that was reached utilized the distinction between internal and external control: Overall policy decisions and the allocation of financial resources were deemed matters of external control and placed under the jurisdiction of the board, whereas such internal matters as admission of students, student discipline, and the conduct of instruction were to be under faculty control.

At about the same time, the power of the board was also challenged from without, by public authorities. In the famous Dartmouth College case, the forces in favor of more state control over colleges and greater public accountability of the boards contended with those in favor of private corporate control. Although the state ruled in favor of public control, the Supreme Court reversed the decision and declared Dartmouth and similar colleges to be private rather than public corporations. Daniel Webster, who argued the case for Dartmouth, "reasoned to the court that the college would lead a precarious existence if it were to be subject to the fluctuations of public opinion or the rise and fall of political parties" (Brubacher and Rudy, 1958, p. 36).

Thus, the Supreme Court paved the way for private corporate control of colleges and the unfettered dominance of business elites on the boards of trustees. Community groups, fueled by the fervor of Jacksonian democracy, began to oppose higher education altogether, calling colleges "seedbeds of aristocracy" (Katz, 1971, p. 10). Legislative subsidies to colleges were greatly reduced, and state laws of incorporation were amended to limit the amount of property that colleges might hold (Brubacher and Rudy, 1958, p. 36). Colleges were poorly attended, and over 80 percent of the colleges founded during the first half of the nineteenth century failed and disappeared (Perkinson, 1968, p. 11). By the early nineteenth century, the educational system was clearly bifurcated into practically oriented and community-controlled common schools and elite colleges administered by boards of trustees that were dominated by business elites. As Jefferson had recommended, "The best geniuses will be raked from the rubbish annually" (Perkinson, 1963, pp. 9–10).

1850–1900: Early Bureaucratization and Professionalism

During the latter half of the nineteenth century, America underwent far-reaching changes at a rapid pace. Industrialization, urbanization, and large-scale immigration transformed both the landscape and the culture. Urbanization proceeded at a faster rate between 1820 and 1860 than during any other period of American history, and the swollen cities were characterized by squalor and chaos. The cultural diversity of the immigrants was seen as a threat, and "foreign values" were blamed for many of the social problems of the period: the urban blight, the poverty, the cultural dislocation, the labor unrest. Extremes of wealth coexisted with extremes of poverty, and class conflict increasingly became both a reality and a concern. The rhetoric of progress was only one side of the period's mentality; the underside of America's reaction to such sweeping changes was fear—fear of diversity, fear of the immigrants, fear of anarchy.

The effect of these changes and attitudes on the educational system was appreciable. One major shift was the new feeling that schooling could no longer be left as a haphazard system of common schools and private colleges, but rather that it had to be centralized, standardized, and controlled by those who were well versed in American values and the needs of industrializing America. A system of American education was increasingly seen as desirable, and the process of centralization and bureaucratization began (Bowles and Gintis, 1976; Katz, 1971; Tyack, 1974).

The particular focus of those in favor of centralization and systematization was the sprawling network of community-controlled common schools. All across America, battles were fought between those in favor of lay community control and the business and professional elites who were leading the drive for consolidation and centralized control. Professionalism arose as a powerful ally of the movement for centralized control. Proponents of centralization and bureaucratization pointed to the poor quality of teaching in many one-room schools, and promised higher standards (Katz, 1971, p. 70).

In addition, incipient bureaucratization was legitimated on the grounds of efficiency and political neutrality. The sheer pressure of numbers in the burgeoning towns and cities, as well as the frequent intrusion of political squabbles into local schools, made standardization and control seem imperative to some, in the interest of taking the schools out of politics. For instance, in Chicago, one new school enrolled 543 students its first year and 843 the next; there were only three teachers, no graded classrooms, and no uniform textbooks (see Tyack, 1974, p. 38). Democracy was seen as inevitably chaotic and inept,[1] and control by a board of "successful men" was proposed, for it was assumed that those who had succeeded could have no vested personal interests to pursue. As one early school management text put it: " 'The businessman chosen from the class of merchants, bankers, and manufacturers . . . and professional men . . . have no personal ends to serve and no special cause to plead' " (Tyack, 1974, p. 140). Such men soon began to shape American educational institutions into a system that was explicitly modeled after the machine or factory, a system designed to achieve correspondence with a fast-industrializing America (Tyack, 1974; Perkinson, 1968; Katz, 1971; Bowles and Gintis, 1976). Some teachers resisted being made functionaries in such a mechanistic system, but their vociferous demands for autonomy were not sufficient to impede the forces of bureaucratization (Tyack, 1974, p. 82, 240).

Although this process of bureaucratization focused initially and most intensively on the system of common schools, which was extensive and highly unstructured, higher education was also transformed and expanded during the late nineteenth century. In addition to an industrial workforce, capitalism also needed more skilled workers at this stage of its development: engineers, managers, technicians, and professionals. The classical tradition in higher education was increasingly seen as decadent scholasticism as a new institution of higher education emerged: the university. Some former colonial colleges, such as Harvard, Yale, and Princeton, evolved into universities as their curricula broadened and as graduate-level instruction became institutionalized. An even more significant innovation was the rise of the state university. After the Civil War, universities receiving regular tax support sprang up throughout the country. These public universities offered a more diversified curriculum, greater educational opportunity to a broader constituency, and greater accountability and relevance to a rapidly industrializing America. State universities "led all classes of people to believe in the value of university education and to wish to attain it" (Brubacher and Rudy, 1958, p. 173).

In addition to universities, colleges and schools that were specialized according to vocational function (rather than by the affiliation of their founders) also emerged. Colleges for teacher training, other professional schools, colleges of engineering, and vocational schools coexisted with universities. In contrast to the increasingly centralized system of primary education, higher education remained "a bewildering array of proprietary, nonprofit, and specialized schools and colleges" (Clark, 1978, p. 107).

However, the differentiated university, private or public, soon became the most viable institution of higher education, and many specialized and professional schools became part of university systems. Classical studies and more vocationally oriented curricula could coexist, albeit in a sometimes conflictual relationship (Jencks and Riesman, 1968, p. 224). This range of diversity and conflicting interests, as well as the growing need for public accountability of the state universities, soon led to an increasingly bureaucratic internal structure, with the growth of a separate administrative staff headed by a president who was accountable to a board of trustees. As Veysey (1965, p. 311) points out; "Bureaucratic administration was the structural device which made possible the new epoch of institutional empire building without recourse to specific shared values."

However, as had been the case with the primary schools, early bureaucratization coexisted with the rising ethos of professionalism among university professors. In the late nineteenth and early twentieth centuries, universities were repeatedly the battlegrounds for struggles over professional autonomy. In these battles, "the basic question was whether the president and trustees or the faculty would determine the shape of the curriculum, the content of particular courses, or the use of particular books" (Jencks and Riesman, 1968, p. 15). Buttressed by an ample administration and bureaucratic structures of control, the governing boards had reopened the question of jurisdiction over internal control that the Harvard faculty had fought for in 1826. At times, these clashes between professors and administrators took dramatic and political form, as in the famed academic freedom cases of the 1890s (Scott and Shore, 1979, p. 110).

By the turn of the century, universities were embracing a more pragmatic and vocational ethos, overtly seeking correspondence with business interests, a correspondence that some businessmen had felt to be lacking.[2] The scope of professional training was expanded to include business administration, journalism, veterinary medicine, social work, forestry, engineering, and so forth. As E. J. James put it in 1906, " 'the state university must stand simply, plainly, unequivocally, and uncompromisingly for training, for vocation. . . . Scholarship is necessary only insofar as scholarship is a necessary incident to all proper training' " (Perkinson, 1968, p. 129). Or, as a New York University professor said even more succinctly in 1890: " 'The college has ceased to be a cloister and has become a workshop' " (Veysey, 1965, p. 61).

1900–1930: Taylorism, Progressivism, and the Rise of Administration

By the turn of the century, American institutions of education had been largely brought into correspondence with the exigencies of industrializing America. Primary education was increasingly structured so as to inculcate the requisite discipline, and higher education was oriented toward providing the appropriate skills: professional, technical, managerial, and agricultural. Moreover, the form of educational institutions was explicitly modeled after the machine and factory. However, contradictions were criticized by communities and teachers for impinging on democratic accountability, on the professional autonomy of teachers, and on the very process of teaching itself.

School boards and administrators responded to their criticisms in a variety of ways that were eventually woven together to create a lasting fabric of educational reorganization. The essence of their response was that the bureaucratic model was sound, but that it needed to be improved, extended, and made more scientific and professional. The rather crude, mechanical bureaucracy had to be transformed into a more streamlined, professional bureaucracy. Initially the analogy had been between schools and factories, but in the early twentieth century a new metaphor began to dominate school administrator's minds: the corporation. It was a new era of capitalist development, and the school system had to respond in order to keep pace with it.

This new, more "modern and rational" bureaucracy had several aspects. First, despite opposition from many teachers, control was centralized into smaller boards more removed from the community. Carnegie and Rockefeller began their respective foundations and imposed a standardization upon educational institutions in exchange for their philanthropy. The creation of a more hierarchical and smoothly functioning system was a paramount concern.

This more systematic bureaucracy involved greater standardization of requirements and grading procedures, a goal that was implemented with the aid of the American Association of Universities, formed in 1900 to "protect the dignity of the degree" (Turnbull, 1972, p. 102). Even more importantly, university administration was to be transformed into a more scientific profession that would combine efficiency with charisma so as to obviate the more deadening attributes of educational bureaucracies. It is an indication of the great esteem in which science was held that scientific training was even presumed to be capable of instilling charisma. The underlying assumption was that if administration could be made sufficiently scientific and professional, professors would respect administrators and more readily accept any infringements on their professional autonomy.

Early attempts to professionalize administration drew upon Taylorism and its rudimentary science of management. However, the crudity of Taylorist attempts to objectify educational outcomes and the compulsiveness with which Taylorist reformers tried to compensate for their lack of expertise aroused substantial faculty opposition and led to complaints that the university " 'cannot follow the definite, precise methods employed by the manufacturer' " (Veysey, 1965, p. 353). However, most university administrators did embrace what President Draper of Illinois called "sane and essential business methods" (Veysey, 1965, p. 354); the task became how to achieve efficiency and control with sufficient sophistication to appease the defenders of a liberal education and professorial autonomy.[3]

A central focus of these more sophisticated attempts to streamline the educational bureaucracy soon became differentiation, both within and between educational institutions. As early as 1890, a National Education Association report on "School Superintendence in Cities" had quoted Herbert Spencer, who said "a differentiation of structure and a specialization of function is the law of all growth and progress" (Tyack, 1974, p. 76). By the early twentieth century, students were being differentiated and tracked into appropriate curricula, the earlier elective system having been greatly eroded.[4] With the growth of the university and the expansion of higher education, college students were no longer exclusively from upper class backgrounds and were not all destined for professional or managerial positions; therefore, more regulation and differentiation and less individual autonomy were in order.

This emphasis on sorting and tracking students drew upon two apparently opposed movements of the time: Progressivism and the vocational education movement. The Progressives called for a "child-centered" education, one that would enable each individual student to fulfill his or her potential and thus become an active participant in both the educational and subsequently the democratic processes. The vocational education movement agreed that there were essential differences among students, but was primarily concerned with categorizing and allocating students to appropriate curricula and occupations. Vocational education proponents soon began to use Progressive ideology as a legitimation for their differentiation of students. The underlying rationale for vocational tracking, however, was the need to differentiate by class background so as to achieve more "efficient" allocation of students to the occupational sector. A 1908 speaker in favor of vocational education was explicit about this when he said: ' "teachers . . . ought to sort the pupils and sort them by their evidence or probable destinies' " (Perkinson, 1968, p. 145). Guidance counseling emerged as an ancillary profession during this period.

Educators soon realized, however, that in order for specialization and tracking to operate effectively and incorporate the idea of "equal opportunity," a more "scientific" method of sorting and classifying students had to be found. By 1920, the search for a more legitimate technology of differentiation was on, and educational testing was being developed.

With the search for a technology of differentiation, science entered into educational policy making with unprecedented fervor. IQ tests, initially developed by Binet in order to discover feeble-minded children, and subsequently used in World War I to facilitate differentiation and ranking of soldiers, soon became the focus of the educators' search. From 1920 to 1921, approximately two million children were tested and accordingly tracked; by 1939, there were over four thousand different tests in circulation. These early tests were far from objective or culture-free: "83 percent of Jews, 80 percent of Hungarians, 79 percent of Italians, and 87 percent of Russians tested as feeble-minded" (Bowles and Gintis, 1976, p. 196).

IQ testing was also from the beginning related to increased vocationalism in the schools;[5] a "scientific" method of assessing "evident or probable destinies" had been found. The internal differentiation of schools became more marked and the process of preparing youth for an increasingly stratified labor market became more streamlined. Corporate capitalism supported the IQ testing movement; the Rockefeller and Carnegie Foundations poured millions of dollars into the development and institutionalization of IQ testing. In return, "American education had accepted the ethics of the emerging corporate order" (Lazerson and Grubb, 1974, p. 50). The ground on which corporate capitalism and the educational establishment negotiated this rapprochement was the presumably neutral one of science; technocracy and the corollary ideology of meritocracy were coming to dominate both educational institutions and society in general as the hope grew that the schools had once and for all been taken out of politics. In 1911, E. Meier expressed aptly this growing faith in science when he said: "The golden rule will be put into practice through the slide rule of the engineer" (Ehrenreich and Ehrenreich, 1979, p. 23).

1930–1980: The Technocratic Administration of Education

The Depression of the 1930s led to an intensification and consolidation of the incipient technocratic administration of education. Cost accounting and efficiency of operation became increasingly important, and institutional survival became increasingly dependent on grants from private foundations and corporations. In addition, the national economic crises and ensuing labor unrest made vocational preparation and rationalization seem an appealing step toward reorganizing society to ameliorate its problems. During the Depression, college enrollments jumped 20 percent because of the inability of the job market to absorb high school graduates (Brubacher and Rudy, 1958, p. 377). Both the public and private sectors extended their control over education during this period to accentuate the testing movement, internal and external differentiation of schools, development of educational research, and centralized coordination aimed at eliminating duplication of offerings and other inefficient allocations of resources.

With World War II and the ensuing Cold War, the emphasis on science and technology and higher education as a crucial component of the growing military-industrial complex further transformed the system of higher education. A massive program of federally funded weapons research during World War II accelerated the trend towards state involvement in higher education. Moreover, the educational system was becoming "a breeding ground for a new labor force of highly skilled scientists, technicians, managers, and workers" (Newt Davidson Collective, 1973, p. 54). Especially after Sputnik in 1957, the search for technological expertise became the new American priority. Functional rationalization took precedence over substantive questioning of ends. In virtually every sphere of life, it was assumed that if technique and means could be sufficiently perfected, progress would be ensured.

Also, the decades after World War II saw an unprecedented expansion of higher education. By the late 1950s, one third of the age cohort was going on to college and, a decade later, almost one half (Bowles and Gintis, 1976, p. 4). With such enormous numbers of students seeking college degrees, differentiation and tracking became crucial to the efficient allotment of graduates into the stratified labor market. In 1948, the Educational Testing Service was set up to streamline and coordinate objective testing (Turnbull, 1972, p. 126). About the same time, the community college was created as a final link in the smoothly stratified system of educational institutions. Community colleges focused on narrow skills training and "cooled out" aspirations for a more liberal college education (Clark, 1960). As A. Etzioni put it in 1970: " 'If we can no longer keep the floodgates closed at the admissions office, it at least seems wise to channel the general flow away from four-year colleges and toward two-year extensions of high school in the junior and community colleges' " (Bowles and Gintis, 1976, p. 203).

However, as in the early phase of bureaucratization, incipient technocratic administration engendered protests, both in the United States and elsewhere. The social movements of the sixties, which were often grounded in the university, attacked the technocratic form of administration for the superficiality of its meritocracy and the depth of its involvement in the military-industrial complex. The ends that technocracy was serving were deeply questioned, as students pointed to moral, political, and environmental problems at home and abroad that technocracy was not only incapable of solving but was also creating or exacerbating. Reform began to proliferate during the late sixties and early seventies: a more "liberal" education, compensatory education, affirmative action, and limited participation by students in university governance.

However, the seventies witnessed disillusionment with partial and co-opted reforms and an intensification of technocratic administration in both educational institutions and society in general. A combination of cynicism, economic recession, and a surplus of technological expertise has legitimated the expansion and consolidation of technocracy. If nineteenth-century bureaucrats responded to early protests by streamlining the bureaucracy and making it more analogous to the corporation rather than the factory, technocracy has embraced a similar rapprochement with technologically advanced industry.

By the late 1970s, a fully evolved structure of technocratic administration had been institutionalized within the educational system. The specific features of this control structure include the following:

Increased Systematization of Educational Institutions
Both within universities and in the educational system as a whole, local autonomy continues to be eroded by centralized control. The system of educational institutions became world-wide in scope, with international agencies such as UNESCO, the International Association of Universities, and the International Institute for Educational Planning beginning to take active roles in educational planning and development by the 1970s. In addition, state, regional, and national boards and commissions continue to be instrumental in determining policy and allocations.

Quantification of Educational Inputs and Outputs
This process has been perfected and extended with the development of standardized tests and computerized data processing. Credentialism has become tantamount to commodification of the educational process. Computerized record keeping and standardized tests continue to be developed, as the National Commission on the Financing of Postsecondary Education and the Education Commission of the States received federal money for this purpose (Newt Davidson Collective, 1973).

Technical Innovation
Educational and administrative technology is being developed at a fast pace in order to aid in the quantification of inputs and outputs, to achieve greater cost efficiency, and to replace imperfect bureaucrats with perfect machines. Computerized systems of record keeping play an even larger role in daily administration, and computer simulation is being perfected in order to aid in decision making (Rourke and Brooks, 1971, p. 181). The implications of such computerized administration transcend mere concern for greater efficiency and raise political questions of centraliza-

tion versus local autonomy: Who gains power and who loses it when such presumably neutral technological innovation is introduced?

Educational technology is also being developed in the area of instruction, for as the Committee for Economic Development advised: "In higher education, the principal source of possible savings is instruction" (Newt Davidson Collective, 1973, p. 89). The National Center for Educational Technology, the Inter-University Communications Council, and the Academy for Educational Development (which published a report called "Higher Education With Fewer Teachers") are developing and perfecting technology to dramatically reduce the number of teachers. Proposals for a "Video University" without teachers or even a campus, as well as the use of cable TV and teaching machines in order to increase class sizes to 2,000 or 3,000 are under consideration. Standardized curricular materials and texts, routinely used in primary and secondary schools, are becoming prevalent in universities as well. Such teaching devices isolate students, accustom them to the use of machines, and greatly facilitate the quantification of inputs and outputs. Human error is perhaps reduced, but so is human interaction, meaningful human dialogue, and the possibility of resistance to control.

Long-Term Planning and "Objective" Decision Making

The underlying rationale of technocracy is the need to plan and to control in order to achieve efficient allocation of scarce resources. Increased collaboration with the state thus becomes a corollary of technocratic administration. Bureaucracy was also concerned with planning, but technocratic planning is qualitatively different, for under technocracy it is assumed that decision making itself is removed from the vagaries of human volition so that it is made scientifically and objectively on the basis of technological imperatives. Computer simulation and modeling veil human choice and political decision making as "assumptions" that are necessary to do long-term planning (Cole and others, 1973). Even the question of which problems are designated as such and how they are defined represent momentous political decisions, although they tend to be viewed as mere technical problems. Such technocratic planning and decision making is by no means limited to the United States, of course, and is in many respects more advanced in both Western (Formerand and others, 1979) and Eastern (Mallet, 1970) Europe, where technocratic reconstruction and protest movements have created a certain uneasy dialectical movement since World War II.

New Professionalism

The profession of teaching is undergoing a transformation under technocracy. Teachers are becoming less professionals and more "experts," whose autonomy is restricted but whose tasks are simplified by the increased use of machine and computer technology and standardized teaching materials. Such technology serves to effect a convergence between administrative and professional (teaching) functions, since administrators and teachers alike become adjuncts of technological rationalization. Teachers function less in order to teach and more in order to differentiate students, and they are amply aided by the appropriate technology. Moreover, technocracy serves to blur the lines of power in the educational hierarchy, since on one level teachers are expert administrators of advanced technology and upholders of the universality of science, while on another level they are mere functionaries implementing a social technology that is centrally devised and controlled. This ambiguous situation of professors under a technocratic system of administration is precisely what was at issue in the Yeshiva case.

The Yeshiva Case: Are Professors Managers?

In 1974, the Yeshiva University Faculty Association (union) filed a petition with the National Labor Relations Board for certification as the exclusive bargaining agent of a unit of Yeshiva's full-time faculty members (*N.L.R.B.* v. *Yeshiva University*, 582 F. 2nd 682 Cir. 1978). The university administration opposed the petition on the grounds that all its faculty members are managerial or supervisory personnel and hence not employees within the meaning of the National Labor Relations Act. The Board rejected the university's contention that its faculty members were managerial employees. It held that faculty members are professional employees entitled to the Act's protection, granted the union's petition, and directed an election. After the union won the election by a substantial margin and was certified, the university refused to bargain. In subsequent unfair labor practices proceedings, the Board ordered the university to bargain and sought enforcement in the Court of Appeals, which denied the petition in 1978 (*Labor Relations Reporter*, 103 F. Supp. II Cir. 1980). The Court of Appeals determined that the faculty of Yeshiva University "in effect, substantially and pervasively operate the enterprise" (*Federal Reporter*, p. 698). When the Board appealed this decision to the Supreme Court, the latter upheld the Circuit Court's decision and denied the Board's petition.

The Supreme Court's majority opinion, delivered by Justice Powell, addresses two main issues. First, the full-time faculty are managerial employees in the sense that they formulate, determine, and put into effect their employer's policies. Justice Powell writes of widespread faculty participation in university governance, stating that with regard to such issues as "faculty hiring, tenure, sabbaticals, termination, and promotion . . . the overwhelming majority of faculty recommendations are implemented" (*Labor Relations Reporter*, 1980). Much of this "evidence," it should be noted, is based on the testimony of Yeshiva deans and administrators. Secondly, Powell contends that faculty members exercise both managerial authority and "independent professional judgment," and that in effect "the faculty's professional interests . . . cannot be separated from those of the institution."

In the dissenting opinion written by Justice Brennan, the sociohistorical context of this labor/management controversy is explored. He cites the curtailment of faculty input into university governance in the face of cost-efficiency pressures, as well as the fact that Yeshiva suffered a financial crisis in 1971–72 that led to a freeze on faculty promotions and pay increases.[6] Brennan concludes that "these economic exigencies have . . . exacerbated the tensions in university labor relations" and that "the very fact that Yeshiva's faculty has voted for the Union . . . indicates that the faculty does not perceive its interests to be aligned with those of management" (*Labor Relations Reporter*, 1980).

In the reasoning of the various opinions concerning the Yeshiva case, at least three educational control structures are referred to. Justice Brennan, in his critique of the majority opinion, contends that the Court's perception of a convergence of interest between faculty and administration is based "on an idealized model of collegial decision making that is a vestige of the great medieval university" (*Labor Relations Reporter*, 1980). As we have seen, such a guild model of collegial decision making, where faculty and students were the university, was never a viable educational control structure in the United States, although it was common in Europe. Justice Brennan goes on to contrast such an idealized model with what he sees as a more realistic one: "The bureaucratic foundation of most 'mature' universities is characterized by *dual authority systems* . . . authority is lodged in the administration but . . . at the same time, there exists a parallel professional network" (*Labor Relations Reporter*, 1980). Here Brennan is referring to the coexistence of professional and bureaucratic control structures within educational institutions, a situation that prevailed, as we have seen, from the late nineteenth century until at least 1930. Although professional and bureaucratic control structures are conceptually distinct, their practical coexistence in educational institutions has led to an analysis of university governance as characterized by "shared authority" (Mortimer and McConnell, 1978; Baldridge, 1971) in which administrative power parallels that of the faculty, occasionally coming into conflict with it. Justice Brennan's assessment of contemporary educational control in this manner is thus aligned with the National Labor Relations Board's definition of faculty/administration relations as dichotomous and adversary in nature.

What Justice Brennan fails to realize is that the Supreme Court's majority opinion refers to neither of the previous two control structures but to a third: the technocratic administration of higher education. Technocracy implies the integration of both faculty and administration into a larger, overarching system whose needs and objectives have priority over those of any subgroup and whose goals are shared by faculty and administration alike. Thus, the majority decision holds that "the faculty's professional interests cannot be separated from those of the institution." It goes on to state that "the concept of 'shared authority' . . . has been found to be 'an ideal rather than a widely adopted practice' " (*Labor Relations Reporter*, 1980).

Thus, both the majority and the dissenting opinions charge the other with clinging to an outmoded model of university governance. What is at issue is the correct interpretation of the administrative structure of contemporary universities. To a certain extent, the majority opinion is correct in distinguishing technocratic administration from earlier forms of professional and bureaucratic coexistence. The fiscal and organizational crisis in higher education has created conditions in which these earlier control structures have been found to be inadequate and are being superseded by new forms of technocratic control. What is less clear, and in fact remains to be decided in the next few years, is the precise shape and nature of the emergent technocratic form of educational governance.

Conclusion

Educational institutions in the United States have developed in relative autonomy from the mode of production and have been characterized by shifting patterns of correspondence and contradiction (Carter, 1976). Different administrative control structures have evolved in order to accentuate correspondence and to minimize both internal and external contradictions. These educational control structures have included: private boards of trustees, professional collegiality, bureaucracy, and technocracy. Each control structure has both dealt with existing contradictions and generated new ones, pointing towards the next control structure.

Technocratic administration is an emergent historical and structural synthesis of professional and bureaucratic forms of administration and control, transcending both forms and implying their gradual transformation, especially de-professionalization (Haug, 1973) and debureaucratization (Eisenstadt, 1959). Technocracy is an organizational control structure based on technical expertise (human or technological) and involving the simultaneous integration of specialized substantive and administrative functions into a comprehensive system of control. Technocratic strategies of administration take the form of technical-instrumental, de-politicized rationality, and seek legitimation of their content on the basis of a new political rationality. As J. Straussman (1978,

p. 11) puts it: "The most obvious assumption in the engineering model of society is that the parameters of public choice are dictated by technological imperatives . . . the 'one best way' approach to public policy."

These technological imperatives are handed down by experts in given areas of specialization: the technocrats. The assumption (but seldom the reality) is that such scientific experts have been lifted above politics by the universalistic force of science: that they are "above politics." Technocratic administration is thus only the most recent of a series of control structures that have all sought legitimation on the grounds of taking the schools out of politics. Technocratic administration substitutes crisis-management for politics; through systems-engineering, environmental complexity and uncertainty can be reduced by increasing system complexity. An important precondition of the success of such strategies is the enlargement and increased sophistication of the intelligence function, rapid information data processing, and planning, as well as the development of appropriate technology to facilitate these functions. Indeed, the presence of a high-powered, sophisticated technical apparatus may give the organizationally useful appearance of power and control, whereas in reality the apparatus may be quite unreliable and vulnerable (Kolko, 1980; Wilensky, 1964).

As an organizational control structure, technocracy is a departure from bureaucracy in several respects. The emphasis on system integration and scientific rationality leads to a transformation of the bureaucratic hierarchy and a modification of bureaucracy's reliance on formal rules. Under technocracy, formal authority tends to coincide more closely with function, so as to introduce a certain diffusion of authority among specialized projects, functions, and subunits (Drucker, 1954, 1977; McGregor, 1960; Berkley, 1971; Luhmann, 1979; Bennis and Slater, 1968). Power becomes defined more in terms of "reason and collaboration" than as "coercion and threat" (Bennis and Slater, 1968, p. 58). The fixed division of labor that is characteristic of bureaucracy is subject to a certain degree of dissolution under technocracy, at least in the higher levels of management, as hierarchical distinctions tend to be replaced by system-wide technical specialties. The imperatives of scientific systems management are sufficiently universalistic that they tend to come into conflict with the rigid bureaucratic division of labor.[7]

The extent to which such a tendency towards universality will supersede the hierarchical division of labor remains an open question at this particular historical juncture, for an equally salient tendency is the consolidation of a "professional/managerial class," an elite group of managers and professional experts, legitimated by an expanded and stratified educational system (Collins, 1980; Ehrenreich and Ehrenreich, 1979; Straussman, 1978).

It is precisely such issues of universalism and elite domination that the Yeshiva case raises. The Supreme Court decision legitimates an actual trend: the integration of professional and administrative functions under the rubric of technocratic systems control. In addition, by calling both professors and administrators "managers," the Supreme Court is effectively circumscribing any democratic, de-hierarchical tendencies that might be present in such a technocratic reorganization of higher education: students and nonprofessorial staff are to be "managed" rather than integrally included in the educational and administrative process. Presumably students are also to be taught, but the teaching function of professors is subordinated to the managerial and differentiating function. Such technocratic professionalism is amply buttressed by the growing apparatus of standardized teaching materials and educational technology.

We have seen that during periods of educational expansion, corollary measures of stratification of educational institutions tend to be instituted. Conversely, it seems that during the present period of crisis and retrenchment in higher education, a certain shift of emphasis towards overall system imperatives and shared interests is occurring: The wagons are being pulled into a circle. However, conflicting interests and demands remain within colleges and universities, as in the society at large, and fiscal emergencies will probably tend to exacerbate them. It seems unlikely that technocratic strategies of adminstration will be sufficient to deal with these conflicts. A more likely contingency is that conflicts of interest will tend to emerge within the university in the years to come: between administrators and professors, and between students and the professorial/managerial stratum. In addition, the growing lack of correspondence between the educational and occupational sectors, most obviously seen in the crisis of overeducation-underemployment, is a central problem for technocratic administrators, and one that has continued to defy diverse strategies of technocratic control.

However, perhaps the de-institutionalization of such conflicts implied by the Yeshiva decision, the removal of these contradictions from the perspective of labor/management collective bargaining, and the jurisdiction of the NLRB may ultimately serve a progressive function. University governance in the next few years will undoubtedly have to deal with groups and individuals whose needs are not being met by strategies of technocratic administration. The resulting conflict within the university may allow the progressive component of technocratic administration to be realized: the nonhierarchical, nonbureaucratic, and universalistic potential of technocracy may become divorced from elitist and system-maintaining dynamics so as to allow for democratic forms of decision making and the use of scientific expertise as a guide to enlightened public policy. Undoubtedly, universities will be strategic and instructive sites of impending social change in the years to come. Perhaps the emergence of a more democratic control structure within the system of higher education and in individual universities will point toward the realization of the tendency towards universality that is embedded in technocracy and lead eventually to democratic structures of self-management and self-determination within the society as a whole.

Notes

1. For instance, as one schoolman put it: "I would as soon think of talking about the democratization of the treatment of appendicitis as to speak of the democratization of schools" (in Tyack, 1974, p. 77).
2. Andrew Carnegie, for instance, said in 1902: "In my own experience, I can say that I have known few young men intended for business who were not injured by a collegiate education. Had they gone into active work during the years spent at college, they would have been better educated men in every true sense of that term. The fire and energy have been stamped out of them, and how to manage so as to live a life of idleness and not a life of usefulness has been the chief question with them" (Callahan, 1962, p. 9).
3. As an example of such complaints by professors, consider the following statement by an anonymous professor in 1907: "There is set up within the university an 'administration' to which I am held closely accountable. They steer the vessel and I am one of the crew. I am not allowed on the bridge except when summoned; and the councils in which I participate uniformly begin at the point at which policy is already determined. I am not part *of* the 'administration' but am used *by* the 'administration' in virtue of qualities that I may possess apart from my academic proficiencies. In authority, in dignity, in salary, the 'administration' are over me, and I am under them" (Veysey, 1965, p. 389).
4. Benjamin Wheeler, president of the University of California, in 1901 expressed a rationale for this erosion of the elective system when he said; "Life has no . . . easy-going elective system, and colleges ought not to have [one]. Life wants men who do things . . . because it is their duty to do them, not because they elect to do them" (in Veysey, 1965, p. 362).
5. In 1916, Lewis Terman made this clear when he said: "At every step in the child's progress the school should take account of his vocational possibilities. Preliminary investigations indicate that an IQ below 70 rarely permits anything better than unskilled labor; that the range from 70 to 80 is preeminently that of semi-skilled labor, from 80–100 that of the skilled or ordinary clerical labor, from 100 to 110 or 115 that of the semi-professional pursuits; and that above all these are the grades of intelligence which permit one to enter the professions or the larger fields of business. . . . This information will be a great value in planning the education of a particular child and also in planning the differentiated curriculum here recommended" (Bowles and Gintis, 1976, p. 197).
6. For instance, he writes: ". . . education has become 'big business,' and the task of operating the university enterprise has been transferred from the faculty to an autonomous administration which faces the same pressure to cut costs and increase efficiencies that confront any large industrial organization. The past decade of budgetary cutbacks, declining enrollments, reductions in faculty appointments, curtailment of academic programs, and increasing calls for accountability to alumni and other special interest groups has only added to the erosion of the faculty's role in the institution decision-making process" (*Labor Relations Reporter*, 1980). Furthermore, he goes on to point out that Yeshiva faculty salaries average 13 percent below those of comparable institutions.
7. See Gorz (1972) and Mallet (1970) as well as various theories of the "new working class" for a fuller analysis of how educated labor tends to come into contradiction with bureaucratic forms of work organization. Speaking of technocracy, Lefort says: "technological developments make human activities increasingly more interdependent and impose a socialization of administration parallel to that of production" (1974/75, p. 51). The result is a certain tendency towards de-hierarchization, but only at the upper levels of the division of

labor. As Lefort puts it: "the engineers and the technicians . . . have a relative autonomy by virtue of their professional knowledge" (1974, 75, p. 42). This relative autonomy is increased as technocracy supersedes bureaucracy, although it is not absolute because of both technological and capitalist imperatives.

References

Bailyn, B. *Education in the Forming of American Society*. New York: Random House, 1960.
Baldridge, J. V. *Power and Conflict Within the University*. New York: Wiley, 1971.
Bennis, W. G., and Slater, P. *The Temporary Society*. New York: Harper & Row, 1968.
Berkley, G. E. *The Administrative Revolution*. Englewood Cliffs, N.J.: Prentice-Hall, 1971.
Bowles, S., and Gintis, H., *Schooling in Capitalist America*. New York: Basic Books, 1976.
Brubacher, J., and Rudy, W. *Higher Education in Transition: A History of American Colleges and Universities, 1636–1968*. New York: Harper & Row, 1958.
Callahan, R. E. *Education and the Cult of Efficiency*. Chicago: University of Chicago Press, 1962.
Carter, M. "Contradiction and Correspondence: Analysis of the Relation of Schooling to Work." In M. Carnoy and H. Levin (Eds.), *The Limits of Educational Reform*. New York: McKay, 1976.
Clark, B. R. "The 'Cooling-Out' Function in Higher Education." *American Journal of Sociology*, 1960, *65*, 569–576.
Clark, B. R. *Educating the Expert Society*. San Francisco: Chandler, 1962.
Clark, B. R. "United States." In J. Van de Graaf, and others (Eds.), *Academic Power: Patterns of Authority in Seven National Systems of Higher Education*. New York: Praeger, 1978.
Cole, H. S. D., Freeman, C., Jahoda, M., and Pavitt, K. L. R. (Eds.), *Models of Doom: A Critique of the Limits to Growth*. New York: Universe Books, 1973.
Collins, D. G. "The Yeshiva University Decision." *Faculty Council Newsletter*, New York University, June 1980.
Cremin, L. A. *American Education: The Colonial Experience*. New York: Harper & Row, 1970.
Drucker, P. *The Practice of Management*. New York: Harper & Row, 1954.
Drucker, P. *Technology, Management, and Society*. New York: Harper & Row, 1977.
Ehrenreich, B., and Ehrenreich, J. "The Professional-Managerial Class." In P. Walker (Ed.), *Between Labor and Capital*. Boston: South End Press, 1979.
Eisenstadt, S. N. "Bureaucracy and Debureaucratization." *Administrative Science Quarterly* 1959, *4* (3), 302–320.
Fomerand, J., Van de Graaf, J. A., Wasser, H. (Eds.). *Higher Education in Western Europe and North America: A Selected and Annotated Bibliography*. New York: Council for European Studies, 1979.
Gorz, A. "Technical Intelligence and the Capitalist Division of Labor." *Telos*, 1972, *1*, 27–41.
Haug, M. "Deprofessionalization: An Alternate Hypothesis for the Future." In P. Halmos (Ed.), *Professionalization and Social Change*, Sociological Review Monograph, no. 20. Keele, England: University of Keele, 1973.
Jencks, C., and Riesman, D. *The Academic Revolution*. New York: Doubleday, 1968.
Katz, M. B. *Class, Bureaucracy and Schools*. New York: Praeger, 1971.
Kolko, G. "Intelligence and Myth of Capitalist Rationality in the United States." *Science and Society*, 1980, *44* (2), 130–154.
Lazerson, M., and Grubb, W. N. *American Education and Vocationalism*. New York: Teachers College Press, 1974.

Lefort, C. "What is Bureaucracy?" *Telos*, 1974/75, *22*, 31–65.
Luhmann, N. *Trust and Power*. New York: Wiley, 1979.
McGregor, D. *The Human Side of Enterprise*. New York: McGraw-Hill, 1960.
Mallet, S. "Bureaucracy and Technocracy in the Socialist Countries." *Socialist Revolution*, 1970, *1* (3), 44–75.
Marx, L. *The Machine in the Garden*. New York: Oxford University Press, 1964.
Mortimer, K., and McConnell, T. *Sharing Authority Effectively: Participation, Interaction, and Discretion*. San Francisco: Jossey-Bass, 1978.
Newt Davidson Collective. *Crisis at CUNY*. New York: Newt Davidson Collective, 1973.
Perkinson, H. J. *The Imperfect Panacea: American Faith in Education, 1865–1965*. New York: Random House, 1968.
Rippa, S. A. *Education in a Free Society: An American History*. New York: Longman Books, 1967.
Rourke, F., and Brooks, G. "The Managerial Revolution in Higher Education." In J. V. Baldridge (Ed.), *Academic Governance*. Berkeley, Calif.: McCutchan, 1971.
Scott, R. A., and Shore, A. *Why Sociology Does Not Apply*. New York: Elsevier, 1979.
Smith, D. *Who Rules the Universities?* New York: Monthly Review, 1974.
Straussman, J. *The Limits of Technocratic Politics*. New Brunswick, N.J.: Transaction Books, 1978.
Turnbull, W. W. "Special Institutions in Systems of Higher Education." In J. A. Perkins and B. B. Israel (Eds.), *Higher Education: From Autonomy to Systems*. New York: International Council for Educational Development, 1972.
Tyack, D. B. *The One Best System: A History of American Urban Education*. Cambridge, Mass.: Harvard University Press, 1974.
U.S. Court of Appeals. "*National Labor Relations Board v. Yeshiva University*." *Labor Relations Reporter* 103, no. 15, Supplement, Feb. 25, 1980.
Veysey, L. R. *The Emergence of the American University*. Chicago: University of Chicago Press, 1965.
Wilensky, H. L. "The Professionalization of Everyone?" *American Journal of Sociology*, 1964. *70* (2), 137–158.

PART III

Structures and Practices

The essays in this section analyze the interrelationship between various structural features of organizations (authority and power, technology, job design, resources, numerical proportions between men and women) and the active responses that people develop to make these structures work for them. The behavior of people cannot be determined by the formal properties of organizations, or by the imputation of some external rationality. Rather, such behavior is an active process of everyday interaction amidst the everyday problems and constraints that organizational structures present.

Michael Lipsky, in his essay on public service bureaucracies, analyzes how street-level bureaucrats, in response to the scarcity of resources and client demand, develop a variety of routines for rationing service. He demonstrates how, under existing structures, it is often dysfunctional for street-level bureaucrats to be more responsive to clients. Service is rationed by increasing the costs to the client—in money, time, information, or psychological burdens and degradations. Agencies are quite aware that such routines result in many eligible people not receiving service; regulations are often consciously intended with this end in mind. Lipsky also reveals the political power relationships involved in waiting or queuing, and the various forms of inequality and bias that result from, or find fertile soil in, the often unconscious patterns of practice of street-level bureaucrats.

Michael Burawoy's study of a contemporary machine shop in Chicago—the very same one that appeared in Donald Roy's classic studies of the 1950s—shows how workers actively participate in transforming their managerially imposed quotas into a game. The game of "making out," though it serves managerial goals of profit, is arranged with a good deal of flexibility by the various parties involved. Burawoy demonstrates how the logic of making out permeates workers' shop floor culture and restructures the patterns of conflict between labor and management. In contrast to some other critical accounts of the labor process, Burawoy argues that work is structured in such a way that workers actively participate in their own consent to domination.

Rosabeth Moss Kanter, in her essay on women and men in a large corporation, develops a dynamic structural analysis of power relations and the variety of behavioral responses to them. As with opportunity, power tends to accumulate in an ascending spiral. Power begets more power. And the powerless tend to be caught in a descending spiral. Kanter's ultimate purpose is to develop organizational strategies for breaking these cycles, especially as they affect women. Thus she focuses on organizational features, such as alliances with sponsors, peers, and subordinates, in an effort to show how women can be caught in cumulative cycles of powerlessness. Stereotypical views of women (e.g., as too nitpicking and bossy) are shown to reflect the preference for men as a preference for power; such views are a behavioral response to powerlessness on the part of women rather than a cause of women's inferior position in most large organizations.

Michael Rustad applies the concept of tokenism in organizations, developed by Kanter and others primarily in studies of corporate and professional women, to the volunteer army, a traditional male enclave both culturally and occupationally. Rustad develops a structural analysis of female recruitment as a "reserve army of labor" in times of male recruitment shortfalls. Such policy exists despite the many proven benefits of female recruits. This context proves to be fertile soil for the dynamics of tokenism (heightened visibility, mistaken identity, boundary heightening), and provides the basis for a range of stereotypical gender-based responses amidst the everyday conflicts and difficulties of army life.

Charles Perrow's study of the accident at Three Mile Island nuclear power plant in 1979 raises serious issues about the organizational possibilities of insuring safety in nuclear systems. Organizational analysis leads him to reconceptualize the very notion of an accident. Accidents in such highly complex, interactive and tightly coupled systems are "normal," in the sense that they are not preventable over time. Failures in warning systems, design and equipment, and operator error are inevitable, take unanticipated forms, and have highly interactive negative effects (negative synergy). Operator mistakes must be viewed as normal and inevitable behavioral responses to systems of such high complexity. Perrow makes a strong case for the argument that the dangers of such technologies are an inherent part of the very organizational systems designed to control them and could not be eliminated by better operator training, safety procedures, or equipment design. The problem is an organizational one, though personnel are often conveniently scapegoated. Perrow's analysis of this particular case sheds light not only on the nuclear power industry as a whole, but has enormous relevance for nuclear weapons technologies, where organizational systems are also highly interactive, tightly coupled, and prone to the same kinds of failures.

14
The Rationing of Services in Street-Level Bureaucracies

Michael Lipsky

Theoretically there is no limit to the demand for free public goods. Agencies that provide public goods must and will devise ways to ration them. To ration goods or services is to establish the level or proportions of their distribution. This may be done by fixing the amount or level of goods and services in relation to other goods and services. Or it may be done by allocating a fixed level or amount of goods and services among different classes of recipients. In other words, services may be rationed by varying the total amount available, or by varying the distribution of a fixed amount. . . .

The rationing of the level of services starts when clients present themselves to the worker or agency or an encounter is commanded. Like factory workers confronted with production quotas, street-level bureaucrats attempt to organize their work to facilitate work tasks or liberate as much time as possible for their own purposes. This is evident even in those services areas in which workers have little control over work flow. For example, police often cannot control work flow because most police assignments are in response to citizen initiated calls.[1] Dispatchers, however, make every effort to permit officers to finish one call before beginning another. Officers often take advantage of this practice by postponing reporting the completion of a call until after they have finished accumulated paperwork. In this way police officers regularize the work flow despite substantial irregularity in requests for assistance.

The way in which work comes to the agency significantly affects the efficiency and pleasantness with which it is accommodated. Official efforts to influence the flow of work vary greatly. They range from the mild advisory of the post office providing patrons with information concerning the times when delays are likely to be longest, to the extreme measures taken by a New York City welfare office that closed its doors at noon rather than admit a greater number of Medicaid applicants than could be processed by available personnel in an eight-hour day.[2]

Reprinted from Michael Lipsky, *Street-Level Bureaucracy* (New York: Russell Sage Foundation, 1980), 87–104, by permission of Basic Books, Inc., Publishers.

Clearly there are costs to clients in seeking services. In both of the above examples agencies seek to inform clients of the costs and the problems they will encounter—in the first instance, if they seek assistance during days when post office patronage is heavy; in the second, if in ignorance of the situation they attempt to apply for Medicaid and cannot be accommodated because of the high intake demand relative to intake workers. In many instances even the failure to inform clients of likely costs in seeking service constitutes a consumer complaint.

The highest costs are borne by potential clients who are discouraged from or forbidden access to bureaucratic involvement. While exclusion from client status is usually accomplished on the basis of legal grounds, the population of the excluded or discouraged includes many whose exclusion is a matter of discretionary judgment. The ineligibility of tenants evicted from public housing, students expelled from school, or welfare claimants deemed uncooperative depends not on fixed criteria alone, but also on interactions with street-level bureaucrats.

The Costs of Service

To analyze individual influence it has sometimes proved useful to recognize the relationship between citizens' influence and their command of personal resources such as money, status, information, expertise, and capacity for work.[3] People who have these resources tend to be more powerful than those who do not. When people have them they enhance personal influence. When workers for public agencies have them they may be used to direct or subordinate clients or discourage clients from further interactions with the agency.

Monetary

Street-level bureaucracies can rarely assign monetary costs for services, since by definition public services are free. However, monetary costs *are* imposed in several instructive instances. In income-providing programs citizens' contributions to the income package may be manipulated as policy. Medicare patients may be asked to pay a higher deductible before insurance provisions become operable. Food-stamp recipients may be asked to pay more for their stamps. The effective taxation of earned income in welfare reduces the number of people in contact with this street-level bureaucracy. Clearly differences in monetary costs serve to ration street-level bureaucrats' services.

Programs sometimes force clients to incur monetary costs that discourage them from seeking service. Acquiring records from other agencies to establish eligibility or securing transcripts for appeals can be costly, particularly if travel is involved. Agencies that keep bankers' hours impose monetary costs on working people who cannot appear without losing wages. Appointments sometimes require parents to seek babysitters. Street-level bureaucracies that seek to minimize these penalties introduce evening office hours, or they provide child-care services.

Time

Just as available time is a resource for people in politics, it is also a unit of value that may be extracted from clients as a cost of service. Clients are typically required to wait for services; it is a sign of their dependence and relative powerlessness that the costs of matching servers with the served are borne almost entirely by clients. It is to maximize the efficiency of workers' time that queues are generally established. A primary reason that clinic-based practice is more efficient than home-based practice is simply that it is patients and not physicians who spend time traveling and waiting. Policemen also allocate time costs by stopping to question young people who, while not guilty of any crime, are judged to require reprimanding.[4]

Some teachers in some school systems make home visits to meet with parents, while others schedule parent-teacher conferences after school on specific days set aside for such purposes. (If there are two parents and one or both work, both are unlikely to be able to meet with the teacher.) These alternative perspectives on parent-teacher conferences measure significant differences in the value placed on time of parents and teachers.

Time costs are often assessed by street-level bureaucrats as delay; they are often experienced by clients as waiting. Bureaucracies can reward clients by expediting service, punish them by delaying service. Court postponements can function in this way, as can an increase in the time between intake interviews and placement on the welfare rolls. Importantly, bureaucracies often have little interest in reducing delay, since more expeditious processing would simply strain available resources.

Assessed time costs may also be experienced as inconvenience, although they are levied as procedure. For example, when an agency refuses to receive complaints over the telephone and requires that they be written, it may cut off complaints lodged frivolously or on impulse, but also discourages complainants who would protest if it were easier.[5] Requirements to complete multiple forms and produce extensive documentation function similarly. It is possible to make an argument that since the real costs of delay and elaborate procedures are the activities foregone while waiting, that is, opportunity costs, it is justifiable that poor people wait longer than the more affluent, since the opportunities foregone are less valued by the society.[6] However, at the very least this elitist view is based on a calculus to the terms of which clients have not consented.

Information

Giving or withholding information is another way in which services may be rationed. Clients experience the giving or withholding of information in two ways. They experience the favoritism of street-level bureaucrats who provide some clients with privileged information, permitting them to manipulate the system better than others. And they experience it as confusing jargon, elaborate procedures, and arcane practices that act as barriers to understanding how to operate effectively within the system. The emblematic carrier of this characteristic is the court clerk who runs his words together in an undecipherable litany to the dominance of court procedures over citizens' rights.[7] At the bureaucratic level the giving and withholding of information is most obvious in examining how agencies manipulate their case loads by distributing or failing to distribute information about services.

Conventionally, analysts assess the demand for services by studying client rolls and visits. (Demands are statements directed toward public officials that some kind of action ought to be undertaken.)[8] If it is recognized that manifestations of client involvement may not fully reflect client interests, analysts contrive ways to assess underlying needs, for example, through attitudinal and census surveys. From this assessment administrators and politicians make claims about appropriate levels of services.

However, if it is recognized that organizations normally ration services by manipulating the nature and quantity of the information made available about services, then it is easily seen that demand levels are themselves a function of public policy. Client rolls will be seen as a function of *clients' perception* of service availability and the costs of seeking services. Client demand will be expressed only to the extent that clients themselves are aware that they have a social condition that can, should, and will be ministered to by public agencies.

When New York City reduced acceptance rates for new welfare cases at seven centers by 17 percent it accomplished this feat by tightening the application process. This meant not only more careful scrutiny of applicants' claims, but also more documentation and inquisition was required, which contributed a separate measure of rationing.[9]

This perspective is illustrated by indices of need for legal assistance for domestic problems. When a sample of Detroit residents were asked if they required a lawyer for assistance with some domestic-relations matters, scarcely more than 1 percent answered affirmatively. It would have been difficult to predict from this survey that approximately 40 percent of the clients of legal aid and neighborhood law offices originally sought help with domestic problems.[10]

Needs become manifest when the institutions that might provide assistance send out signals that they stand ready to assist. The 40 percent of the clients who originally sought help with domestic matters might have been only a small portion of the population that could have benefitted from such assistance. Some who could have used such services may have been deterred from seeking them. Since legal services are vastly underfunded, even more dramatic demonstrations of need might have materialized if more lawyers had been available.

Information about service is an aspect of service. Withholding information depresses service demands. For example, the campaign to reform welfare by dramatically increasing the welfare rolls was based on the view that a political movement could help overcome the stigma attached by potential recipients to welfare status. It could provide the information necessary to realize a substantial increase in the number of recipients.[11] The failure of public welfare agencies to make sure potential recipients receive the benefits to which they are entitled contrasts dramatically with the success of social security and Veterans' Administration benefits. The difference is that the clients of these two income support programs—the elderly, and veterans—are not socially stigmatized.[12]

Client statistics may not indicate much about the objective needs of the client population but they reflect a great deal about the organizations that formally cater to those needs.[13] Thus growing demand for adult continuing education partly exists in the felt needs of the adult population, but the demand also is responsive to the publicity generated by colleges and universities and their desire to attract students and their tuition. The demand for emergency police services exists to an unknown degree, but the introduction of a 911 central telephone number and dispatch system makes it more likely that citizens believe the police will respond quickly. After the system is introduced, the increase in 911 calls will be responsive to organizational factors such as publicity about the service and response time as well as more objective factors such as population growth and changes in the age distribution of the population.

Although the dominant tendency is for street-level bureaucracies to attempt to limit demand by imposing (mostly nonmonetary) costs for services, there are some times when they have a stake in increasing their clientele. They will do this through an analogous rationing process, now directed toward increasing utilization.

Agencies are likely to try to increase their clientele when they are newly established and have to prove their ability to put services into operation. Thus the tripling of service complaints when Boston introduced its Little City Halls program was particularly welcome by its sponsors.[14] Efforts to increase clienteles were generally noticeable when central funding sources launched many subordinate service agencies, which saw themselves competing for funds in the next fiscal cycle. Such agencies would "beat the bushes" for clients in order to demonstrate that they were worthy of future support. Community action agencies and neighborhood mental health centers have been cases in point.[15]

Established street-level bureaucracies may also attempt to increase their clientele if they perceive themselves under attack and calculate that demonstrations of significant service provision, or increases in clientele, might aid their cause. Relatedly, street-level bureaucracies may attempt to increase the number of clients when they are competing against other programs with similar objectives. Such agencies perceive that they are competing for the same client pool, and that only the more successful will survive in the next budget cycle.

This competition also is conducive to quasi-legitimate fraud directed toward making the agencies look better. For example, when drug treatment centers were few they could afford to impose rigorous residential requirements, particularly since clients' commitment to their own rehabilitation was considered critical to therapy. When the number of institutions increased in the early 1970s in response to available funding, and the population of drug users started to decline, to increase their clientele the centers began to relax their enrollment requirements (for example, by accepting clients who previously would have been judged too difficult to help). They also relaxed attendance requirements, so that a treatment bed might be occupied by someone who was not in fact a full-time resident of the center. Besides drug treatment centers, other organizations that have competed for larger shares of a fixed client pool include mental health centers funded in the same city, and academic departments competing for students within a university.

In theory this bureaucratic competition might provide precisely what bureaucracies importantly lack—a substitute for market place accountability. This, of course, is the idea behind educational vouchers. However, the healing effects of competition are too often mitigated by the residual bureaucratic aspects of the competing organizations. Faculty members in academic departments with declining enrollments are still protected by the tenure system, rewards for research (and bringing in research grants), and other factors that protect them from being assessed solely on criteria of service to students. Similarly, educational voucher experiments have foundered on teachers' tenure, union opposition, and parental inability to express preferences within the system for lack of information on the implications of the available choices.

Psychological
Bureaucratic rationing is also achieved by imposing psychological costs on clients. Some of these are implicit in the rationing mechanisms already mentioned. Waiting to receive services, particularly when clients conclude that the wait is inordinate and reflects lack of respect, contributes to diminishing client demands.[16] The administration of public welfare has been notorious for the psychological burdens clients have to bear. These include the degradation implicit in inquiries into sexual behavior, childbearing preferences, childrearing practices, friendship patterns, and per-

sistent assumptions of fraud and dishonesty.[17] Nor have these practices been confined to the "unenlightened" 1950s, although some of the more barbaric features of welfare practice, such as the early dawn raids to catch the elusive "man-in-the-house," are no longer practiced.

To take a modest example, women applying for Aid to Families with Dependent Children at times are required to submit to an interview with lawyers, in which they must agree to assist the welfare department in prosecuting the father of their children. Apparently many women are unwilling to agree to this, since it would jeopardize the tenuous but at least partially satisfactory relationship that they may have with the childrens' father. They fear that the support they currently do receive and the positive benefits of good relations with them would be cut off by alienating the fathers, who may not be making substantial incomes anyway. Applicants are thus forced to lie or risk the loss of an important relationship. The interviews are conducted in a legalistic way with little sympathy for the position of the applicant. Many eligible potential clients do not complete the application process, because they prefer not to suffer these pressures and indignities.[18] Like so many monitoring procedures in welfare, it is unclear if monies recovered through these procedures equal the costs of engaging in them.

Psychological sanctions serve to reduce the demands from clients within the system as well as help to limit those who come into it. The defendant in a lower criminal court who asserts that he or she does not understand the charges will be silenced by the hostile response of the judge or clerk who unenthusiastically attempts to redress the complaint. Teachers, by varying their tone of voice, encourage or discourage pupils from asking questions. A lawyer in responding to clients can communicate the opinion that the inquiry is stupid and the client unworthy of a thoughtful response.

The importance of psychological interactions for rationing service is manifest in the extent to which clients will sometimes seek or approve of service simply because they like the way they are treated. Although they later find against them, sympathetic judges sometimes give thoughtful attention to defendents or complainants with weak cases simply in order to make them feel that they had their day in court. The reported gratitude of citizens who are treated in this way indicate how little people have come to expect from government. It would seem that clients sometimes judge services positively if they are treated with respect regardless of the quality of services. In this connection a study of clients' evaluation of walk-in mental health clinics revealed that "clinic applicants are satisfied with almost any response [from the staff] at first so long as the emotional atmosphere of the contact is comfortable."[19] While seekers of mental health services may be particularly sensitive to the quality of initial client-staff interactions there is every reason to think that these interactions form a substantial part of clients' initial evaluations of schools, courts, police, and other street-level services where there are no clearly defined service products to be obtained.

Queuing

The most modest arrangements for client servicing impose costs on clients. This is evident in the way clients are arranged, or required to present themselves, for bureaucratic processing. Even the most ordinary queuing arrangements—those designed to provide service on a first-come, first-served basis in accordance with universalistic principles of client treatment—impose costs.[20]

Queues that depend upon first-come, first-served as their organizing principle elicit client cooperation because of their apparent fairness, but they may ration service by forcing clients to wait. When clients are forced to wait they are implicitly asked to accept the assumptions of rationing: that the costs they are bearing are necessary because the resources of the agency are fixed. They are also controlled by the social pressures exerted by others who wait. This is one of the functions of the line, waiting room, and other social structures that make it evident that others share the burden of waiting for service.

While resource limitations may be unalterable in the very short run, they are not necessarily immutable. They derive from allocation decisions that consider it acceptable to impose costs on waiting clients. Costs will not be imposed upon clients equally. Long lines processed on a first-come, first-served basis relatively benefit people who can afford to wait, people whose time is not particularly valuable to them, or people who do not have other obligations.

Poor people often suffer in such a system. Not only may clients who appear more affluent get served first because it is thought that the costs of waiting are higher for them,[21] but agencies often paternalistically develop policy as if the costs to the poor were nonexistent. A visit to the waiting room of a welfare office in any inner-city neighborhood is likely to convey the impression that the Welfare Department assumes recipients have nothing else to do with their time. Recipients learn the lesson of people who must seek service from a single source. Like the telephone company, the welfare department is able to pass on to the customer the costs of linking people with service. This system also benefits the average client to the disadvantage of people with extraordinary needs, since initially it has no mechanism for differentiating among clients. However, where the injury to people with extraordinary needs is likely to be severe, as in police work or medical emergencies, the ordering of services is often deliberately structured to search for and respond to this information.

An alternative to the first-come, first-served waiting room or line is the first-come, first-served queue by appointment. This system is also normatively acceptable and theoretically has the advantage of eliminating many of the costs of waiting time. In this queue the costs may appear to be reduced for the average client, but they may still be significant if appointments are crowded together to insure client overlap, as is typically done in health clinics and other medical settings. Crowding appointments may be done for the convenience of bureaucrats whose time is considered more valuable than that of clients, and who thus are guaranteed a flow of clients even if one misses an appointment. The costs of such a queue will also be borne by clients who seek service but cannot afford to wait for it, who are not disciplined enough to make and keep appointments, or who are not sure enough of the likely benefits of service to invest in seeking it. What appears to the street-level bureaucrat as a fair way to allocate time may be seen by the client in the light of past experiences of bureaucratic neglect and taken as a sign that the agency is unlikely to be responsive, or that the problem is unlikely to yield to assistance.

For some clients the costs of waiting may be quite high. In one legal services program approximately 40 percent of eligible clients who received an appointment with a lawyer for the following week did not keep the appointment.[22] This may have been because the problem dissoved during the intervening time, or because merely talking to the intake worker provided a degree of comfort. However, it is equally likely that clients who did not keep their appointments could not keep them but were afraid to say so, were not organized enough to show up at the appointed time, or faced their legal problems without professional advice. Or it may have been that the applicants for assistance interpreted the demand to wait for appointments as a sign that legal services was not likely to be responsive and assumed that, like other public agencies, it would not in the end prove helpful.

In any event, the day a client appears to seek assistance may be the day when he or she is most open to help or the street-level bureaucrat is most likely to be able to intervene successfully. Catherine Kohler Reissman has written about mental health services in an analogous situation. "It is obvious that the disequilibrium created by a crisis is a powerful therapeutic tool that is lost if the situation is allowed to degenerate, through postponement, into a chronic, long-term problem."[23]

Similar to the queue by appointment is the waiting list; clients are asked to wait for what is usually an undetermined amount of time until they can be accommodated. Although it appears to be straightforward on the surface, the waiting-list system has several important latent functions. First, as we have seen in the case of Boston public housing, a waiting list tends to increase the discretion of street-level bureaucrats by providing opportunities to call clients from the waiting list out of turn, or to provide special information that will permit them to take advantage of ways to be treated with higher priority.[24] Waiting lists also permit agencies to give the appearance of service (after all, clients *are* on a waiting list) and to make a case for increased resources because of the backlog of demand.[25] The waiting list appears to record the names of potential clients who are seeking service but cannot be accommodated, although it is obvious to all that many names continue on the list only because the agency has not attempted to discover who is actively waiting and who has long since ceased to be interested.

Some social agencies act as if the waiting list usefully filters potential clients who are truly in need of service and strains out those whose needs are not substantial and who thus drop off. This system of rationing may also provide for a period of time in which spontaneous recuperation may occur, again reserving client spaces only for those who are needy.[26] However, it is uncertain whether continuation on the list is a sign of substantial need or precisely the opposite, a sign that the potential client is successful enough in managing the problem that he or she can wait patiently for services.

A queuing arrangement that maximizes the costs to citizens at the expense of a relatively small number of street-level bureaucrats is employed by lower courts, which typically require defendants to appear on a given day, but notify them only as to the hour they should appear. In a typical situation fifty to one hundred defendants, possibly with a friend or member of their family, must be ready for a hearing or arraignment, with substantial penalties if they do not appear precisely at the beginning of the session (when their names are first called). Here they must wait until the judge arrives, and then wait again while the judge gives priority to defendants in the lockup who may require attorneys, defendants whose attorneys plead that they have to be elsewhere, and defendants whose cases require the testimony of waiting police officers, who themselves are subject to other priorities. Only when [such] priorities are accommodated will the docket be called in alphabetical or some other order.

Defendants may be innocent but by virtue of being arrested are judged guilty enough to pay in time and uncertainty the price that the court exacts for scheduling cases for the primary convenience of the judge. Although practices vary from court to court it is typical that defendants will not be told even approximately when their cases will be called, so that they must wait in the courtroom, possibly for most of the day, until they receive a hearing.[27] The defendant who has waited through such a day has been instructed in the costs of continued interaction with the court system and must consider whether exercising rights or even pleading innocent in a minor matter, although legally valid, is worth the time and irritation. Some court systems have recently recognized that similar problems, including frequent postponements, inhibit witnesses from appearing and testifying in trials. But the same analysis rarely focuses on defendants and their experiences in court.

This queue by roundup is also typical of jury impaneling, where citizens are called for a week of service and must sit in a jury room awaiting assignment, often for several days, perhaps never to be called. The system officially is justified by the fluctuating and relatively unpredictable demand for jurors, and again is premised on the high value placed on the court's time relative to citizens' time. To insure that there are always people ready to serve, more jurors are called than will be required. If the court could tolerate a postponement now and then for lack of available jurors, and if jurors were called to report serially during the week rather than all at once, less time would be wasted for prospective jurors. But such practices could only be adopted if the time of prospective jurors were accorded more value relative to judges' and lawyers' time than is currently the case.

Clients frequently may be quite willing to pay the costs of waiting. Clients undoubtedly understand that there are times when they will have to wait, unless bureaucracies hire enough staff to meet peak demand. And since demand in most street-level bureaucracies is to some degree unpredictable—even schools often have to hire new teachers or shuffle teacher assignments after school has started—it would be too costly to provide services so that waiting would never occur. Waiting becomes injurious and inappropriately costly only under certain conditions.

Waiting is inappropriate when it exceeds the time generally expected for a service. A person may not resent a two-hour wait in an emergency room to receive a tetanus shot if it is clear that patients with more serious claims are being served first. But the same amount of time spent waiting in line simply to hand in forms to renew a driver's license may be exceedingly irritating. Waiting may also be resented as inappropriate when clients have made an appointment, except when the appointment is considered only an approximation of the time of service (as in the case of office visits to doctors).

Still another situation in which clients resent the costs of waiting arises when they wait unfairly. Thus if a favored client gains access to service more easily than others it will be resented by those who are not favored. Sometimes unfairness in waiting time may be so slight as to go unnoticed by clients. A study of black patients in Chicago hospital emergency rooms revealed that compared to whites waiting time was a little more than three minutes, incurred primarily by claimants with nonemergency conditions who sought help when the emergency room was relatively busy. But this cost is not actually trivial. It is worth noting that a modest three minutes or so, *for the 1,105 blacks in the sample alone*, would add up to a full working day for 2,619 people on a yearly basis,[28] a measure of one of the costs of institutional racism for the blacks of Cook County, Illinois.

Routines and Rationing

The existential problem for street-level bureaucrats is that with any single client they probably could interact flexibly and responsively. But if they did this with too many clients their capacity to respond flexibly would disappear. One might think of each client as, in a sense, seeking to be the one or among the few for whom an exception is made, a favor done, an indiscretion overlooked, a regulation ignored.

This dilemma of street-level bureaucrats is illustrated well by the legal services program. Individually, each attorney is obliged by professional norms to pursue fully the legal recourses available to clients. For impoverished clients this presumably means that attorneys should act on clients' behalf irrespective of cost. Only if this assumption is correct could the provision of legal services begin to redress the balance of power in the legal system, which every observer concedes favors those who command legal resources. But if all clients' legal needs were fully pursued there would be no time for additional clients: The dilemma is exquisite. To limit lawyers' advocacy is to deny poor people equal access to the law. To permit unbounded advocacy is to limit the number of poor people who can have such access. Only a reconstitution of the legal system could overcome the dilemma within the current patterns of inequality: either a radical departure in the amount of subsidies for legal assistance for the poor or a radical simplification of legal procedures.

When confronted with the dilemma of serving more clients or maintaining high quality service, most public managers will experience great pressures to choose in favor of greater numbers at the expense of quality. Their inability to measure and demonstrate the value of a service, when combined with high demand and budgetary concerns, will tend to impose a logic of increasing the quantity of services at the expense of the degree of attention workers can give to individual clients. Street-level bureaucrats, however, may devise ways to sabotage management efforts to reduce interactions with clients. The costs of achieving compliance in the face of workers' resistance may sometimes be more than managers want to pay. An example of such worker resistance is related by Robert Perlman in his study of the Roxbury Multi-Service Center. "Confronted with the complexity and number of demands being made on them, staff members resorted to shielding themselves from the mounting pressures. They extended interviews to postpone or avoid taking the next client. They scheduled home visits in order to avoid intake duty."[29]

Whether street-level bureaucrats oppose efforts to limit their interaction with clients, or whether they accept and encourage such efforts as a way of salvaging an unattractive or deteriorating work situation, is perhaps the critical question on which the quality of public service ultimately depends. Although street-level bureaucrats may sometimes struggle to maintain their ability to treat clients individually, the pressures more often operate in the opposite direction. Street-level practice often reduces the demand for services through rationing. The familiar complaints of encountering "red tape," "being given the run-around," and "talking to a brick wall" are reminders that clients recognize the extent to which bureaucratic unresponsiveness penalizes them.

Routinization rations services in at least two ways. First, set procedures designed to insure regularity, accountability, and fairness also protect workers from client demands for responsiveness. They insulate workers from having to deal with the human dimensions of presenting situations. They do this partly by creating procedures to which workers defer, happily or unhappily. Lawyers and judges, for example, generally accept court procedures that insulate them from erratic client demands. Police officials resist instituting (or more properly, reinstituting) a beat system because they are apprehensive that officers would become too involved with neighborhood residents, and thus perhaps engage in biased behavior. For similar reasons they often oppose assigning officers to the areas in which they reside, and they advocate reasonably frequent changes in assignment.

Social workers may be unhappy with the requirement to process endless paperwork rather than spend time providing client services. But whether happy or unhappy with job routines the fact remains that they serve to limit client demands on the system. The righteous objections of critics that routine procedures detract from primary obligations to serve clients are of little account, since in an important sense it is not useful for the bureaucracies to be more responsive and to secure more clients.

Second, routines provide a legitimate excuse for not dealing flexibly, since fairness in a limited sense demands equal treatment. Unresponsiveness and inflexibility reinforce common beliefs already present that bureaucracy is part of the problem rather than the solution, and they further reduce clients' claims for service or assertions of needs.

When routines lead to predictability they may promote a degree of client confidence. As a public defender lecturing his peers on increasing client trust advised: "It's better to tell a client you will see him in two weeks and then show up, than to reassure him by saying, 'I'll stop by tomorrow,' and never show."[30]

But agency practices do not always lead to predictability. When they lead to delay, confusion, and uncertainty they assign considerable costs to clients. At times routines established to protect clients are distorted to minimize contact or services. For example, to insure responsiveness housing inspectors may be required to make more than one effort to contact complainants. However, inspectors may become adept at telephoning complainants when they are unlikely to be home or fail to keep appointments punctually. In Boston this practice "enhanced the prospects of no one being home when the inspector arrived—a practice which when repeated thrice, enabled cases to be dropped."[31]

The significance of practices that subvert predictability, antagonize or neglect clients, or sow confusion and uncertainty is that they are generally *functional* for the agency. They limit client demands and the number of clients in a context where the agency has no dearth of responsibilities and would not in any way be harmed as an agency if clients became disaffected, passive, or refused to articulate demands. Any reduction in client demand is only absorbed by other clients who come forward, or by a marginal and insignificant increase in the capacity of street-level bureaucrats to be responsive to the clients who continue to press.

It is for this reason that we conclude that stated intentions of street-level bureaucracies to become more client-oriented, to receive more citizen input, and to encourage clients to speak out are often questionable, no matter how sincere the administrators who articulate these fine goals. It is dysfunctional to most street-level bureaucracies to become more responsive. Increases in client demands at one point will only lead to mechanisms to ration services further at another point, assuming sources remain unchanged.

The logical but absurd extension of the relationship between demand and services is exemplified by the apocryphal library that reduced costs by closing down. Yet it is a real problem that increased patronage of libraries, museums, zoos, and other agencies providing free goods increases their uncompensated costs when they succeed in becoming more attractive.

Undoubtedly there are dimensions of bureaucratic practice in which increased responsiveness does not add to workers' tasks. Addressing clients politely rather than rudely or indifferently is an area in which greater responsiveness is not necessarily burdensome to the work load. Furthermore, reorganization may result in increasing the responsive capacity of workers. However, most increases in responsiveness—doing more for clients, or even listening to them more—place additional burdens on street-level bureaucrats, who will subvert such developments in the likely absence of any strong rewards or sanctions for going along with them.

There are times when bureaucratic rationing is not simply implicit; limiting clientele or reducing services is the agency's stated policy. In response to reduced budgets or other developments that make client-worker ratios conspicuously high, agencies will reduce the scope of service in several characteristic ways. In reducing services explicitly they will continue to honor the formal norm of universalistic service patterns.

Street-level bureaucracies may reduce services geographically. They may formally narrow the catchment area from which clients are drawn or reduce the number of neighborhoods served by a program. Alternatively, because reductions in service are unpopular, street-level bureaucracies may prefer to reduce the number of centers, effectively cutting services to some areas without formally changing anyone's eligibility. When the borough of Manhattan, for example, consolidated its municipal court system, eliminating district courts in Harlem, it did not formally change access to the court, but informally it substantially increased the costs of using the court system to Upper Manhattan residents.

Services can be limited in terms of clients' personal characteristics. Formally, agencies can change income eligibility levels. Informally, they may limit service by failing to print posters in Spanish or by placing notices in old-age and nursing homes rather than in public housing in order to attract primarily an elderly population.

Street-level bureaucracies also can formally or informally ration services by refusing to take certain kinds of cases. The decriminalization of drunkenness, for example, formally exonerates policemen from dealing with alcoholics (although public disapproval still places pressure on the police to do something about drunks). Informally, departments can limit the clientele if officers choose to ignore public drunkenness, or they can reduce its place in departmental priorities.

Even when limiting services is not explicitly the function of rationing practices, service limitation often is not an unintended consequence of bureaucratic organization. Street-level bureaucrats and agency managers are often quite aware of the rationing implications of decisions about shorter office hours, consolidation of services, more or fewer intake workers, or the availability of information. Consider, for example, the efforts of the Budget Bureau of New York City in 1969 to decrease welfare expenditures. In a document remarkable for our purposes the Bureau suggested several ways to save close to $100 million.[32] In addition to reducing allowance levels, which would supply the bulk of the savings, the bureau recommended four administrative changes. Each would explicitly ration services in some way. A new intake procedure was proposed that would require applicants to be actively seeking jobs prior to the intake interview. This would force people to accept low-wage work, and, it was hoped, "more aggressive utilization of existing leverage over the employables would . . . have a deterrent effect on applications for welfare."[33] The authors recognized that for this innovation to be effective a substantially greater capacity of public employment agencies would be required, but there was no discussion of the costs of achieving this increase.

More frequent recertifications would be conducted to induce recipients who were on the rolls but no longer eligible because of changed circumstances to initiate case closings. (More than half of all case closings were then initiated by clients.) This reform would reduce the time between changes in clients' circumstances and the next reporting period.

Closing seven outreach centers would save some of the costs of running the centers, but more importantly, "larger savings are anticipated from secondary effects. . . . The most important of these is the opportunity *to build up and maintain the maximum legal backlog* between intake and eligibility increasing average backlog from two weeks to a full month."[34] Among other secondary benefits of center closings, the authors of the recommendations expected that "the relative inconvenience to the client of self-maintenance on emergency grants (for which application is normally made at the center more than once a week) may have some deterrent effect on [those] marginally eligible for welfare."[35]

Finally, stronger management audits would introduce greater uniformity in the system and provide better checks on welfare employees, who are portrayed in the document as more interested in enrolling clients than in controlling welfare costs.

Of equal interest are the strategies considered but not recommended. These included reducing intake hours, drastically closing intake centers, and requiring clients to provide increased documentation of birth, wages, rent payments, and other details of eligibility. While these provisions were rejected because they might result in unmanageable backlogs and infringe on clients' legal right to a response to their application within a month, the memo clearly recognizes that these measures would deter application rates by increasing the costs of applying to clients.

Provisions of this memo have been described at some length not because they are themselves remarkable but because they illustrate awareness at the agency planning level of the implications of rationing to limit client demand. It is naive to accept the rhetoric of public officials that their actions have the incidental effect of limiting or discouraging client demands. Rather, the opposite assumption is more useful analytically and more accurate empirically; namely, that public employees and higher officials are aware of the implications of actions taken that effectively increase or decrease client demand. They may deny such intentions publicly, of course, since their jobs require obeisance to norms of public service. They may not favor such policies personally, and they may regret that funding limitations preclude being able to serve more clients. Nonetheless, it is appropriate to assume that public agencies are responsible for the rationing implications of their actions.

In 1976 New York City introduced administrative controls that were credited with reducing the acceptance rate for new welfare applicants by half and terminating 18,000 cases a month. But this was accomplished because eligibles were being turned away "by very negative administration of work and parent-support rules," and because half of those terminated failed to show up for recertification, to respond to mailed questionnaires, or to verify school attendance. Their ineligibility was strictly a matter of difficulty or reluctance to pay the costs of remaining on the rolls until forced to do so. Meanwhile, according to an administrator, welfare centers are "overcrowded," "noisy," and "dirty." Some clients wait four to five hours for service and too often are required to make more than one visit to the center to complete their business. In addition, they don't know the names of people who are serving them."[36] In these and other ways *eligible* clients are asked to pay the costs of seeking relief.

Notes

1. The reactive nature of police work, and police dependence upon citizens in this respect, is stressed in Albert Reiss, *The Police and the Public* (New Haven: Yale University Press, 1971).
2. The latter case is cited by Barry Schwartz, *Queuing and Waiting* (Chicago: University of Chicago Press, 1975), p. 24. This excellent volume provides many insights into issues of priorities in client treatment and the costs of seeking service.
3. See Robert Dahl, "The Analysis of Influence in Local Communities," in Charles Adrian, ed., *Social Science and Community Action* (East Lansing, Mich.: Michigan State University Press, 1960), p. 32.
4. See generally Jonathan Rubinstein, "Suspicions," in *City Police* (New York: Farrar, Straus, 1973).
5. For example, one prosecutor's office that switched from telephone to mail complaint handling in processing white collar crimes experienced a 25 percent reduction in complaints received. Michael Brintnall, "The Allocation of Services in the Local Prosecution of Economic Crime" (Ph.D. diss., Massachusetts Institute of Technology, 1977), chap. 6.
6. See Schwartz, *Queuing and Waiting*, chap. 6.
7. When court clerks use confusing legal language we may call it "bureaucratic language as incantation." M. Edelman, *Political Language: Words that Succeed and Policies that Fail* (New York: Academic Press, 1977), p. 98. But what shall we call the court clerk's chant that strings words together indistinguishably? Perhaps it should be called "incantation as symbolic language." For attempts to deal positively with the rationing effects of legal language, consider the New York state law requiring consumer contracts to be written in clear, understandable language. See *New York Times*, Aug. 11, 1977, p. B1.
8. This is a paraphrase of the definition of demands in David Easton, *A Framework for Political Analysis* (Englewood Cliffs, N.J.: Prentice-Hall, 1965), p. 120.
9. *New York Times*, Sept. 25, 1977.
10. Leon Mayhew, "Institutions of Representation: Civil Justice and the Public," *Law and Society Review* 9, no. 3 (Spring, 1975), p. 403. The discrepancy is so great that it would be difficult to attribute it to differences in the nature of the sample.
11. Richard Cloward and Frances Fox Piven, "A Strategy to End Poverty," *The Politics of Turmoil* (New York: Vintage, 1975), pp. 89–106.
12. Gilbert Steiner, *The State of Welfare* (Washington, D.C.: Brookings, 1971).
13. Kitsuse and Cicourel have written that statistics reflect a great deal about the organizations collecting the statistics. John Kitsuse and Aaron Cicourel, "A Note on the Uses of Official Statistics," *Social Problems* 11 (1963), pp. 131–139. Sometimes the statistics collectors are not the same as those formally charged with providing information about services.
14. Eric Nordlinger, *Decentralizing the City* (Cambridge, Mass.,: Massachusetts Institute of Technology Press, 1972), p. 286.
15. The dynamics of this process are discussed in Michael Lipsky and Morris Lounds, "Citizen Participation and Health Care: Problems of Government Induced Participation," *Journal of Health Politics, Policy and Law* 1, no. 1 (Spring, 1976), pp. 85–111.
16. See the discussion of the psychological implications of waiting in Schwartz, *Queuing and Waiting*, chaps. 1, 8.

17. Virtually every commentary on welfare practices draws attention to the degradation of clients. See Alan Keith-Lucas, *Decisions about People in Need* (Chapel Hill, N.C.: University of North Carolina, 1957); Steiner, *The State of Welfare*; Frances Fox Piven and Richard Cloward, *Regulating the Poor* (New York: Pantheon, 1971), chaps. 4–5.

18. Jeffrey Prottas, *People-Processing: The Street-Level Bureaucrat in Public Service Bureaucracies* (Lexington, Mass.: Lexington Books, 1979). On the continuing relationships between ghetto fathers who have deserted and their families, see Elliot Liebow, *Tally's Corner* (Boston: Little, Brown, 1967).

19. June Grant Wolf, "The Initial Evaluation at a Walk-In Clinic: Applicant's and Evaluator's Perspectives" (Ph.D. diss., Boston University, 1974), p. 76.

20. First-come, first-served "constitutes the normative basis for most forms of queueing." Schwartz, *Queuing and Waiting*, p. 93.

21. Ibid., chap. 6.

22. Carl Hosticka, "Legal Services Lawyers Encounter Clients: A Study in Street-Level Bureaucracy" (Ph.D. diss., Massachusetts Institute of Technology, 1976).

23. Catherine Kohler Reissman, "The Supply-Demand Dilemma in Community Mental Health Centers," *American Journal of Orthopsychiatry* 40, no. 5 (October, 1970), p. 860.

24. See Lipsky, *Street-Level Bureaucracy*, chap. 2.

25. See Jeffrey Galper, *The Politics of Social Services* (Englewood Cliffs, N.J.: Prentice-Hall, 1975), pp. 70–71.

26. Reissman, "The Supply-Demand Dilemma," p. 860.

27. See Schwartz, *Queuing and Waiting*, pp. 26–29.

28. Ibid., chap. 5 and fn. 5, p. 201.

29. Robert Perlman, *Consumers and Social Services* (New York: John Wiley, 1975), p. 77.

30. Speaker, Annual Convention of the National Legal Aid and Defenders Association, Seattle, Washington, November, 1975.

31. Nivola, "Municipal Agency: A Study of Housing Inspectional Service in Boston," chap. 3.

32. "Budget Bureau Recommendations for Savings in the Welfare Budget," March 24, 1969. Unpublished document in author's files.

33. Ibid.

34. Ibid.

35. Ibid.

36. *New York Times*, December 21, 1977.

15
Organizing Consent on the Shop Floor: The Game of Making Out

Michael Burawoy

Making Out—A Game Workers Play

In this section I propose to treat the activities on the shop floor as a series of games in which operators attempt to achieve levels of production that earn incentive pay, in other words, anything over 100 percent. The precise target that each operator aims at is established on an individual basis, varying with job, machine, experience, and so on. Some are satisfied with 125 percent, while others are in a foul mood unless they achieve 140 percent—the ceiling imposed and recognized by all participants. This game of making out provides a framework for evaluating the productive activities and the social relations that arise out of the organization of work. We can look upon making out, therefore, as comprising a sequence of stages—of encounters between machine operators and the social or nonsocial objects that regulate the conditions of work. The rules of the game are experienced as a set of externally imposed relationships. The art of making out is to manipulate those relationships with the purpose of advancing as quickly as possible from one stage to the next. . . .

After the first piece has been OK'd, the operator engages in a battle with the clock and the machine. Unless the task is a familiar one—in which case the answer is known, within limits—the question is: Can I make out? It may be necessary to figure some angles, some short cuts, to speed up the machine, make a special tool, etc. In these undertakings there is always an element of risk—for example, the possibility of turning out scrap or of breaking tools. If it becomes apparent that making out is impossible or quite unlikely, operators slacken off and take it easy. Since they are guaranteed their base earnings, there is little point in wearing themselves out unless they can make more than the base earnings—that is, more than 100 percent. That is what Roy refers to as goldbricking. The other form of "output restriction" to which he refers—quota restric-

---

Reprinted from Michael Burawoy, *Manufacturing Consent* (Chicago: University of Chicago Press, 1979), 51, 57–61, 63–67, 71–73, with permission of the publisher and author.

tion—entails putting a ceiling on how much an operator may turn in—that is, on how much he may record on the production card. In 1945 the ceiling was $10.00 a day or $1.25 an hour, though this did vary somewhat between machines. In 1975 the ceiling was defined as 140 percent for all operations on all machines. It was presumed that turning in more than 140 percent led to "price cuts" (rate increases), and . . . this was indeed the case.

In 1975 quota restriction was not necessarily a form of restriction of *output*, because operators *regularly* turned *out* more than 140 percent, but turned *in* only 140 percent, keeping the remainder as a "kitty" for those operations on which they could not make out. Indeed, operators would "bust their ass" for entire shifts, when they had a gravy job, so as to build up a kitty for the following day(s). Experienced operators on the more sophisticated machines could easily build up a kitty of a week's work. There was always some discrepancy, therefore, between what was registered in the books as completed and what was actually completed on the shop floor. Shop management was more concerned with the latter and let the books take care of themselves. Both the 140 percent ceiling and the practice of banking (keeping a kitty) were recognized and accepted by everyone on the shop floor, even if they didn't meet with the approval of higher management.

Management outside the shop also regarded the practice of "chiseling" as illicit, while management within the shop either assisted or connived in it. Chiseling (Roy's expression, which did not have currency on the shop floor in 1975) involves redistributing time from one operation to another so that operators can maximize the period turned in as over 100 percent. Either the time clerk cooperates by punching the cards in and out at the appropriate time or the operators are allowed to punch their own cards. In part, because of the diversity of jobs, I managed [as a participant-observer] to avoid punching my cards. At the end of the shift I would sit down with an account of the pieces completed in each job and fiddle around with the eight hours available, so as to maximize my earnings. I would pencil in the calculated times of starting and finishing each operation. No one ever complained, but it is unlikely that such consistent juggling would have been allowed on first shift.[1]

How does the present situation compare with Geer? As Roy describes it, the transfer of time from one operation or job to another was possible only if they were consecutive or else were part of the same job though separated in time. Thus Roy could finish one job and begin another without punching out on the first. When he did punch out on the first and in on the second, he would already have made a start toward making out. Second, if Roy saved up some pieces from one shift, he could turn those pieces in during his next shift only if the job had not been finished by his day man. Accordingly, it was important, when Roy had accumulated some kitty on a particular job, that he inform Joe Mucha. If Mucha could, he would try to avoid finishing the job before Roy came to work. Shifting time between consecutive jobs on a single shift was frequently fixed up by the foreman, who would pencil in the appropriate changes. Nonetheless, stealing time from a gravy job was in fact formally illicit in 1945.

> Gus told me that Eddie, the young time study man, was just as bad, if not worse, than the old fellow who gave him the price of one cent the other day. He said that Eddie caught the day man holding back on punching off a time study job while he got ahead on a piecework job. He turned the day man in, and the day man and the time cage man were bawled out.
> "That's none of his damn business. He shouldn't have turned in the day man," exclaimed Gus angrily.
> Gus went on to say that a girl hand-mill operator had been fired a year ago when a time study man caught her running one job while being "punched in" on another. The time study man came over to the girl's machine to time a job, to find the job completed and the girl running another.
> Stella has no use for time study men. She told me of the time Eddie caught Maggie running one job while being punched in on another. Maggie was fired.[2]

These examples suggest that, while chiseling went on, it was regarded as illegitimate at some levels of management.

What can we say about overall changes in rates over the past thirty years? Old-timers were forever telling me how "easy we've got it now," though that in itself would hardly constitute evidence of change. To be sure, machines, tooling, etc., have improved, and this makes production less subject to arbitrary holdups, but the rates could nonetheless be tighter. However, an interesting change in the shop vernacular does suggest easier rates. Roy describes two types of jobs, "gravy" and "stinkers," the former having particularly loose and the latter particularly tight rates. While I worked in the small-parts department, I frequently heard the word "gravy" but never the word "stinker." Its dropping out of fashion probably reflects the declining number of jobs with very tight rates and the availability of kitties to compensate for low levels of output. How do Roy's own data on output compare with 1975 data? Recomputing Roy's output on piecework in terms of rates rather than dollars and cents, I find that during the initial period, from November to February, his average was 85 percent and that during the second period, from March to August, it was 120 percent.[3] During the first six months of 1975, the average for the entire plant was around 133.5 percent. For the different departments this average varied from 142 percent among the automatic screw machines and automatic lathes to 121 percent in the small-parts department, where I worked. The small-parts department functions as a labor reservoir for the rest of the plant because turnover there is high, rates are notoriously tight, and it is the place where newcomers normally begin. Nonetheless, of all the departments, this one probably most closely resembles Roy's Jack Shop in terms of machines and type of work. Thus, overall rates are indeed easier to make now, but my experiences in my own department, where most of my observations were made, bore a close resemblance to Roy's experiences.[4]

What is the foreman's role in all these operations? He is seen by everyone but senior plant management as expediting and refereeing the game of making out. As long as operators are making out and auxiliary workers are not obstructing their progress, neither group is likely to invite authoritarian interventions from the foreman. For their part, foremen defend themselves from their own bosses' complaints that certain tasks have not been completed by pointing out that the operators concerned have been working hard and have successfully made out. We therefore find foremen actively assisting operators to make out by showing them tricks they had learned when they were operators, pointing out more efficient setups, helping them make special tools, persuading the inspector to OK a piece that did not exactly meet the requirements of the blueprint, and so on. Foremen, like everyone else on the shop floor, recognize the two forms of output restriction as integral parts of making out. When operators have made out for the night and decide to take it easy for the last two or three hours, a foreman may urge more work by saying, "Don't you want to build up a kitty?" However, foremen do not act in collusion with the methods department and use the information they have about the various jobs and their rates against the operators, because rate increases would excite animosity, encourage goldbricking, increase turnover, and generally make the foreman's job more difficult. . . .

The Organization of a Shop-Floor Culture

So far we have considered the stages through which any operation must go for its completion and the roles of different employees in advancing the operation from stage to stage. In practice the stages themselves are subject to considerable manipulation, and there were occasions when I would complete an operation without ever having been given it by the scheduling man, without having a blueprint, or without having it checked by the inspector. It is not necessary to discuss these manipulations further, since by now it must be apparent that relations emanating directly from the organization of work are understood and attain meaning primarily in terms of making out. Even social interaction not occasioned by the structure of work is dominated by and couched in the idiom of making out. When someone comes over to talk, his first question is, "Are you making out?" followed by "What's the rate?" If you are not making out, your conversation is likely to consist of explanations of why you are not: "The rate's impossible," "I had to wait an hour for the inspector to check the first piece," "These mother-fucking drills keep on burning up." When you are sweating it out on the machine, "knocking the pieces out," a passerby may call out "Gravy!"—suggesting that the job is not as difficult as you are making it appear. Or, when you are "goofing off"—visiting other workers or gossiping at the coffee machine—as likely as not someone will yell out, "You've got it made, man!" When faced with an operation that is obviously impossible, some comedian may bawl out, "Best job in the house!" Calling out to a passerby, "You got nothing to do?" will frequently elicit a protest of the nature, "I'm making out. What more do you want?" At lunchtime, operators of similar machines tend to sit together, and each undertakes a postmortem of the first half of the shift. Why they failed to make out, who "screwed them up," what they expect to accomplish in the second half of the shift, can they make up lost time, advice for others who are having some difficulty, and so on—such topics tend to dominate lunchtime conversations. As regards the domination of shop-floor interaction by the culture of making out, I can detect no changes over the thirty years. Some of the details of making out may have changed, but the idiom, status, tempo, etc., of interaction at work continue to be governed by and to rise out of the relations in production that constitute the rules of making out.

In summary, we have seen how the shop-floor culture revolves around making out. Each worker sooner or later is sucked into this distinctive set of activities and language, which then proceed to take on a meaning of their own. Like Roy, when I first entered the shop I was somewhat contemptuous of this game of making out, which appeared to advance Allied's profit margins more than the operators' interests. But I experienced the same shift of opinion that Roy reported:

> Attitudes changed from mere indifference to the piecework incentive to a determination not to be forced to respond, when failure to get a price increase on one of the lowest paying operations of his job repertoire convinced him that the company was unfair. Light scorn for the incentive scheme turned to bitterness. Several months later, however, after fellow operator McCann had instructed him in the "angles on making out," the writer was finding values in the piecework system other than economic ones. He struggled to attain quota "for the hell of it," because it was a "little game" and "keeps me from being bored."[5]

Such a pattern of insertion and seduction is common. In my own case, it took me some time to understand the shop language, let alone the intricacies of making out. It was a matter of three or four months before I began to make out by using a number of angles and by transferring time from one operation to another. Once I knew I had a chance to make out, the rewards of participating in a game in which the outcomes were uncertain absorbed my attention, and I found myself spontaneously cooperating with management in the production of greater surplus value.

Moreover, it was only in this way that I could establish relationships with others on the shop floor. Until I was able to strut around the floor like an experienced operator, as if I had all the time in the world and could still make out, few but the greenest would condescend to engage me in conversation. Thus, it was in terms of the culture of making out that individuals evaluated one another and themselves. It provided the basis of status hierarchies on the shop floor, and it was reinforced by the fact that the more sophisticated machines requiring greater skill also had the easier rates. Auxiliary personnel developed characters in accordance with their willingness to cooperate in making out: Morris was a lousy guy because he'd always delay in bringing stock; Harry was basically a decent crib attendent (after he took my ham), tried to help the guys, but was overworked; Charley was an OK scheduling man because he'd try to give me the gravy jobs; Bill, my day man, was "all right" because he'd show me the angles on making out, give me some kitty if I needed it, and sometimes cover up for me when I made a mess of things. . . .

The Dispersion of Conflict

I have shown how the organization of a piecework machine shop gives rise to making out and how this in turn becomes the basis of shop-floor culture. Making out also shapes distinctive patterns of conflict. Workers are inserted into the labor process as individuals who directly dictate the speed, feed, depth, etc., of their machines. The piece wage, as Marx observed, "tends to develop on the one hand that individuality, and with it the sense of liberty, independence, and self-control of the labourers, on the other, their competition one with another."[6] At the same time, the labor process of a machine shop embodies an opposed principle, the operator's dependence on auxiliary workers—themselves operating with a certain individual autonomy. This tension between control over machinery and subordination to others, between productive activities and production relations, leads to particular forms of conflict on the shop floor.

I have already suggested that pressures to make out frequently result in conflict between production and auxiliary workers when the latter are unable to provide some service promptly. The reason for this is only rarely found in the deliberate obstructionism of the crib attendant, inspector, trucker, and so one. More often it is the consequence of a managerial allocation of resources. Thus, during the period I worked on the shop floor, the number of operators on second shift expanded to almost the number on first shift, yet there was only one truck driver instead of two; there were, for most of the time, only two inspectors instead of four; there were only two foremen instead of four; and there was only one crib attendant instead of two or three. This merely accentuated a lateral conflict that was endemic to the organization of work. The only way such lateral conflict could be reduced was to allow second-shift operators to provide their own services by jumping into an idle truck, by entering the crib to get their own fixtures, by filling out their own cards, by looking through the books for rates or to see whether an order had been finished, and so one. However, these activities were all regarded as illegitimate by management outside the shop.[7] When middle management clamped down on operators by enforcing rules, there was chaos.

In the eyes of senior management, auxiliary workers are regarded as overhead, and so there are continual attempts to reduce their numbers. Thus, as already recounted, the objective of the quality-control manager was to reduce the number of inspectors. Changes in the philosophy of quality control, he argued, place increasing responsibility on the worker, and problems of quality are more effectively combatted by "systems control," design, and careful check on suppliers, particularly suppliers of castings. But, so long as every operation had to have its first piece checked, the decline in the number of inspectors merely led to greater frustration on the shop floor.

A single example will illustrate the type of conflict that is common. Tom, an inspector, was suspended for three days for absenteeism. This meant that there was only one inspector for the entire department, and work was piling up outside the window of Larry (another inspector). I had to wait two hours before my piece was inspected and I could get on with the task. It was sufficiently annoying to find only one inspector around, but my fury was compounded by the ostentatious manner in which Larry himself was slowing down. When I mentioned this to him, jokingly, he burst forth with "Why should I work my ass off? Tom's got his three days off, and the company thinks they are punishing him, but it's me who's got to break my back." In this instance, conflict between Tom and the company was transmuted into a resentment between Tom and Larry, which in turn provoked a hostile exchange between Larry and me. "Going slow," aimed at the company, redounds to the disadvantage of fellow workers. The redistribution of conflict in such ways was a constant feature of social relations on the shop floor. It was particularly pronounced on second shift because of the shortage of auxiliary workers and the fact that the more inexperienced operators, and therefore the ones most needing assistance, were also on that shift.

Common sense might lead one to believe that conflict between workers and managers would lead to cohesiveness among workers, but such an inference misses the fact that all conflict is mediated on an ideological terrain, in this case the terrain of making out. Thus, management-worker conflict is turned into competitiveness and intragroup struggles as a result of the organization of work. The translation of hierarchical domination into lateral antagonisms is in fact a common phenomenon throughout industry, as was shown in a study conducted on a sample of 3,604 blue-collar workers from 172 production departments in six plants scattered across the United States:

> Work pressure in general is negatively correlated to social-supportive behavior, which we have called cohesive behavior, and positively related to competitive and intra-group conflict behavior. Cohesive behavior is generally untenable under high pressure conditions because the reward structure imposed by management directs employees to work as fast as they can individually.[8]

The dominant pattern of conflict dispersion in a piecework machine shop is undoubtedly the reconstitution of hierarchical conflict as lateral conflict and competition. However, it is by no means the only redistribution of conflict. A reverse tendency is often found when new machinery is introduced that is badly coordinated with existing technology. Here lateral conflict may be transformed into an antagonism between workers and management or between different levels of management. . . .

Conclusion

Between Geer Company of 1945 and Allied Corporation thirty years later, the labor process underwent two sets of changes. The first is seen in the greater individualism promoted by the organization of work. Operators in 1975 had more autonomy as a result of the following: relaxed enforcement of certain managerial controls, such as inspection of pieces and rate-fixing; increased shop-floor bargaining between workers and foremen; and changes in the system of piece rates—changes that laid greater stress on individual performance, effort, and mobility, and allowed more manipulations. The second type of change, related to the first, concerns the diminution of hierarchical conflict and its redistribution in a number of different directions. As regards the relaxation of conflict between worker and management, one notes the decline in the authority of the foreman and the reduction of tensions between those concerned with enforcement of quality in production and those primarily interested in quantity. The greater permissiveness toward chiseling, the improvement of tooling and machines, as well as easier rates, have all facilitated making out and in this way have reduced antagonism between worker and shop management.[9] The employment of fewer auxiliary workers, on the other hand, has exacerbated lateral conflict among different groups of workers.[10]

These changes do not seem to support theories of intensification of the labor process or increase of managerial control through separation of conception and execution. What we have observed is the expansion of the area of the "self-organization" of workers as they pursue their daily activities. We have seen how operators, in order to make out at all, subvert rules promulgated from on high, create informal alliances with auxiliary workers, make their own tools, and so on. In order to produce surplus value, workers have had to organize their relations and activities in opposition to management, particularly middle and senior management. . . . Workers actively struggle *against* management to defend the conditions for producing profit. For Cornelius Castoriadis, this represents the fundamental contradiction of capitalism:

> In short, it [the deep contradiction] lies in the fact that capitalism . . . is obliged to try and achieve the simultaneous exclusion and participation of people in relation to their activities, in the fact that people are forced to ensure the functioning of the system half of the time *against* the system's own rules and therefore in struggle against it. This fundamental contradiction appears constantly wherever the process of management meets the process of execution, which is precisely (and par excellence) the social moment of production.[11]

But if the self-organization of workers is necessary for the survival of capitalism, it also questions the foundations of capitalism.

> When the shop-floor collective establishes norms that informally sanction both "slackers" and "speeders," when it constantly constitutes and reconstitutes itself in "informal" groups that respond to both the requirements of the work process and to personal affinities, it can only be viewed as actively opposing to capitalist principles new principles of productive and social organization and a new view of work.[12]

But is making out as radical as Castoriadis claims? Or is it, as Herbert Marcuse would argue, a mode of adaptation that reproduces "the voluntary servitude" of workers to capital? Are these freedoms and needs, generated and partially satisfied in the context of work and harnessed to the production of surplus value, a challenge to "capitalist principles"? Does making out present an anticipation of something new, the potential for human self-organization, or is it wholly contained within the reproduction of capitalist relations?[13] We can begin to answer such questions only by examining more closely the relationship between making out and the essence of the capitalist labor process—the simultaneous obscuring and securing of surplus value.

Notes

1. My day man, Bill, never penciled in the time but always got his cards punched in on the clock at the time office. This restricted his room for manipulation; but since he was very experienced on the miscellaneous job, this did not reduce his earnings by very much. When I filled in for him on first shift, I did in fact pencil in the times, and no one complained. This may have been a reflection of my power, since, with Bill away, hardly anyone knew how to do the various jobs or where the fixtures were. By penciling in the times, I reckoned I could earn the same amount of money as Bill but with less effort.

2. Donald Roy, "Restriction of Output in a Piecework Machine Shop," Ph.D. diss., Univ. of Chicago, 1952, p. 240.

3. Ibid., table 4, p. 94.

4. During the week 17 November to 23 November 1975, there were sixteen radial-drill operators in the small-parts department. Their average "measured performances" for the entire year (or for the period of the year since they had begun to operate a radial drill) were as follows (all figures are percentages): 92, 108, 109, 110, 111, 112, 115, 116, 119, 125, 133, 137, 139, 141, 142. The average was 120 percent, which turns out to be precisely Roy's average in his second period. Moreover, the average period spent on a radial drill in the *first eleven months of 1975* among these sixteen operators was of the order of six months, though a number of these operators had probably been operating radial drills for years. The data do not suggest significant differences between the rates on radial drills in Geer's Jack Shop and on radial drills in Allied's small-parts department.

5. Donald Roy, "Work Satisfaction and Social Reward in Quota Achievement," *American Journal of Sociology* 57 (1953), 509–10.

6. Karl Marx, *Capital* Vol. I (New York: International Publishers, 1967), p. 555.

7. I vividly recall being bawled out by a manager who came into the time office long after he should have gone home. He found me going through the books to see how many pieces had been handed in on a particular operation. Second-shift shop-floor management allowed and even encouraged operators to look these sorts of things up for themselves rather than bother the time clerks, but senior management regarded this as a criminal act.

8. Stuart Klein, *Workers under Stress: The Impact of Work Pressure on Group Cohesion* (Lexington: University of Kentucky Press, 1971), p. 100.

9. A similar argument [is] made by Tom Lupton, *On the Shop Floor* (Oxford: Pergamon Press, 1963), pp. 182–83. Though Lupton fails to see the organization of work as the consequence and object of struggles between workers and managers, among workers and among managers, his characterization of the *functions* of the "fiddle" are illuminating.

10. In interpreting these changes we will repeatedly come up against a difficult problem, namely, the degree to which Roy's observations reflect the exigencies of wartime conditions. For example, during the war, government contracts encouraged the overmanning of industry, since profits were fixed as a percentage of costs. Boosting costs did not change the rate of profit. As a consequence, we should not be surprised to discover cutbacks in personnel after the war. Thus, Roy informs us that after V-J Day, just before he left Geer, there was a reorganization in which foremen were demoted and the setup function was eliminated (Roy, "Restriction of Output," pp. 60, 219). Hostility of workers to the company must have been, at least in part, engendered by wartime restraints on union militancy and by the choking-off of the grievance machinery.

11. Paul Cardan (alias Cornelius Castoriadis), *Redefining Revolution* (London: Solidarity Pamphlet 44, n.d.), p. 11.

12. Cornelius Castoriadis, "On the History of the Workers' Movement," *Telos* no. 30 (Winter 1976–77): 35.

13. See, for example, Herbert Marcuse, *One-Dimensional Man* (Boston: Beacon Press, 1964), chap. 1; *An Essay on Liberation* (Boston: Beacon Press, 1969); *Eros and Civilization* (Boston: Beacon Press, 1955), chap. 10.

16
Women and Power in Organizations

Rosabeth Moss Kanter

What does make a difference is *power*—power outward and upward in the system: the ability to get for the group, for subordinates or followers, a favorable share of the resources, opportunities, and rewards possible through the organization. This has less to do with how leaders relate to followers than with how they relate to other parts of the organization. It has less to do with the quality of the manager-subordinate relationship than with the structure of power in the wider system. Early theory in organizational behavior assumed a direct relation between leader behavior and group satisfaction and morale, as if each organizational subgroup existed in a vacuum. However, Donald Pelz, in a study at Detroit Edison in the early 1950s, discovered that perceived influence *outside* the work group and upward in the organization was a significant intervening variable. He compared high- and low- morale work groups to test the hypothesis that the supervisor in high-morale groups would be better at communicating, more supportive, and more likely to recommend promotion. Yet when he analyzed the data, the association seemed to be nonexistent or even reversed. In some cases, supervisors who frequently recommended people for promotion and offered sincere praise for a job well done had *lower* morale scores. The differentiating variable that Pelz finally hit upon was whether or not the leaders had power outside and upward: influence on their own superiors and influence over how decisions were made in the department as a whole. The combination of good human relations *and* power produced high morale. Human relations skills coupled with low power sometimes had negative effects on morale.[1] What good is praise or a promise if the leader can't deliver? As other research discovered, both women and men attach more importance to having a competent, rather than a nice, boss—someone who gets things done. A classic study of first-line supervisors showed that more secure (and hence effective) foremen were those who had closer relationships

---

Reprinted from *Men and Women of the Corporation*, by Rosabeth Moss Kanter (New York: Basic Books, 1977), 168–171, 181–205, by permission of the publisher.

upward in the hierarchy; they had the most frequent exchanges with superiors.[2]

Power begets power. People who are thought to have power already and to be well placed in hierarchies of prestige and status may also be more influential and more effective in getting the people around them to do things and feel satisfied about it. In a laboratory experiment, subordinates were more likely to cooperate with and to inhibit aggression and negativity toward leaders of higher rather than lower status. In a field study of professionals, people who came into a group with higher external status tended to be better liked, talked more often, and received more communications. The less powerful, who usually talked less, were often accused of talking *too much*. There was a real consensus in such groups about who was powerful, and people were more likely to accept direct attempts to influence them from people they defined as among the powerful. Average group members, whether men or women, tended to engage in deferential, approval-seeking behavior toward those seen as higher in power.[3] Thus, people who look like they can command more of the organization's resources, who look like they can bring something that is valued from outside into the group, who seem to have access to the inner circles that make the decisions affecting the fate of individuals in organizations, may also be more effective as leaders of those around them—and be better liked in the process.

Twenty Indsco executives in a sample of managers reached the same conclusion when asked to define the characteristics of effective managers. The question of the relative importance of "people sensitivity," as they put it, provoked considerable debate. Finally, they agreed that "credibility" was more important than anything else. "Credibility" was their term for competence plus power—the known ability to get results. People with credibility were listened to, their phone calls were answered first, because they were assumed to have something important to say. People with credibility had room to make more mistakes and could take greater risks because it was believed that they would produce. They were known to be going somewhere in the organization and to have the ability to place their people in good jobs. They could back up their words with actions. Thus, the ultimate in credibility in the corporate bureaucracy was "the guy who doesn't have to make recommendations; he comes out with a *decision* and all supporting material. Everyone else just says yes or no. . . ."

Credibility upward rather than downward—that is, wider-system power—rendered managers effective, they thought. To have it downward, with subordinates, they must first have it upward, with their own superiors and the people with whom their tasks were interwoven in the matrix. Credibility downward was based on subordinates' belief in their managers' importance, which in turn was based on their political position. People-sensitivity could be an added bonus, but it was considered much less important than power. "Some managers are very successful and very tough," an executive commented. "John Fredericks is as tough as they come but also sensitive to people. His people have gone far, but is that because he's sensitive or because he has clout? It's impossible to untangle." "You can get people to do nearly anything for you if they think you have their interest at heart and will fight for them. They must see that you can produce for them, that the fighting will pay off." And lack of system power could undermine the best of human relations: "Fred Burke came in as an outsider to manage his department, so he didn't know the business and he didn't have the right connections in the company. When he tried to get things from headquarters, he had no clout. Headquarters wanted to talk to the people *under* him because they knew the answers. But sensitive, yes! Christ, I don't know anyone more sensitive than Fred Burke. You've never seen a more sensitive guy; but his people turned against him anyway. They had no respect for him." "What we're saying, I guess," someone tried to summarize the discussion, "is that you need a combination of both—people-skills and credibility." "No," others disagreed. "It's the need to take action that distinguishes effective managers. Having some results at the end of all that people-sensitivity. What good is it if you can't get anything done in Indsco?"

The preference for association with the powerful and the degree to which this preference motivates members of organizations is a function of the degree of dependency built into the organization itself. Where people can do their work rather independently, where they can easily get the things they need to carry out their tasks, where they have a great deal of latitude in decision-making, and where rewards are not so contingent on career mobility, then there need not be the same concern with appropriate political alliances. However, the large, complex hierarchical corporation fosters dependency. . . . In the context of such organizationally fostered dependency, people seem willing to work very hard to reduce it. One way to do this is by allying themselves with the powerful, with people who can make them more independent by creating more certainty in their lives.

Power in an organization rests, in part, on the ability to solve dependency problems and to control relevant sources of uncertainty.[4] This can be true with respect to the system as a whole as well as around individuals. For the system, the most power goes to those people in those functions that provide greater control over what the organization finds currently problematic: sales and marketing people when markets are competitive; production experts when materials are scarce and demand is high; personnel or labor relations specialists when labor is scarce; lawyers, lobbyists, and external relations specialists when government regulations impinge; finance and accounting types when business is bad and money tight.[5] There is a turning to those elements of the system that seem to have the power to create more certainty in the face of dependency, to generate a more advantageous position for the organization. . . .

Alliances: Power through Others

The informal social network that pervades organizations can be very important, as many theorists have pointed out. In a large, complex system, it is almost a necessity for power to come from social connections, especially those outside of the immediate work group. Such connections need to be long-term and stable and include "sponsors" (mentors and advocates upward in the organization), peers, and subordinates.

Sponsors
Sponsors have been found to be important in the careers of managers and professionals in many settings. In the corporation, "sponsored mobility" (controlled selection by elites) seems to determine who gets the most desirable jobs, rather than "contest mobility" (an open game), to use Ralph Turner's concepts.[6] At Indsco, high-level sponsors were known as "rabbis" or "godfathers," two colorful labels for these unofficial bestowers of power.

Sponsors are often thought of as teachers or coaches whose functions are primarily to make introductions or to train a young person to move effectively through the system. However, there are three other important functions besides advice that generate power for the people sponsored. First, sponsors are often in a position to *fight* for the person in question, to stand up for him or her in meetings if controversy is raised, to promote that person for promising opportunities. When there are large numbers of personnel distributed across wide territories, as in Industrial Supply Corporation, there was much advantage to being the favorite of a powerful person who could help distinguish a person from the crowd and argue his or her virtues against those of other people. ("They say the rabbi system is dead," commented a young manager, "but I can't believe we make promotion decisions without it.") Despite a rating system that tried to make the system more open and equitable at lower levels, sponsors could still make a difference. Indeed, one of the problems with not having a powerful manager, Indsco workers thought, was that the manager would not be strong enough to stand up and fight for subordinates in places where they could not fight for themselves.

Second, sponsors often provided the occasion for lower-level organization members to *bypass the hierarchy*: to get inside information, to short-circuit cumbersome procedures, or to cut red tape. People develop a social relationship with a powerful person which allows them to go directly to that person, even though there is no formal interface, and once there, a social interchange can often produce formal results. This could be very important to formal job success in Indsco, to the ability to get things done, in a system where people could easily get bogged down if they had to honor official protocol. One saleman with a problem he wanted to solve for a customer described Indsco as "like the Army, Air Force, and Navy—we have a formal chain of command." The person who could make the decision on his problem was four steps removed from him, not in hierarchical rank but according to operating procedure. Ordinarily, he would not be able to go directly to him, but they had developed a relationship over a series of sales meetings, during which the more powerful person had said, "Please drop by anytime you're at headquarters." So the salesman found an occasion to "drop by," and in the course of the casual conversation mentioned his situation. It was solved immediately. A woman manager used her powerful sponsors in a similar way. Whenever her boss was away, she had lunch with her friends among the corporate officers. This provided an important source of information, such as "secret" salary information from a vice-president. In fact, the manager revealed, "much of what I get done across groups is based on informal personal relations through the years, when there is no formal way to do it."

Third, sponsors also provide an important signal to other people, a form of *reflected power*. Sponsorship indicates to others that the person in question has the backing of an influential person, that the sponsor's resources are somewhere behind the individual. Much of the power of relatively junior people comes not from their own resources but from the "credit" extended to them because there appears to be a more powerful set of resources in the distance. This was an important source of the power of "comers" at Indsco, the "water walkers" and "high fliers" who were on fast tracks because they were high performers with powerful backing. A manager in that position described it this way: "A variety of people become impressed with you. You see the support at several levels; someone seems comfortable with you although he's a vice-president, and he looks you in the eye. You get offered special jobs by powerful people. You're pulled aside and don't have to go through channels. If you can sustain that impression for three to four years, your sphere of influence will increase to the point where you have a clear path for a few miles. You can have anything you want up to a certain level, where the power of the kingpins changes. Here's how it happens. A manager who is given a water walker, knowing that the person is seen as such from above and from below, is put in a no-win situation. If the person does well, everyone knew it anyway. If the person doesn't do well, it is considered the manager's fault. So the manager can only try to get the star promoted, move him or her out as fast as possible; and the manager wants to help accelerate the growth of walkers because someday the manager might be working for them. All of this promotes the star's image." Another rising executive commented, "Everyone attempts to get on the heels of a flier. Everyone who does well has a sponsor, someone to take you on their heels. In my case, I had three managers. All of them have moved but continue to help me. A vice-president likes me. I can count on getting any job up a level as long as he remains in favor."

Those seen as moving accumulated real power because of their connections with sponsors, but they also had to be careful about the way they used the reflected power of the sponsor: "It's an embryonic, gossamer-type thing because four levels up is *far* away, and the connection is very tenuous. It's only a promise of things to come. You can't use it with your own manager, or you get in trouble. The rabbis are not making commitments right now. One guy tried to use his connections with his manager, to cash in his chips too early. The axe fell. He had to go back to zero." Handling relationships with sponsors could be tricky, too. "It's scary because you have to live up to others' expectations. There is great danger if you go up against a godfather. It becomes a father/son issue as well as business. God help you if you are not grateful for the favors given." And, of course, fast trackers can also fall when their sponsors fall if they have not developed their own power base in the interim.

If sponsors are important for the success of men in organizations, they seem absolutely essential for women. If men function more effectively as leaders when they appear to have influence upward and outward in the organization, women need even more the signs of such influence and the access to real power provided by sponsors. Margaret Cussler's and Margaret Hennig's studies of those few women in top management positions in U.S. corporations showed dramatically the importance of sponsorship. A British study concluded that "office uncles" were important in the careers of women in organizations because they offered behavioral advice and fought for the women to be promoted.[7] Ella Grasso, the first woman elected to a state governorship on her own, had a sponsor in John Bailey, who was chairman of the Democratic National Committee from 1961 to 1968. He first spotted her as a political "comer" in the 1950s. Since then he [had] provided advice, campaign help, and introductions to certain circles.[8] At Indsco the same pattern emerged. One woman was brought into her management position at Indsco by a sponsor, a vice-president for whom she had worked as an executive secretary. Her relation to him and the connections she had already made through him made her reception into management quite different from that of other former secretaries. Another secretary who was promoted without sponsorship felt ignored, isolated, and resented after her move, but the first woman's experience was different. Male peers immediately made her one of the gang. During her first week in the new position, she remembered, she was deluged with phone calls from men letting her know they were there if she had any questions, making sure she had a lunch date, and inviting her to meetings.

If sponsors are important for women, they can also be harder to come by. Sponsorship is sometimes generated by good performance, but it can also come, as one of Indsco's fast trackers put it, "because you have the right social background or know some of the officers from outside the corporation or look good in a suit." Some people thought that higher-ups decided to sponsor particular individuals because of identification and that this process almost automatically eliminated women. (There is, indeed, much research evidence that leaders choose to promote the careers of socially similar subordinates.)[9] Men could not identify with women, and very few women currently held top positions. Identification was the issue in these remarks: "Boy wonders rise under certain power structures. They're recognized by a powerful person because they are very much like him. He sees himself, a younger version, in that person. . . . Who can look at a woman and see themselves?" This was a good question. When women acquired sponsors, the reasons were often different from the male sponsor-protégé situation. In one case, officers were looking for a high-performing woman they could make into a showpiece to demonstrate the organization's openness to good women. In another instance, an executive was thought to have "hung his hat on a woman" (decided to sponsor her) to demonstrate that he could handle a "tricky" management situation and solve a problem for the corporation.

Peers
More often neglected in the study of the accumulation of organizational power is the importance of strong peer alliances, although Barry Stein has written about the ways groups can capitalize on the success of a "comer."[10] At Indsco high "peer acceptance," as managers put it, was necessary to any power base or career success. "Individual performers" found their immediate accomplishments rewarded, but their careers stuck . . . because they had not built, nor were seen as capable of building, the kinds of connections necessary for success in ever more interdependent higher-level jobs. "The group needs each other," a sales manager remarked. "To become powerful, people must first be successful and receive recognition, but they must wear the respect with a lack of arrogance. They must not be me-oriented. Instead of protecting their secrets in order to stand taller than the crowd, they are willing to share successes. They help their peers. . . . This is 'leader quality.' "

Strong alliances among peers could advance the group as a whole, as Stein noted in commenting on the fact that certain cohorts sometimes seem to produce all of the leaders in an organization.[11] However, a highly competitive situation could also imbue peer relations with politics and pitfalls. A star performer just promoted to his first management position told me quite proudly how he had just handled his first political battle with a counterpart in his position. One reason he was telling me at such length, he explained, was because he had no one he could tell within the organization. He had decided to take care of the issue by going directly to the other man and working it out with him, then promising him it would go no further. My informant had been the one who was wronged, and he could have gone to his boss or the other person's boss, but he decided that in the long run he was wiser to try to honor peer solidarity and try to build an ally out of the person who had hurt him. "I didn't want to create enemies," he commented. "Some peers look to you for help, to work with you for mutual gain, but others wait for you to stumble so they can bad-mouth you: 'Yeah, he's a sharp guy, but he drinks a lot.' If I had gone against the other guy now, even if I had won, he would have had a knife out for me sometime. Better to do him a favor by keeping quiet, and then he'll be grateful later."

Peer alliances often worked through direct exchange of favors. On lower levels information was traded; on higher levels bargaining and trade often took place around good performers and job openings. In a senior executive's view, it worked like this: "A good job becomes available. A list of candidates is generated. That's refined down to three or four. That is circulated to a select group that has an opportunity to look it over. Then they can make bargains among themselves." A manager commented, "There's lots of 'I owe you one.' If you can accumulate enough chits, that helps you get what you need; but then, of course, people have to be in a position to cash them in."

Subordinates
The accumulation of power through alliances was not always upward-oriented. For one thing, differential rates of hierarchical progress could mean that juniors or peers one day could become a person's boss the next. So it could be to a person's advantage to make alliances downward in the hierarchy with people who looked like they might be on the way up. There was a preference for "powerful" subordinates as well as powerful bosses. Just in the way Bernard Levenson proposed, a manager on the move would try to develop subordinates who could take over, keeping a member of "his team" in place. Professionals and executives needed more junior people loyal to them as much as they needed the backing of higher-level people. Especially higher up, the successful implementation of plans and policies depended heavily upon the activities of those people lower down in the hierarchy who were responsible for the carrying out of day-to-day operations or the translation into specifics of general guidelines. So alliances with subordinates often developed early in careers, anticipating the time when managers would need the support of "their team." There was often a scrambling by managers to upgrade the jobs reporting to them so that they could attract more powerful subordinates. Also, as I have indicated, managers could benefit from speeding up the career of a person already on a fast track.

However, if power was something that not everyone could accumulate, what happened to the powerless?

Accountability without Power: Sources of Bureaucratic Powerlessness

People who have authority without system power are powerless. People held accountable for the results produced by others, whose formal role gives them the right to command but who lack informal political influence, access to resources, outside status, sponsorship, or mobility prospects, are rendered powerless in the organization. They lack control over their own fate and are dependent on others above them—others whom they cannot easily influence—while they are expected by virtue of position to be influential over those parallel or below. Their sense of lack of control above is heightened by its contrast with the demands of an accountable authority position: that they mobilize others in the interests of a task they may have had little part in shaping, to produce results they may have had little part in defining.

First-line supervisors in highly routinized functions often are functionally powerless. Their situation—caught between the demands of a management hierarchy they are unlikely to enter because of low opportunity and the resistance of workers who resent their own circumstances—led classic writers on organizations to describe them as "men in the middle."[12] (However, they are also often "women in the middle.") They have little chance to gain power through activities, since their functions do not lend themselves to the demonstration of the extraordinary, nor do they generate high visibility or solutions to organizational problems. They have few rewards to distribute, since rewards are automatically given by the organization; and their need for reliable performance from workers in order to keep their own job secure limits the exercise of other forms of power. "I'm afraid to confront the employees because they have the power to slack, to slouch, to take too much time," a supervisor of clerical workers said, "and I need them for results. I'm measured on *results*—quantitative output, certain attendance levels, number of reports filed. They have to do it for me." Another one said, "When I ask for help, I get punished because my manager will say, 'But it's your job. If you can't do it, you shouldn't be in that job.' So what's *their* job? Sending me notes telling me it's unacceptable? They're like teachers sending me a report card." First-line supervisors also felt powerless because their jobs were vulnerable during times of recession, while people farther up in the hierarchy seemed secure. They resented the fact that their peers were let go, while higher managers were not. "Why us? Aren't they running the show? Shouldn't they be the ones to suffer if business isn't going well?" And supervisors of secretaries . . . were also rendered powerless by the secretary's allegiance to a boss with more status and clout in the organization.

Occupants of certain staff jobs were similarly organizationally powerless.[13] They had no line authority and were dependent on managers to implement their decisions and carry out their recommendations. Staff programs that managers saw as irrelevant to their primary responsibilities would be ignored. Affirmative action and equal employment opportunity officers often found themselves in this position. Their demands were seen by line people as an intrusion, a distraction from more important business, and the extra paperwork that EEO entailed was annoying. Personnel staff who tried to introduce more rational, universalistic, and equitable systems for job placement for nonexempts also had difficulty selling their programs. . . . These staff activities were seen as destroying a managerial prerogative and interfering with something managers preferred to do for themselves. The aims of personnel people in sending out certain candidates for jobs could conflict with the desires of the manager who would be using the candidate, and when battles resulted, it was often the more prestigious line manager who prevailed.

Regardless of function, people could also be rendered powerless if their own management did not extend opportunities for power downward—if their situations did not permit them to take risks, if their authority was undercut, or if their sphere of autonomous decision-making was limited. There seemed to be a consensus at Indsco that superiors who solved problems themselves or tried to do the job themselves disempowered the managers or professionals under them. Considered ideal, by contrast, was the manager who "never gave anyone an answer; but when you walked out of his office, you had it because he asked you the questions that made you think of it." Many women thus objected to the "protectiveness" that they perceived in their managers, protection that "encased" them "in a plastic bubble," as one put it, and rendered them ineffectual. Anyone who is protected loses power, for successes are then attributed to the helpful actions of others, rather than the person's own actions. Women complained about the "people who want to move walls for me instead of saying, 'Hey, here's a wall. Let's strategize working through it.'" Another said, "You need a lot of exposure to get ahead, a broad base of experience. I don't want to be protected, given the easy management situations, the easy customers, the sure-fire position." And being in a position where decisions were reviewed and authority could be undercut also created powerlessness. A customer service representative faced a situation where she had to tell a customer that she couldn't ship to him because the materials were not available; this was an order that had come down to her. The customer said he would call the immediate manager. The manager backed up the representative, indicating that he would call headquarters but that the rep was right and had the information. So the customer went one step higher in the hierarchy, calling headquarters himself. This time he managed to get a change. Everyone lost credibility, but especially the woman. Nothing diminishes leaders' power more than subordinates' knowledge that they can always go over their heads, or that what they promise has no real clout. A management recruiter advised companies that wanted to ensure the success of new women managers not to inadvertently encourage resistance to the new manager: even seemingly innocuous requests, such as a higher manager asking to be kept informed, could encourage subordinates to bypass the woman and do their reporting higher up.[14]

Powerlessness, finally, was the general condition of those people who could not make the kinds of powerful alliances that helped to manage the bureaucracy. People without sponsors, without peer connections, or without promising subordinates remained in the situation of bureaucratic dependency on formal procedures, routine allocations of rewards, communication that flowed through a multi-layered chain of command, and decisions that must penetrate, as Robert Presthus put it, "innumerable veto barriers."[15] People who reached dead ends in their careers also rapidly lost power, since they could no longer promise gains to those who followed them and no longer had the security of future movement. Powerlessness was also the psychological state of people who, for whatever reason, felt insecure in their functioning as leaders and anticipated resistance rather than cooperation from those whom they were to lead. Indeed, the structural characteristics of modern organizational life tend to produce the symptoms of powerlessness in more and more lower-to-middle managers, supervisors, bureaucrats, and professionals. The chance to engage in the non-routine, to show discretion, to take risks, or to become known, are all less available in the large bureaucracy.

Behavioral Responses to Powerlessness

Controlling Behavior and Close Supervision

Psychoanalyst Karen Horney, in *The Neurotic Personality of Our Time*, described people's neurotic attempt to dominate when they feel anxious or helpless, inferior or insignificant. As a protection and a defense, the psychologically powerless turn to control over others. They want to be right all the time and are irritated at being proven wrong. They cannot tolerate disagreement.[16] In short, they become critical, bossy, and controlling. Some degree of power, in the sense of mastery and control over one's fate, is necessary for feelings of self-esteem and well-being, as Rollo May has indicated.[17] When a person's exercise of power is thwarted or blocked, when people are rendered powerless in the larger arena, they may tend to concentrate their power needs on those over whom they have even a modicum of authority. There is a displacement of control downward paralleling displacement of aggression. In other words, people respond to the restrictivness of their own situation by behaving restrictively toward others. People will "boss" those they can, as in the image of the nagging housewife or old-maid schoolteacher or authoritarian boss, if they cannot flex their power muscles more constructively and if, moreover, they are afraid they really are powerless.

One example of this syndrome comes from research on the leadership style of low-power male Air Force officers. Officers of lower status and advancement potential favored more directive, rigid, and authoritarian techniques of leadership, seeking control over subordinates. Subordinates were their primary frame of reference for their own status assessment and enhancement, and so they found it important to "lord it over" group members. They also did not help talented members of the group get ahead (perhaps finding them too threatening) and selected immediate assistants of mediocre rather than outstanding talent.[18] Similarly, in a French bureaucracy technical engineers in an isolated position with low mobility and low power with respect to directors were, in turn, extremely authoritarian and paternalistic with *their* subordinates.[19]

When people expect to be successful in their influence attempts, in contrast, they can afford to use milder forms of power, such as personal persuasion. Even a little bit of influence is likely to work, and it is so much more pleasant to avoid conflict and struggle. But when people anticipate resistance, they tend to use the strongest kind of weapon they can muster. As Frantz Fanon proposed in *The Wretched of the Earth*, the powerless may come to rely on force, first and foremost.[20] In a series of laboratory studies simulating supervision of three production workers, male subjects who lacked confidence in their own abilities to control the world or who thought they encountered resistance from the mock subordinates used more coercive than persuasive power, especially when resistance stemmed from "poor attitude" (a direct threat to their power) rather than ineptness.[21] We know from other laboratory studies that people are more automatically obedient toward the organizationally powerful than the powerless, regardless of formal position. Subordinates inhibit aggression in the face of power, but they direct more intense aggression to the relatively powerless. Indeed, it can be argued, as a number of other theorists have also done, that a controlling leadership style is a *result* rather than a *cause* of hostile, resistant, or noncompliant behavior on the part of subordinates.[22]

Thus, the relatively powerless in positions of organizational authority also have reason to be more controlling and coercive. If they have less call on the organization's resources, less backup and support from sponsors and managers, less cooperative subordinates, and less influence in the informal power structure, people can only use the strongest tools at their disposal: discipline or threats or maintaining tight control over all of the activities in their jurisdiction. If managers or supervisors who encounter resistance from those they are trying to direct tend to become more coercive in their power tactics, it is a vicious cycle: powerless authority figures who use coercive tactics provoke resistance and aggression, which prompts them to become even more coercive, controlling, and behaviorally restrictive.

At Indsco relatively powerless managers who were insecure about their organizational status tended to give the least freedom to subordinates and to personally control their department's activities much more tightly. (I used formal job characteristics, other people's perceptions, and my own observations to decide who was relatively powerless). These managers made all of the decisions, did an amount of operating work themselves that others in the organization would consider "excessive," and did not let subordinates represent them at meetings or on task forces. They tried to control the communication flow in and out of their department, so that all messages had to pass through them. One manager in a low-power situation, who was considered "tough to work for—too tight," jumped on a subordinate for calling a vice-president directly to ask a question, saying, "*I'm* the one who represents this function to v.p.'s." Another manager with good people working for him wanted to see that all the credit went to him. He wrote a report of his unit's activities that made it seem as though he, and not the salespeople involved, had generated an increase in sales: "By negotiating with the profit center, I saw to it that . . . ."

Sometimes low-power managers and supervisors took over the task and tried to do or direct closely the work of subordinates instead of giving them a free hand, because technical mastery of job content was one of the few arenas in which they *did* feel powerful. Often people get to first-line managerial jobs, for example, because they are good at the operating tasks. Trying to do the job themselves or watching over subordinates' shoulders to correct the slightest deviation from how the supervisors themselves would do it represents a comfortable retreat into expertise from the frustrations of trying to administer when organizational power is low. People can still feel good knowing that they could do the job well—or better than their subordinates. Thus, they are tempted to control their subordinates, keep them from learning or developing their own styles, jump in too quickly to solve problems, and "nitpick" over small things subordinates do differently. All of these things were considered characteristics of ineffective managers at Indsco. However, the temptation to take over the work of the next level down instead of engaging in more general leadership—a temptation that always existed, even for people at the very top, as one of them told me—was succumbed to especially by the powerless.

Conditions of work could intersect with low organizational power to reinforce a tendency toward closeness of supervision. Departments of women clerical workers run by powerless women managers were a case in point. The supervisors were, in turn, managed by men, who gave them detailed orders and little discretion, and the supervisors tended to be in a terminal job and poorly connected to informal power alliances. At the same time, the office setup encouraged a restrictive, controlled atmosphere. The clerical workers were confined to banks of desks in large offices virtually under the nose of the supervisor. These departments were considered among the most tightly run in the corporation. They had the least absenteeism and a decided "schoolroom" atmosphere. In contrast, the conditions of work in sales made it more difficult for even the most control-prone manager to supervise as tightly, since sales people under one manager were often scattered throughout several field offices, and sales workers were legitimately out of the office a great deal of the time. Field sales managers, similarly, operated away from the direct view of their own managers. So the greater freedom of the sales function was empowering all down the line. However, the setting for clerical workers and their bosses made it easier for them to remain powerless.

Rules-Mindedness

The powerless inside an authority structure often become rules-minded in response to the limited options for power in their situation, turning to "the rules" as a power tool. Rules are made in the first place to try to control the uncontrollable; invoking organization rules and insisting on careful adherence to them is a characteristic response of the powerless in authority positions. For one thing, "the rules" represent their only safe and sure legitimate authority, the place where higher-ups are guaranteed to give them backing, because higher-ups wrote or represent the rules. They have few other means to use in bargaining with subordinates for cooperation. As Crozier wrote, "If no difference can be introduced in the treatment given to subordinates, either in the present definition of the job or in the fulfillment of their career expectations, hierarchical superiors cannot keep power over them. Superiors' roles will be limited to controlling the application of rules."[23]

Second, powerlessness coupled with accountability, with responsibility for results dependent on the actions of others, provokes a cautious, low-risk, play-it-safe attitude. Getting everything right is the response of those who lack other ways to impress those above them or to secure their position; and in turn they demand this kind of ritualistic conformity from subordinates, like schoolteachers more concerned about neatness of a paper than its ideas. Secretarial supervisors at Indsco tended to be known for these traits: a concern with proper form rather than a good outcome. Or, as someone else said, "You don't give freedom or experiment with procedure when you're a first-liner. You try to cover your ass and not make a mistake they can catch you on."

Overconformity to the rules and ritual concern with formalities are characteristics of the "bureaucratic personality" identified in Robert Merton's classic essay. Bureaucratic organizations, by their very structures, exert constant pressures on employees to perform reliably within prescribed and predictable behavioral limits. At the same time, routinization of careers within a bureaucracy—the provision of planned, graded, incremental promotions and salary increases—offers incentives for disciplined action and conformity to official regulations. These features taken together, Merton concluded, produced the bureaucrat's substitution of means (the rules, the forms, the procedures) for ends (goals, purposes, underlying rationales).[24]

Melville Dalton also recognized that the powerless hang on to rules, contrasting the "strong" and the "weak" as models of managerial tendencies.

> The weak are fearful in conflict situations and absorb aggressions to avoid trouble. . . .They hesitate to act without consulting superiors and take refuge in clearly formulated rules, whether adequate or not for their footing at the moment. Following their fairy-tale image of the organization as a fixed thing, they suffer from their experience that it is not. This, of course, aggravates their difficulty in grasping the tacit expectations that associations do not want to spell out, when events are troublesome. . . . As they seek to escape dilemmas, their unfitness to act outside the haven of understood rules invites aggression from the strong who are searching for shortcuts in the network of official routes.[25]

Thus, it is those lower in power who become rules-minded, but it is a bit too simple to attribute the concern with rules only to a reactive stance—a general bureaucratic world view. For those with relatively little organizational power but who must lead or influence others, *their control of "the rules" can represent one of their few areas of personal discretion.* They can exchange a bending of the rules for compliance; they can reward their favorites with a lighter application of the rules. However, first the rules must be experienced and honored. Subordinates or clients or workers must know what the formalities are like before they can be grateful for a bit of special treatment. They must see that the manager or supervisor or official has the right to invoke the full measure of the rule. So the persons who concern themselves with the rules both have something that *must* command obedience and have the basis for a form of power through differential application of those same rules. Staff officials without the power or credibility to persuade people in other departments to carry out the *spirit* of new programs (like affirmative action or centralized secretarial hiring) could fall back on their *letter*, burying uncooperative departments in mounds of paperwork.

One Indsco manager who was particularly concerned about protocol, formalities, and proper procedure had come up the ranks the hard way and was still not in a very influential position. He was upset that perquisites and privileges that had taken him long to earn were now automatically given out to younger people. He felt that they took liberties and behaved much too casually. One time, a young person introduced himself to the manager at a company function and then called to make a lunch date. The manager turned him down and then phoned his boss to complain that the young person was trying to get into the executive dining room. However, there were hints of the true feelings behind the manager's complaints. The manager was someone whose only source of power and respect came through the organizational formalities. He counted on being able to control his subordinates by carefully doling out privileges or offering small deviations from the formal rules. If the rules did not mean much anymore, what did he have left?

Territoriality and Domain Control
Merton went on to argue that bureaucrats adopt a domineering manner because whenever they use the authority of their office with clients or subordinates, they are acting as representatives of the power and prestige of the entire structure.[26] Vicarious power—power through identification—Merton seemed to say, breeds bossiness. However, if we look more closely at the organizational structures he described, we can see that this aspect of the "bureaucratic personality" reflects a response to *powerlessness* rather than to power, delegated or otherwise. The organization's concern with regulations reduces administrators' spheres of autonomy, limits their influence and decision-making power. The very provision of graded careers stressing seniority, in which incremental advances are relatively small and all must wait their turn, fosters dependency on the organization, which always holds back some rewards until the next advance. It removes incentives for assertion and reduces people to a common denominator—one in which they did not participate in defining. Unless people can accumulate power through activities or alliances, they face a sense of helplessness and insignificance.

In response to organizational insignificance, officials turn to their own small territory, their own little piece of the system—their subordinates, their function, their expertise. They guard their domain jealously. They narrow their interests to focus exclusively on it. They try to insulate and protect it and to prevent anyone else from engaging in similar activities without their approval or participation as "the experts." Another organizational cycle is set in motion. As each manager protects his or her own domain, the sense of helplessness and powerlessness of other administrators in intersecting units increases. They, in turn, may respond by redoubling their domination over their territory and their workers. The result can be "sub-optimization": each subgroup optimizing only its own goals and forgetting about wider system interests. For example, a worker in Crozier's clerical agency described this territoriality of supervisors. Supervisors were squeezed by higher management, which blamed them for poor morale and delivered speeches and written instructions advising them to pay more attention to leadership. In the worker's view, "They worry too much about their career and the possibility of promotion. They are jealous and awfully competitive. They are also sectarian. Often there is a lot of hostility between sections. . . . Each one of them wants to have his little kingdom."[27]

At Indsco, territoriality seemed more often a response of relatively powerless staff than of line officials. Line officials could turn to close supervision or rules application, but staff had only whatever advantage they could gain through specialized knowledge and jurisdiction over an area of expertise. This was especially clear around personnel functions. The organization was so large that personnel training, management development, and organization development responsibilities were divided up among many different units, some attached to divisions, some attached to the corporation, and some attached to specific functions. Such units often prevented each other from acting by claiming territorial encroachments. The result was that nearly all of them remained narrowly specialized and highly conservative. It was enough to kill a proposal with which other units would have to cooperate if the idea originated in one that was looking temporarily more powerful. There was a parallel problem on the wider system level, where one division was much larger and more powerful than others. Organizational and personnel innovations developed by the major division were rarely adopted by any of the others, even if they proved highly effective, because the other units were trying to protect their own territory as an independent domain.

There were also reflections of territoriality among low-power staff people on the individual level. The tendency was to hang on to a territory that provided legitimacy, even when inappropriate. One staff woman, hired to run affirmative action programs, tended to bring up the women's issue wherever she was, as though she would have no right to participate unless she dragged in her "expertise." Yet, on one occasion she had been invited to join a group of managers because of what she might contribute to general discussions of organizational issues. But she could not let go of her domain, and the managers were sorry they had included her. Similarly, sometimes staff people clung to whatever might help solve their future power issues, regardless of its relevance to present tasks. One manager asked a personnel staff official to send him an older, experienced woman for a position as his administrative assistant. Instead, the man in the personnel department insisted on sending him three ambitious, rather inexperienced younger women, making it clear that personnel matters, such as the decision about which candidates were appropriate, were his domain. However, perhaps there was something else underneath. The three women were ambitious and on the move. If he placed them fast, they owed him a favor, and because they were going to seek to move, they would have to keep coming back to him. Therefore, they were "his" candidates and represented possible future alliances.

Territorial control and domain concerns were also behind much of the treatment of secretaries at Indsco . . . ; but now it also becomes clear that relatively powerless bosses are likelier to be the ones who try to keep strong personal control over secretaries. Those secretaries who were encouraged by their bosses to seek promotions out of the secretarial ranks tended to work for the more powerful bosses.

The behavioral responses of powerless "leaders" to their situations, then, in controlling behavior, rules-mindedness, and territoriality, could make the conditions of work less satisfying for subordinates. To seek a more powerful leader could also be a way of seeking a more empowering, freedom-enhancing environment.

Cycles of Power and Powerlessness

Power rises and falls on the basis of complex exigencies: the organizational situation, environmental pressures, the simultaneous actions of others. However, in terms of individual behavior at least, power is likely to bring more power in ascending cycles, and powerlessness to generate powerlessness, in a descending cycle. The powerful have "credibility" behind their actions, so they have the capacity to get things done. Their alliances help them circumvent the more restricting aspects of the bureaucracy. They are able to be less coercive or rules-bound in their exercise of leadership, so their subordinates and clients are more likely to cooperate. They have the security of power, so they can be more generous in allowing subordinates power of their own, freedom of action. We come full circle. The powerful are not only given material and symbolic advantage but they are also provided with circumstances that can make them more effective mobilizers of other people. Thus they can accomplish and, through their accomplishments, generate more power. This means they can build alliances with other people as colleagues rather than threats, and through their alliances generate more power.

The powerless are caught in a downward spiral. The coping mechanisms of low power are also those most likely to provoke resistance and further restriction of power. The attitudes of powerlessness get translated downward, so that those under a low-power leader can also become ineffective. There was this vicious circle at Indsco: A young trainee was assigned to a "chronic complainer" of a manager, who had had organizational problems and had fallen well below the level of peers in his cohort. The trainee was talented but needed to be channeled. The manager's negativism began to transfer down to the trainee, and the young man started to lose his motivation. Nothing was done to correct the atmosphere. He became less motivated and more critical of the organization. He vented his hostility in nonconformist ways (long hair, torn clothes, general disrespect for people and things). Then people began to reinforce his negativity by focusing on what they observed: he's a "wise guy." They observed the symptoms but never looked at the real problem: the manager's situation. Finally, the trainee resigned just before he would have been terminated. Everyone breathed a sign of relief that the "problem" was gone. The manager lost even more credibility. This just reinforced his negativity and his coerciveness.

Since the behavioral responses of the powerless tend to be so ineffective as leadership styles, it would be the last rather than the first solution of most organizations to give such ineffective people more power or more responsibility. Yet all the indicators point to the negative effects of behavior that come from too little power, such as rules-mindedness and close supervision. Chris Argyris has noted that alienation and low morale accompany management's praise for the reliable (rules-obedient) rather than the enterprising (risk-taking) worker. Studies have shown that turnover varies with the degree to which supervisors structure tasks in advance and demand compliance, absenteeism with the tendency of supervisors to be "directive" and maintain close and detailed control. Yet when supervisors at Sears, Roebuck had responsibility for so many people that they could not watch any one person closely, employees responded to this greater latitude with greater job satisfaction.[28] So perhaps it is meaningful to suggest interrupting the cycle of powerlessness: to empower those in low-power situations by increasing their opportunities and their latitude rather than to continue to punish them for their ineffectiveness, reinforcing their powerless state of mind.

"Power" in organizations, as I am using the term, is synonymous with autonomy and freedom of action. The powerful can afford to risk more, and they can afford to allow others their freedom. The bureaucratic machinery of modern organizations means that there are rather few people who are really powerful. Power has become a scarce resource that most people feel they lack. Although the scramble for political advantage still distinguishes relative degrees of power, the organization places severe limits on everyone's freedom of action. The powerful get more, but they still share some of the mentality of powerlessness.

And women, in large hierarchical organizations, are especially often caught in the cycles of powerlessness.

Women and Power in Organizations

My analysis of the importance of power in large organizations and the behavioral consequences of powerlessness for management styles can help to explain some familiar clichés about women's lack of potential for organizational leadership: "No one wants to work for a woman"; and "Women are too rigid and controlling to make good bosses anyway."

Preference for Men = Preference for Power
There is considerable evidence for a general cultural attitude that men make better leaders. A large number of studies have concluded that

neither men nor women want to work for a woman (although women are readier to do so than men). In a 1965 survey of 1,000 male and 900 female executives, among *Harvard Business Review* readers, over two-thirds of the men and nearly one-fifth of the women reported that they themselves would not feel comfortable working for a woman. Very few of either sex (9 percent of the men and 15 percent of the women) thought that *men* felt comfortable working for a woman, and a proportion of the male respondents said that women did not belong in executive positions at all. A total of 51 percent of the men responded that women were "temperamentally unfit" for management, writing in gratuitous comments such as, "They scare male executives half to death. . . . As for an efficient woman manager, this is cultural blasphemy. . . ."[29] In the survey of nonexempts at Indsco, these workers, too, overwhelmingly agreed with the statement that "men make better supervisors." And they did so while also rejecting the idea that it was "unacceptable" or "unfeminine" for a woman to be a manager, as Table 16-1 indicates. Women managers were aware of this attitude. One woman at Indsco showed me a poster which she considered indicative; it was large and painted in dark, rather foreboding tones. Most of the poster was taken up by the head of a man wearing a workman's cap; he was saying furtively into a telephone, "I just quit. The new boss is a woman."

Yet when it comes to evaluating concrete leadership styles, as used by men or by women outside of organizations, research has found that there is no strong preference for men or general tendency to perceive men and women differently. In one study, subjects were asked to make judgments about male and female leaders exhibiting a variety of styles. The evalua-

Table 16–1
Attitudes of Nonexempt Employees at Indsco about Women as Supervisors†

	Mean rating of agreement with statement on 9-point scale, with 1 = strongly disagree / 9 = strongly agree	
	Men (N = 23)	Women (N = 88)
1. "Men make better supervisors."	7.92	6.50*
2. "It is acceptable for a man to be competitive, but not a woman."	3.51	3.22
3. "A woman cannot be a supervisor and feminine as well."	3.30	3.10

*The difference between the ratings of men and women on this statement was statistically significant ($p < .05$).

†Figures reported by permission of G. Homall from "The Motivation to be Promoted among Non-Exempt Employees: An Expectancy Theory Approach," Masters Thesis, Cornell University, 1974.

tions of men and women did not differ significantly on most variables, including such critical ones as "production emphasis," but there was a tendency to give higher ratings to men than to women when they "initiated structure" and higher ratings to women than men when they showed "consideration," demonstrating some propensity for raters to "reward" people for sex-stereotypical behavior. Another study used a different set of categories but had nearly identical results.

Students and bank supervisors judged stories involving male and female leaders using four different styles. The "reward" style was rated somewhat more effective when used by men, but the "friendly-dependent" style (which the researchers hoped would capture a female stereotype) was rated high for *either* sex when used with the opposite sex. The use of "threat" was considered ineffective for both sexes, though there was a slight but not significant tendency to let men get away with it more than women. It has also been found that people who have once worked for a woman boss are more likely than those who never have to be favorably disposed toward women leaders.[30] And women, as Table 16–1 above showed, are slightly more accepting of the idea of women supervisors and managers than are men. Thus, sex preferences in general seem to play only a very small role, if any, in responding to the style of any specific leader.

Theories saying that women handle power differently from men, that men are the instrumental leaders, oriented toward competition and domination through nature or childhood training, also do not match the realities of adult life in organizations. By the age of ten, for example, leadership in groups does not reflect the use of different strategies of persuasion by females and males. Nor does either sex seem more naturally cooperative or susceptible to social influence from peers.[31] There is as yet no research evidence that makes a case for sex differences in either leadership aptitude or style. A wide variety of investigations, from field studies of organizations to paper-and-pencil tests, indicates that the styles of men and women vary over the same range and that there are no conclusive sex-related strategies.[32] . . . In an organizational simulation using college students, Kay Bartol found that sex of the leader did not by itself affect follower satisfaction, even when female leaders were characterized by high dominance, a trait most likely to "offend" male subordinates.[33] In fact, if sex stereotypes were true, then an argument could be made for the greater capacity of women for leadership roles in organizations, given socialization experiences emphasizing "people-handling" skills. One study showed that members of a business school class ranking high on "masculine" interests, power seeking, and aggressiveness met with less success in large organizations than those with more "feminine" interests in interpersonal relations.

If the much greater desire for men as leaders in organizations does not reflect real sex differences in style and strategy, what does it reflect? As we have seen, people often prefer the *powerful* as leaders. As the Pelz studies at Detroit Edison showed, good human relations skills and sensitivity but low power (a likely combination for women leaders in sexist organizations) could have negative effects on morale.[34] Thus, a *preference for men is a preference for power*, in the context of organizations where women do not have access to the same opportunities for power and efficacy through activities or alliances.

As in the old cliché, everyone likes a winner; in large organizations at least, people would rather work for winners than losers. Perhaps a preference for male managers reflects a "bet" that men are more likely to emerge as winners and power-holders than women. One clever social psychological experiment offers suggestive evidence. Judges were asked to rate paintings supposedly produced by either a man or a woman, with sex of artist varied for different judges. In one condition the paintings were presented as entries in a contest; in a second they were the winning paintings. The women presented as attempting to accomplish were judged less favorably than the men, but those whose paintings had succeeded were evaluated just as favorably.[35] In the great corporate contest, then, subordinates may be "betting" on who is going to be a winner when they respond differently to the idea of women or men as bosses. It is as though followers extend "credit" in the present for imagined future payoffs. This is reminiscent of the Mark Twain tale of the Englishman with the million-pound note. He made a bet with a wealthy man that he could live well forever just on the strength of the note and without using it. Credit was given to him; people vied with each other to supply his wants; and they graciously picked up the bills. He became wealthy and successful—and he never had to cash in the million-pound note. The power that devolved on star performers backed by sponsors at Indsco worked in much the same way. The problem with women was that, first, there were doubts about how far they could go in the corporation, and second, a widespread belief that women could only be individual "movers"—i.e., even if they moved, they could not take anyone else with them.

But power wipes out sex. A woman who does acquire power stops arousing the same level of concern about whether or not she will be wanted as a leader. People who want to attach themselves to power may not even notice sex. On one occasion, a senior Indsco salesman told a long story to colleagues about a problem with a "very, very smart, tough-minded" president of a small company. The president had made good friends among a number of senior Indsco people and therefore managed to get all kinds of concessions. The salesman had to bring this to an end, as well as tell this very powerful client that there would be no credit for the material that had failed when her customers, in turn, used it. . . . It look a long time for the audience to this story to realize that the salesman was saying "she." Some even interjected comments using "he."

The salesman presented the story with such awe of the powerful customer that sex made no difference. He said later that she was someone he would eagerly work for.

The "Mean and Bossy Woman Boss" Stereotype

The other issue around women as organizational leaders also turns out to be a power issue. Perhaps the most blatant picture of the negative American stereotype of a woman boss appeared on the cover of *MBA* magazine in March 1972. *MBA*, distributed to business school students and faculty, devoted this issue, as its blurb indicated, to "Women in Business!" Shown on the cover is a Roy Lichtenstein-style comic-cartoon head of a sultry blond woman with blue eyes, bright red lips, and a low-cut, cleavage-revealing dress. Head thrown back snottily, she is saying, "You're fired!"[36]

And that's what women bosses supposedly do with their authority. No wonder no one wants one.

Abuse of power is only the first in a long list of negative characteristics attributed to women managers over the last few decades by those who don't want them. One survey of 521 young working women just before World War II uncovered so much hostility toward women bosses that even the author, Donald Laird (who thought women belonged behind a typewriter), had to conclude that there was overreaction.[37] Of the women workers, 99.81 percent said they preferred a male boss for reasons such as the following:

1. Women bosses are too jealous. Their positions go to their heads. They boss for the mere sake of bossing, to remind you they are in charge.
2. Women bosses take things too personally. They are not businesslike.
3. Women bosses are overly concerned with efficiency and routine details. They are slaves to the system. They bother about small, petty things.
4. Women bosses supervise too closely. They delegate only superficially.
5. Women bosses find more fault. They are too critical.
6. Women bosses scream to impress people with their importance.

One less prejudiced woman, who had worked for both men and women, reflected on her experiences:

> The two women bosses I've had were very lovely people and were good bosses so far as women bosses go . . . but most women bosses have [this fault, which I call] "old-maid thinking." It is eternally thinking in terms of details, not in terms of the big thing—more interested in the details of the means than in the general significance of the results. A man [gives] me a job to do, and he'll let me do it and not ask how and why and did I check with an "x" or a "v"—which is wasting time and makes me want to yell. Further, a woman boss is so everlastingly curious about my personal business: "when, how many, how late, and who" about my own social affairs. A man doesn't give a hoot just as long as I'm on the job and on my toes when I'm on it.[38]

Laird himself concluded that women make poor supervisors in factories, offices, and even at home because of their tendency to "henpeck" and become too bossy. For evidence he cited, without specific reference, a study showing that being "too dictatorial" was a fault in twice as many women as men in the general population.

Burleigh Gardner, a human relations expert also writing during the war, when women entered formerly closed jobs, found similar complaints by both men and women about women bosses, although he felt that the system forced women into positions where they were likely to fail. His respondents said that women were too emotional, unfriendly, critical, strict, and petty. The National Manpower Council's report on "Womanpower" in the 1950s concluded that women supervisors were said to be more demanding and controlling of subordinates as well as guilty of partiality and discrimination. British surveys show the same thing.[39] And this refrain echoed through my interviews at Indsco.

Stereotypes persist even in the face of evidence negating them. The *real* extent of bossiness among women in authority in organizations may have little to do with the persistence of the stereotype, but this particular portrait has one very important characteristic. *It is a perfect picture of people who are powerless. Powerlessness tends to produce those very characteristics attributed to women bosses.*

A careful look at comparisons between men and women supposedly in the same position shows that what looks like sex differences may really be power differences. It has been hard to test this directly, partly because there are so few women managers, especially in the same organizational positions as men. (Rarity itself, as we see in the next chapter, creates a very different situation for the person who is rare.) One recent investigation, however, did find an organizational setting in which women leaders were more common: high school departments in Florida public schools. The research covered 205 teachers and 40 department heads (25 male and 15 female) in small departments with a roughly equal sex distribution. The first interesting finding was that on the usual measures of leadership style (like taking action, providing emotional support, and so forth), operating styles could not be distinguished by sex. However, there was one statistically significant sex-linked difference in group climate: there was a slightly greater tendency for women leaders to be perceived as generating a tight and controlled atmosphere. Departments headed by men were perceived as slightly higher in "esprit and intimacy"—a good indicator of morale; those headed by women, in "hindrance"—an indicator that the leader was thought to get in the way, to intrude too much, rather than to promote subordinates' autonomy and flexibility.[40] In short, the research uncovered a watered-down version of the bossiness complaint. Where could it have come from?

The difference in atmosphere in the woman-run departments can be traced directly to differences in organizational power of the men and women leaders, although the author of the research did not see this. Mobility prospects, the likelihood that department heads would be moving up in the system, were strikingly different for the men and women in this set of high schools. For one thing, there were no women *above* the level of department head in the whole county. Second, the women seemed to have moved to their last position. They had risen into the headship more slowly than the men; they were older, had put in more time teaching, and had spent a longer time in their previous jobs. At the same time, they had more limited aspirations; one-seventh of the women, in contrast to half of the men, expressed a desire for further promotions. Thus, the men and the women managers were not really in comparable positions. The women were much less mobile and much more powerless. And the powerless are handicapped in leadership.

Women at Indsco in exempt positions where they had organizational accountability or leadership responsibilities were differentially in the most powerless situations. They were primarily first-line supervisors of secretaries or clerical workers or they held staff jobs in personnel or public relations functions. There were no other women with line responsibilities and no women above grade 14, with the exception of a senior researcher. They were more likely to lack powerful alliances, and they reported constantly having to fight off the tendency for the organization to "protect" them by encapsulating them in safe situations. Statistics on the distributions of men and women in organizational functions . . . make clear how common this situation is. Women, when they do achieve managerial or leadership positions, are clustered in the low-power situations. It should not be surprising if they adopt the behavior of the powerless.

It is not only their own relative power that determines the behavior of managers but also the behavior and feeling of powerlessness of those above and below. The relationship with their own superiors is important in shaping the responses of those who supervise too closely. One such generalization about where most women bosses are found is that they are located in tightly supervised and rules-conscious hierarchies. The "female" professions, like nursing, social work, and primary school teaching, all feature close supervisory hierarchies and concern with detail. Government agencies, where more women managers are found than in private business, epitomize bureaucracy in civil service structure, endless red tape, and concern with rules and regulations. Women managers in these settings are likely to themselves be subject to bossy bosses and may take this restriction of their power out on their own subordinates, perpetuating the style downward. Simultaneously, they learn bossiness as a leadership style from their own role models. In corporations like Indsco, where women managers are so rare as to be tokens . . . they themselves may be watched more closely, so that again the restriction of their own latitude of conduct may be transmitted to subordinates.

Simultaneously, powerless feelings of subordinates are translated upward to leaders. Most women managers are likely to manage relatively powerless subordinates: clerical workers, women factory workers, low-level personnel. Powerless subordinates may take out their own frustration in resistance to their managers, provoking them to adopt more coercive styles. The powerless may also resent a boss's advantage, particularly if they think that they could just as easily be the boss. One woman at Indsco who had not attended college was forthright about her hostility toward "credentialed" women brought in to manage her department as a result of affirmative action efforts, while she was still held back. She resented the special treatment they were getting. Women who are jealous of another woman's promotion and try to let her know she's really no better than they may instead provoke her to try to demonstrate her superiority and her control. This is the "lording it over us" behavior some women have complained of in women bosses. From the subordinate's perspective, it is hard to be generously happy about the success of someone getting a chance denied to you. From the boss's perspective, it is hard to share power with people who resent you. The combination of these two viewpoints produces controlling, directive bosses.

Futhermore, people who feel vulnerable and unsure of themselves, who are plunged into jobs without sufficient training or experience, regardless of the official authority they are given, are more likely to first adopt authoritarian-controlling leadership styles. The behavior attributed to women supervisors is likely to be characteristic of new and insecure supervisors generally. Gardner saw this in his World War II studies, when the demands of war production brought inexperienced women into formerly all-male positions. He observed that many people complained about the bossiness of women supervisors but concluded that newly promoted men given supervisory jobs without sufficient training also showed these tendencies.

> Any new supervisor who feels unsure of himself, who feels that his boss is watching him critically, is likely to demand perfect behavior and performance from his people, to be critical of minor mistakes, and to try too hard to please his boss. A woman supervisor, responding to the insecurity and uncertainty of her position as a woman, knowing that she is being watched both critically and doubtfully, feels obliged to try even harder. And for doing this she is said to be "acting just like a woman."[41]

Without the experience or confidence to permit the minor deviations from the rules that in fact make the system work and without enough knowledge and faith in outcomes to loosen control, new managers may be prone to be too directive, controlling, and details-oriented.

In a variety of ways, then, powerlessness stemming from organizational circumstance breeds a particular leadership style caricatured in the stereotype of the bossy woman. This style reflects the situation more than sex, however—if the stereotype carries even a grain of truth—for men who are powerless behave in just the same ways. As Elizabeth Janeway pointed out, "The *weak* are the second sex."[42]

The problem of power thus is critical to the effective behavior of people in organizations. Power issues occupy center stage not because individuals are greedy for more, but because some people are incapacitated without it.

Notes

1. Donald C. Pelz, "Influence: A Key to Effective Leadership in the First-Line Supervisor," *Personnel* 29 (1952), pp. 3–11.
2. Joan E. Crowley, Teresa E. Levitan, and Robert P. Quinn, "Seven Deadly Half-Truths About Women," *Psychology Today* 7 (March 1973); William F. Whyte and Burleigh Gardner, "The Man in the Middle," *Applied Anthropology* 4 (Spring 1945), pp. 1–28.
3. The study of negativity: John W. Thibaut and Henry W. Riecken, "Authoritarianism, Status, and the Communication of Aggression," *Human Relations* 8 (1955), pp. 95–120. The study of professionals: Jacob I. Hurwitz, Alvin F. Zander, and Bernard Hymovitch, "Some Effects of Power on the Relations Among Group Members," in *Group Dynamics*, D. Cartwright and A. Zander, eds. (New York: Harper & Row, 1968). See also R. Lippit, N. Polansky, and S. Rosen, "The Dynamics of Power," *Human Relations* 5 (1952), pp. 44–50; this is a classic study.
4. Michel Crozier, *The Bureaucratic Phenomenon* (Chicago: University of Chicago Press, 1964), p. 164.
5. Charles Perrow has also analyzed the ways in which changing technical requirements affect organizational authority structures in his studies of hospitals. See Perrow, "Hospitals: Technology, Structures, and Goals," in *Handbook of Organizations*, J. G. March, ed. (Chicago: Rand McNally, 1965); and Perrow, "The Analysis of Goals in Complex Organizations," *American Sociological Review* 26 (1961), pp. 854–66. James Thompson made a similar point with respect to business in *Organizations in Action* (New York: McGraw-Hill, 1967).
6. In a system of sponsored mobility, elites or their agents choose recruits early and then carefully induct them into elite status. Ralph H. Turner, "Sponsored and Contest Mobility in the School System," *American Sociological Review* 25 (December 1960), pp. 855–67.
7. Margaret Cussler, *The Woman Executive* (New York: Harcourt, Brace, 1958); Margaret Hennig, *Career Development for Women Executives*, Unpublished Doctoral Dissertation, Harvard Business School, 1970; Michael Fogarty, A. I. Allen, Isobel Allen, and Patricia Walters, *Women in Top Jobs: Four Studies in Achievement* (London: George Allen and Unwin, 1971).
8. Paul Cowan, "Connecticut's Governor Grasso Remembers How She Made It," *New York Times*, May 4, 1975.
9. The evidence that social similarity and compatibility affects a leader's evaluation of followers or subordinates comes from a variety of situations. Borgatta found that high acceptability to a supervisor at the social level was associated with receiving high ratings from him in an all-male sample; Edgar Borgatta, "Analysis of Social Interaction and Socio-metric Perception," *Sociometry* 17 (February 1954), pp. 7–32. A study of staff nurses and their supervisors in three hospitals discovered that friendship with supervisors was a greater determinant of high evaluations than shared work attitudes and values. Ronald Corwin, Marvin J. Taves, and J. Eugene Haas, "Social Requirements for Occupational

Success: Internalized Norms and Friendships," *Social Forces* 39 (1961), pp. 135–40. The cause-effect relationship is not clear in these studies, of course.

10. Stein, "Getting There: Patterns in Managerial Success," Working Paper, Center for Research on Women, Wellesley College, 1976.

11. Stein, "Getting There: Patterns in Managerial Success."

12. Whyte and Gardner, "Man in the Middle." See also Donald R. Wray, "Marginal Men of Industry, the Foremen," *American Journal of Sociology* 54 (January 1949), pp. 298–301.

13. See Melville Dalton, "Conflicts between Staff and Line Managerial Officers," *American Sociological Review* 21 (June 1950), pp. 342–51.

14. Sidney Reynolds, "Women on the Line," *MBA* 9 (February 1975), pp. 27–30.

15. Robert Presthus, *The Organizational Society* (New York: Knopf, 1962), p. 35.

16. Karen Horney, *The Neurotic Personality of Our Time* (New York: Norton, 1937), pp. 163–70.

17. Rollo May, *Power and Innocence* (New York: Norton, 1972).

18. Stanley A. Hetzler, "Variations in Role-Playing Patterns Among Different Echelons of Bureaucratic Leaders," *American Sociological Review* 20 (December 1955), pp. 700–706.

19. Crozier, *Bureaucratic Phenomenon*, pp. 122–23.

20. Franz Fanon, *The Wretched of the Earth* (New York: Grove Press, 1965).

21. B. Goodstadt and D. Kipnis, "Situational Influences on the Use of Power," *Journal of Applied Psychology* 54 (1970), pp. 201–207; B. Goodstadt and L. Hjelle, "Power to the Powerless: Locus of Control and the Use of Power," *Journal of Personality and Social Psychology* 27 (July 1973), pp. 190–96.

22. Thibaut and Riecken, "Authoritarianism, Status, and the Communication of Aggression." Chow and Grusky, in a laboratory simulation with complicated results, found that worker compliance (the degree of productivity and the degree of aggressiveness) shaped supervisory style, especially closeness of supervision and adoption of a punitive style; there were complex interaction phenomena in the data. Esther Chow and Oscar Grusky, "Worker Compliance and Supervisory Style: An Experimental Study of Female Superior-Subordinate Relationships," Paper presented at the 1973 Meetings of the American Sociological Association. Blau and Scott also pointed out that a group's low productivity may be a cause of supervisory style, as well as a result. Peter M. Blau and W. Richard Scott, *Formal Organizations* (San Francisco: Chandler, 1962), p. 50.

23. Crozier, *Bureaucratic Phenomenon*, p. 188.

24. Robert K. Merton, "Bureaucratic Structure and Personality," in *Social Theory and Social Structure*, rev. ed. (Glencoe, Illinois: Free Press, 1957).

25. Melville Dalton, *Men Who Manage* (New York: Wiley, 1959), p. 247.

26. Merton, "Bureaucratic Structure and Personality."

27. Crozier, *Bureaucratic Phenomenon*, pp. 40–42.

28. Chris Argyris, *Integrating the Individual and the Organization* (New York: Wiley, 1964); M. Argyle, G. Gardner, and I. Cioffi, "Supervisory Methods Related to Productivity, Absenteeism, and Labor Turnover," *Human Relations* 11 (1958), pp. 23–40; study by E. Fleishman and E. Harris cited in Charles Hampden-Turner, "The Factory as an Oppressive Environment," in *Workers' Control: A Reader on Labor and Social Change*, G. Hunnius, G. D. Garson, and J. Case, eds. (New York: Vintage, 1973), pp. 30–44. The Sears study was James Worthy, "Organizational Structure and Employee Morale," *American Sociological Review* 15 (1950), pp. 169–79.

29. G. W. Bowman, N. B. Worthy, and S. A. Greyser, "Are Women Executives People?," *Harvard Business Review* 43 (July–August 1965), pp. 14–30. The preference for male bosses was also a finding of National Manpower Council, *Womanpower* (New York: Columbia University Press, 1957), pp. 104–6.

30. The first study is Kathryn M. Bartol and D. Anthony Butterfield, "Sex Effects in Evaluating Leaders," Working Paper No. 74-10, University of Massachusetts School of Business Administration, 1974. The second is Benson Rosen and Thomas H. Jerdee, "The

Influence of Sex-Role Stereotypes on Evaluations of Male and Female Supervisory Behavior," *Journal of Applied Psychology* 57 (1973), pp. 44–48.

31. Eleanor Emmons Maccoby and Carol Nagy Jacklin, *The Psychology of Sex Differences* (Stanford, California: Stanford University Press, 1974), pp. 261, 361.

32. Michel Crozier, *The World of the Office Worker*, trans. David Landau (Chicago: University of Chicago Press, 1971); D. R. Day and R. M. Stogdill, "Leader Behavior of Male and Female Supervisors: A Comparative Study," *Personal Psychology* 25 (1972), pp. 353–60; Cecile Roussell, "Relationship of Sex of Department Head to Department Climate," *Administrative Science Quarterly* 19 (June 1974), pp. 211–20.

33. Kathryn M. Bartol, "Male Versus Female Leaders: The Effect of Leader Need for Dominance on Follower Satisfaction," *Academy of Management Journal* 17 (June 1974), pp. 225–33; and "The Effect of Male Versus Female Leaders on Follower Satisfaction and Performance," *Journal of Business Research* 3 (January 1975), pp. 33–42.

34. Pelz, "Influence."

35. Gail I. Pheterson, Sara B. Kiesler, and Philip A. Goldberg, "Evaluation of the Performance of Women as a Function of Their Sex, Achievement, and Personal History," *Journal of Personality and Social Psychology* 19 (September 1971), pp. 114–18.

36. *MBA* 6 (March 1972).

37. Donald A. Laird, with Eleanor C. Laird, *The Psychology of Supervising the Working Woman* (New York: McGraw-Hill, 1942), pp. 175–79.

38. Laird, *The Psychology of Supervising the Working Woman*, p. 31.

39. Burleigh B. Gardner, *Human Relations in Industry* (Chicago: Richard D. Irwin, 1945), pp. 269–71; National Manpower Council, *Womanpower* (New York: Columbia University Press, 1957), p. 106; and the British reference is Fogarty et al., *Women in Top Jobs*, p. 15.

40. Roussell, "Relationship of Sex of Department Head to Department Climate."

41. Gardner, *Human Relations*, pp. 270–71.

42. Elizabeth Janeway, "The Weak are the Second Sex," *Atlantic Monthly* (December 1973), and *In Between Myth and Morning* (New York: William Morrow, 1974).

17
Female Tokenism in the Volunteer Army

Michael L. Rustad

The United States military, in a sharp break with tradition, expanded and diversified the role of servicewomen in the 1970s. A generation ago the issue facing the services was racial integration. Today the services must cope with sexual integration, not out of choice but of necessity. The end of the draft in 1973 presented the military with the problem of meeting recruitment quotas of over four hundred thousand persons each year. Their solution to make the new volunteer force succeed was to include women in unprecedented numbers. During the 1970s, the United States military enlisted an average of thirty-five thousand women each year. Women took jobs that the Defense Department formerly had considered male domains, such as maintenance, electronics, and telecommunications. These advances, however, can obscure the function women soldiers fulfilled as a reserve army of last resort. The military, after all, included women in significant numbers in order to solve their recruitment dilemma, not as a response to the feminist movement.

This means, on the one hand, that when the unemployment rate is low and male high school graduates are difficult to attract, the military turns to women to fill its ranks. On the other hand, when the unemployment rate is high, the military can recruit highly qualified men with less difficulty, thus less emphasis is placed on expanding the role of military women. In the 1970s, the Defense Department failed to meet its authorized quotas despite outlays of tens of billions of dollars for increased pay, bonuses, and media campaigns. Large numbers of women joining the volunteer military constituted its margin of success. However, in the early 1980s, as the unemployment rate increased, the services met and exceeded their quota of highly qualified males. Consequently, fewer females were recruited. During the first six months of fiscal year 1981, the services recruited 16,300 more qualified males than in the previous year. In the same period, 1,600 fewer female high school graduates were recruited.[1]

In February 1981, the Department of the Army instituted a freeze on the expansion of military women, a policy it termed "Womanpause."[2] In August 1982, an additional twenty-three army occupations were recommended closed to women; these jobs of high civilian opportunity included aerial photography, plumbing, masonry, carpentry, diving, surveying, and quarrying.[3] In November 1982, the Army Policy Review Group recommended a ceiling of 10 percent on the proportion of women (seventy thousand women soldiers). Unfortunately, this instrumental use of military women prohibits natural expansion of their career opportunities; women soldiers are thus confined to permanent token status.

Artificial ceilings like Womanpause guarantee that women will be greatly outnumbered by men in their primary work unit. The army's ceiling of 10 percent female strength means that men outnumber women by a ratio of more than ten to one. Rosabeth Kanter documents the ill effects of tokenism in *Men and Women of the Corporation*. She found that organizations with a ratio of less than fifteen females to eighty-five males set into motion problems of powerlessness and isolation. Token women were unable to generate alliances and support structures that would allow them to fight dominant males. Kanter notes that in any situation where proportions of significant types of people are highly skewed, similar themes and processes can be produced. Kanter hypothesizes that in organizations with a ratio of sixty-five to thirty-five, tokens become minorities. Minority members have the necessary numbers to form allies and action-based identifications.[4]

Khaki Town: The Setting

In Spring 1978, I examined the structure of female tokenism in the United States Army in Europe.[5] Khaki Town is the name I use for the composite of four American military bases in southwestern Germany that provide tactical communications support for more than 234,000 United States troops in Europe. The physical layout of Khaki Town is typical for an American base. Geographically isolated from the neighboring civilian community, the base is a self-contained unit. Service people usually shop at the post exchange and commissary, worship at the "all-faiths" chapel, and live in drab barracks and apartments on base—especially when stationed overseas and confronted with a language barrier. Khaki Town's geographic isolation is thus coupled with cultural distance from the nearby German civilian population. Khaki Town, as it relates to the possibilities afforded by European culture, is like a turtle with a tucked-in head. Therefore, the inhabitants of Khaki Town depend on their immediate environment for cultural sustenance.

From 1975 to spring 1978, nearly three hundred women had been assigned to field-intensive Signal Corps units of Khaki Town. While I did not have access to official military data, my best estimate is that between 70 and 90 percent of the women initially assigned to those units had left their electronic communication specialties by spring 1978.[6] Women were sent to Khaki Town units with little attempt from the higher command to insulate them from the adverse effects of tokenism. Although the United States Army knew of sex-role tensions, it frequently took the stand that women were responsible for any problems that arose. The *Final Report* of the Army Administration Center in 1978 identified the following issues as possible limitations of women: size, strength, grip, arm and leg length, endurance, coordination, aggressiveness, toughness, mechanical ability, pregnancy, and self-image.[7] A passage from the *Final Report* reflects this "blaming the victim" position:

> Sexual fraternization is an inevitable consequence of the widespread integration of women throughout the Army. . . . Cited as especially vulnerable to the problems of sex fraternization are mixed gender teams or small units with remote, isolated missions. Of grave concern are the speculative effects on combat potency. Widespread rage is also feared in stressful situations.
>
> Women are distractive [sic] to men and as long as the ratio of men to women in the Army remains large, many male soldiers if not the majority, will accept women as women, but not as soldiers.[8]

Yet nowhere does the army's *Final Report* bring up the potential benefits of increasing the percentage of military women. Because the average woman recruit is brighter, more likely to have a high school diploma, and less likely to be involved in an early marriage, female recruits are important to the army in maintaining at least some convergence with a civilian population of young adults. Why doesn't the military consider employing more women? Perhaps because a recommendation to balance the proportions of the sexes would contradict the dictates of the reserve army policy. The case study of Khaki Town illustrates the consequences of constraining the number of female soldiers. Paralleling Kanter's study, Khaki Town women soldiers faced isolation from the work culture, heightened visibility, mistaken identity, and opposition from enlisted male culture in the form of paternalism and sexual shakedowns. In addition, these women took on character forms set in motion by the structure of tokenism. The following sections describe how male enlisted culture made it difficult for women to perform female and work roles at the same time.

Isolation from Work Culture

The military male knew his own position and the exact position of everyone with whom he came into contact. The uniform told him where he fit into the whole scheme of things. When a woman wore the uniform her position was marginal. Women were strangers to enlisted male culture and entered unfamiliar domains.

A female entering this situation was evaluated as to her strength, emotional control, and motives for taking a man's job. A forty-year-old sergeant expressed the problem of entering each new job as a stranger:

> I have been in the army now nearly six years and each time I move to another duty station I must prove myself all over again. I must prove that I have the stamina to pull my own weight. Each time they work on you to see whether you can take it, being a woman and all. They would not put all of that bull on a new guy. The common view is that no woman can possibly take it. The only reason why we joined was to get married or run around. We have to break traditional views on women's roles; cope with male supremacy. We have to fill too many roles at one time.

A twenty-five-year-old staff sergeant found that men constantly tested her when she first came to a unit: "If a woman is the first to come to a Company, she must work under the constant scrutiny of males. She must watch out. She must guard every conversation and be careful about who she talks to or runs with."

The typical woman soldier entered an all-male unit with no friendly person to meet and help her. On the contrary, being female tended to arouse ridicule and resentment. A voice-intercept operator expressed the dilemma facing the first women in men's jobs: "We have to prove that we're not enlisted whores or lesbians. Some men prey upon us when we are new to a company for dates. If we go out with them, then we are whores to the other men. If we refuse, we are labeled lesbians."

The following comments of women soldiers represent the widespread feelings of women who had to confront assignments as strangers.

> Women are regarded as novelties or freaks when they first come to a unit.
>
> Supervisors ignore us and hope we'll go away.
>
> Guys expect us to do physically more than we're capable of. They constantly test our capacity as soldiers.
>
> We have to put up with hostile stares by the dependent wives when we go to the commissary, PX (post exchange), and the hospital. They don't know how to take us.
>
> In the beginning of each new assignment immature enlisted men won't return my salutes.
>
> We aren't accepted in the military community. Wives see us as threats and make comments.
>
> We want acceptance as individuals rather than as someone's wife, mother, or lover. They never see us as adults and capable soldiers.
>
> We are treated as sexual objects rather than as competent supervisees.
>
> There are continual complaints about our presence.
>
> Being token women, we have to prove ourselves.
>
> We are overly protected, so we are never given the chance to prove ourselves.
>
> We are categorized. I'm an individual and don't approve of being categorized. They categorize us as "get overs" regardless of our rank and experience.
>
> We are mistrusted by the military community, especially by the married men's wives.
>
> The initial attitude of males is that we are sent here for their pleasure and abuse. We must always be content with that image, before we can get to work.

All respondents were asked, "Do women have to prove themselves in new military assignments, just because they are women?" Eighty-four percent of the females replied affirmatively, versus only one-third of the males. Eighty of the ninety-one women in the sample (88 percent) had seen negative male attitudes thwart women in their military jobs, and 87 percent of the males (108 of 141) had seen women experience difficulties due to negative male attitudes.

Heightened Visibility of Army Women

Women soldiers in Khaki Town experienced what Kanter termed "heightened visibility." Women stand out in the military and are noticed more because of their low numbers.[9] They are intensely scrutinized from both official and unofficial sources. Women are the objects of countless military surveys and human relations seminars—and the subject of rumor, innuendo, and ridicule. In the 1960s, black soldiers were the subject of heightened visibility. Discriminatory conditions led to black rebellion in Camp Lejeune, Mannheim, Long Binh, Kitty Hawk, and other military bases.[10] In the 1970s, a rising proportion of black entrants in the military coincided with a decrease in racial tensions. In 1978, human relations offices in the United States Army in Europe reported that racial discrimination complaints had decreased since the early 1970s by up to 500 percent in some units. During the same period, sexual harassment and sex discrimination complaints increased three to five times.[11] If male-female tension is the emerging crucible for the full expression of enlisted hostility, women are serving the latent function of "scapegoats." When black and white male soldiers realign the boundaries of enlisted culture to exclude women, they unwittingly develop mutual dependencies. Sex-role exclusivism is less dangerous to the military than racial confrontation because women do not have the numbers to fight back.

Military women receive undue attention from special study groups that deal with problems women face—pregnancy, parenthood, and physical stamina requirements. This deflects attention from the enlisted male population. For the Defense Department as a whole, females were almost twice as likely as males to be in the top two categories of military aptitude. In the army, 44 percent of the male recruits did not have a high school diploma versus only 10 percent of the females.[12] In addition, during the first four years of the volunteer force, 608,000 males were absent without leave for a period greater than thirty days. Nearly 25 percent of all enlisted men used drugs or alcohol during work hours at least once per year; one out of four male soldiers missed at least one day of work due to alcohol abuse.[13] In contrast, women were the all-volunteer military's margin of success. They helped to alleviate the problems of numbers, quality, social representativeness, and social control in the volunteer army. Nevertheless, military women were the subject of official concern. The army's Womanpause policy resulted in part from complaints by field commanders that national security was diminished by women's issues such as female clothing, child care, and attrition from physically demanding jobs.[14] The presence of women soldiers drew attention away from the inadequacies of male soldiers, the real "problem" for the volunteer military. Women soldiers made excellent scapegoats because they were alone or nearly alone in their work units. Less than 0.5 percent of females were in senior noncommissioned officer ranks.[15] Thus, not only were women outnumbered, but also they lacked the organizational power to exercise influence and control over their social condition.

In Khaki Town, women soldiers experienced the negative consequences of being seen as a unique management problem. In the army, such visibility is always a disadvantage. To go unnoticed is to escape guard duty, charge of quarters detail, or cleanup details. Women did not have the option of keeping low profiles; their small numbers set them apart. "Being a woman is tough here. It gets pretty bad when your supervisor asks you, 'Well, how do you want to be treated today? Are you on the rag or anything? What you need is a good lay!'"

Sometimes the increased visibility turned into outright hostility. One such incident occurred when a woman was removing a tire from a two-and-a-half-ton truck.

> I was making progress, but I needed a little oil on one of the lug nuts, which had rusted tight. I went into the motor pool to get the oil and when I returned two of my male coworkers had entirely removed the wheel. They left without talking to me, but I overheard one guy say, "I say, equal pay for equal work. Why don't they get women the hell out of the army!"

Mistaken Identity

Another dimension of tokenism found in Khaki Town was the phenomenon of "mistaken identity," or inaccurate attribution. The following examples were cases of mistaken identity found in Kanter's study of women in corporate life: (1) the fact that women are not expected to be doing what they are doing, (2) the surprise that occurs when women are found in "male roles" or realms, (3) the confusion about the difference between work roles and sexual roles.[16]

During the course of my fieldwork in Khaki Town, a case of mistaken identity was reported by the *Army Times*. Apparently, a widespread belief among male soldiers in the Signal Corps and in other units was that female soldiers would not have to remain in their units if war were to occur. Female soldiers were thought to be among the persons who would be evacuated along with dependent wives and children in case of attack. General Bernard W. Rogers, the Army Chief of Staff, affirmed that women soldiers would be deployed in the case of war.[17]

In February 1978, Signal Corps units were being readied for "wargames," which were brief field maneuvers. I observed that several women were not even informed that their units were being deployed. Others were left behind to work in the mail room. In other instances, women were not deployed with their electronic repair teams; instead they were sent to the main site to type or transmit telephone messages. Because all these women had trained for tactical communications, it can be assumed that they were not deployed to be clerks and typists. Yet, supervisors appeared to "mistake" them for maids, clerks, typists, and civilian dependents—or chose not to see them at all.

Such mistaken identity occurred over and over again. Although all ninety-one female subjects had attended special army schools to learn khaki-collared (i.e. the traditionally male field-trained) specialties in communications warfare, twenty-five of them had been assigned to work as mail clerks or at other "pink-collar" jobs. As one of the few male supervisors sympathetic to women stated: "Instead of giving women a chance to perform their duties to their full potential, some supervisors constantly give them boring and demoralizing tasks."

An E-4 telecommunications specialist, one of three women chosen to attend a special military intelligence school, related the following story, which dramatizes the problem that women soldiers were not expected to be doing what they were doing.

> I guess they were not used to having women in the school. The barracks where the women were staying was located a half mile from the rest of the base. One day I was walking to work and was stopped by a colonel in a jeep who yelled, "Hey corporal, get over here. What's the matter down there? Don't you know Army hair-cut regs?"
>
> I replied, "Yes sir, I do!" He started yelling again and I interrupted him. "But my hair-cut is regulation—for a woman!" He started to turn red and then it dawned on him, that he had mistaken me for a man.

A woman radio reporter described how women in her barracks once waited three hours for a general inspection: "The men get inspected first and they forgot all about us!" In another case, a Signal Corps woman was referred to a veterans' hospital in the United States for treatment. At the admissions desk, she had the following conversation with a male administrative clerk:

> *Woman Soldier*: I have been referred here from Fort . . .
> *Clerk*: But you are a female!
> *Woman Soldier*: You must have heard of them before. They are in the army you know!
> *Clerk*: But *we've* never had one before.

The above incident reflects the awkward and serious problem of mistaken identity that females faced in a predominantly male environment. Women had to constantly articulate the soldier role so that they would not be mistaken for helpless females.

Boundary Heightening: Keeping Women Out

Many of the males were anything but happy to have the women in their midst. The men saw the women—especially those who did their Signal Corps jobs well—as a threat to the sanctity of their male universe. Males learned that they could protect "dominant culture" by exaggerating the masculine character of the army. Kanter's study of token women in the corporation revealed that dominant males protected boundaries by emphasizing and exaggerating those cultural elements they shared in contrast to the token. The presence of token women provided the context for revivifying male culture. The importance of male bonds was most pronounced in training programs and at dinners and cocktail parties during training meetings.[18]

The inclusion of women in the Signal Corps created social stresses for both sexes. Beginning with basic training, the women soldiers of Khaki Town found enlisted male culture hostile. An important part of enlisted male culture in the United States Army was the use of a lexicon of vulgar and dehumanizing references to women and sexual intercourse. In basic training, males who did not perform well were labeled "women." Prior to the introduction of women, enlisted culture had begun to change. Janowitz's study, *The Professional Soldier*, first described the slow and continuing transformation of authoritarian discipline in the military to a more civilianized management of soldiers.[19] On the one hand, uncalled for in the new technically oriented military are the coercive disciplinary tactics used in the past. On the other, the traditional male enlisted culture that celebrated physical strength and endurance became outmoded, an inappropriate response to the manners and customs of a bureaucratic military. This shift from raw domination to persuasion, manipulation, and engineered group consensus was therefore viewed by many male soldiers as the death of the "real army."

The military has found that educational level, rather than physical strength, best predicts whether or not a recruit can learn a military job. For the Department of Defense, nearly one-third of its recruits from 1974 to 1979 were male high school dropouts.[20] In contrast, females were ideally suited as a reserve army when it was difficult to recruit qualified males. The inclusion of women then provided the occasion for reviving the swaggering and sartorial enlisted culture that was under attack by contemporary military management. Because women recruits scored higher on military aptitude tests and were better educated, they symbolized the erosion of the old army. Token women provided both the audience and the justification for reasserting hypermasculine values.

One way to protect the boundaries of male enlisted culture was to redefine the roles of women soldiers in traditional terms. The male soldiers of Khaki Town developed two strategies of boundary maintenance: paternalism and sexual harassment.

Paternalism: Sergeant Daddy Warbucks

Some supervisors encouraged women to abandon the struggle to be real soldiers by excusing them from physically demanding jobs. The following account exemplifies how some women received special treatment from supervisors.

It was an uncommonly humid day, and two women were mowing the lawn in front of Khaki Town headquarters. I was inside, in the office of the company commander, when a male colonel called and asked the commander, "Why do you have these women mowing the lawn in this heat?" Fifteen minutes later, two males from another unit appeared in the commander's office and reported that they had been sent to relieve the women.

Despite the trivial nature of this incident, similar examples were remembered by the men. Men would later report to me that they were forced to "take up the slack" for women who could not do their jobs. Significantly, some paternalistic supervisors excused women from male-oriented military duties such as field exercises and war games. It was also apparent that the phenomenon of "mistaken identity" was a thinly disguised strategy to keep women out of traditionally male jobs. Male supervisors did not consider women soldiers integral to their units and did not train them in such duties as guarding the perimeter, assembling radio antennas, and changing tires on two-and-a-half-ton trucks.

Why did men render paternalistic assistance to females? One woman sergeant stated, "Men really feel outdone when a woman performs her duties better than he does." Another woman thought men felt so threatened that they deliberately rigged the work setting so that women would fail. Women soldiers were not really "getting over" as the enlisted men thought. Rather, they were "getting cooled out" of the traditionally male domain under the guise of paternalism.

Sergeant Seducto

More than half of the women (forty-seven) reported that they had been sexually harassed by supervisors. One enlisted woman complained that the way for a woman to get ahead in the army was to sleep with her supervisor. "They'll promote you if they can get down with you," she said. Another woman reported that as soon as she arrived in Khaki Town and took her orders to her sergeant, he looked first at them and then at her. "Sorry about that," he said to her. "No, we can't have an affair. I already have someone."

In Khaki Town, jokes, gestures, and leers could and did occur in any context, both on and off duty. These incidents were not reported to higher command because of the fear of male retaliation, especially from males of higher rank. A mechanic who worked in the Khaki Town motor pool described the continual uneasiness she felt working alone with a group of men who were continually testing her.

> At first they are very apprehensive, the way they are talking to you. You can tell they are talking down to you. I always think to myself, "Here we go again." Then there are others who want to be your friend. Do they want a sexual encounter or do they really want to help?"

Many of the female soldiers commented that they had difficulties with supervisors. One woman related the reality shock of discovering that her soldier role had been sexualized.

> My drill instructor was screwing three of the girls in our class and gave them preferential treatment. He propositioned me, but he turned me off. He really turned me off to the army. I had planned to work hard, but learned you didn't have to be together to get somewhere in the army.

Kanter found that women of the corporation were audiences for tales of sexual prowess.[21] Female soldiers, however, were the very targets of harassment. A great number of women in Khaki Town units commented on day-to-day testing by male soldiers.

> First, I have the biggest problem just being a woman around here. A girl can't be herself without harassment. Males make us feel weird. Many guys will make derogatory comments with sexual connotations to them.
>
> This incident happened when I was in the States. Every time I went into the supply closet, Sgt. ——— followed me. First he tried to put his arm around me. I let him get away with it the first time. I thought maybe he's just a "touchie-feelie" type of person and I don't want to hurt his feelings if he's sincere. Well, one day he grabbed me. I told him, "That isn't the reason why I'm in the army. If you want a piece of ass, look elsewhere."
>
> I don't know about J———. He'll do weird things once in a while. I'll go to the motor pool and he'll grab me around the waist and squeeze me so hard that it hurts. Then he'll let me go and walk away muttering, "Thanks, I needed that." It's weird. I don't quite know how to react.

Social Types of Army Women

The male soldiers of Khaki Town found that they could protect enlisted culture by defining the roles women had to play. A knowledge of the role accommodations of army women is helpful in understanding the deleterious effects of tokenism.

Army woman was really a contradiction in terms according to enlisted males; you were either a woman or you were in the army, according to the stereotype. At the unit level, this was translated by a Khaki Town radio operator as meaning, "If I don't like a certain group of guys because they're too pushy, I am labeled as a 'dyke.' If I date a lot, I'm a whore!" The dyke and whore stereotypes correspond to male prejudices.

The female soldiers in Signal Corps jobs were initiated into two conflicting traditions, female socialization and traditional military culture. Women in these jobs faced a double bind. If they succeeded in their jobs, doubt was cast on their femininity. If they failed, their sex role was affirmed at the expense of their work role. As in Kanter's study, tokens became encapsulated in limited roles that gave them the security of a "place" but constrained their areas of permissible or rewarded action.[22]

Amplifying Femininity

Daddy's Little Girl

Women entering khaki-collar military jobs such as the Signal Corps lack cultural guidelines as to how to adapt successfully. While males have well-developed support systems to teach them how to deal with field duty, encroachments on time, and assaults on identity, women lack a support network.

By simultaneously attempting to fulfill roles as soldiers and as women, the Signal Corps women found that they were subject to the brunt of male discreditation. One solution to the status contradiction of being a woman in a male job within the military is to allow the soldier role to wither away. By exaggerating "femaleness," token females may find willing male role partners such as the "Daddy Warbucks" type. When women voluntarily withdraw their claims to martial roles, male harassment can be neutralized. There is no more reason to heighten boundaries since these women no longer are competing for male jobs.

There are many rewards to "normalizing" relations with male enlisted culture. First, when women give up their claim to the soldier role, they are less threatening to male definitions of femininity. Second, those women who abandon the battle for sex integration and retreat to femininity receive swift male rewards, including attention and assistance, because the feminine role amplification involves few changes in values, attitudes, and definitions for males. A frequent paternalistic gesture extended to women who abandon the soldier role is protection from male-oriented military duties such as field exercises and simulations. The Sergeant Daddy Warbucks-type male supervisors assign the "helpless" to the mail room or to other clerical duties when it is time for the unit to deploy to the field.

A woman supervisor described the patterns of male paternalism as follows:

> We are treated as children by male supervisors who think they have to watch out for us. Male supervisors do not ask individual women to develop their greatest potential. Men ignore suggestions to change these behaviors. Sexist attitudes of older NCOs (noncommissioned officers) and "lifers" create divisiveness among women and limited awareness of military oppression.

The social type of Daddy's Little Girl was generated and patterned by male enlisted culture. Males discouraged women from performing physically demanding jobs. When women were not allowed to function "normally" in Signal Corps work, both males and females considered them to be only "part-timer" soldiers. Resentments and claims that women "get over" ensued when males had to assume extra duty because of the paternalism of supervisors.

The Sexpot

A second form of hyperfemininity is the sexpot role. Some females in Khaki Town tried to resolve the status contradiction of being a woman soldier by emphasizing their sexuality. Certain male supervisors, the "Sergeant Seductos," were always looking for sexual partners among women troopers.

By forming a relationship with her supervisor, a female could find a shield from sexual harassment. Like Daddy's Little Girl, the Sexpot was removed from the most aversive work demands. The Sexpot created divisiveness among Khaki Town women and retarded the growth of female support systems. The other women were distressed by feelings that Sexpots were "getting over" by offering sexual favors to escape demanding tasks. An intercept voice operator said that she lacked confidence in these women: "I don't know what their problem is, but they do lower themselves." An electrical repairer thought that the Sexpots reinforced stereotypes of women soldiers as "whores." A radio operator stated that the few women who do join the army to "run around" created bad first impressions of army women.

Junior enlisted men resented Daddy's Little Girl and the Sexpot because these women did not "pull their share" of extra duty. A platoon sergeant observed that "lots of guys feel that women don't do their share in the field. It is true that certain female soldiers come into the army expecting too much on the side of soft work. Males don't like it when women goes [sic] on sick leave to avoid duty. It means more work to them."

A small but significant number of male supervisors extended equity and, sometimes, goodwill to military women. One such platoon sergeant argued that his women soldiers were his most intelligent and best soldiers. A team chief agreed and thought that men were the "biggest problem" in the integration of women. A sergeant first class observed that most women in the field did their share and saw men "getting over" as well as women. However, nonprejudiced supervisors were an exception in an otherwise resistant male culture. Despite a consensus that females faced formidable barriers, most males blamed women themselves for the problems. Women who occupied the hyperfeminine roles confirmed the suspicion that women could not perform physically demanding jobs. For women still battling to be accepted as soldiers, these women undermined female gains.

Mother
Kanter found that a token woman sometimes became a "mother" to dominant men. The assumption that women are good listeners and easy to talk to made them approachable.[23]

A third form of hyperfemininity found among Khaki Town women was the Mother role, often played by an older enlisted woman. In Khaki Town, a forty-year-old woman reported that junior enlisted men frequently came to her with their "girl friend" problems and even referred to her as "mom." However, she commented that she did not like to be treated as "mother" and preferred to maintain a more distant relationship with males. The Mother role was an effective way to avoid the dyke and whore stereotypes of enlisted male culture. However, if women were imputed to be motherly types, they were not taken seriously as soldiers.

Amplifying the Soldier Role

Super Soldier
The Super Soldier paralleled Kanter's "iron maiden," the stereotyped role into which strong women were placed.[24] The Super Soldier did not submit to either male paternalism or sexual demands. Rather, this type tried to gain acceptance into the male enlisted culture by affecting masculine demeanor and jargon to be perceived as "one of the guys." By attempting to acculturate themselves into the male enlisted culture, these women underplayed their femininity. This style minimized their potential as daughters, seductresses, or mothers.

Physical attributes were deemed important by the woman who tried to play the Super Soldier role. Participation in sports such as softball and touch football was a common recreational activity among these women.

Super Soldiers were often contemptuous of the hyperfeminine Mother or Daughter.

Super Soldiers adhered rigidly to military rules and regimentation. Several of these women were considered the most knowledgeable soldiers in their Signal Corps specialties. Even if women performed their jobs perfectly, acceptance by males was often only superficial. One woman reported that there were limits to the extent that she would play the "one-of-the-guys" role: "I don't have virgin ears. But some of these guys sit and curse all day. Most of the time I roll with it. But if they get really outrageous, I tell them to cool it." If women carried themselves in a masculine manner, they risked the danger of being labeled lesbians. One woman stated, "I have to stick to myself pretty much here. I'd like to play softball for example, but playing softball means automatically that you are gay. I'm not gay, I just like sports, but, no, I can't do that here without a label."

The Lone Ranger of Women's Liberation

Many of Khaki Town's women soldiers were antagonistic toward the women's movement, which seemed beneficial to upper-middle-class women and irrelevant to their military experience. There was a tendency to "personalize" many confrontations with males rather than to attribute them to the problem of being outnumbered. Most of the women soldiers had highly stereotyped notions of the women's movement, and many blamed themselves for their problems in Khaki Town. I observed that only two women viewed themselves as fighters for the rights of women. Both of them belonged to an unofficial chapter of the National Organization for Women. One of the women had an occupational role in the telecommunications field but hoped to transfer to the position of drug and alcohol counselor so that she could have more overall visibility on the base. She felt that women could be taught how to protect themselves against male harassment: "Women can be taught the channels to use if supervisors give them a hard time. We must cope with male supremacy and break the traditional views of women's roles!"

Summary

The women soldiers of Khaki Town faced isolation from work culture, heightened visibility, and opposition from enlisted male culture in the form of paternalism and sexual shakedowns. As a response to these forces, the women of Khaki Town developed two broad patterns of social types that correspond to exaggerated female and soldier roles. Underachieving females discarded the soldier role in the following social types: Daddy's Little Girl, the Sexpot, and Mother. In contrast, over-achieving types included the Super Soldier and the Lone Ranger of Women's Liberation.

In all previous research on tokenism—including Kanter's study of managerial women, Long Laws's analysis of academic women,[25] Spangler's study of women in law schools,[26] and Fuchs-Epstein's study of women in high prestige law firms,[27]—there was no explicit policy consigning women to token status. A hypothetical example illustrates the difference between military tokenism and the other settings. Suppose the American Bar Association arbitrarily limited female membership to 10 percent, as the United States Army has in its "Womanpause" policy. Women law students, who now constitute over 40 percent of each first-year class, would still be pressured to adopt the stereotyped roles of the past.

The latest report of the Assistant Secretary of Defense on *Women in the Military* was commissioned in part to resolve the high level of female attrition in nontraditional work such as the Signal Corps. The Defense Department concluded that women soldiers' difficulties resulted not from the nature of the work itself, but from working alone in a hostile male environment. Female attrition was blamed specifically on the problems of ostracism, sexual harassment, and stereotyping.[28]

The obvious solution to the attrition problem is to increase the proportion of women. With an increased ratio of sixty-five males to thirty-five females, military women would gain power just as women law students did in the 1970s. A more balanced ratio allows women to form coalitions and change the culture of their work group.[29] In 1977, the Army Research Institute known as MAX-WAC (Maximum Women Army Content) conducted a study. After evaluating women in three-day training exercises, MAX-WAC concluded that the proportion of women could be increased up to 35 percent without adversely affecting combat readiness.[30]

The Defense Department, however, decided not to increase the proportion of women. To understand this decision, one must examine the department's motives for including women in nontraditional fields in the volunteer military. The Pentagon has found women volunteers to be extremely well-qualified substitutes for men. The varying need for women "substitutes" depends on the availability of male recruits. For the volunteer military, men are in short supply during good economic times accompanied by low unemployment; conversely, men are in ample supply during periods of high unemployment. As long as military women merely serve as a convenient reserve army of labor for the Defense Department, their career opportunities remain limited by token status and fluctuating job classifications.[31]

Even if the Defense Department were to abandon its current policy of restricting the numbers of military women and the jobs that are accessible to them, key differences between a career in the military and a career in the civilian sector would still exist. Servicewomen, like servicemen, have potentially dangerous jobs that most of us do not want. The restriction of women to "noncombat" jobs and locations has hindered their chances for promotion. The current policy is a red herring. The women of the Signal Corps units in West Germany, for example, face the possibility of death from nuclear weapons, chemical, biological, and radiological agents even in a so-called limited war.

Furthermore, both sexes forfeit some of their civil liberties and human rights when they enter the military. As Sam Ervin said of the military justice system:

> Imagine if you will a system of justice with the burden of proving innocence imposed on the defendant, secret informants, no right to trial, no right to see the evidence, no protection against punishment even when found innocent, no right to legally qualified counsel, no independent judicial review, and no clearly defined rules of what is and is not against the law.[32]

A soldier's personal life is subordinate to the military mission. Frequent mandatory moves impose enormous difficulties on family life and friendships; even "free time" can be interrupted at a moment's notice. Efforts on the part of enlisted service members to form unions that could address these issues are discouraged.[33] In short, without democratization and humanization of the military structure itself, the benefits that *anyone* derives from joining the military are problematic at best.

Notes

1. Department of Defense, Office of the Assistant Secretary of Defense for Manpower, Reserve Affairs, and Logistics, *Background Review: Women in the Military* (Washington: GPO, October 1981).
2. Department of the Army, Office of the Deputy Chief of Staff for Personnel, *Women in the Army: Policy Review* (Washington: GPO, November 1982), 1–11.
3. Ibid., 4-1, 4-20.
4. Rosabeth Moss Kanter, *Men and Women of the Corporation* (New York: Basic Books, 1977), 209–211.
5. The data reported in this chapter was drawn from a larger study. Michael L. Rustad, *Women in Khaki: The American Enlisted Woman* (New York: Praeger, 1982).
6. Commanders of Khaki Town units did not have accurate records of how many women were assigned to their units through the 1970s. At the Assistant Secretary of Defense level, I discovered errors in the estimation of numbers. In general, when commanders were asked about the history of women in their units, they were unlikely to agree on numbers.
7. Department of the Army, *Final Report: Evaluation of Women in the Army* (Fort Benjamin Harrison, Indiana: U.S. Army Administration Center, 1978), 1–5.
8. Ibid., 2–109.
9. Kanter, *Men and Women of the Corporation*, 210–12.
10. David Cortright, *Soldiers in Revolt: The American Military Today* (New York: Anchor, 1975).

11. Estimates were given to me by a "Khaki Town" captain in the Human Relations Office, West Germany, U.S. Army in Europe.

12. Assistant Secretary of Defense for Manpower, Reserve Affairs, and Logistics, March 1980. All-Volunteer Data Base (unpublished tabulations).

13. "Study Shows Extent of Drug, Alcohol Use," *Army Times*, 15 December 1980, p. 1.

14. Department of the Army, *Women in the Army: Policy Review*.

15. Assistant Secretary of Defense for Manpower, Reserve Affairs, and Logistics, All-Volunteer Data Base.

16. Rosabeth Moss Kanter, "The Problems of Tokenism," Paper presented at Wellesley College, Center for Research on Women in Higher Education and the Professions (now Center for Research on Women), 1974, pp. 18–21.

17. Bernard W. Rogers, Army Chief of Staff, *Army Times*, 22 May 1978, p. 1.

18. Kanter, *Men and Women of the Corporation*, 223.

19. Morris Janowitz, *The Professional Soldier: A Social and Political Portrait* (New York: The Free Press, 1960).

20. Assistant Secretary of Defense for Manpower, Reserve Affairs, and Logistics, All-Volunteer Data Base.

21. Kanter, *Men and Women of the Corporation*, 223.

22. Ibid., 230–40.

23. Ibid., 233–34.

24. Ibid., 236.

25. Judith Long Laws, "The Psychology of Tokenism," *Sex Roles* 1 (1975):51–69.

26. Eve Spangler, Marsha A. Gordon, and Ronald M. Piplin, "Token Women: An Empirical Test of Kanter's Hypothesis," *American Journal of Sociology* 84, no. 1 (1978):160–69.

27. Cynthia Fuchs Epstein, *Women in Law* (Garden City, New York: Anchor Books, 1983).

28. Department of Defense, *Background Review: Women in the Military*, 49.

29. Kanter, *Men and Women of the Corporation*, 209.

30. Department of the Army, *Women Content in Units (MAX-WAC)* (Washington: GPO, 1977).

31. We are reminded of Karl Marx's classic analysis of the industrial reserve army. He argued that "the relative surplus population was the pivot upon which the law of demand and supply of labor works. It confines the field of action of this law within the limits absolutely convenient to the activity of the exploitation and to the domination of capital." Karl Marx, "Capital, Volume I," in David McLellan, *Karl Marx: Selected Writings* (Oxford: Oxford University Press, 1977), 481–83.

32. E. Lawrence Gibson, *Get Off My Ship* (New York: Avon, 1978), 292.

33. Ezra S. Krendel and Bernard Samoff, *Unionizing the Armed Forces* (Philadelphia: University of Pennsylvania Press, 1977).

18
Normal Accident at Three Mile Island
Charles Perrow

Accidents will happen, including ones in nuclear plants. But by and large, we believe accidents can be prevented through better training, equipment, or design, or their effects can be localized and minimized through safety systems. The accident at Three Mile Island (TMI) is being assessed in this fashion. The industry started a new training program, the equipment at the Babcock and Wilcox plants is being improved, the design has been modified, the utility chastised—all useful, if minor, steps. Furthermore, to nuclear proponents, such as Edward Teller, the accident proved that the effects can be localized and minimized. It is safe. No one has died as a direct result of radiation injuries in all the years of commercial nuclear plant operation.

But the accident at TMI was not a preventable one, and the amount of radiation vented into the atmosphere could easily have been much larger, and the core might have melted, rather than just being damaged. TMI was a "normal accident"; these are bound to occur at some plant at some time, and bound to occur again, even in the best of plants. It was preceded by at least sixteen other serious accidents or near accidents in the short life of nuclear energy in the United States, and we should expect about sixteen more in the next five years of operation—that is, in industry time, the next four hundred years of operation of the plants existing now and scheduled to come on stream.

Normal accidents emerge from the characteristics of the systems themselves. They cannot be prevented. They are unanticipated. It is not feasible to train, design, or build in such a way as to anticipate all eventualities in complex systems where the parts are tightly coupled. They are incomprehensible when they occur. That is why operators usually assume something else is happening, something that they understand, and act accordingly. Being incomprehensible, they are partially uncontrollable. That is why operator intervention is often irrelevant. Safety systems, backup systems, quality equipment, and good training all help prevent accidents and minimize catastrophe, but the complexity of systems outruns all controls.

Reprinted from *Society* 18, no. 5 (July–August 1981):17–26, by permission of the publisher.

The normal accident has four noteworthy characteristics: signals, which provide warnings only in retrospect, making prevention difficult; multiple design and equipment failures, which are unavoidable since nothing is perfect; some operator error, which may be gross since operators are not perfect either, but generally is not even considered error until the logic of the accident is finally understood; and "negative synergy," wherein the sum of equipment, design, and operator errors is far greater than the consequences of each singly. The normal accident generally occurs in systems where the parts are highly interactive, or "tightly coupled," and the interaction amplifies the effects in incomprehensible, unpredictable, unanticipated, and unpreventable ways. When it occurs in high-risk systems, such as those dealing with toxic chemicals, radioactive materials, microwaves, recombinent DNA, transportation systems, and military adventures, the consequences can be catastrophic. Even a fairly benign system, such as electrical power distribution, can cause considerable harm.

No one who owns or runs a high-risk system wants to consider a classification scheme for accidents that includes a normal accident category. It would be an admission of liability, and for some unknown but finite period of time, an admission of inevitable disaster. The category takes on more meaning when contrasted to preferred ones. I will consider three major categories, although there are others. The best type of accident, for owners and managers, is the "unique" accident, such as the collapse of a building in a giant earthquake, or simultaneous heart attacks for the pilot and co-pilot of an airliner or bomber near a city. No reasonable protection is possible against freak accidents or Acts of God, so no liability can be assigned. They are so rare we need not fear them, and more important, even unreasonable expenditures will not produce a significant reduction in risk. Otherwise, we would build no dams, buildings, airplanes, or armies.

Nevertheless, the unique accident is sometimes contemplated for high-risk, long-lived systems. About halfway into the nuclear power age, it was required that the new plants be built to withstand large earthquakes and the impact of a jet airliner. But even here it was only the reactor building that was so guarded; the auxiliary buildings and the pipelines to it from the reactor building, essential for using radioactive liquids to cool the reactor core in an emergency, are generally not protected. It is easy to imagine the loss of both the main power and backup systems during an earthquake or even a storm. The designs, of course, have not been given destructive testing by actual earthquakes or falling planes. We missed a chance a few years ago when a Strategic Air Command Bomber, flying directly at a nuclear power plant in Michigan, crashed in a stupendous explosion just two miles short of the plant. The pilots at the nearby SAC base were routinely warned not to fly near or over the plant, though they routinely did, at 1000 feet, suggesting it would not have been a unique accident, after all, had it occurred two seconds later.

Because liability cannot be assigned, owners and managers cry "unique" when they can. Failing that, they move to the next most desirable category. This is the "discrete" accident—there was an equipment failure, but it could be corrected and it won't happen again. Generally, discrete accidents—which do occur, indeed are very plentiful in all human-machine systems, and nature itself—involve the failure of one piece of equipment, a limited design error, or an operator error. In a discrete accident, the system responds to that source of error without any significant synergistic developments. Backup systems and isolation devices come into play. While liability can be assigned (nothing should fail, no matter how complex the system), it is generally limited (things will fail, nothing is perfect). More important, the label of a discrete accident is comforting because the system will not be abandoned; it can easily or conceivably be fixed. It will even be "safer" afterwards than before, as with the nuclear power industry after each publicized accident.

At the press conference two months after TMI, Babcock and Wilcox, which built the reactor, argued that this was a discrete accident. There had been an instance of equipment failure, the pilot-operated relief valve, but it was the only instance of this and the system contained planned means to rectify the failure. The actual cause of the accident was the failure of the operators to follow correct procedures after the failure, they argued. If the operators had been on their toes it would have been a trivial event. As we shall see, there were multiple equipment failures, a major design error, and the operators did just what at least some of the experts, some months before, had said they should do. And the event was "mysterious" and "incomprehensible" even to Babcock and Wilcox experts at the site. But management prefers the discrete label to the one that suggests the complexity of the system is at fault.

Discrete accidents allow for operator intervention; the accident itself is comprehensible—someone made a mistake; the equipment failed; the design did not allow for this eventuality—so something can be done. They can also be prevented (to the extent that accidents ever can) by noting warning signals, by using backup or safety systems, and, of course, by rectifying the problem after the accident. Liability can be assessed, but our system of governance and our judicial system is lenient in this regard; "it won't happen again, sir."

The most troublesome category of accidents, both for owners and managers and for the theorist, is the "calculated risk" accident. Liability, where risk is calculated, could easily be assigned, so owners and managers avoid any admissions of calculation, and prefer the categories of unique or, failing that, discrete accidents. Theorists have troubles, too, since on the one hand there is a sense in which a calculation is made of every known risk, making the category vacuous, and on the other hand, there are presumably many unknown risks in complex systems, so calculations are not possible, again rendering the category vacuous. Between these two extremes (more could be done to prevent it since calculations are made, and nothing could be done to prevent it since some things will be incalculable) is a messy but useful area.

Reportedly, the fire that killed the astronauts on the launch pad was considered to be possible, but the level of safety deemed acceptable was below the level of this possibility, so the risk was run. Once it happened, the system was redesigned, perhaps because of the unfortunate publicity rather than a reassessment of the risk calculations, just as the still unburned Pintos were recalled once the government intervened in the private calculation of risk. However, our country was built on risk, as we are hearing lately.

Nuclear proponents are fond of saying that all imaginable risks have been calculated; indeed, they cite this as a major reason for the escalation in plant costs. However, substantial risks that are considered too high to run in new nuclear plants, and thus must be designed out of them, are left to simmer in old plants. In an important decision in 1973, the Atomic Energy Commission ruled that it would not be necessary to "retrofit" existing plants and those to be licensed for the next four years with a backup SCRAM system (an emergency system to halt reactivity). It was economically prohibitive. The Three Mile Island plant lacked a backup emergency core cooling system (ECCS) that is required of newer plants, just as the early ones, such as at Indian Point, New York, require *none*. As we shall see, however, it probably would not have made any difference in the TMI accident.

As suggested, this category is a messy one, open to debate after the fact and hidden from view before it. In any case, the tendency is to classify accidents as unique events, or discrete accidents, rather than calculated risks. Calculated risk accidents that we are able to learn about are generally cataclysmic (that is why we know of them), and thus, like unique accidents, operator intervention is negligible and synergistic effects are irrelevant, though probably present in those few seconds of disaster.

Warnings

Complex human-machine systems abound in warnings—signs in red letters, flashing lights, horns sounding, italicized passages in training manuals and operating instructions, decals on equipment, analyses of faults in technical reports, and a light snowfall of circulars and alerts. Warnings are embedded in construction codes, testing apparatus, maintenance checks, and, of course, fire drills. All personnel are expected to be only indifferently attentive and concerned, so training, drills, reports, and alarms are repetitive, numbing, essential parts of these systems.

Warnings work; but not all the time. We should not be surprised; the very volume of warning devices testifies to this likelihood. If warnings were heeded, we would need only a few modest and tasteful ones rather than a steady drill of admonitions punctuated by alarms and lights.

Yet we stand incredulous when confronted with, for example, the same engine on the same DC-10 aircraft failing twice within a few months (one fatality—a passenger sucked out of the plane); or the cargo doors of DC-10s, after repeated warnings, blowing open three times (the third time a fully loaded plane crashed and all died); or an accident at Three Mile Island that seemed to be almost a simulation of two previous accidents at other plants and fulfilled the predictions of an engineer's hypothetical analysis. Why are warnings not always heeded? There are many reasons, and when we consider the overpopulation of complex, high-risk systems that someone has decided we cannot live without, they are disturbing.

Consider three categories of warnings. First, there are deviations from steady-state conditions that do not activate significant alarms. There was rather a long list of these at Three Mile Island, to be considered later. Each one individually is considered trivial or interpreted in a routine framework. Only hindsight discloses the meaning of these deviations. Second, there are alarms, such as flashing lights or circuit breaker trips or dials reading in the red zone. But operators are accustomed to reinterpreting these alarms as insignificant when they have a conception of the problem which triggered them. Or if the operators have no conception of the problem, the alarm may be attributed to faulty alarm equipment. Since dials sometimes give faulty readings or breakers trip for no good reason even under routine conditions, and since disturbed conditions can create misleading alarms through malfunctioning or complex interactions, the operators may be correct. Alarms, like deviations, always outnumber actual accidents; warnings are in greater supply than actual malfunctions. "If we shut down for every little thing . . . ," the reasoning goes.

Past accidents, mute predictors of future ones, form the third category of warnings. But history is no guide for highly infrequent events. They are not expected to occur again; generally, they don't. Or, there may be compelling economic reasons for continuing to run the risk—as with the DC-10 cargo doors prior to the fatal crash near Paris. Past accidents also fail as warnings if the warning is available to only one part of the system, and that part is only loosely connected to the other parts. This was a major problem at TMI.

Any single plant with a complex technology is likely to be tightly coupled; a disturbance in one part will reverberate quickly to the other parts. But the plant may be only loosely coupled with other parts of its system. Warnings from another plant may not reach it; the mechanisms for transmitting such warnings in the case of nuclear power plants are reasonably redundant and plentiful—the Nuclear Regulatory Commission, the reactor builders, numerous institutes, university centers, and industry bodies all function in this capacity. Indeed, in a crisis, the system comes together tightly; it responded exceptionally well to the TMI accident. They knew that the future of nuclear power was at stake. But under normal conditions they have an interest in minimizing the dangers that exist, avoiding costly shut-downs, and carrying out their separate organizational concerns. These interests buffer the part of the system that experiences a disturbance from the other parts, unless the disturbance is very large and widely publicized. In such a manner TMI was buffered from a technical report prepared by an engineer at another utility, a somewhat similar accident in Europe, and a very similar accident in an adjacent state. All constituted unheeded warnings.

The technical report was prepared by Caryle Michelson, an engineer with the Tennessee Valley Authority, which was considering the purchase of a reactor from Babcock and Wilcox, one quite similar to the two reactors at TMI. Michelson wrote a long memo raising a number of concerns, including a remarkably prescient description of the dynamics of the TMI accident; a LOCA occurs (a loss of coolant accident), a high-pressure injection system (HPI) goes on to maintain pressure in one part of the system, the pressurizer. The pressure rises there, but falls in the reactor core for complex reasons. The operators fear over-pressurizing the pressurizer, because it might "go solid" (become saturated with water and/or steam). Going solid is to be avoided, since it means the reactor must be shut down if it isn't already (SCRAM, or inserting graphite control rods to stop the fission process), and even if it is already, it takes a long time to get it back in operation after going solid, and the utility loses money because it must buy electricity rather than make it. So they "throttle back" on the HPI, but this means less cooling of the reactor core and could lead, in minutes, to damage to the core and even a meltdown.

Michelson's report was sent to the NRC in November 1977; a reply acknowledged they understood the problem, but they kept it to themselves. In April 1978, eleven months before the accident, it was sent to the vendors, Babcock and Wilcox (B&W). There it received normal handling. The engineers read it, considered it, and wrote a reply nine months later, two months before TMI, stating that these matters had all been considered. We do not know what happened to it at the NRC; it seems to have disappeared in their vast files.

Meanwhile, on September 24, 1977, a LOCA occurred at the Davis-Besse plant near Toledo, Ohio. The operators throttled back on the HPI when they saw the pressure in the pressurizer rising, even though it was falling in the core. Fortunately, the plant was operating at only about nine percent capacity, and in a short time they discovered the cause of the accident—a faulty Pilot Operated Relief Valve (PORV)—and bypassed it before any damage to the core occurred. An engineer from B&W, Mr. Kelley, was sent to the plant to investigate the accident. Returning to B&W he gave a seminar on the accident, warning about the improper operator action of throttling the HPI system prematurely, and then wrote a memo suggesting that all units using this kind of equipment be warned about this improper action.

Mr. Kelley's superior, Mr. Dunn, took up the matter and had his memo sent around B&W. Only one engineer responded, and he misunderstood it and dismissed it. Dunn persisted, and the memo, now fathered by a Mr. Novack, made a slow ascent. It was sent over to that division of B&W concerned with customer services, to Mr. Karrasch. He said he gave it to two subordinates, but they do not recall ever seeing it. It was sent there because customer service is traditionally concerned about anything that might unduly interrupt service, and since going solid would, they should review it. (Kelley-Dunn-Novack were concerned about the far more dangerous matter of core damage and meltdown.) No word came from Karrasch, so Novack kept calling. Months went by, and still no answer as to whether they should alert all utilities to this danger. Meanwhile the training department had assured Kelley-Dunn-Novack the operators were, indeed, instructed to not throttle back on HPI in a LOCA, even though they had at Davis-Besse.

Finally, a Mr. Walters met Karrasch at the water cooler and asked about the memo from his people on the engineering side. Karrasch replied, off-handedly, something to the effect that "it's okay, no problem." Mr. Walters pondered the reply as Mr. Karrasch hurried off to a meeting—did it mean there was no problem of going solid, or no problem of uncovering the core, or what? He left the matter hanging. It all came out after the operators at TMI throttled back on the HPI and made a serious accident even more serious. Nineteen months had transpired since Kelly first wrote his memo. B&W then quickly sent out the Kelley-Dunn-Novack memo to all units using this equipment.

To the members of the President's Commission on the Accident at Three Mile Island, this was the familiar curse of a failure in communication, the phlogiston of organizational problems and of many disasters. Warnings were not made available to the proper people; Karrasch, at the least, had failed to communicate with the engineers. Karrasch was more perceptive, if aggressively defensive. There was no failure in communication he insisted; the matter was simply one of low priority. He then went on to suggest the several obvious high-priority matters his office was dealing with, ones forced upon them, the implication runs, by new and pressing NRC safety standards. He was right. Everyone at B&W did what they were supposed to do, with both the Michelson and Kelley memos. Only in retrospect had they assigned the wrong priority. In retrospect we often do.

How many warnings can one heed? The best set of warnings lie among the 2000 Licensee Event Reports (LERs) that are sent by the utilities to the NRC every year. These are required by law, and report significant events that might affect safety. The NRC has gagged on them; no reasonable system for analyzing them exists. The utilities dutifully report these and they sink into the enormous file. What would the operators, even if they were college-trained engineers, do with a steady stream of reports, memos, instructions, analyses that they would be required to remember for years on end, use rarely, and recall instantly in a complex emergency? Only if it had been remembered, along with all the other instructions that continually change, and more important, only if the operators had known it was this type of accident they were experiencing. As we shall see, they did not. Even the experts who were quickly at the scene did not know soon enough.

It is not clear that the system should be more tightly coupled so that warnings, for one thing, should travel faster and create their intended "perturbances." Were the TVA, NRC, Battelle Institute, Brookhaven Labs, university departments, Electric Power Research Institute, Oak Ridge Laboratories, Westinghouse, Combustion Engineering, Babcock and Wilcox, Davis-Besse and TMI and some seventy other plants all wired together into one low resistance circuit, the number of untoward events and immense complexities lying in the nuclear industry would drown them all in signals. Loosely coupled systems have slack, reserve time, and resources. One part of a system can be made to withstand the brunt of a disturbance and protect the others from incessant shocks. Parts can be isolated and even left to fend for themselves. Information is absorbed, summarized, compacted into bits of information in one part that can be sent to the others without inundating them. Centralization is avoided, innovation encouraged.

Such loosely coupled systems are resistant to change from the outside, however. By focusing upon TMI, the President's Commission unwittingly reinforced the survival values of loosely coupled systems—the utility was segregated from the industry, and reprimanded. Indian Point, with its old equipment grandfathered from safety requirements, perched upwind of the millions in the New York metropolitan area, is buffered. Better equipment and training and management at TMI will supposedly take care of the problem, along with a single-headed rather than hydra-headed NRC and some "new attitudes" there. Operators will be flooded with new warnings. But it is normal for the systems to have accidents; warnings cannot affect the normal accident. Tight coupling encourages normal accidents, with their highly interdependent synergistic aspects, but loose coupling muffles warnings.

Whether systems are loosely or tightly coupled, they all face another problem with warnings—the signal to noise ratio. Only after the event, when we construct imaginative (and frequently dubious) explanations of what went wrong, does some of the noise reveal itself as a signal. The operators at TMI had literally to turn off alarms; so many of them were sounding and blinking that signals passed into noise. The extremely detailed log of the accident (accurate to the tenth of a second) put out by B&W performs this merciful winnowing task for us now, selecting out the noise and giving us the signal, with the unspoken admonition "see this reading; *that* was significant." Noisy systems illustrate the banality of the normal accident.

Complex systems are simply not responsive to warnings of unimaginable or highly unlikely accidents. Because they are complex, organizational routines must be carefully followed and off-standard events reinterpreted in routine frameworks. Fortuitous events are always more plentiful than unfortuitous ones, Murphy's law notwithstanding. Most things that go wrong do not matter; the redundancies are plentiful. The "mind-set" that the commissioners referred to so often in their discussions with witnesses allows organizations to go forth without an agony of choice over every contingency. The phrase "I'll believe it when I see it" is misleading, an organizational theorist, Karl Weick notes; it is equally true that "I'll see it when I believe it." The warning of an incomprehensible and unimaginable event cannot be seen, because it cannot be believed. But since it is inconceivable that there were not warnings, investigators, congressional committees, and the superiors of hapless operators dig among the wreckage until they find what can pass for an unheeded warning. But the normal accident is unforeseeable; its "warnings" are socially constructed.

Design and Equipment Failure

It is obvious that designs cannot be perfect or fail-safe, nor can equipment. Everything dangerous would be far too expensive to build and maintain if we required maximum state-of-the-art efforts in equipment and design. Some risk must be run if we wish to have nuclear plants, rail and air transportation, chemical fertilizers, large buildings, military raids, and so on. Even nearly fanatic efforts to reduce risks are insufficient. Given the robustness of most industrial systems, equipment and design failures are not likely to be catastrophic; though they are obviously heavily involved in the 5000 or so industrial-accident deaths we produce in the United States each year. Failures might be catastrophic in high-risk industries, such as the nuclear power industry, especially when the failures are multiple and interacting. Multiple and interacting equipment and design failures abounded in the case of the TMI incident, and several other nuclear accidents or near accidents.

The major piece of equipment failure at TMI was the pilot operated relief valve (PORV). It stuck open. The event was not without prior warnings. There were at least eleven other failures of this key valve at other plants before TMI, including Davis-Besse. The valve had failed once before in TMI Unit 2, and some corrections had been made, but they were obviously insufficient. Furthermore, prior to that failure, it was not possible for the control room operator easily to determine whether the valve was open or closed. After the initial failure, a parsimonious step was taken. A signal was installed, but it only indicated whether a signal was sent to the valve to open or close it, not whether it was actually open or closed. In the March 1979 accident, the indicator said it was closed, while in actuality it was open. Furthermore, the valve had been leaking for some weeks, making check readings from the drain pipe attached to the valve unreliable.

The valve is a particularly crucial one in the pressurized water reactor design of B&W, since the steam generators may boil dry very rapidly—in two or three minutes—rather than slowly, as in the boiling water reactor design built by other firms (15 minutes in one design, and 30 in another). This instance of tight coupling makes core uncovery more likely, though B&W officials argue that it also provides advantages in other kinds of accidents. It also has the distinct commercial advantage of allowing the reactor to continue operating even if the turbine shuts down, thus minimizing expensive down-time.

This advantage was removed after TMI when B&W, following discussions with the NRC, reduced dependence upon this critical valve by having the reactor shut down whenever the turbine tripped. In testimony, a B&W official was reluctant to say that this corrective action signified a design problem in the original B&W equipment, but it would appear to indicate quite a significant one. Thus, there were several warnings, insufficient corrective action, a major failure, and only then, a design change in the system (not the valve).

There were other equipment failures during the accident. Paper jammed in the computer printout, and to get the printout operating, considerable data logging had to be sacrificed. The computer was presumably not designed to handle the volume of a major accident and was one and half hours behind in its printout at one point. There was an error in the instrumentation for the level indicator in the miscellaneous waste holding tank. A check valve was faulty and it let water into the condensate polisher system; this had been noticed before, but the attempt at correcting it had not succeeded. This particular failure probably started the whole accident, but in normal accidents the particular trigger is relatively insignificant; the interaction is significant.

There were serious leaks—the source of which was still unknown some weeks after the accident—in the venting system, allowing unintended radioactive releases to the atmosphere. A safety system was not used because it was not safe; it could easily leak. This was the normal backup system for cooling the reactor by returning liquid from the auxiliary building. Because it could not be trusted, poisonous gas was vented directly into the auxiliary building (and then went to the atmosphere) in a controversial decision, which produced the large radioactive puff. Several people (including a utility official from Metropolitan Edison) testified that leaks in this "safety" system made it a dangerous procedure. That a safety system would be too dangerous to use suggests both a design and equipment failure of some magnitude.

Numerous items were not working at the time of the accident or had failed in the recent weeks. The auxiliary building sump tank had blown a rupture disc some weeks prior to the accident; operators were bypassing the tank (there are no regulations that prohibit this). It complicated the intervention efforts. One operator testified that the plant had tripped twice before in connection with the condensate polishers. In addition, two weeks before the accident there had been a "sizable leak" in the air lines going to the polisher. A pump came on "inadvertently" about a month before the accident, was bypassed, and was still awaiting repair at the time of the accident. Three auxiliary feedwater pumps had been taken out of commission two weeks before the accident and left out, in violation of federal regulations.

There was not just a single piece of equipment failure that might have been bypassed, but equipment failure (and design problems) on a level that should cause concern even in a less deadly, non-nuclear plant, and the presence of warning signals that were not heeded. But the important point is not that Metropolitan Edison was particularly derelict, but that such a state of affairs is fairly normal in complex industrial and military systems. Ammonia plants, a mature part of the chemical industry, had an average failure rate of 10 to 11 shutdowns per year; 50 days of down-time per year; 1 fire per plant every 11 months. The nuclear power industry is extremely safety conscious, compared to most industrial concerns, but it will still have problems such as these, as the large number of accidents indicate. Equipment failures, like accidents, are normal, though not frequent.

Operator Error

From the beginning it was widely believed that operator error was the fundamental cause of the TMI accident. B&W flatly stated this, as did the British Secretary of State of Energy, who cited the cause of the accident as "stupid errors." The conclusion was attributed to the Nuclear Regulatory Commission by the press. The President's Commission on Three Mile Island, in their final report, blamed everyone, but most particularly the operators. They twice note that "the major cause of the accident was due to inappropriate actions by those who were operating the plant and supervising that operation," though problems of design, training, and procedures contributed to operator failure. But they also feel "they should have known" that they were in a Loss of Coolant Accident, "failed to realize" that various problems were due to a LOCA, and were "oblivious" for over four hours to the threat of uncovering the core. (A report prepared by outside consultants, the Essex Corporation, for the Nuclear Regulatory Commission, came to a different conclusion, one that deliberately distinguished the causes of human errors themselves: "The primary conclusion reached on the basis of this investigation was that the human errors experienced during the TMI incident were not due to operator deficiencies, but rather to inadequacies in equipment design, information presentation, emergency procedures and training."

It is not comforting that the most blatant operator error at TMI (though not, it is said, an important cause of the accident) is the one least susceptible to remedial action by educational requirements or training programs. After a routine testing procedure, two valves which were closed for the check were left closed rather than opened. Perhaps some people are more likely to lock themselves out of their houses or cars than others, but educational degrees and training would hardly seem to account for the variations. Such things simply happen. Operating personnel testified that with one or two thousand valves in the plant (making checks on every valve every shift unrealistic) one will expect to find one or two out of position for no good reason at times. One operator testified to personal knowledge of two in the previous year, and about five in the short history of TMI Unit 2.

Some valves are so important that they are locked, and a locked valve book is maintained; but an operator testified that it is "sometimes" not kept up to date. A valve that is checked every shift was once found open despite the check at the beginning of the shift. The problem is aggravated by engineering design where, presumably to save money, indicators do not tell whether the valve is actually open or closed, but only the position of the switch that is supposed to open or close it. Such designs create opportunities for operator error. One minor accident at TMI was caused by an operator inadvertently bumping into some switches while investigating a problem. Not only are there a large number of valves, but frequent testing and maintenance routines require them to be placed in non-normal positions for varying periods of time. Valves in wrong positions have caused and contributed to accidents in other nuclear plants. As long as eternal vigilance is a desideratum rather than a reality, the valve position will continue to cause or greatly complicate nuclear plant accidents.

Errors of judgment by operators are more difficult to analyze (and thus more easy to attribute) because the judgment becomes an error only after the fact. Most cases of operator error in normal accidents are "retrospective errors." Presumably many decisions are made that would be classified as errors according to the books or the training programs, but if they work or cause no problem they will be unnoticed, and thus not lead to a revision of standard procedures. If they work, they are in effect being misclassified as errors by virtue of erroneous procedures in the manuals. The cards are stacked in favor of a declaration of operator error, for operators will not be credited with successful actions which violate procedures, but only charged with those that result in investigated accidents. To aggravate the problem, the system and its procedures are not generally under review, only the operators.

More important, though, is the context of judgment errors. A high pressure spike in the reactor was noted because it automatically brought on a safeguard system. But the operator testified, regarding the spike, that "we kind of wrote it off at the time as possibly instrument malfunction of some sort." This was not an unreasonable conclusion, since instruments *were* malfunctioning. "We did not have a firm conclusion" regarding the spike, he went on, since it appeared and went away with such rapidity. Information about the spike was not widely disseminated at this time because it was neither believed nor understood (though a Senate investigation revealed that at least one person drew the correct conclusion at the time). Such is the common fate of novel signals in normal accidents.

The most significant error, by all accounts, was the failure to maintain the high pressure injection (HPI) system. But consider the context, and the matter of organizational routines and goals. Available readings indicated no problem with the level of coolant in the core; at the time it was not even clear what kind of a Loss of Coolant Action (LOCA) this was. These readings were misleading because of vaporization in the core, but that information was not available. There was no direct way to read the water level in the core, and one B&W official was reluctant to encourage having such an indicator because it would increase other problems (a typical interdependency problem in complex systems). Unaware that there was a danger of uncovering the core, the key danger in nuclear plants, the operators focused upon another danger of considerable magnitude—going "solid" in the pressurizer. They were faced with contradictory indicators. (Even a B&W officer, who blamed the accident upon the operator error of cutting back on the HPI system, said the indicators put on "a mysterious performance.") Pressure was low in the core, but it was thought to be adequately covered, while pressure in the pressurizing vessel was high and getting higher. As the B&W official put it, the pressurizer level should have been going down, but it was coming up, and high pressure injection only *aggravated* it, he added.

The operators did what the Davis-Besse operators had done in a similar accident; they throttled the HPI system back to about half level to prevent going solid. Going solid can cause serious damage to parts of the system, and can easily be avoided by manually overriding the HPI system, and cutting it back. The fear of the operators was shared by some experts at B&W and at least one in the NRC. The reason the Kelley-Dunn-Novack memo was held up and debated so many months was that B&W experts feared that keeping the HPI system on in almost identical circumstances would result in going solid. Subsequent to the accident, experts changed their mind and released the new instructions.

The key problem remains, however. It is not always possible to know just what kind of a LOCA one is in, and when the memo will apply. As one commission member noted, the decision to cut back on HPI has to be taken *before* one can know that it would be the wrong decision, and the B&W engineer testifying agreed. The new instructions may not solve the problem at all, except that they weigh heavily in favor of a more conservative course of action, risking going solid rather than uncovering the core. (In fact, the new instructions proved to be dangerous when followed at another plant several months later, and were revised back to something closer to pre-TMI instructions.)

There were other errors. Operators thought the complex pathways for radioactive wastes led to one tank, but they in fact led to another, which overflowed. The plumbing is so complex that scientists on the President's Commission could not read the tiny details in the chart when trying to trace out parts of the system. A technician was taking a sample to test for radioactivity. The reason they knew the liquid was not radioactive was that he got some of it on his hands, and then they checked *him* for exposure! The operators read on-line display indications of temperatures of 230°, whereas the computer printout (delayed an hour or so) indicated a much more serious 285°, which would have led to a different course of action. (It seems likely here that the operators misread the indicator because a higher figure was not congruent with the interpretation they were working under and which made most "sense"—a common attribute of normal accident behavior.) A supervisor testified he believed there was significant core damage the morning of the accident (Wednesday), but he did not mention this to anyone else at the plant when he talked by phone or when he came in the next day; other plant personnel (and the arriving experts) reportedly did not reach this conclusion until late Thursday, early Friday, or even the next week in the case of some Metropolitan Edison officials. The supervisor testified it would not have made any difference if people had been aware of significant damage, but this is hard to believe. Significant events such as the pressure spike and extreme thermocouple readings of core temperatures were not communicated to key personnel—because they were simply not believed.

The most serious case of possible operator error was the decision to vent radioactive gases (producing the puff and plume over the plant that almost triggered evacuation orders). An NRC officer in the control room at the time believed the venting was the automatic result of excess pressure; the supervisor who ordered it said it was an intended venting, with the concurrence of the NRC officer and prior warnings to civil defense personnel. Most people, including some officials of Met. Ed. and B&W and the NRC, believe that after the "puff" the valve was closed—the pressure having been relieved. But the supervisor testified that after the puff the valve was left open for days, since the level of radioactivity fell off rapidly in the next few minutes.

Defending the venting, the supervisor claimed that he was running low on water being used to cool the system. (A B&W official testified there was plenty of water.) He wanted that water in case the core heated up. (This is puzzling, since he was also sure that the core was stable two days before and had remained stable; indeed, everyone was sure.) He did not trust the backup safety system since its packing and valves might leak if it had to be used to cool the core should the core happen to become unstable. The pressure in the tank had been relieved several times by the previous shift supervisor by brief ventings, and by the present supervisor himself in his shift. Worried about his water reserve, and about the safety system, he decided to try what can only be called a large vent, and when the radioactivity did not continue at a high rate, it became a permanent vent. (Since there are some ambiguities in the published Staff Reports of the Commission, it seems possible that much more radioactive material was released than has been acknowledged. But this is only a possibility.)

Negative Synergy

Of such complexities are normal accidents made. Even in this most studied and documented piece of complex organizational behavior, the testimony is contradictory and the reasoning, elusive. Safety systems are not considered safe; cores are stable but are not considered stable so radioactive venting is risked in a large dose; the supervisor calls civil defense to alert them to the venting and they think he has said that the island is being evacuated, and so on. The closer normal accidents are studied, the more they reveal their potentials for even greater disasters. This is why, after close scrutiny, one can always say, no matter how serious the accident, "it was just luck that saved it from being worse."

Synergy is a buzz word in business management circles, indicating that the whole is more than the sum of its parts, or in their congenial familiarity, two plus two equals five. But minus two plus minus two can equal minus five thousand in tightly coupled, complex, high-risk military and industrial systems. This article has given repeated examples of negative synergy where complex, unanticipated, unperceived, and incomprehensible interactions of off-standard components (equipment, design, and operator actions) threaten disaster.

The observation is hardly novel; engineers frequently test for multiple failures and design against them. But it is significant that in possibly the most dangerous of all our industries, nuclear power generation, there are just two official categories of accidents, simple and complex, and only the first is used in training, since it is impossible to train for the second.

Operator training for accidents is based upon "design-based accidents," that is, those accidents that are anticipated and guarded against through plant design. If one part of the system fails—emergency feedwater, power outage, etc.—a backup system or a means of isolating faulty equipment and bringing other equipment into service is provided for. (This is akin to a "discrete" accident.) What the industry calls a "worst case" accident is one where there are failures not anticipated in the design, and no obvious or tested emergency procedures are available. (This is akin to normal accident.) Multiple-failure accidents are generally "worst case" accidents, because design-based accidents generally anticipate only one major cause. One author notes that "practically all of the reactor accidents that have occurred in the past have been multiple-failure accidents." Multiple-failure accidents are not simulated in training. The number of possible multiple-cause accidents is nearly limitless.

"Normal" accidents, in my terminology, are largely multiple failure accidents, or "worst case" accidents. They are infrequent, but far from rare. The more complex the system, the more likely they are to occur. They may, of course, have a single source; it is not the case that there have to be two or more *simultaneous* equipment or operator failures. But the single source leads to further events which are unanticipated and often unimaginable.

An indication of complexity at TMI is provided by this quote from one supervisor: "I think we knew we were experiencing something different, but I think each time we made a decision it was based on something we knew about. For instance: pressure was low, but they had opened the feed valves quickly in the steam generator, and they thought that might have been 'shrink.' There was logic at that time for most of the actions, even though today you can look back and say, well, that wasn't the cause of that, or, that shouldn't have been that long."

All operators and supervisors testified to experiencing a very unusual situation, and there are repeated indications that an attempt was made to force these situations into normal, routine explanations—the kind called for by the emphasis upon "design-based accidents." This is the significance of the widely reported comment by the NRC commissioners that if only they had a simple, understandable thing like a pipe break they would know what to do, and the (presumably joking) remark that perhaps they should arrange for one since there were standard procedures for handling it.

Testimony from operators as to why discharges were in one tank rather than another, involving back flows, spillovers, a previously ruptured and unrepaired disc, speculation as to the source of water in the sumps, concerns about whether to keep it in the containment building or the auxiliary building, and so on indicate just one part of the system that was difficult to visualize or conceptualize. This was only one of several parts of the system the operators were attempting to deal with and coordinate.

There is unfortunately a good reason for limiting training to design-based accidents rather than normal ones. As the power and size and complexity of plants increase, the permutations will increase geometrically, and so will the perturbations making protection humanly impossible. The recommendation (by Hans Bethe, for one) to marry fusion processes with fission processes in order to extend the life of current fission plants will extend the possible perturbations unimaginably.

The confluence of events is not limited to multiple equipment failures, of course. These will interact with expected operator errors. Equipment or design failures are likely to *elicit* operator errors because they are responding to expected, or routine scenarios, and will misinterpret the unexpected signals. There are several instances of not believing the signals in the TMI accident, and given the occasional unreliability of instrumentation, this is to be expected. When faced with ambiguous events and signals, operators can be expected to construct interpretations around familiar readings, dynamics, and routines, and will have the latitude to discount signals and construct interpretations. But of course, it is the novel interactions, the unexpected, the unimagined, that form the basis of a normal accident. Operators, then, are not conditioned to look for the novel explanation, and training in design failures reinforces the tendency to avert a glance into the unknown. The permutations referred to above make training for novelty, for the normal accident, exceedingly difficult. Prosaic failures—valves left closed, a valve failing to close though the indicator says it has, water in the condensate polisher system—quickly interact to produce the fourth and final characteristic of normal accidents: synergistic effects which are negative for the system and beyond the reach of training and experience.

Future Alternatives

All sorts of things will reduce the risk of discrete and calculated-risk nuclear accidents—revamping the NRC; better operator training, testing, and qualifications; closing of plants near large cities. A meaningful liability system would help. Financial risks from accidents need not be passed on to the rate payer in higher rates, or the public in general through the Price-Anderson Act, which limits the liability of the utility and passes it on to the taxpayer. In addition, warnings help. Some designs are demonstrably safer than others. The Navy may pay more attention to quality control than the private businesses that run most of our utility plants.

But normal accidents, whose origins lie fallow and simmer in the very complexity of the interactive system, waiting upon some failure of equipment, design, or operator action to give them their brief, fierce life, cannot be eliminated. Indeed, they grow with the complexity of the system, including the complexity added by the safety features.

Normal accidents are more likely to be perceived in folk expressions than they are in the technical studies of the labs, the NRC journal *Nuclear Safety*, or the literature on the regulatory process and the sins of the old Atomic Energy Commission. The average person, when she resignedly invokes Murphy's law (if anything can go wrong it will), or notes that "for want of a nail the shoe was lost, for want of a shoe the horse was lost . . . ," or mutters the ubiquitous blanket phrase "accidents will happen," is closer to the truth than the experts. The dominant theme for the experts is the accident that can be prevented by design—"design-based accidents" as they are perversely called. This is what the literature covers. A newer, subdominant theme, popularized by the President's Commission, is the "man-machine" interface, and the lack of attention to the "man." But neither theme is responsive to the key characteristic of tightly coupled, complex, high-risk systems that we pride ourselves on. Synergistic effects of a negative nature are bound to occur. Warnings will not prevent them, nor training, nor equipment and design changes, and intervention is limited.

The defenders of nuclear power are correct that "no energy source can be completely safe." The President's Commission agreed; the only thing to do is to make the risk tolerable. But the degree of risk and the level of toleration have not been tested. The industry is young. The catastrophic potentials—e.g., 100,000 immediate deaths, a poisoned land—have not been given a fair chance to be realized. Unanticipated, unpreventable, incomprehensible, uncontrollable accidents in high-risk systems are sufficiently rare to give us another five or ten years of grace. Then we shall see what is tolerable.

There are always alternatives to systems with catastrophic potential. Periodic, low-cost flooding of sparsely settled flood plains adjacent to rivers is less costly and dangerous than huge dams that tower over densely settled flood plains that people come to consider safe. The argument that "we must have dams" is insubstantial; we can live elsewhere. Our energy crisis does not require building Liquified Natural Gas ships that are the length of three football fields, with control panels that have to be as complicated as those in a nuclear plant. Most of the toxic substances we inevitably spew about are not essential to our lives, but only to private profits or war machines. At the very least let us consider including the externalities, real and potential, in the costs of these goods and services. Thus, for example, each propane gas truck in a city should pay insurance to cover the cost of blowing up a few office and apartment buildings when the truck crashes, the gas flows into the sewers for two or three minutes and spreads, and then is ignited by someone's cigarette near the scene of the accident.

Nuclear plants produce about twelve percent of the United States electrical power now, but we have over twice as much excess peak-demand power standing by in non-nuclear facilities that could be put to use instead. The potential of both conservation and the various forms of solar energy was completely unexpected by most experts and officials.

Decentralized, loosely coupled, low-risk alternatives abound. In these, a serious normal accident does not lie incubating. We get only the irritating but tolerable foul-ups that plague our daily life and our organizations.

PART IV

System and Conflict

The four essays in this section focus on the interaction between specific organizations and the larger social and political systems within which they operate. In particular, emphasis is placed on the relation of the internal modes of authority to the dominant external forms of political power. Organizations are seen as political arenas for the class conflicts inherent in the structure of the political economy. Organizational control is therefore presented as a political resource.

Susan and Norman Fainstein argue that those who blame the bureaucratic irrationalities of public administration for the failures of social and economic programs misperceive the underlying political dynamics of the system. To be properly understood, the successes and failures of bureaucratic performance and administrative accountability must be examined within the parameters set by the distribution of power under the existing political economy. In this regard, the Fainsteins suggest that the relative effectiveness of a government bureaucracy will depend upon its relation to the interests of the capitalist elite. While public agencies are often unaccountable to the general public, they are remarkably accountable to the long-run interests of the corporate system.

In his study of the "iron triangle," Gordan Adams presents a political analysis of the interorganizational decision-making system that governs national security policy. Specifically, he points to the ways in which Pentagon procurement policies serve both the immediate and long-run interests of the large corporate defense contracting industries and their political allies. Beginning with the premise that the nuclear arms race, national security, and United States foreign policy goals are incomplete explanations for the enormous growth of military spending, Adams argues that the expanding power of the contemporary "military-industrial complex" is promoted and sustained by an "iron triangle." Consisting of the organizational machinery of the Defense Department, the corporate defense industry, and key members of Congress (who either have defense plants in their districts or serve on committees that decide on defense funding), the iron triangle is an interorganizational decision-making process that facilitates the flow of money, personnel, information, and influence between its political corners. It operates to reinforce the political power of each, as well as of the whole, and to isolate the process from other parts of the government and the public. The result is a continuing and uncontrollable escalation of the military budget.

Nancy DiTomaso's essay is a case study of the United States Department of Labor in two critical periods of its history: 1869 to 1913 and 1957 to 1973. Illustrating the value of a historical perspective for organizational analysis, she shows that almost all of the decisions concerning the structure of the Department of Labor are linked to major social and political conflicts in the society at large. Initial decisions about the formation and organization of the Labor Department involved political decisions about who should have access to state power; subsequent battles to reorganize in later periods generally reflected a shifting balance in the political alignments of the system as a whole. Traditional ideas about the value of hierarchy and decentralization are seen to depend on political contingencies. DiTomaso thus reveals public organizations to be something more than the products of their environments; they are inherently a part of those environments.

Steven Kelman provides a comparative perspective on the role of government in the industrial workplace in the United States and in Sweden. He focuses on the differences between United States and Swedish compliance patterns and their respective outcomes. Where American government inspectors rely on an "enforcement" or punishment-oriented approach to compliance in an "adversarial" environment, their Swedish counterparts principally resort to normative inducements and the use of representative labor-management groups at both national and shop-floor levels. Kelman shows that the policy makers' choices between these two alternative control systems are functions of the larger context of cultural and political values in the respective systems. Moreover, the Swedish system works in a less bureaucratic manner because Swedish workers, through collective bargaining and national legislation, have won more rights to participate directly in health and safety committees in their workplaces. The primary outcomes of the two systems differ significantly in their levels of hostility and resentment toward regulation. The American system has generated suspicion and resentment between inspectors and employers, but the Swedish system has fostered a cooperative atmosphere of mutual understanding and assistance. A greater trade union role, in short, has led to a less cumbersome, more cooperative, and comparatively effective system of regulation.

19
The Political Economy of American Bureaucracy

Susan S. Fainstein and Norman I. Fainstein

The deficiencies of government bureaucracy in the United States are rooted in the institutional and class context within which the state functions, in other words, the political economy of capitalism. For this reason, diagnoses that blame universal problems of large organizations or idiosyncracies and irrationalities of American public administration for poor governmental performance distort the real situation. The dominant ideology of advanced capitalism, whch stresses the evils of state intervention, colors perceptions of the bureaucratic phenomenon. The attack on the state diverts attention from class privilege and enormous concentrations of private power in the economy. But perhaps even more importantly, it continually propagandizes the idea that state administration is opposed to private business, harassing it at every opportunity and wasting the labor of American citizens through unproductive bureaucrats and bungling interventions. While problems of governmental performance and accountability are real enough, they need to be seen within the totality of the public and private sectors. From this systemic perspective, public failure is frequently produced by private success; government agencies are ineffective because their missions are impossible; and the least controversial bureaucracies are those which smoothly serve the particular interests of capitalism and its dominant class. The task, then, is to reinterpret the shortcomings of bureaucratic performance and accountability within the parameters set by the distribution of power under capitalism.

In doing so, we adopt a Marxist structuralist approach, which, while rooting the failures of American public bureaucracy in capitalism, does not discard liberal democratic values. Thus, we reject both centralized state socialism and conservative market hegemony as solutions to bureaucratic malaise. The discussion begins by summarizing the Marxist interpretation of state administration; it examines the conservative attack

---

Reprinted, with revisions, from *Making Bureaucracies Work*, edited by Carol Weiss and Allen Barton (Beverly Hills, Cal.: Sage, 1980), 279–98, by permission of the publisher.

The authors wish to thank Paul Adams, George Sternlieb, and especially Robert Beauregard for their comments on earlier drafts of this article.

on liberal expectations; it identifies the structurally based cause for alleged bureaucratic malfunction and lack of accountability; then it redefines the bureaucratic problem within the context of American capitalism.

Bureaucracy and Capitalism

Positive liberalism, developed theoretically at the turn of the century and incorporated in New Deal and War on Poverty programs, calls for governmental activity to fill in gaps left by private initiative. The liberal hope is that the harshness of the capitalist market system can be tempered through humane public action. Within this context, the intentions of the state are generally regarded as beneficent, even if its capacity to produce intended results is found wanting.[1]

While liberals have sought to blame governmental malfunction on institutional shortcomings, contemporary Marxist critics have attributed the failings of state interventionism to fundamental contradictions within the political economy. O'Connor (1973) traces fiscal crisis to the demands placed on the state by monopoly capital, which requires government to assume the burden of fostering economic growth (capital accumulation), educating and maintaining the labor force, and co-opting rebellion through the provision of welfare. At the same time, capitalists privately appropriate the return on publicly subsidized investment, leaving the government with insufficient funds to carry out its functions. O'Connor's analysis derives from Marx's characterization of the state as the executive committee of the bourgeoisie, carrying out the collective interests of the property-owning class. Most state expenditure, despite loose employment of the term "welfare state," directly or indirectly subsidizes capitalists. The extent to which the state spends money directly to benefit the populace depends on the degree to which the masses threaten ruling-class interests, forcing the government to respond so as to retain its legitimacy. Miliband (1969) examines the political relationships of capitalist society and asserts that even when socialists capture the government, they cannot act in ways opposed to capitalist interests. Rather, they are bound by the hold which the economic elite has over the entire society—its ideological domination and its ability to threaten economic collapse. In Offe's words (1975: 126), the "very decision-making power [of the capitalist state] *depends* (like every other social relationship in capitalist society) upon the presence and continuity of the accumulation process" (italics in original).

Contemporary Marxist analysts thus make three major points about the capitalist "welfare" state: (1) Its intervention is largely devoted to enhancing the process of capital accumulation rather than directly increasing the welfare of the masses; (2) it provides social benefits only as they are necessary for capitalist legitimation; (3) it is the servant rather than the master of the capitalist class. Massive state bureaucracies therefore arise in response to capitalist needs for nominally depoliticized structures to administer the common interest of the class as a whole.

Conservative opposition to liberal interventionism employs vastly different categories.[2] Rather than questioning the outcomes of bureaucratic activities (who benefits?), conservatives examine inputs (who directs the process? how much does government regulation cost?) and outputs (what is the total benefit?). They agree that the interventionist state cannot succeed in its objectives, but do not blame this result on its capture by the economically dominant class. Instead, they see government as counterproductive in its efforts to regulate the economy; moreover, its attempts at assuring social welfare foster parasitism within both its bureaucratic ranks and its dependent clienteles. Implicit in this critique is the characterization of bureaucracy as a Frankenstein's monster, reified and uncontrollable, operating according to its own autonomous logic rather than rooted in the social structure. State administration is a monstrosity forever trampling on individual liberty. Far from being a way to defend capitalist privilege, the state spawns a new ruling class. Increased socialization of the economy can only mean replication of the Soviet model and the destruction of democratic pluralism and freedom of choice.

Accordingly, the conservative solutions to the problem of bureaucracy under capitalism are privatization and deregulation. Doubts about the responsiveness of the state sector express themselves through proposals for a negative income tax to substitute for state services or educational vouchers to replace centralized public school systems. This mistrust of state administration reflects a Weberian pessimism over social progress under state auspices.

The elements which Weber identified as endemic to bureaucracies—secrecy, lifetime tenure, rigidity—mean that the translation of broad social goals into actual governmental operations is distorted (Gerth and Mills, 1958: 196–204). Organizational maintenance displaces goal attainment as the main activity of bureaucrats (Merton, 1957). The Weberian argument, which underlies most modern sociological analyses, traces bureaucratic functioning to social interests, but it looks only at a narrow range of interests—those directly involved with the bureaucratic organization itself. As a result, it is not so much inaccurate—within its confines it is in fact quite valid—as it is misleading. It is misleading in two respects: first, in its selective factual discussion, which excludes private sector causes and failures; and second, in its definition of categories for analysis.

Public-Private Comparisons

The contention that public bureaucracies are not accountable to outside forces is both theoretically deducible and empirically verifiable within the boundaries of a discussion that looks at the public sector in isolation.

Theoretically, it can be seen that bureaucratic clients have few sanctions over their caretakers and regulators, while politically appointed heads of bureaucracies are restricted from exerting substantial control by the unlimited tenure, expertise, and control over information of their subordinates. The testimony of disgruntled clients and ineffective agency heads corroborates these points.

But using these findings to condemn the public sector means avoiding appropriate comparisons with private bureaucracies. Large businesses, for example the oil companies, are not controlled at the top by representatives of the public nor at the bottom by their clienteles. Moreover, they are accorded rights of privacy not granted the government. In theory, private industry is accountable to its customers through the market. Yet in practice the ability of individuals to choose alternative sources to replace unsatisfactory suppliers is hardly greater in the oligopolistic private sector than in the public domain. The only meaningful choice that remains in either area is boycott—people can opt to go without gasoline or food stamps. The consequences of such a decision, however, are far greater to the consumer than the provider. Where demand is inelastic and supply constrained, consumer sovereignty is a myth regardless of who owns the means of production.

Similarly, corruption within the public bureaucracies is usually discussed without examination of business practices. If public officials prostitute themselves, private businesses buy their services. Moreover, most of the rules for those in government service regarding competitive bidding, lack of favoritism, and refusal to accept emoluments are either nonexistent or unenforced in the corporate world. The hidden tax of corruption affects the public regardless of whether it is paying its costs to the Internal Revenue Service or a privately owned utility company.

Escalating administrative costs for programs are another example of selective use of facts to denigrate public but not private sector operations. The heads of large corporations routinely earn ten times as much as their government counterparts. The theory of the market is that consumers will force companies to reduce their costs by choosing a cheaper alternative. The fact of the matter is that public oversight keeps down the salaries of government officials, while consumer preference has no such effect on corporate management. The private entrepreneur who makes a fortune is applauded for his initiative; the public servant is castigated for his rapaciousness.

The seemingly uncontrollable growth of government has paralleled a corresponding expansion of the monopoly sector of private industry. Large organizations dwarf the individual, regardless of ownership. "Voice" (Hirschman, 1970) has some effect when applied to government—witness the triumphs of the tax revolt—but not when directed against private monopolies except as it evokes government regulation. Neither Marxists nor public choice theorists have presented a convincing alternative to organizational giganticism in an economy based on large-scale production. Enraged citizens have largely blamed government for their misery, not because it is less, but precisely because it is *more* controllable than business, and because the dominance of a capitalist ideology diverts critical analysis from the hegemony of privately controlled organizations.

The differing standards used to judge public and private performance make comparisons of efficiency and effectiveness problematic. The state serves important latent functions which are distorted by commonly used evaluative criteria. Thus, if the government acts as employer of last resort, absorbing the unemployed created by private industry in its drive to cut labor costs, then the low productivity of the public service needs to be seen as a price of capitalism rather than the government alone. Likewise, excessive government expenditure on public works fuels private profit and is generated by capitalist pressure. Ultimately, the translation of cost savings by private industry into profit contributes no more to the general welfare than does government "waste," less so if that waste is widely distributed.

For bureaucracies with a primarily lower-class clientele, the popular criterion for success is a trend toward disappearance rather than good service or growth. Thus, welfare bureaucracies are rarely attacked for inefficiency in distributing checks; rather they are called to account for permitting the rolls to increase. Presumably the best welfare agency would distribute no benefits at all. Now that welfare clienteles are demobilized, the welfare bureaucracies are again more responsive to taxpayer and business groups, the "welfare problem" has been mitigated; the rolls have been cut, and inflation has been permitted to reduce real benefit levels.

The facts of poor public performance therefore seem less self-evident when examined in a context that includes the private sector. But our argument goes further than this. The very way in which the conservative critique is phrased begs certain questions; it is inherently nondialectical and segmented. By seeing public and private as antinomies, the conservative argument attacks the public sector rather than seeing it as a consequence of the political economy of advanced capitalism. Public and private function and malfunction are intimately related, and major reforms of either sector require systemic change in the nature of political control over the economy.

A Redefinition of the Categories of Analysis: Effectiveness

The fact of capitalism has enormous implications for the operation of governmental bureaucracies. Put bluntly, it means that when government acts in the public interest, it maintains and strengthens business institutions and class inequality. Because everyone's life depends on business, responsible governments must create situations conducive to corporate success. In doing so, they divert tax revenues raised from the majority of citizens—the real tax rate is, after all, barely progressive—to the benefit of corporations and their owners. Nationally, defense spending, investment tax credits, and depreciation allowances reward business for pursuing profitability. At the local level, debt, especially bonded debt sold by municipal governments to private owners of capital, provides direct benefits to capitalists: First, they receive a low-risk (and labor-free) return on investment; and second, they profit from public expenditures for economic development which facilitate capital accumulation. On the public side of the balance sheet, however, debt service comes to take over an ever larger chunk of operating budgets. The result is revenue-starved municipal service agencies with declining performance, fiscal stress, and taxpayers' revolts. Washington can print money, so nationally the outcome is inflation and consequent efforts to hold down social expenditures benefiting the lower classes.

Consider an example or two. During the late 1950s, downtown corporations and hotels supported the efforts of the San Francisco Redevelopment Agency to renew a "blighted" neighborhood south of Market Street in order to construct a convention facility—Yerba Buena Center (Hartman, 1974). The direct beneficiaries in the first instance would be the tourist industry and business generally. The city government would be a secondary beneficiary through increased property tax revenue. Thousands of lower-income people were displaced, as were hundreds of small businesses. Since there would be revenue-producing facilities in Yerba Buena (a hotel, garages, and so on), the Redevelopment Agency was able to float bonds without public referendum. For ten years, Yerba Buena Center did not produce any revenue, while its financial obligations were met with municipal and federal resources. Even when the center began to function, it continued to drain the municipal budget, as a second and equally typical case illustrates.

The New York Yankees threatened to leave town unless their stadium was refurbished. "Under duress," the city agreed to expend about $28 million of its capital budget on the job and to grant the Yankees a lease on highly favorable terms. To abbreviate the story, a decade or so later New York City is servicing a debt of $125 million, and the Yankees are making very large profits indeed. Multiply the Yerba Buenas and Yankee Stadiums a hundredfold, and you have a major cause of urban fiscal crisis. The very governments which have continually sought to subsidize business are then charged with inefficient performance by the business class. Municipal bankruptcy is attributed to the high wages and low outputs of working- and middle-class employees or to excessive kindness toward the poor. And the superior performance of private bureaucracies is trumpeted to the citizenry. . . .

The tasks of public agencies are made more difficult by private control of the means of production. We take for granted the fact that profitable activities are monopolized by the private sector; public agencies are left with tasks that produce no financial rewards and are difficult to accomplish, such as housing the poor, cleaning the streets, and educating the mass of the population. To the extent that public operations are relatively labor intensive, they are inevitably susceptible to breakdowns of human organization. Most important of all, government is hemmed in on all sides by private institutions that determine the quality of everyone's life—e.g., the work we do and the wages we receive—and define the environment within which government must function.

Public bureaucracies, in fact, rarely have the ability to control an entire process of production. Thus, the public schools train children for economic success, yet have no control over the requirements of private employers. The Department of Energy is supposed to insure an adequate supply of gasoline, but it cannot even command accurate data from the oil companies, much less itself extract petroleum from the ground and process it. The Department of Housing and Urban Development (HUD) can subsidize low-income housing, but it can neither build units itself nor divert private investment from middle-class suburban development. In each case, the public bureaucracy is inefficient and ineffective. But its problems are foreordained by the conditions under which public agencies operate.

The environments of bureaucracies are defined not only by administrative and legal structures, but also by classes and interest groups, by political milieus of consensus or conflict, by missions which serve the rich and powerful or the poor and weak. Just as inequality and conflict are the "other side" of capitalist economic structures, so too are they central elements in the bureaucratic context. From a Marxist structuralist perspective, the mission, resources, and performance of state administration are the outcomes of political struggle, defined more or less directly by class conflict. The performance of various state agencies will be affected by which class interests they serve and by how well those interests are mobilized. State agencies routinely serve the need of capital, but only serve the lower class when pressured from below. Agencies with lower-class constituencies will be regularly assaulted by upper-class groups for their inefficiency, ineffectiveness, and conflictual operation. Of course, this very attack, combined with lack of cooperation, contributes to agency failure.

We suggest that the relative effectiveness of state bureaucracies will increase as agency activity *corresponds* to upper-class interest. So too will praise for such agencies by powerful political elements. Thus, some bureaucracies will be routinely supported, while others will suffer the continual sniping which further hampers their performance. A brief list of the conditions which make for a "supportive" class environment might look like this:

1. The agency *does not* carry out activities which, if undertaken by business, can produce a profit;
2. *does* increase profitability of capital in general;
3. *does* increase profitability for particular, well-organized fractions of capital;
4. *does not* redistribute material benefits toward the lower classes;
5. *does* contribute to social control;
6. *is not* accountable to lower-class constituencies.

While most cases will be mixed in terms of these six criteria, they do help us differentiate between the environments of, say, the Army Corps of Engineers and the Legal Services Corporation, or the Turnpike Authority and the Community Development Agency. Only political struggle is likely to produce agencies in major violation of the conditions of correspondence. Some past victories over private capital may, however, in a new historical period result in bureaucracies which become more acceptable to the upper classes as their benefits become increasingly obvious. Consider public power and Social Security. Public power was and still is bitterly opposed by private utilities for its violation of our first condition. But in the West, public power agencies have also come to meet the second and third by giving industry the benefits of cheap power. Social Security was initially opposed by business because it had redistributive potential. But the program became shaped so as to facilitate social control without being strongly redistributive and without violating the first and sixth conditions. The lesson of the Social Security Administration, in contrast, for instance, to the now defunct Office of Economic Opportunity (OEO), is that government agencies which assist the poor must also not threaten capital if they are to operate at all well, or even survive longer than the period of mobilization in which they were born.

The relative importance of the several conditions in affecting bureaucratic functioning depends on the overall state of mobilization and consciousness of the classes in capitalist society. Northern European capitalist states differ from the United States in their much greater degree of state planning, in their broader "welfare" activities (e.g., health care and housing), and in the overall higher legitimacy of public administration in the eyes of corporate management (Fainstein and Fainstein, 1978). These differences result in part from European acceptance of a larger realm of public production and of the subordination of particular capitalist interests to those of the whole class, as defined by the state administration itself. The greater viability of Northern European welfare bureaucracies, however, also derives from the far greater strength of working-class parties there than here. The acceptability to the upper classes of redistribution (the fourth condition) depends on a payoff in social control (the fifth condition). Where the lower classes are poorly organized (as in the United States), they can be controlled without redistribution. The point here is that public bureaucratic performance is both a major factor in ideological conflict and is strongly affected by the interplay between agency mission on the one hand and the balance of forces within and between classes on the other.

Lack of Accountability
Accountability, defined as the ability of individuals or groups to monitor and control bureaucratic performance, involves different considerations from effectiveness. In general, the agencies which routinely serve capitalist interests are infrequently criticized as unaccountable, and these include much of the state administration. Put another way, because the Federal Reserve Board and the Department of Commerce act in the public interest as defined by the business class and its dominant ideology, procedural issues about how such agencies are governed do not customarily arise. Indeed, bureaucracies which represent the interests of capital are frequently unaccountable to the electorate. As Friedland, Piven, and Alford (1977) show, economic development agencies, port authorities, pension funds, and the like—bureaucracies which command vast capital resources—are segmented off from the political process, made invisible. So these agencies, at all levels of government, are not part of the accountability problem for the upper classes. Nor are they under much attack from below, since they are effectively obscured by administrative arrangements: Their actual importance and the interests they serve are mystified by the dominant ideology. Agencies which directly serve the interest of capital (called "the economy") are perceived as outside politics and thus outside contests of accountability. No one, in fact, is preoccupied with the activities of these agencies except those interests which can profit directly from their activities.

The accountability problems of state bureaucracies which are not obscured and depoliticized stem from the basic tension between democracy and capitalism. On the one hand, the state is legitimated as reflecting the public interest defined by electoral majorities (albeit through a complex process of representation). On the other hand, the state is fully committed to economic growth at home and security abroad. It must attain these objectives within the context of corporate organization of production and class hierarchy. Moreover, economic growth is required if the upper classes are to maintain their privilege and the lower classes to remain peaceful. Therefore, the state must further capitalist accumulation and must define the public interest as coincident with the interests of capital and the upper classes. In other words, the state must benefit upper-class minorities, while appearing to be controlled by working- and middle-class majorities.

A very important way in which this feat gets accomplished is through the relative autonomy within the state of the administrative apparatus. Legislative debate can center about what the people want, while the state administration looks after what capital needs. In the process, bureaucracies inevitably make policy. While in rare instances, these bureaucracies interpret legislative intent in favor of the lower classes, by far the more usual situation is to go the other way, to put into practice what legislators hesitate to put into words. Thus, the FBI is officially established to fight criminals and enemy spies, but in operation it also acts to intimidate political radicals. State public utility commissions ostensibly intended to control the industry become vehicles for protecting profits. Redevelopment agencies, charged with eliminating slums and blight, end up displacing the poor into even worse neighborhoods.

In each case, when mass mobilization over some egregious event demystifies the operations of the agency in question, politicians declare an accountability problem. The FBI is said to be too independent of the Department of Justice; the utility commission should have a gubernatorial appointment representing public interest groups; redevelopment agencies are required to provide structures for citizen participation. The fault is with the bureaucracy, not with the intrinsic character of the state. The politicians symbolically slap administrative hands and reaffirm the democratic character of government. Accountability problems become pathologies in a healthy democratic body politic. When they are spotted, they are blamed on the bureaucratic phenomenon and duly exorcised. Legitimacy is reestablished.

Another publicly defined accountability problem is that Washington bureaucrats are "too remote" from the electorate, while local government is more easily controlled and responsive. Here again, the definition of the problem must be understood as ideology which obscures or safely redefines the actual situation. The ideology of localism has its roots in the business class and is expressed through conservative attacks on big government and faceless Washington bureaucrats. Business concern over runaway Washington, however, focuses on welfare programs and regulatory activities, not defense spending, central banking, and loan guarantees. Moreover, the distribution of power within the federal system benefits business. Corporations need a strong central government with flexible revenue resources and the capacity to regulate the national economy. At the same time, local governments and thousands of separate jurisdictions permit the upper classes to encapsulate themselves in homogeneous residential areas, thereby escaping the social costs of the lower classes; and local jurisdictions permit corporate flight from onerous taxation or labor organization. Federalism produces a general system of local mercantilism from which business benefits immensely.

Conservatives, particularly in the corporate sector, further object that Washington bureaucracies engulf them with oceans of red tape, requiring endless documentation, thereby adding needlessly to business costs. Here again, some of the objection must be understood as actually based in the substantive programs in question. It is not just red tape but *red* tape when the government tries to control pollution or requires minority employment. Yet there certainly is actual basis for claiming that Washington administrative agencies require disproportionately great amounts of paper work, often for no apparent purpose. The irony here is that Washington red tape proliferates precisely because of the state structure in which the central government cannot direct economic production and does not even control the means of public administration. Facing two markets—one of business and the other of local governments—Washington agencies attempt to implement programs at a distance through the carrot of subsidy and the stick of regulation. Each approach is associated with red tape in the application for funds, monitoring of performance, and proof of compliance. Thus, the very weakness of the central government—an objective of conservatives—contributes to some of the annoying requirements of its administrative agencies, which must depend on regulation as a substitute for operational authority.

Overall then, governmental bureaucracies *are* accountable, if not to the citizens of democratic theory, then to the corporate interests of capitalist practice. While bureaucratic accountability, like bureaucratic performance, does indeed constitute a universal problem of governance, the real problem of the American state system is not unaccountable bureaucracies, but the class to which they are routinely accountable. The problem lies not so much in bureaucracy itself as in the political economy of American capitalism. . . .

Notes

1. The term "state" encompasses both bureaucratic and political roles within the public sector. Our concern here, however, and the scapegoat for most declarations of governmental failure, is with the state bureaucracy (or more correctly within the United States, bureaucracies).

2. The description "conservative" used throughout this article refers to arguments pressed by a variety of bureaucratic critics, who do not necessarily share the same basic social values. Thus, some liberals share conservative doubts concerning the responsiveness of the state sector and press for reduction of the bureaucratic role, even though they may place a higher weight on equality as a social goal.

References

Bowles, S. and H. Gintis. 1976. *Schooling in Capitalist America*. New York: Basic.
Braverman, H. 1974. *Labor and Monopoly Capital*. New York: Monthly Review Press.
Crozier, M. 1964. *The Bureaucratic Phenomenon*. Chicago: Univ. of Chicago Press.
Dahl, R. 1961. *Who Governs?* New Haven, CT: Yale Univ. Press.
Dahrendorf, R. 1959. *Class and Class Conflict in Industrial Societies*. Palo Alto, CA: Stanford Univ. Press.
Djilas, M. 1957. *The New Class*. New York: Praeger.
Fainstein, S. and N. Fainstein. 1978. National policy and urban development. *Social Problems* 28: 125–46.

Friedland, R., F. F. Piven, and R. R. Alford. 1977. Political conflict, urban structure, and the fiscal crisis. *Int. J. of Urban and Regional Research* 1: 447–73.
Gerth, H. H. and C. W. Mills [eds.]. 1958. From *Max Weber*. New York: Oxford Univ. Press.
Hartman, C. 1974. *Yerba Buena—Land Grab and Community Resistance in San Francisco*. San Francisco: Glide Publications.
Hirschman, A. O. 1970. *Exit, Voice, and Loyalty*. Cambridge, MA: Harvard Univ. Press.
Marcuse, H. 1955. *Eros and Civilization*. Boston: Beacon.
Merton, R. K. 1957. *Social Theory and Social Structure*. New York: Macmillan.
Michels, R. 1962. *Political Parties*. New York: Macmillan.
Miliband, R. 1969. *The State in Capitalist Society*. New York: Basic.
O'Connor, J. 1973. *The Fiscal Crisis of the State*. New York: St. Martin's.
Offe, K. 1975. "The theory of the capitalist state and the problem of policy formation." In *Stress and Contradiction in Modern Capitalism*, edited by L. N. Lindberg, et al. Lexington, MA: D. C. Heath.

20
The Department of Defense and the Military-Industrial Establishment: The Politics of the Iron Triangle

Gordon Adams

Introduction

Since World War II, the United States has maintained large, permanent military forces and a global network of security commitments. Despite occasional criticism of national commitments and the level of defense spending—for example, the disarmament movement of the 1960s and the opposition to the Vietnam War—a large military-industrial/national security establishment remains a constant feature of the American political landscape. This establishment, cloaked in national security, seems impervious to criticism and change.

The advent of the Reagan administration brought a dramatic increase in the size and scope of American national security policy. The sudden rapid growth in defense spending caused vocal criticism of defense policies and spending practices. The national debate over defense spending has provided a new opportunity to examine the defense policy process, to view its resistance to outside interference and change, and to explore new directions for American national security policy.

The size and rapid growth of defense spending since 1980 is clear. Between fiscal years 1980 and 1984, the defense budget will have doubled in current dollars and increased 40 percent in constant dollars. In 1984 alone, the defense budget of $270 billion will cost the average American household over $3,000, while the administration's five-year spending plan of $1.6 trillion will cost each household $20,000. By 1988, under current plans, the defense budget will have virtually tripled in current dollars in only eight years.

This rapid growth in spending is unprecedented since 1945. The Reagan military buildup has been the most dramatic peacetime increase in defense spending this nation has experienced. By 1985, defense spending will be at a higher constant dollar level than at any point since the Second World War.

Moreover, defense has become the largest single commitment of taxpayer funds. Roughly 50 percent of each income tax dollar funds military programs: the Defense Department, nuclear warhead programs in the Department of Energy, a part of the National Aeronautics and Space Administration (NASA) spending that serves military purposes, the Veterans Administration, and some proportion of the interest on the national debt incurred as a result of past military spending.[1] In addition, defense spending is a significant portion of federal purchases and research spending. The Defense Department buys 75 percent of all goods and services purchased by the federal government. Moreover, of the roughly $45 billion the federal government spends annually on research and development, 70 percent goes to military-related research and development.

The Reagan administration's commitment to unprecedented peacetime growth in defense spending also encountered widespread domestic and international criticism, opening up the debate about national security. The call for a bilateral nuclear weapons freeze, once a fringe appeal, was supported by as much as 75 percent of the American people, was approved by popular referenda in nine states and many cities, and was endorsed by the United States House of Representatives and by many Democratic politicians. Specific weapons such as the MX missile, mainstay of the Defense Department's effort to build a new generation of nuclear weapons, have been a target of vocal criticism.

This growing critique of defense policy forced the administration, deeply skeptical of arms control, into new arms control talks with the Soviet Union and brought new conflict to an Atlantic Alliance severely divided over the wisdom of deploying new intermediate-range nuclear weapons on European soil. In addition, Americans have grown concerned about the continuing crisis in Central America, persistent problems in the Middle East, and upheavals in the rest of the developing world that could lead to commitment of American troops to overseas combat.

Criticism also has focused on the efficiency of military spending and its impact on the American economy. Repeated investigations of defense spending have exposed flagrant wastefulness and problems with weapon performance—from the M-1 tank that won't drive, to the Bradley amphibious infantry fighting vehicle that can't float, to the four-cent diodes for F-18 simulators that are being bought for $110.[2] These criticisms are heard from conservative (Heritage Foundation), bureaucratic (Defense Department), and liberal (Brookings Institution) voices. They warn that the cost of weapons and the defense budget are out of control and that a crushing bill is mounting—with fearsome consequences for the budget and the economy.[3] The dramatic growth in new weapons purchases, for example, is putting pressure on the federal budget and could actually reduce military readiness; paying for weapons could force cuts in spending for operations, maintenance, and personnel.[4] Moreover, the defense budget may be exacerbating federal budget deficits, high interest rates, and low capital supplies while impeding future industrial investment and the creation of new jobs in the American economy.[5]

The debate over national security and defense spending is more widespread and vociferous than at any time in American political history since 1945. In the past, national security and defense spending issues were left to the experts; now, religious denominations, school children and teachers, civic groups, professional societies, and citizens have entered the debate over nuclear policy, defense budgets, and foreign policy.

The debate, however, has not dramatically changed the defense policy process in Washington. The Scowcroft Commission, appointed in 1983 by President Reagan to examine strategic policy, split the difference in the strategic arms debate, calling for the MX missile to be produced and deployed and, at the same time, for the production and deployment of a missile dubbed "Midgetman," which would substitute for the MX and make its construction unnecessary.[6] Liberal members of Congress known as critics of the administration's strategic policies, such as Representatives Les Aspin (D., Wis.) and Albert Gore, Jr. (D., Tenn.), endorsed this MX decision and urged its approval by Congress. Most dramatically, the call for a bilateral nuclear weapons freeze, passed by the House of Representatives after exhausting debate in spring 1983, was followed by a crucial vote on the MX missile, which would be halted by a freeze. Of the members of the House who endorsed a freeze, ninety-seven also voted *for* the MX program.

In the face of massive spending on new weapons and suggestions that the defense buying process might be out of control, Congress had continued to fund all the administration's requests for weapons procurement. Although Congress reduced the president's request in 1983 and cut the rate of real growth in defense spending from 10 percent to 5 percent, this action proved to be largely a paper exercise. Although the level of budget authority (the right to begin spending money) in 1984 was reduced by over $12 billion from the administration's request, actual outlays (the money to be spent in 1984) were only $5 billion less than what the administration had sought.

Defense policy alternatives offered in Washington stray very little from the administration's program. Despite public criticism of the direction of national security policy and the general sense that greater accountability is needed for defense spending, the policy process has continued to function with little change, operating in virtual isolation from the political process around it.

In order to render defense spending accountable, one needs to understand why it seems so impervious to the normal accountability process of American politics. Three different models can be used to explain the defense policy process; each provides an element that helps to clarify the closed nature of this part of American government.

The National Security Model

From the "national security" perspective, defense policies and budgets are designed through a rational process. A clear, precise definition of the "threats" to the United States (principally the Soviet "threat") leads directly to a rational definition of American military missions as the forces and weapons required to fulfill those missions.[7]

For many analysts of defense policy, the national security model is the only acceptable arena of debate. Commitments, forces, and weapons are subject to some discussion, but the terms of agreement are set in the logic of "threat," world events, and the capabilities of potential adversaries. Debate at this level has provided some isolation for the defense policy process. Cloaked in secrecy, national security arguments provide legitimacy for policy makers who have exclusive access to the secrets. Members of Congress and the public, less privy to the secrets, find they lack expertise and credibility—they are excluded from the policy process.

The nationwide debate over American national security in the 1980s began to strip away the veil of secrecy. Critics of the administration suggested, with growing legitimacy, that the "threats" to the United States were exaggerated and that the defense buildup was based on a series of myths about America's security. The myths purported that (1) the Soviet Union has outspent the United States on defense since 1970, (2) the USSR has a definite "margin of superiority" over American strategic forces, (3) these forces are, as a result, "vulnerable," and (4) the Warsaw Pact dramatically dominates the forces of the North Atlantic Treaty Organization (NATO).[8]

Moreover, it is not clear that a major expansion of weapons spending is actually designed to meet threats to national security. Strategic weapons expansion may fuel an arms race; the expansion of intervention capabilities may lead to war; weapons purchases could cut into funds for military readiness. The "security" model may explain some parts of defense policies and budgets; it may also conceal other sources of policy.

The Bureaucratic Model

A second model of defense policy enriches our understanding of the roots of national security spending and also helps to clarify the imperviousness of the policy process itself. This model focuses on defense policy making as a "bureaucratic" process.[9] Defense budgets and weapons programs, which emerge from bureaucratic self-promotion, inventiveness, and interservice rivalry in the Defense Department, are linked only loosely, if at all, to perceptions of "threat."

In the Defense Department, for example, interservice rivalry among the Army, Navy, and Air Force, leads to competition for funds and, frequently, duplication of weapons systems. The Air Force and the Navy, for example, each purchase several different types of fighter aircraft. Joint fighter programs do not exist.

Inside one service, officials can become attached to a weapon program less for its contribution to security than for its role in ensuring a continued mission for that service. For example, Air Force testimony in the 1970s suggested that the B–52 bomber could survive until the year 2000 as a cruise-missile carrier.[10] Strategic bombers, even those provided with new "stealth" characteristics that would make them less visible on radar, have an uncertain future, given the quality of Soviet air defenses. However, the B–1 bomber is the sole major aircraft program of the Strategic Air Command (SAC). Without the B–1 bomber, SAC's primary mission is the management of land-based strategic missiles. In the 1970s, the SAC was unified in promoting the B–1 over opposition from other parts of the Air Force, from other services, and even from within the office of the secretary of defense.[11]

The contracting practices of the defense bureaucracy also have a direct impact on the cost, size, and contents of the defense budget. David Stockman, director of the Office of Management and Budget, described the Department of Defense as a "swamp of waste" containing some $10 to $30 billion in excessive spending that could be eliminated with no risks for American national security.[12] In 1983 the Grace Commission, appointed by President Reagan to explore waste and savings in federal spending, pointed to roughly $30 billion a year in wasteful Pentagon spending that could be eliminated.[13]

There are many examples of such waste. For instance, 90 percent of all Defense Department prime contracts (in dollar value) are negotiated, not publicly advertised and competitively bid; two-thirds of these are negotiated with just one supplier—"a sole course." After contracts are signed cost control problems plague the Defense Department. Constant renegotiations with contractors change the price, performance, or schedule requirements of most weapons, thus increasing their cost and turning even "fixed price" contracts into "cost plus" contracts. Both the Defense Department and the defense industry lack incentives to keep costs down. Independent testing and cost analysis capabilities in the Pentagon are weak; auditing capabilities are inadequate.

Bureaucratic infighting, self-protection, and inefficiency keep defense spending levels high and directly affect procurement choices.[14] Moreover, the federal government's largest "buying" bureaucracy is committed to defending itself from outside criticism and penetration.[15] The bureaucratic model helps to explain the defense establishment's imperviousness to its critics. The model does not, however, explain why Congress fails to cut back on the rapid expansion of defense spending.

Defense budget and spending decisions cannot be explained solely by "rational" or "bureaucratic" models. The defense policy process is, finally, a "political" process.

The Political Model

This model for defense policies and budgets can be drawn from a more general discussion of the relationship between business and government in American society. The relationship between large corporations and American government has often been described as an antagonistic one, especially from the perspective of business. Business is frequently described as another "pressure" or "interest group" seeking government favors and engaging in a continuous battle to fend off government efforts to control its behavior and activities.[16]

The relationships between these two supposed antagonists in the twentieth century suggests, however, that a more cooperative set of relations has developed. Nowhere is this cooperative connection more apparent than in the defense sector. During World War I, business executives entered the federal government as policy makers, planning virtually all sectors of United States industrial production for the war effort. In addition, the war brought a fledgling aircraft industry into existence. With the end of the war, contractor dependence on government orders became clear.[17] Defense suppliers undertook strenuous efforts to ensure a steady flow of government orders for their products, federal subsidy of their research and development costs, and federal regulation of their behavior.

The emergence of a permanent relationship between the two followed World War II; once again, a surge of orders had expanded the defense industry, and business personnel had played a vital role in war production planning. Since the late 1940s, the Defense Department, which had subsidized construction of a vast military production base, has had a clear policy of maintaining that base in the private sector.[18] The role of the United States as the leading world power provided an apparent justification and focus for continuous defense planning, a large military force, and massive arms procurement. Moreover, the American economy seemed able to contain the expense, absorbing guns and butter in a constant expansion. Within this framework, service bureaucracies and industry officials interacted regularly, and the industry self-consciously developed the capacity to penetrate and influence the policy process.

This constant interaction meets the needs of both participants. Defense Department officials, engaged in self-protection, find useful allies among contractors committed to remaining in the business of defense production. Neither side of this relationship could continue, however, without the active participation of a third player, Congress. Through Congress, the Defense Department acquires the funding that enables the relationship to continue; therefore, Congress must be brought into the relationship as an active participant. The resulting political configuration is a familiar one in American politics: a closeness shared by a federal agency (the Pentagon), its client group in American society (the defense industry), and those in Congress with a special interest in that part of the federal budget (members of armed services committees and defense appropriations subcommittees, and members from congressional districts and states with concentrations of defense spending).

This relationship can be described as an "iron triangle," or "subgovernment," a part of American government that links major interested parties and is isolated from other areas of government policy making.[19] Such triangles exist in other arenas of federal policy making and share four characteristics.

First, a close working relationship in a specific area of policy is shared among three key participants: the bureaucracy, key committees and members of Congress, and a specific sector of American society.

Second, each triangle features an intimate interpenetration between the societal interest and the federal bureaucracy in question. Policy makers and administrators move freely between the two arenas, and policy issues tend to be discussed and resolved among participants who develop and share common values, interests, and perceptions.[20] As the groups in society and the government agency interact, they begin to share policy-making authority; often private sector parties become policy makers and administrators without ever entering public service. Government power and private power become indistinguishable and grow to resemble each other.[21]

Third, such a subgovernment emerges slowly. It is not willfully created in a single moment, but comes into being as a result of constant interaction among its participants. Government bureaucrats help create and maintain a subgovernment. Private industry pursues policies and procedures it desires from the government, and works to maintain the triangle as circumstances change. Shared interests develop between bureaucrats and industry, and disagreements are reconciled through constant interaction.

Fourth, the triangle has a strong tendency to become "iron." Eventually, it becomes isolated from other policy arenas, from Congress, and from the public. The participants exert strenuous efforts to keep it protected.[22] As a result of this gradual isolation, perspectives on policy alternatives narrow, and proposals from outside the subgovernment have no credibility inside. Policy makers and private participants begin to share the assumption that they are acting not only in their own interests, but also in the general "public interest." Ziegler and Peake describe the result:

> In the day-to-day performance of their tasks, administrators see very little of the more general public support which accompanied the establishment of the agency. The only people who are likely to come to the attention of administrators are those whose problems are uniquely a part of the administrative environment. . . . Under such circumstance it is not surprising that the administrator's perception of the public interest is in reality defined by the interests of the regulated parties.[23]

Decisions made for a variety of reasons can be routinely justified in terms of "national security." Behind the veil of national security, the defense iron triangle has unusual power. As Philip Hughes, former deputy director of the Budget Bureau, has described:

> The most relevant consideration is, in blunt terms, sheer power—where the muscle is—and this is a very power-conscious town, and the Secretary of Defense and the defense establishment are a different group to deal with, whether Congress is dealing with them or whether the Budget Bureau is dealing with them.[24]

The continued existence and success of the defense iron triangle depends on a steady flow of information, access, influence, and money. The most crucial actor in this process is the defense industry. Defense contractors are extremely self-conscious about the importance of the political arena to their business success. Defense is big business: The Defense Department contract market amounts to over $100 billion per year. It is also a concentrated and stable business: Most of the top 25 contractors to the Defense Department have been in the business for over 30 years and receive 50 percent of all the contract dollars the Defense Department awards. Finally, it is important business: Many of the leading contracting companies do over 50 percent of their sales with the federal government.[25]

As a result, defense contractors are among the most innovative corporations in finding ways to strengthen their relations with the federal government; they exercise an unusually strong influence over military policy—strategic and conventional alike. Contractor influence, which is unusually difficult to detect, frequently begins at the most invisible level of the weapons planning process: early research and development. The nation's eight leading military research and development contractors—Boeing, General Dynamics, Grumman, Lockheed, McDonnell-Douglas, Northrop, Rockwell International, and United Technologies—received a total of over $20 billion in research and development contracts alone in the 1970s.[26] In addition, these same companies were reimbursed roughly $2 billion for direct corporate investment in research work through the "Independent Research and Development Bids and Proposals" program.[27]

At this crucial early stage, ideas move freely between industry and government, thus giving contractors ample opportunity to influence future decisions. Major contractors are well represented on roughly fifty advisory committees (and hundreds of subcommittees) to the Defense Department and NASA—most notably, the Defense Science Board and the scientific advisory groups of each branch of the military. Membership on key committees gives contractors an opportunity to affect new weapons policies long before the public or Congress is aware of them.[28]

The constant interaction of government and contractor personnel at the research level means that new weapons ultimately bought by the Department of Defense are often created by the firms that stand to gain if these weapons are produced. The *Wall Street Journal* reported, for example, that Boeing was seeking very secret information about plans for land-based missiles from inside contacts at the Pentagon.[29] Early access enables a company to influence future weapons planning at the first possible stage. As one defense industry official described in the late 1960s: "Your ultimate goal is actually to write the R.F.P. [Request for Proposal], and this happens more often than you might think."[30]

Close ties between industry and government are reinforced by a steady flow of employees between the two sectors. In the 1950s, congressional studies showed that more than 1,000 retired military personnel had taken jobs in the defense industry. In the 1960s, this number rose to about 2,000. Between 1969 and 1974, the figure reached 2,000 for the top 100 contractors alone. An examination of the eight leading defense contractors noted above showed that, during the 1970s, 2,000 of their employees transferred either from industry to government or from government to industry. Of the nearly 500 civilians in this group, 34 percent had either worked in or moved to the key research and development offices of the Army, Navy, Air Force, and the office of the secretary of defense.[31]

Examples of the revolving door are numerous. General Alexander Haig, for example, moved from the Army to the presidency of United

Technologies, to secretary of state, and back to an advisory committee with United Technologies. United Technologies employs other government alumni. Clark MacGregor, head of the company's Washington, D.C. office, is a former member of Congress. Hugh Witt, a government relations specialist in the same office, previously worked in the office of the secretary of the Air Force as director of Federal Procurement Policy in the Office of Management and Budget.[32]

T. K. Jones, a former deputy program manager for Boeing, became staff assistant to the Defense Department delegation to the Strategic Arms Limitations Talks (SALT) in 1971, went back to Boeing in 1974 as program and products evaluation manager, and subsequently returned to the Defense Department to work on strategic policy in the Reagan administration. Seymour Zieberg, appointed deputy undersecretary of defense for Strategic and Space Systems in 1977, joined Martin Marietta in 1981 as vice president for research.[33]

The revolving door provides unique access to the defense policy-making process. The *Wall Street Journal* story about Boeing's MX involvement noted that Boeing had obtained its information from a Boeing employee "on leave to work in the Pentagon's Weapons Research and Development Office." Once this employee had read the relevant report, he telexed its substance to a former Defense Department employee working at Boeing's headquarters in Seattle. The newspaper concluded: "The movement of weaponry experts between industry and government jobs, frequently on the same project, facilitates the easy flow of information and tends to blur the distinction between national security and corporate goals."[34]

Research and development access and the revolving door help weapons projects get started. Once underway, a committed constituency grows, and the weapon becomes hard to cancel. Defense contractors use the lobbying resources of their government relations departments to keep the process moving. The contractors' Washington offices are frequently the nerve centers for this effort. From 1977 through 1979, the same eight leading defense companies employed 200 people in their Washington offices and 48 registered lobbyists. According to audits by the Defense Contract Audit Agency, Boeing, General Dynamics, Grumman, Lockheed, and Rockwell International together spent $16.8 million on their Washington offices in 1974 and 1975, an average of $1.6 million each per year. Rockwell alone spent $7 million from 1973 through 1975.[35]

These Washington offices keep track of program developments in the Pentagon and NASA, follow the process of legislation, lobby on Capitol Hill, handle public relations, funnel information back to the company, and negotiate with foreign weapons buyers. Virtually all of the nonentertainment expenditures of these offices, including lobbying activities, have been billed to the government as administrative expenses related to defense contracting.[36]

Congress is an active participant in the defense iron triangle. In principle, Congress's role in the policy process can be extensive.[37] Congress has the capability to conduct oversight on Defense Department activities, and Congress votes on the budget that provides the funding for the Defense Department and its contractors. Because of its critical role, Congress has been the target of lobbying activity, both by the Defense Department and by the contracting industry. Curiously, despite its potential for influence in the policy process, Congress has come to play a highly visible but secondary role. Weapons budgets and the information justifying them are produced by the Defense Department, not by Congress. Congress must react with less information.[38] Moreover, with many weapons contracts already underway, strong bureaucratic commitment, and corporate involvement, Congress has even less room to maneuver.

The net result is that congressional oversight activity, though extensive, seems to have little real impact on the policy process. Hearings on defense procurement waste in the late 1960s, for example, did little to change Defense Department procedure. The same issues are being raised in the 1980s; their effect on the Pentagon procurement process is not yet known. Nevertheless, because of its budgetary role, Congress remains an important focus of activity in the iron triangle.

From the industry's point of view, influence in Congress is crucial. Members of armed services and defense appropriations committees and members who represent defense contracting districts are most important. Committee members jealously guard their jurisdictions, and members from key districts must protect their turf; thus both are appropriate targets for contractor lobbying.

Beyond direct lobbying, contractors also reach members of Congress through campaign contributions.[39] Defense contractor political action committees (PACs) are among the largest corporate PACs in the country. Their contributions are concentrated on members of key congressional committees or members from districts with defense facilities or plants. While a campaign contribution does not mean the member will always vote with the company, it does bring access. Access, in turn, speeds the flow of information and influence in the policy process. Rockwell, for example, carried on a four-year battle to revive the B-1 bomber after President Carter cancelled it in 1977. Among other elements in this campaign, Rockwell's PAC focused its campaign contributions on members of defense appropriations and armed services committees in the House and Senate; nearly all of them voted for the program when the Reagan administration revived it.[40]

Defense contractors also organize grass-roots lobbying campaigns to influence Congress. Because company employees, the communities in which they are located, stockholders, and subcontractors depend on defense contracting for their survival, they are all part of a contractor's grass-roots network. Trade unions such as the United Auto Workers and the International Association of Machinists have many members in defense industries, and their locals often follow a company's call to support its weapons in Washington.

In the mid-1970s, for example, Rockwell International mounted a grass-roots effort on behalf of the B-1 bomber program, then on the brink of cancellation. The company urged its 115,000 employees and the holders of its 35 million shares of stock to write to their Congressmen. The company also asked more than 3,000 subcontractors and suppliers in 48 states to tell their Congressmen that scrapping the B-1 would adversely affect their districts. Rockwell spent $1.35 million on such efforts from 1975 through 1977, an amount that opponents of the B-1 could not have hoped to match.[41]

Conclusion

The political model of defense policy making fills many of the gaps in the explanation left by the national security and bureaucratic models. Through the political model, one can see the policy process in operation over a period of time. National security decisions establish the language, the rationale, and sometimes the screen behind which defense policy and spending decisions are made. While national security is indeed an important policy consideration, it cannot explain the size, scope, and political power of the defense policy apparatus. Bureaucratic explanations add to our understanding of the policy process, but provide only a partial understanding of where and how weapons originate, why they are so hard to stop, and why Congress remains a fairly passive ratifier of funding requests submitted by the Defense Department.

The political model helps answer these questions and displays how the process actually functions. The flow of information, the opening of doors of access, and the opportunities for influence all focus on the single largest piece of federal government buying. Much is at stake; thus, warding off external intervention and public criticism is an important part of the policy process itself. The debate over national security opened up the debate over this policy process. Whether massive public spending for defense actually provides security is dubious. The impact of such spending on the American economy and the substantial sums being wasted are growing concerns. The debate provides the opportunity to institute changes in the way the defense iron triangle functions—to join concerns about the accountability of the policy process with the need for legitimate debate about the requirements of American national security.[42] The defense debate helps one understand how the policy process functions. This understanding may well lead to significant changes in the way national security planning and defense spending will be conducted in the future.

Notes

1. David Gold and Paul Murphy, "Total Military Spending Budget," in *Military Expansion, Economic Decline*, ed. Robert W. DeGrasse, Jr. (New York: Council on Economic Priorities, 1983), 211–37.

2. On the M–1 tank, see contributions by Patrick Oster, Bruce Ingersoll, and John Fialka, in *More Bucks, Less Bang: How the Pentagon Buys Ineffective Weapons*, ed. Dina Rasor (Washington, D.C.: Fund for Constitutional Government, 1983), 34–50. On the Bradley Infantry Fighting Vehicle, see William Boly, "The $13 Billion Dud," in Rasor, *More Bucks, Less Bang*, 13–28. On the diode, see "Millions Found Wasted in Buying Military Spare Parts," *Chicago Tribune*, 11 July 1983, p. 4.

3. George Kuhn, "Department of Defense: Ending Defense Stagnation," in *Agenda '83*, Heritage Foundation, 69–114; Franklin C. Spinney, "The Plans/Reality Mismatch and Why We Need Realistic Budgeting," Defense Department briefing paper (Washington, D.C.: December 1982); U.S. Air Force Systems Command, "The Affordable Acquisition Approach Study" (Washington, D.C., U.S.A.F. Briefing, February 1983); William Kaufmann, "The Defense Budget," in *Setting National Priorities*, ed. Joseph A. Pechman (Washington, D.C.: Brookings Institution, 1983), 39–79.

4. House Armed Services Committee, "Staff Briefing on the FY 1984 DoD O&M Request" (Washington, D.C.: March 1983); Walter F. Mondale to the American Newspaper Publishers Association, New York, N.Y., 26 April 1983, p. 4.

5. See, for example, the appeal from The Bipartisan Appeal to Resolve the Budget Crisis, a business group, for slower growth in defense spending in a letter to William C. Clark, 25 March 1983.

6. *Report of the President's Commission on Strategic Forces* (Washington, D.C.: White House, April 1983).

7. This is, in general, the tone of the introduction to each annual report from Secretary of Defense Caspar Weinberger since the Reagan administration took office. See Department of Defense: *Annual Report of the Secretary of Defense to the Congress, Fiscal Year 1983* (Washington, D.C.: Department of Defense, 1982) and *Annual Report of the Secretary of Defense to the Congress, Fiscal Year 1984* (Washington, D.C.: Department of Defense, 1983).

8. See, for example: Franklyn Holzman, "Are the Soviets Really Outspending the U.S. on Defense?" *International Security* 4, no. 4 (Spring 1980): 86–104; Holzman, "Soviet Military Spending: Assessing the Numbers Game," *International Security* 6, no. 4 (Spring 1982): 78–101; Holzman, "Are We Falling Behind the Soviets?" *Atlantic* (July 1983): 10–18; Richard Stubbing, "The Imaginary Defense Gap: We Already Outspend Them," *Washington Post*, 14 February 1982, p. C-1; Federation of American Scientists, *Public Interest Report* (September 1982); John Collins, *U.S.-Soviet Military Balance: Concepts and Capabilities, 1960–1980* (New York: McGraw-Hill, 1980); and Senator Carl Levin, "The Other Side of the Story" (unpublished monograph, Washington, D.C., May 1983).

9. For examples of this model, see: Morton J. Peck and Frederick M. Scherer, *The Weapons Acquisition Process; An Economic Analysis* (Boston: Harvard School of Business Administration, 1962); J. Ronald Fox, *Arming America: How the U.S. Buys Weapons* (Boston: Harvard Graduate School of Business Administration, 1974); Harvey M. Sapolsky, *The Polaris System Development: Bureaucratic and Programmatic Success in Government* (Cambridge: Harvard University Press, 1972); A. Ernest Fitzgerald, *The High Priests of Waste*, (New York: Norton, 1972).

10. Gordon Adams, "A Bomber for All Seasons," *Council on Economic Priorities Newsletter*, New York, February 1982.

11. Gordon Adams, *The B–1 Bomber: An Analysis of Its Strategic Utility, Cost, Constituency and Economic Impact* (New York: Council on Economic Priorities, 1976).

12. William Grieder, "The Education of David Stockman," *Atlantic* (December 1981): 27–54.

13. U.S. Department of Commerce, President's Private Sector Survey on Cost Control ("Grace Commission"): *Task Force Report on the Office of the Secretary of Defense, Task Force Report on the Department of the Army, Task Force Report on the Department of the Navy, Task Force Report on the Department of the Air Force* (Washington, D.C., July 1983).

14. Fox, *Arming America*; Fitzgerald, *High Priests of Waste*; Peck and Scherer, *Weapons Acquisition Process*; and Richard Kaufmann, *The War Profiteers* (Garden City, N.Y.: Doubleday/Anchor Books, 1972).

15. See, for example, the major effort mounted by the Defense Department and the defense industry to avoid a redefinition of the defense acquisition regulations to make contractor lobbying costs unallowable against defense contracts, as shown in documents released by Common Cause in Spring 1981, and held by Common Cause, 2030 M St., NW, Washington, D.C. 20036.

16. Arthur Bentley, *The Process of Government: A Study of Social Pressure*, 2nd ed (Evanston, Ill.: Principia Press, 1945); E. E. Schattschneider, *The Semi-Sovereign People*, 2nd ed. (Hinsdale, Ill.: Dryden Press, 1975); David Truman, *The Governmental Process: Political Interests and Public Opinion* (New York: Knopf, 1975); and E. Pendleton Herring, *Group Representation Before Congress* (Baltimore: Johns Hopkins Press, 1929).

17. Robert D. Cuff, *The War Industries Board: Business-Government Relations During World War I* (Baltimore: Johns Hopkins Press, 1973); Paul A. C. Koistinen, *The Military-Industrial Complex: A Historical Perspective* (New York: Praeger Publishers, 1980); and Gordon Adams, "Defense Policy-Making, Weapons Procurement, and the Reproduction of State-Industry Relations" (paper presented to the American Political Science Association, Washington, D.C., 28 August 1980).

18. Kaufman, *The War Profiteers*; Fox, *Arming America*; Peck and Scherer, *Weapons Acquisition Process*; James Kurth, "The Political Economy of Weapons Procurement: The Follow-On Imperative," *American Economic Review* 62, no. 2 (May 1972): 304–11; Seymour Melman, *Pentagon Capitalism* (New York: McGraw-Hill, 1970); and Melman, *The Permanent War Economy* (New York: Simon and Schuster, 1974).

19. Among other writers who have explored the concept of such subgovernments, see: Gordon Adams, "Disarming the Military Subgovernment," *Harvard Journal on Legislation* 14, no. 3 (April 1977): 459–503; Lester Salamon and John Siegfried, "Economic Power and Political Influence: The Impact of Industry Structure on Public Policy," *American Political Science Review* 71, no. 3 (September 1977): 1026–43; Joel D. Auerbach and Burt Rockman, "Bureaucrats and Clientele Groups: A View from Capitol Hill," *American Journal of Political Science* 22, no. 4 (November 1978); Grant McConnell, *Private Power and American Democracy* (New York: Knopf, 1967); John Lieper Freeman, *The Political Process* (Garden City, N.Y.: Doubleday, 1955); Douglas Cater, *Power in Washington* (New York: Random House, 1964); and Michael T. Hayes, "The Semi-Sovereign Pressure Groups: A Critique of Current Theory and Alternative Typology," *Journal of Politics* 40, no. 1 (1978): 134–61.

20. Harmon Zeigler and Wayne G. Peak, *Interest Groups in American Society*, 2nd ed. (Englewood Cliffs, N.J.: Prentice Hall, 1972), 180. The authors point out that in such a relationship "agencies and their clientele tend to develop coincident values and perceptions to the point where neither needs to manipulate the other overtly. The confident relationships that develop uniquely favor the interest groups involved. They need only exchange persuasive resources for instrumental policy benefits within administrative markets to satisfy many of their material demands."

21. Harold Seidman, *Politics, Position and Power* (New York: Oxford University Press, 1970), 18. The author points out that "private bureaucracies in Washington now almost completely parallel the public bureaucracies in those program areas where the federal government contracts for services, regulates private enterprise, or provides some form of financial assistance." McConnell, *Private Power and American Democracy*, 244, describes this interpenetration as the process of "privatizing" the state. James O'Connor, *The Fiscal Crisis of the State* (New York: St. Martin's Press, 1973), 66, uses the term "appropriation of a sector of state power by private interests" to describe the same phenomenon.

22. Adams, "Disarming the Military Subgovernment"; Schattschneider, *Semi-Sovereign People*; Hayes, "Semi-Sovereign Pressure Groups"; and Richard Neustadt, *Presidential Power* (New York: Wiley, 1976).
23. Zeigler and Peak, *Interest Groups*, p. 172.
24. Kaufmann, *The War Profiteers*, 248.
25. This is particularly true of General Dynamics, Grumman, Lockheed, McDonnell-Douglass, and Northrop, who are usually among the top ten contractors with the Defense Department.
26. Gordon Adams, *The Politics of Defense Contracting: The Iron Triangle* (New Brunswick, N.J.: Transaction Press, 1982).
27. Christopher Paine and Gordon Adams, "The R&D Slush Fund," *Nation* (26 January 1980); and Adams, *The Politics of Defense Contracting*, chap. 7.
28. Adams, *The Politics of Defense Contracting*, chap. 11. See also, the report of the Defense Department inspector general's office in 1983 on the interrelationship of industry and the Defense Department in the Defense Science Board, as reprinted in the *Congressional Record*, 22 July 1983, pp. S10663–S10677.
29. Kenneth Bacon, "Pentagon Studies How Boeing Got Secret Information," *Wall Street Journal*, 29 February 1980.
30. A North American Aviation official quoted in David Sims, "Spoon-Feeding the Military: How New Weapons Come to Be," in *The Pentagon Watchers* ed. Leonard Rodberg and Derek Sherer (Garden City, N.Y.: Doubleday, 1970), 249.
31. Adams, *The Politics of Defense Contracting*, chap. 6.
32. Ibid., chap. 6 and company profiles.
33. Ibid.
34. *Wall Street Journal*, 29 February 1980.
35. Adams, *The Politics of Defense Contracting*, chap. 9.
36. Ibid.
37. Adams, "Disarming the Military Subgovernment."
38. Now retired Senator Thomas McIntyre (D., N.H.) described the problem he faced as chair of the Senate Armed Services subcommittee on research and development in the face of thousands of Defense Department projects for research and development: "We spend an awful lot of time, but we are lucky if we can take a look at or have a briefing or hearing on, say, 15 percent of those projects." Quoted in Louis Fischer, "Senate Procedures for Authorizing Military Research and Development," in Joint Economic Committee, Subcommittee on Priorities and Economy in Government, *Priorities and Efficiency in Federal Research and Development: A Compendium of Papers*, 94th Cong., 2d sess., 29 October 1976, 26.
39. Adams, *The Politics of Defense Contracting*, chap. 13.
40. Adams, "A Bomber for All Seasons."
41. Adams, *The Politics of Defense Contracting*, chap. 13.
42. Gordon Adams, "Creating Real National Security," in *Alternatives*, ed. Irving Howe, forthcoming.

21
Class and Politics in the Organization of Public Administration: The U.S. Department of Labor

Nancy DiTomaso

I. Introduction

Most analyses of public agencies take their existence for granted and focus instead on the politics of programs and policies. In other words, they have a theory of politics, but not a theory of the state itself. Yet such a theory is necessary if we are to understand the how, as well as the who and when, in studies of public administration. In this article, I address the how of public administration by a case study of the U.S. Department of Labor at two periods in its history. There are two basic points to the analysis: (1) decisions must be made about how public agencies will be organized, and these decisions are subject to a great deal of conflict among those groups that each think they will win or lose critical access to state power, and (2) because early decisions about organizational structure become institutionalized in the political process that follows the development of a new agency, subsequent political battles will be fought over attempts to reorganize.

An ancillary part of the argument is to interpret the meaning of various kinds of decisions about structure. Too often in organizational theory, the principles of administration have been developed in the absence of a particular case, thus leaving the meaning of certain conditional structures ambiguous. For example, within the Weberian model of organizations, hierarchy or centralization of decision making has been taken as the best means to maintain managerial control of subordinates, and alternatively, decentralization has been assumed to be a sharing of power. I will argue in part of this analysis that that is not necessarily so. Indeed, centralization or decentralization are—like many other aspects of organizational structure—subject to contingencies and constraints in both their purpose and their effect.

One of the basic premises on which this argument is built is that if conflict exists between groups within a democratic society, they will be just as concerned about the form of state administration as with its substance. This was certainly true in the U.S. Department of Labor, which was created during a period of intense conflict between management and workers over both the development of trade unions and the organizational control of industry and commerce in the country. Importantly, it continued to be true through other periods of the department's history when working-class and other subordinate groups were making demands on the state that would affect the resources of business and industry.

A second basic premise from which this analysis follows is that state managers do not have blueprints that enable them to know in advance the consequences of particular administrative struggles. Rather, they, like all managers, respond successively to crises as they occur, sometimes reinstituting a program, policy, or structure that had previously been abandoned or sometimes adopting those that had previously been rejected. In other words, they do whatever is necessary to meet the challenges of the day.

II. The Hypotheses

Based on my study of the U.S. Department of Labor, I can offer the following hypotheses about how power is exercised through bureaucratic structures within the state. Because state administration within the United States is part of a democratic governing process, it is subject to demands and constraints from any group that feels it has an interest in what the agency is likely to do. If several such groups are in conflict with each other, the agency itself is likely to be the subject of conflict, and in the playing out of their conflict, they are likely to seek allies to support their claims on the state, thus expanding the constraints with which the agency is confronted. In the formative period of the U.S. Department of Labor, the conflict was primarily between capital and labor, but farmers also were occasionally involved. In the later reorganization of the Labor Department, the conflicting groups were more differentiated: big and small business, craft and industrial unions, and minority groups and their supporters. Conflict erupted over each of the following decision points: who would get to define legitimate goals, the range of legal authority, the size and composition of the budget, the pattern of authority and decision making, and how the recruitment and screening of personnel would be carried out. As each of these decisions was affected by the general structure of control within the agency, a major focus of conflict was the relative centralization or decentralization of the agency at various times and for various purposes, but especially in the later period of reorganization.

Important to our understanding of how conflict over organizational structure shifts to meet new crises or circumstances is that the structure preferred by those in dominant positions was not always centralization and by those in subordinate positions was not always decentralization. Indeed, it depended on what was at stake and who else could make claims to it. Precisely because centralization concentrates power, it also makes it more visible, and when the locus of power is more visible, then the "point of change" is more easily identified. Therefore, centralization is an option preferred by dominant coalitions within organizations only when subordinates are acquiescent. However, when subordinates are pressuring for change, and especially if they have some hopes of succeeding in their demands, decentralization may be seen as a means to fragment power and make it more difficult to change. If pressure for change comes from outside pressure groups instead of subordinates, then a centralized structure that is insulated or buffered from its environment may be the preferred structure. And, within a democratic structure, when a new administration comes to power, the old administration may pressure for decentralization in order to insure its own access and to make reform of the agency more unwieldy. Of course, those who are excluded from the dominant coalition, inside or outside the agency, will pressure for the opposite in each case.

The creation of a Department of Labor was supported by industrial workers and tradespeople, especially those involved in the incipient union movement. It was, at first, opposed by politicians whose primary ties were to business. Opposition was redirected to setting the limits for organizational form and mission and to involvement in selection of personnel and control of the budget. In later years, conflict over reorganization reopened many of the same issues with strong consciousness of the alternative consequences of decisions regarding organizational structure.

III. Formation of the U.S. Department of Labor

The National Labor Union, a short-lived national organization of workers, was the first to demand an "executive department of government in Washington" to protect the interests of labor "above all others." Although "labor," it claimed, "was the foundation and cause of national prosperity," workers had no government agency to represent them (Sylvis, 1872:293). The demand for a department of labor was part of the more general struggle for workers' rights, which was critically shaped in the years from the Civil War to World War I. The major reason workers wanted their own government agency was to identify the sources and the distribution of wealth, as Terence Powderly argued:

> The legitimate aim of the labor bureau is to ascertain beyond the shadow of a doubt what the earnings of labor and capital are in order that justice may be done to both, in order that unscrupulous employers will not have it in their power to rob labor of its just dues, and take all of the profits of the combination of labor and capital for their own aggrandizement. (Powderly, 1890:306)

Workers resisted wage cuts, demanded higher wages and shorter hours, and insisted on their right to know how much wealth their employers made on their labor power.

The state of Massachusetts was the first government to respond to the demands of workers for a department of labor. Massachusetts workers were more organized than any others in the country at the time (perhaps because of the concentration of craftworkers in the state), and they were translating their union activities into the formation of producer cooperatives and into political strength at the polls. After a particularly bitter strike by shoemakers, who were called by one account the "most powerful labor organization in the world" (Lescohier, 1969:8), the political leadership in Massachusetts feared the disaffection of workers. To appease them, the state established the Bureau of Statistics of Labor, whose function was to "collect statistical details relating to all departments of labor in the Commonwealth, especially in its relations to the commercial, industrial, social, educational, and sanitary conditions of the laboring classes" (Wright, 1892 and Pidgin, 1904:7).

General Henry K. Oliver, former state legislator who was involved in the active reform movement in Massachusetts at the time, was appointed to head the new agency. Oliver assumed that a primary goal of the agency was the advocacy for workers. As one of their primary interests was to determine how much wealth employers had so they could know whether they were being paid a fair day's wage, he used the summons power of the agency to study deposits in savings banks. Regarding the incident, the Boston *Commonwealth* reported in 1872, "So the effort now is to abolish the bureau of labor. The struggle between capital and labor is growing bitter—bitter even now on the side of capital. It objects to investigation of its methods" (Reported in Congressional Record, House, April 19, 1884:3141). The enraged employers were unable to get the bureau abolished, but they were successful in their efforts to have Oliver replaced. The government appointed instead Carroll Davidson Wright, a man from a prominent family who had no ties to any labor organization and who had promised to maintain the "neutrality" of the agency.

Wright was to become prominent within the government for his "responsible" role in the collection of statistics on workers. The Massachusetts bureau, under his leadership, became the model for other states. Bureaus were established in Pennsylvania in 1872; Ohio in 1877; New Jersey in 1878; Indiana, Illinois, and Missouri in 1879; and New York, California, Michigan, and Wisconsin in 1883. Wright took the initiative to form a national organization of chiefs of state bureaus of labor, and he used his influence "to frustrate every effort to commit the chiefs to a program of labor reform" (Lombardi, 1942:39). Nevertheless, following the severe depression of 1873 to 1877, which culminated in the most violent and extensive strike the country had ever experienced, he joined with various labor leaders to promote a national bureau of labor statistics.

Legislation to establish such a bureau was modeled on the Massachusetts law and introduced in the U.S. Congress in 1884. A number of issues were discussed in both the Senate and the House; a checklist of some of these is provided in the following remark given in testimony regarding the proposed bureau:

> This is not a question of an eight-hour law; it is not a question of checking the accumulation of great estates in single hands; it is not a question of dividing the products of labor between labor and capital; it is a simple question of having information furnished by public methods and by public instrumentalities to legislators and to other persons interested in these public questions. (Congressional Record, Senate, March 7, 1884:1676)

It was pointed out in the discussions on the bill that each important labor organization in the country demanded a department of labor among its other requests. In the context of the discussion, it was noted also that the secretary of state had requested information on wages, living costs, and production costs from Great Britain, France, Germany, Belgium, Italy, Spain, the Netherlands, Sweden, Norway, and Denmark. The intent was to show that conditions of workers were far better in the United States than in Europe, but similar information did not exist for the United States. In addition, the information was desired to influence the bitterly debated tariff legislation of the time, "in consequence of the agitation in regard to the relations between capital and labor, which has signally marked the last decade" (Congressional Record, House, April 19, 1884:3142). Just as important was the fear among the legislators of what would occur if something were not done to solve "the labor question":

> If the existing rate of wages paid to workingmen in this country can not be maintained, and increased if possible, I despair of the maintenance of the Republic for many generations. (Senator George F. Hoar, of Massachusetts, in Congressional Record, Senate, March 7, 1884:1676)

Much of the discussion on the legislation revolved around where to place the national bureau of labor statistics. Those who assumed there was harmony of interests between capital and labor suggested the functions of the proposed bureau be added to the already existing Bureau of Statistics in the Department of Treasury, which, as the head of the agency noted, was really a department of commerce. (This bureau was the core for the later creation of a Department of Commerce.) Some suggested that it be included in the independent (noncabinet) Department of Agriculture, but this was never taken as a viable suggestion. Wright recommended that the bureau be placed in the Department of Interior, which already housed a bureau for the collection of education statistics. Because there were already committees on education and labor in both the House and the Senate, Wright's suggestion followed the already existing definitions of the proper location of labor matters in the federal government, namely, as social and not as economic issues.

Wright's major concern, then as earlier, was to prevent the agency from becoming "political" in the sense of becoming an advocate for the demands of organized labor. He assumed, like many of the congressional supporters of the legislation, that information on the conditions of workers would neutralize the political demands of workers: "to harmonize and unify existing divergencies between capital and labor" (Grossman and MacLaury, 1975:26). In contrast, a common theme among leaders of organized labor was that the agency would rigidly scrutinize "the means by which employers or moneyed men acquire wealth" and "put a stop to illegitimate profit-taking" (Powderly, 1890:158–160). Despite several forms of reorganization, the Department of Labor was never to take on the major task that workers had envisioned for it. Wright's recommendations, both for the organization and function of the national bureau, prevailed.

After the legislation was passed, labor leaders lobbied for seven months, without success, to get a union person appointed as head of the bureau. Instead, after delaying for many months, President Arthur appointed Wright to the position, while he simultaneously retained his position in Massachusetts. Wright gained increasing favor among government leaders, although he never developed strong ties with organized labor. Among other tasks, he was given responsibility for conducting the national census. In a short time, he became, for all intents and purposes, the adviser to the president on labor matters.

In 1888, his responsibility, along with the structure of the Bureau of Labor Statistics, was expanded again. The primary goal was for Wright to hire assistants to collect information on wages and working conditions in Europe, again within the context of the growing concern over tariffs. According to one congressman, the new legislation made "in other words, a department of industrial statistics" (Congressional Record, House, March 21, 1888:2318) of the bureau. The largest labor organization in the country at the time, the Knights of Labor, continued to lobby in local, state, and federal forums for a cabinet-level department of labor, but to no avail. Wright continued to argue, and continued to be supported by Congress, that the only way to prevent the agency from becoming "political" was to deny it cabinet status and to keep it removed from too close an association with organized labor. The "labor question" itself was a major part of the political agenda of the Congress for years, with many commissions reporting on the causes of strikes and lockouts. Following recommendations of the hearings after the extensive 1886 strikes for the eight-hour day, the Bureau of Labor Statistics was made into an independent, noncabinet Department of Labor, with Wright again at its head. Wright continued in the position for another fifteen years, but his impending retirement worried some of the conservative members of Congress and the business community. Data of central importance to business was collected by the Bureau of Statistics in the Department of Treasury, but major corporate leaders increasingly argued for more extensive information in order to expand markets abroad.

In 1900, the Republican party included a demand for a cabinet-level Department of Commerce in its party platform. The proposed department was to incorporate all of the separate statistical bureaus of interest to business, including as a subordinate bureau the previously created, independent Department of Labor. The legislation was quickly introduced in the Republican-controlled Congress, and hearings began in 1901. In the Senate, support for the legislation was orchestrated by people like Senator Mark Hanna of Ohio, one of the major capitalists in the country. Hanna is noted, among other things, for controlling the political machine in Cleveland, Ohio, and for organizing William McKinley's notorious front-porch presidential campaign against William Jennings Bryan.

The overwhelming concern among business leaders at the time for expanding foreign commerce explains the timing of the proposal for a cabinet-level Department of Commerce, but this only explains in part why the Department of Labor was to be subordinated within the new agency as a bureau. Wright's administration of the Department of Labor was characterized in the hearings on the legislation as "beyond praise," and "perfect." Senator Knute Nelson of Minnesota, who introduced the legislation for the Department of Commerce, also praised Wright, but added, "He is a very able man, but he will not always be with us." Because, Nelson argued, the future head of the Department of Labor may not be "so able and so good as he . . . it is altogether safer for the public service to have a division or a bureau of this kind under some responsible executive department" (U.S. Department of Commerce and Labor, 1904:491).

Hanna was one of several Republicans to argue that the interests of labor and capital are "identical and mutual." To this end, Hanna also argued, contrary to testimony offered by Samuel Gompers, the head of the American Federation of Labor, that organized labor had no objections to the legislation. Hanna argued that the proposed Department of Commerce should incorporate Labor because "a close, effective organization, with one able executive head, is always the best way to accomplish a result" (U.S. Department of Commerce and Labor, 1904:499).

His motivations were not only administrative efficiency, however. He also argued that "there is no interest in the United States today that demands the attention of Congress . . . more" than establishing a Department of Commerce, because "[we] must either find a market for [our] surplus or we must restrict our production . . ." (U.S. Department of Commerce and Labor, 1904:498, 500). Senator Joseph Quarles of Wisconsin, in a magnanimous statement, even suggested that the legislation would move "labor" out of a "tent on the outside . . . right into the mansion alongside of commerce, alongside of capital," so that "the Labor Bureau shall not be an orphan, entirely discredited and unaffiliated" (Congressional Record, Senate, January 28, 1902:1050).

At least some of the members of Congress questioned the motivations of the legislation toward workers. Congressman Dudley Wooten of Texas summarized the intent of the legislation as follows:

> . . . Such men as Morgan and Frick and Baer and . . . represent today the organized greed and tyranny and oppression of corporations and capital in this country. This is the kind of a department that the Republican party asked to be created, and this is the kind of department that the gentlem[e]n are now seeking to create by this bill. . . . (Congressional Record, House, January 17, 1903:908)

He further argued that the proposed legislation was "a deliberate attempt to deny the American laborer his just participation and protection in the organization of the Government" (Congressional Record, House, January 17, 1903:908). At least three attempts were made to simultaneously create a separate, cabinet-level Department of Labor, as well as follow through on the creation of the proposed Department of Commerce to which workers had no objection in principle. The legislation was also a forum for a number of issues regarding the conflicts between labor and capital of the time: immigration, tariffs, regional antagonisms between the North and the South, antitrust proposals, and others. Despite the frank discussions of the interests underlying the legislation, it was finally passed with one symbolic amendment. The new department was called "The Department of Commerce and Labor," but the labor portion of the department was allocated only $184,020 of a total department budget of $8,363,032. Wright continued for a short time as head of what again became the Bureau of Labor Statistics, but all of the secretaries of Commerce and Labor were affiliated with business interests.

For all the previous years, the Department of Labor had been denied cabinet status so that it would not become a "political" agency. What was really implied by this reasoning was to prevent it from becoming an advocate for organized labor. Wright joined with the others who opposed the Department of Labor's being allowed to perform that role. He argued that advocacy for organized labor would make the department an "instrument of propagandism," and "such a course would result in its immediate abolition" (Congressional Record, House, January 17, 1903:905). As business leaders began to recognize their own needs for the information collected by the Department of Labor and as they became increasingly concerned about their ability to control the work of the department following Wright's retirement, exactly opposite logic was used. Administrative efficiency, responsibility, and "dignity" were invoked to explain why the Department of Labor should be made a subordinate part of, but not itself become, a cabinet agency. In other words, as long as the business leaders perceived the agency as primarily symbolic appeasement for the demands of labor, it was isolated from the central operations of the government, although controlled through the screening of personnel, the limitations of its fundings, and restrictions on its legal authority to collect certain kinds of information. In the context of the growing strength of organized labor, when business leaders feared they would lose their control over the agency and when they saw the usefulness of the information that it collected for their own purposes, they proposed to incorporate the department into a centralized cabinet agency, which would predictably be controlled by business representatives. And, of course, they did so on the pretense of representing labor's best interests.

After a decade of political turmoil in which organized labor increasingly gained strength, the joint Department of Commerce and Labor was finally separated into two independent cabinet offices. The Progressive reform movement; the growth of a socialist consciousness among workers that led to the strength of the Socialist party; and the entry of organized labor into party politics all contributed in some important way to the creation of the new cabinet-level Department of Labor in 1913. The legislation creating the department said it would:

> . . . go far to allay jealousy, establish harmony, promote the general welfare, make the employer and employee better friends, prevent strikes and lockouts, stop boycotts and business paralysis, and every year save millions and millions of dollars of losses which result necessarily therefrom. (U.S. House of Representatives, Hearing before Committee on Labor, 1912:5)

Nevertheless, once the department was separated from the control of business leaders, it was again isolated from power. Its jurisdiction was limited, its budget severely restricted, and it was continually treated with suspicion by most administrations. For fifty years after, it remained one of the smallest of cabinet offices, and in the 1940s, there were even attempts to have it abolished.

There is an important difference in the operations of the Department of Labor before and after its incorporation into the joint Department of Commerce and Labor. Organized labor had wanted the agency to investigate the source and distribution of wealth, but as long as the agency had the appearance of being "labor's agency," it only collected information on workers themselves. Within the proposed Department of Commerce, the proposed Bureau of Labor Statistics was to "compile . . . statistics of cities," to report "the general condition . . . of the leading industries," and to collect other "facts as may be deemed of value to the industrial interests of the country" (Congressional Record, House, January 17, 1903:913). After the Department of Labor was made a separate cabinet agency, it became a highly decentralized, fragmented, and ineffectual agency. The few powerful bureaus within it by the late 1950s would not even allow their telephone calls to be handled through a central switchboard (Ruttenberg, 1970). Furthermore, this form of organization for the Department of Labor was strongly supported by conservative politicians and their business allies; various attempts to reorganize the Department of Labor into a more centralized form became a serious issue of conflict, as we shall see in the next section of this paper.

IV. Reorganization of the Department of Labor, 1962 to 1974

Although the identification of "capital" and "labor" as distinct social classes was common around the turn of the century, by the 1960s such terminology had disappeared from government deliberations. Instead, the common language had become "business" and "labor," and in the 1960s, a third group became centrally important in the reorganization struggles within the Department of Labor as well, namely, the "poor." In the 1960s, "poor" was often a euphemism for "black." A number of conflicts among and within these three groups were played out through the Department of Labor. Although "labor" and the "poor" are undoubtedly both part of the working class in the most general sense of the term, various organizations representing the two identified their interests in antagonism to each other during the decade of the War on Poverty.

Conflicts existed between business and organized labor, between organized labor and the poor, between business and the poor, within business (small versus large), and within organized labor (craft versus industrial unions). Although there may also have been conflicts among the poor, these were not an issue for the reorganization of the Department of Labor. The event that brought these conflicts to the Department of Labor was the development of federal manpower training programs. How these programs were organized within federal agencies was understood by all three parties to be an issue of the distribution of power in the country.

The Origin of Federal Manpower Training Programs

At the end of the 1950s and the beginning of the 1960s, workers and employers had distinctive but convergent concerns over employment problems. A plethora of books and articles on automation and the supposed effects of technological change appeared at that time. One account suggests that "anxiety almost amounting to panic" developed "over the reported loss of jobs and escalation of skill demands due to automation" (Crossman and Larner, 1969:176). Workers feared the effects of automation on the elimination of jobs (termed "structural unemployment" by policymakers). Business leaders worried that the skill level of the U.S. labor force prevented the technological changes necessary to compensate for their competitive disadvantage with European economic organizations. These competing concerns were complicated by a close presidential election, a changing administration that had made elaborate campaign promises, and a growing and militant civil rights movement, which was yet to blossom to its full potential. This combination of factors induced policy makers to define federal manpower training programs as a solution to a crisis.

Despite the demands by organized labor that business compensate workers displaced by automation—including guaranteed income proposals—existing economic problems probably had more direct influence on the selection of manpower training programs as a solution to the crisis: an unprecented high unemployment rate during a period of expansion, a second recession closely following the first one (1960 to 1961 and 1957 to 1958), pockets of depression in the midst of overall prosperity, increasing mobility of both plants and workers, as well as the declining competitive position with Western Europe. In this context, a controversy among factions developed within the Kennedy and, later, the Johnson administrations. William McChesney Martin, head of the U.S. Federal Reserve Board under Kennedy, supported the use of more traditional and conservative economic policies, but Walter Heller, Kennedy's chairman of the Council of Economic Advisors, supported the use of Keynesian fiscal and monetary policies. The two positions were reconciled by the Manpower Development and Training Act of 1962 (MDTA), as explained by Sundquist:

> Those who favored an expansionary fiscal policy looked upon retraining as a necessary *supplement*. Those who opposed strong fiscal measures tended to seize upon retraining as a *substitute*. If the economy did not need stimulation to absorb the unemployed, they found themselves reasoning, then jobs for all must in fact exist or would exist if only the unemployed were competent to fill them. If the shortcomings were not in the economy, they could only be in the people. (1968:85–86)

The representatives of organized labor, however, were dismayed with their initial experience with federal manpower training programs. President Kennedy delegated responsibility for the first programs under the Area Redevelopment Act of 1961 to the Department of Commerce. At first Commerce did not implement them at all, and when it did, money was given to nonunion, runaway shops in the South. Despite their strong support for the idea of federal manpower training programs, organized labor was not much more successful in controlling the implementation of programs under MDTA.

Organized labor wanted the training programs to be administered by the Department of Labor, but there was no bureau within the department that could have served their purposes. Each of the three likely possibilities operated as a separate fiefdom within the department. The Bureau of Employment Security (BES) administered the critical unemployment insurance program in coordination with the state employment agencies, but BES was "business's" agency within the Department of Labor (Johnson, 1973:14). The Bureau of Employment Security is an example of centralization within decentralization; all of the major decisions regarding unemployment insurance are made at the state level of government, in close conjunction with employers. Business's interests are protected within the bureau by the Interstate Conference of Employment Security Agencies (ICESA), a government-funded, lobby group for BES. Although BES has field offices in every state and most large cities, organized labor had no desire to expand BES by giving it administrative responsibility for MDTA programs.

Organized labor's strongest ties in the Department of Labor were to the Bureau of Apprenticeship and Training (BAT), which oversees on-the-job training programs in the skilled trades. In that the high salaries of these occupations (especially building and metal trades) depend on limited recruitment, organized labor did not want BAT to administer MDTA because it would have necessitated a major expansion of their programs. A third agency, the Office of Manpower, Automation, and Training (OMAT), was newly created in the advent of MDTA, but it did not have any regional field offices, and its commitments were not well defined at that point. In lieu of any of these three bureaus, organized labor lobbied for the creation of an independent agency to administer MDTA, but was not successful.

Administration of MDTA was eventually shared between BES (for case finding) and another agency over which business had strong influence, the Bureau of Vocational Education (BVE), located in the Department of Health, Education, and Welfare. BVE was another centralized bureau within a decentralized agency; all decisions regarding vocational education, like those in BES, are made at the state level, as part of the "education" responsibilities of each state. BVE implemented the training for the cases found by BES. Despite the continued dismay of organized labor at the administrative arrangement for MDTA, the most immediate cause for their interest in government training programs—high (white male) unemployment—disappeared, so they turned their attention elsewhere for a while.

Manpower training programs, however, offered a solution to another emerging crisis, the civil rights movement, the two major goals of which were "jobs and freedom." The marches in Birmingham in the spring and the "March on Washington" in August of 1963 marked a turning point for the movement. By the end of the year "urban riots" began in a number of cities, and then expanded with fury in the several years to come. The Johnson administration responded with several critical pieces of legislation in 1964, the Civil Rights Act and the Economic Opportunity Act. Job training played a prominent role in both.

The Conflicts of Interest

The administrative arrangement preferred by business leaders when the working class has potential access to critical programs that affect business interests is decentralization. The Bureau of Employment Security and the Bureau of Vocational Education both fit this model, and each is one of the strongest bureaus in its parent agency. In other words, the parent agencies are decentralized, while the purportedly subordinate bureaus are insulated from upper-level administrative control. For this reason, each has also been the subject of conflict between business and labor. Business leaders have always lobbied for various kinds of labor programs to be administered by these bureaus (whenever they could not get them placed in "business" agencies, like the Department of Commerce), while organized labor has always objected. Because the decentralization of BES is understood by organized labor to be advantageous to business, the "federalization" of the bureau has been one of organized labor's continual demands since the inception of the program. Nevertheless, the locus of decision making at the state government level also means that "big" business shares these bureaus with "small" business. At various points in the 1960s, big business withdrew its support for each agency—when its own problems could better be solved nationally—over the objections of small business. Thus, no particular form of organization is as important as whose interests it serves in what context.

Industrial unions, however, seemed more concerned about BES and BVE than craft unions were. The craft unions were happily lodged in the Bureau of Apprenticeship and Training and had made an uneasy peace with BES. During the 1960s, the interests of industrial unions in gaining control over unemployment insurance (and thus over BES) led to a strategy among some unionists to trade off some of BAT's control over on-the-job training for the opportunity for greater union control of BES. This strategy turned out to be ill fated. BAT lost ground over on-the-job training without improving labor's input into the unemployment insurance program.

The conflicts that existed between and within business and labor were complicated in the 1960s by conflicts among . . . business and labor and the poor. For business leaders, when the demands of the poor appeared more threatening than the demands of organized labor and when the skill shortages created by the Vietnam War were of more concern than unemployment insurance (in a tight labor market), they supported a centralized Department of Labor, as long as they themselves controlled it. To solve business's problems with the poor, the Department of Labor was drawn into competition with the Office of Economic Opportunity (OEO), the agency of the poor. The conflict, however, affected the Bureau of Apprenticeship and Training, so the business leaders supporting the new policies solved two objectives by proposing to reorganize the Department of Labor. It was possible for them to do so because of the uneasy relationship that has always existed between unions and minority workers, and hence between unions and the poor. It appears that the business leaders used organized labor's desire to gain control over the Bureau of Employment Security to encourage a conflict between the Department of Labor and OEO's Community Action Agencies (CAAs), and they used minority group suspicion of craft unions to weaken BAT's control of on-the-job training programs. These various conflicts constitute the background against which proposals to reorganize the Department of Labor were made.

The Reorganizations
Conflict among the Bureau of Employment Security, the Bureau of Apprenticeship and Training, and the Office of Manpower, Automation, and Training developed immediately after the passage of the 1962 Manpower Act. The first attempt to reorganize the responsibilities among the bureaus occurred soon after the Birmingham riot in 1963. Secretary of Labor Wirtz appointed a Manpower administrator, John C. Donovan, to coordinate the activities of the three bureaus, and Donovan hired an outside consulting agency, whose recommendations were unsatisfactory to both BAT and BES. The consultant had recommended the dissolution of the field offices of both BES and BAT with a reintegration of their functions into a new, centralized agency called the Manpower Administration, the core of which was to be OMAT. The centralization proposed by this report would have placed the unemployment insurance program under the direct authority of the secretary of labor, and it would have placed the activities of the conservative craft unions under the closer scrutiny of the federal administrators at a time when new demands were being made on federally supported training programs. As the director of Employment Security at the time remarked, "The proposed reorganization would disrupt [existing] relationships and require the development of an entirely new fabric . . ." (memo from Director Robert C. Goodwin, BES, to Secretary of Labor Wirtz, February 1, 1965). In other words, a centralization of authority within the Department of Labor at this time would have decreased the power of those groups that had purposely

created decentralization in order to enhance their power. In this situation, the conservative building trades department of the American Federation of Labor and Congress of Industrial Organization (AFL-CIO) joined with the ICESA, the government-funded, business-controlled lobby, to prevent any reorganization of either BES or BAT. Donovan consequently resigned and a former AFL-CIO research director, Stanley Ruttenberg, took his place—under the condition that he would not support any reorganization of the Department of Labor (see Ruttenberg, 1970:76–78).

As urban riots increased, the Office of Economic Opportunity, which President Johnson had created to solve the problems of unrest, began to create problems of its own. The OEO activities that people in positions of power found most threatening were the organization of voter registration and other forms of political mobilization of the poor. As early as 1965, OEO was charged with "trying to wreck local government by setting the poor against city hall" and with being a "nightmare of bureaucratic bungling" (U.S. Code, Congressional and Administrative News, 1st sess., 89th Cong., 1965:3525–26). The Hatch Act, which restricts political activities of public employees, was extended to OEO, but this did not end the social movement to which OEO was providing an organizational base. Johnson had made OEO a "staff agency" in the White House, purportedly to protect it from congressional interference, but the real intent was probably so he could better control it. When it was evident that even direct White House control was not enough to curtail OEO's political effects, other means were sought. The proliferation of riots made it politically impossible to simply eliminate the War on Poverty, which OEO administered; instead, conservative politicians and their business advisers began taking steps to transfer OEO's programs into the more predictable and more easily controlled cabinet offices. In order to maintain the legitimacy of such an action, those agencies with liberal images, like the Department of Labor and the Department of Health, Education, and Welfare, were targeted to receive the programs. On the one hand, each of the programs and bureaus within them already had defined constituencies and, therefore, constraints on their actions; on the other hand, precisely because they had liberal images, representatives of surbordinate groups had more participation in them. This strategy, therefore, was a risky one for conservative politicians in a precarious political climate.

The President's administrative agency, the Bureau of the Budget, began working behind-the-scenes with the Labor Department to this end, and President Johnson himself began making statements favorable to an expanded Department of Labor. With the prospect of the Department of Labor gaining more power in the federal government, organized labor (especially AFL-CIO) then renewed its efforts to gain control over "its" agency. They supported attempts to centralize control over the various bureaus at the federal level, reinforcing their continual demands to federalize the Bureau of Employment Security.

Two reorganization plans were on the agenda for the Department; the two would have had opposite effects. One was supported by Secretary of Labor Wirtz and Assistant Secretary Ruttenberg. It would have centralized all the manpower training programs from OEO, HEW, and from various parts of the Department of Labor (including the on-the-job training programs of BAT) into a reorganized Manpower administration. This proposal was similar to Donovan's earlier aborted reorganization plan. It was strongly supported by organized labor, even though the craft unions were not anxious to jeopardize their control over on-the-job training. The second proposal was articulated by a 1965 task force headed by George Shultz, dean of the School of Business at the University of Chicago, later to become President Nixon's secretary of labor and President Reagan's secretary of state. This task force proposal recommended separating the U.S. Employment Service (the state employment agencies) from the unemployment insurance program in the Bureau of Employment Security, and increasing the funding from the Department of Labor's general budget for the employment service administrative costs, previously paid for by the tax on employers. The effects of this proposal would have been to insulate unemployment insurance even further from the access of organized labor and to prevent business-provided funds from being tapped for War on Poverty Manpower programs.

Wirtz and Ruttenberg were encouraged behind-the-scenes by the Bureau of Budget staff to pursue their own goals for reorganization in spring 1967. Ruttenberg held secret meetings in which he was assured White House support for the proposal, and Wirtz announced a "realignment" of the Department of Labor later in the year. The primary change in the department was to expand the on-the-job training program and to remove the administration of the new positions from the Bureau of Apprenticeship and Training (and consequently from the craft unions). Although the Interstate Conference on Employment Security Agencies and some unions opposed the change, their opposition was to no avail with the support of President Johnson (and therefore, also by those big businesses who were facing manpower shortages in the skilled trades).

By removing the Bureau of Apprenticeship and Training's control over on-the-job training, the programs could be used to channel unemployed blacks into "accelerated" (meaning shorter time and less training) apprenticeship programs with major corporations who were facing tremendous pressure from the urban riots (symbolized by the summer 1967 riot in Detroit) and who were experiencing shortages of skilled labor during the Vietnam War. The realignment prepared the way for President Johnson's launching of the $350 million on-the-job training program, sponsored by the newly formed National Alliance of Businessmen–Job Opportunities in the Business Sector (NAB-JOBS). The NAB-JOBS program benefited big business at government expense because the federal funds subsidized the training costs for industry to hire the disadvantaged (see U.S. Code, 1st sess., 1967:2576; Ball, 1972:175; and Perry, et al., 1975:187).

Just as important, however, this realignment was another step toward the Department of Labor's taking over the programs of OEO. Three "job creation" programs had already been moved from OEO and transferred to the Department of Labor in 1966, and the placement of the NAB-JOBS program in labor instead of OEO was significant. The Community Action agencies in OEO fought Labor's claims to the War on Poverty jobs programs, but their only support in the late 1960s was "public opinion" and some of the "pro-poverty" legislators. It appeared that the cooperation of organized labor in expanding on-the-job training outside of BAT's control was a means to demonstrate their commitment to minorities and to quell the suspicions of the "poverty" people. In return, they thought they would win approval to centralize unemployment insurance at the federal level.

Wirtz and Ruttenberg interpreted their success in the 1967 realignment as a coup and began to make plans for a more extensive reorganization soon thereafter. They were especially encouraged by the preferential support the Department of Labor was getting—in contrast to OEO, which was coming under increasingly hostile attacks—from the Bureau of the Budget and the White House staff (Ball, 1972:146). They began another series of secret meetings in 1968 with the same people who had planned the 1967 realignment. Their intent was to implement a reorganization plan similar to the one that had led to Donovan's resignation earlier. Assuming that the Interstate Conference of Employment Security Agencies was the primary obstacle to implementing the reorganization (in that the realignment had already neutralized opposition from BAT), Wirtz and Ruttenberg felt confident because they were assured of White House support. Much to their surprise, though, President Johnson rejected their plan to centralize the Department of Labor. In fact, Johnson threatened to fire Wirtz when he announced the reorganization over Johnson's objections, even though the incident occurred only two weeks before the 1968 presidential election. A compromise was finally reached between Wirtz and Johnson: Wirtz's reorganization order would remain in effect, but it would not be implemented until after the election.

When newly elected President Richard Nixon appointed George Schultz, the former task force head, as secretary of labor, Shultz recommended implementing the Wirtz-Ruttenberg reorganization plan on an interim basis. The reorganization that was carried out, however, was actually Shultz's own earlier plan. The effects of the 1969 reorganization were to further decentralize the Department of Labor, which meant greater input from business and less from organized labor. In addition, Nixon moved the Job Corps, the last of the War on Poverty jobs programs, from OEO to Labor. Nixon gave his full support to the NAB-JOBS program and to the Job Corps, both of which had become "for-profit" service delivery programs; all other programs were cut back. Within six months, George Shultz had left the Department of Labor to become head of the Office of Management and Budget (formerly the Bureau of the Budget).

Following the Shultz reorganization, the Department of Labor was said to have "fresh appeal" to employers. The president of the National Association of Manufacturers said that it was "one of the most accessible agencies in this town" (Cooney and Silverman, 1970:140), and a representative of the Chamber of Commerce said, ". . . the business community is pleased with the change of administrations in the Labor Department" (Cooney and Silverman, 1970:140). Nixon then embarked on his revenue-sharing campaign, in which the Manpower Revenue Sharing Bill was to be the first implemented. Organizationally, this legislation meant complete decentralization of all federal programs of interest to organized labor and the poor, because manpower was to be only the first of the revenue sharing bills. Nixon's own director of OEO said, "I know of no way in which the Comprehensive Manpower Bill can be proposed by the President without it being viewed by large segments of the public as a conscious and systematic diminution of the role of OEO . . ." (letter from Donald Rumsfeld, Secretary of OEO, to Robert Mayo, Director of the Bureau of the Budget, August 7, 1969). Despite opposition from organized labor and from "pro-poverty" legislators, the Comprehensive Employment and Training Act (CETA) was passed in 1973, with precisely the effects that organized labor and the poor feared. On the one hand, fewer minority and poor clients were enrolled in the training programs than had been during the War on Poverty days. On the other hand, organized labor ended up with even less access to the administration of the unemployment insurance program and less control over apprenticeship training in the skilled trades. In effect, what was a "double-cross" of the Office of Economic Opportunity by organized labor, turned out to be a "double-double-cross" of organized labor by the conservative politicians and their business allies.

The Department of Labor has remained decentralized and relatively unimportant in the family of federal agencies. Only after the demands of organized labor, in the context of controversy within the business community over the use of economic policies, led to the first federal training programs did the organizational structure of the Department of Labor again become a central concern to business leaders. These programs were first placed in business's agency (the Department of Commerce), and later in "business's bureau" (the Bureau of Employment Security). Within the Department of Labor, the administration of the programs was treated as a separate function from the department's other responsibilities. That the Manpower Administration remained in a separate building, even after the Department of Labor was given a new building during the Nixon administration, is an unobtrusive indicator of the special interest business leaders have in controlling these programs. The Department of Labor became a vehicle for confronting OEO when the demands of the poor posed a more immediate threat than the bargaining table demands of organized labor. At that point, business leaders supported some reorganization of the Department of Labor for their own purposes—which had the appearance of centralization—but organized labor never gained more access to unemployment insurance.

Representatives of organized labor tried at various times to effect organizational changes in the Department of Labor, both to increase their influence in the agency and to increase the agency's power in the government. The intensity of organized labor's concern with unemployment insurance made it possible for conservative politicians and their business advisers to use labor's own motivations against them. The charade of behind-the-scenes negotiations and end-run tactics were convincing. One political scientist concluded that the superior administrative skill of the Department of Labor was too much competition for a poorly managed agency like the Office of Economic Opportunity (Ball, 1972)—just one year before the Department of Labor was itself "internally dismantled." The business community's renewed interest, not the administrative skill of the Department of Labor, gave it the illusion of power in the 1960s.

V. Conclusions

This brief account of two periods in the history of the Department of Labor is intended to indicate the political character of decisions about organizational structure in the public sector. In addition, it has shown that almost all of the decisions about the structure of organizations in the public sector are linked to major social conflict in the society at large. In other words, public organizations are not only shaped by their environments, they are inherently part of their environments and vice versa. Even so, organizations, in the state and elsewhere, are not completely permeable. Once decisions are made and carried out, standard ways of operating are adopted and taken for granted by various constituencies in and out of the organization. Subsequent changes, therefore, also have to be "fought out," in the sense that they raise and are only resolved through conflict. What appear to be obvious alliances and obvious preferences are not always followed. Instead, strategies tend to address the needs of the moment, as long as the group proposing the strategy feels it has the allies and the resources to shape for its own purposes the consequences of whatever actions are taken. No single organizational model is preferred over others. The preferences change with the circumstances.

The issues that most concern the parties to organizational conflict are those that place constraints on or provide opportunities for organizational actors: the definition of goals, budgets, recruitment, and training and the pattern of authority in the organization and in its place within a general organizational network. Politics is always at the core of such decisions, while rationality is always defined by those who benefit most from one alternative or another.

References

Andersen, Gosta, Roger Friedland, and Erik Olin Wright. 1976. "Modes of class struggle and the capitalist state." *Kapitalistate* 4–5:186–220.

Babson, Robert W. 1919. *W. B. Wilson and the Department of Labor*. New York: Brentano's.

Ball, Joseph H. 1972. "The implementation of federal manpower policy, 1961–1971." Ph.D. dissertation, Columbia University.

Cooney, Robert, and Marcia Silverman. 1970. "CPR department study/the Labor Department." *National Journal* 2: 130–41.

Culhane, Charles. 1974. "Manpower report/revenue sharing shift set for worker training programs." *National Journal* 6: 5158.

DiTomaso, Nancy. 1978. "The organization of authority in the capitalist state." *Journal of Political and Military Sociology* 6 (Fall): 189–204.

Dulles, Foster Rhea. 1966. *Labor in America*. 3rd ed. New York: Crowell.

Feagin, Joe R., and Harlan Hahn. 1973. *Ghetto Revolts: The Politics of Violence in American Cities*. New York: Macmillan.

Goldberg, Arthur J. 1961–1962. Correspondence. National Archives.

Greenstone, J. David. 1969. *Labor in American Politics*. New York: Vintage.

Grossman, Jonathan. 1945. *William Sylvis, Pioneer of American Labor*. New York: Columbia University Press.

———. 1973. *The Department of Labor*. New York: Praeger.

Hodgson, James D. 1970–1973. Correspondence. National Archives.

Johnson, Miriam. 1973. *Counter Point: The Changing Employment Service*. Salt Lake City: Olympus.

Kipnis, Ira. 1968. *The American Socialist Movement, 1897–1912*. New York: Greenwood.

Lescohier, Don D. 1969. *The Knights of St. Crispin, 1867–1874*. New York: Anno, and the New York Times.

Levitan, Sar A. 1964. *Federal Aid to Depressed Areas*. Baltimore: Johns Hopkins University Press.

———. 1969. *Program in Aid of the Poor for the 1970s*. Baltimore: Johns Hopkins University Press.

Levitan, Sar A., and Garth L. Mangum. 1967. *Making Sense of Federal Manpower Policy*. Washington D.C.: National Manpower Policy Task Force.

Lombardi, John. 1942. *Labor's Voice in the Cabinet*. New York: Columbia University Press.

MacLaury, Judson. 1975. "The selection of the first U.S. Commissioner of Labor." *Monthly Labor Review* 98, no. 4 (April): 16–19.

Mangum, Garth L. 1968. *MDTA: Foundation of Federal Manpower Policy*. Baltimore: Johns Hopkins University Press.

Metcalf, Evan B. 1972. "Economic stabilization by American business in the twentieth century." Ph.D. dissertation, University of Wisconsin.

Mitchell, James P. 1953–1961. Correspondence. National Archives.

Perry, Charles R., Bernard E. Anderson, Richard L. Rowan, and Herbert T. Northrup. 1975. *The Impact of Government Manpower Programs in General and on Minorities and Women*. Philadelphia: Wharton School of Finance.
Philipson, Morris, ed. 1962. *Automation: Implications for the Future*. New York: Vintage.
Pidgin, Charles F. 1904. *Massachusetts Bureau of Statistics of Labor*. Boston: Wright and Potter.
Powderly, Terence V. 1890. *Thirty Years of Labor, 1859–1889*. Rev. ed. Philadelphia: T. V. Powderly.
Ruttenberg, Stanley. 1970. *Manpower Challenge of the 1970s*. Baltimore: Johns Hopkins University Press.
Shultz, George P. 1969–1970. Correspondence. National Archives.
Sundquist, James L. 1968. *Politics and Policy*. Washington, D. C.: Brookings Institution.
Sylvis, James C. 1872. *The Life, Speeches, Labors, and Essays of William H. Sylvis*. Philadelphia: Claxton, Remsen, and Haffelfinger.
Therborn, Goran. 1978. *What Does the Ruling Class Do When It Rules?* London: New Left Books.
Todes, Charlotte. 1942. *William H. Sylvis and the National Labor Union*. New York: International Publishers.
U.S. Code. *Congressional and Administrative News*. 87th through 93rd Congress, Legislative History, Manpower Development and Training Act, Vocational Education Act, Revenue Act, Civil Rights Act, Economic Opportunity Act, Social Security Act, Emergency Employment Act, and Comprehensive Employment and Training Act. St. Paul, Minn.: West Publishing Co.
U.S. Congress, House of Representatives, Committee on Education and Labor. 1912. *Hearings on H.R. 22913 To Establish a Department of Labor*. Washington, D.C.: Government Printing Office, 1912.
U.S. Department of Commerce and Labor. 1904. *Organization and Law of the Department of Commerce and Labor*. Washington, D.C.: Government Printing Office.
Wilson, William B. 1913–1921. Correspondence. National Archives.
Wirtz, W. Willard. 1962–1969. Correspondence. National Archives.
Wright, Carroll D. 1892. "The workings of the Department of Labor." *The Cosmopolitan* 13, no. 2 (June): 229–236.

22
Bureaucracy and the Regulation of Health and Safety at Work: A Comparison of the U.S. and Sweden

Steven Kelman

The differences between the United States and Sweden in the extent to which fines are used to induce compliance with occupational safety and health regulations and in the extent to which superiors within the agencies supervise subordinates reveal different attitudes toward the kinds of controls that systems ought to use to induce desirable behavior by others.

Control Systems and Societies

Before occupational safety and health became a more important issue at the beginning of the 1970s, inspectors in both countries proceeded similarly. They encouraged compliance by offering employers normative rewards (praise for doing as they should). Fines were almost never used. One problem with this method was that real friendship ties could hardly be expected to grow on the basis of contact as infrequent as that between inspector and employer. In both Sweden and America, inspectors would find the same violations on later visits. Policy makers drew lessons from past failures in developing new strategies.

A classic debate that spans several of the social sciences concerns what kinds of inducements—in particular, rewards or punishments—are more likely to produce desired changes in behavior. Clearly no generalizations can be made across different types of people and situations; what works under some circumstances may fail in others. For normative inducements to function successfully, for instance, the individual whose behavior one seeks to change must regard those seeking to change his behavior as people whose good opinion is valued. In a classic study, Richard Schwartz compared two kinds of Israeli cooperative agricultural settlements, the *kvutza* and the *moshav*.[1] The kvutza was "a large primary

---

Reprinted from *Regulating America, Regulating Sweden*, by Steven Kelman (Cambridge, Mass.: MIT Press, 1981), 195–215, by permission of the publisher.

group whose members engage in continuous face-to-face interaction," where people worked and ate together. In the moshav, people owned land privately and performed only a few tasks together. And in the kvutza, there was no punishment through legal coercion; normative inducements were sufficient to achieve satisfactory compliance with group rules. This system was tried in the moshav, but it did not work. Instead the moshav had to introduce legal coercion to punish transgressors.

When policy makers choose among alternative control systems, they do so in the context of assumptions and experiences they have as members of their society. They begin with assumptions about how likely it is that individuals subject to a law will comply simply because the law expresses the authority of government. In neither America nor Sweden were occupational safety and health policy makers content with existing levels of compliance. There are, nonetheless, degrees of pessimism about baseline levels of obedience to the law. Out of the Swedish *overhet* tradition grows the notion that people ought to defer to the wishes of those in authority. Out of the American liberal tradition grows the notion that it is legitimate for people to define and pursue their own goals, independent of what the state thinks is best for them. But the forces of individual interest, once legitimized, are not easily controlled; there always exists the danger that people encouraged to be self-assertive will fail to see the distinction between doing so when this does no impermissible harm to others and doing so when such harm is done. The traditional problem of European states with established rulers has been to tame those rulers and let people breathe; that of America with its liberal tradition has been to tame the unruly so that other people can breathe.

The Lockean solution was to have people obey decisions made by impartial elected officials or judges, but even under the best of circumstances, obedience on the basis of such an abstract principle was likely to be imperfect. Thus the failure of government to act impartially creates a legitimacy problem for government commands in America. Self-assertive values therefore not only discourage agreement before decisions are made, but also—as comparative crime statistics in America and Europe testify—make it relatively more difficult to get people to comply with decisions once made.

A question was asked in the national inspectors' survey, where at one end of a seven-point scale was placed the statement, "Most employers are law abiding, and try to follow the standards simply because a government agency has issued them," and at the other was the statement, "Without the penalty-imposing powers we have, many employers would simply ignore the standards." The results (table 22—1) indicate that American inspectors have little faith in the automatic acceptance of the law, while Swedish ones are more sanguine. The Swedish results do not show inspectors to be certain of automatic compliance; over half rated most employers at the middle of the scale or worse. But it is the overwhelming

Table 22-1
Evaluation by U.S. and Swedish Inspectors of Employer Compliance

	Scale	U.S. Inspectors (N = 78)	Swedish Inspectors (N = 74)
Most employers are	1–2	9%	18%
law abiding	3	6	26
	4	8	22
Many employers would	5	21	20
ignore standards	6–7	56	15

vote of no confidence American inspectors give employers that stands out.

If policy makers are pessimistic about predispositions to compliance, they are more likely to use punishments than rewards to induce compliance, since those not predisposed to obey the law will generally not be considered deserving of reward. Such assumptions also make the use of normative inducements of any kind less likely since those predisposed to noncompliance will probably be regarded as unlikely participants in a group that may induce compliance. Edmund Burke saw the destruction of deference and other normative means of compliance as the essential evil of liberalism. The use of coercive legal punishment becomes required because other institutions of control can no longer be mobilized. Without deference or other normative means, "laws are to be supported only by their own terrors," Burke warned. "In the groves of their academy," he wrote of the liberal philosophers, "at the end of every vista, you see nothing but the gallows."[2] Foreign observers visiting England during the eighteenth century were struck by the paradox of great concern shown for the rights of the accused and severe punishment for convicted criminals.[3] If this argument is correct, both have a common cause in liberal values. (While attention to rights of the accused is less in Sweden than the United States, punishment for criminal offenses tends to be much lower.)

Out of the overhet tradition in Sweden grew a tendency to deal with conflict by establishing small groups of representatives for the various parties to work out agreements. Another result of this tradition was a belief among modern organizational leaders that they ought to educate members to the beliefs of their leaders. In America it became common to arrange proceedings modeled on adversary trials. American policy makers, when they look at the society around them, not only start off with more pessimistic assumptions about predispositions to compliance but also see a greater tendency to use the legal system to regulate human interactions. Swedish policy makers, on the other hand, not only start off with less pessimistic assumptions about predispositions to compliance but also see a society making far greater use of small groups to regulate human interactions. Thus it is not surprising (though it is obviously not foreordained) that American policy makers chose an occupational safety and health compliance system based on punishments meted out through the legal system when they were dissatisfied with existing levels of compliance. Nor is it surprising that Swedish policy makers chose to use normative inducements, with legal punishments only as a backup. American policy makers don't always choose the means chosen in the case of occupational safety and health enforcement, nor do the Swedes universally choose the methods they chose here either. There are criminal laws in Sweden and areas where social control is achieved primarily through lawabidingness or small group normative inducements in the United States. This is both because dominant values are not universally held and because success or failure at establishing small group-based systems does not follow directly from a general Swedish relative preference for accommodationist institutions and an American relative preference for adversary institutions. Furthermore reliance on punishments through the legal system carries many costs, and for this reason as well, policy makers in America no less than in Sweden have hesitated before using it. But American policy makers may feel they have little choice if they are going to be serious about achieving compliance. In the one other instance of an area of earlier legislative concern that became more important in the late 1960s and where policy makers were dissatisfied with existing compliance levels—environmental protection—there has emerged a similar difference between America and Sweden on the tendency to rely on legal punishments.[4] But again, it is a question of tendencies and predisposition rather than of outcomes that can be predicted deterministically.

The overwhelming majority of the OSHA [Occupational Safety and Health Administration] inspectors questioned in the in-depth survey felt that first-instance sanctions were necessary. Responding to an open-ended question about their attitude toward "the penalty-imposing side of your job," 63 percent of respondents (N = 38) answered that such sanctions were a necessary part of OSHA compliance activities. Those favoring these sanctions did so overwhelmingly because they thought there would be little compliance otherwise. "Teeth are the only way to impress management with the seriousness of the situation," one inspector said. If first-instance sanctions disappeared, replied another, "OSHA would flop—we might as well write it off the books." If the inspector had no power to impose penalties, "they'd laugh at you when you came into the plant," a third stated. Two of the respondents replied with statements paralleling the argument made here. "It's the only means of enforcing the law," said one. "It's the only arm that we have," replied another.

Normative Inducements in Sweden

Deferent values and accommodationist institutions make available various normative inducements for compliance with regulations by employers. The operation of these processes during rule making helps produce a situation where, in contrast to the United States, employer leaders accept the regulations. Employer organizations then help seek compliance by member firms, using either the normative inducement of membership deference to leaders or opinion-formation activities. These are likely to aid compliance, though not to make it complete.

Normative inducements may also be exercised in small groups. The primary feature of the new compliance strategy in Sweden and the main substitute for legal punishments was replication at the plant level of the labor-management small groups used at the national level during rule making and the use of those groups both to monitor performance and to exert normative inducements for compliance. The vehicle was already there, half alive, in the form of existing plant-level worker safety stewards and labor-management safety committees.

The appointment of plant-level safety stewards and safety committees was first encouraged through a 1942 agreement between LO [Swedish Confederation of Labor] and SAF [Swedish Employers' Confederation] on occupational safety and health. Safety committees had by no means been unique to Sweden. Many large American firms have had safety committees. In Sweden unions had also sometimes selected a safety steward, frequently a shop-level union official who also held other union positions, to represent employees in making demands to management. The 1942 agreement required that safety stewards be appointed at all workplaces with ten or more employees and that safety committees be appointed at workplaces with more than one hundred employees.

Initial employer acceptance of the requirement is not hard to explain since the steward's function as it originally appeared was largely to reduce unsafe acts by workers through promoting employee safety consciousness. In the *Instruction for Safety Stewards*, the steward was called on to promote safety and health by becoming "knowledgeable about the safety rules established by the Factory Inspectorate and the employer which apply in the area under his responsibility" and by observing "to what extent these rules are being followed." The steward was "to inform workers about the dangers existing in the particular line of work" and "to emphasize to the workers the importance of having a clean and well-kept workplace, as well as to sharpen consciousness among the workers of how important it is to follow applicable safety rules."[5] Nothing suggested that safety stewards should be doing anything to get new safety devices installed or to increase safety consciousness among employers.

Following the 1942 agreement, safety stewards and safety committees were appointed around the land, but for the next twenty-five years, they maintained what one today might call a "low profile." (In the less discrete vernacular of the time, "nobody seemed to care" about them.) One problem was that most safety stewards did not know much about what made workplaces unsafe or unhealthy. The 1942 LO-SAF agreement had established the Joint Industrial Safety Council designed to educate safety stewards, but its efforts reached only a modest proportion of the target group.

When it was concluded in America that previous occupational safety and health enforcement methods were not working well enough, enforcement was made more punitive. In Sweden, in contrast, the role of the safety steward was revitalized. The first document of the new concern with occupational safety and health in Sweden, the joint LO-Social Democratic program *A Better Work Environment* (1969), made no mention of new legal sanctions for violation of safety and health regulations. Instead the document talked exclusively about giving safety stewards new responsibilities and establishing a special fund to support their education.[6] And the very first piece of legislation passed in 1971 was a law adding a surcharge to employer workmen's compensation premiums to set up a work environment fund that would arrange for such training.

Safety stewards were now going to be the entering wedge at the plant level for the concern with safety and health among national leaders and placed at the center of efforts to achieve compliance. According to the authors of a 1973 Work Environment Fund report, "Even though the work environment is a central issue for labor market organizations, government agencies, and researchers, and even though the mass media now gives the subject extensive coverage, it is doubtful whether occupational safety and health questions have gained a real foothold among workers at the plant level and among the general public. . . . What we must try to do is, by various means, to create an attitudinal and behavioral change."[7] Safety stewards, armed with an education reflecting the values of national leaders, would carry those values to the local level.

This role as entering wedge applied both to employers and to fellow workers. The old view of the safety steward as a person encouraging safety consciousness among workers did not completely die, but in the new view this role extended beyond encouraging the avoidance of unsafe acts to increasing the salience of safety and health such that workers would be unhappy about unsafe conditions. If many complained or even quit, a new inducement, originating in changed worker preferences, would be created for employers to comply with regulations.

Safety stewards would also be able to monitor compliance on an ongoing basis. This new role for stewards in relationship to employers was underscored dramatically when representatives for LO, SAF, and the Joint Industrial Safety Council discussed the planned education drive for safety stewards. At the meeting, LO surprised participants with a clearly articulated insistence that training take place at the plant level with study circles rather than having lectures by company safety engineers or courses away from the plant. The unions wanted course material to include exercises where participants could discuss problems at their own plants and even make inspections of plant conditions as part of the course. (The study circle leaders would be educated centrally.)

A joint committee developed the course material, which was written centrally and used as a basis for local study circles.[8] At the end of each lesson in the material, participants were instructed to tour their own plant to look for troublesome conditions. It was established that the study circles would take place during work time and that employers would pay participants normal wages during time spent on the course.[9] The Work Environment Fund paid for printing the course material and the central education of study circle leaders. From late 1974 through late 1976, the tremendous task of organizing courses for safety stewards at all but the tiniest workplaces was undertaken.

The most dramatic expression of the new role of the safety steward appeared in the revision to the Worker Protection Act in 1974. It allowed safety stewards to stop work temporarily until an inspector could arrive in situations with an "imminent and serious danger for employee life or health."[10] Since its inception, this provision of the law has been used around a hundred times per year.[11] Its significance is largely symbolic, since few employers want to see work continued if an imminent danger exists. But the symbolism is significant: it proclaims the safety steward a person with an important monitoring role.

The revised *Instruction for Safety Stewards* issued as part of a new LO-SAF agreement in 1976 codified the new conception of the steward's role. Although the old instruction from 1942 had referred to the task of the safety steward as being to learn about the functioning safety devices already installed, the new instruction stated that safety stewards should "*monitor* whether safety devices and other hygienic features *are present, are in good condition, and are being used.*" Safety stewards should not only request that safety and health regulations be complied with but they should "participate in following up whether measures have led to the desired result."[12]

The safety committee would be used for providing normative inducements for employers. This required that management sit on the committee. The commentary to the 1967 LO-SAF occupational safety and health agreement stated that it was important that "the very top management of the firm" sit on the safety committee.[13] The 1976 agreement was even more specific and also provided that foremen join the committee.[14] A risk was that safety stewards on the committee would be influenced by employers not to press for compliance, rather than the influence going in the opposite direction. Although that probably happens to some extent, the increased salience in the small group setting of common standards, obedience to the law, and the right to equal treatment, which aid the stewards, works against this.

Enforcement Systems and the Inspection Process

Differences in the enforcement systems in the two countries influence both inspectors and the tenor of their inspections. American inspections are designed more as formal searches for violations of regulations; Swedish inspections are designed more as informal, personal missions to give advice and information, establish friendship ties between inspector and inspected, and promote local labor-management cooperation. Since OSHA inspections are intended as searches for violations, their purpose could be defeated were advance notice given. The *Field Operations Manual* underlines the importance of this point.[15] OSHA's first-instance sanctions system means that even if an employer corrects a violation in front of the inspector, this act cannot influence whether a fine is imposed, a method that contributes to a hostile atmosphere.

In Sweden, whether to give advance notice is left up to the inspector. The course material used to training inspectors says that "there are advantages to giving advance notice of your visit. Then the employer can prepare himself, and the union representative can have time to talk with fellow workers." The material also emphasizes that inspectors should try to create a relaxed attitude during the inspection. During the walk-around, the inspector is instructed, "You can talk about things that don't directly have to do with your mission, in order to create good rapport. Be sure to avoid controversial subjects." Unlike OSHA inspectors who are instructed to take notes constantly during an inspection to record violations, Swedish inspectors are warned that "to write too much during the walkaround can be impractical and irritating. While you're writing, the others will perhaps have nothing to do, or, even worse, will begin discussing some problem, leaving you outside the discussion."[16]

OSHA citations state what sections of the regulations had been violated. A violation might read something like,

> 29 CFS 1926.500(9)(c). Failure to guard wall openings, from which there is a drop of more than 4 feet—openings 2 through 6 not guarded.

Swedish inspectors, in their written inspection notices, are not supposed to refer to violations of regulations but to what steps should be taken. Instead of talking about failure to guard a machine, a written inspection notice would say something like, "A fixed guard should be installed to cover the unguarded transmission."

One of the questions in the in-depth and national surveys was designed to tap inspector enforcement attitudes. At one pole of a seven-point scale was the statement, "It's better for OSHA to be a tough enforcer of the regulations, even at the risk of being considered punitive," and at the other end the statement, "It's better for OSHA to seek to persuade

Table 22–2
U.S. and Swedish Inspectors' Enforcement Attitudes

In-depth survey	
American inspectors	3.4 (N = 40)
Swedish inspectors	5.1 (N = 18)
National survey	
American inspectors	4.2 (N = 78)
Swedish inspectors	4.8 (N = 73)

Note: Responses are on a seven-point scale. Scores less than 4 reveal that inspectors believe that enforcement should be tough—greater than 4, that it is better to persuade.

employers to comply with regulations voluntarily, even at the risk of being considered soft." The mean replies (table 22–2) suggest that American inspectors tend to emphasize enforcement and Swedish inspectors, cooperation.[17] Comments by Swedish inspectors made during in-depth interviews illustrate this point. One said, "I'm not one of those who likes to write too many written inspection notices. I would rather reason together with the employer and the safety steward, and come up with a solution everyone accepts. Writing is so impersonal." Another, "I try to reconcile the parties during the inspection. The first time around I don't try to enforce every point, so as to get our relationship functioning as smoothly as possible." A third said, "I think we can give in on an issue, even if it makes the workplace more hazardous, in order to preserve cooperation. I don't want to destroy cooperation for good."

The Problems with Punishment

The American decision to rely on enforcement based on legal punishment created two major problems: punishment causes resentment, and the use of the legal system increases the transaction costs of achieving a given purpose.

Punishment (in this case, fines) tends to cause resentment because in exchange for the change in behavior, there is no improvement in one's original state but merely an avoidance of worsening. This tends to be perceived as an unfair exchange. To change behavior for a reward, however, means that both the person changing and the agent seeking the changed behavior are better off: the agent because the behavior has been changed as he wishes, and the person changing because an improvement in the original state has been achieved. Elements of OSHA inspections that grow out of the enforcement system described in the previous sections increase resentment further.

Resentment creates two problems. In a democracy, the resentful may

Table 22-3
Inspectors' Perceptions of Employer Attitudes during OSHA Inspections

How Often Do the Employer Representatives:	Most of the Time	Sometimes	Seldom	Almost Never
Seem to be afraid of you when you come in?*	36%	38%	15%	10%
Try to intimidate you?†	0	23	28	50
Try to be overly flattering, just to get on your good side?*	28	26	28	18

Note: Percentages may add up to more than 100 percent because of rounding.
*N = 39.
†N = 40.

act politically against the object of resentment, thus threatening the political future of a program. It also works against voluntary compliance. No sooner did OSHA inspectors move into the field and begin fining employers than the latter began displaying resentment over the treatment they were being subjected to. Table 22-3 displays results from the American in-depth inspectors' survey showing the tense atmosphere surrounding OSHA inspections. Within one year of the effective date of the OSHAct, members of Congress, inundated by protest mail, had introduced some one hundred bills to amend or even repeal the law. In 1972, only a year after the act had gone into effect, the House Select Committee on Small Business held hearings on the effects of OSHA on small business. Later that same year the House Education and Labor Committee and the Senate Labor and Public Welfare Committee held oversight hearings. In 1974 two more hearings in the House and one in the Senate were held. The testimony produced scattered complaints about costs of complying with OSHA regulations, but much of it, and a large proportion of the bitterness, related to how OSHA regulations were enforced. Congressmen presented letters from constituents who complained of the treatment they received.[18]

> A few years ago this type of harassment by the mobsters was considered illegal. Today the U.S. government does it, and it is legal. Please compare the penalty of up to $10,000 fine PER violation of the act with those extended to draft card burners, flag defilers, establishment vandals and other gross disrespectors of property rights and government. As a small business man, my fate is much worse than theirs.

> A criminal guilty of drug, robbery or murder charges is shown more consideration for his Constitutional rights than the owner of a business. For example, an OSHA inspector can enter your place of business without a search warrant. Try that on a drug pusher and the whole thing is thrown out of court.

> If we allow tactics such as we experienced with this U.S. Department of Labor group from Billings, all the lives that were lost fighting Adolf Hitler and his henchmen were lost in vain. . . . We do not expect any special favors or attempts to bend the Laws for us, but we do expect this type of Gestapoism by Government employees to be stopped at once. It violates everything that our country is founded on. The Law Abiding Citizen is afraid to walk the streets of our larger cities day or night because of the Criminal element in our country. Why don't we use this misdirected energy to Restore Law and Order in our country?

The hearings also produced statements lamenting that employers were fined even though they complied with changes that the inspector required. One congressman told the following story:

> [OSHA] came in on Monday, gave them an inspection. The OSHA inspector went through and cited him on 12 minor violations and 2 majors.
> He said, "Mr. OSHA officer, are you going to be in town this week? . . . Will you come back before you leave town and check me out and see if I am up to snuff?"
> The guy comes back on Thursday. . . . He had all the discrepancies corrected. The OSHA inspectors said, "I am really impressed with your attitude. You are really in there pitching. We really appreciate having someone like you. Here is your citation." He got fined $500.[19]

When OSHA asked a small business group to give it the names of members who had protested against heavy-handed inspectors so that the charges could be investigated, not a single complainant was willing to authorize the release of his name. One explained, "I am of the opinion, sadly, that the United States government is not to be trusted. It would not surprise me in the least if the remedial action they speak of would be directed at the source . . . of information, and not at themselves." The response of another employer was similar: "I have little doubt that the Labor Department would use this information in order to seek out our business, discover many violations and close us down. We have worked hard over the past six and a half years to establish our business, and, being in partnership with my parents, I do not feel I could fairly ask them also to risk being put out of business with OSHA officials as judge and jury. Isn't it too bad we have come to this in America."[20]

Resentment at punishment was also expressed through challenges in court to OSHA compliance activities. Violations found by inspectors may be appealed to the Occupational Safety and Health Review Commission, a quasijudicial panel independent of OSHA. When the commission was first formed, its staff estimated that its caseload would be one hundred to two hundred cases a year. Instead it ran about three hundred to four hundred a month.[21] Business also used the courts to display their resentment at OSHA's enforcement system by appeals alleging that key aspects of OSHA's enforcement procedures violated the Bill of Rights. One citation was appealed on the grounds that the provision in the OSHAct allowing the imposition of fines without a jury trial was unconstitutional, and the case went to the Supreme Court, which rejected the argument. The second case to reach the Supreme Court involved a businessman who refused an OSHA inspector entry to his premises, alleging warrantless inspections to be a violation of the protection against unreasonable search. The Supreme Court ruled that warrants were indeed required but established liberal procedures for OSHA to obtain them.[22]

OSHA's political problems resulting from its failure to achieve agreement at the rule-making stage were thus compounded by employers' resentment over its enforcement methods, a combination that spelled serious political trouble. Although outsiders have difficulty influencing bureaucratic behavior during rule making, the use of fines is established by statute, not by OSHA, and it is easier for Congress to intervene here.

Complaints about OSHA's enforcement methods led Congress to try to pass amendments to change these methods. As early as 1972 the House passed an amendment removing firms with fewer than fifteen employees from OSHA coverage entirely, but it did not pass the Senate. In 1973 a similar amendment passed both houses and did not become law only because President Nixon vetoed the appropriations bill to which the amendment was attached. In 1974 an amendment exempting firms with fewer than twenty-five employers was again passed by the House but rejected in the Senate.

Until 1976 OSHA had thus narrowly avoided changes in its enforcement methods. But the precariousness of OSHA's perch was demonstrated by the results of a seemingly small event in the summer of 1976 involving a pamphlet that OSHA had just issued, *Safety with Beef Cattle*. As part of a program to prepare booklets on job hazards for distribution to workers, OSHA had contracted to prepare a series of booklets for farmworkers. Some brochures were designed for workers whose native language was not English; there was no intention to distribute them to, say, Kansas wheat farmers. The first booklet in the series was one of those so written. However, this was nowhere stated on the brochure itself, so as not to offend recipients. Instead, it ended up offending everyone else. To someone not aware of the background, the booklet appeared paternalistic and patronizing; one passage warned farmworkers to be careful lest they slip on cowdung. Outraged newspaper editorials followed.

The booklet was withdrawn, but the damage was done. The uproar occurred just as Congress was debating the year's Labor-HEW appropriation. The coincidence proved to be more than OSHA's standing on Capitol Hill could bear. Amid floor attacks on the agency, the House passed a series of amendments aimed at OSHA enforcement effort. Assessing the situation, OSHA supporters decided some concessions would have to be made. They accepted an amendment exempting from coverage farms with fewer than ten employees and another, hitting at OSHA's fine system in a way no amendment had previously been able to do, prohibiting imposing fines for nonserious violations if there were fewer than ten such violations in a citation.[23]

Supporters of OSHA are unhappy that its enforcement methods have caused resentment among employers, but they have been caught in the American dilemma captured by Edmund Burke: in the absence of other inducements to change behavior, the alternative to punishment is perceived as a massive flouting of the regulations. The dilemma is illustrated by union reactions to proposals that OSHA inspectors be allowed to give employers penalty-free consultation. In order to preserve the principle of first-instance sanctions, whenever an OSHA inspector enters a workplace, it must be to make an inspection. (OSHA personnel may answer questions over the telephone, and many states offer consultation services.) Early on, proposals were made to amend the OSHAct to allow the agency to set up a service to give advice to business. This suggestion appears uncontroversial, yet union spokesmen were so afraid that any dilution of existing policy would destroy compliance that they successfully opposed on-site consultation.[24]

The second problem that resentment causes is that it works against voluntary compliance. Increasing the population of voluntary compliers relative to those who do not comply voluntarily is important for any enforcement system. "The sociological mind reels," John Scott notes, "at the cost of social controls which would have to cope with the unrestrained exercise of amoral human interest."[25] A number of psychological experiments show that people performing a behavior in exchange for some inducement continue spontaneously to engage in the behavior a shorter time after the inducement has ceased being offered than groups performing without benefit of the inducement.[26] Rewards encourage the development of attitudes favorable to voluntary compliance, but the resentment produced by punishment discourages the development of such attitudes. Indeed the dilemma of deterrence is that punishment can actually decrease the sum of compliance by increasing resentment. The evidence from psychological experiments, though not entirely consistent, tends to show that behavior change that punishment brings about ceases as soon as the direct application of the punishment stops unless the punishment of undesired behavior is accompanied by rewarding the behavior one wishes to promote.[27] Alvin Gouldner's *Patterns of Industrial Bureaucracy* is a classic study of the effects of the introduction of a system of formal rules and punishments in a plant where there had previously been few rules. The new system created resentment and produced a situation where employees worked only when someone was watching them.[28]

The greater likelihood that rewards will produce attitude change with respect to the behavior one seeks to encourage than will punishment may be explained in terms of a cognitive dissonance perspective used by some psychologists. Cognitive dissonance occurs whenever there is an imbalance between positive feelings about one object and negative feelings about another object associated with the first one. It is argued that people tend to reduce cognitive dissonance either by becoming less positive to the first object or more positive to the second.[29] For instance, if the Democratic party is associated with support for an increased minimum wage, a Democratic opponent of such a measure will tend to change either his feelings toward it or toward the Democrats. Thus if a person feels positive about a reward he is receiving for a given behavior but initially is indifferent or negative toward the behavior itself, he will experience cognitive dissonance. The dissonance may be reduced by changing his attitude toward the behavior in a positive direction. If a person is being punished for not doing something he does not want to do, there will be a cognitive dissonance; his attitude will remain negative. And if the person is initially indifferent to or only mildly negative toward the behavior, he may become more negative toward it to reduce cognitive dissonance.

The Swedish enforcement system, which uses predominantly normative inducements, has not produced the same resentment among employers. Although it is not true that the use of normative inducements always causes less resentment than use of economic or coercive ones, they do tend in this direction, perhaps because of their propensity to be associated with participation in small groups that provide members with an excess of rewards over punishments. If the safety committee has succeeded in its purpose, employer participants will be receiving more psychological benefits than they are paying costs. In this context, any normative punishment from employee representatives is less resented because its source is a group that bestows, on balance, benefits. Also given the normal conflict of interest between labor and management, it is unlikely that employers would be as stung by criticism as they are pleasantly surprised by praise. Given the status gap between workers and employers, safety stewards will likely seldom give employers a scolding to their face. The main inducements safety stewards probably use, then, are normative rewards.

Certainly there are other reasons beside the Swedish enforcement system for this lack of resentment, but the system is important. The relative lack of resentment could probably not survive its replacement by the American reliance on legal punishment, although any new resentment would probably not attain American levels. In one question on the Swedish in-depth inspectors' survey, inspectors were presented with a brief description of the American enforcement system and asked their reaction to it. Eleven of seventeen respondents thought it a bad one, two were ambivalent, and only three considered it was a good idea. Six of the eleven critical inspectors spontaneously stated that the introduction of such a system in Sweden would lead to increased employer resentment. Responded one inspector plaintively, "If we did that, an inspector could never feel himself welcome at a firm."

PART IV / System and Conflict

The Swedish manual used for training new inspectors warns them to "count on the fact that setting sanctions in motion can create a harder climate for you at the workplace."[30] In 1974 the Worker Protection Act was changed to allow imposition of conditional fines together with orders and prohibitions, and although a significant rise in the number of orders and prohibitions issued occurred, these still constituted a small fraction of 1 percent of the total number of inspections. This increase was accompanied by the appearance, for the first time, of contests of inspections. (Inspector decisions in Sweden may be appealed to agency headquarters and then, as an ultimate step, to the cabinet.) The number of contests has increased steadily from two in a six-month period in 1974 to fifteen in the same-length period in 1976. In Sweden, too, punishment increases resentment.

Another problem created by OSHA enforcement is that the use of the legal system increases transaction costs. Violations must be proven and the accused afforded an opportunity to appeal rulings. This is *a fortiori* so in America, with the great concern for individual rights in proceedings.

In Sweden appeals involve one submission of a letter by the appealing party and a reply by the district. There is no hearing or opportunity for oral examination, and no rules exist for where the burden of proof lies in deciding appeals. Lawyers are almost never involved.[31] In America appeals are first heard by an administrative law judge in the area where the business is located. Proceedings are oral and include cross-examination. OSHA is always represented by a lawyer, and the employer is usually represented by counsel. Burden of proof is on OSHA. A three-member review commission panel in Washington is the next step. It relies on the record developed earlier and on new briefs filed by the parties. Its decisions may in turn be appealed to the court of appeals and from there to the Supreme Court.

Since violations must be proved in order to mete out punishment, OSHA inspectors must be scrupulous about documentation. Inspectors in the in-depth inspectors' survey reported that their supervisors' most common request after reviewing their last ten inspection reports was for documentation. This means taking photos ("I try to get the employer or an employee representative so the employer can't say it was taken at another plant," one inspector noted) and employee statements. For a violation to exist, there must be worker exposure to the hazard, so if a particular machine is not running when the inspector comes through, the inspector must get a worker to say he normally uses it. Consideration of court challenge is the main explanation for a number of policies followed by many area offices. For example, most threshold limit values are expressed as eight-hour averages because often exposure varies widely over different phases of the process cycle, while other times a process is in operation only for a short period each day. Sometimes the inspector sees that exposure is relatively constant or observes that a process cycle is short enough to provide measurements of exposure peaks and troughs without sampling for a full eight hours. In such cases, eight-hour sampling merely increases the time an inspector must spend.

The problem is that if the regulations express a threshold limit value as an eight-hour average, an inspector who has not sampled the full period is open to legal challenge. Thus many area directors are wary about letting inspectors use their judgment on whether a full eight hours is necessary in a particular case, afraid of what will happen when lawyers question OSHA relentlessly about some 18½ minute sampling gap. Four of the fourteen area directors in the area directors' course survey responded that if an inspector had sampled for only six hours, they would insist that zero values be entered for the remaining two hours for the purpose of computing whether the threshold limit value had been exceeded. This means that in some cases where a threshold limit value has been exceeded, legal requirements prevent citation. In contrast, responses to the Swedish national district chiefs' survey showed that in half of the districts, inspectors issued written inspection notices in health cases without doing any sampling at all. (This is not as arbitrary as it may sound. Frequently an experienced person can tell that for a certain type of operation, a threshold limit value will be exceeded where control measures are absent.)

In situations such as these, the issue in any citation appeal may be not whether a hazard exists but whether legal requirements have been followed. To take a bizarre catch-22 type of situation, determining noncompliance with threshold limit values requires sampling, often using devices attached to the employee's body, but such devices may hinder employee movement, leading an employer to claim that the sample was not representative of worker exposure.

Perhaps the most unfortunate results come when legal requirements actually interfere with compliance because they make regulations so hard to understand.

There have been numerous complaints about the incomprehensibility of OSHA regulations, but Assistant Secretary Guenther pointed out that "there is a limit as to how far we can go in paraphrasing or simplifying the language of the standards, because, as you well know, the standards are a legal document in addition to an engineering document."[32]

Although OSHA inspectors may not give on-site consultation, there is no logical reason to believe that during an inspection they should not give employers advice, to the extent of their expertise, on how to correct violations. Yet in 1971 the OSHA legal office stated that if inspectors gave advice and an employer following the recommendations had not succeeded in correcting the problem, the citation could be thrown out in court. By contrast, most Swedish inspectors in the in-depth inspectors' survey responded that they considered giving employers advice as an important part of their job. "An inspector should give examples about how problems can be solved," one said. "Otherwise he's a bad inspector."

The cross-cultural validity of these generalizations about consequences of formalization is illustrated by the infrequent experience in Sweden with orders and prohibitions. The ASV [Worker Protection Board] training manual points out that "an order or prohibition demands more exact documentation. As soon as you suggest that sanctions may be used, you must be more careful about assembling documentation."[33]

The Problem with Normative Inducements

If the problem with using fines to induce compliance is that they produce resentment, the problem with normative inducements is that their success depends on placing the person whose behavior one seeks to influence into a group of relevant others who can influence him. The Swedes have set up institutions to achieve that aim, but success is not assured in any individual case. If this method does not work, compliance based on normative inducements exerts no inducements at all. Hence there arose in Sweden at the end of the period under investigation some criticism against the compliance system. The criticism, not nearly as strong as that in the United States, took an opposite tack. The report on occupational safety and health to the 1976 LO Congress stated that "consequences of violations of the Worker Protection Act are not severe enough."[34] One article in the LO journal was even headlined "Safety and Health Inspectors in the U.S. Have More Power than in Sweden"![35]

The 1976 final report of the State Commission on the Work Environment dealt at some length with sanctions under the new law but proposed no major revisions because "a strong local safety organization is doubtless a much more effective guarantee for compliance with the law than any general criminalization of actions violating the law or the regulations."[36] The committee did recommend, however, that ASV could, at its discretion, issue certain kinds of regulations with first-instance criminal sanctions after a guilty verdict in a trial. But Gunnar Danielsson, ASV director-general, believed that "it is not the idea that most regulations are going to be associated with first-instance sanctions. We must avoid making this law into a criminal law."[37]

Dissatisfaction from unions about primary reliance on normative inducements was expressed through demands to give safety stewards, or safety committees with union majorities, the right to make safety and health decisions. Were these demands realized, the role of safety stewards would no longer be simply to influence employers but to determine factory conditions themselves. LO raised such demands during negotiations for the 1976 LO-SAF safety and health agreement. They were successful in getting the composition of the safety committee changed to give union representatives a one-vote majority (the white-collar union at the plant would be included on the union side as well as the LO union). However, they failed in their central demand. The agreement provided that safety committee decisions involving spending money could be binding only were the vote unanimous, unless the committee was given a certain budget by the firm, in which case the committee could decide on the disposition of the budget by majority vote.[38]

Notes

1. Richard D. Schwartz, "Social Factors in the Development of Legal Control," *Yale Law Journal* 63 (February 1954).
2. Edmund Burke, *Reflections on the Revolution in France*, in *Selected Writings of Edmund Burke*, ed. Walter J. Bate (New York: Modern Library, 1960), 388.
3. Leon Radzionwicz, *A History of English Law and Its Administration* (New York: Macmillan, 1948), 25. The same phenomenon is observable in contemporary America.
4. On this difference, see Lennart Lundquist, *The Hare and the Tortoise* (Ann Arbor: University of Michigan Press, 1979).
5. Arbetarskyddsnamnden, *Allmanna regler for den lokala sakerhetstjanstens organisation* (Stockholm: Tiden, 1948), 50.
6. LO-SAF, *En Battre arbetsmiljo* (Stockholm: Prisma, 1969).
7. *Utbildning och upplysning inom arbetsmiljon* (Stockholm: Rotobeckman, 1973), 42–43.
8. Arbetarskyddsnamnden, *Battre Arbetsmiljo* (Stockholm: Tiden, 1975).
9. LO-SAF, *Overenskommelse om utbildning i arbetsmiljofragor* (Stockholm, 1976).
10. Arbetarskyddslagen, sec. 40(b).
11. "Hundra stopp 1975—och paragrafen anvands mycket mer," *Arbetarskydd* (May 1976): 2.
12. LO-SAF, *Arbetsmiljoavtalet* (Stockholm: Tiden, 1976), 42 (emphasis added).
13. LO-SAF, *Arbetarskydd och foretagshalsovard* (Stockholm: Arbetarskyddnamnden, 1967), 38–39.
14. LO-SAF, *Arbetsmiljoavtalet*, 26.
15. OSHA, *Field Operations Reporting Manual* (Washington, D.C., 1975), chap. V-1.
16. Ture Lindstrom, et al., *Inspektionsmetodik och yrkesskadeutredning* (Stockholm: Stencil, 1975), 7, 9, 11.
17. Differences for the in-depth inspectors' survey are far more dramatic, although the difference between the mean answers for the national inspectors' surveys is statistically significant to the 0.01 level. It is hard to know whether the in-depth or national results should be considered more indicative of inspectors' feelings. Respondents in mail-administered questionnaires may tend to give intermediate, indeterminate responses—that is, to circle "4"—because they had not given the questionnaire as much thought as did the respondents in interviews.
18. These quotations appear in U.S. House of Representatives, Hearings before the Select Subcommittee on Labor of the Committee on Education and Labor, *Occupational Safety and Health Act of 1970 Oversight and Proposed Amendments*, 93d Cong., 2d sess., March–November 1974; and U.S., House of Representatives, Hearings before the Select Subcommittee on Labor of the Committee on Education and Labor, *Occupational Safety and Health Act of 1970 Oversight and Proposed Amendments*, 92d cong., 2d sess., March 1972, pp. 43–44, 173, 399, 1488–1489.

19. *House Labor Hearings* (1974), p. 107.
20. Quoted from Neal Heard, "Undue Process of Law," *Trial* (September 1975): 26.
21. Nicholas A. Ashford, *Crisis in the Workplace* (Cambridge: MIT Press, 1976), 284, 286.
22. *Atlas Roofing Co. v. Occupational Safety and Health Review Commission*, 430 U.S. 442 (1977); *Marshall v. Barlow's, Inc.*, 436 U.S. 307 (1978).
23. Since these were amendments to the year's appropriations bill and not to the OSHAct itself, they applied only for one year and not permanently.
24. See, for instance, the testimony of Jack Sheehan and George Taylor in *House Labor Hearings* (1972), pp. 440–448, 607.
25. John F. Scott, *Internalization of Norms* (Englewood Cliffs, N.J.: Prentice-Hall, 1971), 114.
26. Edward L. Deci, *Intrinsic Motivation* (New York: Plenum Press, 1975), 133–134.
27. Albert Bandura, *Handbook of Behavior Modification* (New York: Holt, 1969), 316–317.
28. Alvin Gouldner, *Patterns of Industrial Bureaucracy* (New York: Free Press, 1954).
29. Leon Festinger, *A Theory of Cognitive Dissonance* (Evanston: Row, Peterson, 1957).
30. Lindstrom, et. al., *Inspektionsmetodik*, 14.
31. Interview with Goran Lindh, ASV.
32. *1972 House Labor Hearings*, 1972, p. 351.
33. Lindstrom, et. al., *Inspektionsmetodik*, 14.
34. LO, *Arbetsmiljo* (Stockholm: Prisma, 1976), 59.
35. Birger Viklund, "Yrkesinspektionen i USA har mera makt an i Sverige," *LO-Tidningen* 57 (February 10, 1977): 13.
36. *Arbetsmiljolag*, 304–305.
37. Interview with Gunnar Danielsson.
38. LO-SAF, *Arbetsmiljoavtalet*, sec. 19, 22.

PART V

Organizational Alternatives and Social Change

The essays in this section analyze a variety of organizations that provide alternatives to hierarchy and bureaucracy. Since no single model provides a comprehensive alternative, or is free from problems of its own, the authors approach their subject with an openness to the problems of alternative organizations, as well as a commitment to more democratic and humane forms. Experience from a variety of settings around the world is analyzed by the authors in an attempt to pose relevant organizational questions for contemporary America.

In their essay, William Foote Whyte and Joseph Blasi analyze alternatives in production organizations of considerably large scale. Their main focus is the worker-owned firm and the dynamics of participation that result from worker ownership. Not all forms of worker ownership are equally conducive to worker control, however, and some even revert back to private ownership and managerial hierarchy. By looking at a range of cases in the United States, in the Mondragón region of Spain, in Israel, and in Yugoslavia, Whyte and Blasi develop a theory of what makes certain worker-owned firms successful and others not. They analyze forms of shareholding, control rights, job redesign, and organizational infrastructure for financial and technical assistance, among others, and conclude with a discussion of the public policy implications of their findings.

In her essay, Paula Rayman looks in detail at the Israeli kibbutz and the evolution of its value system over the course of several generations. The kibbutz movement was profoundly committed to egalitarian and communal values from the beginning, yet recent changes have called into question some of those values. In order to understand this, Rayman analyzes the regional organizations of the kibbutz—the Milouot. The Milouot provides many services and opportunities for members of the kibbutz, yet it also fosters a model of industrialization that undermines some of the original ideals, participation and equality in particular. Rayman insists that any analysis of alternative forms of organization must look at them in the broad context of nation building and production for military bureaucracies and world markets.

Robert Cole investigates one of the most talked-about, and yet one of the most misunderstood, forms of workplace participation, the Japanese quality-control circles. He looks first at the history and philosophy of the job redesign movement in Japan, and some of the American roots of this approach. Then he presents a detailed view of the actual functioning of the quality-control circles, particularly in the auto industry, where the causes of the Japanese productivity edge over American manufacturers have been much debated. Cole's study uncovers many areas of innovation, yet notes that much of this constitutes a form of controlled participation. He concludes with some useful comparisons of participation in the United States and Western Europe.

Michael Smith turns his attention to a much less considered topic in alternative organizations theory, namely how large public bureaucracies can be democratized. He argues that democratic administration is not incompatible with larger forms of representative political democracy, and that organizational democracy could be of benefit to both administrative workers and the public at large. But there are many obstacles to democratization, and Smith analyzes a range of structural features, organizational practices, fears, and rationalizations against such organizational change.

Jane Mansbridge analyzes some of the organizational forms that have been developed by the feminist movement over the past two decades in the United States. She pays particular attention to the consciousness-raising group and the face-to-face consensual form of participatory democracy, since this form had a special relevance to the feminist goals of personal transformation. Yet her own research on small-scale democratic organizations reveals this form to be of only limited value to disadvantaged groups, including women, who tend to participate less than others even in face-to-face assemblies. Mansbridge argues that there can be no single "form of freedom," and that organizational choice depends on the goals and the context, and, in particular, whether or not interests conflict. She concludes with a set of recommendations on representative, participatory, and other forms of organizational involvement.

In the concluding essay of this book, Carmen Sirianni analyzes some of the limitations of holistic participatory work organizations. This form has remained the dominant organizational alternative for egalitarian democrats, partly for good reason. Yet it reveals serious limitations as a general model for achieving equality, democracy, and individual choice on a broad societal scale. Sirianni proposes, instead, a global pluralist model of equality that can accommodate a great variety of forms of work commitment, organizational structure, and participation. He also argues that, to achieve relative equality of work opportunities and flexibility of job commitments, relatively open labor markets and various forms of bureaucratic administration would be necessary. The challenge of Weber, in short, cannot be fully overcome, but it can be redirected in the interests of greater democracy and equality.

23
Worker Ownership, Participation, and Control: Toward a Theoretical Model

William Foote Whyte and Joseph R. Blasi

What happens when labor governs itself? We see both problems and potentialities. If the potentialities are to become realities, we need to review the variety of experiences people have had in employee ownership and labor management relations to arrive at a theoretical framework. Such a framework is essential for guiding us toward the public policy implications of our research.

In the employee-owned firm or worker cooperative production organization, the administration of that firm must provide for two interrelated but conceptually separable functions: organizational governance and the management of work. (This is also true of any other type of production organization, but the distinction is particularly important in designing an unfamiliar type of organization.)

Regarding what the organization *is* and what it *ought* to be, we see members' thinking being shaped by three organizational models: *authoritarian, bargaining,* and/or *town meeting* or *community democracy*. We are not assuming that members have a theoretical model explicitly in mind as they design an organization, live and work in it, and react to it. We do claim that people have implicit models in mind, however vague those visualizations may be, and that they do tend to judge current experience and future plans in terms of such models. Each of the three models has certain strengths and weaknesses. These need to be recognized and assessed so that we can move forward to build a new theoretical model, which may combine some of the features of the three existing models.

Reprinted from *Policy Sciences* 14(1982): 137–63, by permission of Elsevier Scientific Publishing Co. and of the authors.

I. Authoritarian Model

This model comes down to us particularly through the work of F. W. Taylor and his disciples in the scientific management movement (Taylor, 1911). Few executives today would acknowledge that they are followers of Taylor, but they fail to recognize to what extent their present policies and practices in fact follow the basic assumptions of Taylorism. In this model, ultimate control is outside of the workforce, in the hands of key investors, government (if a public organization), or, if within the company, in the hands of the management group.

This model has advantages at least insofar as it makes clear what is to be expected in the management of work. The model sets up a formally structured organization and administration, dividing various functions from each other and linking them together in a hierarchical pattern. It provides for the division of labor, which is necessary for any organization where a variety of tasks is performed, especially when the organization grows beyond what can be handled by a small group. The model also makes clear how discipline is to be handled, since it allocates all the power to the hands of management.

The disadvantages of this model are now well known, but it may be useful to sketch them briefly as a background against which we can examine the other models.

While the doctrine indicates that supervisors and executives have the legitimate right to control work activities because of their expertise, in fact the basis of control becomes *power* rather than *expertise*. Especially in large organizations, those making decisions affecting workers and work activity tend to be so far removed from the scene of action that they have little idea of the work-a-day effects of their decisions.

The model makes no allowance for differences in interests separating workers from management. It is assumed that what is good for management and the investors is good for labor, and the model provides no means whereby labor can challenge this assumption.

Especially as such organizations grow, they tend to become rigid, losing the flexibility required for coping with technological, social, and economic changes.

While some division of labor is necessary for all but the simplest and smallest organizations, the Taylorism model tends to push such division to impractical extremes. The dominant assumption has been that efficiency is best achieved when the work performed by labor is subdivided into small elements so that workers perform repeatedly the same simple operation. Worker and union reactions to this extreme de-skilling of jobs have become painfully apparent in recent years.

The model assumes that thinking will be done by management and that workers serve the organization best when they simply do what they are told. In other words, the model utilizes the muscles and physical skills of workers but makes no mental demands beyond those required to understand the instructions of management. Social researchers, comparing Japanese with United States management, are coming to the conclusion that the ability of a nation exceedingly poor in material resources to overtake resource-rich America is based to a considerable extent on the much fuller utilization of the total human resources of the firm, including the brains of blue-collar workers (Cole, 1979).

The job rights of labor have no formal standing in this model. To be sure, managers may recognize that arbitrary dismissals of workers and shifting of workers from job to job may cause serious production problems, but the restraints here are imposed in terms of efficiency rather than in terms of human rights. Similarly, when layoffs are planned, management may find it advisable to minimize worker complaints by laying off in inverse order of seniority, but here again the guidelines are provided by assumptions about efficiency rather than in terms of rights workers may have acquired through service in particular jobs for a particular period of time.

II. Bargaining Model

In this model, the company is divided into two segments: management and workers, with a union representing workers.

This model has certain clear advantages. It provides for some degree of democratization in the governance of the organization. It recognizes explicitly the interests of labor and provides for representatives of the workers to bargain with management on a wide range of issues.

The model provides some protection against the arbitrary exercise of authority, giving workers a channel of appeal against unfair decisions. Furthermore, in many cases, when local union and management cannot agree on a given grievance, that grievance may be referred to an impartial arbitrator, so that the final decision is taken out of the hands of management.

The model also offers the possibility of establishing collective responsibility among workers, which can be useful to management as well as workers. That is, some management people find it advantageous to work out production and discipline problems in consultation with local union officers rather than having to deal individually with a large number of workers.

On the disadvantage side, it is often argued that the bargaining model undermines managerial authority. While it does indeed place some limits on the exercise of that authority, in a well-established union-management relationship, we generally find contract provisions and unwritten understandings that tend to protect the authority necessary to administer an organization. In the simplest form, such provisions do not allow the worker the right to disobey the orders of his supervisor (except in extreme situations) but protect his right to challenge the legitimacy of an order through lodging a grievance. The standard rule is that you obey, so that the work can go on, but then you follow a judicial process in challenging the order.

We have encountered many bargaining situations in which the two parties seem to be engaged in a zero-sum game. Workers assume that whatever they gain must be at the expense of management, and management people make the same assumption. The bargaining model often tends to produce rigidities that may be so extreme as to threaten the existence of the organization. In the course of the power struggle, with neither party trusting the other, the union pushes for detailed and explicit statements of work rules and work loads. Management may find the accumulation of such rules a severe barrier to the maintenance of a competitive position in the industry. In that situation, management often approaches union leaders in an effort to get their agreement to renegotiate the work rules so as to provide the company with the flexibility necessary to meet changing conditions. Management may even argue that the union's refusal to make these adjustments will make it necessary to close the plant. Since union leaders may have heard the same threats before, they tend to assume that management is bluffing once again. If they are persuaded of the economic necessity of renegotiating the work rules, the union leaders may nevertheless hesitate to embark on this path for fear that the rank-and-file members will accuse them of selling out to management. Thus, the parties may bargain themselves into a self-destructive impasse.

These disadvantages are by no means inevitable. The model can be so adapted as to promote union management cooperation in improving productivity and the quality of working life. We will explore these possibilities later.

III. Town Meeting or Community Democracy Model

In this model, the members of the organization have the power to make decisions. When it comes to voting, the principle followed is one member, one vote.

In the society where civil government is based upon one citizen, one vote, this model for a work organization has an obvious appeal. It fits in with democratic values and with our norms of equal rights for all (Mansbridge, 1973).

The disadvantages of the model are found largely in the major area that it does not encompass: the management of work. In the town meeting, all citizens can indeed participate and have equal voting rights, but the town meeting usually assembles only once a year, except for occasional special meetings. The town meeting, indeed, decides certain policy questions and elects the board of selectmen, but the members of the community do not do the official work of that community. Getting the work done is the responsibility of a few elected officials. Thus, the town meeting model provides no guidance on the division of labor, on the allocation of authority and responsibility, on the need for specialization either because of skill or special leadership competence, on the imposition of disciplinary measures, and so on. Therefore, those who implicitly guide their organizational thinking in terms of this model are left to imagine how a democratic organization would manage work activities. This gap between the theoretical model and the needs of a work organization leads to major confusions, frustrations, and conflicts.

What Happens under Worker Ownership?

Here we will focus our attention on the United States but will draw upon cases from abroad in posing and seeking to answer theoretical and practical questions. In the first place, since we find distinctively different sets of problems shaped by the way the worker-owned organization came into being, we need to separate our analysis for two major types of organizations: those grass-roots organizations created anew where no production or service organization existed before, and those in which worker ownership arises out of the efforts of organizational members and community people to save jobs in a privately owned plant threatened with shutdown.

Grass-Roots Firms

The late 1960s and the 1970s witnessed a burgeoning of small grass-roots production or service cooperatives (Rothschild-Whitt, 1979). Since there is no common register for such firms, and since they are created and sometimes disappear in a short time, we cannot say how many currently exist in the United States, but the number may well be over five thousand. They tend generally to serve local markets and to arise in types of enterprises requiring small amounts of capital per worker. Characteristically, the members of the organization are young people in their twenties and thirties, either single, divorced, or separated, and therefore without heavy family responsibilities. The members are predominantly of middle-class origins. For them, membership in a worker-owned printing company or restaurant is inspired in part by a revolt against the authority that is represented by "the establishment," which they tend to see in terms of large, bureaucratic organizations. In rejecting the individualism of United States culture, they also reject the example of their elders who have secure economic positions.

Members of such grass-roots collectives are in effect struggling with the problem of filling the work organization gap in the town meeting or community democracy model.

The norm of equality among the members is a key principle in structuring the organization, but what it means in practice poses a number of difficult questions. Do equal rights have to be translated into equal participation by members in making decisions? Must all members receive the same pay, without regard to skill or length of service? Or should those who have greater than average family responsibilities receive more money? Should jobs be rotated among the members so that everyone has a chance to perform every job—in spite of differences in levels of skill?

We often find members expressing guilt feelings because they have deviated from the norms of equality to deal with practical problems. For example, as a small worker-owned television repair firm reached the point at which it was becoming increasingly inefficient to have the skilled craftsmen doing their own paper work, they brought in a young woman to do their bookkeeping. They decided indeed to pay her less than the skilled repairmen, but the leader of the organization was concerned with what he assumed to be a violation of democratic principles.

Grass-roots collectives tend to have characteristic problems in the handling of authority. Since the organization comes into being out of a rejection of systems of authority in traditional organizations, members naturally tend to be suspicious of anyone who appears to be giving orders.

The ideal is that all decisions shall be collective decisions. Furthermore, the members correctly recognize that a frequent use of voting in resolving disagreements can undermine group solidarity, and therefore they aim at decision making through consensus. Especially as conditions change and the organization grows, collective decision making can absorb enormous amounts of time and lead to the frustration of the members. The problem becomes especially serious when the organization grows beyond the limits of a small face-to-face group. In the small informal group, even when the members all adhere to the rhetoric that they are all equal and that they have no leader, informal leadership inevitably does arise, so it may be possible to maintain efficiency with group consensus decision making, but the growth of the organization separates people in functions and in space and multiplies the problems of coordination. It is at this point that many previously successful grass-roots collectives tend to break down. The implicit organizational model provides no guidance in the handling of these more complex problems, and they fail to evolve a satisfactory model of their own.

Firms Converted to Worker Ownership

The 1970s were marked by the sudden emergence all over the United States of cases in which employers or employees and community people saved jobs in an impending plant shutdown through buying the plant and establishing a new employee-owned or employee-community-owned company. Contrary to commonly held views that the plants being abandoned are inevitably "lemons," we found that some of the plants being shut down had actually been consistent profit makers but had not yielded a high enough level of profits to satisfy the top management of the conglomerate (Whyte, 1978). In such cases, workers and sometimes also local managers would be satisfied to save the jobs, even if the firm was not making spectacular profits. The problem in such cases is one of transferring ownership so that those who have the major financial stake in the continuation of the firm can become owners. The new firm can then survive even without major technological or local management changes.

In other cases, we have found that the losses of the local plant can be clearly attributed to mismanagement by remote control by conglomerate top executives who have been imposing decisions on situations they do not understand.

In the cases studied by Cornell University's New Systems of Work and Participation Program, we find universally an atmosphere of euphoria at the time of the transformation of ownership and in the early months of employee or employee-community ownership. Over the next months, characteristically, we find growing dissatisfaction, sometimes accompanied by severe conflict. The disillusionment of workers and the resulting conflicts arise out of a failure of management to recognize that an employee-owned firm cannot be managed effectively by following the authoritarian model. Let us consider three examples.

The Mohawk Valley Community Corporation arose out of a divestiture by Sperry-Rand Corporation (Hammer and Stern, 1980; Stern, Wood, and Hammer, 1979). The plant and jobs were saved by an extraordinarily effective area-wide campaign led by the director of the Mohawk Valley Economic Development District and local management people, with the active participation of union leaders. To secure a two million dollar loan from banks and two million dollars in credit from the Economic Development administration, the organizers of the campaign first had to sell nearly two million dollars worth of stock—in a depressed area where unemployment was running over 11 percent. The organizers of the campaign based their strategy on selling the stock in small amounts to large numbers of people. Thirty-five hundred people bought stock, and only about two hundred forty of those were then employed in the Herkimer plant. Management and workers together purchased about 34 percent of the stock, community people holding the other two-thirds.

A month after the dramatic success of this job-saving campaign, four key people from the Herkimer case spoke to a seminar at Cornell. A spirit of brotherly love then prevailed between union leaders and management, both parties sharing the pride in their great achievement. When asked whether his management had made any plans for involving worker participation in decision making, President Robert May shook his head, replying, "We haven't got around to that yet." After a pause he added, "Maybe we should install a suggestion box."

Fifteen months later, when the same cast of characters spoke at a seminar, Whyte met privately with the presidents of the blue- and white-collar workers' unions before the session to ask how things were going. The president of the white-collar union replied, "You ask any worker what it means to work in that plant now. They'll tell you, 'I've got a job.' That's all. Nothing else has changed. This place doesn't run any different now than it did when Sperry-Rand owned it."

The president of the blue-collar workers' union confirmed this general interpretation and added that his union at that time had five grievances ready to go to arbitration—an extraordinary number for a small plant.

In our later contacts with workers and union leaders over a period of months, we found them experiencing increasing dissatisfaction in their relations with management. They also pointed out to us again and again gross inefficiencies in the production operations that they could correct if management were interested in discussing these problems with them.

After a very successful year financially, Mohawk Valley Community Corporation has run into some serious reverses, which have led to a cutting of expenses and reduction of the workforce to the point where it is now down close to one hundred. This decline cannot be blamed exclusively upon the lack of any effective utilization of the brains of the workers. Still, the workers are convinced that the company would be in better shape if they had some input into decision making.

The company seems now clearly on the road back to traditional private ownership. Four members of management have recently purchased enough newly issued shares to give themselves 50 percent of the voting stock and, therefore, absolute control.

In the case of Vermont Asbestos Group (VAG), the hero of the job-saving campaign was John Lupien, the maintenance supervisor, who rallied workers and a few local townspeople and got the assistance of the state agencies in negotiating the purchase of the mine from GAF. Initially, over 80 percent of the stock was owned by members of the workforce, and all of the 170-odd workers bought at least one $50 share.

John Lupien became chairman of the VAG board, whose membership was evenly divided, with seven rank-and-file workers balanced by seven white-collar workers or members of management. A former mine worker, then a representative in the State House, became the fifteenth member.

The ownership and control structure was designed by a local lawyer, Andrew Fields. Neither Fields nor Lupien had any notions about creating economic democracy. Fields described himself with pride as "a little to the right of Barry Goldwater." He believed that the private enterprise system was the greatest creation of the human race since Jesus Christ left this earth, and therefore he boasted that he had tried to set up a structure of ownership and control as close to the private enterprise model as possible.

When anybody asked John Lupien about worker participation in management, he had a stock answer: "If you own stock in General Motors, that doesn't give you the right to run General Motors."

From the outset, worker-members of the board of directors found themselves in an awkward position. Having been elected by their fellow union members, they assumed that they would be responsible to those members and would be reporting to them regarding the deliberations of the board. However, lawyer Fields informed them that all of the board's deliberations must be held strictly confidential, and that nothing could be communicated by the worker-members to the other workers. All communication from the board to the workers would be through official bulletins.

Workers were naturally curious regarding salaries that their company was paying the members of management. Lupien and the company president at first flatly refused to give out any figures. At this point lawyer Fields informed them that his interpretation of the law indicated that they could not withhold such information from the worker-stockholders. Even then, top management did not really open up. The board finally released figures on *salary ranges*, avoiding pinpointing any particular salaries.

At first VAG was fantastically profitable simply because, shortly after the transfer of ownership, the price of asbestos jumped by 63 percent. Within a year, the workers got back more in dividends than they had paid for the stock. Nevertheless, they were not completely satisfied with the situation, as they began to encounter cases in which top management made major decisions without consulting the worker-owners or, in one case, even in direct violation of the expressed opinions of the majority of those worker-owners. The case that seemed to precipitate the sharpest cleavage between worker-owners and management involved Vermont Industrial Products (VIP), a brainchild of John Lupien, who saw the future of the company depending upon its ability to use asbestos tailings (waste) in the manufacture of asbestos board. Since banks were not inclined to put up much money for this purpose, the project could only be financed out of profits. Management's call for a special meeting of stockholders gave workers the impression that their vote would decide the matter. They did indeed vote and solidly defeated the proposal. Then lawyer Fields "clarified" the situation by explaining that such a vote was only advisory to the board of directors and that the board has the legal right to make its own decision on this matter. Lupien then persuaded the board to authorize the project.

It is important to note that this was not simply a situation where the workers were shortsightedly preferring immediate income over the long-term strengthening of the firm. To be sure, the area where asbestos was currently being mined was estimated to run out in about seven years whereas the tailings, already piled far above plant level, could sustain VIP for decades. However, workers opposing Lupien pointed out that in an area adjoining the mine, but owned by the company, geological studies had indicated that there was a fifty-year supply of asbestos. To reach this new source of ore would require substantial excavations, costing millions of dollars. When they expected that the major financing for VIP would be supplied by a bank, some workers said that they had been willing to go along. When the bankers declined to provide such credit, the workers took this as evidence that the VIP project was unwise.

There is no need to render a final judgment on the economic soundness of the VIP plan. The important point here is the way the decision was made. This confirmed for many workers the conclusion that ownership gave them no influence on decision making and, therefore, no reason to own stock in their company if they could get an attractive price for it. When Howard Manosh, a respected local entrepreneur, became aware of the spreading dissatisfaction among the workers, and stepped forward with a tender offer of $1,834 for each share originally bought at $50, he was able in a short time to pick up about 30 percent of the shares. In a proxy contest with Lupien's board of directors, Manosh won fourteen out of fifteen seats and took control. The hero of the job-saving campaign at VAG, John Lupien was then forced out of the company.

When newspapers reported the Manosh takeover, many critics of employee ownership concluded that the case simply demonstrated that American workers were only interested in money and did not care about ownership. Obviously, if the workers had been offered less money for their stock, they would have been less likely to sell, but the circumstances of the case by no means prove that they were indifferent to employee ownership. Having discovered through experience that ownership of a large majority of the shares gave them no influence over major decisions affecting their jobs and their lives, they made a rational judgment that the stock only had a financial value and therefore they should get as much money out of it as possible.

In the South Bend Lathe (SBL) case, our information comes simply from correspondence—from one conversation with President Richard Boulis and from media accounts—but SBL so clearly fits the pattern we are describing as to justify generalizing on the basis of fragmentary information.

SBL is one of the most publicized cases of employee ownership yet to appear, and until recently it had been extraordinarily successful financially. In this conglomerate divestiture case, 100 percent of the stock is coming to be owned by employees through an Employee Stock Ownership Plan (ESOP). As he appointed the trustees who vote the stock, Boulis has been firmly in control up to the present time; the full voting rights will pass to the workforce within a few years.

Our first contact with South Bend Lathe was through a letter Whyte wrote to President Boulis, expressing interest in the case. In his answer, Boulis closed with a sentence that has become one of our favorite quotations: "We tell our people that they have all the advantages of ownership without any of the headaches of management." We wondered then how long it would be before the workers would begin agitating for a share in those "headaches."

When the steelworkers' local union went out on strike in September 1980, Boulis was still running the company as if he had personally owned all of it. He had even declined to let his fellow shareholders know what salary he was paying himself.

Boulis blames the strike on the union, particularly because its higher officers have never forgiven him and the local for trading the pension plan in on an ESOP—and still have a suit in court to rescind that decision. According to newspaper and magazine reports, the union leaders have an entirely different interpretation, which fits far better with what we have seen in similar cases elsewhere.

Warren Brown, writing in the *Washington Post* (September 30, 1980) quotes the following words of a young machinist, Randy Reynolds, who had played an important role in persuading workers to accept the ESOP:

> What we have had there for the last five years is ownership without control. . . . We've bent over backwards since 1975 to make a good product and keep it selling. . . . We've kept our mouths shut—covered up our differences with management to avoid publicity. . . .
>
> But all we got was the same treatment we had before the ESOP, maybe even worse. We made no decisions. We have no voice. We're owners in name only.

According to Boulis, "Employee ownership does not mean employee management. Somebody has to give the orders to make things happen. You can't run a business by committee."

Do SBL workers want to run the company? The *Washington Post* reporter could not find anyone who expressed himself in that way. He gave this interpretation of the prevailing sentiments: "None said he wanted to manage the firm, per se. But they all said that they expected ownership conferred on them a kind of collegial equality with management in which their opinions would be listened to, their views sought."

The *Post* reporter closes his article with Boulis reporting on what he has learned. He says that, when the strike ends, he is going to try "to improve internal communications." He continues:

> When we bought this company, I didn't have time for human relations. I didn't have time to go around patting people on their butts. . . . I didn't think about anything except keeping this business going and making money. But now, maybe I'll find some time for human relations. I guess I'll have to.

Anyone who thinks he can provide effective leadership for an employee-owned company by going around "patting people on their butts" is unlikely ever to learn what it takes to build an effective system of cooperative problem solving. However, several months after the strike, Boulis worked out with the union a program called "share circles" (apparently an adaptation of the Japanese Quality Control Circles), and this opening to worker participation may yet lead to a successful melding of elements of the three organizational models. Nevertheless, when the ESOP is designed exclusively by management (as in this case), it is possible to structure the trust agreement in such ways as to keep legal control in the hands of management indefinitely, in which case opportunities for worker participation will depend upon what management concedes voluntarily or under union pressure.

Is there a way that a firm converted to employee ownership can avoid such frustration and conflicts? That is possible only if the leaders recognize the need to develop a new organizational model which incorporates features from all three models described above. This seems to be going on in the case of the Rath Packing Company headquartered in Waterloo, Iowa.

The Rath Packing Company Case

Rath was once a well-established high quality meat-packing firm, which, at the time of its financial crisis, employed close to three thousand employees. The Rath case differed from the three sketched above in important respects. While in those cases key members of management had led the drive to save the plant, in the Rath case leaders of Local 46 of the United Food and Commercial Workers Union led the campaign. Furthermore, the union leaders were determined not only to save the jobs but also to keep ultimate control in the hands of the workers.

The leaders in the case worked out a complex arrangement in which the union would forego certain previously bargained benefits for its members, putting those funds into an escrow account to be plowed back into the capital structure of the company when it became majority employee owned. They also agreed to a twenty-dollar-a-week payroll deduction over a period of more than two years to enable members to buy newly issued stock, which would constitute 60 percent of the total stock then outstanding. They further arranged to enlarge the board of directors so as to provide a majority of those selected by union leaders.

In arriving at a legal structure of ownership and control, they had the technical assistance of Tove Hammer and Robert Stern of Cornell, who reviewed with the union negotiating committee the experience of other cases of employee ownership emerging out of threatened plant shutdowns and discussed the implications for future worker control of the various ownership arrangements possible under law. This led finally to an arrangement in which workers would put their stock in an Employee Stock Ownership Trust, whose trustees are elected by the workers on a one worker, one vote basis—this being, in effect, an adaptation of one of the main elements of the town meeting or community democracy model. The trustees thus gained majority control over the board of directors.

This was a case where simply a change in ownership would not be sufficient to secure the continuance of the firm. The workers were gaining majority ownership of a firm that was in effect bankrupt. The infusion of new capital from Housing and Urban Development (HUD) and from the escrow fund set aside by workers, plus their twenty-dollar-a-week payroll deduction to buy stock, provided the investment capital necessary to carry out an ambitious modernization program, bringing in more efficient machines, but the company remained in a precarious financial situation. Major improvements in productivity were required to assure the survival of Rath.

After preliminary discussions (by Christopher Meek of Cornell and Warner Woodworth of Brigham Young with union leaders Lyle Taylor and Charles Mueller), Whyte met with Meek and Woodworth, the union leaders, and key management executives to explore the possibility of developing at the Rath Company the kind of joint union-management problem-solving program (Whyte and McCall, 1980) that had been highly successful in private companies through the Jamestown (New York) Area Labor-Management Committee. This led to agreement on a comprehensive program starting at the top with the establishment of a joint steering committee and extending into each of the major departments, which set up joint "action-research teams" to conduct detailed and systematic work on productivity improvements in their departments. Through a technical assistance grant from the regional office of the Economic Development Administration, Meek and Woodworth were able to spend three days per month working with labor and management to stimulate and guide the process of cooperative problem solving. Beginning in February 1981, a Cornell graduate student, Katherine Squire, was in Waterloo to observe action research teams and steering committee meetings, to study the process of change, and to help Meek and Woodworth implement the cooperative program.

This is not simply a matter of arriving at "good communication" between union and management, as is too often assumed by those who hope to see more cooperative relations develop. Research and experience at Jamestown and elsewhere have led to the development of a systematic methodology through which the two parties, starting from their traditional adversarial positions, negotiate agreements first at the company steering committee level to establish the scope and limits of the cooperative program and agree upon the procedures to be carried out as that program is extended into the operating departments.

To distinguish these agreements from the collective bargaining contract, the parties speak of negotiating a *charter* to determine the policies and procedures. While the charter does not have the same legal standing as the union contract, it has the same functions in a different but interrelated area of activity. We might say that the contract governs the relations between the parties in their adversarial roles, whereas the charter governs their relations as they seek to work together on problems whose resolution will determine the fate of the company.

In each department, the action-research team goes through a common series of stages. Members begin with a brainstorming meeting to bring out all of the problems of productivity and quality of working life they face. They then move on in subsequent meetings to establish priorities and to assign responsibilities for the development of information and ideas. Finally, they present for management implementation a proposed solution of the problem studied.

In the early stages of the Jamestown Area Labor-Management Committee, we discovered one major cause for the breakdown of these in-plant cooperative projects. The pattern was that monthly meetings of the plant labor-management committee would be devoted to discussions within which labor members were pointing out problems, making criticisms and suggestions, and management people were trying to respond by saying that they would study the problems and propose actions by the next meeting. In other words, the initiative in pointing out problems and calling for action was in the hands of labor, and the burden in additional work activities and possibly additional expenditures fell entirely upon management. In this situation, management people found themselves overburdened with these new demands. The general result was that they would make some effort to respond to labor's initiatives but would not have sufficient time to do systematic work on all of the problems raised and therefore would constantly be in a position of reporting back less progress than labor had expected. After this process had gone on for some months, labor members, seeing little in the way of concrete results, would begin complaining that the meetings were "just talk and no action" and come to the conclusion that the committee was just another management device to manipulate workers. As management people recognized this growing labor dissatisfaction and came to resent the additional work burden imposed by the process, management would increasingly find occasion to postpone or cancel meetings until the time came when the labor-management committee existed only on paper.

The current Jamestown model and the model being followed at Rath avoid this pitfall by assuring that worker-members of the action research teams participate actively in the study and propose resolution of problems. Furthermore, workers at Rath are involved in an extraordinary range of problems, including the major investment decisions for the purchase of new machines, the redesign of the work flow, and so on. In the Rath case, we see a melding of the community democracy model with the collective bargaining model, where the parties bridge the gap in the community democracy model by filling in policies and procedures for organizing and carrying out the work. This is not to say that the melding process has been easy. Where a high degree of mistrust has existed between workers and management in the past, there will inevitably be occasions when the joint problem-solving process breaks down and workers and management revert to the traditional adversarial role. One of the key functions of the third party providing technical assistance in such cases is to recognize the importance of the negative feelings being expressed, but then to help the parties move back and focus on concrete problems whose resolution will benefit both parties.

Rath also represents an attempted integration of the authoritarian model with the collective bargaining and community democracy models. Here again, the process has not been easy. Since a major shift in power has taken place at the top of the organization, there have been occasions when workers have flatly refused to follow the orders of their foremen and middle-management people. A few of them could not tolerate the change and left the company. Others have assumed that to hold their positions, they must just do what the union leaders tell them to do or what has been explicitly agreed upon by the union and management. Union and management leaders have been seeking to deal with the problems by insisting that workers still are obligated to carry out the foremen's orders.

Of course, the melding of the three models does not leave the main features of the authoritarian model intact. Managers and supervisors must recognize that if they are to function effectively in this new situation, they must exercise their authority in a more participatory fashion than has been customary in the past. Such organizational changes require major learning processes on the part of management as well as on the part of union leaders and workers.

Examination of Well-Established Successful Cases

Up to this point, we have been examining the difficulties experienced by organizations in the United States as they search for a viable model that will support the successful development of worker cooperatives or employee-owned firms. Before drawing general conclusions from those cases, let us examine four examples within which firms structured on the basic principles of the community democracy model (one member, one vote) have successfully maintained themselves over the years.

The U.S. Plywood Cooperatives

The outstanding examples in the United States are found among the cooperative plywood manufacturing firms in the Pacific Northwest. The first such firm was established in the 1920s, and by the 1960s there were as many as twenty-one cooperative plywood companies (Bernstein, 1976). Most of these were started by workers pooling their resources (generally one thousand dollars per member) to start a new firm, but in about one-third of the cases, the worker cooperative rose out of taking over a plant being shut down by a private firm. The firms are characterized not only by equal voting rights but also by equal pay. Everyone gets the same pay for hours worked except the manager, who is hired by the worker-directors and serves the firm on a contract they negotiate with him. Various studies have shown that the plywood cooperatives, over a period of years, have out-performed private plywood firms substantially in productivity and also in the financial rewards of the worker-members. A large proportion of this difference may be accounted for by the smaller number of management and supervisory personnel in the plywood cooperatives. For example, when a private company bought out one of the plywood cooperatives, the first move of the new management was to employ *seven additional foremen* (Greenberg, 1981). In the traditional private firm operating uner the authoritarian model, much of the foreman's job involves policing the workforce, checking when the workers are goofing off, doing careless work, and otherwise reducing efficiency. If workers take over these organization and disciplinary responsibilities themselves, they can save enormous sums of money for their company.

Although the plywood cooperatives have been extraordinarily successful financially, within another ten or fifteen years all of them may have reverted to private ownership. In the mid-1970s, Paul Bernstein reported that the number of firms was down from twenty-one to sixteen, and in 1981, he records the number "close to a dozen" (Bernstein, 1981). Here we have a dramatic demonstration of the "catch-22" situation that worker cooperatives find themselves involved in when ownership is based upon stock. When such a stock ownership plan is adopted (subject to one qualification to be introduced later), the cooperative firm can go out of business either because it fails or because it is highly successful and is unable to transfer stock from one generation of workers to another.

In the plywood cases, the workers have avoided one obvious trap involved in stock ownership plans where there is no limit on the number of shares and, therefore, control tends to gravitate toward higher levels of the company. In all cases, plywood cooperative stock has been limited to one share per worker. However, this has not been a major barrier to the loss of worker ownership in the most successful companies. In the first place, as the firm expands and new workers come in, collective selfishness tends to dominate personnel policies. The original worker-owners recognize that their stock and their stock dividends will increase in value if they decline to dilute their equity by making stock available to the new workers. In this case, the workforce tends to divide into two segments, worker-owners and hired labor, with the predictable consequences in the weakening of labor solidarity.

When a worker-owner retires, he would of course be glad to sell his share of stock to a non-owner worker, but by that time in a successful company, the value of the stock will be far beyond the means of the worker. For example, Bernstein reports two recent cases in which employees sold stock originally purchased for $1,000 for close to $100,000 per share. Since it is only individual private investors or private companies that pay such a price, there is an inevitable tendency for the most successful firms to revert to private ownership. Paradoxically, it is only in the marginally successful firms with such a structure of ownership that the worker-owners have a real possibility of maintaining worker-ownership as the firm passes on from one generation of workers to another.

The Mondragón Cooperative Sector of Spain (Basque Region)
What has become the most dynamic element in Spain's industrial economy had its origin in the small industrial city of Mondragón in the Basque country in 1956 when five men, with support from friends and members of the community, founded the industrial cooperative ULGOR. By 1980, the small beginning had expanded into a system of eighty-seven industrial production cooperatives with close to eighteen thousand worker-members. Mondragón has become Spain's leading manufacturer of stoves and refrigerators and of one type of steel. The cooperatives have also been able to compete effectively in international markets, including winning bids against multinational corporations to build turn-key plants in developing nations (Johnson and Whyte, 1977).

The cooperative production firms have been supported and linked together by the Caja Laboral Popular, a cooperative banking organization that had over 300,000 individual members by 1980. The Caja has provided approximately 50 percent of the capital necessary for the growth of the system and has also provided technical assistance in the creation and development of cooperatives. The cooperatives are also linked together with a cooperative educational system, begun in 1943 under the leadership of Father José Maria Arizmendi. What began as a two-year institution to provide training in industrial skills to young working-class boys has since expanded to serve thousands of students all the way to college degrees in engineering or business administration. Also linked with the system are consumer cooperatives, housing cooperatives, cooperative construction firms, and schools.

At the outset, the production firms were structured in terms of two different organizational models: community democracy and authoritarian, and it was not until almost two decades later that the leaders of the system recognized the inherent contradictions between those two models. The governance of the firm is provided by the application of the fundamental rule of community democracy: one member, one vote.

Equality in voting rights is accompanied by an extraordinarily narrow range of pay differentials, in comparison with those prevailing in private firms. The way this system works out is that the workers at the low end of the pay scale receive somewhat more than workers at the same level in private industry, whereas the top executive receives substantially less. There are no standard provisions for rotation of jobs, but, as the firms have expanded, there have been increasing opportunities for members to move to higher-paying jobs.

The linkage between the firm and the educational system remains throughout workers' careers. When demand for company products slackens, workers, instead of being laid off, may retain their pay while studying, thus encouraging worker self-improvement and also worker commitment to the firm.

When the first firms were established, the leaders of the system believed that, to compete with private industry, they had to organize work in terms of what they took to be the principles of modern industrial management. In effect, they adopted the Taylor authoritarian model with its hierarchy of supervision and control and with assembly lines and other methods of detailed division of labor and job simplification.

In a small organization in which all of the members could readily get together informally to discuss their problems, these frequent face-to-face contacts between the chief executive of the firm and rank-and-file workers opened the way for the kind of informal adjustments that made it possible to harmonize the community democracy model with the authoritarian model. In large organizations, this kind of informal adjustment was not possible. Although the members held ultimate control through electing the board of directors, an annual meeting for that purpose was not sufficient to resolve the contradictions between community democracy and the authoritarian model. It seems significant that the only strike yet to occur in Mondragón production firms took place in the oldest and largest firm, ULGOR. The 1974 strike involved only some 400 members out of a total workforce of 3,400, and it lasted only 48 hours. Nevertheless, the outbreak of this conflict shocked the leaders of the system and precipitated a reassessment of the system's design, leading to two major changes.

Now the leaders of the system reached out to learn of experiences elsewhere in the world in democratizing the workplace itself. This led to rapid changes in some of the firms in the direction of abandoning assembly lines in favor of groups working around a table, moving toward autonomous or self-managing work groups, increasing responsibilities for quality and for the organization of the work for the workers themselves, and so on. In effect, they were reshaping the authoritarian model through introducing elements of democratic governance in the workplace.

The ULGOR crisis also precipitated a move in the direction of the collective bargaining model. From the beginning, workers had elected a Social Council to advise management on matters of personnel policy and social benefits. In contrast to the election of the board of directors for which all members voted together for a given slate of nominees, the representatives on the Social Council were chosen so as to represent particular work groups or departments. The idea was to have one representative on the Social Council for every ten workers but to limit the size of the council to a maximum of sixty members—which meant that in ULGOR each councilor represented fifty members.

Prior to the ULGOR strike, the Social Council tended to be considered ineffective by many workers, and, in fact, the strike arose out of the refusal of a group of dissident members to take their grievance to the Social Council. The ULGOR crisis led to a thorough-going reexamination of the role of the Social Council and to serious efforts to strengthen its influence in the larger firms through giving it power to conduct studies of policies and procedures, with staff assistance, so as to strengthen its recommendations to the management. However, while the scope of the concerns of the Social Council approximate those of a union in a collective bargaining situation, the leadership of the system firmly opposed giving the Social Council any power of decision making. A critical debate on the structure of the Social Council involved the question of who should be its chairperson. From the outset, the chief executive of the firm had also chaired the Social Council, the theory being that this would give the council members direct access to the top executive. Those urging change argued that this arrangement deprived the Social Council of its independence and therefore undermined its usefulness, but their views did not prevail. On the other hand, this reevaluation seemed to lead to a greater tendency of management to consult with the Social Council on all major questions. Furthermore, of course, when a recommendation of the Social Council is rejected by management, the council can call for a special meeting of the general assembly of all worker-members, which then has the power, if it so votes, to overrule management.

Under the Franco regime, unions not ultimately controlled by the state were outlawed, and there was no overt union activity within the cooperatives. With the general democratic transformation of Spain following the death of the dictator, unions have arisen in several of the cooperatives. It remains to be seen whether the growth of unionization will signal a strengthening of the collective bargaining model within the overall system and, if so, the unions may eventually displace the Social Council as representing worker concerns on economic and social questions.

The Kibbutz Cooperative Sector in Israel

In Israel, 100,000 people are organized into small towns or communities called kibbutzim that comprise approximately 3.5 percent of the general population. A kibbutz is basically organized as a community of families governed by a general assembly based on the democratic principle of one member, one vote, exercised through a weekly town meeting.

The type of worker ownership in the kibbutz is unique (Blasi, 1980). It is not based on shares of stock, and there is no membership fee. New kibbutz "neighborhoods" are started with loans and technical assistance from various Jewish agencies and the Federation of Kibbutz Communities after prospective members engage in a substantial period of planning, work in other kibbutzim, and evolution of a socially cohesive group. A kibbutz is owned by its members, but, according to legal charter, a kibbutz cannot be sold and the assets cannot be divided by the members. This is to prevent the "collective selfishness"—such as that of the plywood cooperatives—from destroying the structure of worker-ownership.

The fact that new membership is a social and not an economic decision also means that the kibbutz is substantially more open to a wide variety of individuals who are judged responsible, good workers interested in cooperative ideals. Kibbutzim are organized into a holding company which is affiliated with Hevrat Ovdim (The Workers' Company), a part of the General Federation of Labor—Histadrut or trade union and general labor organization of Israel. If individual members leave, they have very explicit severance pay provisions based on a number of factors. Should the majority of members of a kibbutz decide to dissolve it, short of provisions made for severance and transitional expenses, the assets would return to the holding company for use in continuing the development of the worker-owned sector. The kibbutz has therefore overcome a number of the problems of worker ownership by carefully developing an organization based on membership rights and ownership rights, but restricting the legal ability of owners to do away with worker control and ownership itself. This is really an extension of the community democracy model to a model constitution for economic democracy.

As a cooperative small town, a kibbutz is an amalgam of industries, agricultural branches, membership services branches, and educational institutions. Every member has an equal right to housing, medical care, education for children, food and meals (available in a common dining area or in members' homes), higher education and occupational training, access to a community car pool and (in most communities) unlimited public transportation coupons within the country, occasional overseas vacations, and a paid vacation based on years of membership. Members receive no wages but participate in a series of yearly meetings and in committees which plan how the community's profits will be spent for both industrial and agricultural development and the maintenance of the many services for members. Members do receive annual cash allotments for personal expenses. The community has a commitment to provide employment for all members and, like Mondragón, depends on committees within the cooperative itself and within the federation and affiliated industrial research arms and vocational training arms to develop new industrial or agricultural branches and plan for the transition from one form of enterprise to another. Like Mondragón, which operates its own system of social security, the kibbutzim provide complete social security for their members throughout old age, support for sick or disabled members or those in job transition, and complete medical insurance. Thus, both the kibbutz and Mondragón can be conceived of as systems of labor governance which reduce both the size of government and dependency on government services.

The kibbutzim began in 1910 with the establishment of a successful agricultural worker cooperative in Israel, Degania Aleph. In recent years, while agriculture continues to be pursued, industrial operations have become increasingly important. The 300 industries of the kibbutzim have approximately 15,000 worker-members with sales of $500 million including exports of $144 million.

From the very beginning individual kibbutzim linked themselves together to form kibbutz federations, which function similarly to Mondragón's Caja Laboral Popular in guiding the development of educational and cultural programs and in providing technical assistance, operating management and vocational training colleges, capital through mutual banks, and also liaison with governmental public bodies.

Unlike Mondragón, the workplace and the neighborhood are integrated in the kibbutz. People who work together meet together to discuss community affairs, serve on educational committees that oversee their children's schools, participate in community cultural events, and together elect community economic and social officials and decide community policy. Income is not determined by type of work or by position in an organization, but by membership and the egalitarian ethic.

It is often thought that kibbutzim are characterized by a shared political or religious ideology or a high degree of ethnic homogeneity. Only 15 of the 250 communities are religious (orthodox); the others being secular communities which view Judaism more as a cultural heritage. It is true that 95 percent of the neighborhoods are affiliated through their federations with the Israeli Labor party. Most communities include members from ten to thirty countries, although Sephardic Jews are clearly underrepresented. Today, the kibbutz sector in Israel is one of the most highly educated. It is in the eighth decile in terms of income, and has a living standard similar to the European middle class. On the other hand, we can indeed say that the kibbutzim are characterized by a broad sharing of certain values: a desire to make a central contribution to the Jewish homeland based on social justice and the values of social fellowship, economic cooperation and common ownership, and direct self-management (Blasi, 1980). See Table 23–1 (Leviatan and Rosner, 1980).

The kibbutz attempts to maximize participation while clearly delineating the degrees of authority and the areas of expertise most appropriate for the different participatory institutions. While all plant officials are

Table 23–1
Labor Governance in the Kibbutz

Topic	Plant Committees	Plant Management Board	Workers' Assembly	Kibbutz Committees	Kibbutz General Assembly
Production	—	Suggestion	Decision	Discussion	Confirmation
Investment and development plans	—	Suggestion	Decision	Discussion	Confirmation
Work arrangements	—	Suggestion	Decision	—	—
Technical & professional problems	Discussion	Decision	Information	—	—
Choice of candidates for training	Decision	Suggestion	Decision	Discussion	Confirmation
Election of management team	—	Discussion	Discussion	Suggestion	Decision
Election of other offices	Suggestion	—	Decision	—	—

elected by the plant's worker assembly, the one exception is the plant manager. This person is nominated by the kibbutz-wide nomination committee, discussed by the plant's workers, and then appointed by the kibbutz. The individual may not necessarily come from among plant workers, and the individual is viewed as having a responsibility not only to the workers of the plant but also to the community as a whole.

Within the kibbutz as a whole and in industrial plants and other branches, all coordinating and managerial positions are rotated in order to prevent the creation of a managerial class. These coordinators or officers do not receive any special economic rewards. This rotation is possible and practical for several reasons. First, the kibbutz plans ahead of time for such leadership positions and uses its aggressive system of higher education and vocational training to prepare such coordinators so that a steady pool of expertise exists. Second, research has found that kibbutz plants that abide by the principle of rotation can devote less time to supervision, have better communication channels between managers and workers, more opportunity for advancement, more knowledge of its members about the plant, and a trend toward greater economic effectiveness (Leviatan and Rosner, 1980).

The kibbutz worker-owned sector can be viewed as a laboratory for studying issues of labor governance. Researchers at the Institute for the Study of the Kibbutz and the Cooperative Idea at the University of Haifa have been analyzing the differences between kibbutz forms in their adherence to the various forms of self-management and the effect of these differences on worker satisfaction and the quality of working life in the plants; the researchers are attempting to integrate a focus on the more formal structures of self-management with more informal aspects of workplace organization. Indeed, initial findings indicate that the participation of workers on the shop floor is far more salient in improving the quality of working life than the regular functioning of the plant's Worker Assembly.

Because of pressure put on kibbutz movements to absorb new immigrants and opportunities for increased financial success and expansion, some kibbutzim brought in outsiders (generally Arabs or new immigrant Jewish labor, often Sephardic) as hired labor. All the kibbutz federations consider this a strong violation of ideological norms. In 1975 hired labor represented 65 percent, 24 percent, and 20 percent respectively of the workers in industry of the three largest kibbutz federations. Leviatan and Rosner again have found that the federations without much hired labor have just as successfully organized factories and performed efficiently in a wide range of industries, while those with hired labor have had less formal participation, more supervisory personnel, less trust between workers and management, less rotation, and less involvement of kibbutz members in the life of their community. Notably, this increase in hierarchy occurred among both kibbutz members and hired workers. Since 1975 there has been steadily declining use of hired labor in kibbutz industries and increasing emphasis upon capital investment. This policy has enabled most kibbutz firms to remain small and highly participatory while achieving higher productivity per worker than the average Israeli firm and growing rapidly in sales and exports.

The kibbutz industries have had similar experiences to Mondragón in plant organization. Initially, they too imported assembly line technology in toto, but they are becoming increasingly sensitive to autonomous work and the importance of a detailed community-wide planning of a new industry. Often, jobs are specifically designed for senior citizens. The problem of size has generally not come up except where hired labor was used to create large plants. The size of most kibbutz communities, under one thousand residents, limits its industry. As the table indicates, the relationship between the industry's assembly and the General Assembly is clear. The General Assembly and the Executive Committee of each community—which is made up of coordinators of all major branches and committees and the general economic and social coordinators of the community—are the final authority and devote much time to discussing the effect of industrial decisions on the community and vice versa.

The Yugoslavian Model
The world's largest system of worker cooperatives is found in Yugoslavia where the state has supported the development of industrial firms gov-

erned on cooperative principles (Vanek, 1971, 1975; Adizes, 1971; King and VandeVall, 1978). Here we must not be misled by political ideology. The political leaders of Yugoslavia are avowedly communist and followers of Karl Marx, but Yugoslavian intellectuals claim that they are practicing true Marxism whereas the Russians have distorted the doctrine. In the sense that control of each industrial plant is in the hands of its worker-members on the basis of one worker, one vote, the Yugoslavian economy is the most democratic in the world. To be sure, the state does impose certain regulations and constraints regarding taxes and structure and procedure for governance, and the state establishes certain educational and experiential requirements for anyone who can be elected chief executive of the enterprise, but beyond this, workers govern themselves, meeting in assemblies to elect a workers council, which in turn selects a chief executive and also determines the major policy questions.

Early studies indicate that, while the system was open to worker control, the differences in education and technical expertise were so great that the view of the executive tended to dominate, and worker participation was extremely limited. However, even in cases where the rank and file remained largely passive, there has been considerable rotation in membership in the workers council, so over a period of years a large proportion of the work force gains some experience in participation. Futhermore, following the reform of 1976, Yugoslavian political leaders moved to strengthen worker participation, especially in the larger firms, through stimulating the development of departmental and shop councils to involve workers in participating on topics where they are expert by virtue of the direct working experience.

In Yugoslavia, unions exist and play a rather ambiguous role. Since the firms are thought to be "socially owned," the traditional rationale for an adversarial role of labor against capital is lacking, and designers of the system originally assumed that the union would serve primarily to administer social benefit programs for workers. However, there have been a fair number of work stoppages apparently precipitated by union leaders, and it may be that Yugoslavia is moving toward including some elements of the collective bargaining model into the industrial structure.

Lessons from Successful Cases

Let us now draw upon these successful cases to see to what extent they provide answers to problems we have seen emerging in U.S. grass-roots collectives and in employee-owned firms. We draw the following conclusions:

1. *Job rotation* may have advantages in some cases in broadening the experience of workers and strengthening the commitment to an egalita-

rian ideology, but job rotation clearly is not indispensable for the functioning of an efficient worker cooperative. Any standard pattern of job rotation will prove to be impractical in cases where the firm includes jobs of a wide range of skills and knowledge with those which can be performed only by individuals having special skills and educational background. In fact, in the kibbutzim, while rotation is practiced for general managerial jobs, positions in engineering, chemistry, and other technical specialities are generally not subject to rotation.

2. While *equal pay or pay according to family needs* may be practical in some cases, this is not an indispensable principle for a financially successful worker cooperative. However, since the members themselves have ultimate control over the organization, the pay scale must seem equitable to them. This will mean that the range between the top and bottom pay in a cooperative firm will be substantially less than that prevailing where a company is owned by management or private investors. We can also expect that worker cooperatives will limit the perquisites of management (expense accounts, use of company car for personal purposes, etc.) substantially more than will be the case in private firms. On the other hand, we do not yet know enough to state under what conditions equal pay or pay according to family needs may be practical or even necessary for the survival and growth of the organization.

3. If the cooperative firm is to survive, *control must be based upon labor* rather than upon ownership. In Yugoslavia, the concept of social ownership in effect means that ownership is irrelevant. In Israel, the factory is owned by the kibbutz community, but, except for certain broad questions of the relation of the firm to the community, the factory itself is generally governed by the kibbutz members who work in it. The financial base of the Mondragón system is built upon debt rather than equity. That is, upon entering the firm, the member pays a fee to the cooperative, and this fee is treated as if it were a loan, drawing interest and growing through annual profit sharing. Therefore, short of the financial collapse of the whole Mondragón system, there is no way in which the firms can revert to private ownership.

Control based upon stock ownership seems to presage the eventual transformation of all successful cooperatives into private firms. However, there is a way to maintain a cooperative organization in the long run even with voting based upon stock ownership. In addition to limiting stock ownership to workers on a one share per worker basis (as in the plywood case), rules can be made at the outset for sharing of ownership with new workers and for the limitation on appreciation in the value of the stock by providing additional reward to workers through other devices. For example, a firm could issue one share of voting stock to each worker-member and specify that this share could continue indefinitely to have a nominal value, whereas nonvoting shares could be issued as a means of rewarding workers for improvement of performance of the company. In this case, even if these nonvoting shares could be bought outside the company, this would not change the basic control structure.

4. An *organizational infrastructure* to help financing and to provide technical assistance is essential for development and maintenance of a system of cooperative firms. In Yugoslavia, the whole economy is structured to guide and support worker cooperatives. In Israel, the Kibbutz Federation provides important financial and technical assistance. In Mondragón, the Caja Laboral Popular has been the key organization in financing and guiding growth and in keeping the firms linked together. In the case of the plywood cooperatives, each firm exists as a more or less isolated unit in a sea of private enterprise. To be sure, there is an association of cooperative plywood firms, but the association is relatively weak and not equipped to play the major role of the building and supporting structure we have noted in Yugoslavia, Israel, and in Spain. This means that those in the United States interested in promoting the development of cooperative firms should recognize the need to build an organizational infrastructure, with assistance from universities and government, to provide educational and technical assistance and financing.

5. *Shared values*: In the Yugoslavian, Israeli, and Spanish examples, we find that the cooperatives are built upon a foundation of shared values. This does not mean that all worker-members must share them; rather, it means that the organizational leaders must develop and articulate an ideology that both justifies the form of the organization and guides its development. They must develop the organization mission beyond simply producing goods or services and providing jobs for its members. Furthermore, they must be concerned with linking communal values to concrete policies and practices and to the periodic reassessment of the relationship between theory and practice—so as to assure themselves that they are not trying to implement values that are impossible of realization or, on the other hand, engaging unthinkingly in policies and practices incompatible with their values. In the three foreign systems examined here, we find not only the prominence of shared ideology, but also the commitment to continuing reassessment of the relation of this ideology to the practical problems of organizational maintenance and development.

One of the weaknesses of the plywood cooperatives appears to be the lack of any guiding ideology. To be sure, they did arise out of a culture of immigrants or children of immigrants from Scandinavia, where cooperative values are prominent, but the driving force behind the formation and development of the plywood cooperatives seems to have been much more pragmatic: to create jobs and earn income for worker-members.

In the grass-roots collectives in the United States, we find a common ideology within the leadership group setting up the firm, but all too often this ideology points the organization toward policies and practices that prove to be unworkable. In firms that become employee-owned out of conglomerate divestitures, we find a complete lack of any guiding ideology adjusted to the new situation. In the emergency of the impending plant shutdown, workers are naturally concerned exclusively with saving their jobs. They have only vague expectations regarding how an employee-owned organization might differ from a privately owned firm. Similarly, top management people unconsciously assume that the firm will continue to be operated more or less in terms of the authoritarian model, the main difference being that management will not have to take orders from remote corporate headquarters.

What can be done in situations where a guiding ideology is lacking? Clearly, it will not be helpful to suggest, "Go out and get yourself an ideology." In the divestiture situation, workers, union leaders, and management people should discuss and argue and search for the principles and policies determining how such an unfamiliar type of firm shall be governed. We have seen this process going on in Rath Packing Company.

6. If we assume that workers and management people always have some kind of *organizational* model at least vaguely in mind, and if we assume that these implicit conceptions tend to shape the behavior of those who hold them, then it is important for the people involved to *make the implicit conceptions explicit* and to begin discussion of how to build a model that will be congruent with their values and, at the same time, workable. The three organizational models we have posed at the start of this chapter may be a useful starting point for such a discussion. The new social system emerging out of a worker-management discussion and analysis process may then contain selected elements of these three models, combined with new elements growing out of the experience and ideas of those who are going to live and work under the principles and policies they establish.

Our analysis also suggests the value of a cross-cultural perspective in the design of new forms of organization. In learning from abroad, while recognizing the importance of the unique cultural context underlying any foreign system, we need to extract from that context those *social inventions* that may be adapted and combined with indigenous elements to build American models of worker ownership and participation in management.

Public Policy Implications

In discussing lessons from successful cases, we have concentrated upon what members of employee-owned firms or cooperatives should do to increase the effectiveness of their organizations. While they must bear the primary responsibilities, they are operating in relatively uncharted fields where they need help in mapping the terrain.

Worker-owned firms face the same problems in financing, production, and marketing as small privately owned businesses in an economy dominated by large corporations, but, beyond those familiar topics, members need assistance in understanding the nature of their organization. As we encountered the first cases of divestiture and conversion to employee ownership in the 1970s, it seemed that the actors in each case were responding to the shutdown crisis as if nothing like the ownership conversion they were attempting had ever before happened elsewhere. Now the ideas are more familiar through media reports, but still we find the people concerned having only vague ideas as to what has happened elsewhere in comparable cases. Social researchers and community activists can perform important services by stimulating and channeling the flow of information and ideas so that the people we seek to help can put their own case in the context of other cases. The knowledgeable outsider can thereby help the leaders of the fledgling organization to anticipate at an early stage the problems that will confront them later.

We see the need for building a regional and national organizational infrastructure to provide information, action-research, and technical assistance to worker-owned firms. A few parts of that infrastructure are already in place—but with very precarious financial support. Corey Rosen who, as a congressional staff member, played a major role in the design and passage of the Small Business Employee Ownership Act, recently established (in Arlington, Virginia) the National Center for Employee Ownership. NCEO publishes a monthly informational bulletin, organizes conferences, and stimulates the development of comparative case studies. The Employee Stock Ownership Association (in Washington) also publishes informational materials and conducts conferences for member companies and individual members.

The Industrial Cooperative Association (in Somerville, Massachusetts) provides technical assistance to existing or potential worker-owned firms. The New School for Democratic Management (in San Francisco) provides teaching services especially designed for cooperative organizations and is also involved in technical assistance.

Professors and students in several universities have become active in this field. So far they have had to finance technical assistance out of research budgets. With the Reagan budget cuts especially targeted on social science research, such financing is becoming increasingly difficult to secure. If universities are to play an important role in this field, we will need to devise new programs and new organizational structures. What is needed is an organizational model, similar to cooperative extension in agriculture and rural development, to provide information, ideas, and technical assistance to worker-owned firms—and to small private businesses, which share some of the same problems.

There remains a major gap in available financing for worker-owned firms as well as for research and technical assistance. By law the National Consumer Cooperative Bank is empowered to use up to 10 percent of its funds for credit or technical assistance for worker cooperatives, but having barely escaped extinction at the hands of the budget cutters, has scarce funds available to serve this field. The Small Business Administration is now required by law to avoid discriminating against employee-owned firms in its loan and loan guarantee programs, but the new policy is just going into effect at this writing, so it is too early to judge the importance of support from this institution. While a number of activists are aware of the need for developing cooperatively controlled banking institutions, so far nothing remotely resembling the Caja Laboral Popular or the kibbutzim financial institutions has emerged.

References

Adizes, Ichak. 1971. *Industrial Democracy: Yugoslav Style.* New York: The Free Press.
Bernstein, Paul. 1976. *Workplace Democratization: Its Internal Dynamics.* Kent, Ohio: Kent State University Press.
———. 1981. "Worker ownership and community redevelopment," *The Corporate Examiner* (March).
Blasi, Joseph. 1980. *The Communal Future: The Kibbutz and the Utopian Dilemma.* Philadelphia: Norwood Editions.
Cole, Robert E. 1979. *Work, Mobility and Participation: A Comparative Study of American and Japanese Industry.* Berkeley and Los Angeles: University of California Press.
Greenberg, Edward. 1981. "Industrial self-management and political attitudes," *American Political Science Review* 75 (March):1.
———. 1982. "Producer's cooperative and democratic theory," forthcoming in Henry Levin (ed.), *Industrial Democracy.* Palo Alto: Center for Economics Studies.
Hammer, Tove, and Robert Stern. 1980. "Employee ownership: implications for the organizational distribution of power," *Academy of Management Journal* 23: 78–100.
Johnson, Ana Gutiérrez, and W. F. Whyte. 1977. "The Mondragón system of worker production cooperatives," *Industrial and Labor Relations Review* 31 (October): 18–30.
King, Charles D., and Mark VandeVall. 1978. *Models of Industrial Democracy: Consultation, Co-Determination, and Workers' Management.* The Hague: Mouton Publishers.
Leviatan, Uri, and Menachem Rosner. 1980. *Work and Organization in Kibbutz Industry.* Philadelphia: Norwood Editions.
Mansbridge, Jane. 1973. "Town meeting democracy," *Working Papers for a New Society* 1:5–15.
Rothschild-Whitt, Joyce. 1979. "The collectivist organization: an alternative to rational-bureaucratic models," *American Sociological Review* 44: 509–27.
Stern, Robert N., Hayden Wood, and Tove Hammer. 1979. *Employee Ownership in Plant Shutdown: Prospects for Employment Stability.* Kalamazoo, Mi.: The Upjohn Institute for Employment Research.
Taylor, F. W. 1911. *The Principles of Scientific Management.* New York: Harper & Bros.
Vanek, Jaroslav. 1971. *The Participatory Economy.* Ithaca, N.Y.: Cornell University Press.
———. 1975. *Self-Management: Economic Liberation of Man.* Hammondsworth, England and Baltimore, Md.: Penguin Books, Ltd.
Whyte, W. F. 1978. "In support of voluntary employee ownership," *Society* 15 (September–October): 73–82.
Whyte, W. F., and Donald McCall. 1980. "Self help economics," *Society* 17:4.

24
Collective Organization and the National State: The Kibbutz Model

Paula Rayman

Modern cooperative movements and experiments with collective organization have existed within increasingly centralized national states and within a worldwide political economy shaped by global systems of communication, transportation and markets. Much of the attention social scientists have paid to collectives and cooperatives has focused on the internal community forms of organization such as education, child-rearing practices, and decision-making procedures. However, it is important for students of collective organizations to remember that internal organizational dynamics are deeply influenced by external institutional forces. In turn, it has been the hope of many cooperative movements to effect widespread social change in the larger society.

Within the general literature concentrating on the dynamics between local community and external institutions, an important set of studies has addressed the particular problems confronting communes, cooperative organizations, and other forms of local alternative institutions that attempt democratic, egalitarian norms within a capitalist or state socialist terrain. Rosabeth Kanter, in *Commitment and Community*, reviewed the histories of nineteenth-century American communes and argued that success of these communes depended on their internal solidarity and ability to resist externally imposed norms. David Moberg, in a thoughtful essay assessing American co-ops, communes, and collectives of the 1960s and '70s, suggests that while these experiments have left a mark, they will not achieve continuity or viability until a mass movement gains power to implement their values on a larger scale.[1]

Study of these cooperative experiments raises questions concerning their impact on norms for equality and democracy outside their domain. Moreover, each of these cooperatives offers its own history of reconciling communal values with the traditional culture and ideology of community residents.

Based on Chapter 4 of the author's *The Kibbutz Community and Nation Building*, Princeton University Press, 1982. Readers wishing a more complete view of the Kibbutz role in Israeli society are referred to this text.

From examination of cooperative movements, a picture emerges to reveal numerous modes of penetration that facilitate the incorporation of industrial, urban social norms into communal life. The daily life of cooperative movements and their future direction is significantly shaped by how they meet the challenges of the "iron law of oligarchy" and the push for organizational efficiency.[2] Mass media, fulfillment of national duties (e.g., service in the military), and meeting standardized educational requirements are among the leading carriers of ideas and values. Certainly, one of the most central and effective modes of penetration is the system of economic exchange between the cooperative and the larger environment.

Cooperatives are usually integrated into the economy of national and even international markets. Connection to a noncooperative economic order has great implications for the internal organization of the collective. Patterns of trade and production affect internal patterns of bureaucracy and stratification. In a rural framework, this results in a cash crop economy rather than a self-sufficient agrarian model. A cooperative that competes with external industrial economic enterprises is pressured to import new technologies, which are likely to force a change in the community's division of labor. New modes of production prove to be alienating and de-skilling for the individual worker; furthermore, the emerging work relations establish structural inequality within the cooperative organization as a whole.

In order to successfully compete in the external economic environment, cooperatives must extend sales to international markets. If the labor resources of a cooperative are limited, which is often the case, this may lead to the hiring of laborers from the outside. The introduction of wage labor is disruptive to the collectivist ideology as it brings manager versus worker relations into the daily reality.

Extending sales to international markets poses other problems for the collective. Members of the collective must become skilled professionals in dealing with multinationals and foreign corporations. This limits possibilities for job rotation and forces members, at least temporarily, to assume attitudes not consistent with cooperative ideology. Travel to foreign nations also exposes the member to new forms of consumerism and individualism that are brought home. Unless ideological spirit and internal solidarity are strong, discontent may flourish.

Increasing success in the economic sphere may sow the seeds for dissolution of cooperative social and political spheres. As we move to the case study of an Israeli kibbutz economic regional organization, the Milouot, we will see that the growing advances of the Milouot economic enterprise have caused major problems for kibbutz social structure. This case study allows inspection of the relationship among one kibbutz community, Kibbutz Har,[3] its regional membership in the Milouot, and the Israeli nation.

Background on the Kibbutz

The founding of the first kibbutz in 1909 was the beginning of a collective agrarian settlement movement established to create a Jewish homeland in Palestine. Today, more than three decades after the foundation of the Israeli state, 235 kibbutzim with a population of just over 100,000 constitute about 3.4 percent of the Israeli Jewish population. Geographically dispersed throughout Israel, many are located in military strategic areas due to their history as military outposts.[4]

The realization of collective norms in the kibbutz was greatly aided during the pre-state years and the first decades after statehood by the persistence of cooperative ideology and collective structure in segments of the larger society. First, there has been a continuous, strong network of cooperative institutions directly linked to the kibbutz, including kibbutz federations, agricultural and industrial marketing enterprises, and research and development centers. The Israeli economy, while a combination of private, public, and cooperative ownership, is quite dependent on the public and labor economies that provide over 50 percent of all jobs in the country. The General Federation of Labor, the Histadrut, to which the kibbutzim belong, owns some of Israel's largest factories; through its various trade union, entrepreneurial, social welfare, and educational institutions it covers 90 percent of the Israeli Jewish population. In addition, the kibbutzim are well represented in the national Labor party and other parties of the Left.

However, since the establishment of the state, Israeli society has undergone major transformations, rapidly moving from the "underdeveloped" to almost developed category. The economy expanded enormously during the 1950s and 1960s: The real Gross Domestic Product (GDP) increased over 5 times; private consumption, more than 4 times; and public expenditure, including the military defense sector, over 3.5 times. Between 1950 and 1965, as the population of the country grew from 1.266 million to 2.566 million, Israel's economic infrastructure increasingly reflected that of a developed capitalist nation. Concentration of private capital increased as inequality in income distribution grew. Flow of capital expanded, and international rather than domestic local markets were targeted for trade. New immigration patterns resulted in a more heterogenous, stratified, and class-segregated society. There has been a clear movement away from the pre-state cooperative spirit as more materialist concerns have taken hold.

Understanding this shift in values and economic structure of the larger Israeli society provides a context for examining the structure and direction of a kibbutz regional organization, the Milouot. As the kibbutzim, in part through regional organizations such as the Milouot, strive to meet the requirements of modernization, they confront new tensions between forces of communalism versus individuality, and professionalism versus job rotation. How the kibbutz resolves these struggles is an ongoing process that does not always point in a linear direction. For example, after years of an alternative educational system eschewing national merit tests, the kibbutz high school system recently adopted special preparation courses for the national entrance examinations for universities. On the other hand, Kibbutz Har, to offset the reliance on hired laborers and growth of an industrial managerial elite, recently decided to sell its profitable metal works factory. The following case study of the Milouot provides additional perspectives on how modern collective organizational life and national needs have been integrated.

The Milouot Enterprise

The Milouot enterprise is essentially an economic interregional cooperative based on the economic interests of the area's kibbutz settlements. It was founded in 1960 by twenty-three kibbutzim, representing the three major national kibbutz federations and coming from four regional districts in the western Galilee. In 1975, it had twenty-six share-holding members. The Miloubar central feed mill is jointly owned by two other regional areas of Israel and serves over ninety cooperative settlements in the northern part of the country.

The Milouot's ties to Kibbutz Har are principally economic: broadening of Har's productive base and labor market. In recent years, the economic activity of the Milouot has been enlarged to include educational functions such as job-training programs and nutrition seminars.

Specifically, Har benefits from the Milouot framework in three ways:

1. As an original shareholder, Har receives profit return in the form of rebates or discounts on service costs and in interest on capital shares.
2. Har's agrarian sector is expanded through the various divisions of the Milouot, including the Feed Mill, Cotton Gin, Banana Packing and Ripening Station, Chicken Slaughterhouse, Fruit Grading and Cold-Storage Plant, Research and Development Laboratory, Data-processing Service, and a Citrus and Fruit Products Company, of which the Milouot enterprise is the chief shareholder.
3. By serving as a labor market for Har's members, the Milouot provides job possibilities that are not available within the internal economy (Meshek). There are three categories of kibbutz members who work in the Milouot framework: (a) people that the Milouot requests because of their known skills and talents; (b) people who request to work in the Milouot to expand their job horizons; and (c) people who have a hard time finding a work role in the kibbutz, and thus the kibbutz asks the Milouot to help place them.

This three-pronged relationship to the Milouot has helped Har raise its standard of living, bring technological methods to its agricultural sector, and generally increase the material development of the community.

The members of Har, especially those in leadership positions or in the Milouot framework, have realized that the Milouot has had a strong impact on the individual member settlements. The Milouot has reflected and reinforced the movement away from ideological emphasis toward larger-scale industrialization. The general secretary of the Milouot, a member of Kibbutz Har, gives background on this transition:

> Within "Har" I would say there is a switchover from more idealistic life to materialistic life. . . . We used to work together, to go to meetings together, elect representatives was very important. . . . Today, who cares who goes to a council meeting of the (federation) movement? We just had the election last month and I don't even remember who were the candidates . . . nobody knows and nobody cares. . . . People are much more materialist-minded. I think this is why the place of Milouot is much greater than ever.[5]

It is revealing that many kibbutz members express the attitude that the Milouot "have the kibbutzim," just as industrialization of the kibbutz has caused the "factory to have a kibbutz" rather than a kibbutz having a factory. This expression indicates a realization that Kibbutz Har is now dependent upon the Milouot for its economic stability. The kibbutz is tied to the Milouot's labor and production policies, which are creating an economic definition of regional cooperatives, and reducing the individual community's degree of autonomy.

Organization of the Milouot

Land

The Milouot enterprise serves settlements in the western Galilee and Haifa Bay area, extending from the Lebanese border on the north to the city of Haifa on the south, from the Mediterranean on the west to the central Galilee mountain range on the east. The enterprise is set up at two industrial centers, separate from any inhabited area. The Miloumoz (banana plant) and the Milous (fruit plant) are at the northern center, while the southern center houses the Miloubar (feed mill), Milousiv (cotton gin), Milouof (chicken slaughterhouse), Miloupri (noncitrus fruit plant), Miloumor (research labs), Mioudar (data processing), the central Milouot administration, a petrol station, a store for the sale of Milouot products, and a refreshment stand. Both centers have direct rail connections with the main lines.

The northern and southern centers are located ten minutes and thirty-five minutes respectively by car from Har. Public transportation to neither is direct. Members from Har working at the main southern center team up in car pools. The cars are provided to members holding important positions in the Milouot system and serve as "company cars." Because of the location of the centers, it is difficult for a great number of Har's members to work in the Milouot; in fact, most of the kibbutz members working there come from nearby settlements. It is especially hard for any woman from Har who is breast feeding to work in the Milouot, as she would be separated from her child for a long workday.[6]

Labor
As of 1974, the labor force statistics were as follows: the Milouot employed a total of 982 workers, of which 550 were regular hired laborers, 270 were seasonal hired laborers, and 162 were kibbutz members. Hired laborers working in the northern center came principally from Nahariya, Shlomi, and local Arab villages. Most of the seasonal, temporary hired workers are Arabs and school students off for the summer, while the permanent hired workers are both Sephardic Jews and Arab laborers.

Wages for hired laborers are determined according to fixed scales set by the Histadrut (National General Federation of Labor). Time and a half is paid for overtime and night work. Average wage-rates vary from division to division. In the slaughterhouse, for example, wages are set according to the food-worker scale, which is the lowest in Israel, and metalworkers in the Milousiv cotton gin earn the highest wage rate.

At first, all labor needs for the Milouot were determined independently by the director of each factory or division. Now, the two-sector (hired laborers and kibbutz members) centralized labor power division is in charge of filling labor requirements. Shoshanah Sagay reports on this aspect of her work with Milouot hired labor:

> How do I find them? From the new immigrants. I have connection with absorption centers for new immigrants and I tell them when I need someone. I have connections with the Ministry of Labor. We also find people by way of newspapers. I do not go directly to the villages.

Hired female laborers fill the majority of jobs in the Milouof slaughterhouse, the Miloupri and Milous fruit-packing plants. Their wage levels, reflecting the nature of their jobs, average considerably lower than that of men. Hired Arab laborers constitute 20 percent of the permanent hired labor force and an overwhelming majority of the seasonal work force. Sagay reports that "we (Milouot) are very careful about problems with Arab workers." During the 1973 war, 90 percent of the Arabs showed up for work and were instrumental in maintaining factory output.

Of the nearly 1,000 workers in the Milouot organization, 162 are kibbutz members, mostly in management work roles. Each member kibbutz is responsible for sending a specific number of its members to work in the Milouot every year. The exact number to be sent by each kibbutz is determined by three factors:

1. The extent the kibbutz utilizes Milouot services.
2. The extent of purchases in the Milouot central purchasing organization, the Mishkei Hamifratz.
3. The population of the kibbutz.

According to the three factors, Har was expected to send a total of eight members, seven for the plants and one for regional work. Actually, Har sent six members, four working directly in the Milouot and two in the region. Pressure can be placed on kibbutzim not fulfilling their quota, but compliance is not very rigid. Kibbutz Admit, a relatively new settlement on the Lebanese border, for instance, has the smallest quota of three but could not send even one. Kibbutz Ein Mifratz, with the largest quota of fourteen, sent twelve.

The relationship between the individual kibbutz and the Milouot framework rests on the understanding that member settlements must send workers to maintain their control of the system. Kibbutzniks, therefore, fill all the top managerial positions and many of the skilled work roles. Almost none are in semi-skilled "blue-collar" worker positions. Their work term, which is determined in consultation with their kibbutz economic manager, is usually four years. That is the time allowed for learning the job, producing optimum work, and then training a new member. Not infrequently, however, members stay on after four years, and a few have been at the Milouot for almost its full history. Three Kibbutz Har members are among those who have worked in the Milouot longer than four-year terms.

The relationship between the kibbutz members working in the Milouot and the hired laborers is not merely one of management vis-à-vis the manual laborer. The Milouot managers are members of the kibbutzim, who are the owners of the plants. Thus, kibbutznik Milouot workers are "self-employed" business people, while hired laborers are employees. The Milouot enterprises are controlled by communities in the region, but only a selected group of communities. Workers who are not residents of the cooperative member settlements do not enjoy the same benefits as kibbutznik (and some *mochav*) workers.

The ideological dilemma posed for the kibbutz is well recognized by Milouot Labor Power division heads:

> It's not easy to be the manager and believe in the equality of people . . . it's one of the big problems we face here.

> It's hard to be the bosses. That's something that has to be learned. . . . I always try to keep in mind that here [in Milouot] I am regarded as a boss. . . . They [hired workers] receive salaries from us, we fix the working conditions. The management of the Milouot is not like the management of

private industry, for kibbutz members not even working here make decisions, for the task of the Milouot is to serve the farm [kibbutz] settlements.

The general secretary of Har, in 1975, remarked that the institutionalization of kibbutzniks into managerial positions was one of the most significant influences of the Milouot system on the social reality of the kibbutz. She believed that the more members assumed the tasks of managers, the more they would assume managerial attitudes toward others.

During interviews with kibbutznik Milouot managers, it was suggested that hired laborers are treated better by the Milouot than by other enterprises. In stating that the Milouot had a "distinctive" relationship with hired workers, instances of the ways kibbutzniks try to improve the worker's situation were provided. They included efforts to consult with the hired workers about "social rights" and not just wages, and allowance of input by representatives of the hired labor force into lower-level decision-making processes. The term "social rights" was defined as benefits other than wages provided by the Milouot, such as good insurance coverage, scholarships for workers' children, sending bundles to workers during war time, and special privileges at the Milouot "company store."

Not many alternative work possibilities exist for hired laborers of the Milouot, and most permanent workers stay on the job. After ten years the Milouot gives a worker a watch as a gift. Very few receive training because "the workers in our enterprise are very simple workers" and for the most part "are people without any education." When a hired woman was sent to an inventory course because she "wrote so nicely," it was considered a major achievement.

The situation can be contrasted to the training program available, in increasing numbers, to the kibbutzniks working at the Milouot. Between 1974 and 1977, about twenty kibbutzniks took short courses in engineering, computers, laboratory work, and research—mainly at the Technion University in Haifa. Many of the kibbutzniks who took courses were women who work in the Milouot's laboratories and data-processing center. The less-skilled jobs in these plants—such as key punching—are left to hired women workers. In addition, a number of kibbutzniks have been able to get their B.A. degrees while working within the Milouot.

A final important comparison can be made regarding decision-making opportunities for hired workers and kibbutzniks. The principal decision-making structure resembles that of an individual kibbutz: a general assembly to which all member settlements are invited; a secretariat that meets each week and is composed of the central Milouot management and plant managers; and workers' committees in each "branch" division. In addition, a board of directors meets twenty to twenty-five times a year and is composed of fifteen kibbutzniks: five kibbutz members who work in the Milouot, including the general secretary and four division heads, and ten members elected at large by member settlements. The two-year board term is rotated among the member settlements, with federation affiliations as one criterion; each settlement is assured an opportunity for representation. Aside from the formal decision-making structure, kibbutzniks have an informal structure of maintaining contact and working out problems:

> We are not a mass but only 166 or so people. We know each other. When we eat lunch together we can settle problems. There is a committee of kibbutz workers in the Miloubar [feed mill]. If they have problems the manager of the branch can tell me, since we drink coffee together every morning at 6 A.M.

A sense of camaraderie and unity of purpose guides the kibbutzniks' decisions in the Milouot; they are members of the same club.

Hired laborers belong to various Histadrut labor union groups, depending on their work. If a dispute occurs, they can first turn to their own division's workers' committee, where minor issues are settled. Larger disputes come to the workers' committee that represents all workers in the Milouot and consists of five people. If the dispute is personal, this committee is frequently bypassed, and the problem is taken directly to the head of Hired Labor Manpower. One man represents all the hired workers in the Milouot; he organized the only strike to hit the Milouot, and it began in the slaughterhouse. He is described by the general secretary of the Milouot as "a man from Morocco, who you think is primitive but when you get used to him you see he has natural intelligence." This one representative is the main link between the hired workers and the overall decision structure of the Milouot, in which hired laborers have no representation. In the case of the strike and in other disputes in the Milouot, outside arbitrators have been called in from Histadrut offices in Akko or in Tel Aviv.

A period of difficult negotiation between the management of the Milouot and the hired laborers was in process in the mid-1970s due to the sky-rocketing cost of living in Israel. The hired workers wanted increments as percentages of their salaries, while the management wanted to tie raises to production.

The hired laborers are not battling for inclusion in overall decision making; rather, they are concentrating on wage issues. They have not been enthusiastic about the idea of joint kibbutznik–hired labor cooperative plans, which some kibbutzniks have put forth as a solution to the exclusion of hired laborers from decision-making control. This attitude reflects their rejection of "socialist schemes" and their understanding that the final control of the Milouot would remain with the kibbutzim. It is fundamental to the labor structure of the Milouot that management is not simply in the hands of the 162 kibbutznik workers, but in the hands of the 26 kibbutz community settlements. The Milouot management thus represents the settlement population of 6,000. Only lower-level decision making, within the separate plants, is open to nonmember input.

Capital
Mishkai Mifratz was founded by the kibbutzim in 1948 as a central purchasing organ for kibbutz supplies. In addition to providing this service for individual kibbutzim, Mishkai Mifratz also has serviced purchasing, collection of payments, and other financial functions for the Milouot framework. Fifty-one percent of the founder shares of Milouot are owned by the Mishkai Mifratz purchasing organization, and 49 percent by the 23 original members united in Mishkai Mifratz. Ordinary shares are held by these 23 kibbutzim. The three main sources of investment capital are:

1. Government Development Loans: Accorded the status of "approved enterprises," the Milouot plants are given rights to special development loans and tax exempt status.
2. Bank Loans: These provide about one-third of the investment at regular banking rates.
3. Members' Shares: An initial assessment is made of the capital need of each Milouot project, and members' share capital is fixed at 20 to 30 percent.

Settlements wishing to use the plant's services are asked to participate according to their share of estimated use in the first four- or five-year period. The capital is received by the Milouot from the settlements over a four-year period. Any future increases in share capital come from: (a) other settlements wanting to use a plant's services as full participants; (b) additional capital from members for new projects; and (c) retained profits of the plant, which may be converted into share capital as decided by member settlements.

The principle of *user participation* is the guideline for redistribution of share capital every four years, based upon the previous four-year utilization. If a settlement's use of a plant's services exceeds the average, the settlement must purchase more shares. If such use is below the average, the settlement is eligible for a rebate. Kibbutz Har has approximately 4 percent of the total shares in Mishkai Mifratz; this figure varies according to how much the kibbutz purchases in a given year. The same holds true for the Milouot. Har utilizes the Miloumoz banana plant more than the Milousiv cotton gin, for instance, and its shares would reflect this.

It is impossible to describe financial benefits to member settlements strictly in terms of profit, since the kibbutzim both use the services of the Milouot and are the suppliers of the services. Kibbutz members speak of *achievements* rather than profit. A manager describes the difference between the Milouot system and normal capital enterprise:

> In a normal private factory you can see the difference between the input and output and know the profit. Here you buy chickens from the kibbutz and give a low or high price, which depends on what is best for the kibbutz. You determine the price margin according to what would be best overall for the kibbutz interest.

Although the Milouot system is not the same as other capitalist enterprises, it maintains a pattern of turning the profits from hired labor into assets for member settlements.

Milouot Goals and Functions

The main goals of the Milouot can be summarized as follows:

1. Development of intersettlement cooperation on a broad and solid basis.
2. Development of a regional agricultural industry for the settlements' agricultural produce.
3. Development of modern industrial plants servicing the settlements' agricultural branches.
4. Reduction of production costs of the agricultural produce.
5. Joint endeavors to increase technological knowledge in industry, agriculture, and the settlements' agricultural branches.

In addition, the Milouot framework facilitates communication between the member settlements and the national marketing organization. An information bulletin is sent monthly to the main agricultural branches of each settlement, and regular contact is maintained from the branches to the various Milouot plants. The communication network assures feedback pertaining to the agricultural needs of the settlements and the Milouot.

In addition to the six divisions of the Milouot, two separate companies, the Milous citrus fruit plant and the Miloubar feed mill, were set up in the mid-1960s.

Miloubar

The Miloubar feed mill is unique among the Milouot enterprises for two reasons. First, it is an interregional venture of the Milouot settlement members and cooperative settlements in the Jezreel Valley and Upper Galilee. Second, it is the only Milouot enterprise where kibbutz members constitute the majority of workers, forty-two out of sixty-four plant workers. This is the case since the feed mill is crucial for the running of all the livestock and poultry branches of the member settlements, which would be in serious trouble if it were shut down. It signifies the recognition of the differentiation between the *poalim*, hired workers, and the kibbutz members working in the Milouot. The former, as employees, could call a strike that would cripple the member settlements' economy, while the latter would not act against their own interests. In the Miloubar, hired laborers work primarily in the servicing and repair jobs, while kibbutzniks fill the production jobs.

A closer examination of the Miloubar operation shows how Milouot plants meet their objectives, including how they are linked to national and international organizations. Kibbutz Har's link to the Miloubar is through its poultry branch. In 1974, Har began a new modernized poultry branch, which replaced a failing, nonmechanized setup. It originally purchased twenty thousand chickens from Kibbutz Beit Haemek and started the process of raising them for slaughter.

As a member shareholder of the Miloubar, Kibbutz Har both purchases its chicken feed from the plant and receives a rebate from the plant after "profits" have been determined. In the words of Ishai, head of Kibbutz Har's poultry branch, "Har is a seller of chickens and an owner of the firm that buys the chickens." Thus the cost of the poultry branch and its final income each year take into account the Milouot shares Har holds.

In the first years of Kibbutz Har's early poultry branch, the kibbutz was responsible for getting its own feed and producing the correct mixture, which could often be a hit-or-miss process. Today, the Miloubar offers a wide range of feeds that are produced with advanced technological knowledge and equipment. Transport of the feed is also supplied by the Miloubar, which also offers scientific advisory services to meet the special needs of the branch.

Kibbutz Har is linked through the Miloubar to a wide network of national and international organizations. Together with five other feed mills in Israel, the Miloubar has formed an association that has a technical bureau active in poultry branch and other livestock feed experimentation. The association maintains an experimental dairy herd and fish feed stations. Through the technical bureau the Miloubar cooperates with the cattle and poultry divisions of the Volcani research center, Technion's food technology faculty, and the Fisheries research station. There are many direct ties to the ministry of agriculture.

International links include import and export trade as well as education. The major machine equipment for the Miloubar has been provided by the Swiss company Buehler Brothers. One percent of the production goes for export to European countries. Educational contact is maintained with *Centre de Recherches International de Nutrition et Alimentation* (CRINA) in France, affiliated with Miloubar since 1965, and IFF, a

German research center for food production technology. Contact with the United States Department of Agriculture and private feed production companies is also kept up by Miloubar.

Milouot and the Political-Military Dimension

The Milouot framework provides Kibbutz Har and other member settlements with a structure for maintaining agrarian production during security emergencies and war. The structure for emergency back-up was instituted after 1967 and became particularly important during the 1973 war. It reflects the strengthening of a national emergency network called the Meliah (Organization for Emergency Economy). The chairman of the Meliah is the minister of defense, who supervises all the nation's needs during times of crisis. The general secretary of the Milouot, a member of Kibbutz Har, also is the head of the Meliah functions in the western Galilee region.

Since Israel's army is constituted by the majority of its citizens, when a crisis of war erupts and troops are called up, most of the economy's labor force is absent. It is crucial that arrangements are made to maintain areas of production and essential services. Each Milouot plant has a list of people available in the region who can be substituted for workers if they are called into the army. For instance, the cotton gin plant has issued a questionnaire to all member settlements requesting information on which members have experience in cotton-picking and gin-work activities so they can be called if needed. The 1967 war erupted in the middle of the cotton-planting season, thus causing a serious loss in that industry. Emergency plans were better organized by 1973 so that when war began at the end of the season in 1974, more produce was saved. The head of the cotton gin comments on how emergency plans were put into operation in 1973:

> During the last war my unit was by chance stationed here in the region.... [T]he war caught us just at the beginning of the picking season and it was very difficult.... I knew which kibbutz needed people and which had extra people to help us. Once picking was finished in one place we moved on to the next kibbutz. Our gin was the only one in the country kept running.... Our Arab workers also all came to work and others called to see if we needed help. We got in over one-half the crop and that is how the gin kept running.

There were substantial losses to Milouot members, particularly due to the first days of call-up in the 1973 war. However, the emergency preparations organized in the Milouot protected, as much as possible, the economic interests of member settlements during the crisis. This scale of protection would not have been available without the Milouot enterprise.

This form of economic security is not available to the region's urban and development town residents. By collectivizing resources, therefore, the Milouot has a distinct advantage during a crisis over other residents in the region who are dependent on individual income for their livelihood.

Conclusion

There is little doubt that the Milouot regional organization has been of significant benefit to member kibbutzim. It has allowed the separate kibbutz communities to expand their economies and generally has produced a higher standard of living than otherwise might have been possible. Furthermore, the Milouot at least partially responded to the constraints facing each kibbutz in terms of limitations on land, labor, and capital. The role it plays in terms of security during military crisis is of central importance.

The Milouot has in many ways been a positive force for individual kibbutz members. Providing new occupational positions for kibbutzniks, the Milouot has expanded into areas demanding technical and professional training. Given the push by youth and some of the older members for these kinds of occupations rather than the more traditional manual kibbutz jobs, the Milouot has provided them a new place to look for work while remaining kibbutz members. On another level, the Milouot can simply provide an opportunity for a kibbutznik to get "outside" the confines of small community life for at least a period of time.

However, there have been difficult quid pro quos for the benefits received. On the labor issue, the heavy reliance on hired wage laborers is a basic affront to the essence of kibbutz collectivist principles. The division of labor in the Milouot, moreover, separates the kibbutzniks into a managerial class and the hired laborers into a service/production class. The movement towards kibbutznik professionalism contradicts the traditional kibbutz reverence for manual labor and places deep obstacles in front of possibilities for job rotation. After all, how many individuals can any kibbutz afford to have trained as research scientists, computer programmers, or export sales managers?

The increasing labor specialization and stratification existing in the Milouot organization also raises important questions concerning the relationship of the individual to the community. Politically, participatory democracy cannot work within a stratified workplace where only a certain group, in this case the kibbutz managers, has the power and control to make governing decisions. Wage laborers in this terrain are in the same position as employees of a firm owned by private entrepreneurs. In a more general way, as Adam Smith once remarked, increasing productivity in some narrow sense is often at the expense of the worker's general understanding and awareness. The kibbutz Milouot enterprise is confronting how individuals in a developing industrial society should relate to machines and to each other. Is it inevitable, as Weber suggested, that modern industrial society, as it utilizes individuals more "efficiently," diminishes capacities for individual creativity and cooperation? This runs up against the kibbutz formulation that collectives should offer the best environment for releasing individual capabilities. The regional organization of the kibbutz, while constituting a national success story, places the cooperative movement in confrontation with its internal collective social structure and with a more universal egalitarian ideology.

Notes

1. David Moberg, "Experimenting with the Future: Alternative Institutions and American Socialism," in *Co-ops, Communes and Collectives*, ed. John Case and Rosemary Taylor (New York: Pantheon, 1979).

2. For an excellent discussion of the organizational theories of Michels and Weber, see Nicos Mouzelis, *Organization and Bureaucracy* (Chicago: Aldine Publishing, 1967).

3. Har is a pseudonym for the kibbutz I studied during fieldwork in 1970–71 and again in 1975. While there are dissimilarities among kibbutzim, including size, federation affiliation, and economic base, Kibbutz Har and its regional organizations are representative of kibbutz internal/external relationships.

4. More extensive background on the kibbutz can be found in Chapter 23 by William Whyte and Joseph Blasi.

5. Interview with Milouot General Secretary, May 2, 1975.

6. Hours vary, but the average workday is long: from 6:30 A.M. to 3–4:00 P.M., often with meetings in the evenings. No daycare is provided at the Milouot itself for members or hired laborers.

25
Work Reform and Quality Circles in Japanese Industry

Robert Cole

The Job-Redesign Movement in Japan

Japanese management has increasingly moved toward a focus on employee participation in decision making and small-groupism (*shōshūdan-shugi*). These developments began in the early 1960s and accelerated from the mid-1960s (Yasui 1975, 14–15). The various elements composing these developments incorporated Western management techniques grounded in the social sciences, but also grew quite naturally out of many traditional Japanese social practices. For example, the practice of paying workers for jobs they can do (highly touted in the HEW report as a desired form of job redesign) . . . has been standard in many large Japanese companies for some time. The broad social movement toward "all-employee management participation" included labor-capital conferences, roundtable discussions with employee groups, individuals or groups independently setting goals and communicating them to superiors, zero-defect programs, quality-control circles, and a variety of other volunteer groups, project teams, and task forces.

A particularly interesting characteristic of this development was the leadership provided by high-level management groups.[1] The activities of the Japan Federation of Employers' Associations (Nikkeiren) were especially important. In October 1966 an Abilities First Principles research group was established by Nikkeiren's Labor Management Committee. In the group's report, *Nōryoku Shugi: Sono Riron to Jissen (The Ability Principle: From Theory to Practice)*, released in 1969, it was pointed out that the period 1960 to 1965 had been a turning point in Japanese labor management, as firms shifted from the reward by age and length-of-service system (*nenkō*) to the ability-first system. The report was the first to give a complete description of the change. Many of the factors contributing to this transformation are those we have already discussed: growing

---

Reprinted from *Work, Mobility and Participation*, by Robert Cole (Berkeley: University of California Press, 1979), 132–41, 157–67, 196–204, by permission of the publisher.

labor shortage, rising educational levels, rising technological levels, shifting value system, and so on.

The report defines ability-first management as a matter of discovering the abilities of employees; developing these to the fullest; providing an environment, place, and opportunity for them to be used; and then rewarding them. According to the report all employees should be under the ability-first system, but in fact special attention is paid to white-collar workers, who were viewed as having the greatest potential for introducing change. The ability-first system developed rapidly, in a climate of rapid economic growth, as Japanese firms entered a new stage of large-scale capital prosperity and internationalization after 1966. At that time no one foresaw the recession caused by the successive shocks to the dollar-based world economic system in 1971. As employers sought countermeasures to cope with the increasingly difficult situation caused by these successive shocks, they included in their efforts a reassessment of personnel practices. As a consequence they became increasingly aware of the difficulties encountered in institutionalizing the ability-first principle. Although it was supposed to represent a revolution in enterprise consciousness, in actuality it was no more than a transformation of personnel management. Moreover the system often aroused intense opposition on the part of employees. Older workers, in particular, saw it as a threat to their privileges.

At Nikkeiren's general meeting in 1968 the president of Hitachi Shipbuilding gave a description of his company's experience with all-employee management participation. In the February 1966 issue of *Recruit*, Kawakita Jiro, Kobayashi Shigeru, and Komatsu Sakyo advocated a shift from the administered society to the participation society. Believing he perceived a trend toward all-employee management, the chairman of Nikkeiren, Mr. Sakurada, advocated support for this trend at a top management seminar in August 1970. The theme was that all-employee management participation did not stop at transforming personnel management practices. The slogan "Make Every Man a Manager" (*zen' in keiei*) is attributed to Mr. Sakurada, though apparently it had its origin at Texas Instruments (Jenkins 1973, 195). Other slogans include "Make Every Plant Worker an Engineer." Since this period Nikkeiren has engaged in a wide range of publicizing activities designed to explain and spread this participatory system.

What conclusions may we draw from this description? Notable is the high-level direction given to the spread of these new personnel developments. The mode of diffusion of this software organizational technology parallels the pattern that has been attributed to the Japanese style of industrialization. In the case of physical technology, analysts have been impressed by the rapid diffusion of best practice in Japan. This has been facilitated by various industrial cartel arrangements in the past and by the key role of the Ministry of International Trade and Industry in the postwar period.[2] In the kind of organizational software we are discussing, it is clear that the identification of best practice is more difficult and subject to differing interpretations. Yet whether the selection of a given practice, such as all-employee participation, is in fact "best practice" is less important than the evolution of a consensus that identifies it as such. Nikkeiren, along with other management associations, plays a central role in determining "best practice" at any given time and rapidly diffusing this information to the most important of the potential users.[3]

A variety of surveys of managerial personnel practices confirms that these small group participatory practices are widespread. A major survey of 850 manufacturing firms by the Japan Federation of Employers' Associations in 1968 found that 72.5 percent of the firms were practicing some form of personnel policy emphasizing small groupism. This broke down to 26.1 percent for quality-control circles, 23.2 percent for zero defect, 23.2 percent for improvement groups, and 36.8 percent for management by objective.[4] Since some companies register in more than one category, the total of 72.5 percent is probably more conservatively estimated at about 30 percent, though higher if only large companies were included (Japan Federation of Employer's Associations 1971). Since 1968 these activities continue to be diffused, so that experts estimate a figure closer to 50 percent today. The Fourth Personnel Management Census of the Japan Federation of Employers' Associations repeated the 1968 survey in 1974. They report a sharp increase in the proportion of firms practicing quality-control circles to 39.3 percent, and in those firms having improvement groups to 41.3 percent (extensive discussions of both types follow). Slight increases were recorded for zero-defect groups to 25.8 percent and management by objective to 40.1 percent, with another 12.9 percent of the responses reporting different types of small group activity (Japan Federation of Employers' Associations 1975, 4). These various small group practices contain many of the elements of job redesign as American experts have come to define it.

The Development of Quality-Control Circles

We get a sense of the Japanese capacity to borrow and adapt Western organizational technology to their own needs through a brief tracing of the introduction of quality-control (QC) circles.[5] QC circles may represent the most innovative process of borrowing and adaptation in the personnel policies of large Japanese companies in the postwar period. A QC circle is a relatively autonomous unit composed of a small group of workers, usually led by a foreman or senior worker, and organized in each work unit. It is in principle a "spontaneously" formed study group, which concentrates on solving job-related quality problems, broadly conceived as improving methods of production as part of company-wide efforts. At the same time it focuses on the self-development of workers. This includes: development of leadership abilities of foremen and workers, skill development among workers, identification of natural leaders with supervisory potential, improvement of worker morale and motivation, and the stimulation of teamwork within work groups.

Before 1945 Japan had only moderate experience with modern methods of statistical quality control. William Deming (1970), a recognized expert on the subject, follows the classic definition of W. Shewhart (1931). He defines statistical quality control as "the control of quality through the application of statistical principles and techniques in all stages of production directed toward the economic manufacture of a product that is maximally useful and has a market." Dr. Deming was personally a major influence in the diffusion of statistical quality-control practices in Japan on the occasion of his immediate postwar lectures there. Indeed the Deming Prize was established in 1950 to commemorate Dr. Deming's contribution to the diffusion of quality-control ideas in Japan; the annual competition by major firms for the award serves further to promote the spread of these ideas. Dr. Deming's visit to Japan was part of an early postwar effort by the American occupation to have American statisticians come to Japan and teach American wartime industrial standards to Japanese engineers and statisticians. These efforts were a major factor contributing to the formal adoption of Japanese Engineering Standards (JES) provided for by legislation in 1949 (Tsuda 1977). The Korean War had a further impact on the acceptance of these standards. In order to win military procurement orders from the American military between 1954 and 1961, the quality standards defined by the Defense Department had to be met.

In 1954 Dr. J. Juran, a quality-control expert, arrived in Japan for a series of lectures. He emphasized a newer orientation to quality control, stating that it must be an integral part of the management function and practiced throughout the firm. In practice, this meant teaching quality control to middle management. From 1955 through 1960 these ideas spread rapidly in major firms, but with an important innovation on the part of the Japanese. In the Japanese reinterpretation, each and every person in the organizational hierarchy, from top management to rank-and-file employees, received exposure to statistical quality-control knowledge and techniques, and they jointly participated in study groups, upgrading quality-control practices. This is at the same time both a simple and a most profound twist to the original ideas propagated by the Western experts. Quality control shifted from being the prerogative of the minority of engineers with limited shop experience ("outsiders") to being the responsibility of each employee. Instead of adding additional layers of inspectors and reliability assurance personnel when quality problems arise, as is customary in many U.S. firms, each worker, in concert with his or her workmates, is expected to take responsibility for solving quality problems. This is in contrast to many American firms, where the general rule of thumb is that you do not have workers inspect their own work; implicit here is a basic lack of confidence and trust. It is just one more facet of an extreme division of labor. The implications of the different approaches may be seen in the ratio of inspectors to production workers. For example, at General Motors manufacturing plants we may estimate a ratio of about one inspector for every ten production workers, and in GM assembly plants one for every seven; by contrast Toyota Auto Company estimates the ratio to be one inspector for every twenty-five production workers in manufacturing plants, and one for every thirty in their assembly plants. This is a striking difference with significant cost implications, and both sets of ratios appear to be fairly typical of the industry.

Finally, the large number of inspectors in U.S. firms suggests that there are a large number of rejected items that need to be repaired before they can be further processed. Such is the case. At Ford Motor Company, the rule of thumb has been a 10 percent repair average. That is, 10 percent of their labor is engaged in repairing items that do not meet specifications. This percentage does not appear out of line with the industry average. The Japanese automobile companies, however, are able to rely more on "first time capability" of their employees. Again this cannot help but have significant cost implications.

The major organizational instrument for diffusing quality-control practices in the postwar period was the QC research group, organized in 1948 within the framework of the Union of Japanese Scientists and Engineers (JUSE). JUSE is composed of university professors in engineering and science as well as engineers from leading industrial firms. It is a national nonprofit association dedicated to providing services to participating Japanese companies in the area of quality and reliability. This includes a large number of training programs. JUSE also serves as a major liaison between the private sector and the educational world.

In the early 1960s it was the QC research group within JUSE that took the lead in involving foremen directly in solving quality-control problems and in taking foremen outside their own companies to discuss problems with other foremen (Sugimoto 1972, 6). The low-priced magazine *Genba to QC (Quality Control for Foremen)*, published by JUSE beginning in 1962, was a major factor in stimulating the growth of QC circles. It puts particular emphasis on introducing case-study experiences of given companies to a broader audience of foremen. The magazine, which changed its name to *FQC* in 1973, increased its subscriptions from 6,000 in 1962 to some 70,000 by the mid-1970s. Training programs were begun using not only conventional textbooks but also radio and even television series.

The number of QC circles has grown explosively, from a total of 1,000 registered with JUSE in 1964 to 87,540 by February 1978. With an average of almost ten members a circle, the membership totalled 840,000. Unregistered QC circles are estimated conservatively to total an additional five times the number of registered circles, with a membership of some four million. With the total number of employees in the Japanese labor force standing at thirty-seven million in 1978, this means that approximately one out of every eight Japanese employees was involved in QC-circle activity. These summary figures are undoubtedly inflated because the data do not strictly discriminate between QC circles and some other forms of small group activity such as zero-defect programs, industrial engineering teams, improvement groups, and so on. Nonetheless we are dealing with a movement that has had a significant impact on managerial practices, especially among blue-collar employees in the larger manufacturing firms.

Characteristics of Quality-Control Circles

We may now turn to the details of quality-control practices in Japanese firms. Quality-control methodology is taught to managers in all functions—sales, accounting, purchasing, research, etc. This diminishes the need for specialist quality-control engineers. A key link in introducing quality control to the rank and file has been the intensive training programs given to foremen (commonly thirty to forty hours); the Japanese foreman has traditionally been less of an agent of management than a representative of the workers, so that the upgrading of the status of the foremen and enhanced training were vital for success. The content of QC training programs for foremen, as summarized by Ishikawa Kaoru, a recognized leader in the movement, includes:

1. Administering training as an integral part of the in-company training program which is given to all employees.
2. Teaching simple statistical methods for analysis and how to go about carrying out shop improvements.
3. Teaching in a way that is tied in closely with a given firm's own technology.
4. Emphasizing practical as opposed to academic training, building in the study of real cases.
5. Teaching participative management techniques.

The QC circle, designed, in turn, to link the training of the foreman with the rank and file, turned out to be the most innovative characteristic of the Japanese approaches to quality control.

QC-circle membership usually ranges from three to twenty people with circles of from five to ten members predominating. Ideally, formation and activity of the QC circle are spontaneous, not forced on the employees by management. However, management often plays a behind-the-scenes role (critics would say manipulates), laying the groundwork through educational activities. The central idea is that participants engage in a study process designed to uncover and solve workshop problems. Members get together on a regular basis, learning statistical methods of problem solving and later discussing the selection and solution of actual problems, and setting timetables for completion of each phase of activity. They draw heavily on knowledge and techniques presented in QC textbooks, the examples presented in *FQC*, and their own skill and experience. Meetings are conducted both during regular working hours, with the approval of superiors, and outside regular working hours. Major tools of analysis studied by QC-circle members are the following seven: (1) Pareto diagram (a vertical bar graph ordered according to importance of measurement value), (2) Cause-and-effect diagram (defining effect and reducing it to contributing causes), (3) Histogram, (4) Check sheet, (5) Graph, (6) Scatter diagram, and (7) Control chart. Pareto diagrams, cause-and-effect diagrams, and graphs are the three most commonly used techniques. . . . A further understanding of QC-circle processes may be had from the account of a Toyota Auto Body foreman:

> We think that the first step of analysis is to see whether or not the work is being implemented in accordance with the job standard. Usually, we grasp this phenomenon by plotting the cause-and-effect diagram with the relevant factors, contributing to production being reviewed by one. This is a time-consuming but effective method which involves extensive data gathering by each member of the circle. If the job standard is not strictly followed, it will be fairly easy to discover the cause of defective units. They will arise either from worker error or from inadequate facilities. If worker error is not a problem, tools and materials are checked carefully. If defects still persist in the absence of worker error or material defects, the cause is considered attributable to an inadequate job standard. The task of the QC circle then becomes the development of a new job standard.

The remarkably high level of mathematical training in Japanese public education has been documented through large-scale systematic international comparisons. It means that all Japanese high school graduates have been exposed to a large extent either to the specific statistical techniques taught in the QC circles or to general modes of thinking that parallel them (Husén 1967).[6] In high school, mathematics is a compulsory subject until students graduate, with the standard being more than four hours a week. For non–college bound students math generally accounts for 10.5 percent of the eighty-five credits needed to graduate. Keeping in mind that over 92 percent of the relevant age cohorts now graduate from high school, this prior exposure undoubtedly facilitates the effectiveness of the training workers receive for QC-circle participation once they enter the company.

A study of actual types of improvement activities carried on by QC circles reported by Ishikawa indicates that 50 percent of the activities are concerned with quality control narrowly defined, 40 percent with problems relating to productivity increase and cost reduction, and the remaining 10 percent with safety and other matters. Innovations relate primarily to production technique; there appears to be very little input on product innovation. Some additional characteristics of ongoing QC circles should be mentioned. The QC circle is not a response to specific problems. Rather it is a continuous study process operative in the workshop. Thus the QC circle performs "opportunistic surveillance" for the organization. Thompson (1967, 151) describes this as monitoring behavior which scans the environment for opportunities, does not wait to be activated by a problem, and does not stop its activities when a problem has been found and solved. He suggests that this is a rare quality in organizations, which when present greatly facilitates organizational self-control and increases adaptive capacity.

A survey of QC-circle meeting times found that 40 percent meet once a month, 40 percent twice a month, and 20 percent three or more times a month. The average meeting time is between sixty and ninety minutes. At each circle meeting all members are given assignments which they are expected to complete by the next meeting, using both company and noncompany time. These assignments commonly involve firsthand observation of specific phenomena in the workshop, and collection and analysis of data. At the QC-circle meeting itself, the brainstorming approach operates; each member is encouraged to participate and put forward his ideas. No idea is criticized, and members are encouraged to voice all their ideas no matter how trivial or outlandish they might appear. Selection of study themes or improvement goals and the timetable for achieving the goals is generally done through the initiative of members utilizing Pareto analysis of problems. In some companies, however, management clearly "encourages" the selection of certain themes in as subtle a fashion as possible. One survey reports that 50 percent of projects are selected by workers and 50 percent by management.

Similarly, procedures for overcoming the problems encountered are decided by the QC-circle membership as a whole, with management providing technical assistance as needed and available. All members are expected to acquire new knowledge, techniques, and practices that will help the achievement of the group goals. This is expected to lead to self-development and realization of worker potential. Each circle is formally independent of other circles but may meet with other circles in the company to jointly work on a common problem. Circles in one company are often encouraged to meet with circles in another company to exchange experiences and develop both incentive and new ideas for application (though not necessarily with competitors in the same industry). These visits are often arranged through the QC Headquarters at JUSE. Public demonstrations and awards serve as major devices for popularizing QC circles within the company. Commonly, some provision is made for involvement of top management in these activities. Similar efforts are made outside the company through the numerous QC-circle conventions organized by the QC Headquarters at JUSE. Here companies present their most impressive successes. The number of companies participating in such conventions has expanded rapidly, as has the size of the audience representing still other companies. Again we may say that diffusion of best practice is rapid with respect to the diffusion of the software technology of the QC circle. Furthermore, companies report that a significant incentive for worker participation in QC-circle activity itself lies in their having the opportunity to travel to QC conventions and to present the results of particularly successful cases. These conventions and company visits are intended to revitalize existing circles and prevent ritualism (*manerika*).

With respect to incentives, it is important to note that the financial rewards given to workers who make possible significant savings are quite small. Generally speaking, symbolic payments under $10 are common, with rewards for even the best suggestions, leading say to a patent, seldom exceeding $600. A 1976 JUSE survey of 360 companies reports 52 percent of QC-circle meetings are held outside working hours (commonly after work), or both within and outside, depending on circumstances. Yet a 1971 survey reports that when they are held outside working hours, 24 percent of the circles are not paid any allowance, and in only 60 percent are workers paid their normal overtime rate.

This kind of behavior, in which immediate financial rewards are downplayed, becomes understandable in the context of the lifetime employment system in large firms, where workers closely identify the achievement of their own goals with the achievement of company goals. For a worker to refuse to have anything to do with the QC circles would be seen as a selfish act. That is, an employee is under strong pressure to "voluntarily" participate in QC circles, lest his or her career in the company be jeopardized. Successful participation in QC-circle activities affects management evaluation of employees for salary increases and promotion. This injects a potentially coercive note, but also allows workers an opportunity to demonstrate their talents. On the negative side, even officials of large unions in the private sector, which adopt quite cooperative attitudes toward management's attempts to raise productivity, report that they must keep an eye on management to see that it does not abuse the QC circle by coercing workers to participate. Undoubtedly there is a significant minority of workers who do see the QC circles as coercive and still many more are apathetic. As the practice becomes institutionalized, it is seen more as a policy imposed by management than as spontaneous worker-initiated behavior. "Permanent revolution" is by no means easy to sustain. Perhaps some new form of personnel policy will arise to breathe new life into participatory management, as suggested by Professor Hazama. Toyota Auto found that initial enthusiasm for QC circles waned a few years after their introduction. They were able to reinvigorate them through the channeling of customer complaints through the QC circles. Revitalization is a continual concern.

The major characteristics of the QC circle may be summarized as follows:

1. Foremen training in participative techniques and statistical methods as applied to practical shop problems.
2. Foreman instruction of small groups of workers in their workshop.
3. Emphasis on spontaneous participation of workers and their participation in self-improvement activities.
4. QC circle as autonomous study group operating on a continuous basis.
5. QC circle as a group effort with all members of the circle participating.
6. Extensive staff and managerial assistance to QC circles provided by company.
7. Recognition of circle members through public demonstrations, company awards, and national and regional QC-circle conventions; financial incentives downplayed. . . .

Toyota Auto Body: The Evolution of Job Redesign

Toyota Auto Body is part of the Toyota Motor Company Group. It is one of the 202 companies that belong to the Kyoho Association sponsored by Toyota Motors. The parent company needs little introduction. It is the largest auto producer in Japan, the third largest in the world, and it is rapidly closing in on Ford Motor Company for number two ranking. It has experienced remarkable growth, with production more than quintupling in just the seven-year period from 1961 to 1968—from 200,000 units in 1961 to over one million in 1968. During this same period the number of employees tripled, rising from 12,000 to 35,200.

Toyota Auto Body separated from Toyota Motor Company in 1945 and became an independent company, although closely integrated into Toyota's production system. Of the eleven members of the board of directors, four are from Toyota Motor Company; 40 percent of the company stock is owned by Toyota Motor Company, and sales go almost exclusively to Toyota Motor Company. The company began as a truck body producer but has increasingly moved into passenger car and van production. It has its own production lines for pressing, sheet-metal working, painting, assembling, and shipping. The major facilities are located in Kariya and Fujimatsu which are near Toyota City, the headquarters of Toyota Motor Company. Toyota Auto Body currently employs 5,500 people, of whom some 78 percent are blue-collar production workers. They are all male and this chapter thus deals primarily with male blue-collar workers. The proportion of employees who are blue-collar has shown only a slight tendency to decline over the last eight years. The average age of all employees is 30.9, with 7.1 years of service. Both figures have shown steady increases since the burst of company growth that took place in 1967–1968 and temporarily depressed the average age and length of service. In 1967, for example, the average age was 26.5 and the average length of service 3.9 years. Employees are recruited from various geographical regions. Currently 25 percent are local recruits, 25 percent are from the island of Kyushu, and the remaining 50 percent are recruited from all over Japan.

The specific set of factors that led Toyota Auto Body's management to engage in widespread innovations in personnel policy arose with the completion of its new large-scale plant at Fujimatsu in 1967. As a consequence 1,200 new high school graduates were hired in 1967 and another 1,300 in 1968. These new employees accounted for almost half the total number of blue-collar workers in the company at that time. Although the company had assigned high school graduates to blue-collar jobs in the past, it had never before deployed to the workshop such a large number in one short period. The shortage of middle school graduates led them to rely on the high school graduates to meet their manpower needs. Company management feared that the new employees with a high school education would be dissatisfied with being assigned to the simple repetitive tasks associated with the typical mass-production system. In the past students could assume that going on to high school would assure them of a white-collar job. Furthermore, the high ratio of inexperienced workers to total workers sharply lowered the skill level in the entire company. Finally, the growing labor shortage made it difficult for the company to recruit the kinds of workers desired (middle school graduates). Consequently, they were constrained to make work satisfying for those they did recruit, to reduce labor turnover. The labor shortage also resulted in a declining proportion of new employees coming directly to the company upon graduating from school. The distribution of employees stabilized in the mid-1970s, with the new school graduates accounting for 65 percent of all employees. The rest with prior work experience came mostly from smaller firms. The presence of large numbers of employees who had been socialized in other firms also concerned management.

For all these reasons, but most of all because of the enormous organizational strain associated with the doubling of the number of blue-collar workers, the company decided to design a new mode of personnel administration. The new system was designed to change working conditions and the reward structure in ways that would better meet worker needs as well as raise productivity. The form that this new personnel administration system would take was influenced by Western social science. In particular, management carefully studied McGregor's "Y" theory (McGregor

1960) and Maslow's hierarchical-need theory. The head of the personnel department in the late 1960s, Mr. Nishiyama Daiso, together with Mr. Sabao Tsuyoshi, the general manager of the Fujimatsu Plant, found these ideas applicable to their own situation. Based on a set of inferences drawn from these theories, company officials formulated fundamental principles for human control to be used in the company. They are: (1) trust a man and entrust him with tasks, (2) present the targets so as to stimulate his creative power, (3) train for leadership to enhance the capacity for teamwork, (4) keep in close communication, (5) grasp the personal attitudes of workers, (6) reaffirm company commitment to education and training, and (7) positively perform technical skill training. The system to be described below suggests they have worked hard to operationalize these principles.

Mr. Nishiyama and Mr. Sabao found it necessary to legitimate their new program not only in terms of contemporary social science, but also in terms of the company founder, Toyota Sakiichi. They quote Mr. Toyota's admonition to engage in:

Exploitation: Be ahead of the time and respect new ideas and times.[7]
Harmony: Look for amity and cooperation by sincerity and trust.
Gratitude: Cultivate an enterprising spirit through self-examination and learn the joy of life through labor. (Nishiyama and Sabao 1970)

Further attempts to legitimate the new approach appear in the repeated emphasis in company documents on the need to improve productivity, a need which arose in response to the threat of increased international competition following the opening up of the domestic market in the middle and late 1960s.

Building on the principles of control outlined above, as well as on existing practices and values in Japan, the company laid the fundamental blueprint for the current personnel administration in 1965 and 1966. The first direct steps, taken in 1967, involved increasing the job scope and responsibility of subleaders (assistant foremen) by delegating to the smallest unit (*kumi*), composed of an average of twenty members, the responsibility for plant safety. This function had been previously lodged in a separate group. The next move occurred in 1968 and involved shifting the responsibility for quality control on selected assembly lines down to the individual worker. This entailed giving each worker a button to stop the line when substandard quality products were produced. The new procedure provided for greater accountability by pinpointing the exact location where deficient products were being produced and thus minimizing the chance that they would influence subsequent stages of the assembly line. The company was sufficiently satisfied with the results in terms of contribution to productivity and quality control, as well as contribution to increasing workers' control over their work, to adopt this system for the whole company in 1972. One of the repeated findings of social scientists in the United States is that control over the pace of work is exceedingly important to workers (Blauner 1964, 21, 98–100, 170–71). The button system was designed to encourage workers to believe they drove the conveyor belt, as opposed to being driven by it.

This innovation was not totally successful, however, because the company found that on long lines (of say 350 meters) workers tended to be reluctant to stop the line. The workers feared they would disrupt the system of production. As a result the company, where possible, has now designed the long lines in sections, with a "buffer" of three to five cars after every ten or so stations (one cycle). Thus when a worker presses his button he can stop only a short section of the line, thereby minimizing the disruption of production. We need only contrast this situation to the practices common in U.S. auto firms, in which the right to stop the line is limited to only a very select number of individuals (e.g., plant managers). Moreover, a line stoppage is of such major consequence in many American firms that it is undertaken with great reluctance and must later be justified to still higher ranking officials.

QC Circles

The company became increasingly involved with quality control as part of the policy of the "Toyota family." The first QC circles in Toyota Auto Body were organized in 1964, at the same time that they were introduced into the parent company. With the rapid growth of the automobile industry at this time, and of Toyota Auto Body in particular, the introduction of QC circles may be seen as an attempt to minimize problems of maintaining quality standards, given the large number of new, untrained employees. Second, the QC circles may be seen as the organizational response to maximize control under conditions of explosive growth. The small group activities of QC circles are admirably suited for these purposes.

It became company policy to compete for the Deming Prize, and they achieved the distinction of winning the award in 1970. They were also awarded the gold medal from the QC Circle Headquarters in 1972. By 1976 the company had an impressive total of 763 QC circles operating, up from 285 in 1971. These circles include some 4,000 employees, with almost all blue-collar workers participating. Workers can be members of more than one circle. Circles tend to be organized around a particular job in the workshop, such as the "ceiling-glue group," or the "meter-fitting group." In principle there is voluntary participation. The QC circles are concerned not only with the reduction of goods deficient in quality, but also with almost every other kind of problem, including improvement of productivity, the speed and way of stopping the conveyor belt, job procedures, job training, and human relations problems. The company slogan is "Quality designed by the engineering personnel shall be realized by the production personnel."

When the QC circles first began in the company there were twenty members in each circle, with the foreman serving as leader. It was found that it was difficult to fully involve all workers with such large groups. Gradually the circles were made smaller and in 1968–1969 the foremen were replaced by ordinary workers (who have achieved a specified job-grade ranking). The company discovered that when the foremen were leaders the workers saw the QC circles as an extension of work relations and held back their spontaneous contribution. Since the shift to smaller circles with workers as leaders, company officials believe the circles are making more substantial contributions to increased productivity. The shift toward having ordinary workers as leaders took place in many companies with developed QC-circle programs (in some companies leaders are elected). An attempt is made to rotate circle leadership to satisfy requests for the opportunity to lead a group. The emergence of leadership, however, is not entirely spontaneous. If a worker shows talent in participating and expressing himself, he is approached by a foreman and encouraged to assume the leadership of a QC circle. As the company sees it the number of groups depends on the combination of human needs and physical layout. Whether it be due to worker belief that this is a good outlet for their talents and a chance to demonstrate their worth, or pressure to fulfill company expectations, or some combination thereof, leadership of the circles has not proved a problem. Workers are paid about half the average hourly wage . . . for QC-circle activity after regular hours. The frequency of QC-circle meetings has increased from an average of one a month in 1968 to six a month in 1975.

The discussion thus far might suggest quite autonomous groups, each meeting and setting its own goals and then implementing them. In fact, however, the company carefully coordinates and regulates QC-circle activities. The general QC-circle reports directly to the factory manager and is responsible for company-wide planning for all QC-circle activities. This includes arrangements for extra-company participation in QC-circle conventions to present successful cases. The number of these presentations is now running at some forty a year, up from twenty-two cases a year in the early 1970s. Second, at each departmental level office there is staffing for planning and promoting the QC-circle program in that department. This includes providing the training necessary for workers to participate in the program. At the section level, staff are responsible for implementing the QC-circle training program and running intra-section meetings for QC-circle leaders. Monthly meetings are held for QC-circle leaders to exchange information, select performance themes, and mutually assist in promoting each other's activities. This minimizes obstacles to solving problems when they involve other work stations and sections. A leader council has been established for every section; these councils consist of the workgroup leader, the foreman, and the leader of each QC circle. The council is designed to provide guidance for the activities of QC circles through identification of problems occurring in the implementation of QC-circle activities and for the coordination of QC-circle activities with company policies. Leadership training includes how to conduct a meeting, get workers to express their opinions, and induce participation among workers. Within each department there is a special QC reference room which employees are encouraged to use freely. In each section case competitions are held among QC circles and the best cases are selected for presentation in the monthly company-wide case competition. Unusually successful cases are then presented for the nationwide QC-circle competition. There is considerable competition among circles to participate in these events.

One of the problems that we might anticipate in the operation of QC circles is the absence of necessary technical expertise to solve workshop problems. In part this problem is met by the Industrial Engineering Project Team which is available to every workshop. It has some forty-five members, half of whom are engineers and half of whom are operatives from the shopfloor who have received more than sixty hours of company education. The combination of engineers and operatives in the same team is expected to produce different approaches to problem solving than if the team were made up entirely of engineers. The project team works closely with QC circles, providing on-the-spot specialized analysis of problem areas. In this fashion technical expertise is made available to specific workshops when necessary.

Perhaps the point at which the QC circles depart most clearly from the voluntarist principle lies in the practice of prescribing a fixed number of suggestions to be allotted to each section, based roughly on the previous year's totals (with perhaps some increase over the prior year). A good many of these suggestions for improvements will arise from QC-circle activity. The personnel department officials estimate that group suggestions account for 75 percent of all suggestions (not all of which are from QC circles), with the remaining 25 percent being put forward by individuals. For the best suggestions the company pays a maximum of ¥50,000 ($227) to individuals and ¥60,000 ($272) to groups. The president of the company makes a public presentation annually to those individuals or groups who have been awarded the maximum award. Those receiving the maximum award also receive a two-days-and-one-night study-tour trip. The company even pays ¥500 ($2.27) for individual suggestions and ¥600 ($2.73) for group suggestions that are not accepted. The per capita number of suggestions has risen in the company from 0.29 in 1967 to 3.44 in 1973.[8] One might suspect that the allotment of a suggestion quota would be perceived to be coercive by workers and thus produce quantity rather than quality. Fortunately the company collects data which allow us to develop an indirect measure that sheds some light on this matter. The estimated yearly per capita cost of implementing employee suggestions has risen from $1,245 in 1967 to $3,382 in 1973.[9] If we deflate the 1973 value to allow for the moderate rise in input prices in the transport equipment industry (on an index of 100 for 1967, input prices rose to 120 in 1973), the revised per capita cost for 1973 is $2,817 (Nihon Ginkō 1974, 272). This is a 126 percent increase in the estimated yearly per capita cost of implementing employee suggestions over 1967. However, the number of suggestions per capita reported above rose 1,086 percent between 1967 and 1973. This discrepancy in increase rates suggests that although each individual may be making more valuable suggestions, there is a lot more "noise or static" in the system occasioned by a massive increase of relatively useless suggestions. This suggests that many are pro forma proposals which workers initiate to keep management "off their backs." On the other hand, since the per capita value of employee suggestions (as measured by the rough proxy of cost of implementing suggestions) has increased, the company still finds it to be a productive strategy to set suggestion quotas for each section.

Evaluation of the QC-Circle Program

This leads us to the need for systematic evaluation of company involvement with QC circles. There is no doubt that company officials regard the circles as a major success. They can point to an impressive number of new work arrangements and machinery that originated from QC circle suggestions. In addition there are the increasing number of successful cases presented in nationwide competition and the growing number of QC circles and increasing frequency of their meetings. The rising value of per capita suggestions does not fail to impress them. Company officials also cite the growth in productivity that has occurred in recent years despite a reduction of employees from 6,200 in 1969 to 5,500 in 1972. They point to the trend in the decline of defects per car completed, from 0.95 in 1968 to 0.60 in 1973, the reduction in the man-hours per car processed from ten in 1968 to eight in 1973, and the decrease in the gross frequency of accidents per million work-hours from fifty-three in 1968 to almost zero in 1972. Employee turnover has also declined, with the rate of employee retention rising from 81.8 in 1968 to 91.5 in 1973. Finally, they cite the company morale surveys investigating work satisfaction. These surveys show that the proportion of workers who believe their work is worth doing rose from 29 percent in 1967 (40 percent responded "don't know" and 31 percent reported they were dissatisfied) to 45 percent in 1973 (35 percent "don't know" and 19 percent dissatisfied)[10]. Response to this same question on a national survey showed only 32 percent saying their work was worth doing, with 20 percent reporting "don't know" and 46 percent denying that the work was worth doing. The higher level of job satisfaction suggested by Toyota Auto Body employee responses is particularly impressive, given the apparently alienating qualities of work in the auto industry even in Japan. In a replication of Blauner's (1964) study of alienation by industry, Fujita and Ishida (1970, 199) find the same tendency for workers in the Japanese automobile industry to score extremely high, relative to other industries, in the proportion of workers who feel their jobs make them work too fast, who regard their jobs as dull and tiresome, and who feel their jobs are too simple.

Particularly important for our interest in job redesign is the belief of company officials that through participation in QC circles workers have developed higher and broader skills in the context of improved teamwork.

In 1970, the year the company won the Deming Prize, they cited the following results of their QC-circle activity: better quality, assured delivery dates, and higher profits as the main tangible results; intangible results included enhanced quality consciousness, participation by everyone in quality control, realization of an improved management structure, and development of "thinking workers" (JUSE 1970, 53).

A final indirect measure of the success of management efforts relates to the strength of opposition to existing union leadership in the company. Since the union, as we shall see, has at least passively cooperated with the company efforts, opposition to the union leadership may be seen as one measure of worker acceptance of both the QC-circle concept and a variety of other innovations to be discussed below. The evidence here is clear-cut. The strength of opposition candidates vis-à-vis the incumbent union leadership is almost nil. This suggests the possibility that management policies have had considerable impact in mitigating worker opposition and committing workers to company policies.

At first glance one cannot help but be impressed by the various indicators of QC-circle effectiveness. The interpretation and attribution of causal links is, however, a good deal more complicated than may initially appear. In the first place QC-circle activity accounts for only a small proportion of any employee's working hours. Consequently it is difficult to separate out the impact of QC-circle activities from still other activities that might have influenced morale, number of man-hours per car processed, turnover, union militancy, and so on. It is possible that some significant proportion of the successes mentioned above derived not from QC circles per se but from the variety of innovations that we subsume under the rubric job redesign. . . . It is also plausible that a good number of the recorded changes flowed directly from technological progress. The new Fujimatsu plant allowed for increased economies of scale, and the new equipment permitted a more intensive operation of facilities.

Second, as noted earlier, a major influx of employees took place in 1967–1968. It is only to be expected that initially work relations would be quite disorganized, leading to low morale, high turnover, high accident rates, lowered productivity and the like. As these employees acquired increased experience and skills (i.e., assuming normal learning curves) and the work force stabilized, we would expect that morale would improve, productivity rise, accidents fall, and so on. Moreover, we are dealing here with the survivors of the major employee influx in the late 1960s; those most dissatisfied, and perhaps incompetent, quit or were forced to leave. These employees would tend to be the youngest and least skilled. We know from the company's morale survey that a higher proportion of the youngest employees tends to find their work not worth doing compared to older workers. Notwithstanding the permanent employment system, quit rates at auto firms are quite high by Japanese standards. Based on current experience, Toyota Auto Body anticipates that after one year of employment, 20 percent of new recruits have quit or proven unacceptable for some reason. After an additional year another 15 percent have quit, and after five years they have lost about 50 percent of the original cohort.[11] These figures are for new school graduates and those employees with prior employment. The point is that the large influx of new employees in the late 1960s was followed by a shedding of the more dissatisfied co-workers and the acquisition of more experience by those remaining. This was bound to lead to more satisfied and productive employees. To what extent the data cited above are explained by these phenomena is impossible to evaluate, though I would venture to suggest that these phenomena explain a significant proportion of the recorded changes.

Company officials themselves also recognize that the lack of strong support for opposition union candidates ought not to be overinterpreted. Although they would like to attribute it to the successes of their personnel policies, they recognize that, as a relatively small company, Toyota Auto Body can provide personalized management in a minimally bureaucratic environment. The rural location of Toyota Auto Body further helps it escape from many of the urban ills and frustrations that affect other factory employees. Worker opportunity to purchase their own relatively inexpensive housing near Toyota Auto Body facilities would be one important example.

The extent to which workers accept QC-circle activity is also problematic. We have already seen that the number of suggestions grew much more rapidly than the value of these suggestions as measured in cost of implementation. In the company morale survey in 1975, 30 percent of the workers reported QC circles to be a burden (*omoni ni kanjiru*); the proportion registering dissatisfaction was up from 20 percent in 1972. Union surveys of employees find that quality-control circles increase the physical and mental burdens experienced by workers (Marsh and Mannari 1976, 302). At Toyota Auto Body, such feelings arise from competition between groups and pressure to submit suggestions. Moreover circle leaders report member apathy to be a constant problem.

On the basis of these observations we might conclude that QC-circle activity has had negligible influence. Perhaps we are dealing here with a simple "halo effect," in which increased productivity and worker morale accidentally coincided with the introduction of QC-circle activity. This is quite consistent with Charles Perrow's (1972, 109) conclusion, after an exhaustive survey of organizational research findings, that the impact on productivity of moderately good or bad relations with subordinates appears to be small and difficult to separate from other considerations (though he does not specifically examine the worker-participation literature). The interpretation is also consistent with Hazama's "stimulant" hypothesis.

A further refinement of this view involves recognizing that Toyota Auto Body management is sophisticated enough to understand these relationships (i.e., the at best moderate contribution of QC activity to productivity), but for purposes of worker motivation, they prefer to emphasize the impact of QC-circle activity and other personnel policies. Company success and its attribution, in part, to QC-circle activity becomes part of management ideology designed to legitimate management power. Even if QC circles do not directly raise productivity or do only what industrial engineers can do at least as well, they may increase worker satisfaction and commitment to company goals by allowing for participation. In an indirect fashion this raises productivity by minimizing the likelihood of worker sabotage, worker turnover, and disruptive strikes. Furthermore, even if QC circles are not the cheapest way to solve problems, the workers tend to implement their own changes with enthusiasm. In contrast they will often resent those solutions arrived at and handed down to them by the engineers. This is particularly important in industries such as the auto industry, in which constant model changes and the like require new work layouts at regular intervals.

Let there be no doubt that company officials, based on their own first-hand observation, are sincerely convinced that QC-circle activity is a major factor in company success, and that the system will continue to generate output consistent with management goals. Certainly they have made a major investment of staff and worker time and other resources in QC-circle activity, and they are able to cite many concrete examples of its success. At the shop level QC circles are expected to present evaluations of their performance; for circles claiming to be successful, this typically includes trend charts detailing the decline in the number of defects (or accidents, etc.) observed. The number of reports claiming success rose from 1,222 in 1970 to 1,785 in 1976. Above all, QC circles mean education as it relates to work. The company, as we shall see, has invested heavily in this area. Management also recognizes the major contribution of technology and the new Fujimatsu plant to increased productivity. However, they argue that a momentum was built up as employees worked hard to win the Deming Prize in 1970. This momentum was maintained after 1970 and carefully guided by management (participation in QC circles was not voluntary at this time). QC-circle suggestions were actively solicited and implemented. Management attributes much of the sharp productivity increase in 1971–1972 to these activities. They also report a ratio of inspectors to workers of less than 1:20. . . . Moreover, management reports that the ratio of inspectors to workers was considerably higher prior to the introduction of QC circles, though they do not have data to support this conclusion. It is impossible to judge whether comparable success would have occurred under some other system of personnel administration. Management at Toyota Auto Body does not believe this to be the case, but it may be that the variety of other small-group activities cultivated by Japanese management in this period would have yielded similar results (and did at other companies). According to this perspective QC circles provided a mechanism for the creation of a new mode of worker participation. It was a stimulant in Hazama's sense, but what was important was not the particular statistical techniques of problem solving (e.g., Pareto analysis) but that QC circles served as a vehicle for facilitating worker participation.

Finally, one additional tack to take in evaluating QC circles is to ask whether workers really learn to use the various statistical techniques associated with QC-circle activity. Management reports that all new employees learn the tools of QC as soon as they enter the company. They participate in a one-day course, and there is a more intensive six-day course for those employees who enter the company school. All employees learn the seven techniques. . . . They learn by using them, so that QC-circle activity is not just a matter of the QC leader, who knows how to do it, getting employees to gather data. Yet management reports that although all employees learn to use these techniques there is variation in their ability to apply them. The best workers learn to classify variables to solve production problems. Others simply learn to classify variables. In short, while all learn how to identify problems, many don't learn to deal with the causes of the problem. Although the evidence here is mixed, it does appear that QC-circle activity has sufficiently penetrated the work force so that we cannot simply view it as a technique whereby qualified personnel use ordinary blue-collar workers to gather data for them in simple-minded fashion. . . .

Work Redesign in Japan: An Evaluation

The purposes of this section are twofold. The first is an overall evaluation of work-redesign efforts in Japan seen in comparative perspective. The second . . . involves consideration of our findings for the earlier inferences drawn from our interpretation of the Detroit-Yokohama comparison of job-mobility patterns.

In summarizing characteristics of the rather minimal experience with participatory management in the United States, the HEW task force report *Work in America* (1972, 103–10) delineated the range of decisions in which workers participate. They may determine:

1. Their own production methods.
2. The internal distribution of tasks.
3. Questions regarding internal leadership.
4. What additional tasks to take on.
5. When they will work.

With regard to job content the emphasis in the American literature on job redesign and job enlargement has been on expanding the scope of individual jobs and job rotation in particular. The HEW report also places strong emphasis on the need for profit sharing to be associated with these innovations.

At first glance these foci seem not inconsistent with the descriptions presented in the preceding chapter. To leave the matter here, however, ignores some subtle though, in the last analysis, fundamental differences in the style, content, and direction of participatory management in the two nations.

The Basic Differences
The reorganization of work at Toyota Auto Body is more radical than most U.S. activities in this area. The head of the personnel section summarizes their approach as follows:

> We believe that an individual job and the way it is performed must be activities into which are woven the original ideas of workers, not to be thought of as simply a fixed job which superiors order one to perform. The individual jobs must be carefully thought out with this aim in mind.

We may ask ourselves what obstacles would have to be removed in the United States before we could imagine successful institutionalization of these seemingly utopian assumptions. First, it may be noted, machine design is by and large not a function of each specific company. Rather, it is a highly centralized operation that came into being in the middle of the nineteenth century in the United States. The machine-tool industry developed as a response to the common processes and problems in the production of a wide range of disparate products in a variety of different industries. This technology involved the spread of specialized machines, each designed to insure speedy performance of limited tasks. This presumed a sequential productive process involving large numbers of special-purpose machines, with each one advancing the product one small step further toward its completed form. It was the growing nineteenth-century success in development of machine technology which culminated in the assembly-line system in the early twentieth century. The tendency towards "pre-set tools" which culminated in the revolutionary numerical-control machine technology of the post–World War II period reduced the skills required by the machine operator (Rosenberg 1972, 98–110).

Yet this perspective is based on a conceptualization of technological change exclusively in terms of large-scale innovations. Nathan Rosenberg (1972, 164) notes that much less attention is paid to small-scale, often anonymous, improvements in design and minor adjustments and modifications of practices. Stinchcombe (1974, 8, 17–18, 30) makes the same point in resisting "the easy theoretical distinction between innovation and routine administration." Only by innovation can the routine problems of production be solved. The cumulative impact of frequent small-scale changes can be enormous, and without their consideration approaches to technological change are incomplete. These small-scale changes, often introduced by workers and foremen, are far more critical to raising industrial efficiency than is commonly realized. It is here at the "margins," in short, that workers may have their most significant opportunity of determining production methods. The extent to which the opportunity is exploited may be treated as variable. In this connection, American organizational sociologists generally assume that because a task is routinized, job occupants do not have the potential for nonroutinized decision making. They interpret this situation as one in which job designers are simply responding to a universal organizational logic in situations of high clarity of task objectives, high predictability of expected problems, and high capability in developing regular procedures for handling these problems (e.g., Dornbusch and Scott 1975, 82–83). Our analysis suggests to the contrary that the potential organizational benefits of greater employee discretion may be higher in routinized tasks than is commonly recognized. In this sense American organizational sociologists confuse organizational logic with the political power of engineers to make a particular set of decisions.

Historically in Japan and the United States, as with all successful industrializers, industrialization has been associated with the breaking down of traditional skills. Concomitant with this development has been the separation of work associated with conception (intellectual work) from that associated with execution (manual work). As Frederick Taylor himself wrote:

> Establishing a planning department merely concentrates the planning and much other brainwork in a few men especially fitted for their task and trained in their especial lines, instead of having it done, as heretofore in most cases, by high priced mechanics, well fitted to work at their trades, but poorly trained for work more or less clerical in nature. (Taylor 1947, 65–66, cited in Braverman 1974)

Historically this involved a process of management systematically gathering up knowledge of the work process and then distributing it to individual workers in the form of detailed instructions. Such arrangements do not begin to tap the potential for training and knowledge that workers have. Indeed it is a strategy to systematically denude workers of this potential (Braverman 1974, 84).

Within the Japanese automobile industry the process of breaking down traditional craft skills and substituting semiskilled jobs and assembly-line operations took place in the 1950s and 1960s. Toyota Auto Body did not establish its first fully mass production operation until 1957; at the time the No. 1 Kariya assembly plant was the industry's most modern facility. Now Toyota Auto Body managers are seeking to reverse these historical processes.

In the United States, as a "natural" corollary of having engineers design the basic machinery, the engineers, along with line managers, have assumed responsibility for job design as well (Glueck 1974, 111). Industrial engineers generally adopt the norm that a machine design which breaks the operation down to (cheaper) less skilled operations is a superior one. These are the labor "requirements" which shape their design (Braverman 1974, 199–200). In the American auto industry it is not uncommon to hear industrial engineers talk about the need to design equipment that is "idiot proof." They mean, of course, that it must be designed to minimize any possible interference by those blue-collar workers who must operate it on a daily basis. Toyota Auto Body managers are increasingly questioning these assumptions, and they are doing so in two ways. First they are bringing the industrial engineers into working relationships with the workers and line managers through such activities as QC circles and improvement groups, and secondly they are trying to upgrade the level of worker competence through education; this permits workers to participate more fully in the design of the production process.

The following discussion should give us further insight into the implications of these different strategies. When a persistent quality problem develops the tendency of American auto companies is to turn not only to the inspectors, as noted earlier, but to the engineers, to see if the problem can be designed away. Thus, for example, the American auto producers are increasingly moving away from nut-and-bolt assemblies to rivets. The reason is that nuts must be tightened with just the right torque to insure that they will not loosen when subject to vibration. This has been a significant problem for U.S. auto companies, as reflected in consumer complaints. Unwilling to wrestle with the task of upgrading worker quality, they are turning to rivets, which require considerably less worker skill and discretion. As an alternate solution an auto parts firm began in 1977 to market a newly developed "microencapsulated poxy" that automatically creates a permanent seal when nuts are fastened to bolts. In both developments we see the tendency of the U.S. auto industry to look for technological solutions to their quality problem. A similar response may be seen in the change of types of welding operations for putting panels together. The U.S. auto industry joins exterior body panels by flanging the panels and welding the flanges. The Japanese carmakers often use lap joints with exposed welds where the panels overlap. The flanged joint offers two "advantages": (1) Dimensional control does not require dependence on worker care and skill. (2) Appearance does not require as precise positioning of the weld gun.

The contrast with the Japanese auto industry in these respects is instructive. In terms of design one might call Toyota "backward," since they still rely heavily on nut-and-bolt assemblies and lap joint welding operations. Yet they have consistently produced a superior product as measured by independent quality ratings; it is a more labor intensive operation relying on higher quality labor. They have been able to do so by working to upgrade labor quality rather than seeking to simplify skill requirements whenever quality problems arise. But to present the matter in this fashion conceals the nature of the ongoing process. Because labor quality is high they have fewer incentives to seek out technological solutions which lower skill requirements. This particular example should not be overdone. There has been an enormous amount of technological innovation in the Japanese auto industry over the last decade, often involving the simplification of tasks and including, for example, welding operations. But the primary incentives for these innovations have been the labor shortage, and a desire to reduce physically exhausting and tedious tasks and increase international competitive ability (Koshiro 1977).

Our discussion thus far suggests that a major obstacle to institutionalizing the participation of workers in job design is the conflict with the jurisdiction of industrial engineers. Our conclusion, however, is that the jurisdictional boundaries are not as fixed as at first appears. A second obstacle to increasng worker involvement in job design lies in the attitudes and vested interests of workers, managers, and unions in existing job structures. Grinker and associates (1970, 9) summarize the American situation as follows:

> Even if an industry wanted to alter significantly certain job structures quickly, these patterns have been enforced by unionism and entrenchment of existing workers to the extent that they are almost immutable without cataclysmic consequences, or so most employers and union leaders believe.

Although U.S. manufacturers have a relatively free hand to reorganize jobs below the level of skilled worker, there can hardly be meaningful job enrichment if semiskilled workers are systematically excluded from the job tasks requiring the greatest discretion and responsibility. Monopolization of these tasks by skilled workers is a serious barrier to job redesign. The contrast with the approach adopted by Toyota Auto Body managers is stark. In the context of diffuse job definitions the Japanese manager seeks to organize job duties around qualified individuals. From an employer point of view the costs resulting from ambiguity in job definitions are compensated for by great flexibility in adaptive capacity. The union adopts a hands-off policy. From an employee point of view there is the benefit of having a higher probability of being assigned to jobs that suit one's interest and/or serve company goals. On the cost side there is less protection for the worker in terms of insuring that individual interests will not be sacrificed to company interests. In America, the employer benefits from having clearly defined jobs so that job occupants can be more easily treated as replaceable parts. This provides an important kind of flexibility for employers, though it is, so to speak, a flexibility in using the occupant himself. These differences may reflect the different supply-and-demand functions for labor in the respective nations. Historically labor surplus and weak unions in Japan have allowed employers to take the initiative in constructing job structures. These different strategies may also rest on different conceptions of human nature. In assessing the distinctive job-related worker evaluation strategies practiced by India, Malaysia, Singapore, Pakistan, Canada, and the U.S.A., as compared to ability-based evaluations in Japan and Thailand, Shiba (1973, 65) concludes:

> Those countries relying on job-related evaluation presuppose inequality of human ability and believe that these differences must be recognized and assessed and jobs allocated accordingly. The basic assumption in countries like Japan and Thailand, however, seems to be that human ability is basically constant; that any employee satisfying minimum requirements will, given experience, be able to do any job.

He attributes these differences in perception to the degree of cultural homogeneity in a given society, with the belief in equality of human ability stemming from a more homogeneous cultural base.

It is interesting that the American and Japanese educational systems have been contrasted in exactly the same terms. Cummings (1976) notes the strong egalitarian character of Japanese elementary schools relative to U.S. schools. In contrast to the American schools, which assume that individuals have different abilities, Japanese teachers are less ready to concede the point and act accordingly. Instead they assume that differences in performance result from lack of effort and other factors that can be overcome.

In summary, the HEW report's list of decisions in which workers participate gives us a sense of tinkering, while managers at Toyota Auto Body are acting to enable workers to control the content of the job itself. In the analysis of most Western scholars and engineers, technology is usually designated as the critical causal agent. In line with the heritage of scientific management, work is assigned and jobs designed on the basis of the perceived imperatives flowing from the mechanical processes to be carried out by relating the machine and the man, in a way which maximizes efficiency. This conception limits our capacity to examine all available options, though its dominance, no doubt, reflects the social, political, economic, and cultural conditions prevailing in America. This is not to say conditions are so different in Japan that managers at Toyota Auto Body have entirely succeeded in their efforts to weave worker ideas into the very concept of the job itself. They themselves see this as a policy to be seriously pursued, though hardly at all costs.

The Japanese efforts do have many parallels to the new approaches being explored in Western Europe. In particular, the methods developed at the Tavistock Institute in London and applied in Norway and Sweden through the work of Einar Thorsrud appear quite similar (Emery and Trist 1969; Thorsrud 1969). The emphasis in their approaches is on the development of the organization as an "open socio-technical system" which focuses on the interaction of social and technical factors. The aim is to develop small work groups which maintain a high level of independence and autonomy. As a consequence it is expected that jobs will be enriched, individual responsibility increased, and learning possibilities enhanced. These same statements could be applied to the Japanese efforts.

Controlled Participation

A second characteristic of job redesign at Toyota Auto Body is that the emphasis is not on participation per se, but rather on achieving the consent of workers for policies which management wants to pursue, as well as on guiding workers in the direction in which management would like to see them move. This is apparent in the rhetoric the company uses; the term *sanka* (participation) is not used, rather the focus in on *nattokusei* (consent) and *kobetsu shidō* (individual guidance). Quite apart from rhetoric, the variety of documents and practices discussed in the previous chapter should amply demonstrate this characteristic. We have here a carefully controlled participation in which management often takes the lead informally or formally in initiating policies that workers are then guided to accept and pursue. The operation of the QC circles clearly corresponds to this description, as do the programs for career guidance and life planning. In a similar vein, when asked if the job redesign program at the company was aimed more at the increase of responsibility of each individual employee rather than at employee participation in management, a company official stated:

> Yes, this is correct. We believe that the heavier duties (more important jobs) will enhance employees' motivation to see their jobs as a challenge. We believe that taking jobs with heavier duties is related to employees' participation. . . . The QC circles in our company necessarily result in participatory management because they heighten job quality.

Job redesign occurs in a context of unquestioned management authority at Toyota Auto Body, though the maintenance of this authority is something that the managers self-consciously work very hard to uphold. The belief that they can build increasing responsibility into employees' jobs suggests the considerable trust and confidence that Japanese managers have in their employees. Above all, they do not appear to be concerned that given worker groups will acquire the power to keep their area of work under their own control free from outside interference. Crozier (1964, 153–59) describes such an outcome in a French firm; it is a situation where the power of (maintenance) workers is insured by their exclusive knowledge and the resultant unpredictability of their behavior. There are a number of possible explanations for Japanese management's self-confidence in this regard. The increased responsibility given to workers occurs in a context in which management controls the training, the amount of job rotation, and the content of career patterns. This gives management enormous leverage in preventing the hardening of worker privilege. Furthermore, foremen maintain responsibility for QC circles in their workshop; thus the existing structure of line authority is not threatened. Moreover, management cultivates the ideology of shared organizational goals to legitimize still further its attempt to limit "selfish" efforts devoted to the exclusive enhancement of worker rights and privileges. It is, of course, possible that management may be misreading the situation. There is a line of reasoning about organizational change and worker participation, in particular, which emphasizes its incremental character (Jenkins 1973, 291–93). Small changes work their way through the system gradually modifying structural arrangements, so that in the long run profound changes, often unnoticed in the beginning, end up transforming organizational practices and power relationships. Whether this will be the case with job redesign in Japan is not something we can predict with confidence. As yet management maintains firm control of the innovative process.

Another approach to examining the degree of control management retains over the work process is to directly examine decision-making concerning the determination of the speed of production, the number of items to be produced, and the size of the workgroup. These are crucial decisions for both the firm and employees. We would expect that if job redesign were being implemented in the fashion envisioned by the report *Work in America*, workers would have significant inputs into the decision-making process. Instead we find that at Toyota Auto Body the speed of production, number of units to be produced, and size of the workgroup are decided through consultation at three levels, by the department chief, the section chief, and the supervisor and foreman. These production decisions are made for the section level, not for individual jobs. It is the responsibility of the section chief and lower-level supervisors to set the workpace for the workgroup or individuals where appropriate. Workers and unions have no direct input into the determination of workpace, amount of production, and size of workgroup. To be sure, they can make their views known indirectly through complaints to the foreman if they feel that staffing is inadequate or the workpace too rapid. What about QC-circle activity? Is this not a realm in which they have a direct impact? Apparently this is not the case. Company representatives set the production goals for each workgroup; QC circles act to implement these goals whenever there is a gap between the goal and actual performance. In short, QC circles act in the framework of decisions determined by management.

This leads many Japanese scholars to see QC circles as a device to break worker collective resistance and rebuild group solidarity on the basis of management goals. Our understanding of decision making in organizations must rely heavily on a grasp of the distribution of power in the organization and how power is used. This ought to be a commonplace observation. Yet, while social scientists have treated the subject of power in organizations (e.g., Thompson 1967; Zald 1970), the subject has only recently been receiving more systematic attention (Salancik and Pfeffer 1974, 135–51). The failure to recognize the role of power in organizational decision making is even more apparent in the work of American social scientists studying Japan, many of whom still treat Japan as a consensual society with "bottom-up" participation (Vogel 1975). What our analysis reveals is that the heavy expressive and instrumental reliance on consensus in a Japanese organization is in no way incompatible with the strong exercise of management power and authority.

It is here that Japanese efforts may be clearly distinguished from Scandinavian ones. In the Swedish and Norwegian developments, the aim is to achieve a fundamental change in the basic structure of the organization, with rather open-ended possibilities for worker influence. There is a high level of public discussion, with the dialogue punctuated by concern for democracy and social justice. This has heightened worker expectations. The forward movement has been sustained by labor governments and strong union support. These conditions are not present in Japan and consequently management has been able to proceed without making radical commitments, conceding only those areas in which it is convinced its interests are being fully served. The Japanese effort focused on blue-collar employees in the private sector while as noted the Scandinavian efforts developed more as a national social and political movement. Consequently, the Scandinavian approach included public sector as well as white-collar employees. In the case of the Japanese public sector, strong conflict between the government and public sector unions discouraged any such effort. On the other hand, there is a strong class consciousness and a certain mistrust which interacts with a pragmatic cooperation between management and labor in the Scandinavian private sector that has no counterpart in Japan. This class consciousness focuses attention on relative and absolute wage levels. No discussion of new forms of work organization takes place in Scandinavia without raising important issues of wage equity and giving rise to union and worker suspicion of management motives. These are not significant issues in Japan.

One should not exaggerate these differences. Although the Swedish and Norwegian unions and the social democratic politicians have strongly shaped the public debate and thereby constrained management behavior, they have not been so active at the individual firm level. The central labor union federations fear (especially in Norway) that the existing centralized decision-making process of wage determination would be threatened by the new increase in shopfloor decision making. Consequently, although the unions support the movement in principle, they have adopted a much more passive and defensive role at the firm level than is commonly recognized. This has allowed management to play the dominant role in the articulation of shopfloor participation. Still, there is no doubt that Scandinavian management has been constrained by anticipated reactions from the unions, the social democratic parties, and the workers to an extent that has no counterpart in Japan.[12]

It was not until the late 1970s that some Japanese Socialist party and union theoreticians began seriously to consider *jishu kanri* (workers' self-management) as a new route to increased democratization and socialism (Hori 1977). They see this decentralized approach as an alternative to the centralized Soviet model, advocated by many extreme leftist members of the Socialist party, and as a means to rejuvenate a shattered Socialist party. The popular socialist leader Asukata Ichio, chairman of the Socialist Party, is particularly attracted to the Yugoslav model.

Notes

1. This section, detailing the role of Nikkeiren, draws heavily on the contribution of Nakayama Saburo (1972). Since the book is published by the Japan Federation of Employers' Associations, it may overstate its role.

2. For the prewar period, see Saxonhouse's (1974) discussion of the cotton-spinning industry.

3. Nikkeiren, while analogous in function to the National Association of Manufacturers in the United States (merged with the Chamber of Commerce in 1976), is a good deal more specialized in labor and personnel matters, and more prestigious and powerful in this area.

4. The case of the zero-defect movement (ZD) runs parallel to the evolution of the QC-circle movement to be discussed in the following section. The ZD movement had its origins in the Martin Marietta Company at their Orlando, Florida, plant in 1961, based on their experience in the aerospace industry. The program focused on adopting practices that would reduce accidents, absences, and wasted time. It may be seen as a specialized type of performance-standards program, designed to set quantitative and qualitative performance

levels for employees. General Electric adopted the ZD program in 1963, and the Defense Department advised all contractors to introduce ZD. As of 1965 an estimated 2,500 plants in the United States had ZD programs. The movement does not appear to have experienced notable expansion since that time. It has been criticized in the United States for the implicit coercion involved in "encouraging" workers to sign pledge cards and for leading to resentment among employees who interpreted the program as a criticism of their efforts (French 1974, 223).

In 1966 the Japanese Management Association dispatched a team to study ZD in the United States. Nippon Electric became the first to introduce these practices in 1965, but unlike firms in the United States, in which participation was for the most part voluntary, in Japanese firms all employees joined. ZD programs in Japan experienced immediate popularity and have grown rapidly. They have come to operate increasingly like quality-control circles.

Management-by-objective is an American personnel approach which involves the establishment of goals for individual jobs and the periodic evaluation of performance relative to these goals. In some companies this is a highly autocratic program, while in others employees participate in the setting of goals (French 1974, 384–88). Management-by-objective belongs to that class of performance-standards systems developed in particular for managerial and white-collar positions in the mid-1960s. It became quite popular among many large firms. The approach has been widely discussed and applied in Japan, with a strong emphasis on the participative components.

5. The historical treatment of QC circles in Japan and their functions draws heavily on Ishikawa (1968) and the Union of Japanese Scientists and Engineers (1975).

6. An examination of the guidelines for teaching required mathematical courses in high school shows that among the subjects expected to be covered are:

(1) Change and its recognition

The teacher should enable the pupils, through concrete examples in real phenomena, to express the change in a function's value on a graph and to approach it through the idea of changing ratios. With reference to the above, instruction should be given in the following:

(a) Change in a function's value and differential coefficients. Instruction in functions should be limited to the level of $y = ax^2 + bx + c, y = ax^3$

(b) Terms and symbols: Differential coefficients

(2) Recognition of uncertain phenomena

The teacher should have the pupils develop a statistical way of observation and thinking through the processing of data by means of survey, observations, etc., and through probability tests. With reference to the above, instruction should be given in the following:

(a) Probability of simple events
(b) Simple sampling surveys
(c) Terms and symbols: Trials and events

In addition, teachers are expected to cover one of the following three subjects: vectors and matrices, concepts of linear programming, and electronic computers and flow charts (Ministry of Education, 1976).

7. Exploitation is used in the sense of exploiting opportunities.

8. For purposes of general comparison, we may report that GM runs a fairly vigorous suggestion program that in 1969 elicited 1,037,733 proposals, of which 279,230 were adopted. Seventeen million dollars, an average of sixty-two dollars a suggestion, was paid out to employees for their suggestions. Assuming that most suggestions derived from hourly employees, this works out to 2.4 suggestions proposed per employee. The comparable figures for 1976 show a considerable drop in suggestions proposed, those adopted, and suggestions proposed per employee. The totals are 345,059 suggestions proposed, 95,487 suggestions adopted, and approximately 0.80 suggestions proposed per employee. The

average award increased to $133, but the total amount paid out dropped to $12.6 million. Needless to say, comparing General Motors with a company roughly 1 percent its size has but limited utility.

9. The cost of implementation is at best only a rough proxy for the value of the innovation.

10. The Japanese question was: *Anata no shigoto wa yarigai ga arimasu ka?* (Would you say your work was worth doing?).

11. By comparison it is estimated that in the late 1960s American automakers with facilities in the major northern production centers were losing 60 percent of their entry-level unskilled employees within their first year of employment (Grinker et al. 1970, 53). General Motors loses about 50 percent in the first six months.

12. I am indebted to Professor Sigvard Rubenowitz for the opportunity to meet with his research staff at the Department of Applied Psychology of the University of Göteborg. We had numerous discussions in the summer of 1978 concerning similarities and differences between Swedish and Japanese modes of worker participation.

References

Blauner, Robert. 1964. *Alienation and freedom*. Chicago: University of Chicago Press.
Braverman, Harry. 1974. *Labor and monopoly capital*. New York: Monthly Review Press.
Crozier, Michel. 1964. *The bureaucratic phenomenon*. Chicago: University of Chicago Press.
Cummings, William. 1976. Egalitarian education. Unpublished paper, University of Chicago.
Deming, William. 1970. *Statistical control of quality in Japan*. Proceedings of the International Conference on Quality Control, 1969. Tokyo: Union of Japanese Scientists and Engineers.
Dornbusch, Sanford, and Scott, W. Richard. 1975. *Evaluation and the exercise of authority*. San Francisco: Jossey-Bass.
Emery, F. E., and Trist, E. L. 1969. Socio-technical systems. In *Systems thinking*, ed. F. E. Emery. London: Penguin Books.
French, Wendell. 1974. *The personnel management process*. Boston: Houghton Mifflin.
Fujita, Yoshitaka, and Ishida, Hideo. 1970. *Kigyō to rōshi kankei (The enterprise and labor management relations)*. Tokyo: Chikuma Shobō.
Glueck, William. 1974. *Personnel: A diagnostic approach*. Dallas: Business Publications.
Grinker, William; Cooke, Donald; and Kirsch, Arthur. 1970. *Climbing the job ladder*. New York: E. F. Shelley and Co. Reprinted ERIC Reports, National Institute of Education, U.S. Department of Health, Education and Welfare.
Hori, Masao. 1977. Atarashii shakaishugi e no michi (Road to a new socialism). *Ekonomisuto* 55 (No. 36, August 30): 10–15.
Husen, Torsten, ed. 1967. *International study of achievement in mathematics: A comparison of twelve countries*. New York: John Wiley and Sons.
Ishikawa, Kaoru. 1968. *QC circles activities*. Tokyo: Union of Japanese Scientists and Engineers.
Japan Federation of Employer's Associations. 1971. *Waga kuni rōmu kanri no genkyō (The present situation of personnel management in our country)*. Third Personnel Management Census. Tokyo: Japan Federation of Employers' Associations.
———. 1975. *Waga kuni rōmu kanri no genkyō (The present situation of personnel management in our country)*. Fourth Personnel Management Census. Tokyo: Japan Federation of Employers' Associations.
Jenkins, David. 1973. *Job power*. New York: Doubleday.

PART V / Organizational Alternatives and Social Change

JUSE (Union of Japanese Scientists and Engineers). 1970. *1970 nendo Demingushō jushōsha narabi ni Demingushō jisshishō jushōsha hōkoku kōen yōshi (Announcement of the essential lectures for the 1970 Deming Prize winners as well as the Deming Prize winners for best execution)*. Tokyo: JUSE.

Koshiro, Kazutoshi. 1977. Humane organization of work in the plants: Production techniques and the organization of work in Japanese factories. Paper presented at the Sixth Japanese-German Economic and Social Conference, Düsseldorf, October 3–9.

McGregor, Douglas. 1960. *The human side of enterprise*. New York: McGraw-Hill.

Marsh, Robert, and Mannari, Hiroshi. 1976. *Modernization and the Japanese factory*. Princeton, N.J.: Princeton University Press.

Masutsugu, Eto. 1975. Supuraisusemento nendo no baratsuki taisaku (Measure to reduce variance in splicing cement viscosity). *FQC* 2:41–45.

Ministry of Education, Science and Culture, Japan. 1976. *Course of study for upper secondary schools in Japan*. Tokyo: Ministry of Education, Science and Culture.

Nishiyama, Daiso, and Sabao, Tsuyoshi. 1970. Technical skill evaluation system. *Proceedings*, International Conference on Quality Control, 1969. Tokyo: Union of Japanese Scientists and Engineers.

Perrow, Charles. 1972. *Complex organizations: A critical essay*. Glenview, Ill.: Scott, Foresman and Co.

Rosenberg, Nathan. 1972. *Technology and American economic growth*. New York: Harper and Row.

Salancik, Gerald, and Pfeffer, Jeffrey. 1974. The bases and use of power in organizational decision making: The case of a university. *Administrative Science Quarterly* 19:135–51.

Saxonhouse, Gary. 1974. A tale of technological diffusion in the Meiji period. *Journal of Economic History* 36:149–65.

Shewhart, W. A. 1931. *The economic control of quality of manufactured products*. New York: Van Nostrand.

Shiba, Shoji. 1973. *A cross-national comparison of labor management with reference to technology transfer*. Institute of Developing Economies Occasional Papers Series No. 11. Tokyo: Institute of Developing Economies.

Stinchcombe, Arthur. 1974. *Creating efficient industrial administrations*. New York: Academic Press.

Sugimoto, Yasuo. 1972. The advancing QC circle movement. In *Japan quality control circles*, ed. Asian Productivity Organization. Tokyo: Asian Productivity Organization.

Taira, Koji. 1970. Entrepreneurship, management, and growth of firms: Cases from Japanese business history. Paper delivered at the Conference on Micro Aspects of Development, Chicago.

Taylor, Frederick. 1947. *Scientific management*. In *Compiled writings*. New York: Harper.

Thompson, James. 1967. *Organization in action*. New York: McGraw-Hill.

Thompson, Victor. 1965. Bureaucracy and innovation. *Administrative Science Quarterly* 10:1–20.

Thorsrud, Einar. 1969. *Mot en ny bedriftsorganisasjon (Toward a new performance organization)*. Oslo: Tanum.

Tsuda, Masumi. 1977. Study of Japanese management development practices. *Hitotsubashi Journal of Social Studies* 9 (May): 1–12.

Ueno, Hiroya, and Muto, Hiromichi. 1974. The automobile industry of Japan. *Japanese Economic Studies* 3 (Fall): 3–90.

Union of Japanese Scientists and Engineers. 1975. *QC sākuru kōryō (Main points of QC circles)*. 9th printing. Tokyo: Union of Japanese Scientists and Engineers.

Vogel, Ezra, ed. 1975. *Modern Japanese organization and decision-making*. Berkeley and Los Angeles: University of California Press.

Yasui, Jiro. 1975. Rōdō no ningenka to sanka kakumei (The humanization of work and the participation revolution: A personal view of Japanese efforts). *Nihon Rōdō Kyōkai Zasshi* 17 (May): 2–16.

Zald, Mayer. 1970. *Power in organizations*. Nashville, Tenn.: Vanderbilt University Press.

26
Barriers to Organizational Democracy in Public Administration

Michael P. Smith

Numerous past attempts to restructure American public administrative agencies have floundered because of a failure by proponents of reform to anticipate and prepare for the tenacious resistance to innovation by presently advantaged power holders and the barriers to innovation embedded in the structure and culture of public bureaucracy. Any attempted administrative reform, especially one undertaken in the political world of a public organization, can expect to encounter numerous obstacles to its full or even partial realization. Organizational democracy is no exception.

This essay seeks to identify several potential political, structural, and cultural barriers which are likely to inhibit any concerted attempt to extend organizational democracy to American public administration. Building on the useful definitions of worker participation in decision making in private industry developed by Pateman (1970), the essay develops a set of definitions encompassing the forms of organizational democracy in public administration. Next, it attempts to suggest what actual organizational democracy in public organizations might look like and why it is needed; why rank and file members should enjoy more "organizational democracy."

Once this is accomplished, we turn to our major purpose, the analysis of several major barriers to work democratization in public bureaucracy. . . . The essay concludes by attempting to show that a change strategy that fosters organizational democracy by accretion or encroaching control has some likelihood of long-run success.

Defining Organizational Democracy

The vast literature on work democratization in industry uses the term "democratization" to refer to virtually everything from nonauthoritarian

---

Excerpted from "Barriers to Organizational Democracy in Public Administration," *Administration and Society* 18, no. 3 (Beverly Hills, Cal.: Sage Publications, November 1976): 275–317, and reprinted by permission of the publisher and author. Copyright 1976 by Sage Publications.

leadership styles, to mild forms of worker participation in determining working conditions, to rather extensive forms of worker self-managed enterprises. One recent essay (Garson 1974) identified over ninety different distinctions applicable to participatory work structures. Lest one despair of ever clearing away the underbrush, only three key dimensions of participation are widely applicable for comparative purposes and especially relevant to questions of organizational democracy in public enterprises. These are: (1) the *degree of influence or control over decision making* by individual employees; (2) the *organizational level* at which decisions are reached; and (3) the *type of decision* over which employee influence or control is exercised.

In the analysis which follows, our conceptualization of organizational democracy in public bureaucracy is an extension of the concept of worker participation in managerial decision making in industry developed by Pateman (1970, 67–74). Pateman distinguishes among three forms of participation by individual workers in organizational decision making: pseudo-participation, partial participation, and full participation. She further identifies two levels of management at which particular decisions are reached: higher or enterprise level decisions and lower or workshop level decisions.

By pseudo-participation is meant any management technique which involves no actual modification of the orthodox managerial authority structure, but which is designed to create a feeling of worker participation in decision making. Pseudo-participation includes such techniques as participatory leadership styles by managers, consultative mechanisms, and other symbolic devices used to persuade workers to accept decisions already reached by top management.

Partial participation refers to those decision-making situations in which each individual worker has *influence* over management with respect to making organizational decisions, although management maintains the ultimate right to decide. Pateman (1970, 70) terms such forms of participation "partial" because "the worker does not have equal power to decide the outcome of decisions but can only influence them."

Pateman (1970, 71) uses the concept "full participation" to designate those situations where collective decisions are reached by a group of equal decision makers. In this form of decision making the division between workers and managers breaks down because, in effect, the employees become the managers. Full participation is a process where "each individual member of a decision-making body has *equal power* to determine the outcome of decisions."

Each of these three types of participation is possible at either the day-to-day workshop level of decision making or at the higher level of management that involves decisions about the general policies of the overall enterprise. An employee who is a member of an autonomous or self-managed work group can be said to enjoy full participation in lower-level decision making. An employee who can influence managerial decisions relating to such issues as the pace of work, job redesign, and other matters concerning the organization of work at the shop level is engaged in partial participation at this level. Forms of worker "involvement" short of meaningful before-the-fact influence in lower-level decisions constitute pseudo-participation at this level.

Higher-level decisions refer to the kinds of policy choices involved in "running the business"—e.g., investment policies, plant location and relocation, marketing strategies, and so forth. As with lower-level decisions, worker participation at this level may take the form of either full, partial, or pseudo-participation. For Pateman (1970, 73), pure industrial democracy requires full higher-level participation by employees, directly and/or through representatives, in structures which transfer managerial power and responsibility to the workers themselves. Partial enterprise level participation requires only that the right of employees to influence managerial policies concerning the major ends and means of the enterprise be guaranteed.

In developing a working definition of organizational democracy in public administration, Pateman's distinctions concerning full, partial, and pseudo-participation may be employed as one key dimension of the degree of internal democratization of a public enterprise. Each of these degrees of participation is possible with respect to decisions made at either the lower, the middle-management, or the higher level of a public organization. Decisions at the lower level primarily concern the structure, conditions, and activities of everyday work in public administration. These include such types of decisions as the scope, functions, and authority of public unions; job design and redesign; work schedules; health and safety decisions; employee rights; and other types of decisions sometimes encompassed under the rubric "public personnel administration." Lower-level decisions also include the day-to-day discretion of lower-level workers to specifically implement policy mandates set at higher levels. . . .

Middle-management level decision making in public administration involves the general implementation of policy goals set by higher organizational levels and by external public authority. These decisions encompass functions such as mobilizing human effort and other organizational resources; internal and external communication and coordination; receiving, channeling, and responding to feedback from day-to-day policy implementation activities; and otherwise building cooperation and promoting effectiveness within the enterprise.

Higher-level decision making in public organizations entails an almost infinite variety of types of decisions involving what most generally may be termed the making of public policy. Public policy making involves moral, political, and technical choices about: (a) the proper ends or goals of public organizations, (b) the appropriate political strategy and tactics to achieve these goals, and (c) the suitable technical resources that can expeditiously achieve chosen objectives. Public policy making further involves attempts to obtain adequate knowledge of the social costs or externalities of past public policies as well as the probable intended and unintended consequences of future policy programs. Each of these general types of higher-level decisions must be included in determining the proper scope of influence or control over policy making by members of a public organization.

Why Organizational Democracy?

Why is organizational democracy needed? What can it accomplish? How can it be squared with principles of "overhead" representative democracy? Because the central purpose of this article is to examine why the odds appear to be stacked against organizational democracy, these questions can be treated here only in passing. They are raised nevertheless to show that a case for greater organizational democracy by rank-and-file members of public organizations can be made and, accordingly, that a detailed analysis of the barriers to this kind of structural change is warranted.

The first issue to be addressed is the frequent assumption that organizational democracy in public administration is inherently inconsistent with central tenets of political democracy, insofar as the former is thought to replace the formal authority over the bureaucracy held by popularly elected, representative governmental institutions with internal organs of bureaucratic self-management. In theory, although not always in practice, public agencies are already subject to the authoritative policy choices of publicly elected legislators and executives. The model of organizational democracy envisaged here does not propose to abolish these public officials or to substitute internal democratic controls for already existing formal external control mechanisms, such as legislatures, executives, courts, or elections.

Consider, however, some of the implications of the commonplace observation that the existing external democratic controls often do not work very well in practice. The growing complexity of society and public policy making inevitably shifts political choice into the bureaucratic realm. Public bureaucracy often escapes effective control by elected officials, in any event, whether its internal structure is hierarchical, oligarchic, or democratic. Because this is so, there is no *inherent* reason why accountability must be a zero sum game. To the extent that internal organizational democracy can increase the responsibility and accountability of administrative actions, it may function to "fill in the gaps," so to speak, where external political controls have failed to reach.

Consider just a few such "gaps" where democratic control of administrative behavior through the neat chain of electoral control of public officials, oversight by these officials, and the hierarchical chain of command has failed to materialize: the frequent avoidance of policy issues by political candidates; low voter turnout in primary elections; class biases in electoral participation at all levels; the growth of low visibility special district governments, with little public input and even less control; the growing prominence of expertise; the growing scale and complexity of government at all levels; the daily arbitrary discretionary practices of policemen, schoolteachers, welfare workers, and other lower-level civil servants; the displacement of geographic-territorial service delivery systems by complex functional intergovernmental policy domains. In view of these and other discrepancies between the theory and practice of representative democracy, organizational democracy may be viewed as a supplementary control mechanism that may serve to increase bureaucratic accountability and responsiveness to the extent that it succeeds in infusing each member of the organizational polity with an increased sense of moral responsibility for his or her public choices. If properly structured, organizational democracy may actually increase the effectiveness of public organizations in achieving the broad mandates set down by external public authority, thereby enhancing rather than detracting from the efficacy of elected office holders.

Even in circumstances where no major gaps exist, where external control mechanisms are working relatively well, there is no inherent contradiction between representative democracy and organizational democracy. Worker controlled working units, just like top-management controlled working units, must operate within the constraints set by external public authority. This is true of all political entities, as is the fact that worker controlled units also would be subject to such external constraints as the Constitution and Bill of Rights, the courts, political protest, consumer-citizen-clientele representatives, oversight hearings, ombudsmen, and a myriad of other channels for the participation and representation of stakeholders in the larger polity and society.

As Garson (1975, 24) has noted, the self-management model of organizational control is a mixed system rather than a purely decentralist system. If the workers in a self-managed public organization are to assume moral responsibility for both the positive and negative outputs of a public enterprise, they must be given the moral right to decide on the everyday courses of action that they are to take; but this right is conditional rather than absolute. In an organizational democracy operating in a larger democratic society this right would exist only "within parameters set by representative government," and would be subject to a corresponding right to veto their decisions by other affected stakeholders. Viewed in this light, organizational democracy adds an additional channel for both participation and representation to the larger society. It must still operate within the boundaries set by higher-level representative institutions. It is still constrained by outside stakeholders, who remain free to withhold their consent and raise political issues respecting administrative decisions they do not view as jointly beneficial.

Having addressed this central issue, what else can be said for organizational democracy in public administration? First, increasing opportunities for member participation in responsible decision making can be expected to facilitate the development of members' interpersonal political and social skills—listening, articulating, clarifying, building support. These skills, in turn, can be expected to work against the sometimes abrasive and even hostile relationships that currently exist between bureaucrats and their clients. To the degree that client-consumer-citizen participation structures can be made workable, this same process of social learning may extend to client, citizen, and consumer representatives, thereby facilitating mutual adjustment.

Second, the representative as well as the participatory aspects of organizational democracy may be regarded as a means to avoid the all too frequent tendency of lower- and middle-level administrators to avoid personal responsibility for decision making by passing the buck ever upward. If higher level managers are chosen by or otherwise formally accountable to organizational members, the members become implicated in higher-level management in a more direct and responsible way than they were as mere employees. In a fully developed organizational democracy, the members as well as the clients of an organization gradually could be expected to experience a breakdown of the distinction between the workers who directly contact the public and the managers who make rules and procedures. As mutual reciprocity replaces formal hierarchy as the cement which binds members together as a working unit, each member's responsibility for collective decision making increases. As the sense as well as the reality of decision-making responsibility increases, the public employee is less likely to justify buck passing to himself and less able to justify it to dissatisfied clients or the general public. In this way, increased democratization of public organizations may actually enhance the effective influence of external stakeholders and control mechanisms, by rendering it impossible in principle for a public administrator to pass the buck.

Third, in many complex organizations that are hierarchically structured a good part of the average worker's day is wasted, as much psychic energy that might otherwise be channeled into creative goal achievement is spent coping with pent-up resentments against "the boss" or other sources of low autonomy, job insecurity, and frustration deriving from the hierarchical structure of work. In an organizational democracy, as workers are given increased power commensurate with their right to function as autonomous moral agents, responsible for their own product, the preoccupation with these sources of resentment can be expected to decrease. Once this drain on members' psychic energy is freed, more useful time and energy can be devoted to work itself.

The severe role conflicts experienced by many rank and file public employees (Lipsky 1971, 391–409) constitute an additional source of psychic strain leading to job dissatisfaction and poor performance. Such conflicts arise when the resources provided to the "street level bureaucrat" are inadequate to cope with the expectations that others have concerning effective performance of his role. They also arise when the lower-level bureaucrat's superiors expect him to act in one way and his clients expect him to act otherwise. Organizational democracy in public administration may serve to reduce both of these sources of role conflict. By increasing workers' autonomy, power, and opportunity for creativity, organizational democracy can be expected to increase job satisfaction, thereby increase productivity, and, in turn, maximize scarce resources. More can be accomplished with less. Assuming that the "savings" so realized are poured back into the public enterprise, the problem of inadequate resources can be reduced, and so also the sense of role conflict deriving from this source. Furthermore, in a fully developed organizational democracy there would be no "superiors," strictly speaking, whose authority was derived entirely independently of their nominal subordinates. Thus, "superior versus clientele" conflicts could be expected to decline. Since each member would be directly responsible for his own as well as indirectly for all other organizational outputs, if such conflicts did emerge they would not automatically be resolved in favor of superiors, as now is often the case. In hierarchical organizations lower level personnel commonly "accede" to higher authority in such instances, bouncing their client's problem upward in the hierarchy, with the excuse that responsiveness to the client's particular need "is not my job." As already noted, by definition, organizational democracy is incompatible with such an excuse.

A fourth argument on behalf of organizational democracy in public administration is that it may increase public-bureaucratic contacts, and thereby the vitality of the political process. In the sense that each organizational member is a potential target, organizational democracy creates more visible targets for external sources of political influence and control to contact. Targets not only are more visible, they also are more personally responsible. Contacting public administrators makes good sense under such conditions, since it is reasonable to assume that because no one in the organization is powerless, any direct contact is likely to yield some results. Increased citizen-bureaucratic contacts mean more checks on arbitrary internal decision making and greater accountability to the public.

Fifth, the operation of the Peter Principle may be less likely under conditions of organizational democracy. The practice of internally electing managers would replace the practices of promotion based on time-in-rank or on the cultivation of an upward churning posture, both of which often account for the rise of management personnel to positions for which they are ill suited. Cole's view of leadership under conditions of functional representation is germane in this respect (see Pateman 1970, 37–41). Although day-to-day affairs in a democratically structured public organization would require elected managers to exercise personal judgment, they would be subject to the effective, because reciprocal, scrutiny of other organizational members. Members might advise, criticize, and, as a last resort, recall the representative management. Such an arrangement might well be an effective way to avoid the "training for subservience" which Cole so feared. This participatory organizational aspect of continuous reciprocal advice, criticism, and responsibility might also be a route to more innovative problem solving in complex, multicausal situations, where the more numerous vantage points offered by many heads could be expected to generate more creative options than the judgments of a few.

In summing up, it has been argued that organizational democracy in public administration is worth experimenting with. It may be viewed as a supplementary control mechanism which can serve to develop members' interpersonal skills, decrease the incidence of buck passing, increase job satisfaction and productivity, increase public-bureaucratic contacts, produce more talented managers, and engender more creative solutions to public problems. . . .

Barriers to Work Democratization in Public Bureaucracy

. . . [I]n practice public agencies present several unmistakable barriers to worker participation, especially in higher level decision making. Four characteristics of the institutional and environmental setting of public organizations particularly inhibit the chances for internal democratization of public administration. These include the political needs of public administrators, professional elitism, the folkways of public organizations, and the uncertainty of their environments. To these four properties may be added a fifth barrier—the threat of competition from other less politically costly models of organizational change.

Political Stakes of Public Managers
Politics constrain public administrators. In the interdependent political environment of public bureaucracy, high-level career officials are likely to develop strategies designed to protect their power and affirm their independence from other centers of power. Lacking autonomy and possessing limited resources, public managers spend much of their time in the quest for ever greater "operating room." They feel constrained to satisfy a multiplicity of needs, e.g., the need to secure executive and legislative support; the need to deal with the scrutiny of the mass media; the need to establish working clientele relationships with organized in-

terest groups; the need to deal with a variety of unorganized demands. In the face of such multiple pressures, public managers often pursue self-protective strategies designed to maximize their elbow room. Many of the strategies thus undertaken are incompatible with the goal of work democratization in public administration. The following self-protective strategies are particularly germane.

"Play your cards close to your chest." In a general sense, government secrecy tends to be the norm rather than the exception. Most public organizations have at their core a small circle of trusted and loyal officials with whom information at the disposal of agency heads is fully shared. Beyond this circle, information is often hoarded for fear of leaks, political backlash, or simply loss of control over events. . . .

"Be a team player." This strategy has been used so often by so many agency heads to cope with threatening internal innovations that little comment is necessary. It goes something like this: "In this hostile political environment we must protect our flanks from actual and potential 'enemies' (in Congress, the media, new clientele groups, and the like). We must stick together in the face of competing power centers. Only a united front strategy will allow this agency to survive unscathed. Any reform which encourages internal dissensus (e.g., democratization) will jeopardize our external power position. There will be time enough to discuss such reforms when the environment becomes less hostile (which it never does). For now internal loyalty is necessary. Be a team player."

"The costs of retooling are great." The public manager who is intimately familiar with the personal, professional, and political routines of his colleagues is in a better position to decisively influence agency policy than one who is not. Familiarity with the dynamics of informal organization is often a potent political resource. Since work democratization can be expected to disrupt such familiar routines, administrators wishing to maintain the advantages accruing to them by knowledge of the organization's various standard operating procedures (and their political and psychological basis) can be expected to win allies *within* their organizations by stressing the undesirable costs of change to various participants. . . .

Professional Elitism in the Career Civil Service

Anyone wishing to maintain present power arrangements within public organizations (particularly at the federal level) is in a position to arouse the "self-conception" of professional members of the career civil service in ways that mobilize latent biases against democratic decision-making. Given the present system of recruitment, training, and indoctrination in the career civil service system, it is relatively easy to reinforce predispositions favoring restricted decision making. . . .

The self-conception of the typical career civil servant is shaped by a long period of professional training which places "a relatively high premium on conformity of individual behavior with the norms and mores of the system, and with the purposes of the organization as they are perceived and defined by the system" (Mosher 1968, 152). These mores place heavy emphasis on the value of technical expertise in policy implementation; on the need for specialized education and accreditation as a "union card" granting entry into agency policy-making positions; on rank and status within the profession as hierarchical badges qualifying their possessors to top jobs in the agency; and on deep-seated commitment to the professional discipline. In short, these values amount to a rationale for professional elitism in agency policy making.

Present members of the federal career civil service enjoy a near-monopoly of the top jobs, dominating influence on agency policies, and preferential rewards (Mosher 1969, 150–151). Their experience reinforces their self-conception as rightful guardians of the public interest. To suggest to such persons that members of the general or the collective service can usefully contribute to achieving the goals of the agency by even partial participation in decisions involving political ends and means is likely to fall on deaf ears. They are much more likely to be responsive to appeals to uphold the integrity of their professional expertise. To wit, "If they knew what we know they could legitimately participate. But they don't, so they can't. . . ."

The Folkways of Public Organizations

Over the predictions of some organization theorists (see Berkley 1971)—that because of the increasing education level and professionalization of government service, public organizations of the future will develop a more "thinking and reflective," broad-minded, democratic, and problem-oriented personality type—stands the harsh reality of research on political decision making in public organizations. Here we find a rather less optimistic picture.

Routinized Consultation Practices. Routinized habits and customary procedures for gathering information frustrate the flow of diverse information inputs and evaluations needed to cope with pressing problems. Power holders in many public organizations tend to establish informal consultation patterns sometimes termed the "informal communications system." Often these patterns serve merely to reinforce the ideological or policy preferences of those with the top jobs. In other cases they result from the desire for speed and convenience on the part of administrators operating under time constraints. In either case, over time, such patterns of consultation become ingrained habits and comforting, familiar rituals which practitioners are unlikely to readily relinquish.

Familiar consultation patterns are often converted from means to ends. They become valued for their own sake. They are the most prominent among a variety of "standard operating procedures" (SOPs) which characterize most organizations, but which seem especially prevalent in public organizations. These are the institutionalized folkways which persist for as long as they continue to serve the power needs of organizational elites, the maintenance and survival needs of complex organizations, and the personal identification needs of the most fully socialized organizational members. . . .

The Uses of the Organizational Vocabulary. Bureaucracies are prone to the development of a unique set of concepts and modes of expression—the organizational vocabulary. To the outsider the technical language style by which bureaucrats conceive and depict reality is seen as mindless "gobbledygook." Political analysts have focused on the symbolic uses of this language style. The organizational vocabulary may be used to insulate the administrator from outside pressures by affording him a smokescreen of technical competence which is reassuring to the public. This is doubtless often the case. However, frequent use of the prevailing organizational vocabulary can be as deadening to the critical faculties of the administrator as it sometimes is to the outsider. To facilitate easy internal communication, organizations often develop conceptual frameworks that screen out some aspects of reality and heighten others. These simplifying concepts (e.g., the domino theory) become reified classification schemes. For the users of the organizational vocabulary over time, its categories become "attributes of the real world rather than mere conventions" (March and Simon 1958, 165). As Perrow (1972, 152) observes, "Anything that does not fit into these concepts is not easily communicated.". . .

In addition to the operational codes of particular bureaucracies—shaped by their unique tasks and customs, their cherished forms, and the conceptual frameworks developed to support these—proponents of organizational democracy also must face the emerging ideology of technical problem solving that increasingly has come to characterize any modern bureaucracy. This overarching ideology is an assertion of the general superiority of technical and expert decisions over decisions made by ordinary persons by means of common sense, moral reasoning, or simply subjective human preference. General bureaucratic norms of objective problem identification, efficient selection of technical means, and apolitical policy implementation are antipathetical to any political process for identifying, choosing among, and implementing policies. This is especially true of a democratic political process which demands that moral and evaluational choices of nonexpert organizational citizens and citizens in general be factored into decision making.

. . . [S]ome particular organizational ideologies may be more problematic for the emergence of organizational democracy than others. . . . In public bureaucracy the collective weight of the traditional intellectual baggage of "economy and efficiency," hierarchical control, and the passive public "servant" as principles of public management still encumber the ideological belief system of many public administrators, even though the daily discretionary authority exercised by most top and many middle managers, and even some "street level bureaucrats" (Lipsky 1971), belies such norms. Proposals to partially institutionalize practices which have been regarded as deviations from sound administrative principles are unlikely to penetrate the ideological barriers to change. In public bureaucracy, "built in norms of efficiency and economy, reinforced by public pressures for same, can function as constraints against administrative freedom to experiment with 'less efficient' management styles and processes" (Meade 1971, 176). . . .

Environmental Uncertainty and its Consequences

Some of the "new public administration" literature treats the rapid pace of technological change as a harbinger of more democratic work structures. In capsule form this argument boils down to the assumption that the well-educated new recruits to the public service equate centralization and hierarchy with organizational rigidity. Democratic and decentralized decision-making processes, in contrast, are seen as capable of bringing greater flexibility to public organization. This increased flexibility and sensitivity to turbulence, in turn, is seen as rendering organizations capable of coping effectively with the new environmental problem of "permanent temporariness." The logic of events—i.e., the obvious inability of traditional structures to satisfactorily deal with rapid change—is seen as a potent force which will sweep along even the most hide-bound traditionalist in the winds of change. In short, the pressures exerted by new political forces, by new social values, and by the inexorable march of technological change will force public organizations to reconstruct themselves in ways enabling them to flexibly shift organizational values, goals, techniques, and operating procedures.

While this vision of the organizational future is comforting to persons distressed by the obvious inadequacies of past and present public administration, it is certainly not inevitable. Several difficulties stand out when past organizational experiences are considered.

Fear of Uncertainty. First is the psychological impact of turbulence and uncertainty. The above vision of the organizational future is somewhat overly rationalistic. That is, it assumes that people in organizations who see the futility of the present practices will behave rationally in reconstructing their tools for dealing with a changed situation. But past history is riddled with examples of public men burying their heads in the sand, because of the insecurity, anxiety, and fear of the unknown engendered by a pace of change that they regard as too rapid or too uncertain. Thus, greater environmental turbulence outside a bureaucracy may lead to greater inertia within. Individual members (particularly long-time members who have passed through other turbulent periods) are as likely as not to take a "why take a chance? . . . this too shall pass" attitude. This ostrich-like stoicism is likely to force a heavy burden of proof on change agents on restructuring power arrangements and decision-making practices in public bureaucracy. Avoiding the stress engendered by new internal demands serves to reduce fears of risk and uncertainty. Proponents of work democratization must expect to face the tendency to cope with environmental uncertainty that is seen as "beyond mastery" by retreating into the known and therefore "masterable" elements of one's life—the routine regularities of business as usual. Given the psychological impact of the present social structure, fear of risk and uncertainty is a pervasive phenomenon. To overcome this barrier to organizational restructuring it is necessary to develop an answer to the following question recently posed by Kaufman (1971, 10): "Since some regularities are needed, and all required regularities have unpleasant features, why risk known imperfections for unknown ones?"

Rapid Responses to Turbulence. Perhaps an even greater danger than this ostrich-like posture is the tendency of public authorities to restrict rather than expand decision-making prerogatives in times of actual or perceived external crisis. This narrowing of the circle of key decisions is usually justified by the very arguments which some analysts see as leading inevitably to greater democratization—e.g., "In an environmentally turbulent situation, swift adaptations are required. If we took the time to touch base with a wider circle of sources of information, advice, and evaluation, the situation would have deteriorated. It was necessary to respond rapidly to the runaway pace of change, to a condition of permanent temporariness." In practice, the psychological impact of rapid change often leads to greater short-term centralization, secrecy, and decision-making elitism in public organizations rather than to more decentralization, openness, and democratic participation. . . .

Turbulence and Interest Conflicts. Most public organizations, unlike private ones in capitalistic settings, are confronted with a multiplicity of demands and expectations regarding how public authority ought to be used. The goals of business and industry, while varying somewhat between what Galbraith (1973) terms the "planning sector" (growth, predictability of rate of return on investment, long-term profitability) and the "market sector" (short-term profit), are mainly unidirectional and are far simpler to pursue than are the goals of public organization. Even many proponents of worker self-management in industry do not argue that self-managed enterprises should stop making watches or plywood in order to earn fair profits by increased productivity in favor of, say, ending racial discrimination or even going out of business. (Their quarrel tends to be over the fair and equal distribution of decision-making power and surplus profit rather than the abolition of either.) But these more fundamental and more complex goal conflicts are the very kinds of external demands and expectations that are part of the daily environment of many public organizations. Consider, as one example, the U.S. Department of Housing and Urban Development (HUD). A variety of organized and emergent interest groups expect this agency to subsidize suburban housing development, end discrimination in housing, build public housing, renew cities, relocate displaced families, encourage widespread "citizen participation" in community development, and halt development policies which destroy low-income housing, neighborhood viability, and historically significant buildings. Several of these goals are incompatible when simultaneously pursued. In short, the environments of public organizations are more complex, more turbulent, and more laden with demands than are the environments of most private economic organizations whose main worries are customers and suppliers.

This relatively greater complexity and turbulence poses several major difficulties for proponents of organizational democracy in public administration. In the first place, environmental complexity and turbulence prompts the administrators of many public organizations to frenetically search for ways to simplify, stabilize, and thereby render their environmental pressures more predictable. Greater predictability means greater potential for control of the external environment. But the pressures to simplify a truly complex environment can lead bureaucrats right back into some of the previously discussed oversimplification problems—ideological rigidity, reliance on the familiar, "team player" defensiveness, and the like. Such forms of bureaucratic behavior are likely to lead to the screening out or dismissal of even widely supported worker participation schemes as unrepresentative, "utopian," "faddish," or "lacking in clout."

A second, related difficulty facing proponents of organizational democracy is the widespread practice of clientelism. One of the most reliable methods that administrative agencies have used to stabilize their environment against turbulent external pressures is to find a potentially supportive organized clientele group, cultivate that group's political support, and ultimately co-opt that group formally or informally into the agency's decision-making process. Thus, to return to our earlier example, bankers, home builders, and real estate interests have become supportive clientele groups of the Federal Housing Administration within HUD. The American Legion enjoys similar "consultative participation" in managing the Veterans Administration (Wilson 1973, 317). Once such mutually advantageous marriages have been consummated, and as long as the political advantages remain roughly reciprocal, both the agency and the interest group that has gained this "preferred access" to policy formulation (see Smith 1974, 3–32) can be expected to resist any attempt to restructure the public organization in ways that might jeopardize the relationship. Resistance to change is likely to be especially intense on the part of the threatened interest group. "Interest groups inveigh against changes that disrupt the relationships they have established with the old structure" (Kaufman 1971, 12). In the case of the most well-organized and politically potent clientele groups, the attack is likely to be more than merely verbal. Clientelism, then, may be yet another practical barrier to work democratization in public administration.

Clientelism, as presently structured, may pose theoretical as well as practical difficulties. If organized clientele groups were themselves democratically structured they would not, in principle, pose theoretical problems for proponents of participatory democratic organizations. As Pateman (1976, 13) has observed, "[o]rganizational democracy does not preclude . . . representation of a community council on an enterprise council (or vice versa); both are part of one participatory democratic society." However, many of the currently most successful clientele groups tend to be oligarchically rather than democratically structured. They are run by relatively permanent organizational elites rather than by accountable representatives of the organizational community, subject to the kind of internal accountability mechanisms discussed earlier. They thus constitute a problem in democratic theory as well as a practical obstacle to reform. . . .

Competition From Other Innovative Models

A final barrier to organizational democracy in public administration emerges from the spate of less comprehensive alternative models of organizational change available to administrators forced to restructure public bureaucracy. If the foregoing analysis is valid, it is not difficult to imagine the public manager choosing alternatives such as "project groups," "management by objectives," or "job rotation" rather than consenting to policies designed to extend the right of participation in public policy making to all employees of the organization. These other reforms also address problems of work alienation, agency ineffectiveness, and failure to tap the creative potential of agency personnel. Yet each entails changes which are likely to be perceived as far less threatening to existing power arrangements than internal democratization of decision-making authority.

Consider these three alternatives in turn. Proponents of "organization development" like Bennis and Slater (1968) and Kirkhart (1971, 127–164) advocate the development of a wide variety of temporary, non-career, project-oriented work groups. Such "temporary organizations" are comprised of teams of diverse problem-solving specialists. Work life in the temporary organization is collegially structured. Leadership patterns are situational, growing from the requirements of particular tasks, rather than hierarchically predetermined. Members of the project groups envisioned in Kirkhart's "consociational" model of organizational development are interpersonally as well as technically competent. That is, they have undergone encounter training and other interpersonal experiences designed to build openness and trust and to discourage the development of barriers to collegiality rooted in the social stratification system. Further, clientele representation is a prominent feature of the temporary organizations. Its clients have equal authority with professionals in shaping the ends and means of the project team. Once the temporary organization succeeds in achieving its policy objectives, it simply withers away; its clients are satisfied, and its members move on to other problem areas which require their technical and interpersonal skills (see Kirkhart 1971, 158–161).

Although this model shares some of the goals cherished by proponents of organizational democracy—such as minimum social stratification and collegiality, it contradicts others—such as the formal right to meaningful long-term membership in a relatively permanent enterprise. In any event, it is likely to be perceived as cheaper than democratization by administrators calculating the political costs of organizational change. This is because the main task of a temporary organization is to put itself out of business. Thus, temporary organizations can be grafted onto the permanent bureaucracy in ways that may satisfy critics of agency performance without unduly disrupting prevailing organizational customs and power arrangements. As Perrow (1972, 174) points out, once the problem requiring a project team is solved, the work group may dissolve but "the bureaucracy lingers on." The substantive innovations developed in the temporary organization can then be institutionalized as new routines in the permanent organization. The latter has thereby been shielded from disruptive tendencies within its boundaries which the dynamic but temporary organization has absorbed. Formal and informal power arrangements in the permanent bureaucracy remain basically unchanged.

In similar fashion, the increasingly popular technique of management by objectives (MBO) entails "superiors" consulting with "subordinates" on questions relating to their personal and organizational objectives. This method is often criticized as being a purely symbolic technique designed to reassure lower-level administrators that their views are important while maintaining the power to set organizational objectives in the hands of top managers. But this criticism is somewhat beside the point since, as initially developed by management consultant Peter Drucker, the technique was never intended to decentralize the power to set organizational objectives. Rather, it was a technique designed to encourage top managers in private industry to set measurable goals for persons lower down in their organization to meet. Only then are subordinates granted a fairly high degree of flexibility in determining the best ways to meet the centrally established objectives (Berkley 1975, 310).

This technique is now used with increasing frequency in many public organizations. Since it entails no significant devolution of power to establish agency priorities, but does provide employees with a greater degree of flexibility within which to employ their talents, it is the kind of reform which may be adopted with increasing frequency in the face of demands for pure organizational democracy.

Job rotation is a third relatively cheap organizational innovation. Experience with job rotation indicates that bureaucracies adopting the technique derive both quick short-term benefits in the form of increased satisfaction by workers and lasting long-term benefits in the form of increased loyalty by members and legitimacy for management (see Kaufman 1971, 17). Thus, problems of work alienation and low productivity are likely to be met by increasing use of individual job rotation rather than by more costly systematic reform.

In sum, then, a host of forces conspire against organizational democracy in American public bureaucracy. Public managers pursue self-protective strategies which encourage team playing, restrict the flow of information, and maintain prevailing patterns of advantage. Professional elitism is a prominent feature of the career civil service. Organizational members develop folkways and ideological blinders which limit the possibility of structural reform. The turbulent external environment engenders attempts to control the environment by oversimplification, overreaction, or cooptation. These adaptations tend to exclude the interests of agency employees. Other less costly innovative models stand ready to compete with organizational democracy. To emerge as a new form of public organization, organizational democracy must hurdle many barriers indeed. . . .

Conclusions

What are the implications of the foregoing analysis of barriers to organizational change in public administration? Part of the difficulty in obtaining any comprehensive change is the wide gap between current reality and the proposed ideal. Yet it has often been observed that small-scale, incremental changes can become comprehensive over time without really seeming so. This may well be true in the case of work democratization. Speaking of the long-run comprehensive effect of incremental inroads on managerial prerogatives in the British industrial setting, Kendall (1974) observes that previous gains in the areas of joint control over wages, hours, working conditions, antidiscrimination, and the like "have now become part of the cultural norm, and as a result, are not clearly perceived for what they are." In short, what might have been regarded as unacceptable to policy makers as a single policy has become institutionalized as a result of the cumulative effect of a series of small-scale, but mutually reinforcing, modifications of the existing authority system over time.

If this analysis is correct, it carries some important implications. First, it suggests the prudence of a strategy designed to achieve greater democratization by building on existing practices and policies wherever possible. Such a strategy may diminish fears of change which can trigger formidable structural and cultural barriers to change. Along these same lines, it occasionally may be necessary to downplay the "innovative" and "experimental" labels often invoked when such changes are proposed, no matter how reassuring these labels may be to proponents of work democratization. If a change promising broader participation or control must be "sold," there are many available and accurate labels that can be chosen to emphasize the correspondence of the proposed change to widely shared cultural values such as the expansion and enhancement of ethical autonomy, deliberative choice, and democratic participation.

Second, proponents of more democratic work structures in public bureaucracy must take care in developing alliances with proponents of competing change models. Several questions must first be answered. Does the proposed change promise to extend the scope of partial participation to some particular new type of decision, or is it merely a form of pseudo-participation? If the former, is this a lower or higher level extension? If lower level, is the proposed change likely to reinforce the overall pattern of democratization at this level, or is the scope of its long-term impact likely to be localized, redundant, or otherwise strategically counter-productive? If higher level, is the proposed reform justifiable in the context of the relationship of internal democratization to forms of democratic participation and control in the larger society—e.g., community control, clientele participation, electoral control, consumer representation?

Finally, if a strategy of change by the accretion of small modifications is to succeed, it may well be necessary to pursue a similar strategy in other sectors of the polity and society to avoid a long-run sectoral imbalance. If gains in the democratization of work in industry and genuine citizen participation in the polity do not keep pace with gains registered within public organizations, the incongruence among the sectors may only serve to underline the comprehensive departure of public sector organizations from the rest of the political and social structure. Such a development would threaten to undermine the long-run gains won by pursuing a strategy premised on the assumption that small-scale inroads will in all likelihood become part of the cultural norm. Cultural norms are acquired through a variety of socialization experiences, by a variety of agencies of political socialization (e.g., the family, work structures, political institutions, and the mass media). Unless proponents of work democratization in public administration are willing to support reinforcing goals that enhance democratic participation in other sectors of society, they may encounter considerable backlash from the least-reformed sectors and socialization structures. The hard-won gains obtained by an approach resembling Cole's strategy of "encroaching control" (see Pateman 1970, 60) may then prove to be short lived.

With the stakes of failure high, but the anticipated benefits great—the restoration of each person's full capacity to act as a responsible moral agent—the costs of any political strategy must be carefully weighed. For if, as Cole (1920, 25) argued, "social machinery . . . is the means of either furthering, or of thwarting, the expression of human personality," the human consequences of mistaken political judgments must be consciously considered. To fail to act is to surrender to the present. To act carelessly is to misshape the future.

References

Bennis, W. G., and P. Slater. 1968. *The Temporary Society.* New York: Harper & Row.
Berkley, G. E. 1975. *The Craft of Public Administration.* Boston: Allyn & Bacon.
———. 1971. *The Administrative Revolution.* Englewood Cliffs, N.J.: Prentice-Hall.
Case, J. 1972. "Vision of a new social order." *The Nation* (February 14): 200–206.
Clarity, J. F. 1975. "Workers at two Paris luxury hotels join smoothly in the management." *New York Times* (November 29): 14.
Cole, G. D. H. 1920. *Guild Socialism Restated.* London: Leonard Parsons.
Delaney, P. 1975. "St. Louis tests housing idea: the tenants are in charge." *New York Times* (June 1): 45.
Galbraith, J. K. 1973. *Economics and the Public Purpose.* Boston: Houghton Mifflin.
Garson, G. D. 1975. "Self-management and the public sector." Presented at International Conference on Self-Management, Ithaca, N.Y. (June): 1–28.
———. 1974. "Definitions and distinctions pertaining to work democratization." Presented at International Conference on Self-Management, Cambridge, Mass. (January): 1–12.
Kaufman, H. 1971. *The Limits of Organizational Change.* University: Univ. of Alabama Press.
Kendall, W. 1974. "Workers' participation and workers' control: aspects of British experience." Presented at International Conference on Self-Management, Cambridge, Mass. (January): 1–15.
Kirkhart, L. 1971. "Toward a theory of public administration," 127–164, in *Toward a New Public Administration*, ed. F. Marini. Scranton, Pa.: Chandler.
Lindblom, C. 1959. "The science of 'muddling through.'" *Public Admin. Rev.* 9 (Spring): 79–88.
Lipsky, M. 1971. "Street-level bureaucracy and the analysis of urban reform." *Urban Affairs Q.* 6 (June): 391–409.
March, J. G., and H. Simon. 1958. *Organizations.* New York: John Wiley.

Meade, M. 1971. "Participative administration—emerging reality or wishful thinking?" 169–187 in *Public Administration in a Time of Turbulence*, ed. D. Waldo. Scranton. Pa.: Chandler.

Mosher, F. D. 1968. *Democracy and the Public Service*. New York: Oxford Univ. Press.

New York Times. 1974. "Factory is thriving after being given to workers in Italy." February 8: 34.

Pateman, C. 1976. "A contribution to the political theory of organizational democracy," 3–30, in *Organizational Democracy: Participation and Self-Management*, ed. G. D. Garson and M. P. Smith. Sage Contemporary Social Science Issues. Vol. 22. Beverly Hills, Calif.: Sage.

———. 1970. *Participation and Democratic Theory*. London: Cambridge Univ. Press.

Perrow, C. 1972. *Complex Organizations: A Critical Essay*. Glenview, Ill.: Scott, Foresman.

Presthus, R. 1962. *The Organizational Society*. New York: Vintage.

Redford, E. S. 1969. *Democracy in the Administrative State*. New York: Oxford Univ. Press.

Smith, M. P. 1974. "Pluralism revisited," 3–32, in M. P. Smith, J. James, R. Davidson, G. Orfield, E. Gude, and M. Nadel, *Politics in America: Studies in Policy Analysis*. New York: Random House.

Special Task Force, Department of Health, Education and Welfare. 1973. *Work in America*. Report to the Secretary. Cambridge, Mass.: MIT Press.

Thayer, F. C. 1973. *An End to Hierarchy! An End to Competition!* New York: New Viewpoints, a division of Franklin Watts.

Thompson, V. 1969. *Bureaucracy and Innovation*. University: Univ. of Alabama Press.

Wilson, J. Q. 1973. *Political Organizations*. New York: Basic Books.

Wynia, B. L. 1974. "Federal bureaucrats' attitudes toward a democratic ideology." *Public Admin. Rev.* 34 (March–April): 156–162.

27
Feminism and the Forms of Freedom
Jane Mansbridge

Early in the feminist movement of the late 1960s, it became clear that the forms of organization best adapted to the movement's needs were identical to the classic anarchist forms.

1. The consciousness-raising group and its sister, the action group, had the same role in the larger movement that the anarchist "affinity groups" had in Spain in the civil war. The larger radical feminist organizations adopted a federative form of organization, based on small collectives or cells. In Bread and Roses in Boston, in the Women's Liberation Union in Chicago, in Redstockings in New York, in almost every other

major city in the United States, and even in the Women's Liberation Workshop in London, radical feminists adopted the same form of organization: a voluntary federation of small (six to twelve person) collectives.

2. The radical women's movement consciously avoided creating "stars." Women whom *Time* and *Life* asked to pose for covers featuring the women's movement refused to do so. Other women, giving public speeches, spoke in groups and wore masks to emphasize their collectivity and anonymity. Boston's Bread and Roses had a rule that no woman should appear on television, radio, or in the news without at least one other woman with her. New York's Redstockings censured T. Grace Atkinson when she attracted too much personal attention. Even the National Organization for Women (NOW), traditionally and hierarchically organized, found itself under attack from its members for creating the position of president in which one woman became a formal leader. In the radical women's movement, the conscious avoidance of publicity and unequal status parallels similar concerns raised in the Spanish anarcho-syndicalist revolutionary union Confederación National del Trabajo (CNT), where, for example, certain assemblies decided not to applaud their speakers, on the ground that applause would direct attention to the individual rather than to the substance of the talk.

3. The small collectives and even some large assemblies in the women's movement took their decisions by consensus, not by majority vote. This ensured that each member would then act only on her own commitment. This mode of decision, too, is consonant with much anarchist theory, though not always with anarchist practice.[1]

4. Whenever federated women's collectives had to make joint decisions, they chose the format of a direct, face-to-face assembly attended by all the membership. Anarchist theory also has always inveighed against representation and promoted the face-to-face assembly. Murray Bookchin argues, for example, that the direct face-to-face assembly is the only governmental form that preserves individual liberty. For Bookchin, face-to-face assemblies are the "forms of freedom."[2]

These forms of organization represented a sharp break with the past for many, if not most, of the women who practiced them. The Students for a Democratic Society (SDS) had initiated decentralized, consensual forms in its organization, but the concept never acquired the strength in SDS that it did in the women's movement, and nowhere in SDS did affinity groups play the powerful and all-pervasive role that they played in the women's movement. Nor had most members of the women's movement any previous contact with anarchist theory. The great proliferation of books on anarchism in the paperback bookstores in the mid-1970s came after the women's movement, not before, and may well have been caused, at least in part, by the success of anarchist forms in feminist organization. In short, the theory came after the practice.

Why this strong resemblance, reaching almost to identity, between women's forms and anarchist forms? It is not as if all oppressed groups spontaneously choose anarchist forms. Black groups in the United States, for example, often choose hierarchical forms of organization. The importance to women of the small, egalitarian, consensual collective was, I believe, directly related to one of the major goals of the women's movement—changing women's perceptions of themselves.

The women's movement of the 1960s and 1970s had many goals, most of them aimed at changing the male-dominated institutions that excluded and oppressed women. But unlike most oppressed groups, which can concentrate primarily on external sources of oppression, women had a peculiar relation with their oppressors. Women often loved men, and were loved by them. Women and men often had the same class background. Women and men often worked together intimately in the family. As members of a family, women and men often had the same interests *vis à vis* the larger polity. While some of these characteristics also apply to other relations of domination and subordination, nowhere are the ties so strong as between men and women. This meant that a primary task of the women's movement—perhaps *the* primary task—was to help women change the character of their most intimate relations. Before they could try to seize political or economic power, they had to help one another see their relations with men in a new light, and this required changing their understanding of themselves. For this purpose, the small egalitarian collective provided the necessary high levels of intimacy and support. The antipathy to leaders and the stress on personal commitment rather than subjection to a majority also served to strengthen psyches—to teach women that they could and should respect themselves, that they could and should resist domination.[3]

During the height of the women's movement, several women questioned whether the forms the movement had chosen really promoted its ends.[4] My object here is to question whether those forms, if adopted into the larger society, would serve women's ends.

A movement based on small primary groups—whether Communist cells, anarchist affinity groups, or feminist consciousness-raising groups—can derive great strength from linking the goals of the larger movement to the personal loyalties, expressed commitments, and protection from external culture that a small "primary" group provides. The consciousness-raising (C–R) group allowed six to twelve women to come together informally once a week or so, to share their experiences of being a woman, and, as the Chinese say, to "speak bitterness." They discovered that problems they thought had arisen from the individual peculiarities of their own experience were in fact the same problems that others had, and that those problems were rooted in the systematic oppression of women as a class. In these discussions, each woman discovered that "the personal is political."

Some consciousness-raising groups evolved into action groups—putting out a newsletter, doing guerilla theater, or executing graffiti raids on pornography stores and Playboy clubs. Other groups evolved into personal support groups for the women members, who then did what they could for the women's movement either individually or in other action groups formed for specific purposes. Many C-R groups simply dissolved after a year or so, when their primary purpose of personal evolution was accomplished or when their members moved to other parts of the country.

The radical women's movement of the late 1960s and early 1970s had almost no existence outside of these small consciousness-raising and action groups. But there were thousands of them. The groups had often sprung up spontaneously, and only in the major cities were some of them able to join together into loose, decentralized federations. The strength of such decentralized organization lay in the intense commitment to the goals of the movement that the groups generated, the courage they gave their members to demand changes in the way their friends, colleagues, bosses, husbands, and parents treated women, and the creativity they fostered, not only in poetry, painting, and protest, but also in changing one's own life. Kochen and Deutsch, and also Bennis and Slater, tell us that the more an organization must rely on creativity, innovation, adaptation to change and speed of reaction, the more it benefits from decentralization.[5] When the radical women's movement exploded with new ideas and new energy, that explosion was directly linked to extreme decentralization. It put the women's movement on the front page of national magazines and newspapers, revolutionized public opinion on women's issues from 1968 to 1972, and even brought new words, new usages, and new taboos into the English language.

Yet decentralization was at odds with coordination, particularly at a national level, and particularly over long periods of time. The one women's organization that survived this era and continued to grow, namely NOW, had a relatively centralized structure.[6]

The women's movement's use of consensus also created commitment and solidarity—important virtues in a "fighting" movement. One woman describes the joy of resolving conflict in a meeting right after the women who worked for a radical newspaper had taken over the paper:

> It was such an exciting meeting—almost everybody talked—there were about thirty women in the room—and it went from about a total split to finally someone saying, "Listen, if we can't do that we don't deserve the paper," and then everybody saying, "Right on!" It was one of the few meetings where it goes around and then people just really come together and say "Far out!" You know it's right. It was such a *high* . . . it was wonderful. It was such a high.

But while consensus can inspire and bind together a group of equals with common purposes, it can also suppress real conflict to the advantage of those with greater self-confidence and verbal aggressiveness. Thus, in a mixed group of men and women a consensual procedure may mean that the women subtly lose out.

The same is true for direct assembly government in general. In a government by direct assembly, decisions are made not by representatives, but by the citizens gathered together in a meeting hall. Some New England towns still run their affairs this way; some of these towns are so small that all the adult citizens can come together in one room to vote the amount they will tax themselves and to decide, for example, whether or not to institute zoning, or whether to make parents pay individually when their children ride the school bus. On the radical Left, some "alternative" organizations also run this way, with all members of the workplace making decisions together, in assembly. In the late 1960s and early 1970s I surveyed a number of town meetings and egalitarian workplaces, in order to identify the two most "participatory" for detailed study.[7] Even in the most participatory town and workplace, though, not everyone participated equally in these assemblies. In both settings the working class, the newcomers, the younger people, and those most distant from the polity's centers of communications attended less often and spoke less at the meetings than did the middle class, the oldtimers, the older people, and those who lived or worked near centers of communications.[8]

In both assemblies—the town meeting and the crisis center—women attended meetings as often as men but spoke less. At the town meeting, women spoke only one quarter of the time, made only 8 percent of the major statements of opinion, and initiated not one of the ten controversial exchanges. At the crisis center, with the exception of one extraordinarily verbal woman, women also spoke less. On a checklist of traits and attitudes associated with greater power at the center, women in this workplace fell significantly behind men on only two, but these both involved verbal insecurity.[9]

In short, although ironically women usually do better in academic tests of verbal ability than do men, in a face-to-face assembly, where people must use those verbal skills to influence others, today's women lose out.

The women's movement of the late 1960s and early 1970s demonstrated the strength, at least in some circumstances, of anarchist forms. But before thinking of adapting these forms to the larger polity, women should understand how the forms reflect and perhaps accentuate the disadvantages of those already disadvantaged. In the classic "form of freedom"—the face-to-face assembly—the interests of the disadvantaged, including the working class and women, are not usually protected equally.

This pattern of disadvantage is not confined to women. It recurs for almost all disadvantaged groups. Whenever inequality emerges in a society, the dominant groups will normally have greater influence in setting the norms of that society. It will then be difficult, in the personal, face-to-face atmosphere of an assembly, for the less advantaged to speak out, and their listeners will often discount in advance what they have to say, because their tone of voice and style of behavior does not carry authority.

Moreover, even in the most egalitarian societies certain forms of inequality will probably persist. Some people will continue to live and work closer to the hub of central communications, some will have more friends active in the community, some will have more verbal skills, and some will enjoy responsibility more than others. These people, generally more at ease in the assembly, will either subtly or more crassly dominate the proceedings.

What is to be done about these inequalities depends on whether one assumes underlying conflict or underlying harmony in the community making potential decisions. If on a given set of issues the interests of the members of the polity conflict, then the democratic goal should be to make sure that the interests of the disadvantaged (women, for example) are represented equally.

This is the underlying theory behind what I call "adversary democracy." It is the theory behind majority rule: When no individual is acknowledged to have rights or knowledge superior to any other, and when conflict cannot ultimately be resolved by continuing debate, then all parties will consider the outcome legitimate if each individual has a vote of equal weight and the issue is settled by the preponderance of votes. In adversary democracy, when there is no "right answer," the equal power of each individual is a necessary weapon for protecting interests equally. Accordingly, when interests conflict, referenda and proportional representation will be more likely than open debate in a face-to-face assembly to make the interests of the disadvantaged count equally in the final outcome.

However, if the interests of the members of the polity coincide on a given set of issues, then the democratic goal should be to come to the "best" decision. This is what I call "unitary" democracy, a form of democracy practiced in the West before the seventeenth century, and still practiced in most non-European countries. The theory of unitary democracy assumes underlying common interests among the citizenry. When everyone has common interests, no one's interests are hurt when certain kinds of people participate more than others. Enough people must speak from each vantage point to get all the relevant insights and suggestions onto the table, but this goal does not require equal participation. For example, if the interests of men and women are the same on any issue, it will not hurt women's interests if few women speak, as long as the men and women who do speak express the ideas nonspeakers would have come up with.

This point, however, brings up a second goal of participation. Participation is a device not just for ensuring everyone equal influence over an outcome, but for developing thoughtful, active citizens, who understand when their interests really conflict with those of others, and who are involved enough in their common life to contribute to the greater good of all. If some people rarely or never participate in political life, they are less likely to develop sides of themselves that will be important both to them and to the community. Referenda and representation do not solve this problem. Neither, unfortunately, do face-to-face assemblies. Instead of being encouraged to speak by the theoretically open character of the debate, a habitual non-participant is as likely to be threatened, bored, or otherwise alienated by a face-to-face meeting.

The best response to the goal of self-development is to rely not on large face-to-face assemblies, but on primary-group meetings (twelve persons or less) and on the wide diffusion of small, responsible jobs. Small primary group meetings help people explore what they think about an issue, find support for underdeveloped powers of self-expression and analysis, and develop the initiative for action. Unfortunately, in a context of genuine, irreconcilable conflict, small groups have two drawbacks. They divide minorities so that the minority members cannot give one another adequate support. And they make the enemy human, which can either weaken one's resolve to fight or provoke one to irrational, sometimes destructive, behavior. Thus, for most developmental purposes the small group must have some basis in common interest. In a context of conflict, working within a small group that must negotiate potential conflict with another group helps people become more aware of their real interests. Finally, creating many small jobs with formal responsibility for others helps those who do these jobs become aware of other people's needs and understand different points of view. It also develops self-respect when one does well, and realistic self-criticism when one fails.

If the goal is developing the faculties of the participants, assemblies should try to break up regularly for small-group discussion. This may not increase equality in participation,[10] but it gives each person a greater chance to be active. When the assembly must meet only as a whole, habitual non-participants can sit together, talk quietly among themselves, and possibly meet before and after. These tactics can offset the intimidating character of the larger meeting and contribute to the greater awareness of the disadvantaged.

At one point New York's Redstockings invented a "disk system," by which each woman entering a meeting took twelve disks. She had to spend one each time she spoke and was forbidden to speak after the twelve were spent. This technique had the advantages of making everyone conscious of inequalities in participation and of making the less aggressive members more conscious of their opportunities to speak. It had two disadvantages. First, when interests came into conflict, the tactic was not likely to reduce inequalities of influence. Although everyone at the meeting continued to have one vote, the more powerful always had, in addition, their networks of friends and their command of persuasive rhetoric. Second, in moments of common interest, the tactic probably obstructed ordered and careful debate on the best solution by forcing people with the most to contribute to save their disks rather than making useful, short interventions. It also tended to focus the group's interest on the frequency with which people spoke instead of the quality of what they said.

Redstockings probably instituted this system to achieve a third and final goal of participation—equal respect, or equal status, among the members. If some members consistently speak out while others stay silent, the speakers can gradually become a status elite and the nonspeakers come to feel less than equal. In the radical women's movement of the late 1960s and early 1970s, this concern for equal respect was greater than the concern for either protecting interests equally or developing individual abilities. Women wanted to create communities based on the bonds of friendship, which requires equal respect.[11] "Sisterhood" thus demanded equality, while differences in status tore the bonds apart.

But face-to-face assemblies are not the best vehicle for reinforcing equality of respect. Time limitations and the demands of consecutive debate will always create a distance between the small groups of speakers and the many who are silent—a distance that inevitably grows more pronounced as the assembly gets larger. Small primary groups and the diffusion of small formal responsibilities are more effective tactics for maintaining equal respect than are frequent face-to-face assemblies.

Face-to-face assemblies are less the forms of freedom or equality than the forms of community. Despite all their drawbacks in promoting the equal protection of interests, self-development, and equal respect, assemblies of modest size (say less than 200) can put each member palpably in touch with everyone else. They allow nuances of understanding that can only come from seeing another's face and posture, or hearing the inflections of her voice. They let waves of emotional communion flow as difficult or risky decisions are made; and long after the assembly's end, they bind together the people who were there through the common memory of what they did together. If such meetings continue year after year, they create an accumulation of memories that lets each member see the community as a whole in her mind's eye, feel its many sides and its central pulse, and make its collective good her own.

The organizational forms that feminists use for social change should depend on the context. In external politics, when women's groups make demands on the system that other groups resist, the movement should not try to replace representative institutions with direct democracy. Rather, it should aim its major political efforts at achieving greater representation of women's interests in the areas where they most conflict with those of men. This is not necessarily a matter of having more women in high places. Women legislators do not always represent women's interests better than men do. The women's movement should aim at electing women or men who will represent women's interests best in the major areas of conflict.

In *internal* organization, women's groups should continue to rely on small primary group organization, which contributes to self-development and to mutual support in outside conflict. They should also build extensive experience in formal representation, both for self-development and for the cadre this experience can train for outside conflict. They should not abandon face-to-face assembly, but use it sparingly, primarily to build community. They should be willing to use consensual, face-to-face institutions for issues on which there is an original conflict of opinion but also the possibility of an eventual genuine solution that is in the common interest, and should switch to majority-rule institutions like referenda or representation when a genuine conflict of interest underlies the conflict of opinion.

In short, feminists should not decide that there is only one democratic "form of freedom." They should examine the degree to which interests converge or conflict among the people making a decision, and then choose the institutions and tactics that best fit the underlying distribution of interests.

Notes

1. While I know no published description of decision-making in Spanish collectives, telephone interviews with the authors of three books on the anarchists indicate that anarchist collectives in the Spanish civil war made decisions by consensus when convenient, but had no ideological problem about resorting to majority rule whenever a difficult conflict arose. The authors in question are: Sam Dolgoff, author of *The Anarchist Collective: Worker's Self-Management in the Spanish Revolution, 1936–1939* (Montreal: Black Rose, 1974), Martha Ackelsberg, Department of Political Science, Smith College, author of "Revolution Begins at Home" (forthcoming), an examination of social and political practice in anarchist collectives during the Spanish civil war, and Jerome R. Mintz, author of *The Anarchists of Casas Viejas* (Chicago: The University of Chicago Press, 1982). Fred W. Thompson, a long-time member of the Industrial Workers of the World (I.W.W.), makes the same point regarding the early Wobblies (telephone conversation with the author).

2. Murray Bookchin, "The Forms of Freedom" (1968) in *Post-Scarcity Anarchism* (Berkeley, Calif.: Ramparts Press, 1971), 168. Bookchin concludes:

> The factory committees, which will almost certainly be the forms that will take over industry, must be managed directly by workers' assemblies in the factories. By the same token, neighborhood committees, councils and boards must be rooted completely in the neighborhood assembly. . . . The specific gravity of society, in short, must be shifted to its base—the armed people in permanent assembly.

Against "the intermediary of representatives," see Pierre-Joseph Proudhon in *General Idea of the Revolution in the Nineteenth Century* (1851), reprinted in *The Essential Works of Anarchism*, ed. Marshall S. Shatz, (New York: Quadrangle Books, 1972), 88–89; on "the inherent vices of the representative principle," see Peter Kropotkin, *The Conquest of Bread* (1892), reprinted in Shatz, *The Essential Works of Anarchism*, 205.

3. The power of a small discussion group in helping change behavior was early demonstrated by Lewin in a series of experiments during World War II to discover the most effective way of persuading women to give their children cod-liver oil. See Kurt Lewin, "Forces Behind Food Habit and Methods of Change," *Bulletin of the National Research Council* 108 (1943): 35–36, reprinted in *Group Dynamics: Research and Theory*, ed. Dorwin Cartwright and Alvin Zander (N.Y.: Harper and Row, 1953). More recently, encounter, gestalt, and other therapies have effectively utilized the same technique. On the Chinese use of the small group for directed behavior change, see Robert Lifton, *Thought Reform and the Psychology of Totalism* (N.Y.: Norton, 1962). One might even hypothesize that the more a revolutionary movement demanded internal as well as external change, the more it would rely on small-group organization.

4. See, for example, Jo Freeman, "The Tyranny of Structurelessness," *Berkeley Journal of Sociology* 17 (1972–73): 151–64.

5. Warren G. Bennis and Philip E. Slater, *The Temporary Society* (N.Y.: Harper and Row, 1969); Manfred Kochen and Karl W. Deutsch, "Toward a Rational Theory of Decentralization," *American Political Science Review* 63 (1969): 734–49.

6. NOW adopted the consciousness-raising group, but let it run no more than a limited period of time, and restricted its autonomy. Even in NOW there has always been much controversy over the permissible degree of centralization. NOW remains a great deal less centralized than, say, the NAACP.

7. These cases, and the method of their selection, are reported in my *Beyond Adversary Democracy* (N.Y.: Basic Books, 1980—Chicago: University of Chicago Press, 1983).

8. Mansbridge, *Beyond Adversary Democracy*, 99–111, 184–209, 306–21.

9. "Articulate people intimidate me," and "I express myself well in words." See Mansbridge, *Beyond Adversary Democracy*, 105–06, 191–94. See p. 358 for the checklist of reported personality attributes by gender.

Women at the crisis center spoke less than men in spite of much raised consciousness on the subject. Some of the women at the center, organized in an active and militant support group, had raised the issue of women's lower verbal participation, and many of the men subsequently had made conscious efforts to break themselves of their habits of interrupting women or assuming they as men would speak first.

Don H. Zimmerman and Candace West, "Sex Roles, Interruptions and Silences in Conversations," in *Language and Sex*, ed. Barrie Thorne and Nancy Henley (Rowley, Mass: Newbury House, 1975), 105–29, present evidence that among mixed-sex college-age couples, men commit 75 percent of the "deep interruptions."

10. For example, the crisis center I studied usually broke its large assembly down into small groups of less than 15 people for discussion. However, the one time that I measured speaking in these small groups, the association between advantaged status and speaking was no smaller than in the larger assembly.

11. See Robert Brain, *Friends and Lovers* (N.Y.: Basic Books, 1976), 20; Mansbridge, *Beyond Adversary Democracy*, chap. 2 and 3.

28
Participation, Opportunity, and Equality: Toward a Pluralist Organizational Model

Carmen Sirianni

Political theory has been perennially concerned with the problem of equality. Sociological theory has likewise. As Ralf Dahrendorf has noted, the very first questions that concerned sociology were those having to do with the causes of inequality, whether it was inevitable, and how it could be reduced or abolished.[1] These issues, not surprisingly, have also been at the heart of organization theory from the beginning. It is impossible to read the classical contributions of Weber, Marx, and Michels without recognizing the centrality of such issues as: Is it possible to organize a complex society on more egalitarian and democratic foundations? Weber and Michels, to be sure, had a much more pessimistic answer than Marx and a myriad of other decentralizers, anarchists, communitarians, and egalitarians. And it was Weber and Michels, as well as those who would more directly legitimate the hierarchical principles of capitalist industrial management, who had the most profound impact on the later development of organization theory. Yet what is striking, though also not very surprising, is how tenacious the original questions have remained, and how very much alive are the concerns of democracy, participation, and equality of power and opportunity. A cursory glance at the recent literature in political science and sociology confirms that democratic thought is alive and well, and that equality continues to motivate theoretical debate and empirical research. In the subfield of organizations, these concerns are more vibrant today than they have ever been. The essays in the concluding section of this book represent but a tiny fraction of the innovative thinking, empirical research, and practical experimentation that contemporaries have brought to bear on the classical problems of democracy and equality.

Recent social developments make this quite understandable. The massive entry of women into the labor force and the rise of feminism provide the basis for innovative organizational thinking and strategies. Rosabeth Moss Kanter's classic, *Men and Women of the Corporation*,[2] not only brilliantly analyzes the dynamics of power, opportunity, and tokenism, but articulates an array of organizational strategies that are quite open-ended and far-reaching in their implications—and not just for women but for other groups that experience systematic and often cumulative disadvantages in society. Nor is it an accident that feminist thought has often most forcefully expanded the boundaries of our conception of equality. Yet other developments, as well, pose the questions of democracy and equality with great urgency in the last decades of the twentieth century. Since the late 1960s, blue- and white-collar worker dissatisfaction and rebellion from routinized work have become manifest in a variety of forms in virtually all industrialized countries. Demands for career opportunities and higher education have expanded enormously, opening up a highly visible gap between both expressed desires and demonstrated capacities for educating and training people for intelligent jobs, on the one hand, and the existing system's ability to provide jobs that actually permit workers to utilize their skills and further develop their talents, on the other.[3] On top of this, accelerated capital mobility and technological change have begun to displace massive numbers of people from their jobs and threaten to alter fundamentally the very contours of labor markets and divisions of labor.[4] These developments raise questions of equity as well as survival for those affected and pose, perhaps more profoundly than ever, the issues of who will control and participate in the process of change, and what criteria will be developed for the determination of new job opportunities. And, finally, all of these changes are occurring in the context of a serious ecological crisis that questions both capitalist and state socialist goals of limitless material production and, hence, the basic motivation structures of work and achievement. In short, the quality of life, the meaning of work, the criteria of equity, and the values of democracy are all inescapable issues in the late twentieth century, and they have become more relevant to an organization theory that would creatively respond to the crises with which we are faced.

Yet critical organization theory is confronted with a dilemma. On the one hand, theory and research informed by the values of equality and democracy are more appropriate than ever. On the other hand, none of the previously existing participatory, communal, or egalitarian organizational forms is without serious problems and drawbacks. The challenges of Weber and Michels have yet to be fully confronted. Rothschild-Whitt has analyzed the social costs of small-scale democratic collectivist organizations,[5] some of which (time, emotional intensity) would no doubt persist even if the hostile bureaucratic context were significantly transformed. Rayman analyzes how larger-scale regional organization has seriously constrained or transformed some of the original values of the kibbutz (equality of labor, participation, manual work).[6] Whyte and Blasi note how even in the highly successful Mondragón collectives in Spain, the problems of routine work, hierarchical supervision, and technological constraint remain.[7] Mansbridge points to the limits of the face-to-face consensual organization for the feminist movement.[8] And these are but a few of the problems that have been analyzed by proponents as well as critics of more egalitarian and participatory organizations.

This dilemma of organization theory is, however, not necessarily unresolvable, and a potential solution is emerging—if we keep in mind that there could never be a complete or perfect organizational "solution" to the problems of social life. Disillusion with the failures of past models and the determination to be practically relevant to the complex social world as we know it lie behind the growing appreciation for a more pluralistic conception of the forms of freedom and the principles of justice. No single organizational type is available as an ideal solution. No single distributive principle can determine what is equitable for all social, economic, and political spheres.[9] Yet this need not lead to the abandonment of ideals or the search for more egalitarian and democratic organizational forms. A pluralistic approach, which seeks to articulate systemic interrelationships among a variety of alternative organizational forms and which is not premised on a principled hostility to all aspects of bureaucracy and market exchange, can perhaps provide the basis for a quite far-reaching realization of democratic and egalitarian ideals. Some will no doubt see such an approach as too utopian, and others will argue that it is not utopian enough. This tension is probably inevitable and perhaps represents the healthy realization that none today—not the proponents of traditional hierarchical organizations, not human-relations theorists or neo-Weberians, not Marxists or proponents of small-scale participatory collectives—can rest content that they have discovered the organizational forms and principles that are practical and appropriate, equitable and legitimate in the late twentieth century, or that will survive well into the twenty-first.

An initial sense of some of the problems that face critical organization theorists is revealed by the limitations of the ideal type of participatory egalitarian collective. This ideal type, which in one form or another has been the major point of reference of most radical critiques of hierarchical and bureaucratic organizations in industrial society, has cultural, philosophical, and practical roots that go back through the centuries. It is not difficult to discern the appeal of an organizational type that promises communal and substantive values, personalistic and noncompetitive styles, thoroughly democratic control, little or no stratification, the holistic sharing of tasks, and no systematic division between mental and manual labor. These are some of the deepest values and most enduring aspirations of the human species. And participatory egalitarian collectives have had a practical history that is replete with success along many of these dimensions, at least for some of their members some of the time. As two writers on participatory collectives in the United States in the 1960s and 1970s note:

their importance . . . lies less in the changes they made or failed to make in the larger society than in the experience and training they gave their members. Through the new institutions, many people got their first experience in collective work; they got an opportunity to participate in their organization's management. Members trained each other in sensitivity and skills. . . . Deprofessionalization—making skills less mysterious and more widely available—at times became a reality.[10]

The vision of the democratic organization that holistically shares a wide range of productive tasks in an effort to break down the division of labor is also shared by many critical Marxists, even when they do not necessarily have the same commitment to the small-scale, radically communal, consensual form of it. Recent critiques of the development of the capitalist labor process, and the forms of domination and fragmentation that have shaped that development, take as their point of reference an ideal conception of holism, in which all workers share the full range of functions relevant to their particular sphere of work. Thus, conception and execution are fully reunified, the division between mental and manual labor is overcome, and all workers in each workplace possess a broad enough range of knowledge and skill to enable them to control the "entire production process."[11] Braverman, for instance, indicates what this might entail in the following terms:

> an automatic system of machinery opens up the possibility of the true control over a highly productive factory by a relatively small corps of workers, providing these workers attain the level of mastery over the machinery offered by engineering knowledge, and providing they then share out among themselves the routines of the operation, from the most technically advanced to the most routine.[12]

In his presentation of the outlines of a genuinely democratic socialist alternative in Eastern Europe, Rudolf Bahro presents a very similar picture of labor where "those who construct the machines also worked at them for prolonged periods." He continues:

> we can just as well imagine the everyday situation in a hospital, to take an example from a different sphere, one still more strongly burdened with the prejudices of the traditional division of labor, in which the entire staff consisted of people with full medical training, or other pertinent qualifications, who also took part in all nursing and ancillary work, and in social and economic functions as well.[13]

It is probably no exaggeration to say that this conception of holism, or the model of productive integrity, has become the dominant ideal among contemporary critical Marxists, and the point of reference for virtually all critical accounts of the development of technology and productive organization under capitalism.

It is my basic contention that we can make further progress in articulating the possible organizational forms of a genuinely egalitarian and democratic society only by recognizing the limits of this conception of holism or productive integrity, as it appears in the work of both Marxists and theorists of more radically participatory and communal forms. This is not to say that such organizational forms have no place; far from it. Holistic and participatory collectives have proven their value for many people under a variety of circumstances; under more propitious conditions we could expect them to be more practically viable and organizationally effective in a great range of productive and service tasks. Such organizations will no doubt, in some form or other, remain an important and enduring part of any conception of an egalitarian and democratic society. But only by recognizing simultaneously the limits of such organizational forms can we begin to articulate coherently the range of other organizational possibilities for genuinely democratic control by equal, productive citizens. And only by confronting these limits will we be able to formulate the kinds of inter- and supra-organizational linkages that might be able to sustain relatively egalitarian and democratic outcomes on a societal scale. A credible conception of the latter has yet to be proffered by theorists of either democratic collectives or factory councils, market or state socialism.

In the remaining part of this essay, I will outline some of the limits of the model of productive integrity and indicate some of the organizational problems that remain to be solved, as well as some of the directions in which we ought to look for possible solutions. We are quite far from having a viable model and even from recognizing or agreeing upon all of the important issues. And creative organizational responses to the many problems that remain can only be developed ultimately in practice. Yet theoretical analysis of the experience we already have before us—and the problems we can realistically anticipate in any effort to create more egalitarian and democratic alternatives—remains an indispensable part of both critical thinking and creative organizational strategy.

Along at least three dimensions the productive integrity model appears seriously flawed. First, it does not adequately grasp the problem of *equality* and, in particular, of equality of opportunities for jobs that encourage creativity, learning, and career development. Second, it has an insufficient conception of *individuality* and, in particular, of the variety and flexibility of mechanisms through which workers might arrange their work commitments. Third, it maintains an overly restrictive notion of *democracy* and, in particular, of the range of organizational forms through which people might participate to achieve their goals and protect their interests. From a somewhat different angle, these can be viewed as the problems of opportunity, proportions, and power that are the focal points of Kanter's analysis of men and women in organizations. Let me discuss each of these, in turn, before raising some of the larger issues of markets and bureaucracy.

Relatively equal opportunities for creative work *across* and *throughout* the social division of labor cannot be achieved by a principle of holistic sharing of tasks within particular work units because the amount and type of both routine work and creative work would hardly be commensurate among production units. For instance, the holistic sharing of tasks within retail stores, restaurants, warehouses, garbage collection services—and many other necessary tasks—hardly provides the range of opportunities for creative work, progressive learning, and career development that would be found in universities, medical complexes, research laboratories, architectural firms, publishing collectives, and so forth. In other words, some production units will invariably provide opportunity structures that are far more expansive and far more conducive to learning, creativity, and career development than others. For an organization theory that would not unnecessarily restrict opportunities on the basis of a highly limited notion of the potential talents of the labor force, or an unreflective conception of organizational constraints, this presents a problem.[14] Marxists often get into this bind because they concentrate on the person-machine relationship and the mastery of holistic skills. They also tend to neglect the problem of opportunity structures and career and professional development.[15] Finally, they often ignore the issues that arise in a complex society that produces a vast array of services, many of which have (and will probably continue to have) only limited inherent interest and challenge. More radically democratic and communitarian thinkers get into the same bind because of their primary emphasis on the workplace as community, process as consensus, and achievement as completely noncompetitive and not oriented to careers.

In short, the organizational principle of the holistic sharing of tasks is inadequate from the standpoint of equality, since it cannot provide the basis for relatively equal opportunity structures throughout society. Another way of saying this, in view of the fact that equality could in any case only be achieved in relative terms, is that the principle of productive integrity could conceivably serve to legitimate an organizational structure of considerable and unacceptable inequalities of opportunity. It could provide the foundation for a class-divided society; and various indications suggest that such a structure would be viewed by many as unacceptably unequal[16] and inadequate in terms of opportunities. The narrowness of opportunity structures has been a significant cause of personal frustration and organizational dissolution in many holistic co-ops and democratic collectives that have been constituted by many relatively well-educated people in the United States in recent years, although this factor has gone largely unrecognized and untheorized in sociological studies. Educational reform that genuinely expanded the cultural horizons and learning opportunities of the most disadvantaged groups would no doubt produce even larger cohorts of workers who sought career and professional opportunities much broader than those that would be available in a restaurant, a coal mine, or a plywood firm—whether holistically organized or not. This would be especially true, I think, under conditions of full employment and adequate social services. On the Israeli kibbutz, where commitment to egalitarian and cooperative values was originally quite profound, and various forms of holistic sharing of mental and manual tasks were put into practice, there has nonetheless been a very noticeable dynamic toward individual professional and career development and the expansion of opportunities outside of the communal group or geographic area. Communal work roles have come to be seen by many as too narrow.[17]

Michael Walzer reminds us that, in addition to self-managed cooperatives, there are a variety of ways to reduce inequality at work: the symbolic sharing of the dirty work, the elimination of disrespect associated with certain jobs, or the "rectification of names" of the tasks themselves.[18] Yet he pays too little attention to the question of opportunity structures and career paths, which are surely to remain at the heart of the debate on equality in advanced industrial societies, and accepts too easily that "the class of hard workers" could not be abolished without state coercion.[19] This may well turn out to be true. Yet, on the basis of the current state of organizational thinking, there is no compelling reason to accept fatalistically that the class division of labor cannot be fundamentally altered. Outside of democratic collectivist thought and a fairly narrow conception of market socialism, very little organizational thinking has addressed this issue directly. It will remain an issue for those concerned with achieving greater equality and security because it is difficult to conceive how a democratic society with greatly expanded educational opportunities for all and a commitment to full employment could permanently stabilize sectors of the economy with very narrow opportunity structures, even if self-management and holistic principles of productive integrity were introduced. In short, additional egalitarian strategies and organizational mechanisms would be required.

The productive integrity model also falls short on the question of individuality insofar as its conception (explicit or implicit) of the variety of forms and the flexibility of mechanisms through which people might arrange their work commitments is overly restrictive. It is based on the premise of more or less equal commitments and the fullest sharing of tasks among all members of each work collective. Stated another way, it is the principle of *equal proportions*. As such, it leaves little room for partial, hence unequal, organizational commitments, whether in terms of dedication, time, or learning of skills. But options for partial and unequal commitments are absolutely essential if we are to design a social division of labor that is conducive to a broad pluralism of individual life and work choices or, rather, if we are to expand and enhance those that already exist, especially for some professionals. An egalitarian pluralism, where each individual has options for "a fluid and flexible life course built around work that provides continuous opportunities for learning,"[20] is an emergent ideal in advanced industrial societies that could not be achieved on the basis of fully holistic principles of productive organization.

Given the spatiotemporal limitations of organized social life and the great richness and pluralism of individual needs and priorities for the use of time and resources, people will undoubtedly desire a great deal of flexibility, and require a variety of mechanisms, for their work commitments. Indeed, we can think of many reasons why people would not want to be restricted to a holistically organized productive unit as the performance site for all or most of their creative as well as routine tasks: (1) shifting patterns of friendship, love, and workmate relations over the course of time—and the related problem of emotional intensity in small-scale holistic work collectives;[21] (2) conflicts between family responsibilities and the spatiotemporal constraints of certain jobs;[22] (3) the need for opportunities to test a range of occupational choices by engaging in less than high-level or long-term commitment; (4) the need to minimize workplace commitments in order to pursue various other interests (e.g., art, athletics, travel) that may not currently (or ever) earn one an income. Simple tasks that are not inherently interesting lend themselves particularly well to flexible work arrangements because they are relatively easy to learn and do not require a high degree of continuity for their effective accomplishment. Among the possible social and organizational rationales for flexibly violating the principles of holism and equal proportions are: (1) increased productivity; (2) flexible organizational reponse to demand (e.g., seasonal); (3) technological constraints; (4) the limitation of featherbedding or overstaffing; (5) the enhancement of equality of opportunity, which, as is implicit in the argument above, cannot be achieved without greater flexibility of work commitments than that entailed in the productive integrity model. While a critical organization theory cannot assign priority unreflectively to any of these, and certainly not to productivity, it must consider all of them (and no doubt more) as potentially legitimate reasons for designing and modifying organizations in a less than holistic manner. It cannot dogmatically rule out the possibility that people might choose to organize certain production processes in a relatively rationalized or fragmented manner—if this allows for greater productivity, more free time, or greater options for creative work *in other areas*. Nor can it rule out less than holistic work commitments if they permit desired flexibility and the relative equalization of other work opportunities. In a large-scale democratic polity, these decisions would require a complex calculation of the relative costs and benefits for different groups and individuals of various organizational forms and production strategies. A strict application of holistic principles in the search for a democratic and egalitarian ideal would, without a doubt, create a nightmare of organizational inflexibility incapable of responding creatively to the myriad goals of a complex egalitarian society. A complex calculation of costs and benefits will remain crucial because alternatives must be created in the context of inherited technologies and divisions of labor in a world of extremely uneven development and persisting scarcity. The latter will inevitably leave their imprint on the creation of utopian forms, since the relative costs and benefits of various egalitarian strategies and organizational forms will vary considerably.

The third limitation of the productive integrity model is its conception of democracy. This model presumes that the only consistent and truly democratic arrangement in work organizations is one where fully equal participation and control rights exist for all members, even if representation is necessary because of scale. Equal control rights, of course, are the logical complement of fully holistic sharing of tasks and the breakdown of all mental and manual divisions within the workplace. At the risk of repeating myself, let me say that this is a commendable goal, and one that could no doubt be realized in many workplaces. But in a complex and pluralistic society, it could not be consistently realized in all workplaces, and perhaps not even in the great majority. Thus we require a broader range of democratic forms of workplace organization, one that is consistent with the multiple aims of broad equality and individual flexibility and with the values of solidarity, community, and equal respect.

First, it must be kept in mind that the broadest problems of democratic values and institutions cannot be reduced to workplace relations, even though the latter are a very important component.[23] To a large extent, the productive integrity model simply assumes that democracy on the societal scale requires full-scale participatory democracy in every workplace. But this neither solves the problem of democracy nor sufficiently allows for a pluralist array of individual commitments and organizational forms. Knowledge and control over "the production process as a whole," in the sense usually implied in the productive integrity model (i.e., over the whole of a *particular* production process), in no way directly implies knowledge and control at the societal level. Neither craft knowledge of a particular production process nor even highly advanced scientific knowledge of an entire branch of production provides understanding of global development options. And democratization of knowledge and control at the societal and local community levels can be quite consistent theoretically with various forms of organization in the workplace, with various forms of what Burawoy refers to as the "social and technical *relations in production*."[24] Thus, knowledge and control of the production process as a whole must not be viewed as a naive wisdom that implies a singular, unambiguous form of workplace organization.

If fully holistic principles of organization are significantly modified in order to institutionalize greater opportunities for equality and flexibility, as argued above, the resulting levels of commitment, knowledge, and time would be quite uneven, and in some workplaces greatly so. The singular model of equal participation and control rights in every workplace would, therefore, have to be modified to allow for a variety of forms of participation that simultaneously recognize differential inputs—yet protect the rights and represent the interests of those who might know less, choose to participate less, or choose to participate only minimally. In other words, we need a more pluralistic conception of democratic forms suitable to the great variety of work and time commitments that productive citizens might choose. We cannot premise a democratic system on the intense and complete commitment of every worker to participate in the decisions of every workplace. Where levels of technical knowledge are highly unequal, fully equal control rights would either remain quite formal or become highly irrational in terms of production and the efficient use of resources. Equal distribution of control rights to those whose commitment (to work time and to continuity) varies considerably is not necessarily fair and just. Should the factory worker doing modified assembly tasks ten hours a week, or for a three-month temporary job, have the same control rights as the engineer (or engineer-worker) working on a continuous full-time basis? The answer seems to be clearly negative, although such workers should have control over all aspects of health and safety, grievances, recommendations for technical and labor process changes, and the right to strike. The challenge is not to design the perfect ideal of organizational democracy, and, when it is not realized, alternatively to struggle against complete disenchantment or to blame hostile factors in the bureaucratic environment. Rather, it is to investigate the range of possible democratic organizational forms appropriate to the variety of individual, organizational, and broadly social goals and to evaluate the relative costs, benefits, and unintended consequences of these.

One such cost that will affect the choice of organizational form is time. The scarcity of time is a fundamental aspect of all social organization. All participation in decision-making processes costs time, whether in meetings or in the acquisition of relevant knowledge and information. And time spent in such ways is time not spent on other things that might be of equal or greater value to particular individuals or groups of people. As Robert Dahl has argued, the value of participating in decisions depends on a range of factors: the enjoyment derived from such participation, the importance of the matters being decided and the differences at stake in the alternatives, the likelihood that one's participation will affect the outcome, and the competence of the participant.[25] While participation would certainly be a very salient value in a democratic and egalitarian society, no philosophical or political justification permits considering it an absolute value under all organizational conditions, regardless of the costs.

Thus, a genuinely democratic and pluralist society must recognize the right to limit participation in certain areas of workplace decision making according to agreed-upon criteria. It must recognize the right of individuals *not* to participate directly in certain decisions and, as a derivative, the right of majorities to systematically circumscribe certain participation rights of all but specially delegated representatives. Without the possibility of such restrictions, majorities that might not view direct participation as a priority would be forced to participate or be subject to decisions by unrepresentative minorities.[26] The necessity for calculating the relative importance of participation increases with the expansion of the number of units of which one is a "member." Hence, the more pluralist the work and life options available to people, the more likely that democracy will imply restricted participation rights of various sorts, though the latter by no means rules out general participatory controls when appropriate. Not to recognize the necessity for restrictions, however, is inconsistent with the principles of pluralist democracy.

Many problems would undoubtedly exist with the global pluralist model of equality that I am proposing as a broad alternative to the model of productive integrity. Flexible work arrangements and unequal proportions (of skill, time, commitment, control) would create organizational difficulties (discontinuity, duplication, etc.) and generate tensions with the values of democracy, solidarity, and equality. Any egalitarian and democratic organization theory would have to investigate the variety of ways in which everyday organizational practices sustain or inhibit these broader values. But we must also keep in mind that organizational practices are not reducible to, or fully constrained by, organizational structures; a variety of sources within and outside the workplace (community, family, schools, churches, the state) can nourish the values of democracy, equality, and solidarity.

As Jane Mansbridge has shown, equal power over every sphere or over every decision in a workplace is not a precondition for equal respect, solidarity, or personal growth—all of which can be nourished through multiple sources.[27] Yet relatively equal power must exist in enough spheres if a democratic ethos is to flourish. Transitory orientations to workplaces may tend to undermine solidaristic social relations and even organizational maintenance.[28] Yet arrangements flexible enough to facilitate other work and learning experiences, to mitigate emotional intensity and burnout, and to permit a broader range of interpersonal relations may in fact provide other conditions for mutual support, respect, and stable commitment. Such arrangements may relieve individuals of the all-or-nothing choice of full membership and may lessen the strong tendency of participatory institutions to dissolve after relatively short periods of time—leading in many cases to cynicism about some of the very values that motivated participation in the first place. To premise solidarity and community on every workplace being a *Gemeinschaft* of holistic commitments appears both unimaginative and unrealistic at this stage of urban civilization. Research in alternative forms of organization has pointed to the relative autonomy of different levels of participation, and the significant impact on motivation and satisfaction of even relatively limited forms of job enrichment.[29] Nothing in the empirical literature on political or industrial participation points to the conclusion that high-level or holistic participation by each worker in each unit in which he or she works might be a *necessary* condition for an active and motivated laboring citizenry. And this would seem to hold even more if a greater variety of concurrent options for productive activity and creative work could be institutionalized. It certainly seems feasible, for instance, that an individual with intellectual and participation commitments in one area of professional activity (say architecture or teaching) could perform relatively routine tasks in a factory or in a restaurant for five to ten hours a week and not share in the full range of engineering tasks and planning discussions, or not become a gourmet restaurant cook or go to long-range planning meetings. I do not think we should exclude this or a great range of similar possibilities—or disqualify such an individual *by definition* as an intelligent and engaged citizen, especially if such arrangements facilitate the equalization of opportunities (by more widely distributing routine tasks as well as professional opportunities) and enhance the variety of work options and the flexibility of life scheduling.[30]

In short, the problems to be worked out in a global pluralist model are many. But given the serious limitations of holistic work organizations as a general model, critical organizational research and theory would do well to abandon the search for an ideal participatory form; instead, it should investigate the broad array of organizational mechanisms that might facilitate and impede democracy, community, individual flexibility, and the equalization of work opportunities across the social division of labor.[31]

A more systemic approach oriented toward both interorganizational and intraorganizational mechanisms is thus necessary. Blaming hostile "environmental" factors for the limitations and failures of alternative organizations, while true in many cases, is ultimately an evasion. Critical organization theory has not neglected these interorganizational factors. For instance, many studies show the kinds of larger financial and technical infrastructures that are conducive to worker ownership and self-management. But attention has not focused on the broader conditions and possible institutional mechanisms that facilitate or impede equality of work opportunity on a societal scale. Neither labor market nor state mechanisms have received much explicit attention by theorists of organizational alternatives in the United States. Studies of Yugoslav self-management often do focus on these issues, but this model has clear limitations when it comes to skill and opportunity stratification.[32] Let me briefly argue several theses and indicate a few critical problems that must be addressed in much greater detail by organizational theorists committed to greater equalization of work opportunities.

A free society that institutionalizes a broad range of pluralistic work options to enhance individual flexibility and relative equality *across* the social division of labor (and hence *among* work units) requires a relatively *free and open labor market*, albeit one subject to various forms of democratic regulation. Relatively equal work opportunities and the transformation of the class division of labor cannot be totally administered either through commandist or decentralized planning mechanisms. Fully decentralized nonmarket planning, as I will argue, is impossible; centralized planning, even if it were able to achieve complete control over the labor market (which it has yet to do), would backfire and provide a poor basis for either equality, plurality, or democracy. However, a relatively open labor market in a complex social division of labor inevitably implies a certain degree of segmentation. It implies, in short, a segmented labor market—segmented not necessarily in terms of highly differentiated incomes, benefits, security (as we have today), but in terms of the opportunity structures associated with various positions. The challenge that faces organizational theorists concerned with equality is not to eliminate the labor market, or to redesign all jobs so as to eliminate the very possibility of segmentation. Equality cannot be guaranteed through the structural redesign of all positions. Rather, the challenge is to design a set of complementary social and organizational strategies, and state policies above the level of the individual workplace, so as to prevent or reverse any involuntary or systematic segmentation of the workforce itself. In short, segmentation of *positions* is inevitable in any complex social division of labor, but this need not imply a systematic and unacceptably unequal segmentation of the *people* who fill them. Positional segmentation need not imply class segmentation of opportunities or outcomes.

To prevent a systematically inegalitarian and involuntary segmentation of opportunities and outcomes that traps specific groups of workers in "cycles of disadvantage"[33] is undoubtedly a difficult and complex problem. It becomes even more complex, yet ultimately more tractable, if we institutionalize a wide range of alternative and fluid career patterns ("flexible life scheduling") in the context of a significant reduction of overall working time or of work sharing. Such flexibility would permit people to take significant amounts of time off (e.g., for childrearing), to work only part-time, to opt for the less intense and demanding aspects of a profession for a period of time, to change careers, to sustain multiple and less absorbing career commitments, or to choose more intense commitments in exchange for greater free time later. In short, we could design a range of alternative time cycles for achievement, rather than bestowing disproportionate privileges on the dominant one—to the disadvantage of others. The dominant one is, of course, full-time continuous commitment from early adulthood on, and often entails a surplus of commitment above and beyond this in order to have access to opportunity and security.[34] Without a broad range of alternative time cycles for achievement and fluid career commitments, a significant egalitarian transformation of the division of labor would be impossible. Opportunities would continue to cluster disproportionately around full-time continuous-service positions; the costs and risks of career discontinuities would be too high to encourage the more privileged to accept greater flexibility in the interests of broader access to opportunity. Such resistance could be anticipated even in view of the other benefits of flexibility to those in more advantaged positions. Yet alternative time cycles for work commitment and achievement, like any organizational differentiation, create specific problems of cumulative advantage and disadvantage, as is already shown in part-time work experiments.[35] As long as career movement (vertical or horizontal) and the conditions for further achievement in a complex social division of labor remain important to people—as I think they undoubtedly would even if the organizationally fostered obsession with perpetual upward movement were to wither away—a natural equilibrium state of equal opportunities can not exist. The "struggle for place"[36] and the search for relatively scarce opportunities for comparative recognition would continue within organizational structures dynamically defined by cycles of advantage and disadvantage, which constitute each other. No organizations are without such dynamic cycles, and unlimited advantages are never without disadvantages, even if the balance is far from zero-sum.

Thus a fundamentally egalitarian division of labor would require the continual negotiation and renegotiation of the organizational conditions for achievement and recognition. The parameters of relative advantage and disadvantage would have to be subject to a process of democratic regulation. Regulation, negotiation, and struggle, of course, have been constitutive in the formation and reformation of boundaries in the division of labor all along (e.g., credentialing, licensing).[37] And questions of equity and fairness, often inspired by explicit or implicit commitment to egalitarian values, have been an essential part of this process. In recent years, feminist and civil rights struggles have raised some of the most significant issues about negotiating the conditions for achievement and the parameters of cycles of advantage and disadvantage associated with specific kinds of *positions* in the division of labor (e.g., clerical) and specific *routes of access* (e.g., returning homemaker, compensatory training). They have helped initiate a number of innovative organizational strategies for empowerment and opportunity enhancement. Yet, in the absence of a broader, more powerful and coherent democratic movement, which would challenge the interests that profit-maximizing organizations have in limiting skill and opportunity development in order to enhance managerial control and reduce labor costs, these new strategies will remain limited, and in some cases merely shift disadvantages to other groups.[38]

A relatively egalitarian reorganization of the division of labor thus implies democratic forms of regulation of both internal labor markets and the rules of external access. The latter is particularly crucial if various alternative forms of career commitment are not to result in uncontrolled disadvantages to those who choose them. Various modifications in market and meritocratic criteria would be necessary to offset the cumulative disadvantages of late entry into a particular job market, or reentry, part-time commitment, and other flexible arrangements, even if not *all* relative disadvantages *could* or *should* be eliminated. Conflict over these issues could be expected even in a society with a profound commitment to democratic and egalitarian values. The parameters of cyclical and interactive advantages and disadvantages within and among organizations would remain a contested terrain, since disagreements and differential costs among various egalitarian strategies would undoubtedly continue. Furthermore, what is seen as an equitable rule by some is often perceived as an unfair restriction of opportunity and a disincentive to individual excellence by others. The needs of organizations frequently will conflict with those of individuals. As long as the values of both equity and individuality remain important, conflict within organizations will be inevitable.

Such conflict cannot be eliminated by doing away with markets, and hence the search for relative advantage. Some critics of market socialism argue that equitable and just outcomes could be more or less guaranteed through the structural design of the institutions themselves.[39] But no complex social division of labor, operating under conditions of relative scarcity (which will always exist), can eliminate markets altogether without: (1) severely curtailing the freedom of workers; (2) tyrannizing consumers in its inability to respond adequately to personal consumption needs—or even social consumption; and (3) wasting human and natural resources in a democratically uncontrollable spiral of inefficiency. This has been demonstrated clearly in centrally planned commandist economies, which have nonetheless not been able to avoid introducing, formally and informally, a range of market mechanisms.[40] And the organizational logic would not be radically different if the central planning apparatuses were under greater democratic control. Nor would decentralized planning by worker and community councils be able to avoid similar irrationalities and restrictions without some use of market mechanisms.[41] In such a system, information would be systematically biased toward the unit supplying it; structural incentive to conceal productive reserves, to overestimate required supplies (including labor), and to waste resources would exist; and supply would be unable to adopt flexibly to demand. Any attempt to break out of these inherent organizational inflexibilities by freely negotiating with a variety of potential suppliers or customers on the basis of relative costs and benefits would introduce market calculations into the model. It is instructive, for instance, that the council model of decentralized planning never indicates whether councils are free to go elsewhere with their business if satisfactory arrangements cannot be worked out with other councils. In short, any complex political economy that is democratic, and organizationally flexible enough to respond to the great variety of individual needs in advanced urban civilization, requires market mechanisms of some sort.

Markets, to be sure, raise many serious problems for those committed to equality, social solidarity, ecological balance, and the rational use of productive resources. It is not my purpose to discuss these here, but it should be noted that egalitarian theorists committed to market mechanisms have devoted a good deal of attention to some of the ways these problems can be mitigated. For instance, taxes and subsidies can be used in such a way that prices reflect democratically determined costs and benefits, such as ecological ones; within such a politically regulated framework, markets can serve to reduce waste and promote conservation. Collective purchase can ensure that public needs are not always sacrificed to private consumer demand. Taxes can be used to reduce inequalities among firms or industries that result from different technological capacities or monopoly position, thus separating the allocational from the distributional function of prices. State regulation, along with worker participation, can be used to protect worker health and safety.[42] All of these problems require much more attention than they have received. The primary concern here is how a broad range of market choices in labor and consumption can be maintained without generating an uncontrollable and uncorrectable dynamic toward work rationalization, the unnecessary fragmentation of tasks, and a structural segmentation of the labor force. In short, how can equality of work opportunities be made compatible with market mechanisms?

This question has been given scant attention. Many simply assume that they cannot be made compatible and that either markets must be abandoned or the hope of such equality, relinquished. Others such as Branco Horvat, unlike many earlier proponents of market socialism, are quite aware of the problem of the separation between mental and manual labor and the decomposition of skill. But their hope is founded primarily in technology, along with workers' self-management. The new communications and microelectronics technologies will simply make fragmentation and routine work outmoded and unnecessary.[43] But this will not, in itself, solve the problem of routine work in many areas of production and service or the segmentation of the labor force across the range of work opportunities. In fact, it could very well create a variety of new jobs that are basically routine, even if mentally routine, and that have few learning and career opportunities directly associated with them. New technologies neither eliminate all routine work nor determine the distribution of tasks or the *organizational* conditions for individual achievement, learning, and professional development. Such technologies, to the extent that they do eliminate some of the more routine and dangerous tasks and can be applied flexibly to upgrade work and encourage more holistic work roles, do have great promise. But further organizational mechanisms are required if relative equality of work opportunities is to be institutionalized.

Let me suggest two such organizational mechanisms that appear necessary in some form or other if equality and flexibility of work opportunities are to be achieved. Both would be part of a comprehensive administrative system designed to permit people to combine labor market *choices* with administratively facilitated *choices*; both would guarantee specific *rights* to work and training options that are appropriately *flexible* for individual needs at different stages of one's life and career cycles and are adequately *compensatory* for disadvantages incurred by previous labor market, educational, and training choices. The first is a system of labor market boards at local and national levels, similar in ways to those developed in Sweden.[44] These boards could provide information, placement, certain forms of training, resettlement and displacement allowances (since we cannot assume that workers will never have to be displaced by enterprises that are market rational), and a range of other services facilitating choice, flexibility, and security. The second organizational mechanism is a state-administered sabbatical program with guaranteed minimal rights to extended time off, a flexible range of options for the forms these might take, and perhaps a supplementary taxation system that would allow workers to accumulate further rights to time away from their regular jobs. Such a system would be an extension of social security administration, though time off could be taken throughout one's career, not just at the end of it.

Each of these systems could be complemented by other programs such as artistic sabbaticals and grants for special projects or particular categories of workers; these could be awarded preferentially and/or on a competitive basis. Labor market boards with the functions I have outlined do not seem to present any serious theoretical problems. State-administered sabbatical programs present more serious organizational problems. But, as Fred Best notes of a less ambitious version, "there is no question that a reasonably efficient system could be developed"[45] despite the administrative difficulties and challenges. This is one area that requires much more thought and research by critical organizational theorists, who too often show little interest in how to design or redesign large-scale administrative apparatuses. The latter appear necessary, however, not only to guarantee social welfare rights, environmental protection, resource planning, a more equitable distribution of income, and the like. They appear necessary as well to guarantee rights and facilitate options with the scope and flexibility that would be required to achieve relatively equal work and career opportunities—and to do so in a way that does not undermine the best aspects of market rationality. Serious structural inequalities due to the segmentation of positions in the social division of labor cannot be eliminated by the redesigning of all jobs or by technological innovation. Consequently, the guaranteed right to flexible work and training options over the course of life cycles and career paths must be secured through the state. Yet, since relative equality cannot—indeed, should not—be administered directly, administrative mechanisms should take the form of guaranteeing rights by providing a great array of options. Ultimately, only individual choice, along with political negotiation and struggle within the great variety of organizations in which people work, could actually lead to relatively egalitarian outcomes. But the democratic state can provide the basis, as it often has in the past, for securing individual rights and greater freedom of choice, and for establishing the parameters within which organizational and professional conflicts over the division of labor and the criteria of equity take place.

Administration on this scale, of course, implies bureaucracy—that nagging problem that has persisted since the beginning in organization theory and has defined some of the major lines of debate among Weber, Marx, and Michels. Much subsequent research has clearly demonstrated that none of the classic positions is fully adequate. Yet on the question of the future of democracy and equality, the strengths and limitations of each of them remain instructive. Marx was clearly wrong on the future of the state and bureaucracy (not to mention markets). Neither would wither away in a communist utopia because no society completely beyond scarcity is conceivable.[46] The "rich individuality" and highly variegated work opportunities, which are at the heart of Marx's conception of a fully developed good society, and the egalitarian vision, which is the touchstone of his critique of the capitalist division of labor, would require bureaucratic administration on some scale. Bureaucracy cannot be reduced to domination. Rather, one of its most basic roots is social complexity. Weber, of course, fully realized this, though he often speaks as if complexity is primarily a dehumanized technical issue. But complexity can be viewed just as well from the angle of the richness of life and work options and of forms of social interaction in a technologically advanced and communicatively dense society.[47] Weber was conscious of this to some extent, as he was of the impulses toward substantive equality behind the spread of the social welfare functions of bureaucracy. However, the potential for substantive equality and for the rich complexity of individual choice and social interaction is not emphasized in an organization theory with such profound rationalistic assumptions and such pessimistic concerns over the fate of individuality in an irresistably bureaucratized world.

Marx may have been wrong on the extent to which rich individuality and popular control over complex social and productive tasks could be achieved by participatory means. Today, although many of the criticisms of Weber and Michels are relevant, Marx's stress on participation and workers' control and his critique of oppressive and secretive bureaucracies hardly seem out of place. Perhaps complex democracy cannot exist without bureaucracy. Participatory democratic forms may not be able to replace or even to control legislators and bureaucrats, but these forms have proven their relevance in a variety of organizational contexts. Sweden, Austria, and the Netherlands have used participatory reforms such as citizen advisory councils and written records of administrative deliberations that are open to the public and the press. Their experiences suggest that these innovative reforms, in addition to the legislative oversight on which Weber placed his hopes, can be used to maintain control over bureaucracies.[48] Of course, oligarchy and the tendency for decisions to be made according to the rationales and routines of bureaucrats remain permanent problems. Because of this fact, one can not completely disregard the analyses of Weber, Michels and, more recently, Lipsky. Accountability, however, cannot be secured solely through participatory mechanisms.[49] Yet the variety of existing organizational mechanisms hardly leads to the conclusion that a reasonable degree of accountability is forever beyond our reach. Oligarchy, persistent as it may be, is not wrought of iron.

The goal of relatively equal work opportunities, of a society without in-built structures that impede creative social labor and life-long learning and career development for all who would take advantage of such opportunities, cannot be achieved on the basis of *any* single organizational model. Bureaucracy would be inescapable in such a society for many reasons tied to coordination and regulation; however, I have emphasized the less recognized issues of complexity, flexibility, and equality. The problem of bureaucracy in a society that would attempt a fundamental transformation of the class division of labor ultimately reflects the plurality of individual choices, the richness of social interaction forms that would be available as a regular feature of social organization, and the degree and scope of equality that we would find desirable and appropriate to institutionalize. Developments in contemporary society point to the need to move beyond the profound structural barriers that hinder opportunity, learning, and creative, flexible work for perhaps the majority of our population. How far along the road of an egalitarian transformation we could realistically travel, even under the best of circumstances, remains unclear. Critical organization theorists who consider this question must remain agnostic at this point in time—even if the commitment to equality and democracy requires no tortured justification. However, given our knowledge of organizations, human talent, and creativity, anything less than an open-ended conception of egalitarian possibilities would reflect bad faith at this time. This essay should not be misinterpreted as an argument for complete equality (whatever that would mean) or for a society beyond conflict and the abuse of power. Equality can, no doubt, only be relative and complex. No structural or organizational design could ever fully predict or predetermine how people would utilize and modify structures to their own purposes. But we can continue to think through the problems of organizing democracy and equality only by abandoning the search for the singular ideal. Instead, we must develop a perspective that is simultaneously global and systemic in its conception of social relationships; it must be as pluralistic as the people who would inhabit our organizations and the aspirations they would bring with them.

Notes

1. Ralf Dahrendorf, "On the Origin of Inequality Among Men," *Essays in Sociological Theory* (Stanford: Stanford Univ. Press, 1968), 159–178.
2. Rosabeth Moss Kanter, *Men and Women of the Corporation* (New York: Basic Books, 1977).
3. R. Rumberger, *Overeducation in the U.S. Labor Market* (New York: Praeger, 1981); Beverly Burris, *No Room at the Top* (New York: Praeger, 1983).
4. Barry Bluestone and Bennett Harrison, *The Deindustrialization of America* (New York: Basic Books, 1982).
5. See Joyce Rothschild-Whitt, "The Collectivist Organization: An Alternative to Rational-Bureaucratic Models," *American Sociological Review* 44, no. 4 (Aug. 1979), 509–527.
6. See Paula Rayman, "Collective Organization and the National State: The Kibbutz Model," ch. 24 of this anthology.
7. See William Whyte and Joseph Blasi, "Worker Ownership, Participation, and Control: Toward a Theoretical Model," ch. 23 of this anthology.
See also Ana Gutiérrez Johnson and William Foote Whyte, "The Mondragón System of Worker Production Cooperatives," in *Workplace Democracy and Social Change*, ed. Frank Lindenfeld and Joyce Rothschild-Whitt (Boston: Porter Sargent, 1982), 188 ff.
8. See Jane Mansbridge, "Feminism and the Forms of Freedom," ch. 27 of this anthology.
9. Michael Walzer, in *Spheres of Justice* (New York: Basic Books, 1983), makes a powerful and articulate case for this position.
10. John Case and Rosemary Taylor, eds., *Co-ops, Communes and Collectives* (New York: Pantheon, 1979), 9.
11. Carmen Sirianni, "Production and Power in a Classless Society: A Critical Analysis of the Utopian Dimensions of Marxist Theory," *Socialist Review*, no. 59 (Sept.–Oct. 1981), 39ff. There is a clear basis for this in Marx's own writings, but his conceptions varied along with his changing views of the division of labor itself. See Ali Rattansi, *Marx and the Division of Labor* (London: Macmillan, 1982).
12. Harry Braverman, *Labor and Monopoly Capital* (New York: Monthly Review Press, 1974), 230.
13. Rudolf Bahro, *The Alternative in Eastern Europe*, trans. David Fernbach (London: Verso/NLB, 1978), 280.
14. Though I cannot discuss this in any detail here, it seems to me that the overwhelming conclusion of empirical studies on workplace participation, on IQ and educational achievement and stratification, is that the actual and potential talent in the population at large is vastly greater than what is recognized, encouraged, or rewarded by class-based occupational structures. See, for instance, N. J. Block and Gerald Dworkin, eds., *The IQ Controversy* (New York: Pantheon, 1976); Samuel Bowles and Herbert Gintis, *Schooling in Capitalist America* (New York: Basic Books, 1976).
15. Kanter, *Men and Women of the Corporation*, 259.
16. I am borrowing from Mansbridge's terminology here, realizing that any discussion of equality ultimately requires a fuller clarification of the meaning of "relative equality" and

"acceptable inequalities." See Jane Mansbridge, "Acceptable Inequalities," *British Journal of Political Science* 7, no. 3 (July 1977): 321–36.

17. See, for instance, Paula Rayman's discussion of the regional high school in "Cooperative Movement Confronts Centralization: Israeli Kibbutz Regional Organizations," *Economic and Industrial Democracy* 2, no. 4 (Nov. 1981), 493 ff.

18. Walzer, *Spheres of Justice*, ch. 6.

19. Ibid., p. 183.

20. Fred Block and Larry Hirschhorn, "New Productive Forces and the Contradictions of Contemporary Capitalism: A Post-Industrial Perspective," *Theory and Society* 7 (1979), 379.

21. Rothschild-Whitt, "The Collectivist Organization."

22. Overcoming the sexual division of labor seems clearly dependent on enhancing the flexibility of work commitments outside the home.

23. Sirianni, "Production and Power in a Classless Society."

24. Michael Burawoy, *Manufacturing Consent* (Chicago: Univ. of Chicago Press, 1980), 15.

25. Robert Dahl, *After the Revolution* (New Haven: Yale Univ. Press, 1970), 40 ff.

26. Ibid., 50–51.

27. Jane Mansbridge, *Beyond Adversary Democracy* (New York: Basic Books, 1980).

28. Joyce Rothschild-Whitt, "Conditions for Democracy: Making Participatory Organizations Work," in Case and Taylor, *Co-ops, Communes and Collectives*, 219–221.

29. Paul Blumberg, *Industrial Democracy* (New York: Schocken, 1969); *Work in America*, HEW Report (Cambridge: MIT Press, 1973); Paul Bernstein, *Workplace Democratization* (Canton, Ohio: Kent State Univ. Press, 1976); Daniel Zwerdling, *Workplace Democracy* (New York: Harper and Row, 1980).

30. It is clear from recent research how important these issues have already become. See Fred Best, *Flexible Life Scheduling* (New York: Praeger, 1980); Best, *Work Sharing* (Kalamazoo, Mich.: Upjohn Institute, 1981); Seymour Sarason, *Work, Aging and Social Change* (New York: Free Press, 1977).

31. For Marxists, this would imply abandoning as well the strict division made by Braverman and others between the detailed division of labor in the workshop and the social division of labor, at least where this distinction is used to premise the reduction of class divisions on the total reintegration of productive functions at the level of the individual workplace, or to argue that all fragmented work inevitably fragments and subdivides the people who do it.

32. Josip Obradovic and William Dunn, eds., *Workers' Self-Management and Organizational Power in Yugoslavia* (Pittsburgh: Univ. Center for International Studies, 1978); Ellen Turkish Comisso, *Workers' Control Under Plan and Market* (New Haven: Yale Univ. Press, 1979).

33. This is the central concept in Kanter's dynamic structural analysis of organizations. Its relevance beyond issues of men and women, and even beyond particular organizations, to the social division of labor as a whole is enormous.

34. Such surplus commitment can involve 60–70 hour weeks, or wives willing to take on responsibilities for what Hanna Papanek refers to as the "two-person single career." See Kanter, *Men and Women of the Corporation*, ch. 5.

35. Best, *Work Sharing*, 81. Organizations tend to prefer workers who are lower risk, promise higher- and longer-term benefits, and require less cost (in terms of training, temporary replacement, etc.). These and other factors make cycles of advantage and disadvantage inevitable.

36. See Charles Sabel's use of this concept in his analysis of "careers at work," in *Work and Politics* (New York: Cambridge Univ. Press, 1982), ch. 3.

37. See Sabel, *Work and Politics*, ch. 3; Eliot Freidson, "The Division of Labor as Social Interaction," *Social Problems* 23 (1976), 304–313: and Elliott Krause's articulation of a "political" model of division of labor dynamics in *Division of Labor* (Westport, Ct.: Greenwood Press, 1982).

38. Despite her far-reaching proposals for empowerment and opportunity enhancement, Kanter fails to fully appreciate these obstacles, which have been most clearly articulated, though sometimes overstated, in Marxist analyses of the labor process. In an uncharacteristic reification of organizations as having an imputed rational "interest" in not underemploying their workers and not wasting human talent, she understates the structural obstacles to the broad expansion of opportunities and diffusion of power. Likewise, she underestimates the costs that improvements for one group pose for another, though she is correct to seek changes that potentially benefit organization members more broadly. Greatly expanded opportunities for women in general (secretaries in particular) via bridges between job ladders and job redesign unavoidably raise the question of who will do the typing and what will they be paid. Will managers share in these and other tasks that have less direct payoff for career development? And how will the relatively scarce opportunities for recognition upward be distributed as the pool of talented people with high aspirations and work commitments is considerably enlarged? See Kanter, *Men and Women of the Corporation*, ch. 10; Andrew Zimbalist, "The Limits of Work Humanization," *Review of Radical Political Economics* 7, no. 2 (Summer 1975): 50–59; and some of the obstacles to change discussed in Zwerdling, *Workplace Democracy*.

39. See, for instance, Barry Clark and Herbert Gintis, "Rawlsian Justice and Economic Systems," *Philosophy and Public Affairs* 7, no. 4 (Summer 1978), 324.

40. Wlodzimierz Brus, *The Market in a Socialist Economy* (London: Routledge, 1972); Brus, *The Economics and Politics of Socialism* (London: Routledge, 1973); Alec Nove, *The Political Economy of Soviet Socialism* (London: George Allen and Unwin, 1979); Gyorgy Markus, "Planning the Crisis: Remarks on the Economic System of Soviet-Type Societies," *Praxis International* 1, no. 3 (Oct. 1981), 241–57.

41. See, for instance, the model proposed by Michael Albert and Robin Hahnel in *Socialist Visions*, ed. Steve Shalom (Boston: South End Press, 1983); Albert and Hahnel, *Socialism Today and Tomorrow* (Boston: South End Press, 1981); Sirianni, "The Council Model of Decentralized Planning: A Critical Analysis," in *Socialist Visions*, Albert and Hahnel.

42. Joseph Carens, *Equality, Moral Incentives and the Market* (Chicago: Univ. of Chicago Press, 1981), 187ff; Branco Horvat, *The Political Economy of Socialism* (Armonk, N.Y.: M. E. Sharpe, 1982), 265–272, passim.

43. Horvat, *ibid.*, pp. 249–50, 422–24, 428.

44. John Fry, ed., *Industrial Democracy and Labour Market Policy in Sweden* (Oxford: Pergamon Press, 1979).

45. Best, *Work Sharing*, 82.

46. Sirianni, "Production and Power in a Classless Society," 48–50.

47. In this sense, bureaucracy complements the city in its capacity for effective and expansive time-space distanciation. See Anthony Giddens, *A Contemporary Critique of Historical Materialism* (Berkeley: Univ. of California Press, 1981), 144.

48. Dennis Thompson, "Bureaucracy and Democracy," in *Democratic Theory and Practice*, ed. Graeme Duncan (New York: Cambridge Univ. Press, 1983), 246–49.

49. Sirianni, "Production and Power in a Classless Society," 69; Sirianni, *Workers' Control and Socialist Democracy: the Soviet Experience* (London: Verso/NLB, 1982), 300; Sirianni, "Councils and Parliaments: The Problems of Dual Power and Democracy in Comparative Perspective," *Politics and Society* 12, no. 1 (1983), 83–123; Thompson, "Bureaucracy and Democracy," 248–249.